Ius Comparatum - Global Studies in Comparative Law

Volume 54

Editors
Isabel C. Jaramillo
Universidad de Los Andes
Bogotá, Colombia

Laura Carlson
Department of Law
Stockholm University
Stockholm, Sweden

ISSN 2214-6881 ISSN 2214-689X (electronic)
Ius Comparatum - Global Studies in Comparative Law
ISBN 978-3-030-68493-8 ISBN 978-3-030-68494-5 (eBook)
https://doi.org/10.1007/978-3-030-68494-5

This Springer imprint is published by the registered company Springer Nature Switzerland AG.
The registered company address is: Gewerbestrasse 11, 6330 Cham, Switzerland

Contents

Part III The Soft Medicalization Model

Part IV Self- determination in the Registration of Sex

Part I
Introduction

The Stakes in Sex: Obstacles and Opportunities in Legal Reform for Trans Persons

Isabel C. Jaramillo

Abstract This book comprises chapters from 23 different countries addressing the legal treatment of trans persons specifically with respect to recognition of gender identity through the laws governing civil status. The different chapters clearly demarcate the legal stages the issue of recognition has undergone: denial, suppression, oppression in the form of sterilization requirements and non-recognition, partial recognition and, now, in some countries, almost complete recognition. The chapters also address the different ways forward that can be contemplated by lawmakers everywhere.

For the past two centuries, feminists have struggled to convince us that sex is a marker for discrimination, exclusion and violence. The unapologetic fierceness that the modern state would deploy in policing the boundaries of sex however was impossible to predict. The high costs of the fragile promise contained in belonging to the "right" side of the male/female binary were difficult to anticipate even for trans persons themselves. This book maps national legal responses to gender mobility, including sex and name registration, access to gender modification interventions and anti-discrimination regulations. The chapters here underline the importance of history, culture and legal rules for understanding the operations of the law with respect to discrimination, exclusion, and violence, as well as the stickiness of nature as reason to introduce biology in the legal regulations of human relations and to justify pain and suffering. The scholarship here also reveals how different authorities and civil society became involved in either facilitating or impeding the welfare of trans persons, from judges and legislators, to medical commissions and law students, and from parents to children.

This book is the result of the work of a large number of scholars scattered around the globe. It was not produced with a particular theory or framework in mind. It was initially geared towards "reporting" the civil status of trans persons to the community

I. C. Jaramillo (✉)
Universidad de los Andes, Bogotá, Colombia
e-mail: ijaramil@uniandes.edu.co

I. C. Jaramillo, L. Carlson (eds.), *Trans Rights and Wrongs*, Ius Comparatum - Global Studies in Comparative Law 54,
https://doi.org/10.1007/978-3-030-68494-5_1

of comparative lawyers within the International Academy of Comparative Law in the XX Congress that took place in 2018.[1] As a report, it quite successfully traced national tendencies towards legal self-determination in sex classification and a generous guarantee of rights for individuals expressing diverse gender identities.[2] It revealed the dissemination of a model of protection of rights that not only focuses on formal equality, but addresses the administrative obstacles that trans persons face in their daily lives.[3] It also evidenced the importance of Courts in advancing or obstructing individual rights. As a reporting exercise, however, it was limited in its geographic scope, in the lack of trans personas as authors, and in terms of its timeliness. As to geographic scope, the reports fell short in being globally representative as most reports correspond to countries in the European region and the Americas. Another significant limitation with respect to our group of authors is that only one self- identifies as a trans person. Trans persons have been rightly adamant in their claim for inclusion using the "nothing about us without us" slogan. I personally have been accused of failing to understand the limitations that trans persons face in producing legal scholarship and therefore the privilege they should enjoy in academic settings in speaking about certain topics. As hard as these accusations are to hear for a cisgender woman from the south, that is, accusations about exclusion and privilege uttered by white trans men from the north, for example, this discussion underscores that the academic enterprise is never "neutral" and that each author's trans or cisgender interests drive our interpretations. Our authors are empathetic and concerned as to equality and non-discrimination protections for trans persons and rely heavily on reports and materials elaborated by trans organizations as to understanding this context. In some ways, our authors act more like spokespersons for trans persons: taking no part in defining the "problem" and following instructions in thinking about "solutions". But isn't this distance specifically "part of the problem"? Aren't we exoticizing trans persons and setting them up for exclusion when we fail to think of how we are also limited in our human possibilities when we do not take sex mobility seriously? May we at the same time recognize our cisgender privilege and find the abolition of this privilege to be in the interest for all? I hear myself suspiciously speaking as a man.

A final limitation with respect to our scholarship is its timeliness, restricting its utility in the long term, as legislation and doctrine are changing fast in this field. A notable example of this is the United States Supreme Court's landmark decision exactly 1 month before this manuscript was sent to the publishers, *Bostock v. Clayton County, Georgia*, in which the Court held that an employer who fires an individual merely for being gay or transgender violates Title VII of the Civil Rights Act

[1]For more information on the International Academy of Comparative Law see: https://aidc-iacl.org/ . Accessed 2 July 2020. General reports for the Congress have been published as: https://www.springer.com/gp/book/9783030486747.

[2]The general report was published in the book: https://www.springer.com/gp/book/9783030486747.

[3]Spade (2015) (originally published by South End in 2009).

of 1964.[4] A seminal forerunner to this work is Professor Jen Scherpe's 2015 book, *The Legal Status of Transsexual and Transgender Persons,* which he generously shared with us very early on in the process of thinking about this question.[5] When our national authors where initially approached in 2016, massive changes in the legal landscape of trans persons were already in place, including those countries Scherpe initially covered. Other actors have had greater incentives and resources to keep track of these legal reforms, such as the International Lesbian, Gay, Bisexual, Trans and Intersex Association (ILGA) which has been tracking legal reform affecting trans persons quite extensively since 2015, including 111 countries and 13 territories in their 2017 global report.[6]

The original national reports were consequently rewritten into these chapters addressing the local and transnational debates about legal reform concerning the rights of trans persons. The chapters below reveal the enormous diversity of institutional designs and legal responses to what appears to be a shared diagnosis of the needs and interests of trans persons. For purposes of structure, the difference in approaches to the civil status of trans persons is emphasized, as this was the point of departure for the initial reporting project, and it has been at the heart of the administrative turn in legal reform concerning trans persons.[7] Consequently, we have divided the chapters according to the model adopted by each country with regards to sex changes in the civil registry or official documentation.

Following Scherpe's taxonomy, we use three categories to classify countries in this aspect of their legislation: (1) self-determination; (2) soft medicalization; and (3) strong medicalization.[8] The first group includes countries in which individuals do not need to provide any evidence or support for their claim to change the sex marker in the registry or relevant documents. The following two categories rely on the medical community to establish the sex of the individual throughout her life. The first includes cases in which all that is required is support for the idea that the individual has consulted a professional, either a doctor or counsellor, on the issue of gender transformation, and shows willingness and abilities to undergo the process of becoming an individual of another gender or sex. The second refers to jurisdictions where it is still mandatory to undergo quite invasive surgeries for doctors to certify sex changes that an individual wishes to see formalized in documents. None of the chapters address the criminalization of sexual identity and national legislation prohibiting sexual mobility, though some chapters include accounts of how the issues of sexual and gender transitions were treated prior in their own jurisdictions and reveal quite stringent conditions for trans persons.

---

[4]See Bostock v. Clayton County, Georgia, -U.S-, Slip Opinion No. 17-1618. For a presentation of the legal treatment of trans persons in the United States, see for example, Schroth et al. (2018), pp. 91–126.

[5]Scherpe (2015).

[6]See https://ilga.org/trans-legal-mapping-report. Accessed 2 July 2020.

[7]Spade, *op.cit.*

[8]Scherpe, *op.cit.*

While there is a certain consensus about the advantages of the self-determination model over the other two, and of the soft medicalization model over the strong medicalization model, there is quite a bit of variation regarding the other guarantees, and no exact overlap as to the status model and how the system is perceived as a whole with regards to its ability to protect trans persons. For example, both Argentina and Colombia have embraced self-determination for sex markers in registration. But the amount of violence endured by trans persons in Colombia is much higher than in Argentina. Argentineans also have greater access to health services. The status model does not follow either the federal or centralist configuration of the countries studied, nor the importance of different authorities in furthering changes. Thus, even if the status model is quite relevant and seems to signal the political relevance of trans persons as minorities, it does not provide an understanding of the effects of legal reform or the contextual elements that might support or distract it.

In the following sections of this introductory chapter we: (1) present a review of the literature on the rights of trans persons; (2) explain the main features of each model for the registration of sex and names; (3) present the challenges and paradoxes faced by trans persons in accessing gender modification services; (4) address the reforms of antidiscrimination statutes to include sex identity as a source of discrimination, exclusion, and violence; and, (5) conclude by pointing to the importance of the subversions and displacements motivated by the recognition of trans rights in the realm of family law, and the questions they ignite as to the possibilities of feminist reform based on sex. Before moving ahead, a short note on terminology and authorship is provided, as this definitely has occupied a large part of the conversation about identity and distribution.

1 A Note on Terminology

Feminists have invested a lot of energy in the struggle over representation, the written word being one, but not the only, battlefield.[9] Normalizing the use of "gender" to refer to the characteristics which are socially assigned to individuals on the basis of their "sex" has probably been one of feminism's most important achievements. As noted by Joan Scott in her famous article "Gender as a useful category for historical analysis", "gender" was key to protect research units from accusations of bias. While this move could have had as a consequence the de-politicization of research, it also delegitimized arguments based on "nature" and prevented the construction of males and men as correlates of females and women.[10] In this fight, however, sex became stable, uncontested, and uninteresting as "nature", while gender was carefully scrutinized in its binary operation hoping to

[9]Jaramillo (2007), pp. 16–23. On the role of language in producing the world, I find MacKinnon's and Butler's work most appealing. MacKinnon (1993) and Butler (1990).

[10]Scott (1986), pp. 1053–1075.

and Law from the University of Hong Kong. The contributors in the book are twenty-six, and as the editors clarify, each country was selected because it either represented a region or a model of approaching legal recognition of gender identity. The book includes chapters concerning Italy, Spain, Japan, Hong Kong, Singapore, Australia, Norway, Austria, Brazil, Chile, Greece, Israel, Serbia, Czech Republic, Rumania, and Colombia. It lacks, just us in our case, chapters from any African jurisdiction. The questionnaire used to construct the chapters is similar in many ways to the one used here, but ours also included an emphasis on political actors and mobilization. The only contributor that participated in both projects is Professor Peter Dunne. In the very short introduction to the volume, the editor points out that the purpose of the study was to make visible the most recent developments away from medicalization and towards self-determination in sex, aiming at helping the law to develop without having to repeat mistakes already known. The book concludes with a set of recommendations for policymakers regarding the importance of adopting a self-determination model for sex mobility and providing access to health treatments for all trans persons.

The second study was led by the International Lesbian, Gay, Bisexual, Trans and Intersex Association (ILGA) and first published in 2016 by the organization itself, with a second version released in November 2017.[17] The *Trans Legal Mapping Report* was authored by Zhan Chiam, Sandra Duffy and Matilda Gil González and it "covers the legal situations" of 111 countries and 13 territories. The report contains basic country information about sex and name change through a schematic chart that summarizes for each country whether name and sex changes are possible or not, which norm regulates each issue, and what are the requirements. Information about judicial and administrative decisions is included when available. The 2017 report includes an introduction to international law and the Interamerican System and to the situation of each region in the world with regards to the topics. Interviews of certain activists on the law "in action" or "on the ground" are also to be found. The preface by Zhan Chiam points out that the compilation is intended to circulate information among activists interested in changing the law and therefore, and above all, is an advocacy tool. The preface also celebrates national "advancements" and makes some politically-charged assertions: (1) the document materialized the notion that all studies about trans persons should include them or consult them as experts; and (2) there is no north/south divide that is relevant, as trans persons in all countries endure barriers to legal recognition.

The articles found on different databases concerning the legal treatment of trans persons numbered fourteen published between 2005 and 2016, with more than half published after 2010. Only the three articles from 2005 that use the United States as one of their main, or only, case studies, engage with the problem of conceptualization and criticize the effects of identity in the law.[18] Lloyd and Ohle show how legal discourse produces trans persons as monsters or, alternatively, as sick in order to

[17] Available for free online at: www.ilga.org. Accessed 2 July 2020.

[18] Lloyd (2005), p. 150; Ohle (2005), pp. 237–280; Cowan (2005), pp. 67–96.

deny them basic rights. These authors stress the role of judicial decisions and judicial language in sustaining these images. For Cowan, the comparison between the United States, Canada and the United Kingdom serves to illuminate the usefulness of abandoning the gender/sex difference and the impact of reforms regarding the recognition of trans persons on women.

Most of the articles focused on the functional work that is dominant in the field of comparative law: they use their case studies either to ask others to emulate a good example or to criticize the perversity of the solution adopted. Five articles describe certain cases as examples to follow. In his study of the cases of the United States, Hong Kong and South Korea, Holning describes the decisions by the courts in Hong Kong and South Korea to show possible reasons to change the law on same sex marriage and sex change in the United States.[19] The article by Boyce and Coyle on the 2007 decision of the Supreme Court of Nepal that granted recognition to trans persons and demanded the introduction of a third sex in official documents, similarly, aims at providing activists in other countries with arguments to eventually change their laws in the way suggested by the ruling.[20] The articles by Jiang and Fynes are particularly geared at changing the law in Hong Kong and Ireland, respectively. Jiang uses the cases of Singapore, Japan and the United Kingdom to show the possibility of producing an argument to allow for a sex change for purposes of marriage in the law of Hong Kong.[21] Fynes uses the case of the United Kingdom to argue for change in Ireland. Nonetheless, much in the same vein as Scherpe's work, it recommends that Ireland learn from the mistakes of the United Kingdom and jumps ahead in the recognition of trans persons.[22] Finally, Mrsevic, in his 2016 revision of the legislation in 14 countries around the world, aspires to deliver evidence of the existence of a tendency to accept sex mobility without a diagnosis in order to inspire legal change.[23]

Five more articles reflect on cases which they see as positive but still limited versions of recognition of trans persons. Three of these articles concern the case of India and two the case of the European Union. The articles concerning the case of India stress the importance of pre-European notions of gender and specially the favorable legal and cultural treatment granted to hijras.[24] The most recent ones engage the Supreme Court ruling of 2014, which commanded the introduction of a third sex and the possibility of a sex change.[25] Both articles are interested in the fact that the same Court has refused to decriminalize same sex copulation, while

[19]Holning (2008), p. 67.

[20]Boyce and Coyle (2013), pp. 1–32. It is important to note that the authors do not embrace fully the reasoning used by the Court, as they believe that it relied too heavily on ideas of nature and the natural.

[21]Jiang (2013), pp. 31–73.

[22]Fynes (2014), pp. 31–58.

[23]Mršević (2016), pp. 115–132.

[24]Patel (2010), pp. 835–863.

[25]Swain (2016), pp. 1–6. Kodiyath, S.P. 2015. Deciphering the Dichotomy: Supreme Court of India's Contrasting Jurisprudence on Transgender Rights and Homosexuality. In *N.A.Palkhivala Academy for Advanced Legal Studies and Research.*

admitting the existence of a third sex. The remaining two articles explain the conceptual and historical road traversed in the European Union to recognize the harm in not allowing for a sex change, while at the same time being critical of the distance that has yet to be travelled.[26]

In conclusion, the last few years reveal a particular interest in understanding the legal recognition of trans persons and advocating for a model of self-determination. Comparative law, in these works, helps to reveal frequent mistakes, tendencies and models to follow. Political and theoretical debates are more often treated using individual case studies. In this sense, the present book synthetizes these two tendencies in the literature without being terribly innovative: it is both animated by a functional approach to comparisons and wishes to make some theoretical interventions. More importantly, this work includes chapters on cases mostly unknown to the English and French speaking public and details about the way in which administrative and political apparatuses work to limit possibilities of change. It also reveals gaps in our understanding of the regulatory failures, as neither normalization nor exceptionalization seem to significantly reduce the violence endured by trans persons.

3 Models to Deal with Sex Mobility

We have so far found that countries use two mechanisms to create sex: birth certificates, either produced by the civil registry office or by some other office for the control of population, and identification cards, driving licenses and passports being the most frequently used. Birth certificates have primacy over other documents, as the truth they are expected to contain is generally reproduced in other documents without any need of further proof. For this same reason, the first mechanisms have been harder to change and negotiate than driving licenses and passports, prioritizing the need for certainty in identification over granting rights on the basis of sex.

I propose here the existence of four models to deal with sex mobility.[27] We call the first model the model of "non recognition". The second model we refer to as a model of "strong medicalization" because it demands medical proof of *sex affirming surgery,* including procedures involving sterilization, to make any annotation with regards to change in sex.[28] The third model is a model of "soft medicalization" because it involves doctors in the process of authorizing and accounting changes in sex, but it leaves it to the medical community to decide the criteria it will use. The fourth model, including one-third of the countries covered here, is a model of "self-determination", where individuals are entitled to make the decision about the sex they wish to see reported to others. Each model is described below, including the

[26]Bell (2012), pp. 127–146; Theilen (2016).

[27]Scherpe also has four categories or stages that closely resembles the ones I use here. See Scherpe, *op.cit.*

[28]For a definition of Sex Affirming Surgery see: https://hr.cornell.edu/sites/default/files/trans%20terms.pdf. Accessed 2 July 2020.

justifications used to keep it in place or produce the change the model represents; the focus of legal strategies intending to change the model or that led to the adoption of the present model; and remarks on the operation of the model as available.

The issue of names is also taken up here, identifying three ways of approaching the relationship of names to sex. The first, adopted early on by Germany as a "solution" for the trans persons "problem", supposes that names are gendered and therefore a matter for sex mobility, but that there might be greater flexibility in the regime of names than in the regime of sex. About half the countries in this book adopted first a regime of name flexibilization and later a model of self- determination for sex mobility. The second way does not recognize a relationship between names and sex and therefore allows for name changes through custom or habit and only sets limits on changes for reasons of fraud or criminal intent. The third way deems the relationship between names and sex so strong that it only allows name changes after changes in sex.

Finally, this part reflects on the differences in regulation concerning children's ability to engage in sex mobility and treatment of intersexual conditions as demonstrated by the different national solutions presented in the chapters. As seen from the country chapters included here, the legislation of some countries recognizes that forcing public officials to classify an individual as male or female upon birth may create serious problems for many persons. Some of these countries allow public officials to leave the sex box blank, others allow for sex changes as early as 6 years of age. Most countries, however, neither allow for a third sex nor for sex changes before the age of sixteen.

4 Ground Zero: Non-recognition of Sex Mobility

According to the work of Schroth and others, only four states in the United States still have legislation that prevents individuals from changing the sex they were assigned at the moment of birth: Idaho, Kansas, Ohio and Tennessee.[29] In these states, as infamously used to be the case in England, birth certificates cannot be changed during an individual's life. In England, as Professor Dunne explains, this model was maintained through more than 30 years of litigation in domestic and European Courts. Indeed, as early as 1971, in the Corbett v. Corbett case, the Court decided that a trans woman could not marry a man, even though she had undergone complete sex reassignment surgery, because she could not be considered a woman for marriage. The Court explained that not even gender confirmation surgeries could change the "natural" sex a person is born with. This position was endorsed also in R v. Tan, 1983, where the Court found that a trans woman could be convicted as a pimp, even though this was a male-only crime in British legislation at that time. This position was sanctioned by the European Court of Human Rights in the Rees v. United Kingdom case, in which the Court acknowledged the possible violation

[29] Schroth et al. (2018), pp. 91–126.

of article 8 of the Convention, but found that the conduct of the United Kingdom fell within its margin of appreciation. The limits of this decision were clarified by the Court in its 1992 decision on B v. France, where it found that France violated article 8 of the Convention when refusing to register sex changes while allowing to make many other amendments in the birth certificate of its citizens and registered different sexes for the same person in different documents. Accordingly, the situation of the United Kingdom was exceptionalized as one in which that which was being protected was the accuracy of a document intended to establish circumstances at birth and not to register changes suffered by individuals through life. Not surprisingly, litigation on this topic concerning the United Kingdom is abundant, with more than four cases decided by the Court without any change in the doctrine of the margin of appreciation coloring the regulation of changes in birth certificates.

The difference the European Court of Human Rights was highlighting was a difference emphasized in early comparative law debates that built on the notions of legal families.[30] "Civil status" was a category introduced by the Napoleonic Code to account for individual characteristics that would have "weight" in assigning rights. The proof of civil status was assigned to the office of civil registry, and certificates emanating from the registry were deemed definitive proof. Civil registration, as conjured by the French, nonetheless, incorporated procedures to introduce changes when confronting a mistake or a new fact. Most notable among the new facts demanding changes in the registry were those relating to paternity and marriage. With regards to paternity, changes in the civil registry reflected both cases in which an individual ceased to be the father of someone else, or an individual became a father. These types of changes appear exclusively in the birth registry of the child. In relation to marriage, dissolution of a marriage by death, annulment or divorce, merits inscription in the marriage registry to signal the change from the married status to the status as single person. Changes deriving from "new facts" have been tied up to procedures as simple as a declaration before a notary public of the acknowledgement of an individual as one's own son or daughter, and as complicated as a contentious judicial procedure in which the truth of paternity or marital fault are determined. As noted by those authors in civil law systems, civil registration around the world still follows these basic intuitions.

This civil law approach to the issue of civil status is foreign to those jurisdictions were control of birth information lies with municipal or fiscal authorities and birth certificates are considered only to describe a fact occurring in one moment in time: the birth of a child. From what those authors explain, these systems do not foresee the possibility of facts relating to birth changing, and therefore, have been slow to develop answers to requests in this regard. The most notable case of "conceptual" freeze, as stated above, was the United Kingdom. The UK repeatedly argued that birth certificates in so far as they are only declarative of a fact that could not change, "birth", could not be amended to facilitate the exercise of rights by individuals who had in effect had changed since the moment of birth in relation to one of the

[30]See David and Brierley (1968).

characteristics relevant to the exercise of rights. Denmark, Norway and Sweden, on their part, were presented as having population registrations by fiscal authorities and marking sex in the social security number of individuals. This latter system has proven to be the easiest to change, probably because of its little conceptual baggage: Sweden introduced a law to deal with sex changes as early as 1972, and Norway was recently recognized as the "second best" in protecting the rights of trans persons.

5 Gender Affirmation Surgeries As a Requirement for Changes in Birth Certificates

Ten of the chapters below describe their countries as currently requiring "sex reassignment" surgery as a requisite to obtaining changes in the sex reported in the birth certificate of an individual: Brazil, Chile,[31] Croatia, Czech Republic, Rumania, Serbia, Poland, Taiwan, Turkey and some states in the United States (including the state of Alabama).[32] In all of these countries, sex needs to be registered at birth and this fact may only change if the individual successfully completes sex reassignment surgery, which is the last step in a long path that individuals may take to go from one sex to the other. This way includes different stages of hormonal therapy, openly living as the other "sex" for a period of time, and finally undergoing castration or mastectomy, and reconstruction of sex organs associated to the new sex. During the stage in which the individual lives as the other "sex", he or she may use an assortment of treatments to appear more clearly as "other": definitive depilation of face, legs and arms, voice training, hair implants, prosthetic implants, among others. Though not all stages are mandatory to obtain the sex reassignment surgery, it is crucial to note the amount of "work" that is demanded legally from the individual before allowing annotation of any change.

It is also important to highlight variations existing among these countries with regards to access to sex reassignment surgeries and the indeterminacy attributed to the rule. Thus, in Poland and Rumania, surgeries required to prove sex changes need to be authorized by a judge as they are considered to affect a "personal good" protected by the Constitution. In Poland, the requirement was introduced through a decision by the Supreme Court in 1991. In Rumania, the author explains that the requirement was introduced in a 1996 law that in 2008 was declared constitutional by the Constitutional Court. In Rumania to obtain a change of sex, individuals must first approach an authorized doctor, then must initiate a judicial procedure in order to receive sex reassignment surgery, then need to start a judicial procedure to get a

[31]As explained by Fabiola Lathrop in her chapter here, Chile recently adopted a law that introduced the self-determination model.

[32]Schroth et al. (2018), pp. 91–126.

change in the birth certificate after the surgery has been completed, finally they need to ask for a change in name and ID number.

The authors covering Brazil and Chile, on their part, explain that judges occasionally interpret that changes in sex do not demand gender affirmation surgery. Professor Lathrop from Chile, for example, points out to the importance of strategic litigation led by Professor Lorena Lorca in changing precedent in 24 cases. Lathrop notes that although the requirement is included in Law 4808, the Chilean Constitutional Court interpreted gender identity to be protected implicitly by the Chilean Constitution and explicitly by international law binding on the Chilean State (Judgement 834 by the Chilean Constitutional Court). In Brazil, both changing name and sex in the registry demand a judicial decision, according to Professor Mattos. Judges, in turn, have understood that the only appropriate evidence for them to acknowledge and authorize a name change and sex is evidence of the realization of a sex reassignment surgery. Mattos also explains, however, that some judges have allowed name and sex changes without verifying sex reassignment surgeries. To the contrary, in the case of Turkey, judges over interpret the Turkish Civil Code to mean that the only way to prove there is a just ground for name change, which precedes a sex change, is proving having undergone sex reassignment surgery. Though it is not an explicit requirement for a name change, regulated in 2002, the authors note that judges hardly accept any other evidence to prove that there is a just ground for a name change. The authors also note that notwithstanding the existence of a 2015 case by the European Court finding that the sterilization requirement is in violation of article 8 in the Convention, the *Cour de Cassation* upheld the sterilization requirement in a decision subsequent to the one adopted by the European Court.

In Croatia and the Czech Republic, sex reassignment surgery was introduced as a requirement for a sex change through legislation in 2013 and 2008, respectively. In the case of Croatia, the law demands a certificate from an authorized doctor. The author notes that there are very few of these doctors, and that there are no specialists or clinics that perform these surgeries in the country, making access to sex changes very difficult. The Taiwanese 2008 Directive governing the matter of a sex change is probably the one that most clearly determines the requirement: for cases of male to female transitions, the applicant must prove they have had both penis and testicles removed; for cases of female to male transition, the applicant must prove the removal of breasts and the uterus.

The case of Serbia is interesting because there is no law or regulation explicitly governing changes of sex. The author notes that in Belgrade and Novi, municipal authorities treat a sex change as a correction in the individual's birth certificate if sex reassignment surgery has been completed. The Constitutional Court supported this interpretation in 2012, though it also stated the importance of having a specific law regulating this matter. Professor Jancic explains that the two attempts to legislate on this topic were unsuccessful (2012, 2013).

6 Power to Doctors: The Soft Medicalization Model

Five countries were noted as allowing for a sex change without having to prove the completion of sex reassignment surgery but still requiring a statement by a medical doctor concerning the “condition” of the individual: New Zealand (1995), England (2004), Germany (2011), Austria (2013), Israel (2014), the Netherlands (2014), and Belgium (2017). Again, there are relevant variations amongst these countries: while England requires individuals to prove that they have a gender dysphoria diagnosis, have had at least 2 years of “real life experience” and have the consent of their spouse (2004 Gender Recognition Act), Belgium only brings in a psychiatrist to attest to the time the individual has been struggling with his/her transition when he/she is a minor. In Germany, Austria, Israel and the Netherlands, doctors are in charge of certifying significant changes in sex and prevented from restricting this diagnosis to cases in which sex reassignment surgery has been completed.

Authors of the chapters for Austria and Israel, nonetheless, express their concern that doctors make it very difficult for individuals to obtain certifications of sex changes. Professor Bea Verschraegen, from Austria, explains that according to the 2013 law on this topic, a change in the sex initially registered demands evidence of medical changes adopted by the individual and an expert opinion that the person’s sex will not change again. Though the law requires public officials to keep anonymized statistics on sex changes, Verschraegen has not been successful in locating them, and estimates that not more than ten changes have occurred per year after the enactment of the law. She mentions that there is a perceived lack of consensus among the medical community regarding sex changes. The authors for Israel note that although the 2014 directive by the Ministry of the Interior regarding a sex change establishes that a sex change does not need certification of sex reassignment, the Surgery Committee in charge of giving the required certification is very “conservative and pathologizing” and usually demands more than 2 years of real life experience. The attempt by the Ministry of Health to authorize any medical doctor to certify relevant sex changes for purposes of changes in the registry has been blocked by officials arguing that this was a misunderstanding of the High Court’s ruling in the 2014 case that led the Ministry of Interior to issue the directive regarding a sex change.

The chapter on The Netherlands is careful in explaining the costs associated with a sex changes, mainly derived from the need to submit an expert report to have sex changed in the civil registry. These costs are not covered by the health system or private insurance and span from 60 to 300 euros, and only a few doctors are authorized as experts. Interestingly, though, these are some of the “lightest” reports as they need only certify that the person is convinced and that he/she understands the consequences of the procedure.

7 Self-determination As a Legitimate Source of Sex

Eight of the countries covered in this volume allow for self-determination in establishing sex in the civil registry or population logs: Argentina (2012), Sweden (2013), Denmark (2014), Colombia and Ireland (2015), Norway (2016), Belgium and Greece (2017). The state of Oregon in the United States and Ontario and Alberta in Canada also allow for self-determination. In most cases, reform was introduced by a legislative body. The exceptions are Colombia and Canada, where judges have led the way by introducing rules regarding a sex change and precedent still is the main source of law.

There are also important variations as to the level of protection the model offers to trans persons. Argentina, while being the first legislation to endorse self-determination in sex, or auto identification, still has the legislation most concerned with facilitating self-determination of trans persons and protecting them from police brutality and persecution. Law 26743 of 2012, indeed, establishes a right to gender identity, the duty of registration officials of marking the sex indicated by the person without questions about convictions or proof of such convictions, and the right to obtain treatment to modify gender characteristics. Law 26791 of 2012 establishes the maximum penalty—life imprisonment—for individuals found guilty of killing a person because of her gender identity. Professor Saldivia, the author for Argentina, explains that these views about gender identity and the importance of protecting trans persons from aggression are related to the campaigns against police brutality that followed the transition to democracy in the early 1980's, the relevance of "true" identity in the memory campaigns led by the Plaza de Mayo grandmothers, and advocacy for a depathologization of mental health patients in general.

In every other country, some requirement in addition to free will remains in place. In Sweden and Greece, individuals wishing to change their sex have to show that they are unmarried. In Greece this requirement is related to the non-recognition of same sex marriages. Change of sex produced in this way, nonetheless, is only acknowledged by administrative authorities. Only judicial decisions certifying sex changes are considered binding on all authorities. In Denmark, there is a waiting period of 6 months and a duty to appear in person before the public official twice. This is also the case in Belgium. The 2017 law on gender identity determined that to change sex in official documents, individuals should appear twice before competent authorities, wait 3–6 months, and prove being fully informed about the consequences of the procedure. The Public Prosecutor's office also needs to be notified in case it wishes to raise an objection. In Belgium individuals may request the sex change to be reverted to avoid transphobia or because they felt happier before the change. In Norway, individuals need to contact the Directorate of Taxes for pertinent information, and send back a signed slip confirming they have received proper information. The procedure is only available for Norwegian citizens. In Ireland, similarly, individuals need to declare that they are acting out of their own free will and know the consequences of their decision. In Colombia, individuals need to approach a public notary and have a public deed produced for the registrar to make the change.

8 Name Changes: Not Always a Small Solution

The expression "small solution" in the context of trans persons was introduced in the German doctrinal debate referring to the possibility of introducing flexibility in the regime of naming to allow trans persons to use their identified sex rather than their legal sex in social contexts. As in many of the countries included here, German law restricts naming practices to accomplish two objectives: to reflect the person's sex and to prevent humiliation and ridicule in the case of children. In 1980, a law regarding the change of names and declaration of affiliation to a sex was introduced to allow trans persons to build a social identity somehow separated from their legal identity. The law uses the expression "transsexual imprint" to refer to the cases it addresses and allows individuals to petition district courts to obtain a change in their name to reflect their sex affiliation. For this change to be ordered, the individual needs to present opinions about their case by two experts in transsexualism. Professor Sanders explains that until 1993, individuals had to be more than 25 years old to request a change of name, and until 1996, individuals could be referred to by their legal sex rather than their identified sex. Doctrine strongly advocated that change of sex demanded full sex reassignment. Only since 2011, through a decision of the German Constitutional Court, requirements for a sex change became the same established in the 1980 law for name change.

Belgium, as Germany, adopted this solution for trans persons quite early on already in 1987. Following this law, individuals who felt they wanted to change their forename because their sex did not match the sex in the birth certificate, had to submit a declaration of honor with their request and have declarations from medical experts regarding the individual's experience of sex mobility. Nowadays, though, trans persons who have had their sex changed in the certificate have a right to change their forenames at a reduced rate of 49 euros. As professors Gallus and Verschelden note, other persons interested in changing their forenames can do so if allowed by the Federal Public Service and need to pay 490 euros.

In Colombia, individuals may change their name for free and at will since 1988 without having to state any reason or give justification. Although there are no restrictions in the law regarding the name that an individual may choose, in 1993 the Constitutional Court decided a case in which a public official had denied a request of name change because the individual was choosing a female name while being identified as a man in the birth certificate. In decision T-594 of 1993, the Court affirmed that names were deeply connected to the right to an identity and therefore public officials could not place any restrictions on an individual's choice of name when requesting a name change. This rule covered not only trans persons but also persons wishing to adopt ridiculous or humiliating names. In decision T-168 of 2005, the Court asserted the right of an individual to bear the name of his preferred soccer team over the public official concern as to trademarks and authenticity in the desire to be called in such a ridiculous way. In 2008, the Court explained that individuals that had changed their name once, could change it a second time if the aim was to have their name correspond to their sexual identity. In its most recent decision on the law of name changes, C-114 of 2017, the Court clarified the general right of individuals to change their name more than once but the duty, according to the Civil Procedure Code, of obtaining judicial authorization for the change. One reason for a second name change, as the Court consistently recognized since 2008, could be a change in sex, but the Court recognized in this decision that there could be other circumstances justifying the name change that could be pondered by judges and lead to exceptional authorizations.

In Denmark, a name change was also made accessible to trans persons before adopting a model of self-determination for sex mobility. According to the Act on Names, individual names have to belong to a list of approved names for each sex. Nonetheless, since 2005, the Ministry of the Interior allows changes for people who have been declared "transsexuals" by the Sexology Clinic in Stockholm. After 2009, a report by the Sexology Clinic was deemed unnecessary for a name change. In Sweden, similarly, change of name has been possible in order to reflect an individual's choice of sex since 2009. For this country, however, the change in the very strict regulation of names was introduced by a decision by the Supreme Administrative Court that determined that choice of name could not be restricted by public officials.

England had a flexibility in naming practices that somehow did not bear a relation to the rigidity of the legal system with regards to sex changes in official documents. As covered by Professor Dunne, no formalities are needed to use different names in different life situations: "Under the English Common Law, persons have the right to change their name without undertaking formal legal procedure (provided there is no fraudulent or criminal intent)". But to have a name change acknowledged by government officials a deed poll needs to be executed. These deed polls require either a declaration signed by two witnesses that attest to the fact that the individual is known by the new name rather than by the "official" one; or a request by an organization with which an individual is interacting. Having executed a name change is considered evidence of the real-life experience demanded to obtain a gender recognition certificate after 2004. The USA, according to those authors, has a similar system for name change: individuals may request a change of name by state level courts and in general all they need to do is appear in court. In this case, nonetheless, the authors identify higher risks for trans persons given the power judges have in the common law to impede a name change to "prevent fraud". They also explain that certain states do not allow people in prison or on parole to change names and this significantly affects trans persons who have much higher probabilities of being in these situations.

The same flexibility in naming is attributed to Israel by the authors of that chapter. They state that individuals may freely request changes in their names every 7 years. The term limits may be set aside where special circumstances arise. Israel, on the other hand, retains a soft medicalization model with little access to sex mobility as pointed out above. Taiwan is another example where names can easily be changed. Professor Yi-Chien Chen explains that people change names for a variety of reasons in Taiwan, including following recommendations from fortune tellers regarding bad luck.

The idea that names can be expressive of individual choices is completely absent in some countries where names are so strictly tied to gender and strongly regulated by the state that individuals may only change their names after undergoing a sex change and then only after completing sex reassignment surgery. This is true for Poland, Rumania, Serbia, Turkey and the Czech Republic. In all of these countries, changes in name require a judicial or administrative authorization after corroboration of a "justifiable reason". Those authors point out that judges and other public officials routinely interpret that the only justifiable reason for a man to use a woman's name and vice versa is to have changed her sex. In these countries, a change of sex is only authorized after sex reassignment surgery and this surgery needs judicial authorization. In Brazil and Chile, most judges also interpret that changes in name can only follow a change in sex. In Brazil, a name change to reflect sexual identity was only recently authorized in 2017. As pointed out above, in general these countries also demand sex reassignment surgery before allowing a sex change but judges may decide otherwise, and have done so. Norway is the only country that ties change of sex to change of name and has adopted the self-determination model for sexual identification. In this country, individuals may change their name every 10 years and individuals choosing sex mobility may choose gender neutral names before definitively changing to a name from the other sex.

9 Family Law Effects

Sex plays a crucial role in the regulation of marriage and parenting in most countries. With regards to marriage, the initially question was whether an individual who had undergone gender reassignment surgery could marry according to her new sex. This was the issue in Goodwin v. United Kingdom that in 2002 led the European Court of Human Rights to require England to allow legal recognition of changes of sex in birth certificates. As sex changes started to be legally recognized, the question of the dissolution of marriage by a sex change became crucial, with most jurisdictions establishing an *ipso facto* dissolution of any marriage involving a person who had undergone gender reassignment surgery. As same sex marriage became sanctioned in most jurisdictions represented here, rules demanding the celibacy of trans persons, establishing the dissolution of their marriages or converting their marriages into civil partnerships, were explicitly or implicitly repealed. Only Poland, Greece and Turkey still demand celibacy for a sex change among the countries included here. In England, individuals who are married need to show they have spousal consent to have their gender recognition certificate issued.

Most jurisdictions represented here, on the other hand, determine that sex changes do not affect the birth certificates of any children of trans persons. This rule is criticized for not representing the "truth" of the situation and potentially leading to confusion, especially as erasing traces of sex and name changes becomes a standard way of protecting trans persons from transphobia. There is consensus, nonetheless, that once the parenting relationship is established, changing the name or sex cannot affect the legal bond between the parent and child. Much more difficult to tackle has been those situations of trans men who give birth. The chapter on Israel explains that in one case, sex was legally changed five times to accommodate the fact that according to Israeli law, only women could be mothers and children could not be registered as motherless. Several chapters explain that as sex changes without sterilization become normal, the need to address parenting rules will become more urgent. In the case of a woman who gives birth while married to a trans woman, the co-maternity arrangement adopted by Norway and a few other countries for the case of same sex couples seems to work well enough. Still, it reveals the extent to which legal solutions for lesbians and gays may not be enough for trans persons: "nature" is put to the test in quite different ways.

10 Non-binary Sex Reporting: Dealing with Early Sex Ambiguity and Mobility

As seen above, the experiences of others than trans persons have also reached courts and legislatures. Individuals born with sexual ambiguity and experiences of sex mobility at very early ages have also influenced the regulation of sex. A few countries included here have regulations for such situations. In Argentina, Law 26743 of 2012 establishes that minors may request a sex change with parental support and following rules of progressive autonomy introduced by the Convention on the Rights of the Child. In effect, a famous Argentinean case involved a 6-year-old that was allowed to change her sex. The Norwegian reform of 2016 also allows changing the sex of individuals from zero to 6 years of age. For this age range, however, it demands proving a medical condition. For individuals between 6 and 16 years of age, a sex change is allowed with parental consent and guidance.

The considerations concerning sex interventions at early ages were carefully discussed by the Colombian Constitutional Court in 1999 (decision SU 337 of 1999). The Court confronted the case of a 7-year-old whose mother, under the advice of a medical team, considered it beneficial to subject her to a medical intervention to establish her sex more clearly. The medical team had denied the child surgery based on a 1995 decision (decision T-495 of 1995) by this same Court that argued that surgical interventions on intersexual persons should not be performed until the individual reached the point of being able to give consent. The 1999 Court, in a plenary decision, determined that sex assignment surgeries are not urgent but are indeed very invasive and therefore require the consent of the individual affected, parental consent being important as support and guidance but not enough to proceed with a surgery. The Court took into consideration multiple studies and testimonies to the effect that hormonal and surgical interventions at an early age seem to work more to satisfy societal demands of sexual determination than to help individuals live happier lives. The Court carefully considered the pain and suffering reported by individuals forced to submit to many medical interventions over their first years of age who later on found either that the medical team made a mistake when assigning the sex and working to confirm it, or that in adolescence new facts arose that made initial decisions seem less adequate. Though the Court found that it could not force intersexual persons to lead societal change about sex, it also found that it could force registrars to accept leaving the sex box blank.

The Colombian solution is similar to the one adopted by the 2017 directive of the Ministry of Health in Israel, which establishes that surgeries should always be consented to by the individuals affected unless there is proof of risk to life. Sweden introduced in 2013 a restriction on medical interventions for trans persons at 12 years of age. The only other chapter mentioning this issue was the one on England. Professor Dunne explains that the Committee on the Rights of the Child has advised England to introduce regulations concerning surgeries on intersex babies. The author covering Chile found at least one case in which a 5-year-old was allowed to change her name and sex in legal documents (it is not clear that she was an intersexual person). Most chapters corroborate that the age for engaging a sex change, especially if surgery is involved, is 18 years. Some countries allow 15 years-old to start the process, with additional requirements. Interestingly, however, there is no mention of the practice regarding intersex babies. Most countries do force registrars, and doctors, to choose M or F when issuing birth certificates. Only Germany, Austria, the province of Ontario, and the Netherlands, besides Colombia, are seen as allowing for a blank, an x, or stating that sex is indeterminate in the birth certificate. Denmark allows for an x in passports.

The debate before the Colombian Constitutional Court illustrates the rift between individuals who feel that sex determination is integral to living good lives, and therefore support a sexual binary and emphasize sex mobility, and individuals who believe that sex is/should be ambiguous, and therefore should not matter for society or for legislation. As we will show in the conclusions, most countries allowing for a sex change have not transformed sexually-segregated facilities and educational spaces, sexually-segregated armies, differences in social security regulations, special protections for women, among other relevant consequences of sex. This approach supports the first position; sex should matter but individuals should be able to choose according to their inner experience of how sex matters. The second position is closer to a feminist understanding of how the world should change.

11 Conclusions: The Ideal Model for Sex Mobility

The author writing on Argentina, Professor Saldivia, correctly notes that in these times of biometric identification, the emphasis on security as the value safeguarded by rules on sex identification seems misplaced. Argentinian legislation allowing for choice of sex in birth certificates and other official documents, the model we have called here of self-determination, appears to adequately protect the right of individuals to decide on their belonging to one sex or the other without recourse to doctors, psychiatrists or other experts. This model also diminishes possibilities of humiliation and offense by public officials. It alleviates making decisions about bodily shape and function without proper information, or just to comply with expectations about sex. that constitute heavy burdens on those individuals who certainly are not adequately classified but who are not certain as to the need to proceed by doing dangerous and costly things to "fit in".

The question of intersexual persons becomes most relevant in the context of accepting that legal sex need not correspond to any "biological" reality. As a matter of fact, as pointed out by several authors, the impulse of "biological" conformity normalized sexual reassignment surgeries for intersexual babies and toddlers in countries were adults were prevented from requesting these procedures and not allowed to act as having a sex different from the one they were initially registered with. Detaching sex from "biology" then should also help in reducing the sense of urgency with which the "problem" of intersexuality has been handled up until now. Stressing self-determination could also lead, as established by the Colombian Constitutional Court, to an understanding of the importance of waiting for individuals to have enough discernment to make decisions regarding their own bodies. The need to create a third box for sex or allow sex to be marked as unknown becomes irrelevant or most important, depending on the position one subscribes to concerning the relevance of sex for social life. Indeed, if sex is a matter of choice and self-determination, intersexual persons should feel at ease in deciding for one or the other knowing that they may later change it if their choice does not correspond to their actual experience. This would agree with the idea that self-determination in sex leads to the deconstruction of sex. For those who believe that the self-determination model is proper not because it makes sex irrelevant but because it alleviates bureaucratic burdens for trans persons, then a third sex becomes important to allow intersexual persons to be correctly represented by legal categories. Interestingly enough, countries that currently have regulations concerning a third sex or allow the sex box to not be marked, also have self-determination models for sex.

12 Gender Modification Interventions and Sex Mobility

An important element in the development of the “issue” of trans persons is the technological progress in bodily interventions and the growth of a cosmetic industry that not only embellishes but also modifies bodily shape and function, mostly feeding on women’s anxiety over their appearance and recently also catering to men. In this context, the inner experience of “belonging to another sex” or “being trapped in the wrong body” can be translated into practices of body modification with high costs and, still, associated with high risks. The relevant question becomes then who should bear the costs of these practices of modification. The answer provided by most authors is that national health systems consider gender reassignment surgeries to be included in the mandatory health package. Most authors, nonetheless, point to harsh realities even in this scheme and suggest that health systems should also cover other gender modification costs. Three reasons are implicitly articulated to justify these claims. First, there is the importance of the binary understanding of sex for acceptance into society and the corresponding pain and suffering for not looking the same. Second, there is the poverty endured by most trans persons as a consequence of their difficulties in fitting in. Third, there is the concern that if individuals are not provided with these treatments they may look for the cheapest possibilities available, not always bearing in mind the risks to their health and even their lives.

The Danish chapter nonetheless highlights the contradictions that may derive from adopting a self-determination model for sex and pushing for greater coverage in the health system: once the gender dysphoria diagnostic is abandoned, what would be the justification for massive investments in the individual choices of some individuals? The Danish solution was to leave a diagnostic related to sex mobility in the medial protocols, in the understanding, however, that this is not really a medical condition but rather a life choice. Health systems with greater financial pressures might not be as flexible in this manner. Self-determination models may in fact drive societies to understand choices related to sex mobility as individual choices that should be funded by individuals. This, of course, means not taking any responsibility as a society for the desire to look the same that is at the root of the desperate search for interventions in body shape and function. We need to work on a notion of reparations to work out a scheme that would help complete the transition from strong medicalization models to self-determination models in sex. The limitations identified by our authors in the access of trans persons to gender modification interventions follow. Overcoming these limitations is partially connected to the transformation of the regulations on sex mobility, but other factors also influence access enough to warrant their independent consideration.

13 Surgery As Defilement: The Need for Judicial Authorization

Judicial authorization, as the most significant barrier to access gender modification services from health providers is reported to exist in Turkey, Poland and Rumania. Individuals interested in surgeries that could affect their reproductive functions in these countries need judicial authorization. This requirement derives from the idea that individuals may not dispose over their bodies freely, and therefore only in extenuating circumstances can they proceed with their intentions.

14 Lack of Doctors Trained to Provide Gender Modification Services

In nine countries those authors state that there are no doctors trained to provide gender modification services or that there are too few to meet the number of patients requesting such services. The Austria chapter, for example, notes that although gender reassignment surgeries have been authorized since 1995 –through a decision by the Supreme Court, there are some surgeries that cannot be performed in the country as there are no doctors trained for this (phallus reconstruction is explicitly mentioned as a surgery that cannot take place in Austria). In Croatia there are no doctors that can perform any surgery related to gender. In the cases of Brazil, Denmark and Israel, existing legislation establishes that only authorized providers can offer these services and there are too few providers. In Brazil, there are only five clinics and they are located in the main cities; in Denmark treatment is only authorized at the Sexological Institute in Stockholm, and in Israel only one hospital has the surgery committee needed to authorize procedures although the protocol has existed since 1986. The chapters on Belgium, Ireland, Rumania and the United States also note the scarcity of doctors and specialist teams.

15 Insufficient Insurance Coverage and Lack of Transparency As to Reimbursement

Only two chapters clearly state that gender reassignment surgeries are not covered by their health services: Chile and Poland. In every other jurisdiction included here, gender reassignment surgeries are covered by the mandatory health plan as long as there is a diagnosis. In most cases, the diagnosis is that of "gender dysphoria". In Denmark and Norway, a diagnosis is necessary but it is understood that it is not an illness or mental disorder. In many countries, access to gender modification services is recent, dating from 2012 or 2013, when the most relevant change regarding the recognition of sex mobility was introduced in their legislation. But in countries like

Sweden and Israel, health services have been accessible on paper for much longer: 1972 and 1986, respectively.

Then again, only in Norway and Sweden is it clear that all gender modification interventions deemed necessary are covered by the health system. In Canada, coverage is dominated by the aesthetic/medical binary and therefore only those interventions needed to safeguard the individual's health are included. In Israel it is precisely the need to negotiate across this difference that makes it so difficult for trans persons to access health services in their country. In the United States, interestingly, the mandatory health package for the poorest population—Medicaid and Medicare—includes gender modification interventions, but most doctors in the country and specially those trained, refuse to work for those insurers, turning the guarantee nugatory. In the United States, individuals in prison may access treatment since 2011 as long as they prove having started their life process before entering prison. Since 2016 treatment is also covered for members of the military.

16 Influences Driving Pathologization and Transphobia

Although many chapters suggest that the fact that the health system in a given country does not provide gender modification services is directly connected to recognition of the rights of trans persons under the self-determination model, the case of Serbia is illustrative of the possibility of a strong medical practice that develops privately. Similarly, the chapter on Israel explains that with the 1986 protocol a private practice has developed beyond the publicly funded health system. Austria would provide an example of exactly the opposite path: there are no doctors even if regulation in place since 1995 guarantees coverage. Professor Mattos, for the case of Brazil, points out to the "transphobia" that prevails in the Brazilian health system and that has been documented as a barrier in accessing services that are included in health plans since 2008.The point here is that transphobia is not only connected to the regulation of the civil status of trans persons: it is neither the sole cause of transphobia nor the only step that needs to be taken to transform the current state of things.

The chapters on Poland and Israel reveal how the empowerment of conservative religious authorities may be connected to unleashing a new version of "nature" as an argument against self- determination in sex. Indeed, if the pathologization paradigm-centered science in describing nature, a view of nature in which deviations are represented as diseases, transphobia represents a return to moral disgust and exegesis as reasons to reject certain expressions of the self. In the Christian world, these reasons have organized under the banner of a rejection of "gender ideology", where gender ideology is exposed as holding the notion that sex is not "natural" but rather socially and culturally constructed.[33] Now the natural is not the result of scientific studies but driven by images of God and interpreted by theology.

17 Civil and Penal Anti-discrimination Protections

Concern over transphobia has animated both the introduction of criminal offenses and anti-discrimination regulations to protect trans persons. Three countries have moved in the direction of the criminalization of hate crimes based on gender identity: Argentina, Turkey and Greece. Argentina introduced in 2012 a reform in the criminal code to punish with a life sentence the act of killing someone for her gender identity; Greece introduced in 2013 and 2014 laws punishing discrimination and aggression based on gender identity among other things. In Turkey the Constitutional Court established in 2014 that calling LGBTI persons "perverts" should be considered hate speech for all legal purposes.

Roughly one-third of those countries included here have rules on employment discrimination, prison segregation and use of public facilities, which explicitly incorporate the expressions "gender identity" or "gender expression". In the United States this protection came as early as 1989, when the Supreme Court argued in *Pricewater House v. Hopkins* that gender stereotyping could be understood as a form of discrimination based on sex for the application of title VII. In most countries that have introduced protections for gender identity as a category distinct from sexual orientation, regulation has been introduced much later. Croatia uses the "gender diversity" category in its 2003 and 2008 antidiscrimination regulation and Belgium in 2007 established that discrimination would not be allowed in cases of gender reassignment. In Israel it was not until 2015 that the Supreme Court found that discrimination based on gender identity was forbidden (*Center for Technological Education v. Meshek*), while in Norway the category was introduced in 2017 along with the self-determination model.

Regarding public facilities, our authors express little enthusiasm as to the advances and point to rules that enforce segregation and therefore support violence against individuals who do not seem to fit in the categories. The most pressing issue has been prison segregation for the violence, mostly sexual violence, endured by trans persons. In Canada, Colombia and Israel rules allow for imprisonment in the facilities of the identified or social sex, rather than the legal sex. But both in the cases of Israel and Colombia, the regulation concerning prisons do not seem to work as well on the ground.

---

[33]I found Duncan Dormor's mapping of Christian responses to the issues raised by trans persons very useful. See his chapter in Scherpe, *op.cit:* Dormor, David. Transgenderism and the Christian Church, pp. 28–68. An authoritative position on the Vatican's understanding of the stakes and actors in the confrontation may be found in the Doctrine for the Congregation of the Faith's Letter to Bishops on the Collaboration of Men and Women in the Church and in the World (2004) available at www.catholicnewsagency.com. Accessed 2 July 2020.

Other uses of public facilities have been contested but there seems to be little consensus as to the "solutions". In Denmark and Norway, for example, trans women who have not undergone gender reassignment surgery cannot use public swimming pools, dressing rooms or Spas destined for women only. In England, trans persons in general are prevented from participating professionally in sports.

Every jurisdiction included here acknowledged that sex remained a crucial element in the organization of social life beyond marriage and parenting. The chapters on Turkey and Ireland pointed out to specific ways by which these rules breed transphobia. In the case of Turkey, the legally enforced dress code for public officials is presented as a cause for exclusion of trans persons from public service, while the fact that they are considered mentally unfit to serve in the military excludes them from private service. In Ireland, according to professor Dunne, the consecration of motherhood as a public service in the Constitution translates into a felt need to segregate individuals throughout their lives, making it very difficult for trans persons to operate in this environment. Every other chapter points to the existence of rules that treat men and women differently for social security purposes, for accommodation of motherhood in labor law, and for military drafting.

18 Conclusions

The main purpose of this introductory chapter is to map the legal responses to the issue of the legal recognition of trans persons as developed in the following chapters. Consistent with the existing literature, we find that the law can be as extreme as to rejecting the possibility of changes in sex markers, or as generous as to recognizing that individuals themselves should be able to decide with which sex they identify. Countries in the latter category, though, do not feel that they have reached an ideal regulatory solution yet. Our authors voice concerns over appropriate protocols for health care, exposure to discrimination and violence, which persist even in the face of legislation recognizing self-determination. The need for independent efforts oriented to "fixing" these other systems is palpable: health regulations, criminal sanctions and employment protections proliferate in the search for "solutions" to the marginalization and impoverishment of trans persons. Thus a particular tension is revealed as to the role of law in the production of identity: if the law is indeed so powerful in creating sex, why is undoing law not sufficient for undoing sex? Moreover, if stigma is the result of the law's fixation on the "natural", how come doing away with it is not sufficient for reversing stigma? Part of the answer may lie with the modes as to the dissemination of models of regulation. Some studies have shown that instead of reaching ideological alignment or public opinion support, reforms may be the result of activist bureaucracies, legislators or judges interested in complying with standards fixed by external authorities.[34] For countries that are part of the European Union, the European Court of Human Rights has played a crucial role in compelling changes. The cases of Argentina and Colombia, however, cannot aptly be explained by theories of dissemination. The political work in these countries seems to be done by the notions of transition and the weight they give to identity, true and bodily integrity. These cases could, probably should, be compared to those of Nepal, India and South Korea to check the transition hypothesis and understand its full impact. In particular, these cases could be useful to understanding the power of anti-rights groups in shaping public opinion even against clear legal mandates.

The chapters included here also reveal the urgency of re-examining family law beyond accommodations linked to a gay and lesbian agenda. Indeed, after authorization for marriage and the elimination of celibacy requirements for sex mobility, the issue of parenting has become pressing for trans persons. Three clashing concerns have been expressed by authors: (1) every individual's right to know her true identity, including her provenance; (2) the need for security in identifying the parents of an individual to demand compliance with their duties; (3) trans persons need to be secure in their new identities and avoid stigma and persecution. While the first two concerns are reasons to keep "original" names and sex markers in the birth certificates of children born to trans persons, the third pushes for amending those certificates and introducing information corresponding to the new situation. Beyond the issue of how to keep the record, however, is the question of which facts are relevant to establish parental relations. Currently, legislation assumes that individuals marked as women will contribute with their ovaries and uterus to reproduction, while individuals marked as men will contribute with their sperm. We now know that this is not the only possibility. Our laws need to adjust to this knowledge.

Finally, the scholarship contained here suggests that the trans and inter "issues" could be read as interrogating more broadly the role of sex in our current legal and cultural systems, both as justification for affirmative measures for the advancement of women, and for segregation of men and women. Feminists have been struggling for some time with the challenges posed by this question. It is unreasonable though, in light of what we know now about how sex works to produce pain and suffering, to insist on following the same strategy pursued up to today: some affirmative action plus some segregation. An extension of the notion of parity to every sphere of life should be a plausible model.[35] But the search for alternatives has just begun.

Acknowledgements The author wishes to thank Emilio Lehoucq, Guillermo Estupiñán and Joshua Daza for their extraordinary research assistance. The Law School and Office of the Research Provost at Universidad de los Andes provided the funding necessary to complete this project. The International Academy of Comparative Law was key to articulating a network of authors interested in presenting their cases for an initial report that was presented in the XX General Congress of the Academy. A previous version of this introduction was published in: https://www.springer.com/gp/book/9783030486747.

[34]Taylor et al. (2015).

[35]See Jaramillo (2017), pp. 261–271.

References

Bartra E (2010) ¿Qué encuentro se busca? Breves Cavilaciones sobre el XI Encuentro Feminista y de El Caribe. Debate Feminista 41:197–201
Bell M (2012) Gender identity and sexual orientation: alternative pathways in EU equality law. Am J Comp Law 20(1):127–146
Boyce P, Coyle D (2013) Development, discourse and law: transgender and same-sex sexualities in Nepal. IDS Evidence Rep 13:1–32
Bustamante X (2010) Del XI EFLAC y otros demonios. Debate Feminista 41:165–189
Butler J (1990) Gender trouble. Routledge, New York
Cowan S (2005) Gender is no substitute for sex: a comparative human rights analysis of the legal regulation of sexual identity. Feminist Legal Stud 13(1):67–96
Daune-Richard A-M, Devreux A-M (1992) Rapports sociaux de sexe et conceptualisation sociologique. Recherches féministes 5(2):7–30
David R, Brierley JEC (1968) Major legal systems of the World today: an introduction to comparative law. Free Press, New York
Delphy C (1998) L'ennemi principal: économie politique du patriarcat, vol 1. Éditions Syllepse, Paris, p 180, Coll. Nouvelles questions féministes
Devreux A-M (1985) De la construction féminine aux rapports sociaux de sexe: repères pour une évolution de la définition sociologique des catégories de sexe. BIEF 16:13–23
Elliot P (2010) Debates in transgender, queer and feminist theory. Ashgate, Farnham
Fynes A (2014) A comparative approach to transgender legislation in the UK and Ireland. King's Inns Student Law Rev 4:31–58
Halberstam J (2018) Trans. Oakland. University of California Press, Berkeley
Halley J (2008) Split decisions. How to take a break from feminism. Princeton University Press, Princeton
Holning L (2008) Sexual orientation & gender identity: American law in light of East Asian developments. Harv J Law Gender 31:67
Jaramillo IC (2007) Más allá de la libertad y la expresión: las luchas por la representación. Revista de Jurisprudencia Argentina:16–23
Jaramillo IC (2017) La paridad como forma de pensar la emancipación: oportunidades y límites. In: Bergallo P, Moreno A (eds) Hacia Políticas Judiciales de Género. Editorial Jusbuenosaires, Buenos Aires, pp 261–271
Jiang P (2013) Legislating for transgender people: a comparative study of the change of legal gender in Hong Kong, Singapore, Japan and the United Kingdom. Hong Kong J Legal Stud 7:31–73
Lloyd AW (2005) Defining the human: are transgender people strangers to the law? Berkeley J Gender Law Justice 20:150
Mackinnon C (1982) Feminism, marxism, method and the state: and agenda for theory. Signs 7 (3):515–544
MacKinnon C (1993) Only words. Harvard University Press, Cambridge
Mršević Z (2016) Comparative change in the legal status of transgender persons. Facta Universitatis Law Politics 14(1):115–132
Ohle JM (2005) Constructing the trannie: transgender people and the law. J Gender Race Justice 8:237–280
Patel AR (2010) India's *Hijras*: the case for transgender rights. Geo Wash Int Law Rev 42:835–863
Raskolnikov M (2010) Transgendering Pride. Postmedieval J Medieval Cultural Stud 1(2):157–164
Scherpe JM (2015) The legal status of transsexual and transgender persons. Intersentia, Hong Kong
Schroth PW, Erickson-Schroth L, Foster LL, Burgess A, Erickson NS (2018) Perspectives on law and medicine relating to transgender people in the United States. Am J Comp Law 66(1):91–126. https://doi.org/10.1093/ajcl/avy022
Scott J (1986) Gender: a useful category for historical analysis. Am Historical Rev 91 (5):1053–1075

Sedgwick E (1990) Epistemology of the closet. University of California Press, Berkeley
Spade D (2015) Normal life: administrative violence, critical trans politics, and the limits of law. Duke University Press, Durham
Swain G (2016) Transgenders as the 'other': the politics of transgender community after the historic Supreme Court Verdict. Int Res J Multidisciplinarity Stud 2(2):1–6
Taylor J, Tadlock B, Poggione S (2015) Birth certificate amendment laws and morality politics. In: Taylor JK, Haider-Markel D (eds) Transgender rights and politics. University of Michigan Press, Ann Arbor
Theilen JT (2016) The long road to recognition: transgender rights and transgender reality in Europe. In: Schreiber G (ed) Transsexualität und Neurowissenschaften. De Gruyter, Berlin

'X' Why? Gender Markers and Non-binary Transgender People

Florence Ashley

Abstract Jurisdictions increasingly recognize 'X' as a legal gender marker alongside 'M' and 'F', offering an alternative to those whose gender identity falls outside or in excess of the man/woman dichotomy. This chapter explores the justifications and limitations of 'X' as a gender marker, arguing that it does not place non-binary people on an equal footing to men and women since it serves as a single, catch-all option for a wide range of non-binary identities. The chapter the explores the possibility of expanding the availability of gender markers to reflect the full diversity of non-binary people but suggests that it would be rejected as absurd due to the ongoing role of gender markers in preserving cisnormativity. It concludes that abandoning gender markers may be the only fully inclusive option. For gender liberation to come within reach, we must imagine a future without gender markers.

There are many words used to refer to us. Today, we are most often called non-binary. A few years ago, genderqueer—a term which was brought into usage in the late 1990s (Bulldagger 2006; Roxie 2011)—stood as the prevailing umbrella term for all those of us whose gender identities fell outside or in excess of the categories man and woman. The choice of term is contentious. Some non-binary people argue that we should not be defining ourselves in opposition to the gender binary, whereas others point out that no one can be binary if we realise that there are more genders than men and women. In this latter logic, the gender binary is a belief system that only recognises the existence of men and women, not a reference or property of those two genders. Those who are more attached to the term "non-

Metaphorically a biorg witch with flowers in her hair. I am presently a doctoral student at the University of Toronto Faculty of Law and Joint Centre for Bioethics. I wrote this chapter while at McGill University.

F. Ashley (✉)
University of Toronto, Toronto, ON, Canada
e-mail: f.ashley@mail.utoronto.ca

I. C. Jaramillo, L. Carlson (eds.), *Trans Rights and Wrongs*, Ius Comparatum - Global Studies in Comparative Law 54,
https://doi.org/10.1007/978-3-030-68494-5_2

binary" respond that it brings attention to the pervasive nature of the gender binary and the particular difficulties faced by non-binary individuals in binary societies. Besides "genderqueer" and "non-binary", "gender non-conforming" is also commonly used as an umbrella term, though some believe that it conflates gender identity and gender expression, since gender non-conforming is frequently used to refer to people whose gender expression does not conform to prevailing gender norms despite being men or women. Intra-community discussions on terminology are complex and vary across languages and geographical locations. For instance, French does not have an equivalent for "genderqueer", whereas "non-binary" can readily be translated into "*non-binaire*". Thus, it shouldn't be assumed that my usage of these terms reflects anything more than one common way the words are used in one place and time.

Further complicating the portrait is the falseness of the non-binary/binary binary, as the messiness of gender subjectivity often transcends clear categorisation. Ambiguity and multiple consciousness are familiar features of gender subjectivity. At first glance, the notion of multiple consciousness elaborated by brilliant critical race theorists like Mari Matsuda may seem awkward to apply to gender (Matsuda 1989). Yet perspectives on gender also structure consciousness and many of us experience a form of multiple consciousness as we move through spaces and subcultures which embody different ideologies about gender (Bettcher 2012).

Although I have much affection for the term genderqueer, I will privilege the term non-binary as it is the more common term and movements for the recognition of genders other than man and woman have organised around it in recent years. Perusing Google Trends, it appears that "non-binary" and its alternative spellings ("nonbinary" and "non binary") have come to internet prominence in 2014 and took a clear lead sometime during 2015. Prior to 2014, "genderqueer" was much more common. This is consistent with survey observations. In the 2008 National Transgender Discrimination Survey, "genderqueer" was much more common than "non-binary" as a personal label whereas the 2015 U.S. Transgender Survey showed roughly equal percentages of either labels (Harrison et al. 2011, p. 20; James et al. 2016, p. 44). Based on my anecdotal estimates as a member of non-binary communities, I expect that the trend in favour of "non-binary" as an umbrella term will continue in future surveys, with "genderqueer" being increasingly relegated to the role of individual gender label akin to terms like "genderfluid" and "agender". This is a shift from its initial umbrella nature (Bulldagger 2006).

I do not have a birth certificate that indicates that I am non-binary, let alone one that labels my gender with one of the more specific terms I have used for it in recent years.[1] Would I have changed my gender marker to female had more options been

[1]The affiliation section of my first academic publication spoke of me as "[m]etaphorically, a cyborg witch with flowers in her hair" (Ashley 2018a). I keep a list of things I've called my gender over the years besides man and woman. In very rough chronological order it includes: transfeminine, demigirl, lesbian, femme, high femme, femme fatale, Patron of Evil Deceivers and Make-Believers, non-binary, Ø, queer, ¯_(ツ)_/¯, don't know don't care, aggressively don't care, no, yes, fairie, alien, alienby, tired, so damn tired, agender, a gender, biorg, witch, bitch, Empressor, The Right

available? Perhaps, though it took me a long time to garner enough confidence to assert my non-binary identity. The first label that spoke to me when I began exploring my gender was "transfeminine", a term that highlights my experience as a person who was assigned male at birth but identifies more closely with femininity without necessarily intimating that I identify as a woman. After years of identifying as a woman, I have come full circle, labelling myself to others primarily as transfeminine.

Calling myself a woman was easier. Before I grew into a body that was consistently read as a cis woman's in everyday life, navigating public spaces was difficult. Accessing bathrooms, in particular, can be stressful because of the deeply gendered nature of the space (Herman 2013; Seelman 2016). As I transitioned in law school, affirming myself as a woman meant being more readily welcomed into women's spaces, spaces in which I felt more comfortable and safer. There was enough to explain about being trans without having to defend my everyday choices as a person who isn't a woman yet finds greater fit in women's spaces than men's. It can be challenging to affirm a non-binary identity as a transfeminine person who needs access to spaces, an issue I now try to bring attention to with humour: "Conservatives call me a cross-dresser, but I'm non-binary... does that make me a Mx. CD?"[2]

I was also afraid that I would be denied transition-related care or that my access to it would be unduly delayed. Non-binary people often face delays or refusals of care because clinicians project ambivalence or uncertainty about transition-related care onto them (Spade 2013; Ashley and Ells 2018). Although no public statement has been released on the matter, activists have reported that Finland would no longer allow non-binary people access to transition-related interventions (Kupila 2018). Finland is known as particularly conservative among Nordic countries when it comes to trans healthcare, but their approach reveals a broader lack of recognition with respect to non-binary people. Afraid of navigating the trans healthcare world as a non-binary person, I suppressed my non-binary subjectivity until I had secured all transition-related interventions that I desired at that point in time.

If varied options were offered for birth certificates, I would take them. I am uncertain at this point whether I would prefer having an 'X' or no gender marker at all. Perhaps a 'W' for witch? Or, as I mentioned in a previous article, I would love having the "¯_(ツ)_/¯" emoji as a gender marker (Ashley 2018b). What is not acceptable is being forced into having a male or female gender marker, as I am

Honourable Empressor Florence Ashley, Slayer of Looks and Men, gaygender, activiste insensée, rosebud, this (while pointing at various things), that (also while pointing at various things), good girl, CLiT, *eyeroll*, themme fatale, a ball of chaotic horny energy, feminazgûl, hot, grrl, shut up, trashgender, little shit, gender malcontent, shitposting, annoying, transgenderqueer, genderqueer, dick jokes, revolutionary nonchalance, spite, rage, hurricane, thirst, *lavender smell*, flower, flore, flora, force of nature, divine, transcendent, the unadulterated essence of the sublime, cutiegender, tenderqueer, tenderness, deception, tentacles, unfathomable swirling void, abyss, horny on main, Q3, and a gender not listed here. I regularly update the list.

[2]Mx., pronounced "mix", is a common gender-neutral alternative to Mr./Mrs. I personally favour Ind. and Ent. which are respectively short forms of "individual" and "entity".

neither. I have previously lodged a complaint against the government with the Quebec Commission des droits de la personne et des droits de la jeunesse, the jurisdiction's human rights commission. In parallel, I was very tangentially involved in a lawsuit against the Quebec government which challenged, among other things, the lack of options for non-binary people on birth certificates (Genest 2018). Whether these efforts will effect change remains to be seen, though previous judgements and recent legislative developments across Canada give me hope (Strong 2017; Dearing 2017; Tierney 2018; The Canadian Press 2018a; Zussman 2018). The trial ended over a year and a half ago, but judgment is still under reserve. It will hopefully be released by the time the present book is published.

Gender is complicated, as this short foray into my personal history hopefully shows. Yet, whatever our gender or its story, we all deserve to have identification documents that respect it. The question then becomes: how? What do respectful gender marker schemes look like? This is the question to which we now turn.

1 The 'X' Factor

Recent years have seen the proliferation of jurisdictions that recognise 'X' as an acceptable gender marker in addition to 'M' and 'F'. Increasingly, the option is made available to all non-binary people, though it is sometimes restricted to those people who are intersex (Ghattas 2015, p. 9; OII Germany 2018). In my home country of Canada, Alberta, British Columbia, Ontario, Manitoba, New Brunswick, Newfoundland and Labrador, Northwest Territories, Nova Scotia, Prince Edward Island, Saskatchewan, Yukon,[3] and the federal government have recognised 'X' gender markers in some shape or form (Strong 2017; Dearing 2017; Tierney 2018; Mertz 2018; Zussman 2018; The Canadian Press 2018b; Regina Leader-Post 2019; Gill 2019; McKenzie-Sutter 2019; Grabish 2019). The markers are also available to some non-binary people in Australia, Nepal, New Zealand, and the United States (Knight 2012; Collins 2012; Carpenter 2013; Thomson Reuters 2019).

This option has been a core demand of non-binary movements. Luna Ferguson, an activist, filmmaker, and alienby extraordinaire, has penned many articles explaining why they fought to have an 'X' on their Ontarian birth certificate (Ferguson 2017a, b, 2018). Non-binary activists like Gemma Hickey, Sam K. MacKinnon, Kori Doty, and myself have also fought for the recognition of more gender identities in Canada, along with countless other trans and intersex activists and community organisations (Ashley 2017a; Kassam 2017; Dearing 2017; Grabish 2018). The availability of 'X' gender markers is a step toward the recognition of non-binary identities, and signals to others in society that non-binary identities should be taken seriously.

[3]Yukon Bill No. 5 has received assent but has yet to come into force (Legislative Assembly of Yukon 2017). It will come into force at a time to be determined by the Commissioner in Executive Council.

Identity recognition plays a significant role in wellbeing. Past research has highlighted the relationship between identification documents that correspond to lived gender identity and suicidality, demonstrating that access to concordant identification documents was associated with fewer suicidal ideations and fewer suicide attempts among trans people (Bauer et al. 2015). Disrespect of non-binary people is as common as it is devastating (Ashley 2017b). From a minority stress perspective, lack of respect for gender identity can have an outsized effect on mental health (McLemore 2015, p. 52):

> Confirming one's self-views helps to make the world predictable and controllable, satisfying a psychological need for coherence, providing knowledge about the self, and allowing social interactions to proceed in an authentic and smooth manner. When self-views are not verified by others, people experience negative affect and arousal (e.g., anxiety, depression) and a sense of inauthenticity in social relationships, often disengaging from non-verifying relationships.

As my own story evidences, concealing our gender identity is one of the ways in which non-binary people avoid further invalidation (Losty and O'Connor 2018, p. 54). Expectations of rejection and invalidation are associated with poorer mental health, contributing to the high rates of anxiety and depression in non-binary communities (Rood et al. 2016). Although no study looks specifically at the mental health impact of the unavailability of inclusive gender markers, research on respect for pronouns and chosen name provides a basis for extrapolation consistent with anecdotal reports and community wisdom on the matter (McLemore 2015, 2018; Ashley 2017b; Matsuno and Budge 2017; Russell et al. 2018).

The lack of recognition for non-binary identities on government identification is a form of misgendering and generates further instances of misgendering. Not only do we regularly have to show identification when buying alcohol, entering venues, accessing public benefits and healthcare, and travelling, but the lack of inclusive options makes it harder for non-binary people to have their gender respected in everyday life. If the government doesn't respect us, why would the general population?

2 Free-Form Gender Markers

I would not be satisfied with 'X' as a gender marker. The designation is often used as an *other* or *unspecified* label. On Canadian passports, the 'X' option used to stand for 'unspecified', following the International Civil Aviation Organization standards (Immigration, Refugees and Citizenship Canada). Until 2019, individuals were required to have a gender marker of 'M' or 'F', but could add a printed observation stating: "The sex of the bearer should read as X, indicating that it is unspecified."

Unspecified, placed besides male and female options, suggests that your gender remains male or female, but that you do not wish to specify which of the two you are. Though in my case it may be accurate to say that my gender is unspecified, it is unspecified among a wide range of options beyond male and female. If there are options I can unambivalently declare inapplicable, it is male and female. Thankfully, it is now possible to have a passport with an 'X' gender marker, and the Passport Canada website now refers to this designation as 'another gender', although it continues to mean 'unspecified' under the ICAO standards.

Beyond the specific meaning given to 'X' and the choice of letter, a greater, more fundamental challenge arises. In offering a single letter to those who are neither men nor women, 'X' gender markers place the umbrella of non-binary on the same level as the specific identities of man and woman. But non-binary operates at a different level. The antonym of non-binary is binary, not man and woman. Non-binary operates at a higher level of generality than man and woman, unlike specific non-binary identities such as agender, genderfluid, bigender, and occasionally non-binary itself.

A third gender marker option is progress, but not enough of it. By offering a single box to all non-binary people, the internal differences of non-binary communities are suppressed. Those differences, those more specific gender labels matter. In the 2008 U.S. National Transgender Discrimination Survey, 13% of respondents wrote-in a gender, for a total of 860 write-in responses (Harrison et al. 2011). Many wrote an answer other than genderqueer or non-binary.

A wide range of identities beyond the binary can be found among research participants in academic literature: Agender, Alien, Ambiguously gendered, Ambiguously sexed, Androgyne/androgynous, Anomalous, Bear, Best of Both, Bigender, Birl, Blended, Boi, Both, BRRL, Bulldagger, Butch, Butch dyke, Challenged, Cross dreamer, Dyke, Dyke fag, Dysphoric, Extra, Female boy, Female dyke with a twist, Femisexual, Flexible, Fluctuating gender, FtA, FtX, Gender ambidextrous, Gender atheist, Gender bender, Gender blur, Gender deviant, Gender enhanced, Gender euphoric, Gender fabulous, Gender gifted, Gender neutral, Gender variant, Genderfluid, Gender-free, Genderfuck, Genderless, Genderqueer, Gendertrash, Gendertreyf, Girly male, Grrly boi, Human, In-between/in-betweenie, Incomplete gendered person, Intergender, Intersex/intersexed/intersexual, Jest me, Lesbian, Me, MtA, MtX, Neither, Neutrois, Nongendered, Non-genderspecific, Non-normatively gendered, Other, OtherWise, Pangender, Person, Polygenderal, Post-transgender, Queer, Queerboy, Questioning, Radical, Rebel, Skaneelog, Stud, Third gender, Third sex, T-person, Tranfem, Trannie/Tranny, Trannydyke genderqueer wombat fantastica, Transexed, Transfag, Transfeminine, Transie, Transmasculine, Transweird, Trigender, and Twidget (Harrison et al. 2011; Green et al. 2018; Bradford et al. 2018). An online list maintained by the blog Genderfluid Support boasts 116 distinct identities, many of which differ from those in the preceding list (Genderfluid Support).

Additionally, culturally-specific identities were also reported by the previously mentioned sources (Cameron 2005). Those may or may not be used to the exclusion of man or woman depending on person: Aggressive (Black or African American), Fa'afafine (Samoa), Hijira (Indian subcontinent), Māhū/Mahuwahine (Hawaii), Travesti (South America), Two-Spirit (First Nations). As Sarah Hunt explains (Hunt 2016, p. 5):

> Dominant categories of gender, sex and sexuality have been introduced through colonial processes and institutions, along with other categories such as race. The term 'Two-Spirit' is popularly used by Indigenous people to identify a range of roles and identities which may span, and even complicate, distinctions between gender, sex and sexuality. Indeed, for many Two-Spirit people who identify with a gender identity distinct to their Indigenous culture, these western categories fail to capture the ontologies of gender and sexuality within their own Indigenous language and culture.

The diversity and creativity of responses given in serious surveys and studies that highlight widespread harassment, discrimination, and violence further evidences the attachment that some non-binary people have to their individual gender labels. We spend time and effort to find and develop those identities, which can be of immense psychological importance (Yeadon-Lee 2016; Losty and O'Connor 2018; Pearce and Lohman 2018), and now we can't even have gender markers that reflect and respect that labour? Why do men and women get to have their specific identities represented but not us?

Building on the experiences and expertise of trans activists, the report License To Be Yourself argues along similar lines that "a single third sex/gender option may not sufficiently encompass the full range of gender and sex diversity, including specific regional and cultural identities," suggesting instead an increase in "options for people to self-define their sex and gender identity" (Byrne 2014, p. 21). This argument flows from an equal recognition framework. Likes must be treated alike, and specific non-binary identities are more alike "man" and "woman" than "non-binary" is. Some jurisdictions may be beginning to open up to this line of thought. In a ground-breaking judgment, an Argentinean judge acknowledged the need to recognise individuals' unique gender identity through a multiplicity of gender marker options, applying the Yogyakarta Additional Principle 31 (2017) and granting Lara María Bertolini's request to have her gender recorded as 'femineidad travesti' (Iglesias 2019).

By limiting gender markers to 'M', 'F' and 'X', the law devalues non-binary identities and positions them as less-than binary identities. As D.A. Davis points out (Davis 2017a, p. 237):

> The homogenizing effects of the X marker are not only evident in the extent to which the category obscures differences among non-binary people but also in the extent to which it problematically conflates non-binary gender and intersex status, instead subsuming them within one undifferentiated category.

To overcome this unsavoury suggestion and recognise the formal equality of non-binary people, it is necessary to allow a much broader range of gender markers. At the very least, any letter should be possible given the open-ended nature of gender identities. New gender identities continuously appear. Available letters should include 'M' and 'F' since some non-binary identities begin with those letters, such as "me", "multigender", "femme fatale", and "fairie". Since some identities are represented by characters other than letters—e.g. Two-Spirit is often represented by the numeral '2'—including all ASCII characters would be appropriate. Nothing short of this would sufficiently validate the full diversity of gender identities.

Adventurous jurisdictions may also want to explore non-static and non-visual forms of gender markers. A scratch and sniff gender marker would be a great idea for those who identify particularly with smells—such as the lavender smell I mention in my list of gender terms. For those who are genderfluid or bigender, holographic or movable gender markers—with a little tab that can switch between various letters to represent the gender identity of the day—would be welcome additions.

3 The Absurdity of Gender Markers

I suspect that some of my readers will think I am joking. It may sound absurd, ludicrous, ridiculous. Surely, I can't seriously be suggesting scratch-and-sniff gender markers? Surely the expansive list of gender identities I gave shouldn't be taken so seriously! Even the idea of allowing any letter or ASCII character as a gender marker may seem quite out there.

The sentiment of absurdity impressed upon some by the proposal of free-form gender markers is revelatory of the function of gender markers. If we expect from gender markers nothing more than reflecting or respecting people's gender identities, then free-form gender markers, which push this logic to its extreme, are a matter of course. It is indeed how I have argued in their favour: by showing that they flow from a moral obligation to respect all gender identities equally. However, I do not believe that this is the primary function of gender markers. Rather, the gender marker is a by-product of a social imaginary that centres gender as a legitimate classificatory scheme based on the habitual attitude about gender (Ashley 2018a). Gender markers serve to legitimate and reify the habitual attitude about gender, with trans people being accommodated to the extent that the contemplated reforms don't threaten this expected function.

What is the habitual attitude about gender? Plainly put, it is a set of widespread, fundamental attitudes about gender and its determination: gender is binary, identifiable, invariable, determined by genitals, et cetera (Hale 1996; Bettcher 2007; Ashley 2018a).

That it is an *attitude* rather than a belief is relevant here, because not everyone holding the attitude would, upon reflection, report a corresponding belief. People may treat gender as determined by genitals and categorise others based on theirs in everyday life yet concede that people may not have the genitals usually associated with their gender if asked outright. Similarly, people tend to treat gender as binary as a matter of course when constructing spaces or activities—looking at you, gym class—yet they may similarly acknowledge the existence of non-binary people if asked outright whether they believe more than two genders to exist. Any apparent or actual exception is perhaps acknowledged, but deemed to be marginal (Hale 1996).

Under this attitude, the proposal for free-form gender markers is absurd. Gender is not gender identity, and though non-binary people may deserve accommodation, those accommodations should not come at the cost of undermining the function of gender markers as a binary classificatory scheme. The proliferation of gender markers, and especially the availability of 'M' and 'F' markers for people who aren't male or female, undermines gender markers' ability to track an underlying genital-centric reality, a reality that is closely tied to sexist oppression as well as transantagonistic violence (Ashley 2018a). Compared to 'X', free-form gender markers can't as readily be swept under the rug as an exception, with 'F' and 'M' gender markers continuing to serve as stable categories around which we can legitimately organise society. Whereas 'X' can be left as a fundamentally *othering* category—one that tracks androgyny in the cisgender mind and thus doesn't challenge the visual frame of gender classifiers—the proliferation of gender markers and micro-identifies implies that identities matter beyond merely being *other*. The diversity and individuality of non-binary people is brought to the fore, undermining the conceptual dominance of 'F' and 'M'. Free-form gender markers challenge 'F' and 'M' as stable signifiers of an underlying reality which is putatively deeper than gender identity (Ashley 2020).

When gender markers reflect individual gender identities, including treating partially identifying as a man or woman—as is the case with demiboy and demigirl—separately from male and female gender markers and treating "fairie" as equally deserving of 'F' as "female", the myth of the habitual attitude is severely undermined. "Male" and "female" are no longer special and are even less special insofar as they are but two out of dozens or hundreds of options, rather than two out of three. The proliferation of gender markers threatens bionormative classificatory ideals, hence appearing ridiculous to those who hold the habitual attitude: it defeats the very purpose of gender markers than to have a gender marker scheme that primarily seeks to reflect gender identity rather than gender as understood under the habitual attitude. This, too, explains the reluctance to recognise trans men and women's gender identities or to add an 'X' gender marker. Each, in their own way and to differing degrees, threaten the habitual attitude that underpins gender markers.

4 Cisnormativity Lite

Non-binary lives, and trans lives more broadly, are accommodated so long as they remain a relatively rare exception to an overwhelmingly stable scheme of gender categorisation. Free-form gender markers take the threat posed by 'X' one step further. Because gender markers are always expected to do more than reflect self-identification, the continued existence of gender markers—even as free-form gender markers—is incompatible with a critical trans politics that opposes non-consensual gendering and gender norms more broadly.

Even free-form gender markers perpetuate weakened versions of the habitual attitude about gender and the perceived legitimacy of routine gender categorisation.[4]

[4]By routine gender categorisations, I mean to exclude gendering that arise in response to sexist oppression, such as non-mixed feminist spaces. Unlike routine gender categorisations, such

Commenting on transnormativity, Bradford, Rider, Catalpa et al. highlight how narratives of trans and non-binary identities "legitimize certain transgender experiences" and end up "inadvertently centering cisgender norms and expectations" (Bradford et al. 2018, p. 8). Free-form gender markers maintain cisnormativity lite: although it severely weakens the mapping between gender markers and the habitual attitude, remnants of the habitual attitude's invariability, identifiability, and genital-centric account of gender can be teased out. Moreover, it maintains gender as a uniquely relevant trait for social categorisation.

Firstly, free-form gender markers still require non-binary people to change their gender markers. They are assigned a gender marker at birth and must perform the appropriate dance for the benefits of their cis overlords to have their gender identity recognised. In Ontario and many other jurisdictions, a letter from a clinician attesting to the person's gender identity and the indicability of gender marker changes must be provided. This process subjects transgender people to a long-criticized medicalization of identity: gender identity doesn't stand on its own, but must be proven to an external observer viewed as legitimate by the state (Spade 2013; Vipond 2015; Ashley and Ells 2018; Bradford et al. 2018). This process is burdensome and often costly. Applications frequently cost hundreds of dollars to file, and the clinical assessment can easily cost hundreds of dollars as well. In Quebec, no assessment is typically required for adults but those, who like me have already changed their gender marker once prior to inclusive gender markers options being made available, would have to obtain a similar assessment. By contrast, cis people get to have the gender marker they desire without any cost or any lengthy, and at times dehumanizing, performance of gender variance.

Secondly, free-form gender markers mandate the identification of a unique gender label for each person, which is undesirable. Gender markers require people to identify a single specific gender label, to be kept indefinitely. This dictates that gender can't be identified differently in different contexts for pragmatic reasons and assumes that gender is relatively stable and clear. Yet, non-binary people frequently wish their gender to be identified differently in different spaces, and frequently do not have a stable or clear gender identity.

Non-binary people frequently vary how they communicate and express their gender depending on the space in which they find themselves (James et al. 2016, p. 49). Being identified as trans or queer comes with risks of harassment, discrimination, and violence. These risks vary in shape and magnitude across time and space. Non-binary people must constantly balance safety and recognition, and the balance we wish to strike isn't static. Although I would opt for a unique gender marker on my birth certificate if offered the option, I do not want an 'X' in my passport given the dangers gender variant people face in many countries. Recently, my dear friend and amazing genderbunny Nic Rider travelled to Dubai and shared with me the steps they had to undertake to be read as a gender-conforming cis

categorisations are typically not predicated on a view that gender is a natural category and would not retain their *raison d'être* in a fully egalitarian society.

woman instead of their usual glorious masc self. In Dubai, where same-sex behaviours are criminalised and heavily stigmatised, gender variance is a great risk. Having gender markers at all undermines these kinds of pragmatic, context-sensitive choices and pressures non-binary people into either misgendering themselves for safety reasons or assuming risks which they may not otherwise have assumed.

For many of us, gender is messy, plural, dynamic, and in constant evolution. Some, like me, refuse to figure out their gender and are comfortable with blurriness. Having to commit to a single gender marker stifles my uniquely non-binary creativity. Do I want to be ¯_(ツ)_/¯ or a witch or an alienby? Why do I have to pick? The pressure of having to "figure out" gender is identified in research as a point of tension and anxiety for non-binary people, and free-form gender markers contribute to that (Yeadon-Lee 2016, pp. 25–26; Losty and O'Connor 2018, p. 49; Pearce and Lohman 2018, p. 8). As D.A. Davis points out, adding gender markers "functions to erase much that is disruptive about gender non-conformity, being its multiplicity and incoherence, by imposing norms of essentialism and stability" (Davis 2017a, p. 237). Instead, we should adopt a genderfuck politics and reject "the call to neatly locate ourselves within gender categories" (Ashley 2018b).

Lastly, free-form gender markers retain a strong association between gender and genitals at birth. Though non-binary people may be granted recognition, the standard and presumed normal is that gender is identified by genitals and assigned at birth without the child's assent (Katri 2019). Children's sense of gender does not develop until roughly 3 years old, and yet their gender is noted in their birth certificate shortly after birth. Gender markers remain ciscentric: everyone is assumed to be cisgender until proven otherwise. To the extent that gender markers encode cisnormative associations between gender and genitals, they are antithetical to trans emancipation. The genital-centric account of gender has the consequence of constructing gender as a natural category, facilitating bioessentialist justifications for sexism. The focus on genitalia has dire consequences for intersex people (Starks 2018, p. 220). In Canada, surgeries are routinely practised on intersex newborns, a horrific violation of intersex people's right to bodily integrity which relies on an explicit exception to the Criminal Code provisions on excision and genital mutilation (*Criminal Code*, R.S. C 1985, c C-46, s. 268(3)). These surgeries are legitimated by the state's requirement to clearly identify sex as male or female at birth and are decried by intersex associations, as expressed in the Malta Declaration (2013). Perhaps a solution would be to delay registration of gender until it can be self-declared—Robert Kouri had already pointed to this possibility in the '70s, although he unfortunately dismissed it offhandedly (1975, p. 139). However, a simpler and wiser solution given all I have said up to this point would be to abandon gender markers altogether.

5 Conclusion

A critical trans politics (Spade 2015), which is opposed to all forms of gender oppression, requires the downfall of gender markers. It is unsurprising, then, that critical literature on gender markers has suggested abandoning them instead of expanding the options on offer (Spade 2007, 2015; Needham 2011; Neuman Wipfler 2016; Davis 2017a, b). A proposal for abandoning of gender markers has also been formulated by community organisations (Comité trans du Conseil québécois LGBT 2017). By considering the limitations of both 'X' and free-form gender markers and highlighting how even free-form gender markers reproduce and legitimate cisnormative and sexist social imaginaries, I am adding my voice to theirs.

As Heath Fogg Davis cogently puts it (Davis 2017b, p. 52):

> Eradicating sex markers from our birth certificates, passports, driver's licenses, and state identity cards will not completely uproot sex-identity discrimination and oppression. However, it is an important step that would have profound ripple effects across a wide range of administrative policy venues where these documents are requested and demanded.

Membership in gender categories, and especially legal gender designations, should not routinely be used to distribute rights and privileges. The few legitimate gendered programs and spaces that exist—affirmative action programs and non-mixed feminist spaces, for instance—need only rely on self-identification at the point of entry, and should be understood as compensatory mechanisms in a deeply sexist society which, among other things, thinks so highly of gender that it puts it on birth certificates and identification documents when blood type—a much more medically relevant fact—isn't.

In thinking about civil status, we must not only think about how *doing* civil status can be more or less oppressive, but also discuss how the institution of civil status in and of itself legitimates and maintains oppressive social imaginaries such as gender. Birth certificates and identification documents are minimalistic. Very little information is contained on them, and yet gender is. By listing gender and little more, birth certificates and identification documents suggest that gender is one of the most central characteristics for routine social categorisation. If gender is on birth certificates, then gender must be relevant (Barker 2014). And so long as gender is of routine relevance, gender liberation will remain out of reach. There are no good gender markers, because gender markers will always be tainted by their cisnormative past. If we are committed to material equality, we must imagine a future without them.

Acknowledgements I would like to thank Avery Everhart for calling me a ball of chaotic horny energy; Margot Paquette-Greenbaum because she told me to thank her; Nic Rider for their emotional support; and Ido Katri, Zev Miller, River Shannon, and Isabel Cristina Jaramillo Sierra for their feedback and editorial help.

References

Ashley F (2017a) Projet de loi du Parti Québécois : vers l'inclusion des personnes non-binaires? Ricochet

Ashley F (2017b) Qui est-ille ? Le respect langagier des élèves non-binaires, aux limites du droit. Service Soc 63:35–50. https://doi.org/10.7202/1046498ar. Accessed 2 July 2020

Ashley F (2018a) Don't be so hateful: the insufficiency of anti-discrimination and hate crime laws in improving trans well-being. Univ Toronto Law J 68:1–36. https://doi.org/10.3138/utlj.2017-0057. Accessed 2 July 2020

Ashley F (2018b) Genderfucking non-disclosure: sexual fraud, transgender bodies, and messy identities. Dalhousie Law J 41:339–377

Ashley F (2020) L'In/visibilité constitutive du sujet trans : l'exemple du droit québécois. Can J Law Soc 35(2):317–340

Ashley F, Ells C (2018) In favor of covering ethically important cosmetic surgeries: facial feminization surgery for transgender people. Am J Bioethics 18:23–25. https://doi.org/10.1080/15265161.2018.1531162. Accessed 2 July 2020

Barker MJ (2014) 57 genders and none for me? Reflections on the new facebook gender categories. In Rewriting the Rules. https://www.rewriting-the-rules.com/2014/02/15/57-genders-and-none-for-me-reflections-on-the-new-facebook-gender-categories/. Accessed 2 July 2020

Bauer GR, Scheim AI, Pyne J et al (2015) Intervenable factors associated with suicide risk in transgender persons: a respondent driven sampling study in Ontario, Canada. BMC Public Health 15:525. https://doi.org/10.1186/s12889-015-1867-2. Accessed 2 July 2020

Bettcher TM (2007) Evil deceivers and make-believers: on transphobic violence and the politics of illusion. Hypatia 22:43–65

Bettcher TM (2012) Trans women and the meaning of "Woman." In: Power N, Halwani R, Soble A (eds) The philosophy of sex: contemporary readings, 6th edn. Rowman & Littlefield Publishers, New York, pp 233–250

Bradford NJ, Rider GN, Catalpa JM et al (2018) Creating gender: a thematic analysis of genderqueer narratives. Int J Transgenderism 20:155–168. https://doi.org/10.1080/15532739.2018.1474516. 1–14. Accessed 2 July 2020

Bulldagger R (2006) The end of genderqueer. In: Mattilda AKA, Sycamore MB (eds) Nobody passes: rejecting the rules of gender and conformity. Seal Press, Emeryville, pp 137–148

Byrne J (2014) License to be yourself: laws and advocacy for legal gender recognition of trans people. The Open Society Foundations, New York

Cameron M (2005) Two-spirited aboriginal people: continuing cultural appropriation by non-aboriginal society. Can Woman Stud 24:123–127

Carpenter M (2013) Ten years of 'X' passports, and no protection from discrimination. In *Intersex Human Rights Australia*. https://ihra.org.au/21597/. Accessed 2 July 2020

Collins S (2012) X marks the spot on passport for transgender travellers. New Zealand Herald

Comité trans du Conseil québécois LGBT (2017) Politiques transversales: revendications pour un Québec trans inclusif, Conseil québécois LGBT, Montréal

Davis DA (2017a) The normativity of recognition: non-binary gender markers in Australian law and policy. In: Demos V, Segal MT (eds) Advances in gender research. Emerald Publishing Limited, Bingley, pp 227–250

Davis HF (2017b) Beyond trans: does gender matter? New York University Press, New York

Dearing R (2017) X marks the spot: Gemma Hickey breaks new ground with gender-neutral birth certificate. CBC News

Ferguson JM (2017a) Why I'm applying for a non-binary sex designation on my Canadian birth certificate. Out Magazine

Ferguson JM (2017b) I'll keep fighting until I'm legally recognized as a non-binary Canadian. Huffington Post Canada

Ferguson JM (2018) My non-binary birth certificate a victory for trans community. The Star

Genderfluid Support Gender Master List. In Genderfluid Support Tumblr. http://genderfluidsupport.tumblr.com/gender. Accessed 27 Dec 2018
Genest E (2018) Quebec to be taken to superior court for alleged discrimination against the trans community. The Link
Ghattas DC (2015) Standing up for the human rights of intersex people - how can you help? ILGA-Europe & OII Europe
Gill J (2019) New Brunswick announces third gender marker for birth certificates. CBC News
Grabish A (2018) "I feel like I'm showing a lie": Time for X gender option on Manitoba ID, says non-binary advocate. CBC Manitoba
Grabish A (2019) Manitoba must allow non-binary sex designation on birth certificates: adjudicator. CBC Manitoba
Green J, Denny D, Cromwell J (2018) "What do you want us to call you?" Respectful Language. Transgender Stud Q 5:100–110. https://doi.org/10.1215/23289252-4291812. Accessed 2 July 2020
Hale J (1996) Are lesbians women? Hypatia 11:94–121
Harrison J, Grant J, Herman JL (2011) A gender not listed here: genderqueers, gender rebels, and otherwise in the national transgender discrimination survey. LGBTQ Policy J Harv Kennedy School 2:13–24
Herman JL (2013) Gendered restrooms and minority stress: the public regulation of gender and its impact on transgender people's lives. J Public Manag Soc Policy 19:65–80
Hunt S (2016) An introduction to the health of two-spirit people: historical, contemporary and emergent issues. National Collaborating Centre for Aboriginal Health, Prince George, B.C.
Iglesias M (2019) Ni femenino ni masculino: su documento dirá "femineidad travesti." Clarín
Immigration, Refugees and Citizenship Canada Change the sex on your passport or travel document. In: Government of Canada. https://www.canada.ca/en/immigration-refugees-citizenship/services/canadian-passports/change-sex.html. Accessed 27 Dec 2018
James SE, Herman JL, Keisling M et al (2016) The report of the 2015 U.S. transgender survey. National Center for Transgender Equality, Washington, DC
Kassam A (2017) "The system's violating everyone": the Canadian trans parent fighting to keep gender markers off cards. The Guardian
Katri I (2019) Sex reclassification for gender variant people: from the medicalized body to the privatized self. In: Haider-Markel D (ed) The Oxford encyclopedia of LGBT politics and policy. Oxford University Press, Oxford
Knight K (2012) Nepal's third gender and the recognition of gender identity. Huffington Post
Kouri RP (1975) Certain legal aspects of modern medicine. Sex reassignment and sterilization. Doctorat en droit comparé. Université McGill, Montreal
Kupila S (2018) In Twitter. https://twitter.com/sakriskupila/status/1029442676003930112. Accessed 2 July 2020
Legislative Assembly of Yukon (2017) Bill No. 5: act to amend the human rights act and the vital statistics act
Losty M, O'Connor J (2018) Falling outside of the 'nice little binary box': a psychoanalytic exploration of the non-binary gender identity. Psychoanalytic Psychother 32:40–60. https://doi.org/10.1080/02668734.2017.1384933. Accessed 2 July 2020
Matsuda MJ (1989) When the first quail calls: multiple consciousness as jurisprudential method. Women's Rights Law Rep 11:7–10
Matsuno E, Budge SL (2017) Non-binary/genderqueer identities: a critical review of the literature. Curr Sexual Health Rep 9:116–120. https://doi.org/10.1007/s11930-017-0111-8. Accessed 2 July 2020
McKenzie-Sutter H (2019) People can choose "X" or opt out of including gender on N.S. IDs. *CBC News*
McLemore KA (2015) Experiences with misgendering: identity misclassification of transgender spectrum individuals. Self Identity 14:51–74. https://doi.org/10.1080/15298868.2014.950691. Accessed 2 July 2020

McLemore KA (2018) A minority stress perspective on transgender individuals' experiences with misgendering. Stigma Health 3:53–64. https://doi.org/10.1037/sah0000070. Accessed 2 July 2020

Mertz E (2018) Albertans can now choose "X" gender marker on ID cards, documents. Global News

Needham D (2011) A categorical imperative? Questioning the need for sexual classification in québec. Les Cahiers de Droit 52:71–106. https://doi.org/10.7202/1005512ar. Accessed 2 July 2020

Neuman Wipfler AJ (2016) Identity crisis: the limitations of expanding government recognition of gender identity and the possibility of genderless identity documents. Harv J Law Gender 39:491–554

OII Germany (2018) Geschlechtseintrag „Weiteres" Ist Kontraproduktiv. In: OII Germany. https://oiigermany.org/geschlechtseintrag-weiteres-ist-kontraproduktiv/. Accessed 2 July 2020

Pearce R, Lohman K (2018) De/constructing DIY identities in a trans music scene. Sexualities 22 (1–2):97–113. https://doi.org/10.1177/1363460717740276. 136346071774027. Accessed 2 July 2020

Regina Leader-Post (2019) Marking X for sex designation now an option on Sask. driver's licence. Regina Leader-Post

Rood BA, Reisner SL, Surace FI et al (2016) Expecting rejection: understanding the minority stress experiences of transgender and gender-nonconforming individuals. Transgender Health 1:151–164. https://doi.org/10.1089/trgh.2016.0012. Accessed 2 July 2020

Roxie M (2011) Genderqueer history. In Genderqueer and non-binary identities. http://genderqueerid.com/gqhistory. Accessed 26 Dec 2018

Russell ST, Pollitt AM, Li G, Grossman AH (2018) Chosen name use is linked to reduced depressive symptoms, suicidal ideation, and suicidal behavior among transgender youth. J Adolescent Health 63:503–505. https://doi.org/10.1016/j.jadohealth.2018.02.003. Accessed 2 July 2020

Seelman KL (2016) Transgender adults' access to college bathrooms and housing and the relationship to suicidality. J Homosexuality 63:1378–1399. https://doi.org/10.1080/00918369.2016.1157998. Accessed 2 July 2020

Spade D (2007) Documenting gender. Hastings Law J 59:731–842

Spade D (2013) Mutilating gender. In: Stryker S, Whittle S (eds) The transgender studies reader. Taylor and Francis, Hoboken, pp 315–332

Spade D (2015) Normal life: administrative violence, critical trans politics, and the limits of law, rev edn. Duke University Press, Durham

Starks K (2018) Gender markers on Government-issued identification in Saskatchewan: rights, reform, and jurisdiction in shifting legal landscape. Saskatchewan Law Rev 81:213–426

Strong W (2017) Transgender N.W.T., residents can now change birth certificates to reflect gender. *CBC North*

The Canadian Press (2018a) Saskatchewan to allow people to remove gender designation from birth certificates. *The Globe and Mail*

The Canadian Press (2018b) P.E.I. becomes first province to offer blank space for gender on driver's licences. *CTV News*

Thomson Reuters (2019) These 11 US states are now issuing third gender IDs. *World Economic Forum*

Tierney A (2018) This person just received Ontario's first non-binary birth certificate. *Vice*

Vipond E (2015) Resisting transnormativity: challenging the medicalization and regulation of trans bodies. Theory Action 8:21–44. https://doi.org/10.3798/tia.1937-0237.15008. Accessed 2 July 2020

Yeadon-Lee T (2016) What's the story?: Exploring online narratives of non-binary gender identities. Int J Interdisciplinary Soc Community Stud 11:19–34

Zussman R (2013) Malta Declaration. In: OII Europe. https://oiieurope.org/malta-declaration/. Accessed 2 July 2020
Zussman R (2017) The Yogyakarta Principles plus 10: additional principles and state obligations on the application of international human rights law in relation to sexual orientation, gender identity, gender expression and sex characteristics to complement the Yogyakarta Principles
Zussman R (2018) B.C. now recognizes 'X' gender marker on driver's licence, birth certificate. Global News

Part II
The Strong Medicalization Model

Gender Identity and the LGBT Movement in Brazil

Ana Carla Harmatiuk Matos

Abstract This chapter addresses the legislative, judicial and state policies aimed at trans persons, seeking to critically reflect, from an interdisciplinary approach, on the current Brazilian panorama. As is well known, the violence suffered by the trans population in Brazil is serious; constant violations of trans rights remain unsanctioned. The particularities of the Brazilian legislation are also taken up cursorily here, such as the regulation of the right to name and gender identity; the absence of the "third sex/gender" in registrations; the relationship between the rights of trans persons and of gay, lesbian and intersex persons in the country; and broader discussions about how sex/gender can be viewed as legal categories in the Brazilian context.

Without relying simply on law as offering sole protection and a resignification of the reality of minorities, it must be recognized that law can promote very relevant discussions, reflections and possibilities of inclusion. From this perspective, officializing the name and marital status of trans persons as a gateway to various rights is imperative. This chapter addresses the legislative, judicial and state policies aimed at this especially vulnerable group, trans persons, seeking to critically reflect from an interdisciplinary approach the current Brazilian panorama. As is well

This chapter is based on a report submitted upon the invitation from the International Academy of Comparative Law to analyze the Brazilian conditions about legal recognition of transgender persons. Several students from the Federal University of Paraná's Postgraduate Program in Law were engaged in this project: Andressa Regina Bissolotti dos Santos, Dhyego Câmara de Araujo, Francielle Elisabet, Nogueira Lima, Gustavo Bussmann Ferreira, Jacqueline Lopes Pereira, Lígia Ziggiotti de Oliveira and Marcelo Paulo Wacheleski, along with an undergraduate monitor Yago Paiva and members of the human rights and vulnerabilities research center, coordinated by this author.

A. C. H. Matos (✉)
Federal University of Paraná (UFPR), Curitiba, Brazil
e-mail: adv@anacarlamatos.com.br

I. C. Jaramillo, L. Carlson (eds.), *Trans Rights and Wrongs*, Ius Comparatum - Global Studies in Comparative Law 54,
https://doi.org/10.1007/978-3-030-68494-5_3

known, the violence suffered by the trans population in Brazil is serious; constant violations of trans rights remain unsanctioned. The particularities of the Brazilian legislation are also taken up cursorily here, such as the regulation of the right to name and gender identity; the absence of the "third sex/gender" in registrations; the relationship between the rights of trans persons and of gay, lesbian and intersex persons in the country; and broader discussions about how sex/gender can be viewed as legal categories in the Brazilian context.

1 The Evolution of the Legal Regulation of Sexual Identity in Brazil

In the Brazilian political-juridical context, the advancement of standards considered counter-majoritarian related to sexual and gender diversity has as its paradigm the joint judgment of the Argument of Non-compliance with Basic Precept 132 and Direct Action of Unconstitutionality 4,277, which resulted in the legal recognition of stable relationships between same-sex persons by the Supreme Court through a judgment with general repercussions.

The 'gay marriage' agenda in Brazil initially was brought to the Legislature[1] through Draft Law 1,151 of 1995, proposed by the then deputy Marta Suplicy, a member of the Brazilian Workers' Party (PT—Partido dos Trabalhadores). This draft law remained in place between 1995 and 2001, but the failure in the last attempt to vote it down, at a time when its author was no longer a deputy, eventually resulted in its withdrawal from the agenda, following an agreement among party leaders.

When this legislative project was shelved, the strategy then adopted was to carry out an *advocacy* process[2] of political influence over the actors involved in the judiciary, especially lawyers and legal researchers. Through this, it was possible to form a series of partnerships with lawyers and researchers to formulate doctrines in defense of the legal recognition of stable homosexual relationships, beginning with the hermeneutics of constitutional principles to guiding the interpretation of family law. In this construction, one started to talk in terms of *homoaffective unions*, in harmony with that which was produced in terms of a contemporary family law, or law *of the* families.[3] From such hermeneutic constructions, it was possible to construct judicial precedents to declare the legal effects of these relationships, independently of explicit legislative recognition. It was in a way a joint reaction

[1]The Brazilian Legislature is bicameral, comprising the Chamber of Deputies and the Senate which together form the National Congress.

[2]*Advocacy* is defined here as a practice of political influence within the institutions and over their actors. It is the use of language (such as a rights discourse) and institutionally appropriate positions to influence the political decisions of the actors involved, achieving practical effects in terms of state protection.

[3]Relevant authors that have led this intellectual and academic debate in Brazil include Paulo Lôbo, Maria Berenice Dias, Ana Carla Harmatiuk Matos, and Maria Celina Bodin de Moraes.

between LGBT activism and jurists, to enable the attainment of rights despite the sway and actions of religious and conservative groups over the Legislature. It therefore is a relevant achievement in terms of fighting against heteronormativity, which until then—and still today, to a certain extent—played an important role in the interpretation and application of the laws in the country. The favorable pronouncement of the Court eventually became a paradigm in Brazil, and opened a process of a broader struggle, in which new actions, with new articulations in their surroundings, were litigated.

The Federal Supreme Court recently issued a judgment addressing equal treatment, for inheritance purposes, between spouses and partners, including family entities made up of same-sex persons. The decision was rendered in extraordinary appeals (RE 646,721 and RE 878,694, both with acknowledged general repercussions). The Justices declared article 1,790—which establishes differences between the participation of a partner and a spouse in the inheritance of assets—of the Brazilian Civil Code unconstitutional, reasoning that such a legal order promotes a hierarchy between families, thus violating the principles of equality, of the dignity of the human being as a person, and of proportionality.

The Extraordinary Appeal 646,721 specifically addresses inheritance in relation to persons of the same sex. Based on the argument that there is no discriminatory element capable of justifying differential treatment between spouses and partners irrespective of sexual orientation, the Court concluded by extending the inheritance rights irrespective of sexual orientation.[4] The Federal Supreme Court has consequently become a privileged stage around the political struggle over sexual and gender rights. A series of lawsuits are currently pending before the Court regarding issues central to the agenda of the main groups of the Brazilian LGBT movement. These can be organized into three groups:

1. The continuity of the discussion about *homosexual/homoaffective families*;
2. The recognition of the existence and the necessary combat against *homophobia*, through criminalization; and
3. The right to juridical and social recognition of gender identity to trans gender persons.[5]

This third group is relevant here and comprises three actions. The first is the Extraordinary Appeal (RE) 670,422, commenced in October 2012, with a judgment initiated in April 2017 and finalized in August 2018, reiterating the possibility of gender change in the civil registry of trans persons without the need of sex reassignment surgery or the registration of the trans sexual condition in cases in

[4]Available at: http://www.stf.jus.br/portal/cms/verNoticiaDetalhe.asp?idConteudo=342982. Accessed: 20 May 2017.

[5]This discussion can be seen from the dissertation developed by Andressa Regina Bissolotti dos Santos, under the guidance of Ana Carla Harmatiuk Matos, addressing the trajectory of the LGBT movement in its search for rights and in relation to the law. This dissertation was defended and approved on March 30, 2017. Cf. Santos (2017).

which the applicant did not opt for the surgery.[6] The second is the Extraordinary Appeal (RE) 845,779, commenced in October 2014 and had its general repercussion recognized in November of the same year, discussing the possibility of compensation for moral damages resulting from the embarrassment suffered by a trans person who was prevented from using a bathroom consistent with her gender in a shopping mall in the city of Florianópolis (SC) and which judgment was initiated in November 2015.[7] The third is the Direct Action of Unconstitutionality (DAU or, in Portuguese, ADI) 4,275, which called into question Article 58 of Law 6,015/73, in order to allow changes of name and sex in the civil registries of trans persons and that, in our opinion, was properly judged, from February 28 to March 1, 2018, in order to dejudicialize the rectification procedures and facilitate them without the need to present psycho-pathological reports.[8]

All three of these actions reached the Federal Supreme Court in 2011 after the legitimacy of same-sex unions was recognized. This means that these decisions worked not only as a manifestation in relation to a specific issue, but as an institutional opening giving relevance to the guidelines of the LGBT movement, which remains stagnant in other spaces, such as the Brazilian Legislative Branch. Another example of a joint struggle of different minorities was that with respect to state and municipal educational plans. Taken by conservative discourses to deprecate what they called a 'gender ideology'—meaning, in this vein, any attempts to discuss gender and sexuality in schools—it has resulted in a necessary joint action of feminists, homosexuals and trans persons. The way by which the advancement of gay, lesbian, feminist, and other minority rights, such as the rights of trans persons, articulates is arguably complex in Brazil, often involving joint actions and opening of spaces. On other occasions, however, it can produce exclusionary discourses that reinforce the marginalized and even *abnormal* image that is socially attributed to the trans experience.

[6]Acompanhamento processual. RE 670422. Available at: http://www.stf.jus.br/portal/processo/verProcessoAndamento.asp?incidente=4192182. Accessed: 23 Jan. 2017.

[7]This is what in practice has been understood as the declaration of the State on the social recognition of the gender identity of transpersons. Acompanhamento processual. RE 845779. Available at: http://www.stf.jus.br/portal/processo/verProcessoAndamento.asp?incidente=4657292. Accessed: 23 Jan. 2017.

[8]Acompanhamento processual. ADI 4275. Available at: http://www.stf.jus.br/portal/geral/verPdfPaginado.asp?id=400211&tipo=TP&descricao=ADI%2F4275. Accessed: 4 May 2018.

2 The Impact of the LGBT Movement and Trans Activism

The avenues through which rights related to gender identity in Brazil have emerged are strongly related to the work of the Brazilian LGBT Movement. The literature analyzing the development of this movement[9] constantly points to the intimate relationship the movement has established with rights and with the discourse of rights. The LGBT movement in Brazil initially began as a homosexual movement. At that time, the focus was on the identity of the *homosexual*. It began in the late 1970s, on the Rio-São Paulo axis, at a time when trans gender and gay identities did not yet differ in the national context.[10] The development of this identity perception, in which homosexual and trans gender experiences would clearly be differentiated, occurred during the 1980s and mainly the 1990s. It can be glimpsed in the changes passed by the movement's nomenclature, from a *homosexual* movement to a *LGBT* movement. In this sense, trans identities only began to figure in the nomenclature of the movement in 1995, when it came to be identified as GLT (gays, lesbians, and transvestites).[11] It is interesting that they started using the expression *transvestite* and not the *trans sexual* nomenclature or the more recent *trans gender* term. As the literature clarifies, transvestite has a Brazilian and/or Latin American *feminine* identity. It is marked by a transgressor experience of gender that is related to other markers, such as race and an experience of body construction in street spaces.[12] The trans person—who can be either she or he—experiences, on the other hand, a gender dissidence whose meaning speaks to medical knowledge, although from resignification and a contest for the term.

The mobilization by trans persons in Brazil starts from this specific Brazilian experience, that is *transvestite*. Many activists still identify themselves from the transvestite identity, even though they act in conjunction with other trans gender experiences under the mantle of the expression '*trans*'. Trans activism is the protagonist (with the support of other organizations) of the legal modifications in the Brazilian legal order regarding gender identity, which has mainly occurred through litigation and the judiciary.

In the national legislative context, it is important to point out that although judicial success has been achieved with the DAU 4,275, there is intense action and discussion around Draft Law no. 5,002 of 2013. Known as the Law João Nery, it provides for the right to gender identity and proposes to modify Article 58 of Law 6,015 of 1973 (Public Registration Law) in order to allow the rectification of information concerning name and sex directly in the notary—therefore, through the extrajudicial route. Therefore, there is intense action by trans activists for the construction of the current form of juridical regulation of gender identities. But

[9]Simões and Facchini (2009). Also: Facchini (2003), pp. 79–127. And further: Green (2000), pp. 271–296.

[10]Simões and Facchini (2009).

[11]Facchini and França (2009), pp. 54–81 and 62.

[12]Pelúcio (2005), pp. 217–248.

such action has been painful, as it meets strong resistance in the current context, especially in the National Congress. Hence, the counter-majority character of the Federal Supreme Court is thought to be based on political expectations. Alongside that, there is a constant need to deconstruct the biologicizing and pathologizing visions with which our law often conceives transgressive gender identities.

3 The Legal Recognition of Trans Persons' Sexual Identity

3.1 The Current State of Affairs

According to the research project "TransMurder Monitoring" by the NGO Transgender Europe, Brazil leads the world ranking of countries where trans persons are most often murdered.[13] In spite of this problem, the current Legislature has not offered enough specific normative support for the guidelines considered central in this subject. On the other hand, it is possible to observe that substantial juridical transformations in themes related to gender and sexuality have been driven in different spheres, which often are not directly submitted to the majoritarian political process. It should be noted that until 1997, when the Resolution 3,482 of the Federal Council of Medicine, authorizing gender modification surgery, was presented experimentally in Brazil, the juridical treatment of the trans population oscillated between indifference and repression.

Although local experience ranks legislation as the primary source of law, the judicial branch is commonly asked to confirm the values enshrined in the 1988 Constitution of the Federative Republic of Brazil in favor of LGBT citizenship. In short, many trans persons were able through litigation to change name and gender in their birth records, sometimes without the need of proof of surgery and/or hormonal treatment. Following the route of litigation, a trial (currently suspended) in the Federal Supreme Court on the use of bathrooms according to sexual identity began in 2015. In March 2018, the Supreme Court, on an occasion considered remarkable for the LGBTI movement, decided through an Direct Action of Unconstitutionality (DAU 4,275) in favor of registry modification of trans persons (who so wish) via an non-judicial procedure, without the requirement of surgeries, medical and/or psychological reports, being sufficient as a self-declaration, in a constitutionalized interpretation of the Public Registration Law and in light of what the Pact of San José de Costa Rica prescribes.

In addition to this recent case, a request for measures, initiated by the Public Defender of the Union—was filed prior to the DAU trial and therefore suspended pending this action. The case has been processed by the National Justice Council, in which the judicial review body is asked to advise the civil registry offices in order to process the requests for rectification without judicial intervention and without

[13] Transgender Europe (2016).

requiring gender modification surgery, in the form of Article 110 of Law 6,015/1973 (Public Registration Law), which foresees the possibility of corrections regarding recorded inaccuracies easily noticed. Now that the DAU has been judged as appropriate and the request for measures has been closed, the National Council of Justice issued Appointment No. 73/2018, standardizing the procedures to be followed by the notaries, in order to avoid administrative inconsistencies that may occur in the vast Brazilian territory.

It is also apparent throughout this chapter that spheres linked to the Executive Branch and other institutional bodies from which standards (in the broadest sense) have been created have provide relevant content for this analysis. In this sense, ministerial ordinances from secretariats linked to the various federative entities, presidential decrees, and internal guidelines compose relevant elements of a set of movements that make up the legal scenario in terms of sexual orientation and gender identity. Thus, gender modification surgeries through the Brazilian public health system are possible. Another peculiarity is the use of the social name, which will be better explained below. It is noted, however, that despite some institutional advances trans persons are not sufficiently made visible and welcomed in government programs.

4 The Lack of Specific Legislation for Trans Persons

In Brazil no bespoke laws deal specifically with the civil recognition of *gender identity* of trans persons, especially with regard to the right to name and rectification of *sex* designative (a term used to attest both, biological sex and gender of persons, and that legally integrates the civil status of natural persons[14]) in their respective birth registers. This is why these rights, until the judgement of the DAU 4,275, were gradually being conquered through litigation based on an interpretation of the Public Registration Law mentioned above and in light of constitutional principles, such as the dignity of the human person.

In the Brazilian federal context, some normative acts have already been issued in order to authorize the use of the social name by trans, transvestite and trans persons—for example, users of the Public Defender's Office (Resolution 108, dated May 5, 2015); professionals enrolled in the Brazilian Bar Association (Proposition 49.0000.2014.001585-2 of the Federal Council of the Brazilian Bar Association); citizens who access the direct, autarchic and foundational federal public administration (Decree 8,727 of April 28, 2016), among others.[15] These

[14]As can be seen in Ventura (2010).

[15]Informações consolidadas em Direito Homoafetivo: consolidando conquistas (Consolidated information on Homoaffectionate Law: Consolidating achievements). Available at: http://www.direitohomoafetivo.com.br/normatizacoes.php?a=7&p=3#t. Accessed: 8 Feb. 2017.

minor fields, although endowed with high symbolic value, cover however only small portions of the population—mainly representatives of certain social strata.

More recently, the Ministry of Education issued Resolution No. 1/2018, which delimits the use of the social name of transvestites and trans persons in civilian school records, including for persons under the age of 18, provided that the request is made by their legal representative. Decree No. 9.278/2018, in turn, regulated the addition of the "social name" to identity cards (RG), a measure that, however, is not capable of deleting the original name of the previous civil registry.[16]

The fundamentals pointed out by trans persons are needs of adequacy of name, personality right, identity and self-recognition. It is well-known that a *social name* is the name by which trans persons and transvestites prefer to be called in daily situations instead of their officially registered names that do not reflect their gender identity. This Brazilian particularity was originally implemented based on internal regulations of universities and municipalities, at the state and municipal levels, and, officially, the Federal University of Amapá (UNIFAP) was the pioneer in its adoption in 2009. However, this is not sufficient for full citizenship and the legal recognition of rights.

For the formalization of the first name change, one can search for help by extrajudicial means or, more commonly, by judicial means. Until recently, prior to the decision given in the DAU 4,275, the administrative change was based on Articles 58 and 110 of the Public Registration Law, as well as on the general guardianship clause of the human person with protection for personality and on the Principles of Yogyakarta. In 2015—that is, prior to the pronouncement of the Supreme Court on the issue, in constitutionality control—the Public Defender in Bahia succeeded in an administrative request, at which time this institution emphasized that the rights of third parties would also be safeguarded after the rectification of the first name, since the identification numbers of other documents, such as Identity Card and Individual Taxpayer Registration Number Card, would not be modified.[17] Through this action, it was possible to change the name of a trans person without filing a lawsuit.

The second way, most widely used until 2018, of changing the name of a trans person is therefore by filing a lawsuit for changing the civil register. The requirements that must be met in the initial petition are those contained in Articles 55, 58, 109 and 110 of the Public Registration Law. When the request is based on Article 109 of the Public Registration Law, a trans person must provide evidence that supports the claim for modification, complement or reuse of his/her first name. The lawsuit for name rectification requires the opinion of the Public Prosecution Service about the case. The decision, of a constitutive nature, can be appealed before the State Court of Justice and when no other appeals are made (*res judicata*), a warrant for drawing-up, complementing, and rectifying the register will be issued. A further

[16]Brasil (2018). The identification bodies will have until March 1, 2019 to update their systems in order to adopt the new standards established by the decree.

[17]BN Justiça (2015).

plea may be drawn up on the basis of Article 110 of the same law. A trans person can then argue about the need to change or correct the first name, without an extensive burden of proof, in case of a material error. Still, for changing a name the argument found in the single paragraph of Article 55 of the Public Registration Law is still feasible, which highlights the modification in the hypothesis of exposing the person to ridicule.

At the beginning of the changes, doctrine and practice on the subject were based on biological discourses, now appropriated by conservative political fronts, linking the alteration of the name to the presence or not of female or male genitals and sex organs, not even considering the possibility of the civil registry revealing gender and not biological sex.[18] This view supported the decisions extinguishing the case by the "legal impossibility of the request" (article 485 of the Brazilian Civil Procedure Code[19]), but is being progressively overcome.

When the request is judged, the person's submission to gender modification surgery has relevant weight regarding the authorization (or not) for first name change. We summarize below the arguments favorable to the possibility and that can appear together in the judicial decision:

1. Article 3, items I, III and IV, of the Brazilian Federal Constitution, points out that the foundations of the Republic are the construction of a free, fair and solidary society (I), the eradication of poverty and marginalization, as well as the reduction of social and regional inequalities (III); the promotion of the good of all, without any form of discrimination. These fundamentals reiterate the importance of the formal first name's alteration in the civil registry in order to eliminate the discrimination against the trans person whose original name is not in accordance with his/her gender identity.[20]
2. Article 5, items II and X, of the Federal Constitution, are corollaries of freedom. While item II indicates that there is no illegality when there is no prohibition to change the name, item X protects the personality rights by ensuring the

[18]In this sense, Campos (1977), p. 347.

[19]"Art. 485. The judge shall not decide on the merits when: I – he/she rejects the initial application; [. . .]" (this author's translation).

[20]As an example, some excerpts from the Special Appeal 100,839-8-SP, judged by the Superior Court of Justice: "Civil law. Special resource. Transsexual undergoing sexual reassignment surgery. Change of first name and sex designation. Principle of the dignity of the human person. [ ] – The affirmation of the sexual identity, comprehended by the human identity, contains the realization of the dignity, in what concerns the possibility of expressing all the attributes and characteristics of the gender immanent to each person. For the transsexual, having a dignified life means to see his/her sexual identity recognized, from the psychosocial point of view, reflecting the real truth he/she experiences and that is reflected in society. [. . .] Ultimately, affirming human dignity means for each one to manifest his/her true identity, which includes the recognition of his/her real sexual identity, observing respect for the human person as an absolute value. [. . .]" (this author's translation) (REsp 1008398/SP, Rel. Ministra Nancy Andrighi, Terceira Turma, julgado em 15/10/2009, DJe 18/11/2009. Available at: https://ww2.stj.jus.br/processo/revista/inteiroteor/?num_registro=200702733605&dt_publicacao=18/11/2009. Accessed: 7 Mar. 2017.

inviolability of intimacy and honor, with a guarantee of compensation in case of moral damages.

3. Articles 55 and 58 of the Public Registration Law (6,015/1973) generally demonstrate the legal possibility of requesting first name change.[21]
4. The first name on the registry should correspond to a criterion of person's self-recognition. It configures violation of human dignity to subject a person to an identity that does not match his/her self-perception. However, there is a dissonance of understanding among the Brazilian courts: while some of them subordinate the modification of the name to the gender modification surgery,[22] others authorize the request based on the understanding that the gender identity is a social construction, unrelated to biological sex.[23]
5. The first name should be changed after gender modification surgery, as an extension of the health treatment to the person who presents "gender dysphoria", in accordance with Articles 196 and 199 of the Federal Constitution.

---

[21]In this case, mention is made of some sections of the judgment of the Special Appeal 73,799-: "PUBLIC REGISTRATION. CHANGE OF SEX. EXAMINATION OF CONSTITUTIONAL MATTERS. IMPOSSIBILITY OF EXAMINATION IN THE ROUTE OF SPECIAL REMEDY. ABSENCE OF PREQUEST. SUMMARY N. 211/STJ. CIVIL REGISTRY. AMENDMENT OF PRENOM AND SEX. JUDICIAL DECISION. AVERBATION. CHARTERARY BOOK. [...] The combined interpretation of arts. 55 and 58 of Law 6,015/73 grants legal protection for the operated transsexual to obtain judicial authorization for the change of his/her first name, replacing it by public and notorious nickname by which he/she is known in the environment in which he/she lives. 5. Failure to legally understand the request made in the exordial means to postpone the exercise of the right to personal identity and to subtract from the individual the prerogative to adapt the registration of sex to his/her new physical condition, thus preventing his/her integration into society. 6. In the bookkeeper's book, it should be recorded, in the margin of the registration of the person's name and gender, that the changes made were the result of a judicial decision. 7. Special appeal known partly and provided." 3 (this author's translation) (REsp 737.993/MG, Rel. Ministro João Otávio de Noronha, 4ª Turma, julgado em 10/11/2009, DJe 18/12/2009).

[22]As an example, it is observed the judgment of the Civil Appeal 0909159-11.2012.8.26.0037 by the Court of Justice of the state of São Paulo which, in 2014, understood that the modification of the transman's name (FTM) should be dependent on transgenitalization surgery. (Available at: https://esaj.tjsp.jus.br/cjsg/getArquivo.do?cdAcordao=7371273&cdForo=0&vlCaptcha=niFzw. Accessed: 7 Mar. 2017).

[23]The Santa Catarina State Court of Justice authorized the change of the name of transman (FTM), even without the neofaloplasty surgery. Check the excerpt of the decision (this author's translation): "Rectification of the name and gender in the civil registry makes it possible to exercise the acts of civil life and to live in society without embarrassment or discrimination, and guarantees the author's right to human dignity, sexual identity, psychic integrity and sexual self-determination. The rectification of the civil registry cannot be conditioned to the transgenitalization surgery, which has a high cost and imposes risks, because what is sought is the psychic sexual identity. [...]" (TJSC, Apelação Cível n. 2015.015342-4, de São José, rel. Des. Domingos Paludo, j. 05-11-2015. Available at: http://app6.tjsc.jus.br/cposg/pcpoSelecaoProcesso2Grau.jsp?cbPesquisa=NUMPROC&Pesquisar=Pesquisar&dePesquisa=20150153424. Accessed: 7 Mar. 2017).

On the other hand, judicial decisions in which applications for change of first name are rejected, do so based on two main arguments regarding merits, which are as follows:

1. The principle of immutability of the civil registry must prevail in the face of the request of first name alteration made by a trans person.[24]
2. Even if the person has undergone gender modification surgery, his/her first name should not be changed, since the civil registry must reflect the "truth of the facts", which is the correspondence of the first name with the genetic data of the person.

Aside from this scenario, it is emphasized again that in a recent judgment of the Direct Action of Unconstitutionality under No. 4,275, filed by the Attorney General's Office in 2009, seeking a constitutional interpretation of Article 58 of the PRL able to facilitate first name and sexual designative rectifications by trans persons, the final result was the dispensability of medical and/or psychological reports and any other requirements for the interested parties to obtain the desired change of their civil registry, besides determining the dispensability of the action (even if through voluntary jurisdiction) before the Judiciary. This decision, a historic conquest, was addressed to the trans persons movement, since it gave a constitutional interpretation that de-bureaucratizes the procedures for documentary rectifications, which also meets the guidelines recommended by the IACHR in the Advisory Opinion No. 24/17.[25] As the minutes of the trial were officially published on March 9, 2018, according to the Brazilian Official Gazette, the effects (*erga omnes* and binding on other organs of the Judiciary and the direct and indirect public administration) of the Supreme Court decision become immediate and extended to all the Brazilian territory.

Among the actors who have been involved in the debate are non-governmental organizations and other institutions that have publicly announced that they are in favor of trans persons' right to change their names, some of whom also acted as *amici curiae*[26] in the case. Some of these actors include: Brazilian Institute of Family Law (IBDFam); Sexual Diversity Advocates Group (GADVS); Brazilian Association of Gays, Lesbians and Transgenders (ABGLT); Dignity Group—for the Citizenship of Gays, Lesbians and Transgenders; Integrated Laboratory on Sexual and

[24]On this basis, the Court of Justice of Paraná dismissed an appeal of a trans person. Here, an excerpt of the decision: "Given its importance as an individualizing character and element of personality, the inalterability of the name is the rule in the Brazilian legal system, which enshrines the principle of immutability of the name." (this author's translation), available at: https://portal.tjpr.jus.br/jurisprudencia/j/11704668/Ac%C3%B3rd%C3%A3o-1091843-7. Accessed: 13 Mar. 2017).

[25]This advisory opinion can be fully accessed through: http://www.corteidh.or.cr/docs/opiniones/seriea_24_esp.pdf.

[26]It is about the possibility of third parties being in a lawsuit that discusses the topic about which they act, have knowledge or provide information that may assist in the Court's reasoning. About the subject: Bueno (2012).

Gender Diversity, Policies and Rights (LIDIS); Latin American Center on Sexuality and Human Rights (CLAM); and Federal Council of Psychology (CFP).[27]

The present moment is one of uncertainty regarding the standardization of registration procedures in the country, mainly because an important issue was not the subject of deliberation expressed in the Supreme Court pronouncement: The rectification of the first name and of the sexual designative in the civil registry as for children and adolescents. If following the guidance of the Inter-American Court of Human Rights, through Advisory Opinion No. 24/17, used as a benchmark in the DAU 4,275 judgment (in addition to the Pact of San José, Costa Rica), the right to gender identity will also apply to children and adolescents who wish to submit requests to modify their civil records, according to their self-perceived gender identity, by administrative means, with due representation. This is, by the way, the understanding of the specialized legal literature. Cases of successful registration of children and adolescents through the Judiciary are still scarce. In this sense, the sentence pronounced by the State Court of the State of Mato Grosso, in 2016, is noteworthy.[28]

5 Legal Regulations for Intersexuals and the Possibility of a "Third Sex"

No legal regulations or judicial activity explicitly address the issues of intersexuals and of a third sex currently in Brazil. Intersex persons are historically not recognized nor have much representativeness in the social movements and in judicial requests for rights, which contributes to a situation of greater vulnerability. However, the emerging visibility of the demands related to this population has been built mainly in communities that proliferate on the Internet, as is the case of the page "Intersex Visibility" ("Visibilidade Intersexo", in Portuguese) in the social network Facebook, which has just over 4700 followers. It should also be mentioned that in a decision handed down by the Court of Justice of Acre, the name and gender changes of an intersex 3-year-old child were authorized. The request was made by the Brazilian Bar Association (Order of Attorneys of Brazil—Acre Sectional). According to reports,[29] the child's condition was only discovered after his birth, when a genetic test was performed.

Moreover, the legal possibility of a 'neutral gender' or 'third sex' does not exist to date in Brazil. There is no law on the subject, nor judicial discussion concerning the issue in the higher courts. In fact, the discussion about the rights of trans persons in

[27] About this actor, it is important to emphasize that professionals in the area of Psychology in Brazil are articulated for the depathologization of transsexuality. More details about events and projects: http://site.cfp.org.br/tag/transexuais/. Accessed: 14 Mar. 2017.

[28] BBC (2018).

[29] Bassette (2018) and Lucon (2018a).

Brazil has basically taken place in terms of the possibility of shifting from one sex to the other—consequently in binary terms. The beginning of a discussion about intersex experiences in Brazil may be signaling a closeness to the debate about 'third sex' or 'neutral gender'. It begins to question the violence that constitutes medical interventions, especially surgical, in the bodies of intersexual children, who are forced to undergo a series of treatments without even understanding why, and without being able to express themselves about interventions in their own bodies.

The intersex movement is still novel in Brazil. Some central groups in the LGBT struggle have incorporated intersex guidelines into their agenda—such as the Dignity group, a non-governmental organization based in Curitiba and with national incidence, mainly through the participation of its members in the Brazilian Association of Lesbians, Bisexuals, Bisexuals, Transvestites and Transgender (ABGLT). However, a properly intersexual activism is still incipient. No groups with high incidence, national or regional, are observed.

6 The Stakes in the Legal Regulation of Sexual Identity

The Brazilian Federal Constitution and other national legislation have several statements corresponding to rights and duties directed to individuals based on the designation of gender in the civil registry. This is the case, for example, with respect to maternity and paternity leave—the first modality is for pregnant women designated as women at birth, and the second is designed for those parents who are recognized as "men" on the basis of their sex. There is a severe discrepancy between these benefits given that maternity leave is guaranteed by Article 7, item XVII, of the Federal Constitution, for a period of 120 days (which may be extended to up to 180 days), while paternity leave is granted for a maximum period of 5 days, according to Article 7, item XIX, of the Federal Constitution, in accordance with Article 10, § 1 of the Temporary Constitutional Provisions Act (ADCT).[30]

These rules, however, have been relaxed by judicial decisions in lawsuits filed by homosexual male couples wishing to exercise paternity by adoption or assisted human reproduction.[31] In this line of thinking, homosexual lesbian couples should not be treated differently, in order to allow two adoptive mothers to enjoy the maternity leave benefit. In Porto Alegre, capital of the state of Rio Grande do Sul, the birth of a trans couple's son was reported, stating that Anderson, the trans man who gave birth to the child, was granted his maternity leave, while his girlfriend, Helena, got the paternity leave.[32] However, no official statistics on cases such as

[30]On May 3, 2016, the then Brazilian President Dilma Roussef instituted the "Extension Program of the paternity leave for the servants ruled by Law No. 8,112/1990" (this author's translation), extending the benefit period to 20 days.

[31]CNJ (2015).

[32]Boechat (2015).

this—trans parents seeking the benefit to enjoy time with their child(ren)—are available.

Another notorious distinction in the legal system concerns the compulsory military enlistment that occurs in Brazil only for those designated as men at birth (according to Law 4,375/1964). Only in 2012, through Decree 12,705, the permission was extended to female military officers to act as combatants of the Brazilian Army in areas previously restricted to male military personnel. It is important to note that in April 2017, the First Federal Court of Barueri sanctioned the Brazilian Army with compensation for material and moral damages caused by officers of the corporation to a trans student at the time of her enlistment.[33] It should be emphasized that this case is apparently the first one in which the Army was sanctioned for discriminatory conduct; more specifically, transphobia.

The present topic can also be illustrated by the differentiation present in the social security system, in which the right to retirement, with respect to both time of contribution and age, has different material criteria in relation to the sexes. That is, to grant the retirement pension benefit, different deadlines are required, depending on whether the insured is designated as a man or a woman at birth. According to § 7, item II, of Article 201 of the Federal Constitution:

> Art. 201. The social security will be organized in the form of a general regime, of a contributory nature and obligatory affiliation, observing criteria that preserve its financial and actuarial balance, and will attend, under the terms of the law, to:
>
> [...] § 7° Retirement is guaranteed in the general social security scheme, according to the law, obeying the following conditions:
>
> [...] II - Sixty-five years of age, if male, and sixty years of age, if female, being reduced the limit in five years for rural workers both male and female and for those who carry out their activities in family economy regime, included in these category the rural areas producers, the artisan miners and the artisan fishermen. (this author's translation)

In accordance with the constitutional provision Law 8.213/1991, its Article 48 provides that "retirement by age shall be due to the insured person who, after expired the period of grace required by this Law, completes 65 (sixty-five) years of age, if male, and 60 (sixty), if female" (this author's translation), which is also reiterated by Article 51 of Decree 3,048/1999, in verbis:

> Art. 51. Retirement by age, once the required period of grace is met, will be due to the insured who turns sixty-five years of age, if male, or sixty, if female, being reduced these limits to sixty and fifty-five years of age for rural workers, respectively men and women, referred to in letter "a" of item I, letter "j" of item V, and items VI and VII of Art. 9 caput, as well as for the insured artisan miners who prove to work in a family economy regime, as defined in § 5 of Art. 9. (this author's translation)

According to the National Association of Transvestites and Transsexuals (ANTRA), 90% of the transvestite and trans population are forced into prostitution because of the prejudice suffered in formal workplaces and because of school

[33] Lucon (2017).

dropout, which, in turn, impairs the qualification of trans persons and cyclically impedes their insertion into the labor market.[34] There consequently is repeated neglect of the trans segment, something that is attempted to be minimized, at first, by the recognition of gender identity, through the feasibility of rectifying official identification documents (which, for its turn, refers to previous topics).

Nonetheless, certain projects of regional initiative have been developed to help trans persons (and/or other LGBTI) in obtaining substantive protection. One—and perhaps the one with the greatest institutional notoriety—is the "Projeto Reinserção Social Transcidadania" ("Transcity Social Reinsertion Project"), of the São Paulo City Hall, which "aims to strengthen professional placement, social reintegration and recover of citizenship for the LGBTI population in situation of vulnerability, attended by the Coordination of Sexual Diversity (CADS)" (this author's translation).[35]

7 Current Debates Before the Brazilian Legislature and Judiciary

Several avenues have been pursued in the search for recognition of rights for trans persons: legislative, judicial, and even administrative. Within the legislative scope is the Draft Law (PL) 5,002 of 2013, known as João Nery Law or Law of Gender Identity. On the internet page of the Chamber of Deputies, where the PL is currently located, it is clarified that the law provides for the right to gender identity and amends Article 58 of Law 6,015, dated December 31, 1973.[36] The PL was presented to the plenary of the Chamber of Deputies on February 20, 2013 and since then it has undergone several modifications, such as joining and unjoining to projects of diverse laws, archiving and unarchiving. It is important to note that the Brazilian legislature has never approved any law to expand the rights of LGBT persons, since the first proposal in 1995 (PL 1,151, about the regulation of civil union between persons of the same sex) to this day. For that reason, it is possible to affirm that the political force of the groups opposed to these rights is extremely strong on the National Congress, being unlikely that the approval of this project or others related to the theme will occur in the next years.

The largest extensions of rights have taken place from the Brazilian Judiciary. Currently, three lawsuits concerning the rights of trans persons are filed in the Federal Supreme Court. The first is Extraordinary Appeal (RE) 670,422, which was legally admitted in October 2012 and considered to be of general repercussion in 2014. This appeal had its judgment initiated in April 2017 and finalized in August

[34]Cazarré (2015).

[35]Prefeitura De São Paulo (2019).

[36]For further details see the original proposal, available at: https://goo.gl/riTQZB. Accessed: 7 Apr. 2017.

2018. It discusses the possibility of gender change in the civil registry of trans persons without the need for gender modification surgery,[37] and without the record of a trans person status in the civil registry of those persons who have not been operated but who wish to have their names rectified. The Brazilian Institute of Family Law (IBDFAM), the ANIS—Institute of Bioethics, Human Rights and Gender, and the Public Defender's Office of the Union were accepted as amicus curiae in this case.

Another case mentioned once again is Extraordinary Appeal (RE) 845,779, distributed in October 2014 and whose general repercussion was recognized in November of the same year. Its trial began in November 2015, and since July 2018 it is concluded for the Rapporteur, Justice Roberto Barroso. It discusses the possibility of compensation for moral damages resulting from the embarrassment suffered by a trans person who was prevented from using, in a shopping mall, the bathroom consistent with her gender.[38] In practice, this RE has been understood as being at the moment of enabling the State's declaration on the social recognition of the gender identity of trans persons, as well as on the right of these persons to use bathrooms consistent with their gender. This apprehension of the concrete case, in a critical perspective, seems to demonstrate a marked state interference in a context that, in theory, is not exactly measured as legal: although public space toilets are, as a rule, separated into booths suitable for men and for women, there is, to our knowledge, no explicit regulations (as a law or resolution) that determine the use of toilets in these terms, being this configuration reiterated, therefore, through a rule not written in codes.

A third lawsuit related to this topic, also cited in this chapter, is the Direct Action of Unconstitutionality 4,275, which was proposed by the Attorney General's Office, legally admitted in July 2009 and judged between February 28 and March 1, 2018. This DAU referred to the possibility of changing name and sex in the civil registers of trans persons, calling into question the constitutionality of Article 58 of Law 6,015/1973, thus bringing it very close to the content of Law 5,002/2013. The initial request by the Attorney-General of the Republic was accepted, and the Federal Supreme Court, in a majority decision, considered that it is possible to change name and gender in the civil registry even without performing a surgical procedure of sex reassignment/gender modification or hormonal or pathological treatments. This allows interested person the possibility of the change being made directly in the civil registry, giving interpretation to Article 58 of the Public Registration Law according to the Federal Constitution and the Pact of San José of Costa Rica (in addition to expressly refer to the Advisory Opinion No. 24/17 of the IACHR), exercising, in addition to constitutionality control, the control of conventionality, therefore. Regarding this case, the Brazilian Institute of Family Law (IDFAM), the

---

[37] Acompanhamento processual. RE 670422. Available at: http://www.stf.jus.br/portal/processo/verProcessoAndamento.asp?incidente=4192182. Accessed: 7 Apr. 2017.

[38] Acompanhamento processual. RE 845779. Available at: http://www.stf.jus.br/portal/processo/verProcessoAndamento.asp?incidente=4657292. Accessed: 23 Jan. 2017.

Group of Lawyers for Sexual Diversity (GADVS), the Brazilian Association of Gays, Lesbians and Transgenders (ABGLT), the Dignity Group—for the Citizenship of Gays and Lesbians, the Integrated Laboratory on Sexual Diversity and Gender, Policies and Rights (LIDIS), the Latin American Center on Sexuality and Human Rights (CLAM), the Federal Council of Psychology and the Public Defender's Office of the Union were accepted as amici curiae.

In an administrative session also held on March 1, 2018, in the analysis of the consultative request under No. 0604054-58.2017.6.00.0000, the Superior Electoral Court expressed its opinion on the interpretation to be given to the term "sex" contained in Article 10, paragraph 3 of Law No. 9,504/1997,[39] which should be read as *gender*, understanding that both trans men and trans women can be inserted in their respective female and male quotas for the candidacy for political positions before the Chamber of Deputies, the Legislative Chamber of the Federal District, the Legislative Assemblies and the Municipal Councils.

In addition to the judicial scope, it is worth mentioning what has been happening in the administrative sphere. Several federal universities were already approving the internal use of the social name of trans persons. On April 28, 2016, the then president Dilma Rousseff signed Decree n. 8,727, which provides for the use of the social name and the recognition of the gender identity of transvestites and trans persons in the scope of the direct, autarchic, and foundational federal public administration. Also, on March 22, 2018, the Plenary of the Superior Electoral Court approved that trans electors may use the social name in their voter's card.[40] In general, therefore, it is possible to affirm that there is the possibility of progressive rights being recognized gradually in the near future, but that the organization and articulation of groups that oppose to this have been of concern for trans activists.

8 Final Considerations

From the foregoing it is possible to observe that the recognition of trans persons in Brazil is recent. The LGBTI movement, mainly as far as the trans category, only gained greater prominence from the 1990s. Since then, the Brazilian legal system has been a space for discussions and changes regarding the guarantee of the rights of trans persons. These changes occur mainly within the scope of the judiciary and in contrast, the legislature still shows itself mostly against the demands of LGBTI citizenship.

[39]"Article 10. Each party or coalition may register candidates for the Chamber of Deputies, the Legislative Chamber, the Legislative Assemblies and the Municipal Councils in a total of up to 150% (one hundred and fifty percent) of the number of seats to be filled except: [...] § 3o Of the number of vacancies resulting from the rules set forth in this article, each party or coalition shall meet the minimum of 30% (thirty percent) and a maximum of 70% (seventy percent) for each sex." (This author's translation).

[40]Lucon (2018b).

The quest for these rights revolves around the recognition of gender identity. Currently, those self-determined trans persons can proceed to extrajudicial rectification of name and sex designative directly at the Civil Registry Service, regardless of surgical or hormonal treatment. This achievement occurred within the scope of the Federal Supreme Court, with the judgment of the Direct Action of Unconstitutionality (ADI) n. 4,275, and was followed by the Appointment n. 73, of the National Council of Justice. However, Brazil is still strongly marked by transphobia, as evidenced by the number of murders and the difficulties these persons face in accessing their basic rights. This form of self-identification is still often treated as a pathology. In addition, although the Single Health System (SUS) currently offers gender modification surgery and hormonal treatments, there is great bureaucracy, few resources, and entrenched prejudice.

Added to this is the difficulty in carrying out eventual treatments and surgeries for young persons, when necessary, besides the possibility of social recognition according to the gender with which they identify themselves. The rectification of registration according to the sex/gender identity for minors is also a matter of debate, because, if not allowed via the Civil Registry Service route, it then would depend on the judicial process. And although gender modification surgery is no longer required for change in civil registries, this factor is still considered decisive (or highly valued), as can be seen by the history of the national decisions. Thus, although there are many difficulties, the LGBTI movement, the support of various institutions and the demonstration through the internet, have helped to increase visibility and publicize the rights of trans persons.

References

Bassette F (2018) Mãe muda na Justiça nome e gênero de filho que nasceu com dois sexos. Veja. https://veja.abril.com.br/brasil/justica-determina-nome-e-genero-de-crianca-intersexo-de-3-anos/. Accessed 4 May 2018

BBC (2018) A história da primeira criança transque conseguiu alterar os documentos no Brasil. G1, May 11, 2018. https://glo.bo/2G5Qu7m. Accessed 5 May 2019

BN Justiça (2015) Sem ação judicial, Defensoria consegue efetuar mudança de nome e sexo de transexual. http://www.bahianoticias.com.br/justica/noticia/52592-sem-acao-judicial-defensoria-consegue-efetuar-mudanca-de-nome-e-sexo-de-transexual.html. Accessed 6 Mar 2017

Boechat B (2015) Casal transexual dá à luz menino em Porto Alegre e planeja casamento. G1. http://extra.globo.com/noticias/brasil/casal-transexual-da-luz-menino-em-porto-alegre-planeja-casamento-16746233.html. Accessed 7 Apr 2017

Brasil (2018) Decreto n° 9.278, de 5 de fevereiro de 2018. http://www.planalto.gov.br/ccivil_03/_Ato2015-2018/2018/Decreto/D9278.htm. Accessed 4 May 2018

Bueno CS (2012) Amicus curiae no Processo Civil brasileiro: um terceiro enigmático. Saraiva, São Paulo

Campos AMde (1977) Comentários à Lei de Registros Públicos: das disposições gerais do registro civil de pessoas naturais (arts. 1 a 109), 1st edn. Jalovi, Bauru, p 347

Cazarré M (2015) Preconceito afasta transexuais do ambiente escolar e do mercado de trabalho. EBC. http://www.ebc.com.br/cidadania/2015/11/preconceito-afasta-transexuais-do-ambiente-escolar-e-do-mercado-de-trabalho. Accessed 7 Apr 2016

CNJ (2015) Casais homoafetivos conseguem licença-maternidade na adoção de crianças. http://www.cnj.jus.br/noticias/cnj/80257-casais-homoafetivos-conseguem-licenca-maternidade-na-adocao-de-criancas. Accessed 7 Apr 2017

Facchini R (2003) Movimento homossexual no Brasil: recompondo um histórico. Cadernos AEL 10(18/19):79–127. http://segall.ifch.unicamp.br/publicacoes_ael/index.php/cadernos_ael/article/view/73. Accessed 15 July 2013

Facchini R, França IL (2009) De cores e matizes: sujeitos, conexões e desafios no Movimento LGBT brasileiro. Sexualidade, salud y sociedad (revista latinoamericana) 3:54–81, 62

Green JN (2000) "Mais amor e mais tesão": a construção de um movimento brasileiro de gays, lésbicas e travestis. Cadernos Pagu 15:271–296

Lucon N (2017) Estudante transexual que foi exposta durante alistamento militar receberá indenização de R$ 60 mil. NLUCON. http://www.nlucon.com/2017/04/estudante-transexual-que-foi-exposta.html. Accessed 7 Apr 2017

Lucon N (2018a) Justiça do Acre autoriza criança intersexo de 3 anos a mudar nome da documentação. NLUCON. http://www.nlucon.com/2018/04/justica-do-acre-autoriza-crianca-intersexo.html. Accessed 4 May 2018

Lucon N (2018b) TSE aprova que pessoas transe travestis poderão utilizar nome social em título de eleitor. NLUCON. http://www.nlucon.com/2018/03/tse-aprova-que-pessoas-trans-e.html. Accessed 4 May 2018

Pelúcio L (2005) Na noite nem todos os fatos são pardos: notas sobre a prostituição travesti. Cadernos Pagu (25), julho-dezembro de 2005, pp 217–248

Prefeitura De São Paulo (2019) Projeto Reinserção Social Transcidadania. http://www.prefeitura.sp.gov.br/cidade/secretarias/trabalho/cursos/operacao_trabalho/index.php?p=170430. Accessed 7 Apr 2017

Santos ARBd (2017) Movimento LGBT e direito: identidades e discursos em (des)construção. Dissertação de mestrado. Direitos Humanos e Democracia. Programa de Pós-Graduação em Direito da Universidade Federal do Paraná

Simões JA, Facchini R (2009) Na Trilha do Arco-Íris: do movimento homossexual ao LGBT. Editora Fundação Perseu Abramo, São Paulo

Transgender Europe (2016) TransMurder monitoring. http://transrespect.org/en/idahot-2016-tmm-update/. Accessed 20 Mar 2017

Ventura M (2010) A transexualidade no tribunal: saúde e cidadania. Uerj, Rio de Janeiro

The Legal Status of Trans Persons in the Republic of Croatia

Nenad Hlača

Abstract This chapter presents the basic legal framework for the recognition of the rights of trans persons in the Republic of Croatia. It explains how the Constitutional Court and Health bureaucracies have developed tools to facilitate access to gender confirming treatments and surgeries, as well as the registration of changes of name and sex. It also explains, however, that the main issue concerning trans persons in Croatia today is the lack of doctors trained in the surgical and emotional aspects of gender transitions.

In the legal system of the Republic of Croatia, a series of legal texts explicitly prohibit discrimination and thoroughly elaborate on gender equality. In this sense, Article 3 of the Constitution explicitly mentions, *inter alia*, freedom, equality, gender equality, respect for human rights and the rule of law as the highest values of Croatia's constitutional order. The rights and freedoms of citizens are to be consistently protected regardless of the person's gender. Article 14 of the Constitution reads as follows:

> All persons in the Republic of Croatia shall enjoy rights and freedoms, regardless of race, colour, gender, language, religion, political or other conviction, national or social origin, property, birth, education, social status or other characteristics. All persons shall be equal before the law.[1]

In addition to the Constitution, the Anti-Discrimination Act explicitly mentions gender as one of the reasons for promoting equality of citizens as the highest value of

[1]Constitution of the Republic of Croatia, OG—Official Gazette, n. 56/90, 135/97, 8/98 [consolidated text], 113/00, 124/00 [consolidated text], 28/01, 41/01 [consolidated text], 55/01 [correction], 76/10, 85/10 [consolidated text] and Change of the Constitution of the Republic of Croatia (National Constitutional Initiative) OG, n. 5/2014 Constitutional Court Decision n. SuP-O-1/2014.

N. Hlača (✉)
Faculty of Law, University of Rijeka, Rijeka, Croatia
e-mail: nenad.hlaca@pravri.hr

I. C. Jaramillo, L. Carlson (eds.), *Trans Rights and Wrongs*, Ius Comparatum - Global Studies in Comparative Law 54,
https://doi.org/10.1007/978-3-030-68494-5_4

the constitutional order.[2] This Act expressly prohibits discrimination on grounds of personal or family status, health status, genetic inheritance of gender identity and expression or sexual orientation. Due to the complexity and importance of the legal order of the Republic of Croatia, Article 1 of the Anti-Discrimination Act is cited here in its entirety:

1. This Act provides for the protection and promotion of equality as the highest value of the constitutional order of the Republic of Croatia, creates prerequisites for the realization of equal opportunities and regulates protection against discrimination on the grounds of race or ethnic affiliation or colour, gender, language, religion, political or other belief, national or social origin, property, trade union membership, education, social status, marital or family status, age, health condition, disability, genetic heritage, native identity, expression or sexual orientation.
2. Placing of any person, or a person related to that person by kinship or other relationship, in a less favourable position on the grounds referred to in paragraph 1 of this Article shall be, within the meaning of this Act, deemed to be discrimination.
3. Placing of a person in a less favourable position based on a misconception of the existence of the grounds referred to in paragraph 1 of this Article shall also be, within the meaning of this Act, deemed to be discrimination.

The Labor Law[3] also expressly prohibits discrimination with respect to gender and sexual orientation, marital status or family responsibilities. The Gender Equality Act is another document that prohibits discrimination,[4] and its Article 6 proclaims:

> Discrimination on the basis of gender (hereinafter: discrimination) shall mean any normative or real, direct or indirect differential treatment, exclusion or limitation based on one's gender which renders more difficult or denies equal recognition, enjoyment or exercise of human rights of men and women in political, educational, economic, social, cultural, civil and any other sphere of life. Any discrimination on the basis of one's marital or family status and sexual orientation shall be forbidden. Any incitement of another person to discrimination shall be considered an act of discrimination under this Act.

The Croatian Ombudsman for Gender Equality has been established based on the authority of the Gender Equality Act. The Ombudsman for Gender Equality is an independent body that is obliged to submit a report to the Croatian Parliament once a year.

[2]Anti-Discrimination Act, OG 85/2008.

[3]Labor Act, consolidated text, OG 137/2004.

[4]Gender Equality Act, OG 116/2003, 82/2008.

1 Constitutional Referendum on the Definition of Marriage

Croatia as a member of the Council of Europe, starting from the principle of subsidiarity, enjoys wide discretion with respect to its judicial judgments. However, judgments of the European Court of Human Rights considerably contribute to the growing trend of accepting a new transgender identity after gender change. Since moral judgments are based on tradition and value systems, national authorities have autonomous authority to prescribe the preconditions for marriage, even though these legal provisions need not be in the exclusive domain of discretion—within the margin of appreciation. Gender identity also includes the right to sexual orientation and sexual life, as well as the recognition of legal effects/rights to post-operative trans persons. However, it should be noted that according to the latest census data, the Croatia is a predominantly Catholic country, and based on the views of its citizens it is a country that shares traditional values that were publicly obscured during the Communist era.

In a sovereign and independent, democratic state, citizens are expected to participate in the public political life and are free to create initiatives and fight for their goals. In this context, the Act on referenda and other forms of personal participation in the state and local and regional self-government has opened up the possibility of direct citizen participation.[5] The citizens' initiative "In the Name of the Family" encouraged the holding of the state constitutional referendum on December 1, 2013, whereby 65.87% of Croatia's citizens voted for a new constitutional definition of marriage. The announcement of the Constitutional Court's constitutional referendum on the definition of marriage was published in 2013.[6] Once the referendum was passed, the Constitutional Court made the Decision on the conclusion of the process of reviewing the constitutionality and lawfulness of the referendum held on December 1, 2013, based on which the Article 62 of the Constitution was supplemented with a new paragraph into the Constitution that introduced the definition of marriage as a union between a woman and a man.[7]

In the following year, the Croatian Parliament adopted the Same-Sex Life Partnership Act.[8] This Act regulates life partnerships of same-sex couples, the principles, conclusion and termination of life partnerships, the procedures by the competent bodies related to the conclusion and termination of life partnerships, the keeping of a register of life partnerships and the legal effects of life partnership

[5]Act on referenda and other forms of personal participation in the state and local and regional self-government, OG 38/2009.

[6]Communication of the Constitutional Court of the Republic of Croatia on the Citizens' Constitutional Referendum on the Definition of Marriage, OG 138/2013.

[7]Decision on the conclusion of the process of reviewing the constitutionality and lawfulness of the referendum held on December 1, 2013, in which Article 62 of the Constitution of the Republic of Croatia is supplemented by the new paragraph 2, n.: SuP-O-1/2014 of January 14, 2014, OG 5/2014.

[8]Same-Sex Life Partnership Act, OG 92/2014.

(Art. 1). A life partnership is defined as a family life relationship between two persons of the same sex, concluded before a competent body, pursuant to the provisions of this Act. An informal life partnership is a family life relationship between two persons of the same sex who have not concluded a life partnership before a competent body, provided the relationship has lasted no less than 3 years and from its beginning has met the requirements prescribed for the validity of a life partnership.

The existence of an informal life partnership is demonstrated in the same manner and under the same requirements as a common-law marriage relationship. In the case of a dispute between the partners, the existence of an informal life partnership is to be proven before the competent court. An informal life partnership which meets the requirements referred to in this Act leads to personal and material effects to which the provisions of this Act (with the exception of Article 38) apply *mutatis mutandis* in the field of personal rights, relationships related to children, and the property relations of the life partners. An informal life partnership is to lead to the same effects in the fields of inheritance, the tax system, pension insurance, the social welfare system, compulsory health insurance and healthcare, rights and obligations concerning employment relations, access to public and market-related services and public law status as those granted to a common-law marriage relationship by separate regulations governing those fields.

2 Regulation of Civil Status and Name

The 1993 Act on State Registers provided in its Article 9 the option of subsequent registry of sex change. [9] In 2013, the Parliament of the Republic of Croatia stipulated with its new Article 9a a more detailed condition that sex change as a change of data is entered into the birth registry by means of a decision of the competent authority following the opinion of the competent body regarding the sex change or life in another gender identity in accordance with medical documentation. This Act stipulates that the manner of collecting medical documentation is to be prescribed by a special regulation.[10]

3 Regulation of the Gender Identity

The Constitutional Court concluded, in a case initiated by a person for the protection of the right to life in another gender identity, there had been ineffective decision-making in the request for the realization of rights in the area of personal life in the

[9]Act on State Registers, OG 96/1993.

[10]Act on amendments and additions to the Act on State Registers, OG 76/2013.

sense of Article 35 of the Constitution, which has led to extended uncertainty with regard to the gender identity of the person. The Constitutional Court stated the following: "In the Republic of Croatia there is a legal right to enter a sex change into the birth registry in the case of 'life in another gender identity'."[11] This was followed by the Ministry of Health's Regulations on the Manner of Collecting Medical Documentation and Determining the Conditions and Assumptions for a Sex Change or Life in Another Gender Identity.[12] The same Ministry published in 2015 in the Official Gazette a list of experts who have experience in work with transsexuals and are competent to formulate an opinion in the National Health Council's proceedings about gender change or life in another gender identity.[13] The Ministry also provided detailed Professional guidelines for the creation of opinions of health care workers and psychologists on the establishment of terms and conditions for changing gender and life in another gender identity.[14]

4 Conclusion

The fundamental problem of trans persons in the Republic of Croatia is that there is no developed practice in surgical procedures of gender change and there are no specialized clinics. Persons are forced to pay for these procedures at foreign clinic interventions from their own funds. The Croatian Health Insurance Fund, through which health insurance rights are exercised, does not cover the costs of sex-change operations, but only the costs of hormonal therapy and psychological support. Despite these positive steps, it appears that the by-laws of the Ministry of Health that have been passed recently have not provided the complete legal framework for effective protection.

The Constitutional Court of the Republic of Croatia in a 2014 judgment correctly concluded that the boundaries between the positive and negative obligations of the state are not accurately defined. In determining whether or not there is such a

[11]Constitutional Court Decision of 18 March 2014, U-IIIB-3173/2012, OG 46/2014.

[12]Regulations on the Manner of Collecting Medical Documentation and Determining the Conditions and Assumptions for a Sex Change or Life in Another Gender Identity, OG 132/2014.

[13]List of experts who have experience in work with transsexuals and are competent to formulate an opinion in the National Health Council's proceedings about gender change or life in another gender identity, NN 59/2015.

[14]Professional guidelines for the creation of opinions of health care workers and psychologists on the establishment of terms and conditions for changing gender and life in another gender identity, OG 7/2016.

commitment, there is a degree of proportionality that needs to be established between the general interests of the community and the individual's interest, whereby the state should enjoy a certain discretion.[15] The final conclusion is that the legal status of transsexual and transgender persons in the Republic of Croatia is still under reconstruction.

[15]Constitutional Court Decision of March 18, 2014, U-IIIB-3173/2012, OG 46/2014.

The Civil Status of Trans Persons in the Czech Republic

Zdeňka Králíčková

Abstract This chapter presents the regulation of sexual identity in the Czech Republic. It shows that notwithstanding the recent reform of the Civil Code to address the civil status of trans persons, this reform dates from 2012, the possibility of a change in the registered sex still is conditioned on the divorce or cancellation of registered partnership, and gender confirming surgery as well as sterilization. The Constitutional Court failed to examine the petition of an individual who desired to change his sex but not to undergo surgery for not having exhausted available remedies. Parliament has neglected to approve Bills responsive to expert criticisms of the 2012 Civil Code reform.

It is necessary to stress that the current legal regulation in the Czech Republic with respect to change of gender identity is still firmly based on involuntary divorce of marriage or cancellation of registered partnership, as well as involuntary surgery and sterilization. However, a broader discussion is occurring on this topic within the LGBT community, and among legal and medical experts and in the general public as well.

The legal developments concerning trans persons in European countries, the recent case law of the European Court of Human Rights and other aspects have been recently considered by a group of deputies of the Parliament of the Czech Republic. A new legislative draft is pending that aims to change the legal regulation of marriage in the Civil Code that was passed in 2012. This draft would have a significant impact on the regulation of gender identity due to revisions of the definition of marriage. Once the amendment on gender neutral marriage is passed, involuntary divorce of marriage or cancellation of registered partnership would no longer be conditions for gender modification.

In addition, there is a second pending draft by the Ministry of Justice which goes even further: it proposes to radically shift the concept of gender modification in both

Z. Králíčková (✉)
Masaryk University, Faculty of Law, Brno, Czech Republic
e-mail: zdenka.kralickova@law.muni.cz

I. C. Jaramillo, L. Carlson (eds.), *Trans Rights and Wrongs*, Ius Comparatum - Global Studies in Comparative Law 54,
https://doi.org/10.1007/978-3-030-68494-5_5

the Civil Code and the Act on Specific Health Services. Involuntary surgery and sterilization would no longer be among the key words concerning gender modification any more. A change in gender identity would be possible by a statement lodged at the registry office. There is much criticism and negative opinions in this respect, especially by the Czech Sexology Association.

Time will show how the Parliament deals with the drafts. The issue has been hotly debated by experts as well as ordinary people, which is of course nothing new. Traditional institutes—the concept of marriage and the civil status of person—are at stake, which is very sensitive for society.

1 Trans Persons Under Current Czech Law

The Czech Republic is a country with a continental civil law legal system. *The Constitution of the Czech Republic (Constitution)*[1] and *the Charter of Fundamental Rights and Basic Freedoms (Charter)*[2] form a part of the constitutional order of the Czech Republic. Recognizing the inviolability of the natural rights of man, the rights of citizens, and the sovereignty of the law, proceeding from the universally-shared values of humanity, both the Constitution and the Charter protect human rights, namely human dignity and liberty, equality of fundamental rights and basic freedoms regardless of gender, race, colour of skin, language, faith and religion, political or other conviction, national or social origin, membership in a national or ethnic minority, property, birth, or other status. Finally, according to the Charter, everyone has the right to the protection of his or her health. Citizens shall have the right, on the basis of public insurance, to free medical care and to medical aids under conditions provided for by law (Article 31 Charter).

For understanding the legal regulation of trans persons' sexual identity it is necessary to list other sources of law, mainly international treaties[3] and the Acts as follows:

[1]Act No. 1/1993 Sb., as amended. The English translation available at: http://www.psp.cz/en/docs/laws/constitution.html. Accessed 15 Nov 2018.

[2]Act No. 2/1993 Sb., as amended. The English translation available at: http://www.usoud.cz/fileadmin/user_upload/ustavni_soud_www/Pravni_uprava/AJ/Listina_English_version.pdf. Accessed 15 Nov 2018.

[3]The Article 10 of the Constitution provides as follows:

Promulgated treaties, to the ratification of which Parliament has given its consent and by which the Czech Republic is bound, form a part of the legal order; if a treaty provides something other than that which a statute provides, the treaty shall apply.

- *Convention for the Protection of Human Rights and Fundamental Freedoms;*[4,5]
- *Convention for the Protection of Human Rights and Dignity of the Human Being with regard to the Application of Biology and Medicine: Convention on Human Rights and Biomedicine;*[6]
- *Convention on the Rights of Persons with Disabilities;*[7]
- *Convention on the Rights of the Child;*[8]
- *Civil Code (CC),*[9] that establishes civil status (Section 15 ff. CC) and regulates civil law aspects of change of sex (see Section 29 CC);
- *Act on Register Offices, Name and Surname (AR),*[10] that regulates registration of a child, his or her name, surname, sex etc. and consequences of sex change;
- *Act on Population Records and Birth Numbers,*[11] that regulates administrations of information of the state citizens, theirs husbands, wives, registered partners, children and issuing and changing of Birth Registration Numbers;
- *Act on Specific Health Services (ASHS),*[12] that regulates medical aspects of sex change;
- *Act on Equal Treatment and on the Legal Means of Protection against Discrimination and on Amendment to Some Laws (the Anti-Discrimination Act),*[13] that defines more precisely the right to equal treatment and prohibition of discrimination.

2 The General Legal Regulation of Civil Status

According to the *Convention on the Rights of the child*, a child has to be registered in the Book of Birth (Vital Register). *The Act on Registry Offices, Name and Surname* provides that both the Book of Birth (Vital Register) (Section 14 AR) and the Birth Certificate (Section 29 AR)[14] must contain

---

[4]A statement of the Foreign Office, No. 209/1992 Sb.

[5]Regarding the case law of the International Court of Human Rights see Kmec et al. (2012).

[6]A statement of the Foreign Office No. 96/2001 Sb.

[7]A statement of the Foreign Office No. 10/2010 Sb.

[8]A statement of the Foreign Office No. 104/1991 Sb.

[9]Act No. 98/2012 Sb., as amended. The English translation of the original text is available at: http://obcanskyzakonik.justice.cz/index.php/home/zakony-a-stanoviska/preklady. Even though the Civil Code has been amended, the amendment is not relevant to the issue in question. Accessed 15 Nov 2018.

[10]Act No. 301/2000 Sb., as amended.

[11]Act No. 133/2000 Sb., as amended.

[12]Act No. 373/2011 Sb., as amended.

[13]Act No. 198/2009 Sb., as amended. The English translation available at: https://www.ochrance.cz/fileadmin/user_upload/DISKRIMINACE/Antidiscrimination_Act.pdf. Accessed 20 Feb 2018.

[14]If there is a mistake in the Book of Births, the Book of Marriages, the Book of Registered Partnerships or the Book of Deaths, the Registrar is allowed to correct it. See Section 50 AR "*Correction of erroneous or incorrect data*".

(a) the name, or names, and surnames of the child,
(b) the day, month and year of birth of the child,
(c) birth registration number, place of birth and sex of the child,
(d) name, or names, surname, or surnames, date and place of birth, birth registration number, nationality (state citizenship) and place of residence of the parents.

A child can be registered only as female or male. The sex of the child is recognizable not only from "information about sex", but from the name, surname and from the birth registration number of the child according to the *Population Records Act.*[15] A change in gender identity made in accordance with law must be registered as well (see "an additional record of a sex change", Section 17a AR). The change is accompanied by the change of a name and a surname and birth registration number of the trans person. For details see below.

The Act on the State Citizenship of the Czech Republic[16] regulates the state Citizenship, which complements civil status in the Czech Republic. The civil status can be proved by public documents (in Czech "veřejná listina") which are Birth Certificate, Marriage Certificate, Certificate on Registered Partnership and finally Identity Card (in Czech "občanský průkaz").

Besides public law registration of a child, the *Civil Code* provides further attributes of the civil (personal) status:[17]

(a) name and surname (Section 77 CC)
(b) legal personality (Section 15/1 CC)
(c) legal capacity (Section 15/2 CC)[18]
(d) domicile or residence (Section 80 CC)
(e) family status: single, married to an opposite sex spouse, registered with the same-sex partner, divorced, widowed, adopted etc.

3 The Legal Regulation of Sex/Gender

Within the process of the child's registration into Book of Births (Vital Register), the Registrar must enter the child's sex into the Book of Births with the letters "F" or "M". The Birth Certificate must also contain such information (Section 10/3 AR).

[15] Act No. 133/2000 Sb., Population Records Act and Act on Birth Numbers, as amended. It means that the birth number shows the sex of every person. See the role of the number "5" added to the month of birth below in the examples:

Male-to-female: if a man was born on the 1st January 2000, his birth number is 00-01-01/xxxx. After a sex change it would be 00-51-01/xxxx.

Female-to-male: if a woman was born on the 1st January 2000, her birth number is 00-51-01/xxxx. After a sex change it would be 00-01-01/xxxx.

[16] Act No. 186/2013 Sb., On the Citizenship of the Czech Republic, as amended.

[17] According to the legal doctrine, the civil status (in Czech "osobní stav člověka") is traditionally understood as a personal legal position towards other people from which status rights and duties (non-proprietary ones) are derived. See Frinta (2014), p. 152.

[18] A person can be limited in their legal capacity by the court (Section 55 ff. CC).

There is no gender-neutral or third-sex possibility. Regarding the lack of intersex legal regulation there are voices of critics at the web pages of LGBT organizations.[19] However, experts, mainly doctors, are quite restrictive and conservative.[20]

As to the registering of an additional sex change, the *Act on Registry Offices, Name and Surname* (17a AR) provides as follows: "An additional record of sex change shall be made to the Book of Birth on the basis of a certificate issued by the health service provider who is required to notify the registry office within 3 working days of the date of sex change. The day of sex change is the day shown in this confirmation."

4 The Legal Regulation of Names

As already mentioned, *the Act on Registry Offices, Name and Surname* provides that both the Book of Birth (Section 14 AR) and the Birth Certificate (Section 29 AR) must contain the name, or names, and surnames of the child. There are many rules covering this (Section 62 AR). Mainly, it is provided, that:

> Any existing name can be entered into the register book in the correct orthographic form. It is not possible to write the names garbled, dull and homemade. A natural person of a male cannot register the name of a woman and vice versa. The registry office will not write down the name if it is known that name is used by the sibling if the siblings have a common parent. If doubts arise as to the existence of a name or its proper form, the physical person is required to produce a document issued by an expert witness.

Any person is allowed to change his or her name (Section 72 AR). *The Act on Register Offices, Name and Surname* provides that:

1. The name, or names, or surname, or more surnames, which the natural person is obliged to use, may be changed to a natural person only upon his or her application, or the application of his or her legal representatives.
2. A change of surname shall be permitted, in particular, if the surname is derogatory or ridiculous, or if there is a serious reason for doing so.
3. A change of name shall not be permitted if a man requests a change of his name to a woman's one or, conversely, if a chosen name is not existing, is grievous, diminished, domestic or it is a name of a living sibling of the joint parents. If doubts arise as to the existence of a name or its proper form, the applicant shall be required to produce a document issued by an expert witness.

[19] See Anonymus (2018) and Intersexualita (2018).

[20] For instance, see Zvěřina (2014).

Finally, there are special provisions regulating a change of a name in relation to sex change (gender reassignment). *The Act on Register Offices, Name and Surname* states (Section 72/5 AR) that:

> At the request of a natural person and confirmation of the provider of health services, the registry office shall permit the change of the name or names and the surname
>
> a) to a neutral name and surname when treatment for gender reassignment has been initiated; or
> b) to another name, if applicable, name and surname, if the treatment for sex change was completed.

5 The Legal Regulation of Family Status

The Civil Code provides legal regulations determining who is a child's mother (Section 775 CC) and father (Sections 776 ff. CC).[21] The child, and even an adult, can be adopted and become a part of a new family *(adoption natura imitatur)* by judicial decree (Sections 794 ff. CC). Marriage can be concluded only by persons of the opposite sex. This traditional approach was not changed by the Civil Code (see Section 655 CC). However, there is a pending draft aiming to change the entire concept of marriage as discussed below.

People of the same sex are allowed to enter into registered partnerships regulated by *the Act on Registered Partnership.*[22] Registered partnerships are in some aspects similar to marriage (maintenance duty between the partners and ex-partners) and in some to cohabitation without marriage (no duty to live together, no duty to be faithful to each other, no duty to help each other, no community of property, no common tenancy of a flat by operation of law, no protection of family dwelling and no institution of the things forming a common household). Regarding partners as parents, they have no right to adopt a child together (or to become step-adopters) or to become common foster parents.[23] According to the pending draft discussed below, *the Act on Registered Partnership* should be cancelled.

---

[21]For more see Hrušáková et al. (2017).

[22]Act No. 115/2006 Sb., as amended.

[23]The same was provided by the Family Act No. 94/1963 Sb. (cancelled by the Civil Code).

6 Specific Legal Regulations Governing Sex and Gender Modification

The Civil Code,[24] the primary source of status rights, uses in relation to changes in sex the terms "individual" or "human being" (in Czech "člověk") and provides as follows (Section 29 CC):

1. Sex change of an individual takes place by surgery while simultaneously disabling the reproductive function and transforming the genitalia (sexual organs). The date of the sex change is presumed to be the date indicated in the certificate issued by the health care provider.
2. Sex change does not affect the personal (civil) status of an individual or his or her personal and property situation; however, marriage or registered partnership terminate. The rights and duties of a man and woman whose marriage terminated to their common child and their property rights and duties at the period following the termination of marriage are governed, by analogy, by the provisions on the rights and duties of divorced spouses to their common child and on their property rights and duties at the period following the divorce; a court shall decide, even of its own motion, on the care each of the parents will take of their common child thereafter.

As mentioned above, the *Civil Code* as *lex generalis* allows a person to change sex (in Czech "člověk"). That is, *Civil Code* does not define such a person in connection with his or her state of health nor does it stipulate *expressis verbis* the condition of a permanent disparity between the psychological and physical gender ("Sexual Dysfunctional Disorder") in contrast to *the Act on Specific Health Services* discussed below. According to the legal doctrine, a wider concept of any person

[24]The Civil Code was passed after quite a long preparatory period. It is interesting that "Principles and Starting points of the Civil Code" did not contain anything regarding the change of sex. See Eliáš and Zuklínová (2001). Neither its predecessor, the Act No. 40/1964 Sb., Civil Code, did regulate such an issue.

However, the first published version of the Civil Code, the so-called "White Book", contained a regulation of the change of sex. For more see Eliáš and Zuklínová (2005). The text of the Section 33/1 Draft was as follows: "Changing the sex of a person through medical and cosmetic interventions is taken to occur on the day that will be confirmed by the appropriate health facility as the day of the change." It is important that neither the reproductive function nor the transformation of the genital organs were mentioned in the text.

Finally, another published version of the Civil Code, the so-called "Blue Book", provided quite differently. See Eliáš and Zuklínová (2008). The text of the Section 28/1 Draft was as follows: "Changing the sex of a person occurs by surgical intervention while disabling the reproduction function. It is considered that the day of the change of sex is the date stated in the confirmation issued by the health service provider."

The explanatory report (memorandum) to the two above mentioned drafts cited the Québec Civil Code (CCQ) without further elaborating on the relevant change. For more see CCQ-1991—Civil Code of Québec. In: *LégisQuébec* [online]. Available at: <http://legisquebec.gouv.qc.ca/en/ShowDoc/cs/CCQ-1991>. Accessed 1 Feb 2018.

(in Czech "člověk") regulated in the *Civil Code* suggests that the official sex is exclusively associated with the biological sex and does not allow the psychological choice of sex.[25]

7 The Act on Specific Health Services

The Act on Specific Health Services[26] uses the term "transsexual patient" (in Czech "transsexuální pacient"). In harmony with *the International Statistical Classification of Diseases and Associated Health Problems* by the WHO, it refers to "Sexual Identification Disorder".[27] The possibility of changing sex is exclusively tied to a person who has a persistent mismatch between mental and physical sex. *The Act on Specific Health Services* as *lex specialis* is quite restrictive.

The Act on Specific Health Services provides in its Part 4 Changing sex of transsexual patients as follows (Section 21 ASHS):

1. By changing the sex of transsexual patients, for the purposes of this Act, it is understood the exercise of health care for the purpose of the change of sex by a surgical intervention while disabling the reproductive function. A transsexual patient means a person who has a persistent mismatch between mental and physical sex ("Sexual Identification Disorder").
2. Gestational surgical procedures may be performed on a patient

   (a) which has been clearly identified as having a sexual identity disorder and demonstrated the ability to live permanently as a person of the opposite sex, and

---

[25]For more details, see Doležal (2013a), p. 342; Dobrovolná (2014), pp. 191 ff.; Frinta (2014), pp. 145 ff.

[26]The former Act No. 20/1966 Sb., on Popular Health-Care, as amended by the act No. 548/1991 Sb., provided for the first time the possibility of "transgender surgery" as follows (Section 27a):

(1) Physical interventions in the reproductive capacity of individuals, castration, stereotactic surgery and transsexual surgery shall be carried out only on the request of the person to be performed and, after approval by a commission of professional consisting of attorney, at least two physicians with specialization in the relevant field and two other doctors not participating in the medical intervention.

(2) Before the application is made, the person shall be duly informed by the physician of the nature of the medical intervention with a warning of the risks and any adverse consequences associated with it.

Before the amendment to the Act on Popular Health-Care, there was a "practice" under "internal instructions" by the Ministry of Health published in Journal of Ministry of Health No. 1-2/1971 and 1-2/1980 (in Czech "Věstník"). Regarding history, see Těšínová et al. (2011), pp. 160–161.

[27]See the Statement of the Czech Statistical Office No. 495/2003 Sb., On the International Statistical Classification of Diseases and Associated Health Problems (ICD-10), the 10th revision, disease "F 64", in Czech "MKN-10", "poruchy pohlavní identity". Tableární část. In: *Ústav zdravotnických informací a statistiky ČR* [online]. Available at: <http://www.uzis.cz/cz/mkn/index.html>. Accessed 15 Feb 2018.

(b) who has not got married or who has not entered into a registered partnership or similar relationship of the same sex abroad, or he or she proved that his or her marriage or registered partnership or similar bond has been terminated.

3. Surgical procedures aimed at changing sex are performed on a patient who has reached the age of 18 years, on the basis of

(a) his or her written requests; and
(b) positive opinion of the expert commission/panel.

8 The Recommended Procedure

The Ministry of Health issued *The recommended procedure for surgical interventions aimed at sex change in transsexual patients (The Recommended Procedure).*[28] It uses the terms "people with disorders of sexual identity" (in Czech "osoby s poruchami pohlavní identity") and provides in its Preamble as follows:

> The implementation of surgical interventions aimed at sex change is part of a complex therapy for people with disorders of sexual identity, the goal of which is to achieve a lasting sense of satisfaction in the sexual role and the associated mental satisfaction. For people with a diagnosis of transsexuality a surgery along with hormone therapy and RLE (Real Life Experience) are an effective procedure.

According to some experts,[29] it is necessary to stress that *the Act on Specific Health Services* does not use the term "transforming the genitalia (sexual organs)" but "change of sex" which is less invasive and more sensitive towards the patients and in harmony with *The Recommended Procedure.*

As for details, *The Recommended Procedure* provides that surgical procedures aimed at the sex change of transsexual patients are surgical interventions aimed at achieving sex reassignment while at the same time preventing the reproduction function. These surgical procedures are:

(a) Female-to-male: mastectomy (reduction mammaplastics), hysterectomy, bilateral ovariectomy, meta-idioplasty, faloplasty, scrotoplasty and urethroplasty, and
(b) Male-to-female: orchiectomy, penectomy, vaginoplasty, clitoridoplasty and labioplasty.

Other conditions upon *The Recommended Procedure* are as follows. A sex change can be done to the patient:

[28]File No. 29991/2012, published in Journal of Ministry of Health No. 8/2012 (in Czech "Věstník"), for more see http://www.mzcr.cz/Legislativa/. Accessed 1 Nov 2017.

[29]See Frinta (2014), pp. 150–152.

(a) for whom a complete disorder of sexual identity has been clearly established—transsexuality,
(b) who have been shown to have the ability to live in the opposite sex for at least 12 months (RLE),
(c) which, if the state of health allows, has been using the relevant hormonal preparations for the past 12 months at least,
(d) who has not been married and/or who has not entered into a registered partnership or similar relationship abroad, or he has proven that his/her marriage or registered partnership or similar relationship was cancelled,
(e) who has reached the age of 18, and
(f) who has a demonstrable awareness of the nature of surgery, the surgeon's options, the duration of hospitalization and possible complications.

Finally, *The Recommended Procedure* provides that a sex change can be done to the patient:

(a) upon his written request,
(b) on the basis of medical reports confirming that all required examinations and diagnostics have been carried out, and that the patient meets the required criteria, and
(c) after approval by an expert commission/panel established by the Ministry of Health.

The criteria demonstrating the patient's readiness are:

(a) demonstrable progress in the transition to a new role, and
(b) provable progress in dealing with family, at work, positive changes in personal life to improve mental well-being, satisfactory management of social maladaptation problems, psychoactive substance abuse, drug overuse, psychotic disorder, and suicidal tendencies.

From the abovementioned legal sources, it is possible to conclude the following conditions the patient must meet for sex reassignment:[30]

(a) age over 18 years,
(b) family status: single, divorced, cancelled registered partnership, widowed etc. (not married, not registered),
(c) written request of the patient,
(d) unambiguous determination of a sexual identification disorder,
(e) demonstration of the ability to live permanently as a person of the opposite sex, and
(f) positive opinion of the expert commission (panel).[31]

---

[30]The law does not provide that the patient should be a Czech state citizen. The existence of (minor) children is not a legal obstacle to a sex change.

[31]Regarding the expert commission (panel), *the Act on Specific Health Services* provides (§ 22/6 ASHS) that:

In practice, the following steps must be taken:[32]

(a) diagnostics: examinations that indicate that a person feels fit to another sex,
(b) the decision-making process: the phase after the diagnosis, the person decides in relation to the recommendations of the specialist doctor,
(c) real life test (RLT): a test phase in which a person tries to live in a role of the opposite sex (he or she can change his or her name and surname to neutral one); it is a test of the correctness of his or her decision,
(d) hormonal therapy: it is approached after several months of the testing phase (the recommended duration is about 1 year), and
(e) operation: the procedure itself follows after the legal and administrative steps.

As regards the starting of the process of the sex change, *the Act on Specific Health Services* provides (Section 23 ASHS) that:

1. Sex changes may be initiated if the patient or guardian of the patient has given his or her written consent immediately prior to commencement of the change, and
2. The provider shall provide confirmation to the patient and to the guardian of the patient about the implementation of sex reassignment.

In this respect, as it was already mentioned above regarding the regulation of the name and surname, *the Act on Register Offices, Name and Surname* states (Section 72 AR) that:

> At the request of a natural person and confirmation of the provider of health services, the registry office shall permit the change of the name or names and the surname
>
> a) to a neutral name and surname when treatment for gender reassignment has been initiated; or
> b) to another name, if applicable, name and surname, if the treatment for sex change was completed.

If a natural person does not request a change of a name and surname after the change of sex, the registry office shall enter the surname in accordance with the rules of the Czech Grammar in the form corresponding to the new sex; regarding the name, the registry office shall not enroll anything in the Book of Birth and makes a notification to the court.

The expert commission, after examining the application, shall draw up a written expert opinion in which it assesses whether all the conditions for the change of gender are fulfilled; it shall also indicate the period of validity of the opinion, taking into account the urgency of the intervention of the medical intervention. A positive opinion on making a sex change requires the approval of all members of the expert commission. In the event of an agreement of all members being missing, the expert commission will describe in its opinion the reasons which led to it. The expert commission submits to the Ministry of Health an expert opinion in three copies and a copy of the record of the meeting.

[32]For details see Fifková (2002), pp. 43 ff.

9 The Act on Register Offices, Name and Surname

Other public law aspects of the sex change must be mentioned. First of all, *the Act on Register Offices, Name and Surname* regulates additional records of the sex change and provides as follows (Section 17a AR):

> An additional record of sex change shall be made to the Book of Birth on the basis of a certificate issued by the health service provider who is required to notify the registry office within 3 working days of the date of sex change. The day of sex change is the day shown in this confirmation.

10 The Population Records Act

Then, the *Population Records Act*[33] provides that the trans person must be assigned with a new birth registration number as follows (Section 17/2): "The change of the birth registration number shall be made when . . . (d) the sex has been changed."[34] The process is followed by issuing a new Identity Card[35] and a new Passport[36] because of the new name, surname, sex, and birth registration number.

11 Access to Medical Treatments

As mentioned above, the sex change is available to those who have the diagnosis of the "Sexual Identification Disorder" according to *the International Statistical Classification of Diseases and Associated Health Problems* by the WHO.[37] That is why the sex change is covered by the public insurance.[38] It includes as follows:

(a) diagnostics: examinations that indicate that a person feels fit to another sex,
(b) the decision-making process: the phase after the diagnosis, the person decides in relation to the recommendations of the specialist doctor,
(c) real life test (RLT): a test phase in which a person tries to live in a role of the opposite sex (he or she can change his or her name and surname to a neutral one); it is a test of the correctness of his or her decision,
(d) hormonal therapy, and
(e) operations.[39]

---

[33] Act No. 133/2000 Sb., Population Records Act and Act on Birth Numbers, as amended.
[34] See No. 16 and mainly the examples.
[35] Act No. 328/1999 Sb., On Identity Cards, as amended.
[36] Act No. 329/1999 Sb., On Travel Documents, as amended.
[37] See *supra* note 28.
[38] See Fifková (2002), p. 110.
[39] *Ibid.*

However, "cosmetic treatments", which include for instance epilation, breast augmentations, insertion of prosthetic testes, voice therapy and thyroid eminence elimination, are paid for by the patients.[40]

12 The Current Discussions

Many experts[41] express opinions in the scholarship on the *Civil Code* that the law regulating sex changes was passed without proper analyses, a wider discussion[42] and mainly without the knowledge of the modern regulations abroad, the case-law of constitutional and supreme courts, and societal trends.[43]

The identified key problems with respect to trans persons are as follows:

- pathologization of trans persons,
- forced divorce or cancelling of registered partnership,
- forced surgery, and
- forced sterilization.[44]

According to some lawyers,[45] the future amendment to the *Civil Code* should replace the wording "transforming the genitalia" (sexual organs) into a less invasive "sex change" which can be for instance only hysterectomy (for FtM) and orchiectomy (for MtF).

---

[40] See Weiss (2010), p. 463.

For details and criticism regarding the pathologization of trans persons, see Havelková (2015), p. 132.

[41] For the historical background, in particular the period before 1989, and the period after the fall of communism in Czechoslovakia in 1989, statistical data, the current regulation and its criticism, mainly regarding pathologization of trans persons, see Havelková (2015), pp. 125–145.

For further criticism of the current legal regulation, see Doležal (2013a), pp. 332–346; and Frinta (2014), pp. 145–156.

[42] However, there has been an ongoing serious discussion on the website of the Journal of Medical Law and Bioethics (in Czech "Časopis zdravotnického práva a bioetiky"). See articles mentioned below.

Agha (2013), Baršová (2013), and Doležal (2013b, c).

[43] See for instance the Recommendation to the Council of Europe Member States by the Commissioner for Human Rights in Council of Europe. Human Rights and Gender Identity. In: Council of Europe [online]. Available at: <https://rm.coe.int/16806da753>. Accessed 20 Feb 2018.

See also The Yogyakarta Principles on the Application of International Human Rights Law in Relation to Sexual Orientation and Gender Identity. In: The YOGYAKARTA PRINCIPLES [online]. Available at: <http://www.yogyakartaprinciples.org/>. Accessed 13 Feb 2018.

[44] See the proceedings from the conferences held at Masaryk University, Brno, for instance "Dny práva 2017"—"Day of Law 2017" and "COFOLA 2018" available at: https://www.law.muni.cz/content/en/proceedings/. Accessed 1 Feb 2018.

[45] See Frinta (2014), pp. 150–152. The author speaks about *cruelty* towards trans persons and is in favor of interpreting the legal regulation *largo sensu* instead of *stricto sensu*.

Regarding *the Government of the Czech Republic,* let us mention just an analysis of the current situation.[46]

Finally, the activities of *the Ombudsman (Public Defender of Rights)* (in Czech "Veřejný ochránce práv") should also be mentioned, especially the criticism regarding forced sterilization.[47] As regards military service, there are no official data, however, some experts reported a case from 2004 of discrimination against a MtF post-operative trans woman who applied for a job in the Czech Army.[48]

Last but not least, we should mention criticism made by LGBT organizations, mainly "Trans*parent",[49] "Proud"[50,51] and *the Collective Complaint by the Transgender Europe (TGEU)* jointly with *ILGA-Europe* and two international non-governmental organizations to the Council of Europe.[52]

---

[46]Details available at https://www.vlada.cz/assets/ppov/rlp/vybory/sexualnimensiny/CZ_(analyza_web.pd.). Accessed 1 Feb 2018.Unfortunately, the data downloaded for the purposes of the National Report presented at the 20th International Congress of Comparative law, Japan, Fukuoka, 2018, are no longer accessible.

[47]See Nucená sterilizace transgender lidí je v rozporu s lidskými právy, rozhodl soud. In: *Ombudsman* [online]. 28.7.2017 [2018]. Available at: <https://www.ochrance.cz/diskriminace/aktuality-z-diskriminace/aktuality-z-diskriminace-2017/nucena-sterilizace-transgender-lidi-je-v-rozporu-s-lidskymi-pravy-rozhodl-soud/>.

See Evropská komise zveřejnila první zprávu o zavedených opatřeních na podporu LGBT rovnosti. In: *Ombudsman* [online]. 23.6.2017. Available at: <https://www.ochrance.cz/diskriminace/aktusality-z-diskriminace/aktuality-z-diskriminace-2017/evropska-komise-zverejnila-prvni-zpravu-o-zavedenych-opatrenich-na-podporu-lgbti-rovnosti/>. Accessed 17 Feb 2018.

[48]See Pechová (2007). Noted according to Havelková (2015), p. 142, Note No. 130.

[49]TRANS*PARENT strives for the empowerment, social justice, promotion of rights and positive social changes for the benefit of trans men, women and other non-cis persons. The organization was founded in Prague in the spring of 2015 by a group of trans activists in response to the urgent need to create a support space and change policies to promote advancement of transgender equality. TRANS*PARENT thus works towards understanding and acceptance of trans and non-cis persons on both the social and the legislative level. For more see https://www.transparentprague.cz/english. Accessed 12 Feb 2018.

[50]See file://PROUD-cz_trans-healthcare_ILGA-report_FINAL.pdf. Accessed 1 Feb 2018.Unfortunately, the data downloaded for the purpose of the National Report presented at the 20th International Congress of Comparative law, Japan, Fukuoka, 2018, are no longer accessible.

[51]*Closing Recommendations* (available in English) were available in *Report on Trans People and their Experiences with Health Care and Legislation*. Prague: Platform for equality, recognition and diversity (PROUD), 2012. Available at: http://proud.cz/o-proudu/dokumenty.html. Accessed 1 Feb 2018.Unfortunately, the data downloaded for the purpose of the National Report presented at the 20th International Congress of Comparative law, Japan, Fukuoka, 2018, are no longer accessible.

[52]For details see *Report on Implementation by the Czech Republic of the Recommendation CM/Rec (2010)5 of the Committee of Ministers of the Council of Europe on measures to combat discrimination on grounds of sexual orientation or gender identity*, supported by ILGA-Europe's Human Rights Violations Documentation Fund in the framework of the project "*Implementing the Council of Europe's Recommendation on LGBT Rights*". This project was financially supported by the Dutch Government Department for Gender & LGBT Emancipation of the Ministry of Education, Culture and Science. Prague: Platform for equality, recognition and diversity (PROUD), 2012. Data were available at: file://Proud-cz/Report_implementation_LGBT_Council-Europe.pdf. Accessed

According to one sociological study,[53] gay organizations operating in the Czech Republic devote almost all their time to the organizing of leisure activities in the form of trips, sporting events or debates. Almost none of them work with awareness-raising (educational) or political activities in relation to the majority of society. Additionally, many gay organizations are at least nominally declared to be gay-lesbian, although there are hardly any lesbian women among their members. Given that the functioning of these organizations usually depends only on a very limited number of individuals, few of them actually have a long-term character and form of a civic association. This causes great difficulty in mapping the development of the community and addressing it in terms of policies that are of direct concern (e.g. information on means of protection against discrimination, HIV prevention, etc.).[54]

13 The Jurisprudence of the Constitutional Court

The Constitutional Court of the Czech Republic has recently refused to grant a petition for appeal by a person requesting that his birth registration number be changed to a neutral or "at least" female form and for a change, or cancellation, of the provisions of the relevant laws that regulate this issue as seen above.[55] The complainant had the "male" sex recorded in his personal documents (Birth Certificate, Identity Card, etc.), which he had not identified with since his early childhood, feeling like a person without an assigned sex. If he had to "choose" between the male and female sex, he would prefer the female one, although he did not consider himself to be a woman. He did not feel the need to have female genital organs, and therefore rejected surgical intervention that would result in his losing reproductive function as prescribed by the law. The facts that he had the male sex recorded in his personal documents and that his birth registration number identifies him as a man, brought him mental frustration according to an expert opinion. The Ministry of the Interior repeatedly informed the complainant that the official sex change and a new birth registration number assignment could not occur without his submitting a confirmation of the implementation of the sex reassignment under the legislation in force.

1 Feb 2018.Unfortunately, the data downloaded for the purpose of the National Report presented at the XX International Congress of Comparative law, Japan, Fukuoka, 2018, are no longer accessible.

See Complaint from 27th April 2015, Case Document No. 1, Registered at the Secretariat on 30th March 2015. In: Council of Europe [online]. 27.4.2015. Available at: <https://rm.coe.int/CoERMPublicCommonSearchServices/DisplayDCTMContent?documentId=09000016804835f1>. Accessed 1 Feb 2018.

[53]See Císař and Vráblíková (2012).

[54]However, there is no doubt that increasing social support of LGBT rights influences the decision-making process of courts and legal regulation of "sensitive" matters. For more see Kozubík and Wintr (2016), pp. 34–47.

[55]See Resolution of the Constitutional Court from 15th November 2016, No. III. ÚS 3376/16.

The Constitutional Court found the complaint inadmissible for the failure to exhaust available remedies. The Court found that the complainant should have first sought protection of his rights in proceedings before administrative courts. It added that by dismissing the complaint without prejudice that there is no danger of *denegationis iustitiae* in relation to the complainant. If the complainant fails to gain effective protection of his rights in the administrative proceedings, he will be able to file a new constitutional complaint in which he will be able to raise all the objections contained in his current complaint.

14 Pending Legislative Drafts

As mentioned above, the legal developments concerning trans persons in European countries, the recent case law of the European Court of Human Rights and other aspects have been widely discussed in the Czech Republic these days. The first significant step to improve the situation of trans persons was the above-mentioned first draft by a group of deputies of the Parliament of the Czech Republic which was lodged in reaction to criticism of the current legal regulation in 2018.[56] The pending draft aims to change the provisions of marriage and sex change in the *Civil Code*. This pending draft is seen by some as progressive and modern, but others view it as a step towards undermining traditional family values. A more correct term could be *alternative*.

As mentioned above, the Civil Code provides that "[m]arriage is a permanent union of a man and a woman formed in a manner provided by this Act" (Section 655 CC). Should the pending draft be passed, the relevant Section would provide that "[m]arriage is a permanent union of two people formed in a manner provided by this Act." In addition, the pending draft would not change the current regulations governing that affiliation will not be used for establishing parentage of same sex couples. There should be no gender-neutral parentage in gender-neutral marriages. Regarding the sex change, the regulation of forced divorce would be cancelled. It means that the marriage would not be terminated due to sex change.

This pending draft should amend *the Act on Specific Health Services* as well. The new provision would be that "[g]estational surgical procedures may be performed on a patient which has been clearly identified as having a sexual identity disorder and demonstrated the ability to live permanently as a person of the opposite sex" (new Section 21/2 ASHS). The text "(b) who has not been married or who has not entered into registered partnership or a similar relationship of the same sex abroad, or who has proved that his or her marriage or registered partnership or similar bond were terminated" would be repealed as would also the Act on Registered Partnership.

---

[56]Parliament of the Czech Republic, Chamber of Deputies, Parliamentary term No. VIII., Draft No. 201/0.

Some revolutionary changes should also come about with the second legislative draft that is pending.[57] The Ministry of Justice has proposed a radical amendment to the *Civil Code* in relation to the latest case law of the European Court of Human Rights in 2018.[58] Individuals should be able to change their sex/gender by simply making a statement at the registry office where they would "only" submit a confirmation of a sexologist that they suffer from a disorder of sexual identity. The doctor who issues the confirmation of the disorder of sexual identity would not send it to the appropriate registry office but would provide it to the trans person concerned who might or might not subsequently make a statement of the sex change before the registry office.

If this second draft was adopted, the provision in *Civil Code* would be as follows (Section 29 CC):

1. A person who has attained 12 years of age and who has a persistent inconsistency between the mental and registered sex in the Book of Birth or other record under another legal regulation has the right to change the sex.
2. One's sex can be changed by a personal statement before the registry office. The statement must be accompanied by a confirmation that the person has a persistent mental disparity between his mental and registered sex, which is issued to him or her by a doctor specialized in the field of sexology or with a special professional competence in the field of sexology. For a person under the age of fifteen, the consent of his or her legal representative is required.

According to the Ministry of Justice, the current legislation on the sex change of a human making it only possible with the simultaneous elimination of the reproductive function and the transformation of the sexual organs is in direct contradiction with the case law of the European Court of Human Rights. The Ministry of Justice considers that:

> The draft will have a positive impact on the sexual minority of trans persons. These people suffer from a disorder of sexual identity ("Sexual Identification Disorder"), while the effective legal regulation does not respect their true sexual identity and for its legal recognition an invasive surgery is required, including the sterilization of the person, which is a disproportionate interference with physical integrity and, for some, it is impossible to be carried out.

Finally, according to the Ministry of Justice, the current legislation is discriminatory, since a trans person whose true sex is not legally recognized without having undergone the surgical interventions is still legally regarded as a person of the sex which he or she does not feel affiliation. This means, among other things, that even the documents of the trans person do not correspond to his or her real gender, and the trans person is thus subjected to very unpleasant situations in the normal life where

[57] For more see http://www.ceska-justice.cz/2018/06/navrh-ministerstva-spravedlnosti-lide-budou-mit-pravo-menit-pohlavi-bez-chirurgickeho-zakroku/. Accessed 22 Feb 2019.

[58] For details see official web pages of the Government of the Czech Republic, https://apps.odok.cz/veklep-detail?pid=KORNAZWHY3ZN. Accessed 22 Feb 2019.

he or she is to present his or her documents but data such as the name, surname, sex, and birth registration number recorded in these documents do not usually correspond to the appearance, behaviour, and generally. to the social role of the person. There may be situations in which a person will be discriminated against as a result of this discrepancy, for example, when being recruited, in communication with the authorities, etc. According to the Impact Report on the proposed draft, the new regulation should affect about one thousand persons.

Several sexologists opposed this pending draft. They argued in particular that sex is not an "optional discipline", and that the Draft assumes that expert opinions on the required sex change will be issued "practically on hold, which a real sexologist would not do" because "we work and communicate with some of these people very long, perhaps for two years. It's no easy job."[59] On the other hand, the pending draft was supported by the Ombudsman.[60]

15 Conclusions

As mentioned above, there are several significant problems in the current legal regulations concerning trans persons and gender identity in the Czech Republic. Beside the more general ones, as for instance no relevant research and serious discussion, involuntary divorce of marriage or cancellation of registered partnerships, involuntary surgery and sterilization, let us mention assigning a new birth registration number to trans persons. This issue is said to be a remnant of the communist past when there were no insurance numbers as the state provided health care for everybody free of charge. Some experts[61] think that the new birth registration number may be a real problem for trans person as there would not have "legal continuity" and they would have to disclose his or her "old birth number" and thus "the previous sex" to prove "legal continuity" in relation to various public and private persons. Finally, problems also arise for trans entrepreneurs who run business as individuals and for anybody who pays taxes using "tax identification number/VAT ID" (in Czech "DIČ") containing the numerical information about sex. On the other hand, legal and medical experts may still remember a case widely publicised when a sex change carried out according to "the old practice"[62] allowed a convicted criminal to go free due to the fact that she was given a new birth registration number after the original birth certificate number was expunged from

[59]For the statements of the head of the Czech Sexology Association, Jaroslav Zvěřina, see https://www.info.cz/cesko/vlada-ma-problem-sexuologove-odmitaji-vydavat-posudky-na-zmeny-pohlavi-bez-operace-39984.html. For more information see the website of the Czech Sexology Association at http://www.sexuologickaspolecnost.cz. Accessed 22 Feb 2019.

[60]See https://zpravy.aktualne.cz/domaci/sterilizace-by-nemusela-byt-podminkou-pro-uredni-zmenu-pohla/r~595980bcfd6411e8a7f60cc47ab5f122/v~diskuse/. Accessed 22 Feb 2019.

[61]See Havelková (2015), p. 142.

[62]For the legal development see *supra* footnote no. 27.

the records. This is not an out-of-date topic. Recently, the Ombudsman deputy drew attention to the risk of false criminal record statements in cases where offenders underwent a sex change.[63]

As already mentioned, the new Czech legal regulation of gender modification is not seen by many as optimal. It is a question of what it should be. Looking at the laws of the surrounding states (Germany, Austria, Slovakia and Poland), we find out that they are different, or sometimes quite distinct. It should be appreciated that after the fall of the Iron Curtain the Czech legislators began to deal with the issue of trans persons not only when amending or adopting health regulations (in 1991 and 2011), but also when adopting the Civil Code (2012). The fact that the Civil Code, which was passed after a long preparatory phase and wide discussion, should be fundamentally altered, is worrying. Civil Codes as pillars of private law should not be changed daily, or very often, when it comes to conceptual questions. However, if the new legislation enshrined in the Civil Code reflects developments in the European legal systems and the case law of the European Court of Human Rights, then it is undoubtedly appropriate to welcome efforts to carry out changes in the area of trans persons. As already indicated, for example, the Czech Sexology Association sees the proposed changes as problematic and refuses to issue confirmations that should be submitted by trans persons at registry offices when applying for a sex change on the basis of the forthcoming amendment to the Civil Code. Some experts think that this "resistance" to changes will contribute to the fact that in the future the legal regulation of trans persons will be absolutely liberal, i.e. that gender identity will be simply a matter of choice.

References

Agha P (2013) Trans jako výzva symbolickému uspořádání společnosti. Časopis zdravotnického práva a bioetiky 3(1). http://medlawjournal.ilaw.cas.cz/index.php/medlawjournal/article/view/40. Accessed 1 Feb 2018

Anonymus (2018) Změna pohledu na úpravy nejednoznačných genitálií. In: Translidé [online]. http://www.translide.cz/nejednoznacne-genitalie

Baršová A (2013) Skalpel a duše. Ke změně pohlaví podle nového občanského zákoníku. Časopis zdravotnického práva a bioetiky 3(1). http://medlawjournal.ilaw.cas.cz/index.php/medlawjournal/article/view/43. Accessed 1 Feb 2018

Císař O, Vráblíková K (2012) LGBT aktivismus v České republice: historie, organizace a aktivisté. In: Heinrich Böll Stiftung [online]. https://cz.boell.org/sites/default/files/studie_lgbt_v_cr.pdf. Accessed 1 Feb 2018

Dobrovolná E (2014) In: Lavický P (ed) Občanský zákoník I. Obecná část (§ 1-654). C.H. Beck, Praha, pp 191 ff

Doležal A (2013a) In: Melzer F, Tégl P (eds) Občanský zákoník. Velký komentář, § 1-117. Svazek 1. Obecná ustanovení. Leges, Praha

[63]For details see https://www.ochrance.cz/aktualne/tiskove-zpravy-2015/ministerstvo-neresi-riziko-vydavani-nepravdivych-vypisu-z-rejstriku-trestu/, http://www.ceska-justice.cz/2015/07/sabatova-upozornila-na-riziko-nepravdivych-vypisu-z-rejstriku-trestu/. Accessed 22 Feb 2019.

Doležal A (2013b) Konstrukce identity v právním diskurzu. Dvojí pojetí bytí. Časopis zdravotnického práva a bioetiky 3(1). http://medlawjournal.ilaw.cas.cz/index.php/medlawjournal/article/view/42. Accessed 1 Feb 2018

Doležal T (2013c) Judikatura Evropského soudu pro lidská práva v oblasti problematiky "translidí". Časopis zdravotnického práva a bioetiky 3(1). http://medlawjournal.ilaw.cas.cz/index.php/medlawjournal/article/view/44. Accessed 1 Feb 2018

Eliáš K, Zuklínová M (2001) Principy a východiska nového kodexu soukromého práva. Linde, Praha

Eliáš K, Zuklínová M (2005) The Draft Civil Code. The Draft of a Working Group. Ministry of Justice, Praha

Eliáš K, Zuklínová M (2008) Občanský zákoník. Version for the Government meeting. Ministry of Justice, Praha

Fifková H (ed) (2002) Transsexualita: diagnostika a léčba. Grada, Praha, pp 43 ff

Frinta O (2014) In: Švestka J, Dvořák J, Fiala J (eds) Občanský zákoník. Komentář. Svazek I (§ 1 až 654). Wolters Kluwer, Praha

Havelková B (2015) The legal status of transsexual and transgender persons in the Czech republic. In: Scherpe JM (ed) The legal status of transsexual and transgender persons. Intersentia, Cambridge, p 132

Hrušáková M, Králíčková Z, Westphalová L (eds) (2017) Rodinné právo. Učebnice, 2nd edn. C. H. Beck, Praha

Intersexualita (2018) GLBTI Poradna [online]. http://glbtiporadna.unas.cz/intersexualita.php. Accessed 1 Feb 2018

Kmec J, Kosař D, Kratochvíl J, Bobek M (2012) Evropská úmluva o lidských právech. komentář. C.H. Beck, Praha

Kozubík J, Wintr J (2016) Ústavní soudy a práva gayů a leseb – veřejné mínění jako determinant rozhodnutí soudů? Jurisprudence 5:34–47

Pechová O (2007) Transsexuální lidé v kontaktu s veřejnou správou [online].Translide.cz. http://www.translide.cz/translide-a-verejnasprava (cit. 26. 2. 2021)

Těšínová J, Žďárek R, Policar R (2011) Medicínské právo. C.H. Beck, Praha, pp 160–161

Weiss P (ed) (2010) Sexuologie. Grada, Praha, p 463

Zvěřina J (2014) Pohlavní příslušnost by neměla být volitelná. In: Česká justice [online]. 25. 5. 2014. http://www.ceska-justice.cz/2014/05/jaroslav-zverinapohlavni-prislusnost-by-nemela-byt-volitelna/. Accessed 1 Feb 2018

Gender Modification in Poland: A Case Law Phenomenon in a Civil Law Country

Michal Wojewoda

Abstract This chapter presents the evolution of the case law of Polish courts and highlights the most important issues concerning the situation of trans and intersexual persons in Poland. While recognizing the significance of judicial activism, the author admits that the current situations has many disadvantages and cannot be considered as satisfactory.

1 Introduction

There is no written law concerning gender modification proceedings in Poland. Nevertheless, as from the 1960s, the Polish judiciary has successfully tackled this issue. Certain procedures were set out that can be followed by trans persons in order to change their civil status with regard to the officially recorded sex. This eventually could lead to a reassignment of gender, typically accompanied by a change of name. The peculiarity of this situation consists in the fact that Poland is a civil law country in which courts have no legislative powers. Although no written regulations expressly provide for the change of sex, such proceedings do take place in Poland due to the case law. This chapter presents the evolution of the case law of Polish courts and highlights the most important issues concerning the situation of trans and intersexual persons in Poland. While recognizing the significance of judicial activism, the author admits that the current situations has many disadvantages and cannot be considered as satisfactory.

Sex (gender) is one of the elements of the civil status in Poland. According to the Law on Civil Status Acts of 2014,[1] a person's sex is recorded in the birth act.[2] There

[1]The law of 28 November 2014, consolidated text: Dziennik Ustaw [Official Journal] (hereinafter O.J.) 2020, item 463, hereinafter cited also as: the "2014 Law".

[2]See Art. 60 point 3 of the Law on Civil Status Acts.

M. Wojewoda (✉)
Faculty of Law and Administration, University of Lodz, Lodz, Poland
e-mail: mwojewoda@wpia.uni.lodz.pl

I. C. Jaramillo, L. Carlson (eds.), *Trans Rights and Wrongs*, Ius Comparatum - Global Studies in Comparative Law 54,
https://doi.org/10.1007/978-3-030-68494-5_6

are only two possibilities—every individual is either male or female. When a baby is born, the medical personnel assisting the delivery are obliged to fill in a birth card, which is an official medical certificate describing various characteristics of the child, including sex.[3] The child's sex is decided according to external biological features (the biological sex). The birth card is then submitted to the local Civil Registry Office and it constitutes the basis for recording the child's sex in the birth act (the legal sex).[4]

The problem of trans persons consists in a clash between the biological/legal sex (as recorded in the Civil Status Register) and their actual gender identity as based on deep internal feelings and psychological experiences (the psychological sex). In Poland, the situation of trans persons—in terms of gender modification possibilities—is not regulated by any specific legislation. There exists a legal lacuna here. For many years the legislator regarded transsexualism as a marginal issue apparently not worthy of regulation. With the passing of time the problem has become more vocal but at the same time it has always been a delicate and politically sensitive matter. Still, the Polish legislator did make one serious attempt to regulate the issue in question. On 15 September 2015 the Sex Reconciliation Act was adopted by the Parliament.[5] However, the (non-overturned) veto of the Polish President resulted in the Act never coming into force.[6]

Lacking any special written law, it is the judiciary that tackled the problem. As early as in the 1960s, the Polish courts began to recognize the right of trans persons to apply for a change (reassignment) of their legal sex. Invoking some general substantive rules and applying universal procedural mechanisms, the courts have equipped trans persons with fairly effective (though perhaps cumbersome) tools as presented in this chapter.

Interestingly, despite the fact that the case law is not directly "anchored" in any express regulations devoted specifically to the problem, the possibility of reconciling the legal sex (as recorded in the Civil Status Register) with the personal sex identity has never been seriously questioned in Poland. It is rather the conditions for such a "sex change" (sex reassignment) and the corresponding procedures that are disputed by the legal doctrine,[7] courts, politicians and by various non-governmental organizations which promote (or oppose) the rights of trans persons.

The Polish case law concerning trans persons has evolved significantly over the past 50 years. Some initial concepts have been replaced by new ones. This replacement—in the opinion of many commentators—does not necessarily mean progress.

---

[3]See Art. 54 section 2 of the Law on Civil Status Acts. The official template of the birth card is an attachment to the ordinance of the Minister of Health of 7th December 2017, O.J. 2017, item 2305.

[4]See Art. 53 section 1 of the Law on Civil Status Acts.

[5]For the text of the Act as adopted by the Parliament, see http://orka.sejm.gov.pl/proc7.nsf/ustawy/1469_u.htm (last accessed: 11 August 2019).

[6]More information about this "aborted" piece of legislation will be given *infra*.

[7]There exists abundant literature concerning the situation of trans persons in Poland, see the bibliography cited by Ostojska (2014), pp. 286 *et seq*.

The evolution of the judicial activism in this respect will be discussed in some detail below. Before that, however, the general normative background of the change-of-sex cases will be discussed. That is because, despite the lack of express legislation on the subject, the case law concerning trans persons is often seen as somehow "rooted" in the Polish Constitution of 1997.[8] Additionally, since Poland is a part of the international community and a member of the European Union and the Council of Europe, which organizations widely recognize the rights of trans persons, it is important to say a few words about the impact of international instruments on the local situation.

2 The Constitutional Background and International Sources

Although the Polish Constitution[9] does not specifically address the change-of-sex issue, it does contain a number of provisions that concern, albeit indirectly, the situation of trans persons. It is vital to recall these provisions as they shape the general legal background against which the discussion on transsexualism should be conducted. One should begin with Art. 33 of the 1997 Constitution which solemnly declares the principle of sex equality:

1. "Men and women shall have equal rights in family, political, social and economic life in the Republic of Poland.
2. Men and women shall have equal rights regarding, in particular, education, employment and career promotion, and shall have the right to equal compensation for work of similar value, to social security, to hold offices, and to receive public honours and decorations."

The above principle is further supported by a non-discrimination rule that can be found in Article 32 section 2 of the Constitution, which states that "[n]o one shall be discriminated against in political, social or economic life for any reason whatsoever."

Another interesting provision, directly referring to the concept of sex (gender), is Art. 233 of the Constitution. It deals with the special regulations that can be enacted when martial law or a state of emergency is declared. The provision in question makes it clear that even under such exceptional circumstances: "Restrictions on human and citizen freedom and rights solely on the grounds of race, sex, language, religion or lack thereof, social origin, birth and property are unacceptable."

---

[8]See authors cited by Ostojska (2014), pp. 151–152.

[9]O.J. 1997, No. 78, item 483. The Republic of Poland is a parliamentary democracy. The written Constitution of 2nd April 1997 is the superior law in Poland. The other sources of binding rules in Poland are: ordinary statutes, regulations based on statutory delegation, acts of local law (in limited areas) as well as international conventions and the law of the European Union (to which Poland has belonged since 2004). The consistency of the legal system in Poland is controlled by the Constitutional Tribunal.

Apart from the above cited provisions, the Polish Constitution of 1997 includes even more important rules. It is especially Articles 30 and 47 of the Constitution that squarely place the issue of gender modification in a constitutional context. Article 30 guarantees the respect of personal dignity of every human being: "The inherent and inalienable dignity of the person shall constitute a source of freedoms and rights of persons and citizens. It shall be inviolable. The respect and protection thereof shall be the obligation of public authorities." Additionally, Article 47 guarantees the protection of private and family life: "Everyone shall have the right to legal protection of his private and family life, of his honour and good reputation and to make decisions about his personal life."

The second general point of reference for gender identity questions in Poland is international law and especially the European Human Rights Convention of 1950 (ECHR to which Poland acceded in 1991[10]). The recent case law of the European Court of Human Rights (ECtHR) seems to require that every democratic country should envisage some procedure to be followed by trans persons with regard to their gender modification. It must be recalled that, after some initial hesitation (perceivable in older rulings), as from 2002 the ECtHR has made it clear that—in light of Art. 8 ECHR that guarantees the respect of private life—all Member Countries (including Poland) should possess adequate procedures that make the change of legal sex possible.[11] In Poland such proceedings do exist but—due to the 'spontaneous' (judicial) way in which they have been developed—their shape is not very clear. Admittedly, that poses certain problems with regard to the above ECtHR requirements.[12]

Acknowledging the importance of the legal considerations presented above, it has to be said that the gender modification judgments by Polish courts rarely cite the 1997 Constitution, the ECHR or the ECtHR case law. Naturally, since Poland is not a common law country, every court ruling must be based on some written rule. Therefore, the judiciary does refer to certain regulations (both substantive and procedural). These regulations—which are meant to constitute (substitute) legal basis for particular judgments—will be discussed *infra*. However, as an introduction, the concept of the civil status and its registration in Poland will be shortly presented as it is exactly in this context that the trans person cases are decided.

[10]O.J. 1993, No. 61, item 284.

[11]See, in particular, judgments delivered in the following cases: *Christine Goodwin v. the United Kingdom* of 2002 (application No. 28957/95; http://hudoc.echr.coe.int/eng?i=001-60596); *I. v. the United Kingdom* of 2002 (application No. 25680/94; http://hudoc.echr.coe.int/eng?i=001-60595); *Grant v. the United Kingdom* of 2006 (application No. 32570/03; http://hudoc.echr.coe.int/eng?i=001-75454), and *L. v. Lithuania* of 2008 (application No. 27527/03; http://hudoc.echr.coe.int/eng?i=001-82243) (last accessed: 11 August 2019).

[12]Cf. remarks in Conclusions *infra*.

3 Regulation of the Civil Status in Poland

The Law on Civil Status Acts of 28th November 2014 introduces a legal definition of the civil status to the Polish legal system. It can be found in Article 2 section 1, which reads: "The civil status is a person's legal situation, expressed by the individual personal characteristics, as shaped by natural events, legal actions or judicial decisions, or decisions of the authorities, which is demonstrated in civil status acts." After confronting this definition with other provisions of the 2014 Law,[13] one can draw the conclusion that the civil status notion embraces the following elements: first name(s), surname, family name, date and place of birth, sex, names and surnames of parents as well as the indication of marital status. Accordingly, in the light of current legislation, the dominant view in the Polish legal doctrine is that civil status is a private law notion reflecting both family elements (filiation, marriage) as well as personal aspects (name, sex) of the individual's legal position.[14]

The civil status as such—being a collective term including various elements—is considered to be one of the 'personal goods', i.e. strictly personal values, commonly recognized and respected in society and protected by the law.[15] This does not preclude the possibility of treating some of the civil status components as independent personal goods deserving separate protection. That concerns, in particular, the name and surname but also the (sense of) sex identity. The civil status of natural persons is recorded in the Civil Status Register which—as from 1 March 2015, when the 2014 Law came into force—is run in an electronic version. The Register has a national reach. Individual entries are made by the Civil Registrars in any of the Civil Registry Offices scattered throughout the country. Such offices are organized by local authorities (communes). Currently, there are almost 2500 Civil Registry Offices in Poland.

During the lifetime of an individual there might occur various changes of their civil status, which should be duly recorded. For each such change—in order to make an entry in the Civil Status Register—adequate procedures must be followed. It is important to remember that civil status changes are always a consequence of some legal fact that has occurred in the life of an individual. Sometimes it is a court judgment (e.g. in case of divorce or the judicial finding of paternity), on other occasions it is a decision of the Civil Registrar (e.g. when the name or surname is

---

[13] It is particularly useful to take cognizance of Articles 60, 88 and 95 of the 2014 Law, which name the components of the three types of civil status acts drawn up under Polish law (birth, marriage and death acts), as well as Art. 49 of the 2014 Law, which describes the contents of the certificate of civil status issued on the basis of data included in the Civil Status Register.

[14] See Wojewoda (2014), pp. 17 *et seq*. This approach is also accepted by the Supreme Court, see e.g. the judgment of 10 January 2019, II CSK 371/18.

[15] The examples of personal goods are given in Art. 23 of the Polish Civ.C. The list is not exhaustive and includes: health, freedom, dignity, freedom of conscience, surname or pseudonym, image, confidentiality of correspondence, inviolability of home as well as scientific, artistic and inventive activities.

changed in administrative proceedings[16]). Some changes of civil status may also be effected by voluntary acts performed in front of the Registrar (e.g. entering into marriage or acknowledging the paternity). Typically, any change of civil status is effective only for the future (*ex nunc*) and is recorded by means of the so called 'supplementary annotation' which is added to relevant civil status acts.[17]

It is worth highlighting that all entries in the Civil Status Register are declaratory. Nevertheless, the role of the Register is crucial in practice, as transpires from Art. 3 of the Law on Civil Status Acts. The provision in question proclaims a general rule that civil status acts are the sole evidence of the events recorded therein. This means that proving, in any kind of proceedings, somebody's death, filiation, marital status or sex always requires an official certificate (a birth, marriage or death certificate) issued from the Register. These certificates constitute faithful reflections of relevant civil status acts.

Article 3 of the 2014 Law further explains that in order to correct any untrue statements that may potentially appear in a civil status act, a proper court ruling is always required. Several different possibilities come into play in this respect. To take one example, a civil status act can be annulled by the court if it describes an event not consistent with facts or if there are defects reducing the probative value of the act.[18] Another instrument used to eliminate false records from the Register (without annulling the whole act) is the judicial correction of the civil status act, as regulated in Art. 36 of the 2014 Law. This concerns acts that were drawn up wrongly from the very outset. The correction judgment is given in non-adversarial proceedings initiated by a motion of an interested person. The petitioner must prove that some data was wrongly presented in the Register. When the judgment becomes final, the correction is introduced into the Register and it has a retroactive effect (effectiveness *ex tunc*).

The above court procedures aimed at annulling or correcting civil status acts, must be distinguished from the situation when clear mistakes (e.g. spelling errors) are found in the Register. If—in the light of other civil status acts or official documents deposited in the Register—the mistake is obvious, then a "technical correction" may be effected. It is done in a simplified manner (without court's intervention) by the Civil Registrar who can act even on its own motion.[19]

---

[16]Cf. remarks in a respective section *infra*.

[17]In case of marriage, the change of civil status is considered to be so important that a separate marriage act is created.

[18]See Art. 39 of the Law on Civil Status Acts.

[19]Art. 35 of the Law on Civil Status Acts.

4 The Original Concept of Change of Sex: The Birth Act Correction

After sketching this broad legal background, it is time to explain in more detail how the Polish judiciary addressed the problem of persons applying for the reassignment of their legal sex. One can distinguish two phases here. What was proposed initially was *a direct correction of the birth act by the court*. This approach was later replaced by a different idea which consists in *a judicial recognition of sex identity to be then recorded in the Civil Status Register by means of a supplementary annotation* (and not through correction of the act).

It all started with a judgment by the Voivodeship Court of Warsaw handed down on 24 September 1964,[20] which undoubtedly was of a precedential character. The court, acting as a court of second instance, dealt with the motion of a trans woman who—further to gender modification surgery undergone in another country—sought to change her legal sex from male (as officially recorded) to female. Persuaded by medical experts' opinions, which confirmed that the petitioner's psychological sex was feminine, the court decided that the birth act should be accordingly corrected. The motives of the judgment made it clear that primacy had to be given to the actual sex identity over the biological sex as recorded at the time of birth. Importantly, although the court applied the correction procedure,[21] it did it only *per analogiam* underlining that the birth act was drawn up correctly and the change of sex should have effect only for the future, i.e. from the time of the surgical intervention.

The above judgment attracted a lot of scholarly comment, which generally was favourable.[22] It took, however, more than a decade before a first official pronouncement by the Polish Supreme Court was made with regard to the possibility of changing sex by trans persons. In its judgment of 25 February 1978,[23] the Supreme Court approved the practice of using the non-adversarial correction proceedings in order to effect the change of legal sex of a trans person. Once again it was underscored that the procedure is to be applied only by analogy and that the correction is effective exclusively for the future. An important novelty consisted in the Supreme Court's observation that, in exceptional cases, the change of legal sex could be effected without a former surgical intervention, provided that the actual sex identity of the person in question is permanent and irreversible.

As far as the lower courts were concerned, the 1978 Supreme Court judgment paved the way to the correction of legal sex in a growing number of cases. What is more, the exception envisaged by the Supreme Court—concerning the absence of

[20]II Cr 515/64.

[21]The court acted on the basis of Art. 26.3 of the 1955 Decree 'Law on Civil Status Acts', which was then in force and which envisaged judicial correction of civil status acts in a similar manner that Art. 36 of the current 2014 Law does.

[22]The judgment of the Voivodeship Court in Warsaw and the doctrinal reaction thereto is described in some detail by Ostojska (2014), pp. 93–98.

[23]III CZP 100/77.

gender modification surgery—did, in fact, become a rule. This approach, while accepted by psychiatrists and sexologists, who emphasized the therapeutic effect of the judicial change of sex on their patients, was sometimes criticized in the legal scholarship.[24]

An unexpected halt in the development of the jurisprudence concerning trans persons took place a decade later. In its judgment of 22 June 1989,[25] the Supreme Court solemnly proclaimed that transsexualism is not a valid reason to correct the designation of sex in the birth act of the interested person. The fact that the original civil status act revealed the biological sex of the child in compliance with its external sex features led to the conclusion that the act was drafted correctly. This, is turn, precluded the possibility to use correction procedures that are reserved only for cases in which the civil status act was faulty *ab initio*. The judgment was handed down by the extended panel of seven judges and it was officially declared to be a 'legal rule' of the Supreme Court. Such rules are entered into a special book and they must be followed in the future by other (regular) panels of the Supreme Court. Indeed, the restrictive view taken in 1989 was soon reiterated in another ruling of the Supreme Court dated 8 May 1992.[26]

5 A New Concept: The Writ for Recognition

The fears that the judicial change of sex would not be possible anymore were dispelled in another judgment of the Supreme Court, which was handed down on 22 March 1991.[27] But this time, a completely new approach was adopted with respect to the situation of trans persons. The inapplicability of the correction procedures, proclaimed by the 1989 ruling, was not challenged. The Supreme Court indicated an alternative way for the change of legal sex.

The adherence to a given gender identity was declared one of the 'personal goods'—a special legal category that is protected by the law. Some of these goods—e.g. health, freedom, honour, personal image or name—are listed directly in Art. 23 of the Polish Civil Code (Civ.C.).[28] Others are occasionally discovered by the courts (e.g. voice, family tradition) or they are named by the legal doctrine (e.g. civil status). Accepting that the adherence to a given gender identity, or—as it is put in more recent writings—gender identity as such, is a protected personal good entails that there must exist effective legal instruments which will guard this value and help realize it. In its 1991 ruling, the Supreme Court decided that—lacking special statutory provisions on the change of sex—the procedure that should be

[24]See authors cited by Ostojska (2014), pp. 104–107.

[25]III CZP 37/89.

[26]III CZP 40/92.

[27]III CRN 28/91.

[28]The Civ.C. of 23 April 1964; consolidated text: O.J. 2020, item 1740.

followed is a general 'writ for recognition' action, regulated in Article 189 of the Polish Code of Civil Procedure (C.C.P.).[29] The provision in question reads: "The plaintiff may request the court to determine the existence or non-existence of a legal relationship or a right if they have legal interest therein."

It is worth highlighting that the above rule provides only a general and strictly procedural tool to be used in numerous situations when various substantive issues are at stake. This time the said mechanism was indicated by the Supreme Court as a proper way to protect gender identity. It is submitted that the legal interest of a trans person, which interest—according to Art. 189 C.C.P.—is an important criterion necessary to launch every 'writ for recognition', consists here in the need to eliminate an existing clash between the psychological sex (usually reflected in the plaintiff's look and behaviour) and the legal sex as demonstrated in the Civil Status Register and in the identity documents. Such clash results in serious legal uncertainty concerning the trans person's position in society. Accordingly, the task of the court is to establish (recognize) what the 'real' sex of the plaintiff is. To this end medical opinions are needed. That is why various experts are usually called during the proceedings.

The formal confirmation of the 'real' sex of the plaintiff in the court's judgment allows for the designation (reassignment) of the 'new' sex in the Civil Status Register. This, in turn, opens the door for the change of name of the applicant (see *infra*). The last step is the replacement of identity cards and other personal documents. They should be re-issued with the new data showing the sex officially recognized by the court and the changed name.

This new approach, endorsed by other rulings, both of the Supreme Court[30] and courts of lower instances, may—at first glance—appear similar to the original concept of the correction of a civil status act. There are, however, several important differences which need to be highlighted.

5.1 *Peculiarities of the 'Writ for Recognition' as a Method to Change the Legal Sex*

Unlike the correction proceedings which are envisaged by the Law on Civil Status Acts,[31] the recognition action has a different legal basis. On the substantive level, the Civil Code provisions concerning the protection of personal goods come in to play

[29]The C.C.P. was enacted on 17 November 1964; consolidated text: O.J. 2020, item 1575.

[30]See e.g. the Supreme Court judgments of 22 September 1995, III CZP 118/95, of 6 December 2013, I CSK 146/13 and of 10 January 2019, II CSK 371/18.

[31]It should be clarified here that the original 'correction' concept was used by the judiciary under previous regulations which were: first the 1955 Decree and later the 1986 Law on Civil Status Acts. The court correction of a civil status act was envisaged, respectively, in Art. 26 of the 1955 Decree and in Art. 31 of the 1986 Law. An analogous procedure is now regulated in Art. 36 of the current 2014 Law.

(Articles 23 and 24 Civ.C.) and on the procedural level it is Art. 189 C.C.P. (already cited) that allows for the determination (recognition) of a legal relationship or a right. Let it be reiterated here that these legal bases are only 'makeshifts' adopted by the Supreme Court for lack of provisions directly devoted to the problem of trans persons. It is not surprising, then, that—being a substitute solution—the path indicated by the Supreme Court in its 1991 ruling is open to some criticism.

First of all, it should be noted that the 'writ for recognition' is launched in adversarial proceedings. In this type of civil process, the plaintiff (a trans person) is required to name the defendant against whom the writ is addressed. It is not easy to resolve, though, who should be summoned in this type of case. The Supreme Court originally held that the role of defendants should be taken by parents of the plaintiff or—if they are both dead—by a special curator appointed by the court. This may create uncomfortable situations in the courtroom with parents feeling 'accused' by their children. Apart from that, notwithstanding any medical evidence confirming the psychological sex, parents do not always sympathize with the position of plaintiffs and not infrequently they want the case to be dismissed.

In one of its relatively recent rulings of 6 December 2013,[32] the Supreme Court tried to refine its view concerning the defendant party. It was suggested that if the plaintiff has children and/or is married, it is the spouse and children who should be obligatorily acting as defendants. In such a situation, parents are not mandatory participants of the proceedings. When arriving at this conclusion, the Supreme Court put forward an argument that the consequences of the potential change of sex go far beyond the individual interest of the plaintiff. They also bear heavily upon the legal situation of his/her children and spouse and that is why these persons must participate in the proceedings.

This concept did not find popular acceptance, though. In its judgment of 15 December 2017,[33] the Appellate Court in Łódź rejected the view that children of a given trans person must participate in the change-of-sex proceedings. The judges deciding the case adhered to the former view that the plaintiff should rather indicate his/her parents as defendants. On the one hand, it was recalled that parents are named in the birth act which is supposed to be annotated with the information about the reassigned sex (if the claim is successful). This—in the opinion of the appellate court—makes them directly involved in the case. On the other hand, it was stressed that birth acts of children are not changed in any respect. The change of sex does not modify the parent-child relations, which means that children need not participate in the proceedings.[34] This very position was upheld by the Supreme Court after reviewing the case in cassation proceedings. In the judgment of

[32] I CSK 146/13.

[33] I ACa 531/17.

[34] However, let us observe in passing that, as it will be explained below, from the substantive point of view the sheer fact of having children and, especially, being married may be seen as a negative condition for the change-of-sex judgment.

10 January 2019[35] it was reiterated that the role of defendants in the change-of-sex cases must be attributed exclusively to parents of the plaintiff (or, if both parents died, to a curator appointed by the court). It was also admitted by the Supreme Court that, in fact, even parents have no direct interest to appear in the process. They are summoned for strictly procedural reasons. It is because the 'writ for recognition' case (Art. 189 C.C.P.), being a typical adversarial case, obligatorily requires a defendant.

The second characteristic feature of the current concept used by the Polish judiciary to protect rights of trans persons concerns the way of introducing the information on the reassigned sex into the Civil Status Register. It must be underlined that the judgment recognizing the real (psychological) sex of the plaintiff does not lead to the correction of the birth act. It only paves the way for making an appropriate supplementary annotation which is put on the margin of the act and which reflects the change of the civil status effective for the future. After the annotation is made, the adjusted civil status of an individual is revealed in all new excerpts issued from the Register. In case of trans persons, an annotation concerning their change of sex, introduced into the original birth act, has this effect that all birth certificates issued in the future will show the reassigned sex. The short (simplified) version of the certificate will show only the current data, whereas the full version will show both original and new data (side by side).

6 The Conditions for the Judicial Change of Sex

After explaining the procedure in which the case is heard, it is time to consider the particular conditions for the judicial change of sex. In the absence of clear statutory provisions, these conditions must be inferred from the case law of the Supreme Court (and courts of lower instances).[36] There are two types of positive prerequisites—formal and substantive ones. In order to win the case, the plaintiff should make sure that all these prerequisites are met and that no negative conditions are present.

6.1 Formal Conditions

The formal conditions are linked with the procedural requirements. Further to Art. 189 C.C.P., the interested person should file a writ for recognition of their real (psychological) sex. It is crucial that the plaintiff correctly indicate the defendant party. As explained, this role is generally reserved for the plaintiff's parents (see

[35]II CSK 371/18.

[36]This case law is broadly analyzed in literature, see e.g. Holewińska-Łapińska (2010); see also Grzejszczak (2013).

above). If the interested person starts a wrong type of proceedings (e.g. instead of the writ for recognition, the correction of the birth act is demanded further to Article 36 of the Law on Civil Status Acts) or if there is no indication of defendants, the case may be dismissed for formal reasons.[37]

A short mention about fiscal requirements should also be made here. As has been said earlier, a writ for recognition of the sex identity is perceived as an instrument of protecting the personal goods. This type of action falls within the competence of the district court. In such cases, in order to start the proceedings, an initial fee of PLN 600 must be paid.[38] Additionally, in the course of the process the plaintiff will normally be charged with the costs of medical opinions. Still, upon a properly justified request, the person who is not in a position to pay the costs may be granted exemption (full or partial) from court fees and expenses.

6.2 *Substantive Conditions*

It is even more difficult to identify the substantive conditions of a successful court action concerning a change of sex. As indicated below, the necessary prerequisites are not clearly determined. Interestingly, there might also appear some local variations (in certain appellate circuits) with regard to particular conditions.

The most vital and universally recognized condition seems to be *the total, permanent and irreversible adherence to a given sex* (that is opposite to the legal sex originally shown in the birth act. This means that the protection of sex identity is dependent on finding what that identity really is. It is also significant that initial references in case law to the personal '*sense of* sex identity' are nowadays replaced by mentions of sex identity as such. This linguistic refinement is perceived as an indication that the court's assessment must be objective[39] and it should not be limited to the plaintiffs' declarations based on their subjective experience only. Additionally, the court should be persuaded that the interested trans persons are prepared to live in the new (reassigned) sexual role until the end of their days.

In order to examine all these elements, medical experts are called upon to give opinions concerning the plaintiff's sex identity. These opinions are usually decisive for the judgment. Still, it is not enough that transsexualism is confirmed by the expert. One can also distinguish another, supplementary condition for a successful change-of-sex case. The analysis of case law demonstrates that it is generally expected that *the plaintiff's outlook should be typical of persons belonging to the sex* which—allegedly—is the real sex of the individual in question. This does not

[37]See e.g. the judgment of the District Court in Sieradz of 2 February 2017, I C 50/16.

[38]This is a fixed fee applicable in cases for the protection of personal goods. The fee seems moderate. For comparison—in 2020 the minimum monthly salary in Poland (for a full-time job) was PLN 2600 gross (about PLN 1900 net).

[39]See Ostojska (2014), pp. 130 and 172–173.

mean that full surgical adaptation is necessary (some legal and ethical problems concerning such surgeries are taken up below). What is usually needed is at least hormonal treatment that would help acquire the look of a man or woman (respectively). Also, in trans men cases, a proof of the plaintiff's mastectomy significantly facilitates the recognition of the male sex. Still, the courts' practice in this respect is sometimes erratic and, admittedly, it may differ in various parts of Poland.

6.3 *Negative Prerequisites*

As far as negative conditions for the change of legal sex are concerned, one can tentatively mention two considerations. The first is *the marital status of the plaintiff*. Available statistics demonstrate that, by and large, only single trans persons apply for the recognition of their psychological sex. However, should the plaintiff be married, the aforementioned 2013 Supreme Court ruling strongly suggests that the existence of marriage must entail the dismissal of the case. It was observed in reasoning of the ruling that a potential change of sex of a married person does not annihilate the marital bond, which—from now on—would exist between two people of the same sex. Since homosexual marriages are not allowed in Poland,[40] the change of sex of a married person must not be allowed.

The same 2013 judgment hints at the presence of a second negative condition, which is *the welfare of children* of a trans plaintiff. As was explained by the Supreme Court:

> When making a decision [on the change of legal sex] it is important to consider not only the trans person's desire to reconcile the legal sex with their psychological sense of sex identity, but also the circumstances concerning the child, namely its readiness to accept a situation in which it is expected to perceive its parent as a person of another sex than the sex attributed to this parent at the time of conception and birth, as well as – perhaps – in the upbringing of the child at some stage in its life.

The above Supreme Court's guidance is a clear indication that whenever the child's welfare might be seriously disturbed by the recognition of the 'new' sex of its parent, a negative judgment should be handed down in the change-of-sex proceedings.

Having said this, it should also be clarified that the court must always make its own evaluation of facts and of experts' opinions. In particular, the unfavourable attitude of the defendants with regard to the plaintiff's demand is not, by itself, a sufficient reason to dismiss the case. Still, it is obvious that especially parents (but also children) may shed proper light on the day-to-day behaviour and habits of the plaintiff. Their testimonies are therefore important. They can prove helpful when

[40] Cf. Art. 18 of the Polish Constitution and Art. 1 of the Polish Family and Guardianship Code of 1964 (consolidated text: O.J. 2020, item 1359).

deciding whether the adherence to a given sex is really total, permanent and irreversible.

7 Access to Treatments

Since one of the conditions for a successful change-of-sex case is (at least) a hormonal treatment undertaken by the plaintiff, a few words should be devoted to the problem of access to various treatments by trans persons. Transsexualism, according to international standards, deserves medical treatment.[41] Trans persons need medical assistance in many respects. This includes not only hormonal therapy or adaptation surgeries but also a need for various medical tests as well as professional consultations with specialists such as sexologists, psychologists, endocrinologists or even oculists.[42] These needs have not been acknowledged by the Polish legislator. Currently, transsexualism as such does not justify access to any dedicated medical procedures within the public health system (financed by the State). This means that, generally, patients must pay full cost of all special treatments.[43] On the other hand, if a trans person has adequate financial resources and is determined to get appropriate help and advice, receiving it is not a serious problem. There are numerous medical institutions offering professional help.[44]

It must be mentioned, however, that not all procedures are equally accessible, even with payment. In particular, an important legal and ethical problem exists concerning adaptation surgeries aimed at changing (adapting) the external sex organs of trans persons. As demonstrated in various studies, a majority of trans persons feel to be 'strangers in their bodies' and they are ready to take various steps to address this problem. At least a part of the trans population expresses the need for a full surgical adaptation.[45] Still, it must be remembered that this kind of intervention leads to infertility, which result is irreversible. Consequently, it can be seen as an example of a severe bodily injury in the meaning of criminal regulations. In cases of such injuries, the consent of the injured person does not eliminate the criminal character of the act. Thus, an adaptation surgery may be seen as illegal even if performed upon a clear request of the patient. That is why, for fear of criminal prosecutions, doctors often decline to perform adaptation surgeries in Poland unless

[41]See the International Statistical Classification of Diseases and Related Health Problems, Chapter V, No. F64.0, http://apps.who.int/classifications/icd10/browse/2016/en#/F60-F69 (last accessed: 11 August 2019).

[42]Śledzińska-Simon (2013), p. 176.

[43]Łojko (2010), pp. 45–61.

[44]Using the Internet fora, trans persons exchange information about specialists in the Abramowicz et al. (2017), p. 151.

[45]See the study by Kryszk and Kłonkowska (2012), pp. 236 *et seq.*, cf. *Sytuacja społeczna osób LGBTA. Raport za lata 2015/2016* [Social situation of LGBTA persons. The 2015/2016 Report], *op.cit.*, pp. 146–150.

a judgment on the change of sex has already been issued.[46] This criminal context may also be one of the reasons why judiciary does not require a surgical intervention as a precondition for the recognition of the 'real' psychological sex. As it was already mentioned some hormonal treatment will usually do.

8 Intersexual Persons

There is neither any gender-neutral nor "third sex" possibility in Poland. Still, there is a narrow margin of "intersexual persons" whose sex is ambiguous and difficult to ascertain at the time of birth, as they possess both male and female sexual features. In cases of intersex newborns, the task of deciding the child's sex lies with the medical personnel that assists the delivery. In doubtful cases, the predominant (external) sexual features would decide which sex is marked on the birth card.[47] The data from the card is later copied to the birth act in the Civil Status Register.[48]

However, the psychological sex of the person in question, as built up and expressed in the future years, can turn out to be different than that registered. Unfortunately, the situation of intersex persons is not regulated by the law either. This problem attracts less attention than the trans persons' cases. Also here, it is the judiciary that has elaborated some practical answers to questions which arise when the psychological sex turns out to be different from the biological sex "chosen" for the child, by medical staff, at the time of birth. Interestingly enough, in this sort of cases there is less controversy concerning the available legal procedures. If it is clear that the sex 'chosen' for the child is not consistent with its psychological sex and the adherence to the latter is permanent and irreversible, it is commonly agreed that the original entry in the birth act should be *corrected by the court in non-adversarial proceedings*. The long established medical and judicial practice in this regard is not seriously disputed, even though it differs from the concept applied nowadays in trans persons' cases.

The Supreme Court allowed the correction of the birth act of an intersexual person as early as in 1958.[49] It was argued before the Court that already at the time of birth there was a clear preponderance of biological male features of the child, which meant that ascribing the child to the female sex was a serious mistake. As it was explained, material mistakes in the civil status acts are corrected in special

[46]In legal doctrine, the prevailing view seems to be that, despite the side effect of making the individual infertile, the adaptation surgeries serve a strictly medical purpose, connected with the well-being of the trans person in question, and as such they must be seen as legal, see Knyziak (2016), pp. 54 *et seq.*

[47]See Gawlik et al. (2016).

[48]See Art. 53 and 54 of the 2014 Law on Civil Status Acts.

[49]See the Supreme Court judgment of 14 November 1958, 2 CR 798/58.

non-adversarial court proceedings.[50] This type of proceeding has been used in other cases, too, in which the original decision concerning the biological sex, as indicated in the birth act, was challenged by intersexual persons.

It is submitted that the Supreme Court judgments of 1989 and 1992 (discussed above), which stopped the use of correction procedures with regard to trans persons, did not concern intersex people. The availability of correction proceedings in the latter type of cases was endorsed by one of the recent Supreme Court rulings of 6 December 2013.[51] It is not totally clear, though, whether the birth act correction should have a fully retroactive effect here. The change of entries in the Civil Status Register usually takes place with regard to grown up intersexual persons whose actual sex identity can be conclusively ascertained. However, the resulting correction and the indication of a 'new' sex in the birth act opens the question concerning the time period in which a given individual played a different social role (officially being a person of the opposite sex). Admittedly, it is difficult to solve this kind of problem without the intervention of the legislator.

9 Regulation of the Name

Gender modification procedures—whether concerning trans or intersexual persons—bring about only a partial solution. They lead to making proper entries in the Civil Status Register by means of additional annotation (trans persons) or by means of correction (intersex people). But the only element of the civil status which is thus adjusted is the sex (gender) of the individual in question. One of the unresolved problems is the change of name/surname. It is important to remember that in the Polish language both first names and surnames usually clearly tell to which sex a given person should be assigned.

Under Polish law, a legal change of first and/or family names of an individual can take place in many different situations. The most obvious examples concern marriage, divorce or filiation proceedings when such change is collateral (incidental) to other changes of the individual's civil status. In such cases, appropriate legal provisions provide a comprehensive regulation for all aspects of the situation.

In addition to the above examples, a specific Act on the Change of Name and Surname, dated 17 October 2008,[52] introduces a general possibility for changing the name or surname upon a motion of an individual. The case is then decided by a Civil Registrar in administrative proceedings (with no judicial involvement). The main

[50] In the 2014 Law on Civil Status Acts it is Art. 36 but a similar provision was present also in former regulations.

[51] I CSK 146/13.

[52] Ustawa o zmianie imienia i nazwiska, consolidated text: O.J. 2020, item 707.

condition for a successful motion is "important reasons" demonstrated by the petitioner, which reasons should duly justify the requested change.[53]

The lack of provisions on the change of gender identity in Poland is mirrored by the absence of any dedicated legislation concerning the change of name/surname of trans and intersexual persons. Not surprisingly then, in practice, all interested persons make recourse to the 2008 Act. The change of name according to administrative rules of the said Act will generally be possible but *only after the gender modification judgment is given* by the court. Thus, the "important reason" that allows for the change of name/surname in this instance is not the transsexualism/intersexualism as such but an appropriate court ruling confirming the "new" sex of an individual.[54] When this ruling becomes final, the change of sex can be recorded in the Civil Status Register and, consequently, also the name or surname can be adjusted.[55]

10 Current Discussions

The present situation in Poland concerning the rights of trans persons does not seem satisfactory. The change-of-sex procedures that are applied by courts are not based on any clear statutory regulations. This judicial activism attracts criticisms from many angles. Firstly, constitutional objections are raised with regard to the role of the courts. It has to be reiterated that, according to the Polish Constitution of 1997, case law is not a valid source of legal rules. Secondly, what is criticized is the actual choice of legal tools which—after provisional adaptations—are used to help trans persons. Thirdly, there is a lot of uncertainty as to the detailed conditions upon which the legal change of sex is dependent. This uncertainty is further aggravated by some variations in judicial approach in different parts of Poland. Last but not least, an alarming legal gap has recently become evident in connection with the discussed issues. A 2016 case of a trans man who never underwent the adaptation surgery and after the change of legal sex delivered a child (formally acting in the masculine role) demonstrated that the Polish legal system is not prepared to deal with such situations. The court faced serious difficulties deciding who (and in which sex role) should be named, in the birth act, as parents of the child.[56]

---

[53]Article 4 of the 2008 Act gives examples of such important reasons, which include the change of name/surname that is disgraceful or the adoption of a name/surname actually used by the petitioner.

[54]Cf. Ostojska (2014), p. 137.

[55]Sometimes a trans person is given a new name by the court as a part of the change-of-sex judgment. This practice is doubtful, though, because of the lack of appropriate legal basis. The idea of a judicial adjustment of the name and surname of trans persons, which would constitute a part of the change-of-sex proceedings, was accepted in the 2015 Sex Reconciliation Act but the Act never came into force, see remarks in the next section.

[56]See the judgment of the Appellate Court in Wrocław of 7th March 2016 (I ACa 1830/15) commented by Boratyńska (2016).

In these circumstances, it is not surprising that, for a number of years now, continuous demands for the regulation of the trans persons situation have been voiced in Poland. The most active actors in this respect include—the "Trans-Fuzja" Foundation[57] and the association "Kampania Przeciw Homofobii" ("Campaign Against Homophobia"—a LGBT organization with a national reach[58]). It is worth mentioning, too, that the Polish ombudsmen also supported various efforts that aimed at regulating the change-of-sex procedures.

The situation of trans persons in Poland acquired extra publicity in 2011 when Anna Grodzka (a trans woman) was elected member of the Polish Parliament, being the first openly trans person holding this position.[59] It was during her term in office that important legislative steps were taken leading to the acceptance by the parliamentary majority of a new law in the discussed area. On 15 September 2015 the Sex Reconciliation Act[60] was adopted with a view to finally dispelling doubts concerning the procedures and conditions for the change of sex in Poland.[61] The cornerstones of this piece of legislation—which, in the end, never came into force—may be summed up in the following points:

(a) The 2015 Act envisaged special proceedings for persons whose sex identity was different from their legal sex as recorded in the birth act. Sex identity was legally defined as a fixed and intensively felt experience of one's own sexuality, which may be compliant or not compliant with the person's sex indicated in the birth act. The title of the Act was meant to underline that the issue in question was not the 'change of sex' but rather the reconciliation of the legal sex with the actual sex identity (when these two categories are not in line).
(b) The petitioner applying for gender modification was expected to possess full capacity for legal acts, which meant that they should be of age (over 18 years old) and not legally incapacitated. Moreover, the petitioner could not be married at the time of initiating the case.
(c) The proceedings envisaged in the 2015 Act were of non-adversarial character and the only mandatory participant thereof was the petitioner (thus parents and children would not be directly involved). In order to secure uniformity of decisions, all cases based on the Act were supposed to be heard by a single court in Poland, namely a division of the District Court in Łódź (central Poland).
(d) The motion for the sex reconciliation should be supported by two independent opinions of medical experts (sexologists, psychiatrists or psychologists), which should clarify what is the actual sex identity of the petitioner.

---

[57]See the internet site of the foundation—http://transfuzja.org/.

[58]See https://kph.org.pl/.

[59]Cf. the Wikipedia entry concerning Anna Grodzka, https://en.wikipedia.org/wiki/Anna_Grodzka (last accessed: 11 August 2019).

[60]The text of the Sex Reconciliation Act (hereinafter: "the 2015 Act"), as adopted by the Polish Parliament, can be found at: http://orka.sejm.gov.pl/proc7.nsf/ustawy/1469_u.htm (last accessed: 11 August 2019).

[61]A short commentary to the 2015 Act was prepared by Boratyńska (2015).

(e) The court was expected to give its judgment within 3 months from the time of filing the motion. This short deadline appeared feasible since the only mandatory evidence that had to be taken during the proceedings was the personal testimony of the petitioner. This testimony would be assessed in the light of expert opinions already accompanying the petitioner's motion. Naturally, if needs be, the court could call extra witnesses or consult other experts—of the court's choice—to confirm the sex identity of the petitioner.

(f) Had the motion for the reconciliation of sex be successful, the court was expected to order that a new birth act ought to be issued. This act would indicate the sex of the petitioner in compliance with the sex identity confirmed in the proceedings. Further to an appropriate request made in the same proceedings, the petitioner would be given new first names plus, if applicable, the grammatical form of his/her surname would be adjusted to reflect the changed sex.

As already mentioned, the 2015 Sex Reconciliation Act did not enter into force because it was vetoed by the Polish President according to his constitutional prerogatives. The main reasons for the veto concerned the alleged diversion of the Act from the prevailing court practice in the change-of-sex cases. What was criticized was:

- the simplification of evidence (the judgment could be based on private opinions without a clear obligation to hear sworn court experts);
- the faulty statutory definition of sex identity, which lacked the referral to permanence and irreversibility of the petitioner's situation;
- the possibility of several sex changes during the lifetime of an individual, and
- the abandonment of any requirements concerning former hormonal treatment and/or the adjustment of the external appearance of the petitioner.[62]

The arguments were also put forward that the 2015 Act made it possible for a trans person to get married with an individual of the same biological sex which the petitioner had before the sex change. Furthermore, fears were voiced that such married couples could also adopt children. It is important to realize, though, that as far as the last-mentioned fears and reservations are concerned, they are equally applicable with regard to the existing court practice, which has prevailed in Poland for more than 50 years now.

The presidential veto was not overturned by the Parliament (although the Constitution allows for it) partly for formal reasons—the legislative works concerning the veto were just not completed before the end of parliamentary term in November 2015. The newly elected Parliament, in which conservative forces prevailed, has not taken any initiative in the discussed area. As the governing right-wing party remained in power also after the 2019 elections, it is very unlikely that such initiatives will come up in the foreseeable future.

[62]See the press coverage of the veto at: http://prawo.gazetaprawna.pl/artykuly/897813,uzasadnienie-do-weta-prezydenta-ustawa-o-uzgodnieniu-plci-moze-prowadzic-do-destabilizacji-norm-spolecznych.html (last accessed: 11 August 2019).

It has to be noted in passing that Poland has preserved a traditional (conservative) model of family law. The cornerstone of the system is monogamous, heterosexual marriage. As it was already mentioned, no same-sex marriages are allowed. There are no registered partnerships either (no matter if homo- or heterosexual). Repeated campaigns of gay and lesbian movements, supported by a more liberal part of the Polish society, never resulted in any change of law.[63] In effect, there is an interesting contrast between the situation of trans persons, which for many years—due to judicial activism—have enjoyed the possibility of the sex change, and the situation of homosexuals who never succeeded in getting any legal concessions. In the light of the law, same sex relationships are treated as informal, factual unions that—with some minor exceptions—are completely irrelevant from the legal point of view.

Still, after the failure of the 2015 Act, the gay and lesbian movements continue to act hand in hand with trans persons. The mission of various non-governmental organizations active in this area, such as the association "Kampania Przeciw Homofobii" ("Campaign Against Homophobia"), often combine the promotion of interests of both transgender and homosexual persons. They concentrate on combating discrimination and prejudice based on sex identity and sex orientation. They also keep on fighting for appropriate legal regulations in this field.

11 Conclusions

As demonstrated above, the situation of trans persons in Poland is rather complex and far from clear. On the one hand, for more than 50 years the judiciary has been ready to assist trans persons—in one way or another—in their attempts to reconcile the legal sex with their gender identity. On the other hand, up to now no written law has been put in place so that the rights of the above minorities could be properly respected. In consequence, the position of trans persons seems unstable and, at least to some extent, open to subjective treatment on the part of judges. This situation—in the humble opinion of this author—hardly conforms to proper democratic standards.[64]

References

Abramowicz M, Bulska D, Górska P, Kryszk K, Mazurczak J, Rawłuszko M, Soral W, Strzałkowska A, Świder M, Winiewski M (2017) Sytuacja społeczna osób LGBTA. Raport

---

[63] Still, it is not uncommon for the Polish nationals to enter into various institutional homosexual relations abroad (e.g. same sex marriages or registered partnerships).

[64] To attenuate the situation, under the aegis of the Polish Ombudsman a special (non binding) guide was prepared for lawyers with the view to streamlining the judicial practise with regard to sex reassignment cases, see Adamczewska-Stachura and Pilch (2020).

za lata 2015/2016 [Social situation of LGBTA persons. The 2015/2016 Report]. In: Świder M, Winiewski M (eds) Warszawa, p 151. https://kph.org.pl/wp-content/uploads/2017/11/Sytuacja-spoleczna-osob-LGBTA-w-Polsce.pdf. Last accessed 26 Feb 2021

Adamczewska-Stachura A, Pilch P (2020) Postępowania w sprawach o ustalenie płci. Przewodnik dla sędziów i pełnomocników [Sex reassignment procedures. A guide for judges and attorneys]. Warszawa. https://www.rpo.gov.pl/sites/default/files/Postepowania_w_sprawach_o_ustalenie_plci.pdf. Last accessed 26 Feb 2021

Boratyńska M (2015) Ustawa o uzgodnieniu płci a przygody transseksualistów w próżni legislacyjnej [Sex Reconciliation Act and the adventures of transsexuals in the legal vacuum]. Prawo i Medycyna 3

Boratyńska M (2016) Prawo i Medycyna 4

Gawlik A, Bielska-Brodziak A, Krawiec G (2016) Dzieci bez płci. Jak polski prawodawca rozwiązuje problemy osób interseksualnych [Children without sex. How the Polish legislator has addressed problems of intersexual persons], cz. 2: "Zasady przypisywania płci prawnej" [vol 2: Principles of establishing the legal sex]. Prawo i Medycyna 3

Grzejszczak R (2013) Transpłciowość w świetle badań [Transsexualizm in the light of research]. In: Dynarski W, Śmiszek K (eds) Sytuacja prawna osób transpłciowych w Polsce – raport z badań i propozycje zmian [Legal position of trans persons in Poland – research report and proposed changes]. Warszawa. http://transfuzja.org/download/publikacje/sytuacja_prawna_osob_transplciowych_w_polsce.pdf. Last accessed 11 Aug 2019

Holewińska-Łapińska E (2010) Sądowa zmiana płci. Analiza orzecznictwa z lat 1991–2008 [The judicial sex change. The analysis of the case law for the years 1991–2008]. In: Ślebzak K (ed) Studia i analizy Sądu Najwyższego [Studies and analyses of the Supreme Court], vol 4. Warszawa

Knyziak I (2016) Legalność zabiegu adaptacyjnego (zagadnienia prawnokarne i cywilnoprawne) [Legality of adaptation surgeries (criminal and civil law issues)]. Państwo i Prawo 9:54 et seq

Kryszk K, Kłonkowska A (2012) Sytuacja społeczna osób transpłciowych. Analiza danych z badania ankietowego [Social situation of transgender persons. Analysis of survey data]. In: Sytuacja społeczna osób LGBT. Raport za lata 2010/2011 [Social situation of LGBT persons. The 2010/2011 Report], Warszawa, pp 236 et seq. https://www.kph.org.pl/publikacje/Raport_badania_LGBT_do_netu.pdf. Last accessed 11 Aug 2019

Łojko N (2010) Finansowanie zabiegów związanych z dostosowaniem płci psychicznej do płci fizycznej w Polsce [Financing procedures concerning alignment of psychological and physical sex in Poland]. In: Śledzińska-Simon A (ed) Prawa osób transseksualnych. Rozwiązania modelowe a sytuacja w Polsce [Rights of trans persons. Model solutions and the situation in Poland]. Warszawa, pp 45–61

Ostojska J (2014) Sądowa zmiana płci [The judicial sex change]. Doctorate thesis, Warszawa. https://depotuw.ceon.pl/bitstream/handle/item/1014/S%C4%85dowa%20zmiana%20p%C5%82ci_Joanna%20Ostojska.pdf?sequence=1. Last accessed 26 Feb 2021

Śledzińska-Simon A (2013) Sytuacja prawna osób transseksualnych w Polsce [Legal position of transsexuals in Poland]. In: Dynarski W, Śmiszek K (eds) Sytuacja prawna osób transpłciowych w Polsce – raport z badań i propozycje zmian [Legal position of trans persons in Poland – research report and proposed changes]. Warszawa, p 176

Wojewoda M (2014) Kilka uwag o definicji 'stanu cywilnego' w nowej ustawie Prawo o aktach stanu cywilnego [Some remarks on the definition of 'civil status' in the new Law on Civil Status Acts]. Metryka 2:17 et seq

The Civil Status of Trans Persons Under the Romanian Legal System

Daniela-Anca Deteşeanu and Cristina-Mihaela Nicolescu

Abstract This chapter highlights some essential landmarks concerning the conditions of recognition of the civil status of trans persons under the Romanian legal system. It shows that the medical and legal transition of trans persons in Romania represents a process full of uncertainties. The absence of an adequate legal framework and a lack of unity of the practice (also, from the medical, administrative and legal points of view) jeopardize the private lives of trans persons. Therefore, in some situations, the protection offered by the national authorities can prove at best to be illusory.

Under the Romanian legal system there are no specific regulations concerning trans persons, nor are there any clear medical, administrative or judicial procedures configured. However, without any doubt, medical modification to the gender with which a trans person identifies is allowed, as well as the legal recognition of the new gender identity. If a trans person obtains a favourable judicial decision, based on which the necessary changes have been made in the civil status acts, being issued a new identity card, then, in principle that person can enjoy the legal consequences of his/her new gender identity, in all areas of social life. As to the coverage by the national health insurance system of gender modification treatments and surgery, there is no convergent point of view within the competent authorities.

In Romania, issues related to trans persons are not highly debated. Officially, only few cases are documented. A possible explanation consists in the rather conservative character of Romanian society, with traditions, Christian morals, the church etc. playing an important role in the configuration of the collective mindset. However, a

One version of this chapter was previously published in Romanian in ANALELE UNIVERSITĂŢII DIN BUCUREŞTI – SERIA DREPT (AUB – DREPT), ISSN: 1011-0623, C.H. Beck Editions.

D.-A. Deteşeanu (✉) · C.-M. Nicolescu
Faculty of Law, University of Bucharest, Bucharest, Romania
e-mail: daniela-anca.deteseanu@drept.unibuc.ro; cristina-mihaela.nicolescu@drept.unibuc.ro

I. C. Jaramillo, L. Carlson (eds.), *Trans Rights and Wrongs*, Ius Comparatum - Global Studies in Comparative Law 54,
https://doi.org/10.1007/978-3-030-68494-5_7

number of human rights NGOs constantly champion for the defence and promotion of LGBT rights at the national level.

From the legislative point of view, there is no specific regulation dedicated to issues related to trans persons, only a few scattered provisions being identifiable concerning the modifications on the civil status acts and the administrative change of the name of natural persons.

This chapter highlights some essential landmarks concerning the conditions of recognition of the civil status of trans persons under the Romanian legal system, with the necessary main phases covered in order to make the medical and legal gender transition.

1 Regulation of Civil Status

Romania is a parliamentary democracy, having its foundation in a written Constitution (adopted in 1991, revised in 2003). The Romanian Constitution[1] also determines the relationship between international and national law. Considering the relationship between the Constitution and the international human rights law, art. 20 par. 1 of the Constitution provides that the interpretation and the application of the constitutional provisions concerning the citizens' rights and liberties shall be made in accordance to the Universal Declaration of Human Rights, the covenants and other treaties to which Romania is a party. Considering the relationship between international human rights law and the rest of the normative system (the national laws *infra* Constitution), the international regulations concerning human rights have priority, except when more favourable provisions are provided in the Constitution or the national laws.

In this context, and having in mind the object of this chapter, the relationship between the Romanian legal system and the European Convention on Human Rights and Fundamental Freedoms (ECHR)—ratified by Romania under the Law no. 30/1994—must be emphasized. The position of the international law doctrine is that the provisions of the ECHR, together with the jurisprudence of the European Court of Human Rights (ECtHR) represent an indestructible unity, being directly applicable in the Romanian national law and by the national judges, having a superior legal force than the national law. This position has been validated by the Romanian courts, starting with the Constitutional Court and going to the regular courts of law. More

[1]According to article 1, par. 4 of the Romanian Constitution: "The State is organised based on the principle of the separation and equilibrium of powers – legislative, executive and judicial – within the frame of a constitutional democracy." The Parliament is the supreme representative organ of the Romanian people and the only legislative authority of the country. The constitutional Romanian system establishes, as guardian of the Constitution, an independent judicial authority—the Constitutional Court. The Court decides on the constitutionality of the laws, the international treaties, the regulations of Parliament and the Government ordinances (art. 142 and the following of the Constitution).

specifically, the ECtHR case-law including those concerning sexual minorities, trans persons etc., shall have priority vis-à-vis national legislation. However, even if, as already mentioned, the Romanian tribunals often invoke the ECHR case-law, the Romanian legislation is not harmonised with the European jurisprudence in this matter.

1.1 Romanian Family Law and Civil Status Generally

The Romanian Constitution provides some general principles concerning family law: art. 26 of the Constitution provides the obligation of public authorities to respect and protect the family life, art. 48 determines the general principles representing the foundation of the family law,[2] while art. 49 frames the special rules of protection and assistance of children and young people. The main law that regulates the family relations can be found in the Civil Code, adopted under the Law no. 287/2009, in force since October 1st, 2011—Book II "On Family" (arts. 258–534).[3] The Law no. 71/2011 for the application of the new Romanian Civil Code abrogated the ancient Family Code (adopted under the Law no. 4/1953). According to the legal definition—art. 98 of the Civil Code—"the civil status is the right of a person to individualize itself, within its family or in society, by its strict personal qualities deriving from the acts and deeds of civil status".

The relevant doctrine considered that the civil status comprises of the following elements: the gender of the person (men or women); filiation (from marriage; born out-of-wedlock; with unknown parents; adopted); the matrimonial status (married; not married; divorced; widowed; remarried); the relation with the relatives; age etc. (Ilie, 2016, 112 and the following; Reghini, Diaconescu, Vasilescu, 2013, 197 and the following). Therefore, under the Romanian legal system, the *gender*, as a factual attribute of the person and anatomic reality, is part of the civil status of the natural person. From birth until death, the civil status is governed mainly by imperative legal provisions, therefore, not by the will of its holder. No person can directly modify his/her civil status. Nevertheless, there are available certain possibilities to perform some acts, having, as effect, a modification of his/her civil status.

In order for a natural person to acquire a certain civil status, some circumstances must intervene as the law attaches some consequences concerning the civil status to such circumstances. The following are considered sources of the civil status:

---

[2]The principle of the marriage freely consented by the spouses, the principle of equality of spouses, the right and the obligation of the parents to ensure the development, the education and the instruction of the children, the principle of equality of children in front of the law, irrespective if they are born out of marriage or out of wedlock.

[3]After the adoption, in 2009, of the Romanian Civil Code, the Juriscope Institute of Poitiers and the Faculty of Law of the University of Bucharest reunited in a project under which the code was translated into French. The translation of the Romanian Civil Code in French has been published by Dalloz publishing house, in 2013.

- the law;
- the facts concerning the civil status (the birth and the death);
- the legal acts concerning the civil status (manifestations of will which create or modify the civil status; for example, the marriage, the legal act of recognising the filiation, etc.);
- the court decisions granted in civil status legal actions (for example: the determination of filiation, the contestation of paternity, the annulment or the dissolution of marriage, the approval of adoption etc.)

1.2 Competent Authorities

The competences related to the civil status belong mainly to the *local public authorities*, respectively the local councils/the General Council of Bucharest Municipality, the local community public services for the evidence of persons, as well as the civil status public officers from the city halls or other administrative units where there no other local community public services for the evidence of persons—art. 3 par. (1) of the Law no. 119/1996 regarding the acts of civil status, as republished.[4]

According to art. 3 par. (2) of the same law, the following are competent as civil status public officers:

(a) Mayors of the municipalities, departments of Bucharest, cities or communes;
(b) Heads of the diplomatic missions or consulates of Romania;
(c) Commanders of vessels or aircraft; and
(d) Civil status officers designated by order of the ministry of national defence or, as the case may be, ministry of administration and internal affairs.

1.3 Proof of Civil Status

As a general rule, civil status is proven by the *acts of birth, marriage or death*, recorded, according to the law, in the registers of civil status, as well as by the certificates of civil status, which are issued based on such registers. From the point of view of their probative value, it must be emphasized that the acts of civil status are considered *authentic deeds* which prove, until deemed false, the validity of those registered by the civil status officer based on his/her personal acknowledgments, and, until a contrary prove exists, for the other entries—art. 99 par. (2) of the Civil Code. The certificates of civil status are the documents which attest, either integrally or partially, the acts of civil status. They can be originals or duplicates. Given the indivisible character of the civil status, the legal solution provided by art. 99

[4]Republished in the Official Gazette of Romania, Part I, no. 339 of May 18, 2012, with the subsequent amendments.

par. (3) of the Civil Code, in accordance to which "the judgment regarding the civil status of a person is opposable to any other person, as long as there is no other newer judgment deciding the contrary", is logical.

By exception, according to art. 103 of the Civil Code, the civil status can be proven, before a tribunal, by any means of evidence, in the event:

(a) No civil status registries existed;
(b) Civil status registries have been lost or destroyed, in all or in part;
(c) It is impossible to acquire the civil status certificate or the civil status act extract from abroad; or
(d) The drafting of the civil status act was omitted or, as the case may be, refused.

1.4 Changes to the Acts of Civil Status

Changes in the content of the acts of civil status are subject to review by the tribunals, under a judicial procedure based on which the acts of civil status can be, as the case may be, annulled, amended or modified—art. 100 par. (1) of the Civil code. By exception, the rectification of the acts regarding the civil status and the mentions to them can be done under an administrative procedure, ex officio or upon request, only based on a decision of the mayor from the city hall which keeps the act of civil status—art. 100 par. (2) of the Civil code.

2 Specific Regulations Concerning Trans Persons

Under the Romanian law system, there are no specific regulations concerning the status of transpersons, neither are clear medical,[5] administrative or judicial procedures configured. Some disparate and incomplete provisions can be identified in the Law no. 119/1996 regarding the acts of civil status, as republished, as well as in the Government Ordinance no. 41/2003 regarding the acquiring and the administrative change of the name of natural persons.[6]

Therefore, according to art. 43 letter (i) of the Law no. 119/1996, "mentions can be recorded in the acts of birth and, whenever necessary, in those concerning the marriage or the demise, concerning the changes occurred in the civil status of a person, in the following cases: [...] the change of the sex, after the final court decision". Also, according to art. 4 par. (2) letter (l) of the Government Ordinance no. 41/2003: "The applications for the change of the name are considered grounded

[5] Clear guides of intervention, explicitly assumed by the Romanian professional organs, helping the physicians to perform their duties, are inexistent.

[6] Published in the Official Gazette of Romania, Part I, no. 68 of February 2, 2003, with the subsequent amendments.

in the following cases: [. . .] when a person was granted with the change of sex, under a final court decision and that respective person requests an adequate forename, presenting a medical document from which his/her sex results".

These legal provisions have been subject to an *a posteriori* constitutional control, with respect to the provisions of art. 22 par. (1) regarding the right to life and physical and mental integrity, corroborated with art. 34 par. (1) regarding the right to the protection of health and art. 26 regarding the private, intimate and family life, of the Romanian Constitution. By Decision no. 530 from May 13, 2008,[7] the Constitutional Court considered that the objections raised are not grounded, stating as follows:

> The mentions which are registered in the acts of civil status based on a court decision are exclusively related to the legal nature of these acts, as well as to the legal status of the person, having as purpose a correct record of the population. Considering this legal regime of the acts of civil status, the Court holds that the approval of the change of sex by a final court decision (. . .) is necessary for the registration of the mentions regarding the changes occurred in the civil status of a person, therefore one cannot consider it an intervention of the tribunals in the private life of a person, as the author of the exception suggested, as such person would decide on this matter. Therefore, the change of sex represents an option of that respective person, having effects on his/her social status, which is related to the public order.

Regarding the *wording used in this field*, it must be mentioned that the incomplete provisions from the legislation are limited to the use of the expression "change of sex". For this reason, no legal concept can be distinguished.

In medical practice, Romanian psychiatrists constantly used the diagnosis of "sexual identity disorder", as defined in *DSM IV – Diagnostic and Statistical Manual* drafted by the American Psychiatry Association (ACCEPT Study, 2014, 11). After 2013, a tendency to use the phrase "gender dysphoria"/"gender identity disorder" can be observed.

With respect to the national regulations against discrimination, it is worth mentioning the Government Ordinance no. 137/2000 regarding the prevention and punishment of all forms of discrimination,[8] the frame-regulation in this field, and which configured the general legal frame meant to ensure the guarantees for the observance of the principle of equality between citizens, the exclusion of privileges and discrimination. Among the criteria enumerated in art. 2 par. (1) of the ordinance are mentioned sex and sexual orientation, any discrimination whatsoever (distinction, exclusion, restriction or preference) based on these reasons being prohibited.

The prohibition of the discriminatory treatment based on sex or sexual orientation can be also found in other legal documents regulating certain areas. For example, according to art. 663 par. (2) of the Law no. 95/2006 regarding the reform in medical care[9] "a physician, dentist, the nurse/midwife cannot refuse the medical care/health

[7]Published in the Official Gazette of Romania, Part I, no. 526 from June 11, 2008.

[8]Republished in the Official Gazette of Romania, Part I, no. 166 from March 7, 2014.

[9]Republished in the Official Gazette of Romania, Part I, no. 652 from August 28, 2015.

related treatments based on ethnic, religious or criteria related to sexual orientation, or on other discriminatory criteria, prohibited by the law".

3 Legal Requirements for Changing Legal Gender

Under the Romanian legal system, a trans person is allowed to make the medical gender transition towards the gender with which he/she identifies, as well as the legal recognition of the new sexual identity. Given the scarcity of legal regulations in the area, the steps that must be performed by a trans person for resolving both the medical and the legal issues can only be inferred, taking into account the crystallised medical, administrative and legal practices. In brief, the *stages* are the following:

- *A psychiatric evaluation* is necessary attesting that the person fulfils the criteria for the diagnostic of gender identity disorder (transsexualism) and can initiate the hormonal treatment for the change of the secondary sexual characteristics;
- *Judicial approval for gender modification surgery,* even though the condition does not result *in terminis* from the law, physicians willing to provide such medical services condition them on the existence of a court decision.
- A court decision allowing the modification of the acts of civil status, following the change of gender.
- The change of a trans person's first name, through an administrative procedure;
- *The attribution of a new personal numeric code – CNP*;[10]
- *The registration of the corresponding mentions in the acts of civil status and getting the new identity cards.*[11]

Some courts considered the performance of surgery interventions on genitals as a precondition for a change in the acts of civil status, even in the hypothesis when a person already acquired, according to the reality, the status of "man", with which he identified himself for some years already, in the social life. In our opinion, these court solutions collide with the ECtHR case-law in the field (*A.P., Garçon et Nicot v. France*—April 6, 2017), where the Court ascertained a breach of art. 8 ECHR (the right to private life), from the perspective of the obligation imposed to the applicants,

[10] According to art. 15 Letter (d) of the Government Decision no. 1375/2006 for the approval of the Methodological Norms for an unitary application of the legal provisions concerning the record, domicile, residence and identity cards of the Romanian citizens (published in the Official Gazette of Romania, Part I, no. 851 from October 17, 2006), a new CNP shall be attributed to the same person if the applicant changed his/her gender. It must be emphasized that, in the Romanian legal system concerning the acts of civil status, besides the sex criteria, the gender identity is evidenced through the first name and the first figure of the personal numeric code.

[11] According to art. 19 par. (1) letter (i) of the Government Emergency Ordinance no. 97/2005 regarding the record, domicile, residence and the identity cards of the Romanian citizens (republished in the Official Gazette of Romania, Part I, no. 719 of October 12, 2011), in case of change of sex, the community public services for the record of persons shall issue a new identity card.

to make an intervention and an irreversible medical treatment, which, in opinion of the Court, signifies to condition the full exercise of the right to protection of the private life by waiving the full exercise of the right to respect of physical integrity. Therefore, one cannot impose an obligation to be subject to a surgery for the change of gender upon the right of a natural person to self-determination (entering in the field of application of art. 8 ECHR).

Considering these coordinates as given by the ECtHR case-law, one could anticipate the judgement that this Court issued in the two cases against Romania, where the applicants (X, respectively Y) invoked the infringement of art. 8 ECHR for the refusal by Romanian authorities to modify the registration regarding their gender, the name and the personal numeric code in their act of civil status, for the reason that they did not perform a surgery for the conversion of their gender (ECtHR, judgement X. and Y. v. Romania—2145/16 and 20607/16, January 19, 2021).

There are no express regulations concerning the age, the matrimonial status (which means that, theoretically, even a married person can use the medical and legal procedures for the change of gender),[12] inexistence of the natural or adopted children etc. During the procedures in front of the tribunal, apart the written evidence (medical documents gathered during the preliminary phases of the gender conversion process), usually the applicants also use witnesses, respectively close persons (friends, colleagues from work) who can provide to the court useful information about the gender identity showed by the trans person in his/her social life. In addition to such means of evidence, the applicants, depending on each case, presented to the court personal photos in various social hypostasis. (ACCEPT Study, 2014, 22).

4 Legal Provisions Regarding Names

4.1 General provisions regarding the name

Under the Romanian legal system, the name is an attribute for the identification of the natural person, being composed of the family name (surname) and the first name. The surname is acquired by the effect of filiation and can be modified in case of change of the civil status, as provided by the law, while the first name is determined at the date when the birth has been registered, based on the statement regarding the birth. Under the conditions provided by the Government Ordinance no. 41/2003, the Romanian citizen can change either their first name, or their surname, or both, through an administrative procedure.

[12]In respect to the situation of an existing marriage, see our comment under Sect. 7.

4.2 Change of Name in Case of Trans Persons

The Romanian law recognises the effects of the gender change through a medical intervention, both in case of the name, and in case of the civil status. Regarding the name, the procedure to be followed should be exclusively administrative, but it must be emphasized that, unfortunately, the courts' practice in the field is not unitary. Therefore, some courts[13] admitted the count regarding the approval of the medical intervention for the change of sex, based on the medical expertise presented, but rejected the count concerning the change of name, correctly grounding their solution on the provisions of the Government Ordinance no. 41/2003 (the change of name shall be done only through an administrative, not a judicial procedure).[14]

According to art. 4 par. (2) letter (l) of the above-mentioned ordinance: "the application for the change of name is considered as grounded in the following cases: [...] when a person has been granted the change of sex through a definitive court judgment and requires a corresponding first name, presenting medical documents showing his/her sex". According to a document issued by the National Institute of Forensic Science *Mina Minovici*, "as a matter of principle, such kind of expertise is requested only after the medical intervention (...). The medical intervention is irreversible and, consequently, it involves only a formality with respect to the medical act, which has as objective only to ascertain the reality of the intervention which, in an affirmative case, implies, also, the recommendation to change the civil gender". (ACCEPT Study, 2014, 25).

The administrative procedure requires, in principle, lodging a reasoned application to the community public service regarding the record of persons. In this case, the change of the first name shall be performed through an administrative order.[15] A new birth certificate shall not be issued, as in case of the modification of the acts of civil status through judicial means, but the new first name shall be recorded, as a new mention, on the act of birth.[16]

However, some tribunals also granted the change of the applicant's first name, therefore voiding from legal effect the provisions of the Government Ordinance no. 41/2003. The general reasons which ground the legal solution concerning the change of the first name of a trans person gravitate around the following arguments: once granted the change of gender from female to male or vice-versa, a logical correspondence also must exist concerning the first name of such person.

[13]In order to protect the private life of trans persons, most of the documents/web pages do not provide for their personal data, the name of the courts or the precise date when the decision was granted.

[14]It was shown in the argumentative part of the court decision that the applicant, due to the surgery for the change of sex, shall be able to change the first name through an administrative procedure.

[15]According to the data provided by ACCEPT Study (p. 13), "in the period between 2007 and 2012 9 applications for the change of the first name have been registered at the national level, under the administrative procedure", by trans persons.

[16]Art. 13–15 of the Government Ordinance no. 41/2003.

5 Access to Treatment and Health-Care Services

In Romania, trans persons have access to hormonal treatments and medical services for gender modification, but it has to be emphasized that, in practice, all the process prove to be at least difficult, especially because of the lack of information, of clear procedures, as well as the lack of specialists duly qualified in working with trans persons.

As mentioned before, most medical units condition the performance of the surgery for the change of sex upon a prior court decision. Even more, in some cases, that in his/her application in front of a court, the applicant (the trans person) requests the court to grant, through its decision, the commencement of the necessary hormonal treatment. It is true that in other cases, the applicants have lodged with the court's file medical letters from the qualified physicians—endocrinologist—showing that the person has already started the hormonal treatment, its duration and the fact that the treatment generated some changes—some of them irreversible (ACCEPT Study, 2014, 19–20). From an evidentiary perspective, the psychiatric expertise represents, without any doubt, the most important proof to be administered in front of a court. The psychiatrist is called to attest that a person fulfils the criteria for the diagnosis of gender identity disorder (transsexualism).[17] The court stated in one case as follows: "As it results from the deed concerning the psychiatric evaluation, the applicant meets the criteria for a diagnosis of gender identity disorder, and, during the evaluation, we could not identify other psychiatric symptoms, current or significant in the past, that would attribute the identity disorder to other psychiatric condition".

Regarding the coverage, by the health insurance system of the treatment and surgery for gender modification, it must be emphasized that, over time, the institutions competent in this field (the Ministry of Health, the National House for Health Insurances, medical units) offered contradictory answers to the question if the medical services related to the medical transition are or not covered by the national budget for health insurances (ACCEPT Study, 2014, 13). Nevertheless, the tendency seems to be that of covering such medical services within the national budget, under condition that the psychiatric expertise attests the fact that the operation of gender modification is the most suitable solution for the particular situation of that respective person, in order to improve his/her social life, being the only remedy for transsexualism.[18]

---

[17]In the opinion of the well-known professor dr. Ioan Lascăr, the surgeon who performed the first intervention for the change of sex in Romania, "the transsexualism is a psychiatric disorder, and its treatment is performed by surgery"—the interview was published in the newspaper "Adevărul" from 18 January 2014.

[18]As it is known, in the case *Van Kück v. Germany*—Judgment from 12 June 2003, case no. 35968/97, the ECtHR did not analyse the right of the applicant to have reimbursed per se the expenses, and it did not determine any positive obligation of States concerning the coverage of the expenses incurred with the treatment and the surgeries for gender modification.

6 Gays, Lesbians and Trans

Under the Romanian legal system, the family is based on the act of marriage, as defined by art. 259 par. 1 of the Romanian Civil Code “the freely agreed union between a man and a woman, concluded as provided by the law”. In addition, par. 2 of the same article grants the right of *a man and a woman* to marry and form a family. Any doubt regarding a possible interpretation of art. 259 par. 2 of the Civil Code in a larger sense has been clarified by art. 277 which provides explicitly that the marriage between persons of the same gender is prohibited.

In accordance with the same article, the interdiction has effects in the area of private international law, meaning that in Romania such marriages cannot be recognized, even if they have been duly concluded abroad:

(a) Marriages between persons having the same gender, when concluded abroad, either by Romanian citizens, or by foreign citizens;
(b) Civil partnerships between persons of different genders or even between same gender, concluded abroad, either by Romanian citizens, or by foreign citizens.

In other words, except for the marriage between a man and a woman, the Romanian Civil Code, in its current drafting, does not allow for any other form of marriage or registered partnership, either between persons of the same gender, or between persons having a different gender. This traditionalist view is not currently weakening, nor is it evolving towards a wider conception concerning the marital unions. Even if such position might seem surprising, given Romania’s international obligations and its attachment (at least from a legal point of view) to the European values, it is somehow justified by a traditional and religious social layer.

On the one hand, a debate has been launched in the public space by the traditional organisations, which proposed a constitutional review, in order to modify art. 48 of the Romanian Constitution[19] (“The family”) in the sense that, similarly to the relevant article of the Romanian Civil Code, the constitutional text must specify expressly that the marriage is the union *between a man and a woman*. The referendum was organised on 6 and 7 October 2018, the scrutiny not being validated, due to the insufficient participation (21.1% of the registered persons).

On the other hand, the debate has been reinforced by a request made by a homosexual couple to have their union, concluded abroad, recognised in Romania. Under this frame, an unconstitutionality exception has been raised in front of the Romanian Constitutional Court (file no. 78D/2016), concerning art. 277 of the Romanian Civil Code (the non-recognition of the same sex marriages concluded abroad). On 18 July 2018, the Constitutional Court, in its plenary section, granted its decision concerning the exception of unconstitutionality of art. 277 par. (2) and (4) of the Civil Code, stating that these provisions:

[19] Art. 48 par. 1 of the Romanian Constitution provides that the family is based on the freely concluded marriage between spouses, on their equality and on the right and obligation of the parents to guard on their children and to ensure their education and instruction.

> [C]annot constitute the legal base for the Romanian competent authorities to refuse the right of stay, on the Romanian territory, of the spouse – citizen of a EU member State and/or a third state, same-sex person, who is bound by marriage legally concluded on the territory of a EU member State, with a Romanian citizen, having the domicile or residence in Romania, or citizen of a EU member State who has the right of residence in Romania, for the reason that the Romanian national law does not provide for/recognize the same-sex marriage.

By a majority, the Constitutional Court decided in favour of the exception of unconstitutionality and stated that "the provisions of art. 277 par. (2) and (4) of the Civil Code are constitutional if they allow the right of stay on the Romanian territory, under the conditions provided by the European law – of the spouses – citizens of EU member States and/or citizens of third States – from the same-sex marriages, concluded in an EU member State"—Decision no. 534 of 18 July 2018.[20] One can observe that in the above-mentioned case, the Constitutional Court gave its opinion exclusively for the point of view of the possibility to grant the right of stay on the Romanian territory, without touching so far the thorny matter of the non-recognition, completely, of the personal and patrimonial effects generated by the same-sex marriages duly concluded abroad.

In this context, it must be mentioned that under the Romanian legal system there are no regulations dedicated to intersex persons. One court has held as follows regarding the outstanding condition for the conclusion of marriage, the gender difference:

> The gender difference is an essential element for a marriage to be concluded. If a severe genital malformation involves a gender non-differentiation, the solution is the absolute nullity of the marriage; consequently, the courts must determine, on a case-by-case basis, if a genital malformation represents or not a lack of sexual differentiation, which prevent the sexual relations between spouses.[21]

According to a local newspaper, in 2011 an inter-sex baby was born in a hospital in Bacău city. Even if the baby had characteristics of both sexes, in the birth certificate was registered as a girl, based on the clinical examination made by the obstetricians and paediatricians, and the child was subject to a correction surgery.[22]

7 Stakes in Gender

If a trans person obtains a favourable court decision based on which the necessary changes on the acts of civil status can be performed, being issued a new identity card, that person can make use, in principle, of all legal consequences of his/her new identity in all sectors of the social life, whereas the new sexual identity is part of the

[20] Published in the Official Gazette of Romania, Part I, no. 842 of October 3, 2018.

[21] Supreme Court, Civil Section, decision no. 1196/1972, available in the Compendium of decisions for the year 1972, pag. 199.

[22] Article published in the newspaper Deşteptarea from Bacău, available on the web page: http://www.desteptarea.ro/nou-nascut-hermafrodit-in-bacau/ (web page consulted on August 10, 2017).

civil status. Therefore, the person who suffered a surgery for the change of sex shall be able to marry a person of the opposite gender to the one resulted from the surgery. Nevertheless, it must be emphasized the fact that there is an obligation of information of the future spouse about this circumstance, otherwise the marriage can be nullified for *dolus* (fraud).

If the person who undergoes gender modification surgery is already married, the issue as to the fate of the ongoing marriage should be raised. Given the fact that under the Romanian legal system, only the heterosexual marriage is authorised, it is obvious that a marriage between two persons of the same sex legally cannot continue. Some authors considered that due to the lack of an express regulation and by applying the general rules, the solution should be either the caducity of the marriage, while others choose the termination of the marriage from the date when the registration concerning the change of gender is made in the registry of civil status (Avram, 2016, 42).

With regard to *public pensions*, it must be emphasized that, in the Romanian legal system, the limit of age for retirement is different, respectively 65 years for men and 63 for women, according to art. 53 par. (1) of the Law no. 263/2010 regarding the unitary system of public pensions.[23] We were unable to identify in the Romanian legislation in force some provisions/instructions which provide a possible algorithm to determine the age of retirement for trans persons, considering the periods of contribution as man, respectively as woman.

Concerning *military service*, in Romania, starting 1 January 2007, the execution of a compulsory military service has been suspended. According to art. 1 of the Law no. 395/2005,[24] "the Romanian citizens, men or women, who meet the conditions provided by the legislation in force, can perform, on a voluntary basis, any form of military service, without discrimination". It is interesting to mention that, only in case of men, the law provides the obligation that, within a 6 months period from the moment of celebration of the 18th anniversary, to present to the military centers in order to be registered in the military evidence.

In the context of the analysis of the reverberations produced by the legal recognition of the new sexual identity, it worth mention an under-law regulation, respectively the Order of the Ministry of Sports and Youth no. 1.058 from 24 April 2003 for the approval of the Technical Norms regarding the medical examination of the sportspersons.[25] In Annex no. 2 to this order the *medical and sport contraindications* are provided, the transsexualism (point 52) and the hermaphroditism (point 53) being mentioned among the definitive/final contraindications.

[23]Published in the Official Gazette of Romania, Part I, no. 852 from December 20, 2010, as modified and reviewed.

[24]... regarding the suspension, in time of peace, of the compulsory military service and the transition to a voluntary military service, published in the Official Gazette of Romania, Part One, no. 1155 of December 20, 2005.

[25]Published in the Official Gazette of Romania, Part One, no. 327 of May 14, 2003.

8 Conclusions

As seen from all the above-mentioned elements, the medical and legal transition of trans persons in Romania represents a process full of uncertainties. The absence of an adequate legal framework and a lack of unity of the practice (also, from the medical, administrative and legal points of view) jeopardize the private lives of trans persons. Therefore, in some situations, the protection offered by the national authorities can prove at best to be illusory.

The organisations championing for the observance of trans persons' rights have synthetized, over time, a series of recommendations addressed to the competent public authorities, aiming to improve the legal and institutional framework, so that:

- Trans persons have better access to the legal recognition of their gender identity;
- A separation exists between the medical transition and the legal transition;
- Access of trans persons to the medical assistance for transition based on an informed consent is assured;
- The emphasis is on the private relationship specialist-trans person, instead of an institutional intervention (ACCEPT Study, 2014, 43).

Gender Identity, National Identity and the Right to Self-Determination: The Peculiar Case of Taiwan

Yi-Chien Chen

Abstract This chapter examines the contested legal field of sex/gender issues in relation to trans rights in Taiwan, taking the intimacy recognition case as an example. First, Taiwan's political democratization, the women's movement and gender equality movement will be set out in order to answer the question of what were the conditions for Taiwan to become one of the most LGBT friendly countries in Asia? Second, the Wu-Wu trans marriage case will be analyzed to demonstrate the limits of the current binary male-female legal categories and explore whether the legal recognition of two trans persons' marriage adequately encompasses their genderqueer identity. Third, the current status quo of the administrative procedures and practices regarding gender change registration and lastly, reform suggestions will be explored.

Built on the rich results of the democratization of intimacy by the women's movement, growing demands for protection of non-heteronormative relationships and nonbinary sex/gender identities have played out vividly in the recent social-legal activism in Taiwan, pushing it to become the first nation in Asia to legalize same sex marriage in May 2019. Less known however is the Wu-Wu trans marriage case in 2013. Both parties were trans women, though at the time of marriage registration they held national identification cards with different sex marker (one female, one male). The Wu case demonstrated the limitation of the current binary female-male legal categories in Taiwan and openly questioned whether the legal recognition of marriage between two trans persons adequately encompassed their own fluid sex/gender identity. Unlike in some Euro-American countries, there is no specific law regulating gender modification surgery or sex change registration in Taiwan. These are done through administrative regulations, everyday bureaucratic practices, civil servants' discretion, civil society activism which I call 'the Taiwanese way', flexible and pragmatic. In the process of becoming oneself and building intimate

Y.-C. Chen (✉)
Graduate Institute for Gender Studies, Shih Hsin University, Taipei, Taiwan
e-mail: yichien@mail.shu.edu.tw

I. C. Jaramillo, L. Carlson (eds.), *Trans Rights and Wrongs*, Ius Comparatum - Global Studies in Comparative Law 54,
https://doi.org/10.1007/978-3-030-68494-5_8

relationship on one's own terms, trans couple exercised the right to gender self-determination and called upon the Taiwan state for recognition. On the way to being noticed and recognized as a long self-ruled independent island country, Taiwan strives to meet the international human rights standards, including 'the right to self-determination', which then acts as a link between trans persons and their state to take actions.

Legalized marriage for same-sex couples was enacted by legislation effective 24 May 2019.[1] This law allows a same-sex spouse to adopt the birth child of his or her spouse but did not specify any additional family rights, including joint adoption rights. On that same day, hundreds of same sex couples filling the local household registration offices grabbed international media attention as Taiwan became the first country in Asia to legalize same sex marriage. I was interviewed and asked so often by international journalists why Taiwan was the first in Asia, and what was our next step? The Marriage Equality movement is actually only a small part of a larger democratization of intimacy project/movement launched by feminists and LGBT rights activists and it began much earlier and will certainly not end here.

This chapter examines the contested legal field of sex/gender issues in relation to trans rights in Taiwan, taking the intimacy recognition case as an example. First, Taiwan's political democratization, the women's movement and gender equality movement will be set out in order to answer the question of what were the conditions for Taiwan to become one of the most LGBT friendly countries in Asia? Second, the Wu-Wu trans marriage case will be analyzed to demonstrate the limits of the current binary male-female legal categories and explore whether the legal recognition of two trans persons' marriage adequately encompasses their genderqueer identity. Third, the current status quo of the administrative procedures and practices regarding gender change registration and lastly, reform suggestions will be explored.

1 The Special Status of Taiwan: National Identity in Question

Taiwan is a young constitutional democracy whose official name is the 'Republic of China' (hereafter R.O.C.), at times confusing as there also exists the 'People's Republic of China' (hereafter P.R.C.), also known as China. There are five branches in the central government, including Executive Yuan, Legislative Yuan, Judicial Yuan, Examination Yuan and Control Yuan. The written R.O.C. Constitution was first put into effected in 1947 in China (now the P.R.C.). The then-ruling party nationalist party (KMT) had lost the civil war to communist party and retreated to

[1]The Legislative Yuan of Taiwan, acting in the final hour before the May 2019 deadline set in the Judicial Interpretation No. 748 dated on May 24, 2017 by Grand Justices, passed "Enforcement Act of Judicial Yuan Interpretation No. 748" on May 17, enacted by the President Tsia on May 22, effective on May 24.

Taiwan. The Constitution was modified seven times in Taiwan (R.O.C.) afterwards, modifiable originally by National Assembly, later changed to be Legislative Yuan.[2] Martial Law was lifted in Taiwan in 1987. The Democratic Progressive Party (DPP) currently holds a legislative majority and Tsia Ing-wen is currently serving as the president since May 20, 2016, the first female leader of the nation.

When President Tsia sworn in, Taiwan received much international attention, both because her party DPP historically holds an independent separatist political view from China, and because she is the first woman leader in the modern Chinese history including both ROC. and PRC. In Asia, Tsia's becoming national leader story remains unique since many of the women leaders in other Asian countries came into power as they are daughters or wives of powerful male politicians.

2 Democratization of Intimacy: Ground for LGBT Rights Movement

In the early 1980s, feminists and women's groups in Taiwan sought to challenge restrictive gender roles, privileges of men/fathers/husbands/sons, assumptions of possessiveness that they saw as inherent to marriage. Feminist theories pointed out the many ways by which traditional marriage has disadvantaged women through legal, social, cultural, economic, and physical control (Chen 2010). The regulation of marriage residency offers a good example of the relationship between culture, law, and the state. The Chinese saying "marrying a cock, following a cock; marrying a dog, following a dog" describes the patriarchal family norm literally, in the dominant cultural imagination of the family. When a woman gets married, she marries into her husband's extended family and becomes a ghost belonging to this family even after death. The cultural norm was represented in the Civil Code and before the 1998 family law reform it read: the designated residency during the marriage is the residency of the husband.

Thanks to feminists, women's groups, women lawyers and the suffering parties in some landmark legal cases, the Civil Code was gradually reformed away from the male-preferred provisions to gender neutral ones. These changes include parental rights, child custody, marriage property, surname of the children, and etc. The man woman bond family norm, where men as husbands and fathers enjoy more rights than women in the marriage, is now transformed to be two-person joint/

[2]See Additional Articles of the Constitution of Republic of China, Article 12: Amendment of the Constitution shall be initiated upon the proposal of 1/4 of the total members of the Legislative Yuan, passed by at least 3/4 of the members present at a meeting attended by at least 3/4 of the total members of the Legislative Yuan, and sanctioned by electors in the free area of the Republic of China at a referendum held upon expiration of a 6-month period of public announcement of the proposal, wherein the number of valid votes in favor exceeds one-half of the total number of electors.<http://law.moj.gov.tw/Eng/LawClass/LawAll.aspx?PCode=A0000002> (last visited on July 1st, 2019).

partnership family model.[3] The less important gender specific roles in marriage become, the easier it is for same sex couples to enter the 'marriage' institution. In addition, Gender Equity Education Law was passed in 2004, requiring that all schools shall not discriminate against students on the basis of their gender, gender temperaments, gender identity, sexual orientation in teachings, activities, assessments, rewards and penalties, benefits, or services. This law intends to insert the educational moments at all levels of school to educate students what law cannot change immediately, social understanding of LGBTIQ people. The Gender Equal Employment Law was reformed and renamed (originally titled Two Sexes Equal Employment Law) in 2008 to expand the protection to employees who are discriminated against at work on the basis of gender identity and sexual orientation.

3 Taiwan Experiences International Isolation

The sources of law in Taiwan includes international treaties (in theory and in practice contested), the Constitution (additional articles of the Constitution, and interpretations of Grand Justices), codes (civil, criminal, administrative, labor...), regulations (including administrative regulations and directive orders), and administrative practices. Taiwan is not a member of United Nations and often is rejected at most of the major international organizations and meetings due to the objection of China (P.R. C.).[4] Taiwan along with other 14 members founded the "Unrepresented Nations and People Organization (UNPO)" in 1991 and its Members are indigenous peoples, minorities, unrecognized States and occupied territories to defend their political, social and cultural rights, to preserve their environments and to promote their right to self-determination.

Recently Taiwan has ratified three major international treaties, the International Covenant on Civil and Political Rights, International Covenant on Economic, Social and Cultural Rights, The Convention on the Elimination of all Forms of Discrimination Against Women (CEDAW). For CEDAW, Taiwan has issued three national

[3]The image of the 'family' in the civil code of Taiwan on its face/on book is now far less "patriarchal" than it was enacted in 1930, and yet still very "heterosexual". As C.J. Chen in "Marriage as Heterosexual Patriarchy and Privilege" (2010) argued: feminist legal reform weakened marriage's function as a patriarchal institution, but simultaneously created an invisible cage. Women's oppression in and through marriage remains. Indeed, the marriage residency legally is now to be decided through negotiation of the spouses, but the cultural norm remains and dictates how people negotiate. Furthermore, marriage maintains heterosexual hegemony's authority and reinforces this authority by delivering privileges to married couples and by making adultery a criminal offense. Thus, a reformulation of the concept and institution of intimate citizenship based on the principle of "anti-compulsory heterosexual marriage" is necessary and far more urgent than other countries.

[4]Two recent examples are Taiwan was not invited to WHO meetings and world aviation meetings where one would think health and aviation security should be the last place the world can afford "exclusion" practices.

reports respectively in 2009, 2013, 2017. Although Taiwan cannot fully complete the ratification process due to its internationally isolated status, Taiwan's Legislative Yuan has enacted three Treaties' Implement Acts for the first two in 2009 and for CEDAW in 2011. In another words, in order to fight and survive the international isolation, Taiwan volunteers to follow the international rules via making the international treaties a part of Taiwan's domestic legal system.

The Executive Yuan of Taiwan established the task force-level Committee of Women's Rights Promotion (CWRP) on May 6, 1997, incorporating the advocacy and proposals of representatives from women's organizations, scholars and experts into the country's highest decision-making mechanisms. The Executive Yuan underwent reorganization on January 1, 2012 and the CWRP was expanded and became the Gender Equality Committee (GEC). On 1 January 2012, the nation's first authoritative unit dedicated to gender equality—the Department of Gender Equality (DGE)—was established. GEC is currently staffed by DGE and helps in integrating gender equality policies across various government bodies and directing central and local governments as they put gender mainstreaming into practice.

There were many debates on the legal status of the DGE before it was finally decided that it would be under the GEC. DGE is established to govern the gender equality issues but since it is under GEC as an administrative resource, it fails to have the real power to demand other ministries also under the Executive Yuan to work together as was planned. In 2014 the GEC proposed to change the executive practices of requiring completion of gender reassignment surgery to change legal gender, it came so close that the Ministry of Health and Welfare agreed to forgo the medical requirement and promised to further work with the Ministry of Interior on details. Although nothing really came through later, still the GEC and DEG proved to be possible driving forces of change, certainly also depending on the people on the committee.

4 Law and Society

As Taiwan is a young democracy, the Taiwanese are still learning how to be active in participating public affairs, and cautiously trusting the legal system, as are also more specifically trans persons. Marriage equality is a working-together project, done by trans persons suffering on a daily basis, couples and families, activists, the concerned general public and the state, which claims to pursue freedom and equality, and set its feet far away from China. Law is actually not so influential in Taiwanese everyday life, and law can send out a message regarding freedom and equality, but it cannot completely change the way people think about LGBT. As a factor in forming a civil young constitutional democracy, law certainly plays a crucial role, but we should not overestimate the effect of the law itself.

Responding to queer critiques of the pursuit of same sex marriages, many trans persons are not so naive to believe that everything will be normal now after marriage equality. It is not the answer to all LGBT rights issues, rather it is one of the basic conditions for new political and social possibilities to emerge. The most important thing for many LGBT couples is to have a smooth everyday life after all. Law could send out important messages, those messages could let LBGT people feel more grounded, but these are only the first step, no more or no less:

> I think law is just a threshold that means at this point, you can enter the life of marriage, but after that how will you lead a life (過日子)? Even you can marry, have children and form a family, but how will you face the reality in this society, the way this society has been treating the sexual minority people? I am thinking of this aspect. (T.)

> Law might protect people, but it is not going to happen only because the same sex marriage is approved and all the sudden the opposing ones think gay are normal people, they still think gays are different, who do things we cannot approve ever, this is deep inside in their thoughts. (F.)[5]

5 Wu-Wu Trans Marriage: The Trans Marriage Challenged

It is best and easiest to view Wu's trans marriage first as an example to illustrate the Taiwanese arbitrary legal regulation of sex/gender/sexual identity as categories, and to understand that the current heterosexual hegemony in the Taiwanese legal regime is not flawless. Jiyi Wu and Yiting Wu were both registered males at birth and who underwent gender reassignment surgery in July 2012, 3 months before they registered for marriage. Prior to their marriage registration, Yiting Wu collected all the documents she needed (the related administrative order and the required documents will be explained and discussed in next section) and went to Household Registration Office (hereafter HRO) and registered her current gender, female shown on her newly issued national identity card. Then Jiyi Wu, a man, and YiTing, a woman legally recognized by the state now, went to HRO to register their marriage. After they got married, Jiyi Wu then with all the required documents changed her gender from male to female in the HRO, also recognized by the state and got her new identification card. The government in June, 2013 issued a letter to them and questioned the legality of their marriage and threatened to invalidate it.[6]

Since there is no law regarding such issues for trans persons at all, the reality for the trans community is that each individual has to find and fight along the way, maybe through intensive media exposure and advocacy or relying on the kindness of individual civil servants who make favorable decisions in specific questions raised by the trans community at that time as presented. There are no central laws or rules, only administrative practices which could be monitored or sometimes pressured to

---

[5]An in-depth interview with ten participants in Taiwan was conducted in 2016–2017 on same sex partnership and its legalization, Interview file is with author. Please see Tang et al. (2019).

[6]The case received a lot of international media attention as well, <https://blogs.wsj.com/chinarealtime/2013/08/09/taiwan-reinstates-transgender-couples-marriage/> (visited on Aug. 8, 2017) The letter please see the document with Author with the permission of parties at stake.

change practices by the activists or NGOs. Gender/Sexuality Rights Association Taiwan was established in May 1999 with the aims to promote rights of sexual minorities in the aspects of family, education system, politics, economy and law. The previous version of the sex change registration requirement administrative order in 2007 was negotiated and improved through the protest of the Gender/Sexuality Rights Association Taiwan and other activists.[7] This means flexibility sometimes for creative trans persons and activists, but also suggests potential arbitrary governmental decisions negative to trans persons. This is rather Taiwanese in its flexible and pragmatic way. I often wonder if it is because Taiwanese people are used to be left alone to creatively run their lives without the intervention of the state or because Taiwan is left out by the international communities for so long that the Taiwan bureaucratic state is used to finding spaces for tactic survival.

6 Two-Wives Marriage Legally Sustained

Wu and Wu's trans marriage (the parties named it themselves in the interview) received lots of media attention both domestically and internationally and stirred public discussion about the marital rights of LGBT people in Taiwan. They are both women recognized by the state and are married to each other. In the pride march and in some press conferences they also call themselves "Two wives troop"(兩妻部隊, playing Chinese word pronunciation game with same pronounced word sea and land amphibious force). They were both very conscious and vocal about the trans activism and LGBTIQ movement in Taiwan.

After a public hearing and a closed-door consultation meeting, the Ministry of Interior found no law and no legitimate ground to invalidate the marriage, concluding that the marriage was valid as it was between a man and a woman legally at the time of registration. The Ministry of Justice also announced that a 1994 administrative directive letter explained that a change of gender during a legally recognized marriage does not affect a person's marital standing and the person's relationship with his or her offspring.[8] When people go to HRO to register a marriage, civil servants usually check the parties' ID cards for the opposite sexes, without any medical examination requirement. When people undergo gender reassignment surgery, there is no direct link between the hospital and the HRO for a change of sex.

[7] 2007 年 10 月 16 日內政部發布的內授中戶字 0960066142 號函釋 (A administrative letter numbered 0960066142, issued by Ministry of the Interior of Taiwan on 2007.10.16). It required trans not only to remove sex organs but to rebuild the desired sex organs in order to do the sex change registration.

[8] Again, no law exists regarding gender modification procedures and related status change or any obligation and rights. We only have administrative letters and orders in Taiwan regarding gender modification issues. That means, whenever there is a case, communications between the citizen and the administrative agencies, or between agencies will then start. When there is a question from the citizen, there will be answers from the administrative agency, if the agency thinks it can handle it.

The birth sex, the legal sex registered, the way how people identify themselves both psychologically and physically, and how people express their identified gender are all separate and distinct aspects. The then heterosexual legal system before 24 May 2019 only recognizes one possibility, female to male heterosexual union, and Wu and wu's marriage brought their intimate union to the Taiwanese society and proved to the state that other possibilities do exist. Questions and challenges remain after the 24th of May when a separate law governing same-sex marriage was enacted: Was Wu's marriage a same-sex marriage or a heterosexual marriage? Should there be any marital disputes, is the civil code or the "Enforcement Act of Judicial Yuan Interpretation No. 748" the governing law?

7 Gays & Lesbians and Trans: Legal Advancements or Backlash? Social Acceptance

Huang Mei-yu and her partner of 7 years Yu Ya-ting held the first Buddhist wedding ceremony performed by a highly-respected Buddhist master Shih Chao-hwei on 13 August 2012. According to "Changing Attitudes toward Homosexuality in Taiwan, 1995–2012" (Cheng et al. 2016), overall social tolerance toward LGBT people has increased, which is mainly due to cohort succession and partly to intra-cohort changes in attitudes. Improvement in education and liberal values related to divorce, prostitution, and gender roles act as mediators for the cohort differences in tolerance. In addition, women and the university-educated have more liberal attitudes toward homosexuals than men or the least-educated in recent years. Christians were not especially intolerant toward homosexuality in 1995 but became significantly less tolerant than other religions by 2012.

After more than one hundred LGBT local groups discussion forums around Taiwan, Taiwan Alliance to Promote Civil Partnership Rights (TAPCPR)[9] in 2012 advocated publicly three proposals for same sex couples and families, coined under the umbrella concept of 'multiple ways to form families' (多元成家): marriage, partnership and multiple-person family. However, only the marriage equality (same sex marriage) proposal gained enough political support and was made a motion to the Legislative Yuan by DPP Congresswoman Zhe in 2013. On the other hand, the three proposals were not correctly understood by the general public and mainstream media, the 'multiple ways to form families' was thus misunderstood and misused by the opposing religious groups to be symbols for promiscuity of homosexuals.[10]

---

[9]The first year of the civil partnership project was within the Awakening foundation, which was also one of the leading feminist foundations in the Marriage Equality Alliance in 2016. Later Civil partnership project started to run as a single-issue NGO in their second year.

[10]The opposing same-sex marriage groups often use 'multiple ways to form families' to lead general public to believe that the controversial proposals are in discussion in the legislative Yuan, the truth is only marriage equality proposal is on the table at this moment. Please also see the Q and A from Marriage Equality Alliance <http://equallove.tw/questions/8>.

8 Full Range Legal Activism: Administrative, Legislative and Judicial

In November 2016, the death of an openly gay university professor Bi, of French origin, triggered legislative action again. When DPP congresswoman Yu brought the civil code amendment to allow same sex marriage to the Legislative Yuan, a marriage equality alliance was quickly formed by Taiwan Tongzhi Hotline Association, Taiwan LGBT family rights advocacy, Awakening foundation and other two queer organizations.[11] There was before this only one marriage equality single issue advocate group. Taiwan Tongzhi Hotline Association, the biggest LGBTIQ organization in terms of budget and personnel, mainly does community service for LGBT individuals. Awakening foundation is a feminist NGO founded in 1982 and focuses on women's rights issues and gender and law/policy in general. Its expertise in law reform is certainly unique in the alliance. To say marriage equality is on the top of the LGBT movement agenda in Taiwan is an overstatement. Marriage equality pursuit is more a collective reaction to the structural disadvantages of LGBTIQ individuals and the same sex couples and families.

Not only was a Civil Code amendment bill to allow same-sex marriage awaiting in the Legislative Yuan for cross-party consultations as backed by the professional opinions of Judicial Yuan, but the Council of Grand Justices in Taiwan also heard a constitutional challenge applied by the Taipei City government and a gay rights activist (represented by TAPCPR lawyers) concerning same-sex marriage in a publicly broadcasted session on 24 March 2017. Finally, on May 24, Judicial Yuan declared that not allowing same-sex marriage is unconstitutional, and that it was within the legislative competence to decide in what form to effect the decision, either amending civil code or enact/introduce a new law within a 2-year period.[12] The question remained: when? how equal?[13]

9 Backlash by the Religious: Referendum

Following the 2017 Grand Justices ruling, progress on implementing a law was slow due to strong opposition from conservative and religious groups and government inaction. In February 2018, the Alliance for Next Generation's Happiness, opposed

[11]This alliance later registered on May 1, 2020 as Taiwan Equality Campaign. <https://equallove.tw/about> (last visited on June 20, 2020).

[12]The Council of Grand Justices in Taiwan rarely heard constitutional challenge in publicly broadcasted session and it is the first time in the Taiwanese legal history that it issued an English abstract of the decision on May 24th, 2017.

[13]Author's essay on what this Judicial interpretation means to the future legislative actions, please read "Not only same sex marriage" (不只是同婚) in 107 Forum in Women's and Gender Studies, 2017.10.

to same-sex marriage, proposed holding a referendum on the issue of same-sex marriage and LGBT inclusive education, which requires collecting about 280,000 signatures (1.5% of eligible voters) for the initiative to be presented to the voters. On the other hand, a group in favour of same-sex marriage and LGBT inclusive education at school level rallied to submit its own questions as to the same issues in the same referendum. At the end, through mobilization from both sides, though unequally, Taiwanese society has experienced the most troubled time regarding LGBT issues related information, many ungrounded rumors, misinformation against sexual minorities, both in printed media and social medias.

On 24 November 2018, Taiwanese voters approved the three initiatives launched by the Alliance for Next Generation's Happiness in the referendum and rejected the two pro-LGBT initiatives.[14] Two of the initiatives are to prevent recognition of same-sex marriages in the Civil Code and opting for a separate law to protect same-sex unions. The Government confirmed that the Grand Justices ruling would be implemented and that the referendums could not support unconstitutional law. Taiwan's administrative Yuan proposed a draft on 21 February 2019 titled "The Enforcement Act of Judicial Yuan Interpretation No. 748" for same-sex marriage. Religious groups counter proposed with "The Enforcement Act of Referendum No. 12," draft that defines same-sex unions as non-marital relationships. As the world knows by now, finally the even more compromised version of "The Enforcement Act of Judicial Yuan Interpretation No. 748" passed and won Taiwan the reputation of Asia's first nation to legalize same sex marriage. The reality is this version of the law was far from being as comprehensive as the 2016 civil code amendment brought by DPP Congresswoman Yu.

These advancements or backlash against same sex marriage came before the legal advancements regarding trans persons' civil status. Not enough attention was given to the proposal by the Ministry of Health and Welfare in 2013 to remove surgery as a legal requirement for change of sex legally, and due to governmental inaction no progress has been made to-date.

10 The Regulation of Civil Status and Sex: Female or Male

Sex is a category within civil status, along with parenthood, marital status, residency address, etc., all of which are shown in the personal ID. Taiwanese have a very complicated national ID card in comparison to many Euro-American countries. At

[14]In the referendum, three initiatives proposals read: "Do you agree with using means other than the marriage regulations in the Civil Code to protect the rights of two people of the same gender to build a permanent life together?"

"Do you agree that the marriage regulations in the Civil Code should define marriage as between a man and a woman?"

"Do you agree that during the elementary and junior high school stage, the Ministry of Education and schools at all levels should not implement same-sex education as stipulated in the Gender Equity Education Act's implementation rules?"

the time of this writing, a newly-designed digitalized national identification card has been discussed, possibly birth sex will not be shown in the future. Sex is assigned by a doctor at birth based on genitals, then the parents of the newborn present the medical document and register the birth of the child to the local district Household Registration office (HRO) in each county. It can be changed later also in the same office, as managed under the Civil Status Division in the Ministry of Interior.

One can present the following documents and change the civil status in the local district HRO. According to the executive directive letter (NeiShouZhongHu NO. 0970066240) issued by the Ministry of Interior in 2008, in the case of a male to female trans, one needs two evaluation reports by psychiatrists, and the medical examination report of the completion of removal of the penis and testicles issued by any qualified hospital. In the case of female to male trans, one needs two evaluation reports by psychiatrists, and the medical report of the completion of removal of the female organs, including breasts, uterus, ovaries.[15] During the period between 1998 and December 2016, 666 people changed their sex status in Taiwan according to the statistics by the Ministry of Interior.

There is no particular law and legal regulation concerning issues for trans persons. The only regulation clearly written is the executive (directive) letter issued by the Ministry of Interior to direct its subordinate governmental agencies regarding the civil status change. Scholars have argued its lack of legality and possibly violation of the constitutional right of trans persons. However, it is the current existing administrative practice.

There is no gender-neutral and/or "third-sex" possibility in Taiwan. Sex is considered as an important characteristic of personal being, and there are only two options, namely male and female. Transgender as an additional possibility, and for time being, the best option would be a separate category. For example, according to "Regulations Governing the Detention of the Aliens" enacted on 12.01.2015, article 3 paragraph 2: male detainees shall be separated from female detainees in detention centers. If a detainee is found to be a trans person, he/she will be detained separately in a solitary room in detention center (according to the gender showing on his/her identification certificate). There are cases in the university dormitory trans students were put in an individual room after a long discussion with students involved.

Taiwan Adolescent Association on Sexualities advocated to add "大" ('big' literally translated) or "跨" (trans) option besides male and female binary options in the civil status registration. The scholarly research on the subject commissioned by the Ministry of Interior in 2013 suggests that in the short term, the government should drop the sex shown in the ID all together, and keep the record in the household registration only. In the long term, the team suggests adding "social gender" next to the existing "biological sex" category in the household registration record. The research report also proposed that for intersex people, parents can choose

[15]On 2008, 11/3 "NeiShouZhongHu NO. 0970066240" was issued by the Ministry of Interior. It is a directive order from the superior governmental agency to answer certain specific questions raised by the subordinate agency.

not to register at all, and wait until the intersex baby becomes adult to decide or until surgery is completed.[16]

11 Prohibition of Discrimination Because of Gender Identity or Sexual Orientation

There are legal rules that prohibit discrimination based on gender identity or sexual orientation in education, employment, labor law, housing act. . .etc. The first was the Gender Equity Education Act enacted in 2004, "the school shall provide a gender-fair learning environment, respect and give due consideration to students, faculty, and staff with different gender, gender temperaments, gender identity, and sexual orientation."[17]

The Act of Gender Equality in Employment as amended in 2008 states that employers shall not discriminate against applicants or employees because of their gender or sexual orientation in the course of recruitment, screening test, hiring, placement, assignment, evaluation and promotion; in the case of holding or providing education, training or other related activities; in the case of holding or providing various welfare measures; in the case of paying wages; in the case of retirement, discharge, severance and termination.[18]

12 The Legal Regulation of Names

Names are easily changed in Taiwan, and the governing laws are the Household Registration Law and Name Act.[19] Many Taiwanese change their names because fortune tellers advise such in order to change their fate or bad luck (the law reads: the

[16] A Comparative Study of Gender Change System for Trans (各國跨性別登記制度), <http://www.ris.gov.tw/c/document_library/get_file?uuid=a8d8e8df-b7e3-4a35-a7c5-49d30e7634e2&groupId=10157> (visited on July 1, 2019)

[17] Schools shall be subjected to a fine not less than 10,000 New Taiwan Dollars (US$323) and not more than 100,000 (US$3225) New Taiwan Dollars in violation of the following: the school discriminates against students during recruitment or evaluation of applications for admission, in its instruction, activities, assessments, rewards and penalties, benefits, or services on the basis of his or her gender, gender temperaments, gender identity or sexual orientation. Article 12, Gender Equity Education Act <http://law.moj.gov.tw/Eng/LawClass/LawParaDeatil.aspx?Pcode=H0080067&LCNOS=%20%2012%20%20%20&LCC=2> (visited on Aug. 4, 2017).

[18] Article 7–11, Chapter II Prohibition of Gender Discrimination of Act of Gender Equality in Employment, <http://law.moj.gov.tw/Eng/LawClass/LawParaDeatil.aspx?Pcode=N0030014&LCNOS=%20%20%207%20%20%20&LCC=2oj.gov.tw/Eng/LawClass/LawParaDeatil.aspx?Pcode=N0030014&LCNOS=%20%20%207%20%20%20&LCC=2> (visited on 04.08.2017).

[19] Household Registration Act<https://law.moj.gov.tw/ENG/LawClass/LawAll.aspx?pcode=D0030006>, Name Act, <http://law.moj.gov.tw/Eng/LawClass/LawContent.aspx?PCODE=D0030011> (visited on 07.09.2017).

applicant's given name is unflattering or has an excessively long romanized form, or there are other special considerations). One simply needs to go to Household Registration Office and apply, which is also the case for trans persons. However, changes may be granted only three times, again also the case for trans person. No requisites are imposed to obtain changes.

13 Stricter Regulation Though No Requirement of Surgery?

In 2012 Advisors of Human Rights Advisory Committee in the presidential office proposed amending the trans gender change registration.[20] The Ministry of Health and Welfare called a meeting to discuss this subject in December 2013 and concluded that gender identity is a basic human right and shall be respected with no requirement to remove sexual organs. The review committee of the CEDAW second nation report has also concluded that the government is to follow this conclusion and put it into practice, to invalidate the executive order as to the removal of sexual organs as legal requirement for sex change.[21]

In 2014 the GEC proposed changing the executive practices of requiring gender modification surgery to change sex, and the Ministry of Health and Welfare actually agreed to forgo the medical requirement and promised to further work with the Ministry of Interior on details. On 24 December 2014, Legislative Yuan Congressman Ding along with other 20 parliamentarians proposed abolishing the current executive directive letter on gender change, and asked the Ministries of Interior and of Health and Welfare to work out an alternative procedure. They reached again the conclusion to abolish the surgical requirement with some conditions: (1) there will be a sex change review committee to be in charge of applications; (2) sex change can be done after one is over 18 year old, once in a life time; (3) 6 months reflection waiting period after the review of the case application, and held a press conference to announce this general direction with a one month deadline for a result. On 16 January 2015, the internal meeting within two ministries was held and reached the same basic conclusion: discussion to be continued.[22]

The latest news is that the Ministry of Interior will propose a draft to replace the executive direction, there shall be three stages in proceedings of sex/gender changes: (1) Application of sex change with two evaluation reports by psychiatrists,

---

[20]Please see the meeting record on 06.13.2012 <http://www.president.gov.tw/Page/321/8/總統府人權諮詢委員會第八次委員會議>.

[21]The Review of Taiwan's Second National Report on the Implementation of CEDAW, Conclusion and Comments of the review committee, 26 June 2014 <http://www.gec.ey.gov.tw/News_Content.aspx?n=D9EB035103686D4C&sms=B1994CB005CB173C&s=2F3CD146B97C0A37>.

[22]In a document issued on 02.03.2015 from Executive Yuan to Legislative Yuan regarding the gender change issue, please see <lci.ly.gov.tw/LyLCEW/agenda1/.../LCEWA01_080702_00292.doc> (visited on Aug. 15, 2017).

(2) Committee review of the application, organized by experts from Ministries of Justice, Interior, and Health and Welfare (3) 6 month waiting period before one goes to register in Household Registration Office. The proposal contains "no children", "not in a marriage", "once in a life time" requirements. Several Trans NGOs immediately had a press conference and condemned the even stricter requirements as a step backward from the current situation.[23] In 2017 CEDAW third National Report from the government reads: this subject is under discussion. Very disappointedly, the discussion goes on and lives of trans persons remain the same. Control Yuan has issued a letter of warning to the Ministry of Health and Welfare for its continuing neglect of intersex persons and at the time of this writing, there is no further information from that Ministry.

14 Trans Activists and NGOs

The actors involved in the debate include LGBT organizations, trans organizations, certain members of political parties, scholars, respective gender equality committee board members, etc. The Intersex, Transgender and Transsexual People Care Association (性別不明關懷協會) has been vocal in the issue of removing surgery as a legal requirement for change of gender registration.[24] Taiwan Trans Butterfly Garden (蝶園), the first trans NGO in Taiwan, has been more cautious about the conditions of the above proposal. Does this entail more governmental regulation despite no surgery requirement as one proposal by the Ministry of Interior reads, will there be a committee formed by all areas of experts to oversee the change of sex registration matter? Transgender Punk Activist (跨性別倡議站)[25] echos that stated by Trans Butterfly Garden along with Tozhi Hotline Association (台灣同志諮詢熱線), Sexuality Rights Association (性別人權協會), the center for the study of Sexualities in Central University[26] etc., in carefully dealing with governmental intervention in the matter of change Trans' civil status matters and advocate more publicly-informed decision-making procedures.[27] The conservative religious groups are against it and there are different debates within the trans community as well.

[23] Sex Change Registration Stricter in the future? , Hao Chung Wang <http://www.coolloud.org.tw/node/81399> (visited on Aug. 15, 2017).

[24] Intersex, Transgender and Transsexual People Care Association <http://www.istscare.org/gender-recognition-opendoc/>.

[25] Transgender Punk Activist Taiwan <https://transgenderpunk.wordpress.com/>.

[26] Center for the study of sexualities in Central University <http://sex.ncu.edu.tw/>.

[27] The Joint Announcement of Trans Groups on 2014.12 <http://www.coolloud.org.tw/node/81233>.

15 The Right to Self-Determination

In the process of becoming oneself and building intimate relationship on one's own terms, trans couples exercised the right to gender self-determination and called upon the Taiwan state for recognition. On the way to be noticed and recognized as a long self-ruled independent island country, Taiwan strives to meet the international human rights standards. It is 'the right to self-determination' which links the trans and their state to take actions.

The Wu-wu trans marriage is legally sustained and recognized by the Taiwanese government. They followed every bit of the administrative orders and procedure to finally be registered as married and change their respective birth sex to fit with their own gender identity. In the mind of general public and some civil servants, their actions were considered to be manipulative and finally 'get away with law'. However, I find it exactly the opposite. Wu and Wu knew the current administrative procedures very well after years of dealing with civil servants and the bureaucracies at school, at work and the local household registration office. They did every step correctly according to the regulations at the time and actually put themselves subordinate to the state. Although Juyi Wu is clear about her gender identity and underwent gender reassignment surgery, she went to the household restoration office with her birth sex, male, with her partner to register marriage. She intentionally put herself under the rule of the state. One can argue that instead of showing her genderqueer identity, she recognized the rule of binary sex category existing at the time in the civil code and registered as husband to her spouse. It is the State that did not fully comprehend the potential changing nature of human bodies and identities, it is the State that deliberately ignored the existence of various genders.

Sadly, the complex status of Taiwan as a nation resonates with the current plight of trans persons. Taiwan is often listed in the international law textbooks as a 'special' case, a unique status quo, with China (P.R.C.), recognized by the most powerful nations in the world, claiming Taiwan is a part of China but with the reality that Taiwan is a self-ruled island nation with its own jurisdiction and people. Gender incongruence is defined as "a marked and persistent incongruence between an individual's experienced gender and the assigned sex", whereas Taiwan's marked and persistent national identity incongruence continues to exist between how it identifies itself and how the international norm views Taiwan. Living within this self-rule island nation for decades, my analysis is inspired not only by the decades of efforts to decolonize the fields of queer and transgender studies, but also by how Taiwanese collectively experience isolation and arbitrary decisions of international community with very limited room for right to self-determination.

The sexual minority communities in Taiwan have requested in many cases their governing state to recognize their mere existence and demand protection. The binary legal system that constrains the life opportunities available to diverse gender- and sexual-minority communities must change immediately, and through responding to its people, the Taiwan state acted many times to reassure its state power, to gain legitimacy to rule the nation, and by signing up the international treaties on its own terms Taiwan state needs to take further action to realize its promise to become a full rule of law nation which protects its people without discrimination based on sexual orientation and gender identity.

Reference

Chen C-J (2010) Marriage as heterosexual patriarchy and privilege. J Womens and Gend Stud 27:113–199

Cheng Y-h A, Wu F-CF, Adamczyk A (2016) Changing attitudes toward homosexuality in Taiwan, 1995–2012. Chinese Sociol Rev 48(4):317–345. https://doi.org/10.1080/21620555.2016.1199257

Tang DT-S, Khor D, Chen Y-C (2019) Legal recognition of same-sex partnerships: a comparative study of Hong Kong, Taiwan and Japan. Sociol Rev. https://doi.org/10.1177/0038026119858222

Civil Status and Trans Persons in Turkey

Yalçın Tosun and Candan Yasan Tepetaş

Abstract This chapter examines the legal status of trans persons within the framework of Turkish law. It explains that even if homosexuality is no longer a crime, homophobia and transphobia are widespread in the country. The law ignores the existence of LGBTI+ individuals and a vast majority of government officials and media view homosexuality as a biological disorder and an illness which should be treated. At the same time, trans persons are in a vulnerable and marginalised position. The lack of domestic legal protection for trans persons results in the limitation of their fundamental rights as citizens.

The 2018 Turkey Progress Report issued by the European Commission[1] noted that "there are serious concerns on the protection of the fundamental rights of lesbian, gay, bisexual, transgender and intersex people".[2] Notably, LGBTI+ persons face various forms of discrimination in many different areas.[3] Even though

[1]As a candidate country for accession to the European Union (EU), Turkey is harmonizing its legislation with the EU.

[2]European Comission, *Turkey 2018 Progress Report*, COM (2018) 450 final, p. 39, (*Turkey 2018 Progress Report*), available at https://ec.europa.eu/neighbourhood-enlargement/sites/near/files/20180417-turkey-report.pdf (20.05.2019).

[3]LGBTI Equal Rights Association for Western Balkans and Turkey, available at http://www.lgbti-era.org/content/turkey (30.08.2017); also see, ILGA-Europe Rainbow Map 2019 Annual Review (*Rainbow Map 2019*) in which Turkey ranked the second most restrictive country on LGBTI+ rights among 49 countries in Europe, available at https://www.ilga-europe.org/resources/news/latest-news/10th-rainbow europe-confirmed-stagnation-and-regression-lgbti-equality (20.05.2019).

Y. Tosun (✉)
Istanbul Bilgi University, Faculty of Law, Civil Law Department, İstanbul, Turkey
e-mail: yalcin.tosun@bilgi.edu.tr

C. Y. Tepetaş
Istanbul Bilgi University, Faculty of Law, Private International Law Department, İstanbul, Turkey
e-mail: candan.yasan@bilgi.edu.tr

I. C. Jaramillo, L. Carlson (eds.), *Trans Rights and Wrongs*, Ius Comparatum - Global Studies in Comparative Law 54,
https://doi.org/10.1007/978-3-030-68494-5_9

homosexuality is not criminalized, the social tolerance for LGBTI+ persons is very low, and regrettably, homophobia and transphobia are widespread in the country.[4] The law ignores the existence of LGBTI+ individuals and a vast majority of government officials and media view homosexuality as a biological disorder and an illness which should be treated.[5] At the same time, trans persons are in a vulnerable and marginalised position. The lack of domestic legal protection for trans persons results in the limitation of their fundamental rights as a citizen.

This chapter examines the legal status of trans persons within the framework of Turkish law. In this vein, it begins with the legal regulation of civil status.

1 The Legal Regulation of Civil Status

Civil status refers to issues related to the law of persons and family law, including name, nationality, age, sex,[6] marital status, kinship and other life events such as birth and death.[7] Accordingly, sex is considered as a category of civil status in the Turkish legal system. The Turkish Civil Code (TCC) is the principal legal source dealing with the regulation of civil status. The provisions on civil status are of a mandatory nature since they deem to pertain to public policy.[8] In addition to the TCC, the Civil

[4]In a 2013 study of Pew Research Center, only 4% of respondents in Turkey rated homosexuality as morally acceptable, 12% as not a moral issue, and 78% as morally unacceptable, see http://www.pewglobal.org/2013/06/04/the-global-divide-on-homosexuality/ (26.08.2017). In an another study, 84% of the respondents in Turkey did not want to live with LGBTI neighbours, see V. Yılmaz, S. Bırdal, "*LGBT Rights in Turkey: The Long Road to Tolerance*", available at http://www.e-ir.info/2012/12/14/lgbt-rights-in-turkey-the-long-road-to-tolerance/ (26.08.2017). A survey conducted in 2012 by KONDA, a research company in Turkey, introduced that only 11.2 % of the respondents answered that homosexuality should not be considered as a crime, see http://konda.com.tr/wp-content/uploads/2017/03/KONDA_1205_TOPLUMDAKI_AYIP_GUNAH_VE_SUC_ALGISI.pdf (26.08.2017). Another survey conducted by the same research company in 2018 established that 23,6% of the respondents do not tolerate LGBTI+ persons in their neighbourhood, see http://www.hurriyet.com.tr/kelebek/hurriyet-pazar/toplumsal-ruh-halimiz-guvensiz-tepkili-icedonuk-41225188 (26.05.2019).

[5]For instance the statement of Aliye Kavaf, Turkish Minister of State responsible for Women and Family Affairs, see Amnesty International, 'Not an Illness nor a Crime': Lesbian, Gay, Bisexual and Transgender People Demand Equality, 2011, London, p. 5, available at https://www.amnesty.org/en/documents/EUR44/001/2011/en/ (25.08.2017). Also a Turkish newspaper entitled "Akit" called a LGBTI+ NGO as a perverted organisation, see *Rainbow Map 2019, Turkey,* available at https://www.ilga-europe.org/sites/default/files/turkey.pdf (20.05.2019).

[6]The Turkish language does not distinguish between the terms of sex and gender. Instead, "biological sex-*biyolojik cinsiyet*" and "social aspects of sex-*toplumsal cinsiyet*" are the terms used to refer to sex and gender.

[7]K. Oğuzman, O. Seliçi, S. Oktay-Özdemir, *Kişiler Hukuku (Gerçek ve Tüzel Kişiler)*, Istanbul 2015, p. 105; C. Şanlı, E. Esen, İ. Ataman-Figanmeşe, *Milletlerarası Özel Hukuk*, Istanbul, 2016, pp. 383-384; Serozan, p. 480.

[8]Oğuzman, Seliçi, Oktay-Özdemir, p. 106.

Registration Services Act (CRS)[9] and the Regulation on the Application of the Civil Registration Services Act[10] set forth the issues related to the registry of civil status.

Civil status is determined in accordance with the official register kept by the state.[11] The General Directorate of Civil Registration and Nationality, which is affiliated to the Ministry of Inferior, is in charge of maintaining the civil status register. Extracts of the records may be issued by the civil registration directory of each district.[12]

The records of civil status register constitute complete proof of the facts evidenced by them, unless their content is shown to be incorrect.[13] The state is liable for losses which occur in the exercise of the registration of civil status.[14] The liability of the state is considered strict liability, i.e. regardless of fault, intention or negligence.[15]

When a child is born, the sex/gender to be registered, which can only be female or male, is solely determined by biological sex characteristics of the newborn. An identity number is also attributed to the new born.[16] There is no gender-neutral and/or "third-sex" possibility under Turkish law. Also, there is no legal regulation on intersex persons. Intersex persons are marked as male or female in the birth certificate. Accordingly, intersex persons may undergo surgical interventions before the age of eighteen.[17] These interventions can be performed by the consent of their family. On the other hand, intersex persons are also allowed to consciously choose their gender and go through an operation.[18] Since this is still an untreated area, no further information can be reported here.

Under Turkish law, any record in the civil status register can be changed only by a court judgment.[19] The competent court is the court at the place of residence of the

---

[9]Law numbered 5490. It is published in the Official Gazette numbered 26153 and dated 29.04.2006 and entered into force on 29 April 2006.

Currently, a Draft Law on the amendment of some provisions of the CRS has been submitted to the Plenary of the Grand National Assembly of Turkey on 25.07.2016. The text of the Draft Law is available in Turkish at http://t24.com.tr/files/20170725161348_nufus-hizmetleri-ile-bazi-kanunlarda-degisiklik-yapilmasina-dair-kanun-tasarisi.pdf (25.07.2017).

[10]It is published in the Official Gazette numbered 26355 and dated 23.11.2006.

[11]Arts. 36-37 TCC.

[12]Under Art. 37/2 TCC, Turkish consulates in foreign states could be entitled to act as a civil status officer.

[13]Art. 7 TCC. This principle is also emphasized in Art. 43 CRS.

[14]Art. 38 TCC.

[15]Oğuzman, Seliçi, Oktay-Özdemir, p. 151.

[16]Art. 7 CRS.

[17]Kurtoğlu, p. 84.

[18]LGBTI Equal Rights Association for Western Balkans and Turkey, available at http://www.lgbti-era.org/content/turkey (30.08.2017).

[19]Art. 39 TCC, Art. 35 CRS.

In detail, see T. Ansay, "Law of Persons", in *Introduction to Turkish Law*, Eds. T. Ansay, D. Wallace JR, 6th edition, Ankara 2011, p. 92; Oğuzman, Seliçi, Oktay-Özdemir, pp. 147–150; Serozan, p. 489.

2 The Lack of Legal Protection for LGBTI+ Persons Under Turkish Law

The Turkish Constitution does not expressly mention gender identity and/or sexual orientation as grounds for non-discrimination. Even though Art. 10 of the Constitution[34] regulates the equality principle and contains an open-ended list of groups which should be treated equally before law, this list does not contain any reference to either sexual orientation or gender identity.[35] The Constitutional Court held in its judgments of individual applications that even if it is not explicitly stipulated in the Constitution, discrimination based on sexual orientation is also prohibited.[36] More importantly, in 2014 the Constitutional Court ruled for the first time that referring to LGBTI individuals as "perverts" constitutes hate speech.[37] The European Comission against Racism and Intolerance (ECRI) recommends to the Turkish authorities to

[34] Art. 10 of the Constitution reads as follows: "Everyone is equal before the law without distinction as to language, race, colour, sex, political opinion, philosophical belief, religion and sect, or any such grounds. Men and women have equal rights. The State has the obligation to ensure that this equality exists in practice. Measures taken for this purpose shall not be interpreted as contrary to the principle of equality. Measures to be taken for children, the elderly, disabled people, widows and orphans of martyrs as well as for the invalid and veterans shall not be considered as violation of the principle of equality. No privilege shall be granted to any individual, family, group or class. State organs and administrative authorities are obliged to act in compliance with the principle of equality before the law in all their proceedings." For the translation, see https://global.tbmm.gov.tr/docs/constitution_en.pdf (18.08.2017).

[35] LGBTI+ NGOs and human rights organizations sytematically demand that the Art. 10 of the Constitution be amended to include "sexual orientation" and "gender idendity". In detail, see Mcclaın and Waıte-Wrıght (2016), pp. 176–177; LGBTT Hakları Platformu, *Yogyakarta İlkeleri Işığında 1892 Anayasası Raporu Analizi*, Istanbul 2010, pp. 11–12; SPOD Anayasa Çalışma Grubu, *LGBT Yurttaşların Yeni Anayasaya Yönelik Talepleri*, Istanbul 2012, pp.12, 21 ff.; Contribution from Turkey (KAOS GL & SPOD & Pembe Hayat & Ilga-Europe & ERA) to ILGA Europe's submissions to Progress Reports of the European Comission, 18 May 2016, available at https://www.ilga-europe.org/sites/default/files/enlargement_review_turkey_2016.pdf (10.08.2017).

However, even in the Constitution reform of 2014, the majority of the Parliament did not accept the proposal regarding the inclusion of "sexual orientation" and "gender idendity" to the Constitution, see ECRI, *Report on Turkey*, Fifth Monitoring Cycle, 4 October 2016, (ECRI, *Report on Turkey*), p. 35, para. 98, available at http://www.coe.int/t/dghl/monitoring/ecri/country-by-country/turkey/TUR-CbC-V-2016-037-ENG.pdf (25.08.2017).

[36] The decision of the Turkish Court of Constitution, *Sadıka Şeker*, application no: 2013/1948, dated 23.01.2014; the decision of the Turkish Court of Constitution, *Kamil Çakır*, application no: 2013/997, dated 15.10.2014, the decision of the Turkish Court of Constitution, *Metin Çetinkaya ve Maide Çetinkaya*, application no: 2013/1280, dated 28.05.2014.

[37] The decision of the Turkish Court of Constitution, *Sinem Hun*, application no: 2013/5356, dated 08.05.2014. The decision is available in English at http://www.constitutionalcourt.gov.tr/inlinepages/leadingjudgements/IndividualApplication/judgment/2013-5356.pdf (10.08.2017).

ratify the Protocole No. 12[38] to the European Convention on Human Rights (ECHR).[39] Yet, the state has not taken any action so far to do so.

In 2015, the United Nations Universal Periodic Review on Turkey noted that "domestic legal provisions do not explicitly discriminate on the basis of sexual orientation and/or gender identity. However, there are numerous examples of discriminatory applications of the laws being against LGBT persons".[40] The fact that Turkey does not have any domestic regulation which expressly prohibits discrimination on the grounds of sexual orientation and/or gender identity contributes the emergence of human rights violations of LGBTI+ individuals.[41] The recent legislative changes, including the Law to Protect Family and Prevent Violence Against Women[42] and the

[38]As Turkey is a codified civil law country, statute law (*lex scripta*) is the primary source of law. Equally, the Constitution, international conventions which are of equal status to law if they have been duly put into effect, codes, statutory decrees, regulations and by-laws are the applicable legislation. In accordance with Art. 90(5) of the Constitution, if there is a conflict between the laws and international conventions on fundamental rights and freedoms, the provisions of international conventions shall prevail. Within the context of this chapter, it is worth to outline that Turkey, being a member of Council of Europe, has been a party to the European Convention on Human Rights (ECHR) since 1954, ratified most of its Protocols but except the Protocole No. 12 to the ECHR and recognized the compulsory jurisdiction of the Court in 1990. Turkey ratified also the International Covenant on Civil and Political Rights (ICCPR) and the Convention on the Elimination of All Forms of Discrimination against Women (CEDAW). The ECHR is Turkish Law numbered 6366. It is published in the Official Gazette dated 19.03.1954.

[39]ECRI, *Report on Turkey*, p. 13, para. 2.

[40]International Gay and Lesbian Human Rights Commission - Submission to the United Nations Universal Periodic Review on Turkey, Human Rights Violations of LGBT Individuals in Turkey, January/February 2015, pp. 2, ("United Nations Universal Periodic Review on Turkey"), available at http://www.iglhrc.org/sites/default/files/uprSubTurkey.pdf (15.07.2017).

[41]In detail, see Y. ÖZ, *Study on Homophobia, Transphobia and Discrimination on Grounds of Sexual Orientation and Gender Identity, Legal Report: Turkey*, p. 7 ff., available at http://www.coe.int/t/commissioner/source/lgbt/turkeylegal_e.pdf (20.07.2017); N. Karadağ, *Cinsel Azınlıkların Bireysel Hakları*, Istanbul 2008, pp. 120–122; KAOS GL, LGBTI News Turkey, IGLHRC, *Human Rights Violations of LGBT Individuals in Turkey, Republic of Turkey - Submission to the United Nations Universal Periodic Review*, November 2014, available at http://ilga.org/wp-content/uploads/2016/02/Shadow-report-16.pdf (20.08.2017); European Comission, *Turkey 2016 Progress Report*, COM (2016) 715 final, p. 76, available at https://ec.europa.eu/neighbourhood-enlargement/sites/near/files/pdf/key_documents/2016/20161109_report_turkey.pdf (25.08.2017); ILGA-Europe, Annual Review of the Human Rights Situations of Lesbian, Gay, Bisexual, Trans and Intersex People in Europe 2017, pp. 230-236, available at https://www.ilga-europe.org/sites/default/files/Attachments/annual_review_2017_online.pdf (08.07.2017); KAOS GL, *2015 Cinsel Yönelim ve Cinsiyet Kimliği Temelli İnsan Hakları İzleme Raporu*, available at http://www.kaosgldernegi.org/resim/yayin/dl/lgbt__insan_haklar__raporu_kaosgl_2015_1.pdf (20.08.2017); M. Göregenli, *2016 Yılında Türkiye'de Gerçekleşen Homofobi ve Transfobi Temelli Nefret Suçları Raporu*, Ed. M. Köylü, Kaos GL Publication, 2017, p. 13 ff, available at http://www.kaosgldernegi.org/resim/yayin/dl/nefret_suclari_raporu_2016.pdf (20.08.2017); Mcclain and Waite-Wright (2016), p. 160 ff.; ECRI, *Report on Turkey*, p. 24, paras. 51–52.

[42]Law numbered 6284. It is published in the Official Gazette numbered 28239 dated 20.03.2012.

2014's amendments[43] to the Criminal Code[44] do not contain any reference to sexual orientation or gender identity.[45] The hate crime law introducing protection on the grounds of gender identity and sexual orientation has never been enacted.[46] The Law on Human Rights and Equality Institution of Turkey[47] providing for the establishment of a human rights committee was adopted. But, the references to sexual orientation and gender idendity on the initial draft law were not incorporated at all to the adopted law.[48]

It would thus seem that the law ignores the existence of LGBTI+ persons,[49] This denial which is accompanied by a low social tolerance[50] leads to the various forms of discrimination in many different areas.[51] Furthermore, the state of emergency declared after the coup attempt of 15 July 2016 leads the restriction of fundamental

[43]These amendments implemented by the Law numbered 6545. It is published in the Official Gazette numbered 29044 and dated 28.06.2014.

[44]Law numbered 5237. It is published in the Official Gazette numbered 25611 and dated 12.10.2004. An unofficial English translation of the Law is available at http://www.wipo.int/edocs/lexdocs/laws/en/tr/tr171en.pdf (15.08.2017).

Regarding this issue, also see ECRI, *Report on Turkey*, pp. 14–15, para. 11; Göregenli, pp. 21–22.

[45]LGBTI+ NGOs and human rights organizations demand also anti-discrimination and hate crime legislation recognising gender identity and sexual orientation as grounds for special protection and also the revision of the existing laws on violence against women. See, K. Ördek, "The Social Experiences of Trans People in Turkey", in *Transrespect versus Transphobia*, Eds: C. Balzer, C. Lagata, J. S. Hutta, 2015, (ÖRDEK, 2015), p. 72, available at http://transrespect.org/wp-content/uploads/2015/08/TvT-PS-Vol9-2015.pdf (25.08.2017); GÖREGENLİ, pp. 8–9.

[46]Art. 122 of the Criminal Code regulates the discrimination and hate crime. However, this provision is deprived of being effective and applicable since it was regulated poorly. See, ECRI, *Report on Turkey*, Fifth Monitoring Cycle, 4 October 2016, pp. 13, para. 4; p. 14, para. 8, available at http://www.coe.int/t/dghl/monitoring/ecri/country-by-country/turkey/TUR-CbC-V-2016-037-ENG.pdf; Aytekın Inceoğlu (2015), p. 56 ff.; U. Karan, *Uluslararası İnsan Hakları Hukuku ve Anayasa Hukuku Işığında Eşitlik İlkesi ve Ayrımcılık Yasağı*, Istabul 2017, pp. 189–192; Göregenli, pp. 7–8, 22.

[47]Law numbered 6701. It is published in the Official Gazette numbered 29690 and dated 20.04.2016.

[48]See, ILGA-Europe, Annual Review 2017, p. 230; ECRI, *Report on Turkey*, p. 15, para. 14 and p. 18, para. 27; European Comission, *Turkey 2013 Progress Report*, COM (2013) 700 final, pp. 58–59, available at https://ec.europa.eu/neighbourhood-enlargement/sites/near/files/pdf/key_documents/2013/package/tr_rapport_2013.pdf (25.08.2017); SPOD, *2012 Cinsel Yönelim ve Cinsiyet Kimliği Temelli İnsan hakları İhlalleri İzleme Raporu*, 2013, pp. 43-44, available at http://www.spod.org.tr/docs/hak_ihlal-son-1.pdf (25.08.2017).

Regarding the demands for the inclusion of gender identity and sexual orientation to the relevant law, the Minister of Justice stated that they would not prefer to make such inclusion according to their political attitude, see Göregenli, p. 8.

[49]Amnesty International, 'Not an Illness nor a Crime': Lesbian, Gay, Bisexual and Transgender People Demand Equality, 2011, London, available at https://www.amnesty.org/en/documents/EUR44/001/2011/en/ (25.08.2017); ÖZ, p. 6; Göregenli, p. 24.

[50]ECRI, *Report on Turkey*, pp. 34–35, para. 97; ILGA-Europe Annual Review, p. 236.

[51]For a recent study, see Yılmaz and Göçmen (2016), p. 470 ff.

rights in the name of anti-terror measures and security.[52] For instance, the Governorship of Ankara issued an order to ban all the LGBTI+ events for an indefinite period of time for the reasons of public security, protection of public health and morality and protection of other's rights and liberty.[53] Following these developments, LGBTI activists filed a law suit against the Governorship's order.[54] However, pride marches and other pride events in different cities of Turkey including Istanbul have been banned by public authorities.[55]

Notably, the lack of special legal protection triggers the violations of fundamental rights and freedoms of trans individuals in Turkey as well as the discriminatory treatments, hate crimes, attacks, murders and police brutality against them.[56] Trans persons are in a vulnerable and marginalised position in Turkey.[57] According to a 2016 data, Turkey has the highest number of trans murders in Europe.[58] Nevertheless, Art. 29 of the Criminal Code on the "unjust provocation" by the victim continues to be exercised for the penalty reduction.[59] As investigations are not held properly and the penalties are not deterrent, the number of trans murders is dramatically increasing. A report of 2009 prepared by LGBTI Right's Platform to be submitted to the CEDAW clearly underlined that the right to life of trans persons is at stake.[60] The brutal murder of *Hande Kader*, 23 years-old trans woman and a

[52]ILGA-Europe Annual Review 2017, pp. 233-234; *Turkey 2016 Progress Report*, p. 76.

[53]*Turkey 2018 Progress Report*, p. 37; http://www.kaosgl.org/page.php?id=24993 (1.7.2019).

[54]http://www.kaosgl.org/page.php?id=25016 (1.7.2019).

[55]*Rainbow Map 2019, Turkey,* available at https://www.ilga-europe.org/sites/default/files/turkey.pdf (20.05.2019).

[56]ILGA-Europe Annual Review 2017, pp. 232–236; *Turkey 2016 Progress Report*, p. 76; ECRI, *Report on Turkey*, p. 24, para. 51; ILGA Europe's Review of the Human Rights Situation of LGBTI People in Turkey, Contribution to the 2015 EC Progress Report, available at https://www.ilga-europe.org/sites/default/files/ilga-europes_submission_to_ec_2015_progress_report-turkey.pdf (20.07.2017); SPOD, *LGBTİ'lerin Hukuk ve Adalete Erişimi*, Haziran 2016, pp. 118–135, available at http://www.spod.org.tr/docs/SPoD-lgbtilerin-hukuk-ve-adalete-erisimi-2015.pdf (20.08.2017); KAOS GL, *2015 Cinsel Yönelim ve Cinsiyet Kimliği Temelli İnsan Hakları İzleme Raporu*, p. 4 ff., available at http://www.kaosgldernegi.org/resim/yayin/dl/lgbt__nsan_haklar__raporu_kaosgl_2015_1.pdf (20.08.2017); TGEU, "Istanbul Trans Pride: TGEU Calls on Turkey to Protect Basic Human Rights", available at http://tgeu.org/istanbul-trans-pride-tgeu-calls-on-turkey-to-protect-the-rights-of-trans-people/ (20.08.2017); Engın (2015), pp. 849–853; ÖZ, pp. 44–48; Mcclaın and Waıte-Wrıght (2016), pp. 165–166; Göregenli, p. 13 ff.

[57]Ördek (2015), pp. 64–65.

[58]This data is taken from the Trans Murder Monitoring (TMM) Project, available at http://transrespect.org/en/idahot-2016-tmm-update/ (25.08.2017).

[59]European Parliament Resolution of 14 April 2016 on the 2015 report on Turkey, Text adopted: P8_TA (2016) 0133, para. 24, available at http://www.europarl.europa.eu/sides/getDoc.do?pubRef=-//EP//TEXT+TA+P8-TA-2016-0133+0+DOC+XML+V0//EN (20.08.2017). M. Doğan, "LGBTI Individuals Face Countless Problems in Turkey", available at https://lgbtinewsturkey.com/2015/05/15/on-idahot-lgbtis-face-countless-problems-in-turkey/ (26.08.2017); Engın, p. 843; Göregenli, p. 22.

[60]LGBTI Right's Platform, Shadow Report on Turkey Submitted to the 46th Session of tahe Committee on the Elimination of all forms of Discrimination Against Women, "Discrimination and Violence Against Women on Basis of Sexual Orientation and Gender Identity", August 2009, p. 5, available at https://www.outrightinternational.org/sites/default/files/CEDAW_TURKEY_Thematic_LBT_WOMEN.pdf (25.08.2017).

well-known LGBTI+ activist, regrettably underscores that the situation has not changed.[61]

While homosexuality and transgenderism are not criminalized in Turkey, the Criminal Code and the Law on Misdemeanours[62] continue to be a source of discriminatory and arbitrary practice against trans persons.[63] Also, the Law on Road Traffic[64] is often used for the arbitrary detention of trans women.[65] Moreover, the terms "general morality", "public decency", "public order", "obscenity", "immodesty" and "protection of the family", which are to be found in various provisions of Turkish law, are mostly interpreted by judicial and administrative bodies to restrict the rights and freedoms.[66] Last but not least, in 2015 the Court of Constitution affirmed that apart from 'sexual intercourse by the connection of a man and woman's genitals', all other sexual intercourse types are identified as unnatural.[67]

---

[61]Hande Kader was murdered brutally on 12 August 2016. For a news account, see https://lgbtinewsturkey.com/2016/08/20/the-hande-kader-murder-no-one-hears-our-voice/ (25.08.2017).

[62]Law numbered 5326. It is published in the Official Gazette numbered 25772 and dated 31.03.2005.

[63]V. Eşsız, Devletin Eli, Beli, Sopası: Anlatılmamış Sürgünden "Kabahatlere" Türkiye'de Trans Bedeninin Denetimi, *in Cinsellik Muamması, Türkiye'de Queer Kültür ve Muhalafet*, Istabul 2012, pp. 215–218; Contribution from Turkey (KAOS GL & SPOD & Pembe Hayat & Ilga-Europe & ERA) to ILGA Europe's submissions to Progress Reports of the European Commission, 18 May 2016, available at https://www.ilga-europe.org/sites/default/files/enlargement_review_turkey_2016.pdf (10.08.2017); *Turkey 2013 Progress Report*, p. 59; ÖZ, pp. 45–46; Göregenli, pp. 21–24.

[64]Law numbered 2918. It is published in the Official Gazette numbered 18195 and dated 18.10.1983.

[65]In the case of *Cemal Duğan*, the Turkish Court of Constitution held that the detention of the applicant on the basis of gender identity did not constitute discrimantory treatment nor violation of the right to respect for private life (The decision of the Turkish Court of Constitution, *Cemal Duğan*, application no: 2014/19308, dated 15.02.2017).

[66]EŞSIZ, pp. 217-219. For instance, see Art. 125 of the Law on Public Servants; Arts. 225 and 226 (4) of the Criminal Law; Arts. 33 and 41 of the Constitution.

Furthermore, the case of LambdaIstanbul LGBT Solidarity Association constitutes a solid example where the court of first instance had decided to close down the organization as it went against the morality of Turkish society (Beyoğlu 3rd Civil Court, numbered 190/236, dated 29.05.2008). Fortunately, the Turkish Court of Cassation overtuned this decision, see the Turkish Court of Cassation, 7th Civil Chamber, 25.11.2008, File No: 2008/4109, Decision No: 2008/5196 (Kazanci database). On this issue, see Hammarberg (2011), pp. 80, available at https://www.coe.int/t/Commissioner/Source/LGBT/LGBTStudy2011_en.pdf (20.08.2017).

Also, the European Court of Human Right (ECtHR) decided in the judgment *KAOS GL v. Turkey* case that the seizure of the copies of the magazíne KAOS GL on the grounds of its content which had been found contrary to the "*protection of public moral*" amounts to a violation of Art. 10 ECHR. See, ECtHR, *KAOS GL v. Turkey*, application no: 4982/07, dated 22.02.2017, (http://hudoc.echr.coe.int/eng?i=001-168765).

[67]The decision of the Turkish Court of Constitution, 01.04.2015, File No: 2014/118, Decision No: 2015/35, (http://www.resmigazete.gov.tr/eskiler/2015/04/20150418-10.pdf).

The employment rights of trans persons are also at stake.[68] The discriminatory practices in education and employment usually lead trans persons to the sex industry.[69] The provisions of the Law on Civil Servants[70] regarding dress code or acts incompatible with the dignity of the official post are often used as a ground of expulsion from their post.[71] In 2012, a police officer was dismissed because of his perceived gender identity.[72]

With regard to health services, trans persons' access to health services are very limited in practice. Even though there is no legal regulation prohibiting trans persons to access to health services, the misconduct of medical experts or the refusal of medical treatment may happen.[73] The lack of domestic legal protection for trans persons results in the limitation of their fundamental rights as a citizen.

Military service is mandatory for all male Turkish citizens. Longtime, homosexuality was considered as a mental disorder under Turkish Armed Forces Regulation and homosexual persons were found unfit to serve.[74] The Regulation of Turkish Armed Forces was amended in 2013[75] and the classification of mental illness was removed. However, as employers in Turkey look for the status of military services,

[68]For a recent report on the employment of trans women in Turkey, see http://www.transkadinlarinistihdami.org/en/project-report (20.08.2017); also see, A. Öner, *Beyaz Yakalı Eşcinseller, İşyerinde Cinsel Yönelim Ayrımcılığı ve Mücadele Stratejileri*, Istanbul 2015, p. 93 ff.; M. Göregenlı, T. Ş. Serdengeçti, *Situation of Lesbian, Gay, Bisexual, Transgender and Intersex Employees in Private Sector in Turkey*, Ed. M. Köylü, Istanbul 2015, available at http://www.kaosgldernegi.org/resim/yayin/dl/de_ozel_sektr_calisani_lgbti___ingilizce.pdf (20.08.2017); M. Göregenlı, Y. Öz, *Situation of Lesbian, Gay, Bisexual, Transgender and Intersex Public Sector Employees in Turkey*, Ed. M. Köylü, Istanbul 2016, available at http://www.kaosgldernegi.org/resim/yayin/dl/kamu_calisanlari_eng.pdf (20.08.2017).

[69]Ördek (2015), p. 64.

[70]Law numbered 657, dated 14.07.1965, published in the Official Gazette numbered 12056 and dated 23.07.1965.

In fact, Art. 125(E)(g) of this Law introduces a ground which allows for dismissal if a civil servant is found "to act in a shameful and embarrassing way unfit for the position of a civil servant".

[71]In detail, see Göregenli, Öz, p. 23 ff.

For the decisions of the administrative courts and the Council of State, see http://www.kaosgl.org/sayfa.php?id=5985 (20.08.2017).

[72]United Nations Universal Periodic Review on Turkey, p. 5.

[73]For a news account on a case of a medical expert of a state hospital who refused to treat a trans person, see http://t24.com.tr/haber/trans-hastayi-tedavi-etmeyen-ayrimci-doktora-ceza,326897 (20.08.2017). In this case, the Turkish Medical Association issued a notice againt the medical expert.

[74]The Turkish Armed Forces' Physical Capabilities Regulation, issued in 1986, listed homosexuality as an "advanced psychosexual disorder," a mental illness. In detail, see https://www.al-monitor.com/pulse/originals/2015/11/turkey-military-gay-rights-homosexual-picture.html (20.08.2017) and for the examination process which was highly debatable, see http://www.bbc.com/news/magazine-17474967 (15.08.2017).

[75]For the Amended Regulation, see Official Gazette dated 05.02.2013 and numbered 28550.

the status of "unfit to serve in the military" cause barriers to access to employment.[76] In this respect, the case of Halil İbrahim Dinçdağ, a football referee who expelled from the profession because of his unfit status to serve in the military constituted a landmark case.[77] Furthermore, under the Discipline Law of the Turkish Armed Forces,[78] homosexuality is still regulated as a reason for army officers for the expulsion from the army.

While same-sex relationships are increasingly accepted across the world, Turkey does not recognize same-sex marriage or civil unions for same-sex partners. Under Turkish law, marriage is only be established between a man and a woman.[79] Since this is considered as the essential element of a legal marriage, its lack causes a non-existent marriage without any legal consequences.[80] Subsequent to full gender recognition, which carries out the amendment of gender/sex marker in the register, a trans person could marry a person of the opposite sex. If the trans person does not obtain full gender recognition, he/she shall not have such right.[81]

Except marriage and engagement, Turkish law does not regulate any form of legal unions. Accordingly, cohabitations, including of same-sex persons, are *de facto* permissible, but they are not legally recognized. Thus, no legal consequences have been attributed by law. For instance, same-sex partners are deprived of legal inheritance rights, next-of-kin status or right to a joint adoption.[82] Still, Turkish law of obligations may offer some solutions for the unions of same-sex partners.[83]

Article 41 of the Turkish Constitution provides that the family is the cornerstone of the society.[84] This perception of family is based on the permanent committed

---

[76]"The Case of S.C.: Discrimination in Employment", 2 December 2013, available at http://lgbtinewsturkey.com/2013/12/02/case-of-s-c-discrimination-in-employment/ (20.08.2017).

[77]For a detailled information and an analyze of this case, see https://lgbtinewsturkey.com/2013/11/29/case-of-halil-ibrahim-dincdag-discrimination-in-employment/ (22.08.2017).

[78]Official Gazette dated 16.02.2013 and numbered 28561.

[79]Even though the TCC does not provide that, a marriage is only be established between a man and a woman, certain provisions of the TCC, namely Arts. 124, 134, 136 indicate that it can be concluded by two persons of different sex. Moreover, Art. 2 of the Marriage Regulation describes marriage as "a legal contract concluded between a man and a woman with the intention to establish a family before [an] authorized marriage officer in the required procedure". For a detailled information on the issue, see C. Yasan, *Milletlerarası Özel Hukukta Aynı Cinsiyetten Kişilerin Birliktelikleri*, Istanbul 2013, pp. 57–74; also, see Başoğlu and Yasan (2011), p. 321.

[80]K. Oğuzman, M. Dural, *Aile Hukuku*, Istanbul 1998, pp. 88–89; Dural, Öğüz, Gümüş, *Aile Hukuku*, pp. 69, 75; Yasan, pp. 72–73.

[81]Atamer (2005), p. 68; Atamer (2015), p. 325; Atamer, Taşkın, p. 761. However in the case of Barış Sulu and Aras Güngör, the authorities refused to grat a marriage license even though the couple is of opposite sex. For a news account, see http://www.kaosgl.org/page.php?id=9271 (29.08.2017).

[82]In detail, see Yasan, pp. 63–74; C. Yasan, "Eşcinsellerin Evlat Edinmesi", in *Prof. Dr. Belgin Erdoğmuş Armağanı*, Istanbul 2011, pp. 895–908.

[83]In detail, see Yasan, pp. 66–71; Başoğlu and Yasan (2011), pp. 325–326.

[84]Art. 41 of the Constitution reads as follows: "Family is the foundation of the Turkish society and based on the equality between the spouses. The State shall take the necessary measures and establish

relationship of two persons of the different sex in the form of marriage. In contrast to the ECtHR judgments,[85] the right to family life is only granted to two persons of different sex and same-sex de facto unions have been regarded as a breach of Turkish moral values.[86]

3 The Development of Specific Legal Regulations Concerning Trans Persons

Prior to 1988, there was no legal regulation in Turkey regarding the legal status of trans persons. Yet, the issue came before the courts.[87] The landmark case was the application of *Bülent Ersoy*, a famous Turkish singer.[88] In this case, the Turkish Court of Cassation rejected the application and held that the laws in force did not confer to individuals the right to choose their gender, and except intersex persons, nobody may undergo a gender confirmation surgery and change the sex/gender mark in the register.[89] One of the statements of the court unfortunately deserves to be highlighted, which reads as follows, "one could only pity the applicant for the loss of her male sexuality without being able to transform into a real woman". Both the conclusion and the reasoning of the court were heavily criticized.[90]

---

the necessary organization to protect peace and welfare of the family, especially mother and children, and to ensure the instruction of family planning and its practice. Every child has the right to protection and care and the right to have and maintain a personal and direct relation with his/her mother and father unless it is contrary to his/her high interests. The State shall take measures for the protection of the children against all kinds of abuse and violence".

[85]ECtHR, *X.Y.Z v. United Kingdom*, application no: 21830/93, dated 22.04.1997, (http://hudoc.echr.coe.int/eng?i=001-58032); ECtHR, *Schalk and Kopf v. Austria*, application no: 30141/04, dated 22.11.2010, (http://hudoc.echr.coe.int/eng?i=001-99605); ECtHR, *Vallianatos and Others v. Greece* applications nos: 29381/09 and 32684/09, dated 07.11.2013, (http://hudoc.echr.coe.int/eng?i=001-128294); ECtHR, *Oliari and others v. Italy*, applications nos: 18766/11 and 36030/11, dated 21.10.2015, (http://hudoc.echr.coe.int/eng?i=001-156265); ECtHR, *Aldeguer Tomas v. Spain*, application no: 35214/09, dated 14.09.2016, (http://hudoc.echr.coe.int/eng?i=001-163660).

[86]Kurtoğlu (2009), p. 85, available at http://cins.ankara.edu.tr/aycak.html (15.07.2017).

[87]For the decisions of Turkish courts of first instance which decided in favor of the change of gender mark in the civil status register, see Will and Öztan (1993), pp. 235–237; Öztürel (1980), pp. 169–270.

However, the Court of Cassation sytematically upheld these decisisons of lower courts in case they had been appealed, see Will, Öztan, p. 236.

[88]The circumstances giving rise to the case of Bülent Ersoy in brief, see Kurtoğlu (2009), pp. 83–84; Zengin (2014a), pp. 160–166.

[89]The decision of the Turkish Court of Cassation, 2nd Civil Chamber, 21.01.1982, (Yargıtay Kararları Dergisi, 1982, pp. 323–336); the decision of the Turkish Court of Cassation, 2nd Civil Chamber, 27.03.1986, (Yargıtay Kararları Dergisi, 1986, pp. 112–1126).

[90]In detail, see N. Kocayusufpaşaoğlu, *Türk Hukukunda Transseksüeller Nüfus Kütüğündeki Cinsiyet Kaydının Düzeltilmesi İçin Dava Açabilir mi ?*, İstanbul, 1986, pp. 9–66; Burcuoğlu

The legal recognition of preferred gender was eventually made possible in 1988 through an amendment to Art. 29 of the former TCC.[91] Even though the updated version of Art. 29 of the former TCC was the first explicit legal provision addressing the legal recognition of preferred gender, it was also criticized. Especially the lack of the prerequisites of the gender confirmation surgery and the emergence of a same-sex marriage for a certain period were debatable in the legal doctrine.[92]

Currently, the legal status of trans persons is regulated under Art. 40 TCC, enacted in 2002. Yet, on 29 November 2017 the Turkish Constitutional Court annulled the requirement of compulsory sterilisation provided by Art. 40 TCC[93] and this decision became effective on 20 March 2018 by its publication in the Official Gazette.[94] Thus, Art. 40 TCC, entitled "*sex change*", reads as follows:[95]

> A person who wants to change his/her sex has to apply to the court personally and ask a permission for a sex reassignment. For the permission to be given, the applicant must have reached the age of 18 and must be unmarried. Besides he/she must prove with an official health report issued by an education and research hospital that he/she is of transsexual nature, that the sex reassignment is compulsory for his/her mental health.

In case it is confirmed by an official health board report that a sex reassignment surgery was effected based on the permission given and in accordance with the purpose and medical methods, the court will decide for the necessary changes to be made in the civil status register.

In contrast to Art. 29 of the former TCC, Art. 40 offers a more detailed rule.[96] It sets out the requirements both for the gender confirmation surgery and the change of

(1986), p. 439 ff.; Atamer (2005), pp. 65; Atamer (2015), pp. 315–316; Wıll and Öztan, pp. 228–235.

[91]This ammendment is provided by the Law numbered 3444.

The updated versión of Art. 29 of the former TCC provides as follows: "A person who was capable to provide a report of a health commission conforming that she/he had undergone a gender reassignment surgery might apply to the court to change the sex/gender mark in the register. In case the applicant is married, the spouse would be given due notice of such an application and the marriage would terminate upon the final and conclusive decision of the court ordering the change in the register. If the couple have children, the court should also decide which of the parents would be entitled to have the custody of the children." For the translation of the provision, see Atamer, p. 66.

[92]In detail, see Kocayusufpaşaoğlu, p. 255, 251 ff.; Will, Öztan, p. 239 ff.; Atamer (2015), p. 316; Zevkliler (1988), pp. 264 ff.; Güven (1997), pp. 45, 59 ff.; M. Dural, T. Öğüz, *Türk Özel Hukuku, C. III, Aile Hukuku*, Istanbul 2013, p. 122 ff.

[93]The decision of the Turkish Court of Constitution, 29.11.2017, File No: 2017/130, Decision No: 2017/165, (http://kararlaryeni.anayasa.gov.tr/Karar/Content/541c15e5-cca0-4b1b-bee7-63fa0e24a29e?excludeGerekce=False&wordsOnly=False). For the press release in English, see http://www.constitutionalcourt.gov.tr/inlinepages/press/PressReleasesofJudgments/ConstitutionalityReview/46.html (20.05.2019).

[94]Official Gazette numbered 30366 and dated 20.03.2018.

[95]For the translation, see Atamer (2015), pp. 317–318.

[96]Art. 40 TCC of 2002 has largely been influenced by the German Gender Recognition Act (Transsexual Act – *Transsexuellengesetz).* See, Atamer (2015), p. 315, n. 4; Sağlam (2004); Turan Başara (2012), pp. 249–250.

sex/gender mark in the register. Still, the requirements to obtain the legal recognition of preferred gender, which will be outlined below, are problematic.

Article 40 TCC falls within the provisions concerning the civil status register and it adopts the usage of "*transsexual nature*" without including any definition. It should be noted that Turkish law does not define transsexual either. According to the court practice and the scholars, transsexual refers to all persons who suffers from an unconformity between their sex designated at birth and their gender identity.[97] It is also worth to mention that Art. 40 TCC is the only provision regulating the legal status of trans persons. In Turkish law, there is no specific and fully comprehensive statute dealing with the issue.[98]

4 Procedure and Requirements for the Legal Recognition of Preferred Gender

Pursuant to Turkish law, the legal recognition of preferred gender occurs on the basis of judicial procedure. According to Art. 40 TCC, the legal recognition starts with an application to the court to get the permission to gender confirmation surgery. The competent court is the court at the place of the residence of the applicant. The individual should apply to the court in person. It is not required that the applicant should be a Turkish citizen.[99]

For the permission to be granted by the court, had required an applicant

- to be over 18 years old;
- to have sufficient mental capacity;[100]
- to be unmarried;
- to be of transsexual nature;
- and the gender confirmation surgery should be essential for his/her mental health.

The last two preconditions must be proved with an official health report from the health board of an education and research hospital. Additionally, in a decision of 2011, the court also required that the applicant should submit a copy of criminal record.[101] If all these preconditions are satisfied, the court allows access to the

[97] Atamer, p. 66; Atamer (2015), p. 318; Sağlam; p. 462, 464; Sert, p. 261.

[98] The fact that the legal status of trans persons was not regulated in a separate and special law but included in the section of the TCC on the civil status register is subjected to criticisms. See, Sağlam, p. 457; Güven, pp. 57–58; Dural, Öğüz, Gümüş, *Aile Hukuku*, p. 122.

[99] Güven, p. 66; Wıll, Öztan, pp. 249–250; Atamer (2015), p. 323; Atamer, Taşkın, pp. 747–748.

[100] Although not explicitly stipulated in Art. 40, it is also required that the applicant must enjoy sufficient mental capacity, see Atamer (2015), pp. 321–322; Atamer (2005), p. 66; Atamer, Taşkın, p. 741; Sağlam, p. 460; Güven, p. 63; Turan Başara, p. 252; SERT, pp. 259–260; M. Dural, T. Öğüz, *Türk Özel Hukuku, C. II, Kişiler Hukuku*, Istanbul 2013, para. 629.

[101] The decision of the Turkish Court of Cassation, 2nd Civil Chamber, 04.10.2011, File No: 2010/11100, Decision No: 2011/14833 (Kazanci database). This requirement is criticized by the LGBTI

surgical intervention. The applicant may undergo the surgery at any hospital in Turkey or abroad.[102]

Following the gender confirmation surgery, the second judicial step starts. The person needs to apply again to the court in order to obtain the recognition of the preferred gender in the civil status register. The court would decide to order the necessary amendment in the register if it is confirmed by an official health report that the gender confirmation surgery was performed based on the permission given and in compliance with the purpose and medical methods. In case the person has undergone an unauthorized surgery (probably abroad, without prior court permission), the Turkish Court of Cassation confirmed that he/she would still be able to apply to the court the recognition of the preferred gender in the civil status register.[103]

It would not be possible to state that there is a standardized legal procedure in respect of the legal recognition of preferred gender.[104] The first instance courts' decisions depend on various issues, including the place where the court is located, the perspective of the judge and whether the applicant is a trans woman or trans man.[105] Once the court grants the application, the administrative authorities perform the necessary amendment to the civil status register. This amendment only concerns the sex/gender marker in the register, the identity (citizenship) number of the person does not change.

After the amendment in the register, the person receives a new identity card[106] and should apply to the relevant authorities for the issuance of new documentation such as passport, driver's license or diploma.[107] However, the requests of individuals regarding the renewal of their educational certificates (diplomas) have been

---

acitivists and scholars see, http://bianet.org/bianet/toplumsal-cinsiyet/134935-cinsiyet-degisikligi-icin-sabika-kaydi (26.08.2017); Atamer, Taşkın, pp. 743–744.

However, in the recent decisions of the Court such requiremenet has not been imposed, see Atamer, Taşkın, p. 744.

[102] Atamer (2015), p. 324; Atamer (2005), p. 67; Atamer, Taşkin, p. 749.

[103] The decision of the Turkish Court of Cassation, 2nd Civil Chamber, 13.12.2010, File No: 2009/19039, Decision No: 2010/20942 (Kazanci database). Also in a decision of 2009 the Court held that even though the requirements of Art. 40 TCC were not satisified, the recognition of a German Court decision in respect of the change of name and legal confirmation of preferred gender of a Turkish citizen does not contravene Turkish public policy (*ordre public*), see the decision of the Turkish Court of Cassation, 2nd Civil Chamber, 21.12.2009, File No: 2009/9678, Decision No: 2009/22090 (Kazanci database). For further information, see Atamer (2015), pp. 322–323; Atamer, Taşkın, p. 746; Atamer (2005), p. 67.

[104] S. Hun, "Trans Bireylerin Geçiş Süreci ve Hukuka Genel Bir Bakış", in *Trans Danışma Merkezi (T-DER), "Veri Toplama Raporu: Yeniden Doğdum"*, Ed. B. Sulu, Ankara 2014, (Hun, 2014), pp. 23, 29–30; Ördek, 2016, p. 94.

[105] HUN, 2014, p. 23.

[106] The Turkish identity cards which were coloured pink or blue to refer to female or male were abondoned starting from 2016.

[107] New personal documentation would be issued in accordance to the normal renewal procedures which would include potential fees.

denied by the secondary educational institutions[108] and universities.[109] This practice is incompatible with the judgments of the ECtHR[110] and the Resolution of the Parliamentary Assembly of the Council of Europe.[111] This constitutes also a huge burden on the individuals for full participation in employment.[112]

5 Deficiencies Related to the Existing Procedure and Requirements

Taken as a whole, Art. 40 TCC on the legal recognition of the preferred gender does not respect the human rights of trans persons, the system prescribed is not transparent, nor easily accessible. In fact, this provision reflects a heteronormative approach based on the biological and dualistic understanding of sex.[113] To begin with, the reasoning of Art. 40 TCC states that "the person must not be married in order to ensure that the institution of family is not undermined by persons whose gender is ambiguous". The expression "*ambigious*" used herein clearly provides that the law maker in the first-place treats transsexuality as a pathology/disorder, which should be treated.[114] This point of view is also underlined when the access to gender confirmation surgery requires a court decision ascertaining that such surgery is compulsory for the "*mental health*" of the applicant. The law establishes the pathologization

[108]Art. 76(2) of the Regulation of the Ministry of Education on the Secondary Educational Institutions regulates that any amendments to be made in the diplomas pursuant to a court decision shall be endorsed in the existing one. For a news account, see http://www.birgun.net/haber-detay/translara-serh-li-diploma-100861.html (27.08.2017).

[109]For a news account on a pending case filed on 28.01.2017 against Marmara University, see http://www.hurriyet.com.tr/ecenin-diploma-savasi-40502872 (27.08.2017).

[110]ECtHR, *van Kück v. Germany*, application no: 35968/97, dated 12.09.2003, (http://hudoc.echr.coe.int/eng?i=001-61142); ECtHR, *B. v. France*, application no: 13343/87, dated 25.03.1992, (http://hudoc.echr.coe.int/eng?i=001-57770); ECtHR, *Christine Goodwin v. U.K.*, application no: 28957/95, dated 11.07.2002, (http://hudoc.echr.coe.int/eng-press?i=003-585597-589247).

[111]Resolution 2048 (2015) of the Parliamentary Assembly of the Council of Europe, "Discrimination against transgender people in Europe", text adopted by the Assembly on 22.04.2015, para. 6.2.1, available at http://assembly.coe.int/nw/xml/XRef/Xref-XML2HTML-en.asp?fileid=21736&lang=en (20.08.2017). Also, see HAMMARBERG, p. 13, 85.

[112]Hammarberg, p. 90.

Respectively, a trans man who is not able to exercise his profession because of the refusal of the renewal of his diploma filed a law suit. For a detailled information on the case, see S. Hun, "LGBTİ Bireylere Yönelik Eğitim Hayatındaki Ayrımcılık: B.E.T. Diploma Değişikliği Davası", in SPOD, *LGBTİ'lerin Hukuk ve Adalete Erişimi*, Haziran 2016, pp. 100–107, available at http://www.spod.org.tr/docs/SPoD-lgbtilerin-hukuk-ve-adalete-erisimi-2015.pdf (20.08.2017).

A court of first-instance recently ruled that the endorsement procedure is against the right to respect for private life, see the 5th Chamber of the İzmir Administrative Court, dated 17.03.2016, File No: 2015/738, Decision No: 2016/439 (HUN, 2016, p. 107).

[113]Hun (2015), p. 316; Zengin (2014b), p. 66; Kurtoğlu (2009), p. 81 ff.; Atamer, Taşkin, p. 755.

[114]Hun (2015), p. 315; Kurtoğlu (2009), p. 84; Zengin (2014a, b), p. 170 ff.

of trans persons.[115] The gender confirmation surgery is considered as a necessity for a particular medical problem.[116] This necessity must be confirmed by an official health board report of an an education and research hospital, which may be issued up to 2 years of examination.[117] The health board consists of medical experts from psychiatry, endocrinology, urology, gynaecology and reconstructive surgery.[118] The process includes psychotherapy sessions, hormone intakes and a real-life test.[119] To note, the report of the health board constitutes an expert opinion under Turkish law, thus it is not binding on the court.[120]

Article 40 TCC subjects the legal recognition of preferred gender to an extremely strict and lengthy medical control without really taking into account trans persons' expectations, desires and feelings in respect of their bodies.[121] On the one hand, the law completely ignores that gender identity is an issue of self-identification and it should not be dependent on a medical diagnosis.[122] On the other hand, the fact that many cities in Turkey do not have education and research hospital or required medical experts causes also serious impediments for trans persons to access to health care.[123]

---

[115]Hun (2015), p. 317; Kurtoğlu (2009), p. 84.

[116]See, Scherpe and Dunne (2015), p. 619; Hammarberg, p. 105.

[117]Zengin (2014a, b), p. 55; Ördek (2015), p. 65; Atamer, Taşkin, pp. 730–731, fn. 17.

However, in a decision of 2006, the court pointed out that following the psychiatric examination lasting for "*four years*", the gender confirmation surgery found compulsory for the mental health of the applicant, see the decision of the Turkish Court of Cassation, 2nd Civil Chamber, 13.02.2006, File No: 2005/17485, Decision No: 2006/1343 (Kazanci database).

[118]Atamer (2015), p. 319; Atamer, Taşkın, p. 729, Sağlam, p. 463.

[119]Regarding the assessment procedure in detail, see Atamer (2015), pp. 319–321; Atamer, Taşkin, pp. 730–731; Zengin (2014a, b), pp. 58–60.

To note, the medical experts use the standarts of World Professional Association for Transgender Health (WPATH), see Atamer (2015), pp. 319–320. However, trans persons have serious concerns regarding the therapy sessions and they argue that the aim of this process is "*to fit trans individuals in the heteronormative standarts of Turkish society*", see Zengin (2014a, b), p. 63. In parallel, see Hun (2015), p. 316.

[120]Atamer (2015), p. 322; Atamer, Taşkın, p. 730; also see, Sağlam, p. 463; Turan Başara, pp. 250–251.

[121]Zengin (2014a, b), pp. 58, 64; Ördek (2015), p. 66.

[122]Resolution 2048 (2015) of the Parliamentary Assembly of the Council of Europe, paras. 6.2.1 and 6.2.2; Hun (2015), p. 318; Scherpe, Dunne, pp. 6653–655.

For a more detailled discussion of the issue, see Theilen (2014), pp. 328 ff.; Sørlie (2017), pp. 178–179.

However, the ECtHR concluded in its latest decision *A.P., Garçon et Nicot v. France* that the states parties had a wide margin of appreciation in deciding whether to impose the requirement of a prior psychological diagnosis, see ECtHR, *A.P., Garçon et Nicot v. France,* applications nos: 79885/12, 52471/13 and 52596/13, dated 06.07.2017, paras. 138-144, (http://hudoc.echr.coe.int/eng?i=001-172556).

[123]Ördek (2015), p. 65; Ördek (2016), pp. 93, 106–107; Hun (2015), pp. 316–317; also, ee Hammarberg, p. 111.

Besides, prior to the Turkish Constitutiobal Court's judgment in 2017 Art. 40 TCC required a compulsory sterilisation to get access to gender confirmation surgery. This requirement seriously contradicted with trans persons' rights of human dignity, bodily integrity and private life; thus, it has been severely criticized.[124] It was certainly not in line with human rights and international tendecies[125] and contravenes the Resolutions of the Parliamentary Assembly of the Council of Europe.[126] However, the Turkish lower court decisions, which granted the legal recognition even though this requirement had not been satisfied, were usually upheld by the Turkish Court of Cassation.[127] In fact, in the judgment *Y. Y. v. Turkey*, the ECtHR declared that the requirement of permanent infertility as a pre-condition to undergoing gender confirmation surgery is incompatible with the right to respect for private life (Art. 8 ECHR).[128] The argument of Turkey, which suggested that this pre-condition was necessary to protect both the public interest and the interests and

---

[124]Karadağ, pp. 105–106; Sağlam, pp. 464–469; Turan Başara, pp. 255–256; Hun (2015), p. 317; Hun (2014), pp. 23–24; Kurtoğlu (2009), p. 85; Atamer (2005), p. 67; Atamer (2015), pp. 320–321; Atamer, Taşkın, p. 731 ff.; Ördek (2016), p. 89, 94, 97; Ördek (2015), p. 72; also, see ECRI, Turkey Report, p. 36, para. 103; Scherpe, Dunne, p. 650; Lee (2015), p. 118 ff.

Still, a Turkish scholar suggests that it would be more appropriate if the requirement of permanent infertility is not imposed prior to accessing gender confirmation surgery, but to register the sex/gender marker change in the register, see SERT, p. 262. However, it should be noted that such surgeries could not be always medically possible, or simply not desired by trans persons, see Commissioner of Human Rights of the Council of Europe, "Human Rights and Gender Identity", Strasbourg 29 July 2009, CommDH/Issue Paper 2009(2), (Comm/DH Issue Paper 2009), pp. 8, available at https://rm.coe.int/16806da753 (28.08.2017).

[125]For instance, the countires such as Germany, Sweden, Austria, Denmark, Spain, Ireland, Portugal, Hungary, United Kingdom, Malta and Netherlands do not impose sterilisation as a requirement for legal recognition, see Hammarberg, p. 87; *A.P., Garçon et Nicot v. France,* para. 71; Scherpe, Dunne, pp. 643–646; Lee, pp. 139–148.

[126]Resolution 1728 (2010) of the Parliamentary Assembly of the Council of Europe, "Discrimination on the basis of sexual orientation and gender identity", text adopted by the Assembly on 29.04.2010, para. 16.11.2, available at http://assembly.coe.int/nw/xml/XRef/Xref-XML2HTML-EN.asp?fileid=17853&lang=en (28.08.2017); Resolution 1945 (2013) of the Parliamentary Assembly of the Council of Europe, "Putting an end to coerced sterilization and castrations", text adopted by the Assembly on 26.06.2013, available at http://assembly.coe.int/nw/xml/XRef/Xref-XML2HTML-en.asp?fileid=19984&lang=en (28.08.2017); Resolution 2048 (2015) of the Parliamentary Assembly of the Council of Europe, para. 6.3.1; also see, HAMMARBERG, p. 13.

[127]For instance, see the decision of the Turkish Court of Cassation, 2nd Civil Chamber, dated 20.04.2006, File No: 2005/20746, Decision No: 2005/5916 (Kazanci database); Atamer (2015), p. 320, fn. 20.

[128]ECtHR, *Y.Y. v. Turkey*, application no: 14793/08, dated 10.06.2015, (http://hudoc.echr.coe.int/eng?i=001-152779). In detail, see Dunne (2015), pp. 646–658; Atamer (2015), p. 321; Atamer, Taşkin, pp. 733–738.

health of trans persons[129] reflected the desire of the state to protect and reinforced the binary understanding of sex in the society.[130]

Regrettably, subsequent to the judgment of *Y. Y. v. Turkey* which is dated 10.06.2015, the compulsory sterilisation prescribed by Art. 40 TCC has not been abolished until 2017. In fact, after the judgment *Y. Y. v. Turkey*, the Court of Cassation confirmed the lower courts' decisions, which have held that the applicant must be permanently deprived of the capacity of reproduction.[131] In doing so, the courts violated Art. 90(5) of the Constitution stating that if is there is a conflict between the laws and international conventions on fundamental rights and freedoms, the provisions of international conventions shall prevail.[132] This compels the individuals to make a choice between compulsory sterilisation or legal gender recognition.[133] In other words, the sterilisation requirement is forced by the state and trans persons' personal desires, expectations and self-determination has not been taken into consideration. This indicates that the state continues to utilize the legal recognition process as a heteronormative corrective measure.[134] The lawmaker and judges consider that trans persons needed to be 'fixed' through surgery.[135] The legislative proposal introduced in 2015 and the most recent judgment of the Turkish Constitutional Court, will be addressed below.

Moreover, Art. 40 TCC provides that the applicant must have reached the age of 18 and must be unmarried. Regarding the age requirement, in extraordinary circumstances where a delay might cause serious problems, the court could allow the persons under the age of 18 to access to the gender confirmation surgery.[136] However, the existence of extraordinary circumstances represents a higher standart. Since there is no reported case, we may only speculate that this could occur in a case of suicide attempt, or severe psychological trauma. In order to ensure the well-being of trans persons and to reduce the problems they might face in accessing to education or employment, we believe that without proving any extraordinary circumstances,

---

[129] *Y.Y. v. Turkey*, paras. 74, 80.

[130] In parallel, see Hun (2015), p. 316; Kurtoğlu (2009), p. 85; also see, D. Ferhat, "Data Collection Report: 'I Was Reborn'", in *Counselling Centre for Transgender People Association (T-DER), "Data Collection Report: I Was Reborn"*, Ed. B. SULU, Ankara 2014, p. 46.

[131] The decision of the Turkish Court of Cassation, 18th Civil Chamber, dated 02.03.2016, File No: 2015/23063, Decision No: 2016/3697 (Kazanci database); The decision of the Turkish Court of Cassation, 18th Civil Chamber, dated 30.04.2015, File No: 2014/18452, Decision No: 2015/7159 (Atamer, Taşkin, p. 738).

[132] Atamer, Taşkin, pp. 738–739.

[133] ÖZ, p. 44; Dunne (2017), p. 10; also, see *A.P., Garçon et Nicot v. France*, paras. 131–132, 135.

[134] Regarding this issue, see S. Agıus, C. Tobler, *Trans and Intersex People- Discrimination on the Grounds of Sex, Gender Identity and Gender Expression*, European Comission-Directorate General for Justice, June 2011, pp. 19; Dunne (2017), p. 9.

[135] Dunne, p. 650; Hun (2015), p. 317, also, see Scherpe, Dunne, p. 639.

[136] Kaya (2008), p. 73; Başara, p. 251; Atamer (2015), p. 321; Atamer, Taşkın, p. 740.

the trans persons would be able to start the legal process at an earlier age,[137] especially if the best interest of the applicant requires so.

As regards to the requirement of not being married, it is interpreted that the applicant should not be married at the time of the application.[138] The fact that Turkish law denies same-sex marriage and excludes any alternative recognition of same-sex unions is the main reason of this requirement.[139] This also offers that if the applicant is married, divorce is required so as to prevent an existing marriage becoming one of the same-sex. In fact, the reasoning of Art. 40 TCC states that the law maker aimed to "impede the breakdown of the institution of the family, which is the foundation of the society by persons whose sex is ambigious and to ensure psychological and moral values by preventing a person from changing his/her sex while he/she is still married and shares a common life with children and spouse". However, in case the person is married, this requirement does not consider either trans persons' or their families' well-being[140] but introduces a mandatory divorce under the pretext of protecting the Turkish family structure. It thus seems that this requirement reflects society's primary interest to enforce the binary understanding of sex.[141] Thus, it is also criticized by scholars.[142]

Lastly, Art. 40 TCC provides that the court allows the application if the gender confirmation surgery has been effected "in accordance with the purpose and medical methods". Regrettably, the Turkish Court of Cassation interpreted this requirement as "full" gender reconstructive surgery imposing the reconstruction of relevant genital organ.[143] This constitutes an infringement of bodily integrity and private autonomy, thus seriously contravenes human rights of trans persons.[144] As stated above for the compulsory sterilisation requirement, this also compels the individuals has to choose between a full gender reconstructive surgery or legal gender recognition.[145] Trans persons' personal desires, expectations and self-determination has not been taken into consideration. The lawmaker and judges assume that persons must

[137]In this respect, it has been suggested that the end of the puberty period would be a more convenient choice, see Güven, p. 62.

However, we accept that the age limit for legal recognition is a sensitive issue. In detail, see Scherpe, Dunne, pp. 625–629.

[138]Atamer (2015), p. 322; Atamer, Taşkin, p. 741; Güven, p. 65; Sağlam, p. 461; Turan Başara, pp. 252–253; Sert, p. 265.

In this respect, also see the decision of the Turkish Court of Cassation, 2nd Civil Chamber, dated 11.05.2010, File No: 2009/2171, Decision No: 2010/9487 (Atamer, Taşkin, p. 741).

[139]See, Scherpe, Dunne, pp. 632–633.

[140]Regarding the impacts on the families and children, see Comm/DH Issue Paper 2009, p. 9.

[141]Agıus, Tobler, p. 19.

[142]Atamer, Taşkın, pp. 742–743; Hun (2015), p. 348; in contrast, see Turan Başara, p. 253.

[143]The decision of the Turkish Court of Cassation, 2nd Civil Chamber, dated 13.02.2006, File No: 2005/17485, Decision No: 2006/1343 (Kazanci database).

[144]Atamer (2015), pp. 750–759; Ördek (2016), p. 97; Hun (2015), p. 318, Ördek (2015), p. 72; also, see Scherpe, Dunne, p. 639 ff.

[145]Atamer, Taşkın, p. 757.

be cured for a "proper" male or female identity, which should be in line with the "normal" gendered stereotypes.[146] A recent case on the issue before the Turkish Constitutional Court, will be addressed below.

6 Legal Challenges to the Existing Law

Subsequent to *Y. Y. v. Turkey* judgment, two different legislative proposals in respect of Art. 40 TCC was submitted by a member of the Turkish Parliament, namely Mahmut Tanal from the Republican People's Party. The first proposal, submitted on 24 November 2015, suggested the abolishment of "permanent infertility requirement".[147] This proposal mentioned that the legislator's prejudice is apparent in the reasoning of Art. 40.[148] It was also pointed out that Art. 40 violates the "right to reproduce" protected under the ECHR, CEDAW and the Constitution. Additionally, it was asserted that the relevant provision contradicts Art. 20 of the "Recommendation CM/Rec (2010)5 of the Committee of Ministers to member states on measures to combat discrimination on grounds of sexual orientation or gender identity" dated 31.03.2010.[149]

The second proposal, submitted on 8 January 2016, was pertinent to the abolishment of the requirement of "not being married".[150] In this proposal, attention was drawn to the Hammarberg Report. This Report provides that it is necessary to "remove the requirement of being unmarried, or divorce for already married persons, as a necessary condition for the legal recognition of a trans person's preferred gender".[151] Nevertheless, since Turkish law only recognizes that the marriage should be established between a man and a woman, this proposal alone would not be sufficient, and a comprehensive legal reform is certainly needed for the abolishment of the requirement.[152]

Both proposals were submitted to the Commission. However, there has yet been no progress regarding their implementation. On this issue, further positive steps are certainly needed. In addition to these proposals, same Member of Parliament, Mahmut Tanal, submitted three other legislative proposals regarding the social

[146]Atamer, Taşkın, p. 758; Hun (2015), pp. 317–318; also, see Scherpe, Dunne, pp. 647–650; Dunne (2017), p. 20.

[147]See, the proposal no. 2/237 to modify the TCC (no. 4721), http://www2.tbmm.gov.tr/d26/2/2-0237.pdf (28.08.2017).

[148]Ördek (2016), p. 90.

[149]This provision offers that "prior requirements, including changes of a physical nature, for legal recognition of a gender reassignment, should be regularly reviewed in order to remove abusive requirements."

[150]See the proposal no. 2/642 to modify the TCC (no. 4721), http://www2.tbmm.gov.tr/d26/2/2-0642.pdf (28.08.2017).

[151]Recommendation no. 5(3), see Hammarberg, p. 13.

[152]Atamer, Taşkın, p. 743, also, see Scherpe, Dunne, pp. 633–634.

security and employment rights of trans individuals. To begin with, the process to ensure that the trans women, without the need to file a law suit, could also benefit from the orphan's pension paid to the orphan girls is ongoing.[153] In this respect, it was proposed on 23 November 2015 that the Law on the Turkish Republic Retirement Fund[154] would be amended in order to allow the persons who obtained legal recognition of preferred gender to make their claims retroactively.

Secondly, a modification proposal to the Labor Law[155] in order to protect the employment rights of trans individuals was submitted on 6 January 2016.[156] This proposal suggested that Art. 30 of the Labor Law shall be amended in order to impose an employment requirement of a certain number of trans individuals in the private and public sectors.[157]

Thirdly, on 15 May 2017, an amendment to the Law to Protect Family and Prevent Violence Against Women was introduced. It was put forth that taking into consideration the medical and psychosocial needs of trans and intersex persons, modifications should be made to expand the definition of family to cover the non-marriage unions in order to put them under the social security coverage.[158]

On the other hand, the permanent infertility requirement, i.e. compulsory sterilization, prescribed by Art. 40 TCC has been taken to the Turkish Court of Constitution due to a plea filed by a court of first instance in Edirne.[159] On 14 June 2017, the Court decided to examine the constitutionality of this provision in respect of substance.[160] The requirement of having a gender confirmation surgery which has been effected "in accordance with the purpose and medical methods", i.e. having a full surgery in regard to the reconstruction of relevant genital organs, has also been taken to the Turkish Court of Constitution.[161]

On 10 October 2015, the Court decided to examine the constitutionality of these two requirements in respect of substance. Finally, on 29 November 2017,[162] the

[153]Atamer and Taşkin (2015), pp. 772–773.

[154]Law numbered 5434. It is published in the Official Gazette numbered 7235 and dated 17.06.1949.

[155]Law numbered 4857. It is published in the Official Gazette numbered 25154 and dated 10.06.2003.

[156]See, the proposal no. 2/611 to modify the Turkish Labor Law (no. 4857), http://www2.tbmm.gov.tr/d26/2/2-0611.pdf (28.08.2017).

[157]See the proposal no.2/611 to modify the Turkish Labor Law (no. 4857), http://www2.tbmm.gov.tr/d26/2/2-0611.pdf (28.08.2017).

[158]See the proposal no.2/1721 to modify certain Legal Acts, https://www.tbmm.gov.tr/develop/owa/tasari_teklif_sd.onerge_bilgileri?kanunlar_sira_no=211603 (28.08.2017).

[159]For a detailled information, see http://kaosgl.org/page.php?id=21001 (29.08.2017); https://www.opendemocracy.net/north-africa-west-asia/sinem-hun/legal-recognition-of-transgender-people-in-turkey-will-court-seize- (29.08.2017).

[160]See, http://www.anayasa.gov.tr/icsayfalar/gundem/detay/genelkurul/773.pdf (29.08.2017).

[161]Ördek (2016), p. 97; Atamer, Taşkın, pp. 751–752.

[162]See, http://www.constitutionalcourt.gov.tr/inlinepages/press/PressReleasesofJudgments/ConstitutionalityReview/46.html.

Court rendered its judgment.[163] The Court decided by majority to abolish the permanent infertility requirement,[164] but not the requirement of having a gender confirmation surgery which has been effected in accordance with the purpose and medical methods.[165]

In the first judgment, The Court of Constitution decided that the permanent infertility requirement set forth in Article 40§1 TCC violated Constitution and annulled the provision.[166] According to the Court of Constitution "there is no reasonable balance between the restriction imposed on the relevant persons' physical and corporal existence as well as her/his private life and the aim sought to be reached, such a restriction constitutes a disproportionate interference.[167]" In addition, the Court stated that requiring a precondition such as permanent infertility for gender reassignment might create severe and irreparable results. Consequently, Article 40§1 TCC has been annulled for violating Article 13, 17 and 20 of the Constitution.

In the second judgment of the Court of Constitution, Article 40§2 TCC is requested to be annulled on the grounds that violation of corporal and spiritual existence of individuals. Article 40§2 provides that where is certified by an official medical board that a gender reassignement surgery has been performed in accordance with the purpose and the medical techniques, based on the authorization granted to this end, the court shall decide to proceed with the rectification of the civil registration codes. The Court of Constitution decided that the provision requiring the gender reassignment surgery is regulated to protect the public order and it does not constitute a violation either for individual freedom or private life. In conclusion, the Article 40§2 of TCC has been found not to violate Articles 13, 17 and 20 of the Constitution, therefore the request for its annulment has been dismissed.[168]

---

[163]For news accounts, see https://bianet.org/kadin/lgbti/192050-aym-cinsiyet-gecisinde-uremeden-yoksun-olma-sartini-kaldirdi (03.12.2017); https://www.cnnturk.com/turkiye/anayasa-mahkemesi-cinsiyet-degistirmede-o-sarti-kaldirdi (03.12.2107).

[164]The decision of the Constitutional Court, 29 November 2017, File No: 2017/130, Decision No: 2017/165.

[165]The decision of the Constitutional Court, 29 November 2017, File No: 2015/79, Decision No: 2017/164.

[166]See, http://kararlaryeni.anayasa.gov.tr/Karar/Content/541c15e5-cca0-4b1b-bee7-63fa0e24a29e?excludeGe rekce=False&wordsOnly=False.

[167]See, http://kararlaryeni.anayasa.gov.tr/Karar/Content/541c15e5-cca0-4b1b-bee7-63fa0e24a29e?excludeGe rekce= False&wordsOnly=False.

[168]"[A]ssumption of the fact that a transsexual person can make a change in the sex section of her/his civil register without undergoing a gender reassignment surgery will cause a difference between a person's biological sex and the sex stated in her/his civil register. In other words, it will create a de facto legal situation that contradicts the person's biological sex. Further, if not gender reassignment surgery is required, a person might change his/her sex in the civil register just to enjoy or refrain from certain rights that are recognized by the legal order distinctively for the opposite sex. This would negatively affect the social life and hence the public order, and it could create an obstacle for individuals to enjoy their rights and freedoms properly." See, http://kararlaryeni.

However, there might be trans persons choosing not to undergo this reassignment surgery for personal reasons or healthy problems making the surgery impossible. As stated in the raport of 'Human Right and Gender Identity' of Council of Europe, it is not proportionate for the state to prescribe same treatment for all trans persons.[169] In fact, the process of gender transition and the legal recognition of preferred gender are essentially independent issues and should be regulated separately.

7 Major Consequences of the Legal Recognition of Preferred Gender

7.1 The Regulation of Names

Under Turkish law, a name is a personal right that is under the protection of personality. The general rule relating to change of name is regulated in Art. 27 TCC. Pursuant to this provision, a person may request from the court to change his/her name if there is a justifiable reason (just ground).[170] Justifiable reason is neither defined nor restricted in law. In accordance with the principle of good faith, if a person has a just ground to bear a name different from his/her original, the change of name would be allowed.[171] The judge, taking into consideration all the relevant circumstances and the applicant's psychological, emotional and moral interests, would decide if there is a justifiable reason or not.[172] In court practice, if a person has already been known by his/her family and social circle by the name he/she wants to assume, this constitutes a justifiable reason unless there is a violation of

anayasa.gov.tr/Karar/Content/0c609e7e-58be-45f4-97b0-470caa6f3777?excludeGerekce= False& wordsOnly=False.

[169]"[M]edical treatment must always be administered in the best interests of the individual and adjusted to her/his specific needs and situation. It is disproportionate for the state to prescribe treatment in a "one size fits all" manner. The basic human rights concern here is to what extent such a strong interference by the state in the private lives of individuals can be justified and whether sterilisation or other medical interventions are required to classify someone as being of the one sex or the other." See, Comm/DH Issue Paper 2009, pp. 8.

[170]Oğuzman, Seliçi, Oktay-Özdemir, pp. 116–118; Serozan, p. 483; Ansay, p. 98.

[171]Oğuzman, Seliçi, Oktay-Özdemir, p. 117.

[172]Oğuzman, Seliçi, Oktay-Özdemir, pp. 116–117; also, see the decision of the Turkish Court of Cassation, 18th Civil Chamber, 22.10.2007, File No: 2007/7881, Decision No: 2007/8649 (Kazanci database).

mandatory rules.[173] The individual does not have the right to adopt any name he/she desires.[174]

The legal recognition of preferred gender is considered as a justifiable reason so trans person is allowed to change his/her name in accordance with Art. 27 TCC.[175] Equally, the court practice confirmed that the legal recognition of preferred gender in the civil status register provides a justifiable reason for change of name.[176] However, it is worth mentioning that following the legal recognition, a change of name is not an obligation and a trans person may continue to use his/her original name, especially if it is a neutral name.[177]

On the other hand, it is suggested that a trans person may also change his/her name without the legal recognition of preferred gender.[178] Even if this is true in theory, a trans person still needs to establish the existence of a justifiable reason for a change of name. We believe that in such case, the establishment of a justifiable reason would be more difficult[179] and the willingness of the judge to allow the change would have a crucial role.

As pointed above, the change of name is only possible by a court judgment.[180] The civil status officer should participate in such proceeding.[181] The court shall hear both the civil status officer and the witnesses of the applicant which should be at least two. The proceeding lasts for a minimum of 6 months. Once the court allows the application, the relevant amendment shall be made by the authorities and the new name should be announced officially.

---

[173] The decision of the Turkish Court of Cassation, 18th Civil Chamber, 12.04.2011, File No: 2011/2391, Decision No: 2011/4931 (Kazanci database); The decision of the Turkish Court of Cassation, 18th Civil Chamber, 26.06.2012, File No: 2012/6324, Decision No: 2012/8146 (Kazanci database); The decision of the Turkish Court of Cassation, 18th Civil Chamber, 30.04.2015, File No: 2014/18248, Decision No: 2015/7152 (Kazanci database); The decision of the Turkish Court of Cassation, 18th Civil Chamber, 13.01.2016, File No: 2015/5694, Decision No: 2016/347 (Kazanci database);

[174] N. EKŞİ, *Vatandaşlık Hukukumuzda Türkçe Olmayan Ad ve Soyad Meselesi*, Istanbul 2008, p. 67.

[175] Atamer (2015), pp. 325; Atamer (2005), pp. 68; Atamer, Taşkın, pp. 761; Sağlam, p. 460; Güven, p. 67; ÖZ, p. 45; Sert, pp. 263–264; Turan Başara, pp. 257–258; Wıll, Öztan, p. 451.

Art. 40 TCC on the legal recognition of preferred gender does not contain any provision regarding a change of name, thus the general provision relating the change of name is applicable.

[176] The decision of the Turkish Court of Cassation, 18th Chamber, 01.12.2008, File No: 2008/11648, Decision No: 2008/12671 (Kazanci database); the decision of the Turkish Court of Cassation, 18th Chamber, 17.06.2002, File No: 2002/4281, Decision No: 2002/6855.

[177] SERT, pp. 263–264.

In fact, like the case of Bülent Ersoy, in some cases the individuals prefer not to change their legal name after the legal recognition of preferred gender, see Will, Öztan, p. 450.

[178] ÖZ, pp. 45.

[179] In parallel, see Wıll, Öztan, pp. 251–252.

[180] Art. 27 TCC; and Art. 35 CRS.

[181] Art. 36 CRS.

Prior to the decision of the Constitutional Court,[182] Art. 36(1)(b) CRS provided that a law suit for an amendment or rectification in the civil status register regarding a specific issue should be brought once. However, the court practice and scholars accepted that the emergence of a justifiable reason is not subjected to a time limit and a reason which occurs later may also be a just ground for a re-change of name.[183] Consequently, a trans person may be allowed to re-change his/her name depending on the establishment of a justifiable reason and within the limits of the principle of good faith.

7.2 Access to Treatments

Starting from 23 October 2013, Turkey's healthcare system covers the expenses of the gender confirmation surgeries, including breast implants and genital surgeries.[184] The individuals may benefit from the public health insurance in accordance with the relevant procedure prescribed by social security regulations. Yet, public health insurance has deficiencies. It does not cover neither hormone intakes nor the surgeries performed in private hospitals.[185] As for private health insurance companies, they still deny covering gender confirmation surgeries.[186]

Only a few medical experts in the state hospitals are comptent enough to properly perform gender confirmation surgeries. Thus, trans persons mostly prefer to undergo gender confirmation surgery in private hospitals.[187] Given that many trans persons do not have sufficient financial support and that public health insurance do not cover surgeries performed in private hospitals, the burden on the individuals to access to treatments is still pertinent.[188]

Lastly, it has been reported that one of the major state hospitals in Istanbul has decided not to perform compulsory sterilisation surgeries[189] under the pretext of

[182]The Turkish Court of Constitution, 30.03.2012, File No: 2011/34, Decision No: 2012/48.

[183]The decision of the Turkish Court of Cassation, 18th Civil Chamber, 06.05.2008, File No: 2008/3994, Decision No: 2008/5513 (Kazanci database); The decision of the Turkish Court of Cassation, 18th Civil Chamber, 27.05.2002, File No: 2002/3480, Decision No: 2002/6028 (Kazanci database); The decision of the Turkish Court of Cassation, 18th Civil Chamber, 20.01.2003, File No: 2002/11187, Decision No: 2003/48 (Kazanci database); B. TUNÇ DEMİRALP, *Uygulamada Nüfus Davaları ve Yargılama Yöntemi*, İstanbul 1993, p. 83.

[184]The Social Security Institution of Turkey, an oficial paper dated 23.10.2013, numbered 10463188/3878389-17074768, titled "sex reassignment surgery".

[185]Atamer, Taşkın, p. 750.

[186]Atamer, Taşkın, pp. 749–750.

[187]Atamer, Taşkın, p. 750.

[188]Ördek (2015), p. 65; Ördek (2016), pp. 89, 106–107; Hun (2015), pp. 316–317; also see Hammarberg, p. 111.

[189]For a news account see, http://www.cumhuriyet.com.tr/haber/saglik/751942/Homofobik_karar.html (06.07.2017).

inconvenience suffered by other patients and the permanent lost of genital organ of the applicant.

8 Conclusion

The authors of this chapter believe that in respect of the legal recognition of preffered gender, the recommendations[190] introduced by LGBTI+ activists and ILGA Europeshould be taken into consideration by the government and the lawmaker. In this regard, Turkey should enact a separate law on the legal recognition of preferred gender for which the Argentina Gender Identity Law of 2012 should be used as a model.[191]

References

Atamer YM (2005) The legal status of transsexuals in Turkey. Int J Transgenderism 8(1):65

Atamer YM (2015) The legal status of transsexual and transgender persons in Turkey. In: Scherpe JM (ed) The legal status of transsexual and transgender persons. Intersentia, Atamer, p 324

Atamer YM, Taşkın D (2016) Transseksüellere İlişkin Hukuksal Düzenlemeler: Uygulama, Anayasa ve Avrupa İnsan Hakları Sözleşmesine Aykırı Yönler ve Revizyon Teklifleri. Yargıtay Dergisi 42(4):760

Aytekın Inceoğlu A (2015) Türk Ceza Kanunu'nun 122. Maddesinde Düzenlenen Nefret ve Ayrımcılık Suçunun 'Nefret Suçu' Kapsamında Değerlendirilmesi. Legal J Law 13(150):56 ff

Başoğlu B, Yasan C (2011) National Report: Turkey. Am Univ J Gender Soc Policy Law (19):321

---

[190]See, *Contribution from Kaos GL, SPoD, Pembe Hayat, ILGA-Europe and ERA to Turkey's Report 2016*, pp. 4, available at https://www.ilga-europe.org/sites/default/files/enlargement_review_turkey_2016.pdf (15.08.2017). In terms of rights and equal treatment of trans and intersex persons, these reccommendations read as follows: "The government should be urged to

- Pass a law that allows trans people to undergo a gender reassignment procedure without demands of sterilisation, unmarried status, and other discriminatory points of the Civil Code.
- Introduce legal regulations to recognise the preferred gender identity based on self-determination.
- Apply the ECHR decision on Y.Y. vs. Turkey case to reform Article 40 of Turkey's Civil Code.
- Develop inclusive social policies and national employment strategies in order to provide equal opportunities in social services, benefits and employment opportunities for trans and intersex persons.
- Report and monitor a nationwide consensus on school drop-outs of trans and intersex children; hence, to come up with national strategies about how to solve the relevant problems.
- Apply European Directives on Goods and Services, and Employment to provide equal access and treatment, also for trans and intersex persons.
- End arbitrary implementation of the Misdemeanour Act Law against trans persons".

[191]For the English translation of the Argentina Gender İdentity Law, see https://tgeu.org/argentina-gender-identity-law/ (15.08.2017).

Burcuoğlu H (1986) Prof. Dr. Necip Kocayusufpaşaoğlu'nun 'Türk Hukukunda Transseksüeller Nüfus Kütüğündeki Cinsiyet Kaydının Düzeltilmesi İçin Dava Açabilir mi?' Adlı Eseri ve Buna Bağlı Olarak Yargıtay 2. Hukuk Dairesinin 27.3.1986 T. ve E. 651, K. 3256 Sayılı Kararı Üzerine. İstanbul Barosu Dergisi 60(7-8-9):439 ff
Dunne P (2015) Commentary: YY v. Turkey: infertility as a pre-condition for gender confirmation surgery. Med Law Rev 23(4):646–658
Dunne P (2017) Transgender sterilisation requirement in Europe. Medical Law Rev:9
Engın C (2015) LGBT in Turkey: policies and experiences. Soc Sci 4:842–843
Güven K (1997) Cinsiyet Değişikliği ve Hukuki Sonuçları. Gazi Üniversitesi Hukuk Fakültesi Dergisi 1(1):45
Hammarberg T (2011) Discrimination on grounds of sexual orientation and gender identity in Europe, 2nd edn. Council of Europe Publishing, Strasbourg, p 80
Hun S (2015) Türk Medeni Kanunu'nun 40. Maddesi Somut Norm Denetimine Tabiyken: Trans Geçiş Sürecinde 'Bekletmeler'in Trans Öznelliklere Etkisi. Ankara Barosu Dergisi 4:316
Kaya M (2008) Türk Hukukunda Cinsiyet Değişikliği ve Hukuki Sonuçları. Ankara Üniversitesi Hukuk Fakültesi Öğrencilerinin Fakültelerine Armağanı:73
Kurtoğlu A (2009) Sex reassignment, biological reproduction and sexual citizenship in Turkey. Fe Dergi 1(2):85
Lee R (2015) Forced sterilization and mandatory divorce: how a majority of Council of Europe Member States' laws regarding gender identity violate the internationally and regionally established human rights of trans people. Berkeley J Int Law 33(1):118 ff
Mcclaın M, Waıte-Wrıght O (2016) The LGBT community in Turkey: discrimination, violence and struggle for the equality. Creighton Int Comp Law J 7:176–177
Öztürel A (1980) Transseksüalizm ile Hermafrodizmde Yasasal Tıpsal ve Adli Problemleri. Ankara Üniversitesi Hukuk Fakültesi Dergisi 37:169–270
Sağlam İ (2004) Türk Medeni Kanunu Madde 40 Üzerine Bir Değerlendirme. Ankara Üniversitesi Hukuk Fakültesi Dergisi 8(3–4):459
Scherpe JM, Dunne P (2015) The legal status of transsexual and transgender persons- comparative analysis and recommendations. In: Scherpe JM (ed) The legal status of transsexual and transgender persons. Cambridge, Intersentia, p 619
Sørlie A (2017) Governing (Trans)parenthood: the tenacious hold of biological connection and heterosexuality. In: Otto D (ed) Queering international law: possibilities, alliances, complicities, risks. Taylor & Francis, Milton Park, pp 178–179
Theilen JT (2014) Depathologisation of transgenderism and international human rights law. Human Rights Law Rev 14:328 ff
Turan Başara G (2012) Türk Medeni Kanunu'nun 40. Maddesi Kapsamında Cinsiyet Değişikliği ve Hukuki Sonuçları. Türkiye Barolar Birliği Dergisi:249–250
Will MR, Öztan B (1993) Hukukun Sebebiyet Verdiği Bir Acı- Transseksüellerin Hukuki Durumu. Ankara Üniversitesi Hukuk Fakültesi Dergisi 43(1-4):235–237
Yılmaz V, Göçmen I (2016) Denied citizens of Turkey: experiences of discrimination among LGBT individuals in emplyment, housing and health care. Gender Work Organ 23(5):470 ff
Zengin A (2014a) Sex under intimate siege: transgender lives, law and state violence in contemporary turkey, Ph.D. Thesis. Universiy of Toronto, Toronto, pp 160–166
Zengin A (2014b) Sex for law, sex for psychiatry: pre-sex reassignment surgical psychotherapy in Turkey. Anthropologica 56(1):66
Zevkliler A (1988) Medeni Kanun ve Cinsiyet Kargaşası. Türkiye Barolar Birliği Dergisi (2):264 ff

Part III
The Soft Medicalization Model

Civil Status and Trans Persons in Austria

Bea Verschraegen

Abstract This chapter highlights the Austrian legal framework of the civil status, sex as a category of law, the legal embodiment of trans persons and the process regarding the change of sex, the name of a trans person, the family law effects and early sex ambiguity. It explains the complexity derived from the federal nature of the State, and the little interest afforded to the issue by the political system. It also shows, however, how, step by step, society has become better acquainted with and cognizant of trans persons and the need for the possibility of changes of sex. The Austrian Administrative and Constitutional Courts must be given credit for the fact that a change of sex no longer requires surgery. The procedure for the change of sex reflects the burdens that go along with it, but also demonstrates the understanding of all suffering caused, if no change of sex were permitted by principle.

The legal situation of trans persons in Austria is perceived as issues of sex and gender and thus indirectly linked with the traditional binary sex model on which e.g. marriage, registered partnership, parenthood and the name formerly were based. These core issues in civil law are however also shaped by fundamental principles and human rights (equality, prohibition of discrimination etc). Civil status is conceived as a notion proper to Civil law. By attributing civil status to a person, the law assigns rights and duties accordingly, and until recently, as limited to the binary model relating to male or female sex. Deviations from this model historically have been considered by the legislator and society as a marginal issue concerning minority groups. Public interest in changing the legal situation has been absent and thus the democratic process in acting for the interest of vulnerable minority groups has proven to be slow and reluctant. The Austrian legal system with competences of the Federation and the States on the one hand, and the hybrid distribution of legislative and executive power on the other, has contributed to a certain lack of transparency. Hence, the conditions of the recognition of the civil status of trans

B. Verschraegen (✉)
University of Vienna, Vienna, Austria
e-mail: bea.verschraegen@univie.ac.at

I. C. Jaramillo, L. Carlson (eds.), *Trans Rights and Wrongs*, Ius Comparatum - Global Studies in Comparative Law 54,
https://doi.org/10.1007/978-3-030-68494-5_10

persons are embedded in a legal order that reflects the tensions necessarily linked with a multilevel system of law and competences. This chapter highlights the legal framework of the civil status, sex as a category of law, the legal embodiment of trans persons and the process regarding the change of sex, the name of a trans person, the family law effects and early sex ambiguity.

1 The Legal Framework of Civil Status

The legal framework of civil status is highly complicated and hybrid. Its roots go back to the first half of the twentieth century[1] and necessarily was linked with the laws enacted by the Third Reich after the Anschluss of Austria to the German Reich in 1938. It took a long time to detangle the various sources of law and their contents from policy measures that were regarded after the Austrian Declaration of Independence of 27.04.1945 as unacceptable in a democratic society.

Today Austria is based, as all other countries in continental Europe, on a civil law system. Next to constitutional laws, federal and state laws (*Gesetze*), ordinances (*Verordnungen*),[2] instructions (*Weisungen, Erlässe*),[3] EU primary and secondary law, international treaty law, also customary law and especially case law, developed by the ECtHR, the CJEU and the Austrian Constitutional Court, play an important role. Particularly in the context of civil status, the various forms in which and by whom law is enacted are important as they reflect the democratic law-making process. Administrative authorities can themselves enact administrative law

[1]Austria became part of Nazi Germany in 1938 and ceased to exist. After the Second World War, i.e. in the Second Republic of Austria, the *B-VG* entered into force again (1945). A Constitutional Law was enacted according to which any reactivation of National Socialism was put under severe punishment (*Verfassungsgesetz vom 8. Mai 1945 über das Verbot der NSDAP [Verbotsgesetz]*), StGBl. (*Staatsgesetzblatt*), No. 18/1945, https://www.ris.bka.gv.at/Dokumente/BgblPdf/1945_13_0/1945_13_0.pdf. The State Treaty (*Staatsvertrag betreffend die Wiederherstellung eines unabhängigen und demokratischen Österreich*) with which an independent and democratic Austria was re-established, entered into force on 05.06.1955, BGBl. [Bundesgesetzblatt, FedGaz] No. 152/1955). Further important constitutional laws were enacted, such as the Federal Constitutional Law of 26.10.1955 on Austrian Neutrality (*Bundesverfassungsgesetz vom 26. Oktober 1955 über die Neutralität Österreichs*, BGBl. No. 211/1955), the Federal Constitutional Law of 04.03.1964 (*Bundesverfassungsgesetz vom 4. März 1964, mit dem Bestimmungen des Bundes-Verfassungsgesetzes in der Fassung von 1929 über Staatsverträge abgeändert und ergänzt werden*, BGBl. No. 59/1964, amendments BGBl. No. 168/1968, BGBl. I No. 2/2008) with which certain provisions of the Federal Constitution (version 1929) were amended and the European Convention of Human Rights was retroactively allocated constitutional status. See for a historical overview Stelzer (2014).

[2]Ordinances are general legal acts, i.e. addressed to the community and enacted by administrative authorities. Such authorities can also issue decisions (*Bescheide*) in concrete cases.

[3]An instruction is an internal legal administrative act, it can be issued by an administrative organ and be directed to subordinate organs, or by an administrative authority directed to subordinate authorities or their employees, and specifies the way how to proceed.

(addressed to the authorities) and deliver decisions (binding to the party/parties at stake). Importantly, the change of sex and its requirements are not embodied in a formal legislative act, but in instructions or mere recommendations issued by the executive branch. This implies that local authorities have a certain margin of appreciation and practice regarding the registration of the change of sex that varies from state to state. Access to treatment depends on availability, and health coverage on the qualification as necessary medical or cosmetic treatment.

Several layers of authorities are involved in matters of civil status (i.e., gender, name), its regulation and judicial review. The Federation has powers of legislation and implementation i.e., in civil law affairs (*Zivilrechtswesen*; Art. 10(1)6 B-VG) and in matters pertaining to civil status, including the registration of births, marriages and deaths, and change of name (*Personenstandsangelegenheiten*; Art. 10 (7) B-VG).[4] The authorities responsible for the registration of the civil status of a person are organized on the state level and their administrative decisions are, in the last instance, basically open to legal review by the Austrian Administrative Court and the Austrian Constitutional Court.[5] When it comes to the family law effects (e.g. parenting, child custody, name issues) ordinary courts come into play.

Civil status (*Personenstand*) in the sense of the Act PS 2013 is the status of a person within the legal order. The status recurs to criteria of family law and includes the name of a person (§ 1(1) Act PS 2013).[6] These criteria are of private law nature, whereas the registration and the issuing of official documents regarding birth, name etc are a matter of administrative law. This hybrid nature of civil status exemplifies how the enactment of laws regarding civil status falls into the competence of the legislative bodies of the Federation, whereas the administration of civil status, including the responsibility for the registry is a task of administrative authorities on the municipal level.[7] The competent supervisory authority is the Federal Ministry

[4]The Act on Personal Status (footnote 10), the Act on the change of family names and first names (footnote 11), the Ordinance on Personal Status (footnote 8) as well as the Instructions addressed to the Registry Offices (footnote 9, and the Austrian Civil Code (atCC; footnote 12) exemplify the exercise of this federal power.

[5]The Austrian Constitutional Court (*Verfassungsgerichtshof, VfGH*) decides on violations of constitutional law (especially the Federal Constitutional Law [atFC]), national fundamental rights as entailed i.e., in the BLFR 1867, the ECHR and the EU-Charter. Both the ECHR as well as the EU-Charter have constitutional ranking. See VfGH 14.03.2012, U 466/11; U 1836/11. The Austrian judicial system has two tracks: One is known as the ordinary judicial system (*ordentliche Gerichtsbarkeit*), which decides on civil and criminal matters—starting from the District Courts (*Bezirksgerichte*) to the Regional Courts (*Landesgerichte*) and the Courts of Appeal (*Oberlandesgerichte*) up to the Supreme Court of Justice; the second track are the courts of public law: The Federal Administrative Court (*Bundesverwaltungsgericht*), the nine State Administrative Courts (*Landesverwaltungsgerichte*), and the Federal Finance Court (*Bundesfinanzgericht*) up to the Austrian Administrative Court (*Verwaltungsgerichtshof*) and the Austrian Constitutional Court (*Verfassungsgerichtshof*).

[6]Birth, marriage, registered partnership and death (§ 1(2) Act PS 2013), as well as change of sex or name, are legally relevant situations which touch upon civil status.

[7]The Central Computerized Civil Register (CCCR; *Zentrales Personenstandsregister, ZPR*), is managed by municipality and municipal associations (*Gemeinde & Gemeindeverbände*), as registry

of the Interior. The head of the Ministry enacts all relevant internal instructions, such as the Ordinance on Personal Status (OPS 2013[8]) as well as the Instructions addressed to the Registry Offices (IRO 2019[9]). The motivations and arguments underlying such instructions are hardly accessible to the public.

The Federation enacts the legal provisions, both substantive and procedural, which touch upon the civil status, such as the Act on Personal Status (Act PS 2013[10]) and the Act on the change of family names and first, i.e., given names (Act CN[11]). Substantive law provisions relevant to the civil status are embodied in civil law. According to the Austrian Civil Code (atCC[12]), every person has the right to a name (§ 16 atCC) that enjoys particular protection (§ 43 atCC). This right is regarded as a general right to protection of personality (*allgemeines Persönlichkeitsrecht*). The protection is granted with regard to the family name from birth on (§ 155 atCC) and with regard to the given name as soon as it was chosen or assigned (§ 13 Act PS 2013).[13] Some important substantive law provisions regarding the name of persons and marriage for example, are dealt with i.e., in the atCC, the Marriage Law (atML[14]) including its 1. Ordinance on the Implementation of the Marriage Law (1. OML,[15] ranked as a law[16]).

The procedure regarding matters of civil status is basically administrative by nature, e.g. the change of name on the administrative track is regulated in the Act

---

offices or, as the case may be, by the competent Austrian representative authorities (*österreichische Vertretungsbehörden*).

[8]*Verordnung der Bundesministerin für Inneres über die Durchführung des Personenstandsgesetzes 2013 (Personenstandsgesetz-Durchführungsverordnung 2013—PStG-DV 2013)*, BGBl. II No. 324/2013, recent amendment BGBl. II No. 59/2019.

[9]*Durchführungsanleitung für die standesamtliche Arbeit (DA)*, April 2019, BMI-VA1300/0112-III/3/b/2019, amending BMI-VA1300/0018-III/4/b/2018, followed by the Instruction (*DA*), November 2019, BMI-VA1300/0415/III/3/b/2019, supplemented by the information with regard to the entry of sex, Reference No. 2020-0571.947.

[10]*Bundesgesetz über die Regelung des Personenstandswesens (Personenstandsgesetz 2013—PStG 2013)*, BGBl. I No. 16/2013, recent amendment BGBl. I No. 104/2018.

[11]*Bundesgesetz vom 22. März 1988 über die Änderung von Familiennamen und Vornamen (Namensänderungsgesetz—NÄG)*, BGBl. No. 195/1988, recent amendment BGBl. I No. 105/2019.

[12]*Allgemeines bürgerliches Gesetzbuch für die gesammten deutschen Erbländer der Oesterreichischen Monarchie (ABGB)*, JGS (*Justizgesetzsammlung* from 1780-1848) No. 946/1811, recent amendment BGBl. I No. 148/2020.

[13]The procedure to follow is regulated in the Act CN. See in particular § 2(1)(8-9) Act CN.

[14]*Gesetz zur Vereinheitlichung des Rechts der Eheschließung und der Ehescheidung im Lande Österreich und im übrigen Reichsgebiet. Vom 6. Juli 1938*, dRGBl. (German Reichsgesetzblatt) I S 807/1938, recent amendment BGBl. I No. 59/2017.

[15]*Verordnung zur Durchführung und Ergänzung des Gesetzes zur Vereinheitlichung des Rechts der Eheschließung und der Ehescheidung im Lande Österreich und im übrigen Reichsgebiet (Ehegesetz). Vom 27. Juli 1938*, dRGBl. I S 923/1938 (*1. DVOEheG*), last amendment BGBl. No. 566/1983.

[16]According to § 2 *Rechts-Überleitungsgesetz (R-ÜG)*, StGBl. No. 6/1945 (as amended by BGBl. I No. 100/2003). The R-ÜG is a constitutional law from May 1, 1945 on the restoration of law and order in Austria.

CN, and matters of civil status are dealt with in legal sources that are both addressed to the persons and the authorities (e.g. Act PS 2013).

2 Sex As a Category of Law

Sex is also a crucial aspect of the civil status of a person. The law does not define, however, under which conditions a person is considered as male or female, nor is there any law in the strict sense of the word that deals with trans persons or with a person opting for the third sex. Administrative practice and judicial review, therefore, determine how to proceed when it comes to sex as part of the status of a person. Nonetheless, for the purpose of employment, military service, education, pension, access to health services, and family law issues, e.g., adoption or recognition of paternity, the registered sex is decisive.

The sex of a person is determined by the physician or the midwife as the medical experts. The civil registrar who registers the birth of a child (§ 11 Act PS 2013) has no right to question the sex[17] and is, therefore, bound to register what was determined by the medical staff at the time of birth.

Amendments at a later stage, e.g., in case of change of sex, are covered by § 41 Act PS 2013. Any amendment of the registry must refer to legal consequences of the amendment for the civil status and must, if necessary, specify the date of effect of such consequences (§ 11(3) Act PS 2013). In practice, the change of sex in the registry requires the evidence of measures, by which the change of sex was achieved (for details of the process see Sec. 4).

Up until very recently, neither Austrian law nor Austrian practice provided for a gender-neutral or "third sex". It seemed to be entirely uncontested that the law be based on a binary sex system, i.e., male/female. The Austrian Administrative Court[18] as well as the Austrian Constitutional Court[19] held that the Austrian legal system and also society do not doubt that a person is either male or female, i.e. *tertium non datur*. Further, according to the previous Instructions addressed to the Registry Offices (IRO 2018),[20] the persons involved in the birth announcement (*Anzeige der Geburt*) and in the authentification of birth (*Beurkundung der Geburt*) had basically two options: male / female. However, the Austrian Constitutional Court decided on 15.06.2018 that based on Art. 8 ECHR, the term "sex" (*Geschlecht*) as mentioned

[17]Kutscher and Wilpert (2018).

[18]In its judgment of 30.09.1997, 95/01/0061, the VwGH held that a person can only be of male or female sex, referring to the judgment of the ECtHR, 17.10.1986, no. 9532/81—*Rees/UK* and to Art. 12 ECHR.

[19]VfGH 03.12.2009, B 1973/08.

[20]See footnote 9; for the text see Kutscher and Wilpert (2018); for the current legal situation see Sec.7.

in § 2(2)(3) Act PS 2013 is not confined to male or female, but can be understood and must be interpreted to include alternative gender identities.[21]

Despite the introduction of the "third sex" based on decisions delivered by the Austrian Constitutional Court[22] and the Austrian Administrative Court,[23] even fundamental parts of the Austrian legal system still adhere to the principle that a person is either male or female.[24] A considerable range of laws distinguishes between the two sexes (male / female). The issue extends further to large parts of the legal system: In addition to marriage, parentage and child custody, the social security system is founded on the binary model and distinguishes between the female and male persons in order to protect their interests. The FedLET[25] prohibits gender-based discrimination of women in the field of employment. Differences in treatment in order to protect women (e.g. maternity protection) or to promote equal treatment with men, different pension age for men and women to name just as an example, are measures regarded as necessary. Military service, a duty limited to men, is uncontested in Austria. Therefore, areas such as labor law, military service, general public health and security ought to be adapted. In short, it would certainly not suffice to introduce a specific prohibition of discrimination against persons for reasons of their gender-neutral or third sex.

How the decisions should be implemented and to what extent the legislation must be changed, is a controversial question.[26] Given the current legal basis or rather lack

---

[21] VfGH 15.06.2018 G 77/2018. The Austrian Constitutional Court referred to the Bioethik Kommission (see footnote 58), which suggested that a third option ought to be envisaged, be it as a third sex ("inter", "diverse") or as an unspecified alternative to the binary model male/female ("open", i.e. to be specified or "X"). The Austrian Constitutional Court decided on the occasion of a decision made by the State Administrative Court for Upper Austria (Landesverwaltungsgericht Oberösterreich; LVwG OÖ), which dismissed a request made by a person to have the entry of his sex in the civil registry changed from "male" to "inter", in eventu to "different", in eventu to "X", in eventu to "indeterminate", in eventu to a similar term, in eventu to delete the registration of the male sex. The petitioner issued a remedy to both the Austrian Administrative Court and the Austrian Constitutional Court, which proved to be successful. According to the recent supplement of the *DA* (November 2019), see footnote 9, each individual concerned can now request the entry "diverse", "inter", "open" or the deletion of any gender specification, yet a correction of the entry "male" or "female" into "diverse", "inter", "open" or the deletion of such entry requires an expert opinion.

[22] VfGH 15.06.2018 G 77/2018, see footnote 21.

[23] VwGH 14.12.2018, Ro 2018/01/0015.

[24] See e.g. Art. 7(3) atFC ("equality of men and women"), Art. 26(1) ("suffrage by men and women", same Art. 23a, 60 atFC, Art. 95 atFC ("suffrage [. . .] by the male and female provincial citizens"), Art. 12 ECHR ("Men and women of marriageable age have the right to marry and to found a family").

[25] The Framework Equality Directive 2000 was implemented in Austria by the Federal Law on Equal Treatment (FedLET, *Gleichbehandlungsgesetz, GlBG*; BGBl I No. 66/2004, latest amendment BGBl. I No. 16/2020). This law also does not contain any specific provision regarding transgender persons, but generally prohibits gender-based discrimination (§§ 1 FedLET et seq.). In light of Austria's obligations under international treaty law and EU law, the protection of this law can arguably be extended to transgender persons as well.

[26] Dengg and Schranz (2018), (277).

of legislative activity, it is up to the courts and the administrative authorities to interpret the law according to the principles laid down in the Austrian Constitutional Court's decision of 15.06.2018.[27] Based on this decision, the Ministry of the Interior issued new Instructions.[28] Any change as fundamental as the introduction of a third option necessarily requires, however, a fundamental change of the legal foundations of the State, its laws and of legal thinking. It seems wise to opt for a legislative reform which needs to pass parliament, instead of entrusting this demanding task to administrative stakeholders, given that legal security and uniform implementation of rules as opposed to divergent practices between administrative authorities of the states are in the best interest of the persons concerned. Furthermore, the distinction between male and female is also drawn in the Constitution itself, necessitating amendments by legislation.

However, no such legislation has yet been passed. One can, at this stage, only assume why: Apart from the current political situation,[29] the introduction of a gender-neutral or third-sex is certainly not a widespread issue of general discussion. Political interest of the general public is lacking. The lobby groups deal with the issue, and so do specialists, who have discussed i.e., the judgment delivered by the German Federal Court of Justice (*Bundesgerichtshof, BGH*) of 10.10.2017 by which the "third sex" was recognized.[30]

The Instruction of 20.12.2018[31] lays down rules on the procedure to be followed for the change of sex and regarding sex ambiguity. It[32] distinguishes the change of

[27]VfGH 15.06.2018 G 77/2018. See footnote 21, and i.e., Dengg and Schranz (2018), p. 272, also VwGH 14.12.2018, Ro 2018/01/0015.

[28]BMI-VA1300/0528-III/4/b/2018 with the heading "*Verwaltungsangelegenheiten—Sonstige; Personenstandswesen. Erkenntnis des VfGH vom 15. Juni 2018, G 77/2017-9, zu § 2 Abs. 2 Z 3 PStG 2013—Umsetzung zu Varianten der Geschlechtsentwicklung ("3. Geschlecht")*; BMI-VA1300/0145/III/3/b/2019, followed by a supplement in 2020, see footnote 9.

[29]An Interim Government was appointed in May 2019 which remained in office until the new government was appointed in January 2020.

[30]APA, Deutschland erlaubt das dritte Geschlecht "divers", in Die Presse 14.12.2018, online: https://diepresse.com/home/ausland/welt/5546206/Deutschland-erlaubt-das-dritte-Geschlecht-divers. Accessed 1 Mar 2021; BGH 10.10.2017, 1 BvR 2019/16. The "*Verein intergeschlechtlicher Menschen Österreich*" strongly criticized the implementation of the judgment of the Austrian Constitutional Court by the federal administration, whereas the joint press release from VIMÖ, Plattform Intersex Österreich and HOSI Salzburg had welcomed the judgment, see Haller, Sieg für Alex Jürgen*: Intersex-Aktivist erkämpft dritte Option, 29.06.2018, online: http://www.hosi.or.at/2018/06/29/sieg-fuer-alex-juergen. Accesses 1 Mar 2021. Critical voices deplore that the required medical expertise cannot be drawn up by a doctor of one's own choice, but must be issued by an external VdG-Board and therefore produces a deterrent effect. For this very reason, the City Counsellor in charge with issues of anti-discrimination J. Czernohorszky (Social Democrat) of the City of Vienna and M. Lindner (MP Social Democrat), spokesman for equal treatment, diversity and LGBTI, demanded a review of the implementation and wish to include persons concerned in such process. See APA, "Drittes Geschlecht": SPÖ über Innenministerium "empört", in Die Presse 27.12.2018, online: https://diepresse.com/home/innenpolitik/5552066/Drittes-Geschlecht_SPOe-ueber-Innenministerium-empoert. Accessed 1 Mar 2021.

[31]See footnote 28.

[32]BMI VA1300/0528 III/4/b/2018.

the registration of sex under § 41 Act PS 2013 from the registration of sex on the occasion of birth. In the former case, the sex shall, upon request and on the basis of a reasoned medical report drawn up by a VdG-Board, be changed to "diverse" (*divers*); in the latter case the sex remains "open", i.e. incomplete until the sex can be identified.[33]

For persons with a variant of sex development, i.e. a gender identity disorder (*Variante der Geschlechtsentwicklung (VdG)*), the sex as registered in the CCCR and mentioned on certificates regarding civil status can be changed into "inter", "diverse" or "open" or can remain unanswered, and, as the case may be, re-changed into male/female according to § 41(1) Act PS 2013. Yet, the need for an expert opinion for all non-binary options[34] does not sufficiently take into account the decision of the Constitutional Court because no real weight is attached to the right of self-determination. It is up to the VdG-Boards to draw up a reasoned report. VdG-Boards are interdisciplinary and multi-professional medical expert groups, set up by the Ministry of Health. Persons concerned cannot consult a specialist whom they trust, but are confined to contact a VdG-Board. Such Boards are not established all over Austria,[35] which implies that persons concerned may face travel and cost contingencies in addition to the fact that they may find it difficult to consult specialists they do not know.[36]

3 Legally Changing Sex and the Obstacles Encountered

Austria has up until today not enacted any specific law regarding the change of sex. The Instruction of the Ministry of the Interior of 27.11.1996 on Transsexuals[37] referred to the lack of consensus between the various Austrian Ministries, the Constitutional Service of the Federal Chancellor's Office and medical experts on

[33]See Hübsch, Deutscher Bundestag verabschiedet Gesetz für drittes Geschlecht, ÖStA 2019, 59 et seq; for details see also Sec. 7.

[34]See Instruction 2019 and its supplement (footnote 9).

[35]See the roadmap from the Ministry of Health, https://www.sozialministerium.at/Themen/Gesundheit/Nicht-uebertragbare-Krankheiten/Sexuelle-Gesundheit.html, at Empfehlungen zu Varianten der Geschlechtsentwicklung.pdf, VdG-Boards, 58 ff and 78. Accessed 1 Mar 2021.

[36]Cf. i.e., Humer, Dritter Geschlechtseintrag in Dokumenten: Gutachtenzwang statt Selbstbestimmung, 27.12.2018, online: https://www.ots.at/presseaussendung/OTS_20181227_OTS0029/dritter-geschlechtseintrag-in-dokumenten-gutachtenzwang-statt-selbstbestimmung. Accessed 1 Mar 2021; APA, "Drittes Geschlecht": SPÖ über Innenministerium "empört", in Die Presse 27.12.2018, online: https://diepresse.com/home/innenpolitik/5552066/Drittes-Geschlecht_SPOe-ueber-Innenministerium-empoert. Accessed 1 Mar 2021.

[37]The Austrian Constitutional Court annulled certain provisions of the Instruction of the Ministry of the Interior of 27.11.1996 on Transsexuals (36.250/66-IV/4/96), because they did not meet the requirements of a statutory instrument (ordinance), see VwGH 27.02.2009, 2008/17/0054 and VfGH 08.06.2006, V 4/06.

the medical aspects of transsexualism. All Ministries involved agreed that at least a solution ought to be offered to those persons who had undergone a gender confirming surgery with the goal to achieve at least an outward appearance of the opposite sex. They further agreed that for the time being a legislative initiative seemed inappropriate in view of the various solutions found in foreign legal systems and the obviously low number of persons concerned.[38]

As already indicated, the legislator has been quite reluctant to introduce laws regarding sex changes, leaving the adaption of the law to judgments by the Higher Courts to the executive branch. It seems that the Vienna Anti-Discrimination Office for same-sex and transgender lifestyles (VADO; *Wiener Antidiskriminierungsstelle für gleichgeschlechtliche und transgender Lebensweise, WASt*), who is in close contact with various lobby groups, approves of this situation, because informal, i.e., not legally binding rules are, of course, more flexible to handle and offer more possibilities to change the policy, if necessary. It goes without saying that the elaboration of a law and any amendments thereof must pass parliament and the outcome may produce undesired results due to the political influence which accompanies each elaboration of a law.

Depending on the Federal State at stake, the Federal State/city/municipality provide for platforms to deal with discrimination of same-sex and transgender lifestyles. In Vienna, the VADO serves as interface between the LGBT-community, politicians, and administrative authorities[39] and offers counselling, support, and education, takes awareness-raising actions, organizes conferences, is engaged in national and international networks and cooperates closely with the relevant Ministries. The Austrian-Bavarian Association for Transidentity and Intersexuality (*Österreichisch-bayrische Gesellschaft für Transidentität und Intersexualität*), to name one example, serves as an important contact point where persons concerned can ask for advice using the hotline of the association.[40] Numerous blogs of lobby groups, associations and individuals have been posted in which transsexualism, gender identity, the transformation process and the real life experience are described, showing how society and commerce react to the growing awareness towards transsexualism, and how big the diversity within the groups and among the various associations is.[41] These are very different, but policy-wise important contributions, because they make apparent what could or should not be considered by politicians and the legislator. A range of associations, working groups and platforms in Austria[42] are also important forums, which can—in the long run—influence the way how transsexuality is perceived and should be dealt with.

---

[38]The Instruction on Transsexuals of 1996 stated that this assessment, originally dating from the early 80ies, is still accurate, see VfGH V 4/06.

[39]See WASt (ed.), Trans*Identitäten (broschure, 2013).

[40]See http://www.trans-austria.org/trans-austria.

[41]http://www.schweigsamer.at/; http://www.thinkoutsideyourbox.net; http://community.transgender.at/.

[42]E.g. http://www.hosiwien.at/links/; http://www.verein-ausgesprochen.at/; http://dievilla.at/; http://www.queerconnexion.at/; http://www.regenbogenfamilien.at/infos/regenbogenfamilien-2/; http://www.transx.at/; http://transmann-austria.at/; http://www.trans-austria.org/trans-austria/;

The media has published articles on the current well-being of transsexual persons, in which a widespread transphobic attitude is described, causing distress to the persons concerned.[43] Despite differences, the histories of same-sex marriage and the legal position of trans persons share many similarities, the former's evolution is further linked with trans persons in so far as always the role of sex and its attributions male/female have been one of the core issues. It was only in the 1990s that the issue of sexual orientation of homosexual persons slowly emerged in Austrian (political) discussions, the legislator seemed more than hesitant to move quickly.[44] Again the Austrian Constitutional Court acted step by step to remove discriminatory provisions relating to gender-biased legal rules and thus urged the legislator to amend the legislation accordingly. In lieu of legislative implementation, the Ministry of the Interior released instructions addressed to administrative authorities.[45]

The development of the legal recognition of the same sex-status reveals a spirit which is quite distant, if not even hostile, to any divergence from a traditional binary model. Whether this also applies to transsexuals is hard to say. Possibly, family members of trans persons who have never dealt with the condition may feel uncomfortable when faced with the situation, but also trained personnel, such as medical doctors, therapists and social workers who during their career were not trained accordingly[46] may find it difficult to become accustomed to new developments. Aggravating is the fact that many fail to distinguish between transsexual persons on the one hand and homosexual persons on the other. These are two very different categories of persons with different needs and accordingly different legal provisions apply to them. The comparison drawn in the manuscript is explicitly limited to the deep-rooted traditional binary model and similarities in the history of their legal progress.

---

http://tabera.at/; http://www.queeramnesty.at/; http://transgender.at/index.html; http://ilga.org/; http://www.plattform-intersex.at/; https://queeriosity.at/.

[43]See Der Standard, 10.05.2017: Tragler, Was Transsexualität mit psychischer Gesundheit zu tun hat.

[44]It was only in 2010 that the Law on Registered Partnerships (*Eingetragene Partnerschaft-Gesetz*) was enacted, which was followed by decisions from Austrian supreme courts, i.e., the Austrian Constitutional Court declaring specific provisions as unconstitutional. On 04.12.2017, the Austrian Constitutional Court decided that the marriage must be accessible to same-sex persons and registered partnership to persons of different sex, see VfGH G 258/2017 e.a.

[45]As well as including an Instruction containing restrictions for international same-sex couples, whose domestic law does not provide for a same-sex marriage and who wish to get married in Austria. In such case, the request would have to be rejected. The Instruction might have violated the prohibition of discrimination, but the issue has been solved early July 2019 by the legislator who enacted an amendment (BGBl I No. 72/2019) of the Austrian Private International Law Act, (§ 17 (1a)) thereby avoiding such discrimination.

[46]Information provided by Mag. Wilhelm, VADO (WASt) on 08.08.2019.

Currently, adjustments to the third sex, more specifically i.e., the access to toilets is a controversial issue.[47] Some worry that the insistence on the binary system might lead to a never-ending hurdle-race and might encourage violence against intersex persons. At the basis of this debate was a school in Bavaria (Germany), which provides for toilets for persons belonging to the third sex. I.e., in Lower-Austria, some companies are in the process of installing adequate facilities for intersex persons.[48]

As demonstrated above, the legal status of trans persons and the procedure to change their registered sex is shaped by administrative practice and judicial review. The historical development is essential to understand the legal standing of trans persons, which is why it will be summarized briefly: According to the 1996—Instruction, a transsexual, post-surgery person could request the change of the data pursuant to § 16 Act PS 1984[49] in force at the time of the Instruction and obtain a margin note on the sex change. The authorities, however, first sought scientific advice on the successful change of sex and sometimes refused the change of data. Only the given name of a person could be changed without such surgery. The Austrian Administrative Court, taking into account the case law[50] of the ECtHR as well as the case law of the CJEU, did at the time still require a surgery through which the primary genital organs were to be removed, but held that a transsexual person after the change of sex has the right to marry. The question, whether a married person can have his changed sex registered, was affirmed by the Austrian Constitutional Court in 2006.[51]

In view of this background, the main question to be solved by the Austrian Administrative Court on 27.02.2009 was whether a surgery removing the primary genital organs was a mandatory condition for the registration of the change of sex. The facts were as follows: A male to female transsexual requested a change of sex in the official registry. She claimed to have reached a clear outward appearance of the other sex and underlined that her feeling of belonging to that sex would with high probability not change anymore. However, surgery would cause a long-term sick leave which would most probably lead to the termination of her contract as a leading manager in an international group company and thus seemed unreasonable. The

[47]APA, Drittes Geschlecht erobert Österreichs Uni-Alltag, in Der Standard 04.06.2018, online: https://derstandard.at/2000080913648/Drittes-Geschlecht-erobert-Oesterreichs-Uni-Alltag. Accessed 1 Mar 2021

[48]See Streimelweger, Erstes WC für das dritte Geschlecht, 21.08.2018, online: https://www.noen.at/melk/melk-erstes-wc-fuer-das-dritte-geschlecht-intersexualitaet-astrid-niedermayer-kathrin-piegler-110824760. Accessed 1 Mar 2021.

[49]See meanwhile § 41(1) Act PS 2013.

[50]VwGH 30.9.1997, 95/01/0061; ECtHR 17.10.1986, no. 9532/81—*Rees / UK*; ECtHR 27.09.1990, no. 10843/84—*Cossey / UK;* ECtHR 25.03.1992, no. 13343/87 – *B. / France*: Violation of Art. 8 concerning recognition of transsexuals; CJEU 30.04.1996, C-13/94, *P. / S. and Cornwall County Council*, confirming discrimination due to unequal access to employment and working conditions of a transsexual.

[51]VfGH 08.06.2006, V 4/06.

authorities dismissed the request. The Austrian Administrative Court referred to its judgment of 30.09.1997 in which it had already pointed to a psychological component (feeling of belonging to the other sex) and came to the conclusion that if such a feeling most probably and largely remains irreversible and provided such feeling is expressed by an outward appearance of the opposite sex, the Austrian legal system does not impede the registration of change of sex in the official register.[52] Since then, sex re-assignment surgery is no longer required for a legal change of sex. The expert opinion confirming that the person has reached "a clear outward appearance of the opposite sex and forecast that the feeling of belonging to that sex will with high probability not change anymore" suffices to have the sex (and name) changed in the official registry. Therefore, Austrian law has been in accordance with more recent case law of the ECtHR, notably *A.P., Garçon and Nicot / France*[53] for nearly a decade, in that the undergoing of an operation (in casu: compulsory sterilization) is no condition for the recognition of sexual identity and for the change of the name.

4 The Legal Procedure Regarding Change of Sex

It is nowadays uncontested that changes of the civil status by change of sex no longer require surgery in which primary genital organs are removed.[54] The change of the formal registration of sex on the occasion of birth is possible in accordance with § 41 Act PS 2013, i.e., following an investigative procedure (e.g. by procurement of an expert opinion), during which the chosen name can already be changed in a gender-neutral first name. The rule provides that the registry office (*Personenstandsbehörde*) must change the registration if it has become incorrect. This applies to names and to the sex. The authority is deemed to issue a copy of the CCCR on request of the person at stake. Once the change of sex is registered, the given name can be changed, a new birth certificate is delivered without mentioning the change of sex. Based on this new birth certificate a series of other certificates and documents can be applied for and must be provided (e.g. police registration form, citizen certificate, passport, driving license).

According to the IRO 2019, the requirements for the change of sex can usually only be confirmed by a reasoned expert opinion.[55] The Instruction refers in this context to the decision of the Austrian Administrative Court of 27.02.2009.[56] Neither the decision nor the IRO 2019 specify who exactly is supposed to qualify

---

[52] VwGH 27.02.2009, 2008/17/0054.

[53] ECtHR 06.04.2017, no. 79885/12, *A.P., Garçon and Nicot/France*.

[54] See VwGH 27.02.2009, 2008/17/0054.

[55] The text of the IRO 2019 reads: "Dies kann in aller Regel nur durch die Einholung eines Sachverständigengutachtens ausreichend geklärt werden".

[56] VwGH 27.02.2009, 2008/17/0054. The decision itself does not specify who exactly is supposed to write such an expert opinion.

for the elaboration of such an expert opinion, but it must clearly be an experienced expert. The findings of a psychiatrist, a psychotherapist[57] or a clinical psychologist, which states that the person has reached a clear outward appearance of the opposite sex, and that the feeling of belonging to that sex will with high probability not change anymore, suffice. The Austrian Bioethics Commission has published a comprehensive report on intersex and transidentity in 2017, in which all requirements are explained in depth.[58] In Vienna, legally not only a municipality, a city, but also a Federal State, the Municipal Department charged with Matters of Trade Law, Data Protection and Civil Status (*Magistratsabteilung 63*) sets up requirements for persons born in Vienna in accordance with the suggestions of the Commission and in accordance with the Recommendations issued by the Ministry of Health:[59]

- the declaration that the person has the feeling to belong to the other sex and that this feeling is probably irreversible, and
- the declaration that the person has the outward appearance of the opposite sex.

The diagnosis "transsexualism" is no longer required since the autumn 2020. However, as the jurisdiction of administrative authorities is divided between the Federation (*Bund*), i.e. the relevant Ministry of the Interior and the Ministry of Health, and the Federal States (*Länder*), i.e., the competent organs to issue instructions applicable on their territory, the registry offices of the States may apply different standards according to which the case law, in particular the case law of the Austrian Administrative Court and of the Austrian Constitutional Court on sex re-assignment, is transformed in detail. Registry offices decide on applications to change the civil status, i.e. change of the sex. Depending on how they transform the leading decision of the Austrian Administrative Court of 2009, practice may vary from State to State. The State Government of Vorarlberg for example has instructed the municipal authorities to temporarily reject a change of sex based on a

[57]Kutscher and Wilpert (2018): the authors explicitly state that a report on a surgery (if at all), a medical report or a psychotherapeutic report substantiating that a clear outward appearance of the opposite sex is reached and forecasting that the feeling of belonging to that sex will with high probability not change anymore, suffices. From different psychotherapeutic angels see e.g. Silbermayr (2018), pp. 482–492; Günther (2015), pp. 113–124; Kunert (2013), pp. 34–46.

[58]Bioethik Kommission, Intersexualität und Transidentität. Stellungnahme der Bioethikkommission: access via https://www.bundeskanzleramt.gv.at/themen/bioethikkommission/publikationen-bioethik.html. Accessed 1 Mar 2021.

[59]*Empfehlungen für den Behandlungsprozess bei Geschlechtsdysphorie bzw. Transsexualismus nach der Klassifikation in der derzeit gültigen DSM bzw. ICD-Fassung*, released on 20.06.2017, replacing the previous Recommendations from 1997, see https://www.sozialministerium.at/Themen/Gesundheit/Nicht-uebertragbare-Krankheiten/Psychische-Gesundheit/Transsexualismus-Geschlechtsdysphorie.html. See also https://www.oesterreich.gv.at/themen/dokumente-und recht/Aenderung-der-Geschlechtszugehoerigkeit.html. . Accessed 1 Mar 2021.

psychotherapist's reasoned statement, claiming it does not meet the criteria of a "specialist medical report".[60]

The law does not limit the number of times the sex can be changed. One would assume that without the necessity of genital surgery persons might be inclined to change their sex more than once. This is not the case. How many "regretters" practice deals with is unknown. Possibly, in out of 10 cases less than one person regrets the sex re-assignment.[61] Accurate statistical data are, however, not available. But as has been described already above, the entire treatment may not only take a long time, medical specialists who treat the patient and accompany him/her for a considerable period of time are to my mind extremely cautious before giving a favorable opinion. Liability on the one hand as well as the reputation on the other are influential factors regards the standards applied by them. None of them is interested in a newspaper heading reporting that the medical doctor, the clinical psychologist and/or the psychotherapist came to an erroneous opinion. If, therefore, they face a "regretter" all experts will be extremely reluctant to take such a situation lightly. The legal procedure for a re-change is the same as the original procedure, provided no genital surgery was performed which is, of course, irreversible. Yet, even in this case a re-change ought to be legally permitted, if the current requirements are met.

5 Medical Perspectives: Access to Treatment and Health Coverage

The Austrian Bioethics Commission distinguishes in its report between "intersex"[62] and transgender.[63] From a medical point of view, *intersex* resp. "disorders of sex development" (DSD) is proposed, as defined by congenital conditions in which development of chromosomal, gonadal, or anatomical sex is atypical. The term transgender refers to persons who can be assigned to a specific gender, but they do not identify with that gender. Hence, their gender identity does not coincide with their biological sex. While these terms cannot be found in statutory law, case law and administrative law reflect the terminology.

[60]Förtsch, Im Auftrag diskriminiert? 14.04.2019, online: https://www.vol.at/im-auftrag-diskriminiert/6168726. Accessed 1 Mar 2021. However, already the „Letter Transsexuality" 2007 BMI-VA 1300/0013-III/2/2007 issued as an Instruction by the Ministry of the Interior considers a psychotherapist competent to provide an expert opinion for a change of sex.

[61]Practice refers to "regretters", when a person regrets the sex re-assignment. Statistical data are not gathered, therefore the estimation remains a random one. In addition, regretters will hardly consult the same psychotherapist, if they really opt for a re-change of their sex (information provided by Mag. Wilhelm, VADO [WASt] on 08.08.2019).

[62]Austrian Bioethics Commission (footnote 58), 11.

[63]Ibidem (footnote 58), 15.

The Federal Ministry of Health and Women's Affairs[64] released its Recommendations for the treatment and care process regarding persons suffering from gender dysphoria, i.e. transsexualism according to the classification of the current DSM / ICD-edition,[65] reflecting by and large the Standards of Care for the Health of Transsexual, Transgender, and Gender Nonconforming People,[66] and the Diagnostic and Statistical Manual of Mental Disorder, Version 5 (DSM-5).[67] The Recommendations were elaborated by a multi-professional, interdisciplinary expert group in co-operation with representatives of the Ministry of the Interior in charge of matters of civil status, and deal with the treatment and care process for persons who reached the age of majority and suffer from transsexualism, i.e., gender dysphoria. The Recommendations are also expressly directed to the authorities in charge of the civil status register and highlight § 41 Act PS 2013, according to which registrations shall be amended, if they have become incorrect, recommending criteria that reflect the decision of the Austrian Administrative Court of 27.09.2009:[68] The change of sex does not require sex surgeries, but a statement from either a medical expert, a clinical psychologist or a psychotherapist on the diagnosis of the medical condition, the prognosis regarding the sustainability of the condition and the declaration regarding the outward appearance. It is important to mention that the Ministry of Health has no competences in matters of civil status; its recommendations are legally not binding. Recommendations as the one at stake used to be published after deliberations in the Austrian Health Council (atHC, *Oberster Sanitätsrat, OSR*).[69]

The Council as well as the Ministry deal with the health of persons and follow international guidelines for determining diseases and disorders. Hence, the focus is quite different from the one of other official bodies. Yet, some lobby groups have

---

[64]*Ministerium für Frauen und Gesundheit*, meanwhile the Federal Ministry of Social Affairs, Health and Consumer Protection (*Bundesministerium Soziales, Gesundheit und Konsumentenschutz*), i.e., the Ministry of Health.

[65]See footnote 59.

[66]Elaborated by the World Professional Association for Transgender Health (WPATH), 7th Version, Atlanta/USA (2011).

[67]Of the American Psychiatric Association, May 2013. See pp. 1-2 of the Recommendations (*Empfehlungen*).

[68]VwGH 27.02.2009, 2008/17/0054.

[69]The Austrian Health Council (atHC) is an independent consultative committee of the (former) Ministry of Health and Women, introduced on the basis of § 8 Law on Federal Ministries, regarding matters that fall within the competence of the Federal Minister (*Bundesgesetz über die Zahl, den Wirkungsbereich und die Einrichtung der Bundesministerien (Bundesministeriengesetz 1986—BMG)*, BGBl. No. 76/1986 as most recently amended by BGBl I No. 61/2018. The atHC is composed of voluntary members, in particular experts in the fields of medicine, psychology, care, science, the Austrian Medical Chamber, the Austrian Chamber of Pharmacists, social security and public health services. The atHC consults the Minister, gives non-binding opinions on question of fundamental nature in the context of "current state of medical science", delivers expert opinions and recommendations. No online information is available anymore. The atHC has not been staffed since the new government took office in January 2020.

strongly criticized the pathologisation of transsexuals and thus the recommendations drawn up by the Ministry of Health,[70] similar to how some groups would like to have the classification by the ICD-10 (version 2016)—"Mental and behavioural disorder", more specifically F.64 "Gender identity disorder", removed from the list, in order to reach a de-pathologisation and to avoid the stigma. Although the goals are well-intended and reasonable, one should in any case make sure that the patients are medically and therapeutically well-supported, when they envisage, go through and reached sex re-assignment. It seems hard to imagine how this can be realized without the appropriate therapies.[71] Although it may well be that an agreement is reached on the ICD-11 to declassify transgender identity as a mental disorder in its global list of medical conditions or to rename it as "gender incongruence", the need for support of persons concerned continues to exist. Surely the missing conformity of outer appearance and documents, especially during the "real life experience" is a burden that should not be underestimated. Some persons also experience the legal requirements for sex re-assignment as a real harassment or an enormous burden to say the least.[72] Others criticize that transgender persons are considered as mentally ill and strive at avoiding such pathologisation.[73] Voices of trans persons describe their sadness and loneliness,[74] the transformation process,[75] or discrimination at school.[76] Reports differ, however, significantly. A female to male transsexual person reports

---

[70]See footnote 59.

[71]See recently Dengg and Schranz (2018), p. 272 (277).

[72]Schlosser, Transidentität: Der lange Weg zum richtigen Körper, in Medical Tribune 17.05.2017, online: https://medonline.at/2017/transidentitaet-der-lange-weg-zum-richtigen-koerper/. Accessed 1 Mar 2021.

[73]Wiener Verein Trans X, österreichische Vereinigung Trans X. See also Berger-Kolb/Sekerovic, TLP: Transsexualität ist keine Krankheit, 30.01.2017, online: https://www.meinbezirk.at/innsbruck/c-gesundheit/tlp-transsexualitaet-ist-keine-krankheit_a2007314. Accessed 1 Mar 2021. See also Kaiser, Über das Pathologisieren von Transsexuellen, in Der Standard 30.10.2011, online: http://derstandard.at/1319181481300/Weltgesundheitsorganisation-Ueber-das-Pathologisieren-von-Transsexuellen. Accessed 1 Mar 2021.

[74]E.g. Treichler, Transsexualität: Die Geschichte von Gaby und Gabriel, in Profil 11.01.2017, online: https://www.profil.at/gesellschaft/transsexualitaet-geschichte-gaby-gabriel-7933875. Accessed 1 Mar 2021.

[75]Schweiger, Herbst, Ein Transmann beantwortet alle Fragen, die ihr euch vielleicht nie gestellt habt, in VICE 28.02.2016, online: https://www.vice.com/de_at/article/9bm7dp/fragen-an-einen-transmann-192. Accessed 1 Mar 2021.

[76]Stanic, "Wie eine Allergie". Aus Henrik* wurde Hannah*: Warum eine Direktorin ein Transgender-Kind nicht an ihrer Schule haben wollte, online: http://www.dasbiber.at/content/wie-eine-allergie. Accessed 1 Mar 2021. Further Rieger, Transgender-Kind ist in Montessori-Schule unerwünscht, in Kurier 17.07.2017, online: https://kurier.at/chronik/niederoesterreich/transgender-kind-ist-in-montessori-schule-unerwuenscht/275.106.289. Accessed 1 Mar 2021; Fabry, Ausgrenzung: Montessorischule im Visier des Volksanwalts, in Die Presse 20.07.2017, online: http://diepresse.com/home/bildung/schule/5255640/Ausgrenzung_Montessorischule-im-Visier-des-Volksanwalts. Accessed 1 Mar 2021.

that the sex re-assignment was no obstacle in the professional environment of a police officer.[77]

The Recommendations deal with the treatment and care process as follows:[78]

- Diagnostic Process for the determination of gender dysphoria, i.e. transsexualism: In this process the nature and the extent of the discomfort or uncomfortable feelings caused by the discrepancy between the subjective sex role and the sex determined at birth shall be determined in a diagnostic process consisting of a psychiatric diagnosis, a clinical psychological diagnosis and a psychotherapeutic diagnosis. The aim is to ensure that the medical condition will continue to exist on a long term basis and to determine indication for further treatment. One of the three experts, appointed by the patient, shall summarize the suggestions reflecting a clear consent among them.
- Treatment confirmation: The patient can demand a stamped confirmation from the treating expert (including his/her address). The confirmation of the diagnosis and the relation between the treatment and the outward appearance has a validity amounting to maximum 2 years.
- Therapeutic process: From the consent between the experts follows the treatment according to the individual state of suffering of the patient. The treatment has the goal to improve the psychic and social situation (self-care, working capacity, development of enduring perspectives for life and relationships, realistic sexual expectations etc) as well as the strengthening of the patient's identity. In case psychic, social and / or somatic disorders are at stake, the patient shall be treated by a clinical psychologist, a psychotherapist, and a psychiatrist or by another medical expert.
- Previous to the hormonal treatment: If the patient strives for a hormonal treatment the diagnostic process shall be followed by a urological-gynecological examination and a risk screening in order to check whether there are any contraindications. Depending on the case, a cytogenetic examination may be indicated as well. Any contraindications shall be paid regard to in the medical, clinical psychological or psychotherapeutic treatment. In addition, a statement shall be made by the clinical psychologist OR the psychotherapist, followed by a psychiatric control examination together with a joint indication of the three experts regarding the further treatment process from the perspective of psychic and somatic aspects of treatment. The leading expert shall summarize the statements reflecting a clear consent among the experts.
- Hormonal treatment: Only if an indication for the inducement of somatic treatment is confirmed a hormonal treatment shall be started. This treatment must be

---

[77]See Kartik, Dieser Polizist lebte im Körper einer Frau, in Trans-Cop, 04.05.2017.

[78]Ministerium Frauen Gesundheit, Empfehlungen für den Behandlungsprozess bei Geschlechtspdyphorie bzw. Transsexualismus nach der Klassifikation in der derzeit gültigen DSM bzw. ICD-Fassung (20.06.2017), Recommendations, pp. 3–7. See recently Heidinger, Türk, Arbeitsgruppe Varianten der Geschlechtsentwicklung (2019): Empfehlungen zu Varianten der Geschlechtsentwicklung; Wien: BMASGK.

medically checked on a regular basis. At the same time the medical, clinical psychological or psychotherapeutic treatment shall be continued, if the situation so requires. The intent is at this stage to accompany the "real life experience" of the patient. Usually, hormonal treatment takes about 1 year, and if the patient then wishes, the genital surgery can be performed. Yet, an assimilation to the desired sex role can be performed without previous hormonal therapy as well, e.g. in case of a mastectomy.

- Previous to surgeries: If the patient desires a sex re-assignment surgery (SRS) a further psychiatric control examination shall be carried out and a statement shall be drawn up either by a clinical psychologist or by a psychotherapist. The leading expert shall summarize the statements, whereby the summary shall reflect a clear consent of the experts regarding the continuous and independent wishes of the transsexual and the desired sex role. Based on this statement, the indication for a surgery is confirmed and the patient can be referred to the medical experts qualified for sex surgeries.
- Documentation: The entire treatment process must be documented according to the state of the art.
- Surgery: The surgery/surgeries is/are carried out and operation findings shall be documented.
- Postoperative: After the surgery/surgeries a medical, clinical psychological and/or psychotherapeutic treatment should be offered to the patient.

Access to treatment is necessarily coupled with the question who will bear the costs of the treatment.

The Austrian Supreme Court has dealt with this issue in a couple of decisions. In an alimony proceeding decided in 1995 by the Austrian Supreme Court, a petitioner aimed at the attribution of costs caused by his change of sex. The Court explicitly affirmed transsexualism as a medical condition.[79] In 1996 the Austrian Supreme Court dealt with the question, whether the psychotherapeutic treatment which accompanied a surgery to change the sex, i.e. removal of the primary genital organs is to be considered as a treatment covered by the health insurance. The main argument was the qualification of transsexuality as medical condition, which requires that the wish of the person to belong to the sex corresponding his/her mental and, following the surgery, his/her physical condition must be respected.[80]

Hormonal treatments are regarded as a treatment necessary in case of sex re-assignment. All costs are covered by the National Health Service. The same applies to sex re-assignment surgeries by which the primary genital organs are removed. Other measures, such as beard depilation may well be considered as cosmetic treatments, to be paid privately. The medical diagnosis is a fundamental requirement for any treatment covered by the National Health Insurance.

---

[79] OGH 21.12.1995, 3 Ob 570/95.

[80] OGH 12.09.1996, 10 ObS 2303/96s.

In Vienna, such surgeries are either performed by a specialist in plastic surgery or in urology. At present, no phallus constructions are done in Austria, because either specialists are not available or no assistant doctors with the necessary proficiency are available during the week-end. Therefore, such surgeries are performed, if at all, abroad (e.g. in Münich). Surgeries in Austria are at present limited to male-female surgeries.[81] Provided, no doctor performs such a surgery in Austria, the Austrian Insurance might cover the costs. Upon intervention by the Austrian Ombudsman Board which referred to the obligation under EU law[82] to authorize a surgery in another Member State, if it cannot be performed in Austria, the Styrian Health Insurance Fund assumed the costs of the surgery performed in Germany in one particular case.[83]

While, as a rule, Social Insurance has covered both the domestic surgeries and the hormonal treatment, it only pays cost contributions with regard to psychotherapy. This can potentially create an important financial burden on the patients, because without a need for surgery, psychotherapy before, during and after the sex re-assignment can prove to be extremely important depending on the case at stake.[84] Especially since a surgery is no longer a mandatory requirement for the legal change of sex, support by psychiatrists, clinical psychologists and psychotherapists—in practice the patients are usually supported by a psychotherapist—is of overall importance. If namely the number of "regretters" would also rise, this might indicate that medical support before, during and after sex re-assignment might not have been dealt with according to the state of art, which can raise liability issues.

In 2015, the first Transgender-Centre (TGCI) at the University Hospital Innsbruck was set-up. The interdisciplinary Centre advises persons with gender identity disorders.[85] The Centre considers it vital to avoid pathologisation of the issue and cares for around 80 patients of whom around 50% are unemployed.

[81]Information provided by Mag. Wilhelm, VADO [WASt]) on 08.08.2019.

[82]See Directive 2011/24/EU of the European Parliament and of the Council of 9 March 2011 on the application of patients' rights in cross-border healthcare OJ L 88, 45, recital 31, Art 8.

[83]See Volksanwaltschaft, Bericht der Volksanwaltschaft an den Nationalrat und an den Bundesrat (2018), Kontrolle der öffentlichen Verwaltung, 74 et seq., online https://volksanwaltschaft.gv.at/downloads/72sag/PB-42-Nachpr%C3%BCfend.pdf. Accessed 1 Mar 2021. The report 2019 of the Volksanwaltschaft (Austrian Ombudsman Board) confirms that further actions shall be taken to strengthen the interest of intersex persons, https://Volksanwaltschaft.gv.at/downloads/cbhfk/PB 43_Kontrolle öffentliche Verwaltung 2019.pdf, 58.

[84]Information provided by Mag. Wilhelm, VADO [WASt]) on 08.08.2019.

[85]Report from Arora, Transident: Vom Mann zur Frau werden oder umgekehrt, in Der Standard 22.04.2017, online: http://derstandard.at/2000056315440/Transident-Vom-Mann-zur-Frau-werden-oder-umgekehrt. Accessed 1 Mar 2021; see also http://tirol.orf.at/news/stories/2838027/. Accessed 1 Mar 2021.

6 The Name of a Trans Person

The name of a person is an expression of his/her personal identity and is perceived by law and by individuals as of outmost importance. In practice, transsexuals who are in the process of sex re-assignment, more specifically during the "real life experience"[86] are recommended, but not obliged to determine a gender-neutral name.[87] The recommendation might serve the purpose to improve the integration of the person in view of his/her future change of sex in professional life and society. It is not possible to request a change of the given name to the intended one before the change of sex, because a request to change a given name not corresponding to the sex of that person is to be refused.[88]

The Act CN[89] provides detailed rules on the requirements for a change of the name upon request (Art. 2 Act CN), explicitly providing in § 2(2)(3) Act CN for the case that the name of a person shall be changed, if the given name does not correspond to the sex, e.g., when the sex was re-assigned after the determination of the given name. Art 3 Act CN contains rules according to which a request to change the name shall not be granted, among those is a 10-year barrier after a previous change of name with a counter-exception in Art 3(1)(8 in fine). The determination of a gender-neutral first, i.e. given name is based on Art 2(1)(10) Act CN. Yet, this provision is not mentioned in the counter-exception of Art 3(1)(8) Act CN, i.e. a new request to change the name after the change of sex shall not be granted before 10 years have elapsed. From a formal point of view, a person who opted for a gender-neutral name during his/her real-life experience and wishes to change the name (again) after the change of sex would be barred from doing so during a period of 10 years.

This issue is controversial. Based on a literal interpretation, the next change of name could not take place before 10 years have elapsed.[90] Some argued, however, that the law has an unintended legal loophole, in which case the further change of a given name following a change of the sex should be granted notwithstanding the 10-year barrier.[91] A third option consists of a request of the person to have the name changed "for other reasons". In sharp contrast to the first and the second option the third option is fee-based, because the change is (deemed to be) purely based on the

[86]See in particular Sec. 4.1. and 4.3.

[87]The determination of a gender-neutral first name is based on § 2(1)(10) Act CN and states that the change of a name is allowed, if) (10) the person who requests the change can credibly demonstrate that the change of the family name is necessary to avoid unreasonable disadvantages regards economic aspects or his / her social relations, and these disadvantages cannot be avoided by other means.

[88]See § 3(1)(8) Act CN).

[89]See footnote 11.

[90]See Kutscher and Wilpert (2017).

[91]See Michel (2008), pp. 100–111 (109).

personal wish of the person.[92] Weighing the interests of the person during and after his/her transition against the interests of the State, to limit the number of changes in order to avoid abuses, the balance clearly swings in favor of the applicant, who should be able to change the name after the change of sex any time and free of any costs.

During the post-World War II era, the public debate on the law of names focused primarily on the equal treatment of men and women, especially the right of women to decide for themselves which name they shall carry when they marry. Neither sexual orientation nor the change of sex with or without consequence with regard to the name have been on the political agenda in the past century. It is, therefore, not surprising that transsexuals and gender identity have certainly been no political priority. This is also reflected in the way how the legislator has been dealing with the situation of transsexual persons and how little transparent the rules on the change of names are dealt with in the law.[93]

7 Family Law Effects

Regarding the effects of a change of sex on an existing marriage, the Austrian Constitutional Court[94] found that the question whether the marriage after the change of sex could or could not be challenged, could not (and cannot) be decided by an administrative authority. Therefore, with regard to the marriage the sex re-assignment has in principle no impact on the validity of the marriage, unless a party takes action to have the legal relationship dissolved. The same holds true for a registered partnership. Further, the relationship to the children remains unchanged from a legal point of view, e.g. paternity is not questioned, if the sex of the father is changed in the register.[95] Although these questions were decided in the context of change of sex, there seems to be no convincing reason, why the family law consequences of the change of sex on the basis of the binary model should apply, when a party opts for the third sex.

[92](§ 2(1)(11) Act CN). This provision was introduced with an amendment to the Act CN (see footnote 11) in 1995, BGBl. No. 25/1995. At the same time, it was provided that the change of the name "for other reasons" shall be fee-based (§ 6 Act CN). The legislative materials explain the reason for this financial burden. Whereas the change of the name pursuant to § 2(1)(10) Act CN is based on reason that deeply touch upon the personality of a person, the change of the name "for other reasons" pursuant to § 2(1)(11) Act CN is based on the personal wish of the person, see AB 49 BlgNR 19. GP 10. The fees amount currently to 163 Euro (Federal administrative levies) and 382,60 Euro (fees), see the overview in Kutscher and Wilpert (2017).

[93]See e.g., critical comments by the Verein für transgender Personen, Namensänderung, online: https://www.transx.at/Pub/Recht_Vornamen.php. Accessed 1 Mar 2021.

[94]VfGH 08.06.2006, V 4/06.

[95]OGH 21.4.2009, 10 ObS 29/09a SZ 2009/50.

In 2017, the Austrian Constitutional Court decided that § 44 atCC, according to which a marriage could only be concluded between persons of different sex, was discriminatory and the wording "of different sex" was repealed.[96] In this author's opinion, this implies that persons registered as of the third sex and trans persons (regardless of a change of sex) can marry any other male, female or person of the third sex or register a partnership with any such person without facing legal obstacles.

Female to male transsexuals who did not undergo a surgery, but limited their sex re-assignment to hormonal treatment and accompanying medical, psychologic and psychotherapeutic treatment, who became pregnant and gave birth gained public attention by media reports. The interruption of the hormonal treatment may well imply conception, because the basic ability to conceive has not been eliminated. This happened, apparently for the first time in Austria, in February 2017.[97] The question which arises is whether the biological mother, who is legally a male, should be considered as the mother of the child,[98] put differently whether the registered sex has an impact on the legal nature of the parent who gives birth to a child. According to § 143 atCC the mother is the woman who gave birth to the child. This definition reflects the Roman principle "*mater semper certa est*". One may assume that the legislator did not consider the situation in which a man gives birth to a child. According to this legal principle "he" is the biological mother. Perhaps the most stringent argument in favor of the registration of the man who gave birth as the mother of the child are the best interests of the child: The child has a fundamental right to know his/her origins.[99] Therefore, the man who gave birth to the child could be mentioned as the mother of the child in the birth register (and on the birth certificate of the child). If one considers sex re-assignment a matter of personal identity which can be changed without an irreversible surgery, the idea that identity of a person in the sense of gender is one issue, parentage in the sense of sex is another, might be more readily accepted.

After the change of sex, a person born as a woman and who is male after the change of sex cannot validly recognize paternity.[100] It is further open for discussion,

---

[96]VfGH 04.12.2017 G 258/2017. The same was held regards the wording "of equal sex", as provided for in the Law on Registered Partnerships, BGBl. I No. 135/2009, most recently amended by BGBl. No. 161/2017 and repealed the restrictions as from 31.12.2018. Since 01.01.2019, same sex couples can enter a marriage with one another and couples of different sex can contract a registered partnership.

[97]See report from Hubmann, Erstmals in Graz: Schwangerer Mann bringt Kind zur Welt, Kleine Zeitung 25.02.2017, online: http://www.kleinezeitung.at/steiermark/graz/5175017/Exklusiv_Erstmals-in-Graz_Schwangerer-Mann-bringt-Kind-zur-Welt. Accessed 1 Mar 2021; further report from Hubmann, Mann bringt Baby in Graz zur Welt: Darüber diskutiert man in Österreich, Kleine Zeitung 26.02.2017, online: http://www.kleinezeitung.at/steiermark/graz/5175340/Aufreger_Mann-bringt-Baby-in-Graz-zur-Welt_Darueber-diskutiert. Accessed 1 Mar 2021.

[98]Dengg and Schranz (2018), p. 272 (278).

[99]Art. 8 Convention on the Rights of the Child, Art. 8 ECHR, Art. 1 Federal Constitutional Law on the rights of the Child.

[100]Kutscher and Wilpert (2018).

whether a person registered as "inter", "diverse", "open" or without any indication and who gave birth to a child is to be regarded as the mother of the child. At present, the arguments forwarded above in the interest of the child could speak in favor of the person who gave birth to child. Yet, this allocation is by no means mandatory. It might well be that the best interests of the child are best served by treating facts as they are, i.e. born by person "inter", "diverse", "open" or without any indication, as parent of the child, notwithstanding the current provision in the atCC (§ 143). It seems too early to prefer the Roman principle to other solutions. As a variety of contexts, among them e.g. surrogacy, where parenthood is highly controversial,[101] clearly demonstrate, a majority opinion on this issue is not in sight. Furthermore, whether a female to male transsexual person, who is pregnant and then gives birth to a child, could claim maternity leave for example, has so far not been decided. One may assume that both in the interest of the pregnant person and of the child maternity leave should be granted.

8 Non-binary Sex Reporting

The sex of a person is determined by the doctor or the midwife as the medical experts. The civil registrar who registers the birth of a child (§ 11 Act PS 2013) has no right to question their determination of sex.[102] For this determination upon birth, the outer appearance of the child at birth is decisive. The registered sex is binding for all authorities and bodies and appears on the birth certificate.

If the sex of a person is unclear at birth—a situation which concerns an estimated 30 cases per year[103]—the registration must remain incomplete and the sex on the birth certificate remains to be specified (*offen*) until the sex can be identified. Such statement only serves the purpose to indicate that the registration is still incomplete, it does, by no means, imply a "fourth" category of sex.[104]

In this context, the question arises how the child should be named. Selecting a gender-neutral name is recommended, whereby the parents must respect following criteria: They are bound to choose a name within the range of first names permitted by Austrian law,[105] § 13(2) Act PS 2013 provides that unusual given names or given

---

[101]Verschraegen (2019), p. 266 ff.

[102]Kutscher and Wilpert (2018).

[103]The Austrian Ombudsman Board (2020) Report 2019, 61 f. See also the latest supplement to the instruction of November 2019, BMI-VA1300/0145/III/3/b/2019. The most recent recommendations regarding gender identity disorders of newly borns, children and young people were presented by Heidinger, Türk, Arbeitsgruppe Varianten der Geschlechtsentwicklung (2019): Empfehlungen zu Varianten der Geschlechtsentwicklung; Wien:BMASGK.

[104]See also footnote 33.

[105]The Austrian Statistics Service (*Statistik Austria*) is an independent non-profit institution incorporated under public law and provides services for the Federal Statistics. See *Bundesgesetz über die Bundesstatistik*, BGBl. I No. 163/1999 as amended most recently by BGBl. I No. 32/2018. It

names that are contrary to the best interests of the child shall not be registered. The registry office shall in such case inform the guardianship court (§ 13(3) Act PS 2013). This choice is only a limited one and creates doubts as to the proportionality of such requirement.[106]

9 Conclusions

Step by step, society has become better acquainted with and cognizant of trans persons and the need for the possibility of changes of sex. The Austrian Administrative and Constitutional Courts must be given credit for the fact that a change of sex no longer requires surgery. The procedure for the change of sex reflects the burdens that go along with it, but also demonstrates the understanding of all suffering caused, if no change of sex were permitted by principle. Surely, legal recognition of the third sex in a society which has grown up in the tradition of a binary model demands a perspective quite different from the one which most of us have been familiar with. The adaptation of existing law to the standards set up by the Austrian Constitutional Court requires legislative steps at least regarding fundamental issues, such as the change of the Constitution to name one example.

The hybrid legal system and the jurisdiction allocated both to the Federation and the States leads to different rules with different requirements regarding the change of sex as well as regarding the registration of the third sex. Persons affected by these territorial deviations face considerable hurdles, not to mention the difficulties caused by a system of VdG-Boards lacking balanced distribution as they were appointed by the Ministry of Health in certain parts of the country, but not throughout the country.

In this author's opinion, the case law of the Austrian Constitutional Court and of the Austrian Administrative Court, together with the practice, in particular the Recommendations issued by the Ministry of Health[107] on 20.06.2017 after having consulted the atHC, reflect a spirit which is basically tolerant towards persons who wish to have their sex re-assigned. Contrary to other legal systems no mandatory sex re-assignment is required. Instead, the continuous therapy and supervision of the patient appear to safeguard his/her best interests. Early sex ambiguity has been treated as medical condition in a society based on a binary model. Therefore, the

---

publishes the usual first names determined in Austria on a yearly basis. The first name needs not, however, correspond to what is usual in Austria. If a foreign first name is chosen, the applicant must prove that the name is usual in the country in which the chosen name is a usual option. See also Greif, Doing Trans/Gender. Rechtliche Dimensionen (2005) 166. A declaration from a foreign representation authority will suffice.

[106] Judge Walsh in his concurring opinion to ECtHR 25.03.1992, no. 13343/87 – *B. / France* § 6, did not consider this as an "unreasonable request". Unfortunately, the ECtHR did not deal with this question. See also the remark made by Greif (2005) Doing Trans/Gender. Rechtliche Dimensionen, 84 note 321.

[107] See footnote 59.

possibility to wait with the registration of sex has convincingly been considered preferable to an early sex assignment surgery.

Acknowledgements I wish to express my thanks to Mag. Wilhelm, head of WASt (Wiener Antidiskriminierungsstelle für gleichgeschlechtliche und transgender Lebensweisen), to W. Eder, Dipl. Päd., MSc, psychotherapist in Traunkirchen (Upper-Austria), and to Dr. E. Silbermayr, psychotherapist in Vienna, who gave me valuable information and many important insights into the situation and the treatment of transgender persons. L. Kiparski, Mag. U. C. Schreiner and Dr. M. Komuczky supported me obtaining documents and finding unpublished legal sources for the answers to the questionnaire submitted to the General Reporter before the World Conference. Last but not least, I owe sincere thanks to A. M. Kriechbaum who performed valuable editorial work regarding the second last, substantially new, but reduced version.

References

Dengg A, Schranz J (2018) Das dritte Geschlecht. RdM 2018(6):272-280

Günther M (2015) Psychotherapeutische und beratende Arbeit mit Trans*Menschen. Erfahrung, Haltung, Hoffnung. Verhaltenstherapie & psychosoziale Praxis (VPP) 2015(1):113–124

Kunert C (2013) Werden wollen, wer man wirklich ist. Transsexualität als konstitutionelle Geschlechtsinkongruenz – ein personenzentrierter Standpunkt. Person. Internationale Zeitschrift für Personenzentrierte und Experienzielle Psychotherapie und Beratung 17(1):34–46

Kutscher N, Wilpert T (eds) (2017) Das österreichische Personenstandsrecht, 2nd edn. Manz, Vienna. 27th update, I E 1, 188, note 34

Kutscher N, Wilpert T (eds) (2018) Das österreichische Personenstandsrecht, 2nd edn. Manz, Vienna. 28th update, I B, 18 note 7

Michel U (2008) Unveränderlichkeit des Namens. ÖStA:100–111

Silbermayr E (2018) Transidentität – Aspekte für die psychodramatische Arbeit im Einzelsetting. In: Kern S, Hintermeyer S (eds) Psychodrama – Psychotherapie im Einzelsetting. Theorie und Praxis des Monodramas. Facultas, Vienna, pp 482–492

Stelzer M (2014) An introduction to Austrian constitutional law, 3rd edn. LexisNexis, Vienna

Verschraegen B (2019) Leihmutterschaft – Zum Recht auf Elternschaft. iFamZ (4):266-271

Trans Persons in Belgium

Nicole Gallus and Gerd Verschelden

Abstract The development of a recognition and protection of gender identity and trans persons in Belgium has taken place through several different corollaries, from judge-made law to statutory law, from judges to the civil registrars, from medical requirements to self-determination, and from a binary to a non-binary or fluid conception of gender. This chapter explores these legal developments in Belgium at length, as well as proposing steps forward.

The Belgian legal framework regarding trans persons has evolved immensely over time. Medical conditions were abolished in favor of the principle of self-determination. Major drivers underlying this development were the increasing scientific knowledge surrounding transgenderism, human rights and, in general,

Professor Gallus is responsible for the sections addressing Civil Status (Sect. 1), Access to Treatment (Sect. 7), Trans Parents (Sect. 10) and Stakes in Sex (Sect. 11)

Professor Verschelden is responsible for the introduction and conclusion, as well as those sections addressing the specific Belgian Legal Regulations concerning Trans Persons (Sects. 2 and 2.4), Terminology and Definitions (Sect. 3), the Legal Regulation of Name and Sexual Identity (Sects. 4 and 5), Gender Neutral and/or Third Sex (Sect. 6), the Current Discussion (Sect. 8), Gays & Lesbians and Trans and Intersex Persons (Sects. 9 and 12). The author wants to express his sincere gratitude to student-researcher Leander Van Driessche, for his help updating this chapter.

N. Gallus
Université libre de Bruxelles, Bruxelles, Belgium

Comité Consultatif de Bioéthique de Belgique, Bruxelles, Belgium
e-mail: nicole.gallus@ulb.ac.be

G. Verschelden (✉)
Institute for Family Law, Ghent University, Ghent, Belgium

Gender Team, Ghent University Hospital, Ghent, Belgium
e-mail: gerd.verschelden@ugent.be

I. C. Jaramillo, L. Carlson (eds.), *Trans Rights and Wrongs*, Ius Comparatum - Global Studies in Comparative Law 54,
https://doi.org/10.1007/978-3-030-68494-5_11

the growing awareness of the phenomenon and the accompanying shift in social norms.

This evolution, starting in the 1960s, can be summarized as follows:

- *From judge-made law to statutory law.* The Belgian rules to facilitate a sex change were originally developed *praeter legem* by the judiciary through the lower case-law. It lasted until 2007 for the legislature to intervene. The 2007 Transsexuality Act[1] was replaced in 2017 with the Gender Recognition Act.[2] In 2019, this Act was partially deemed unconstitutional.
- *From judge to civil registrar.* The 2007 Transsexuality Act changed the legal procedure from a judicial to an—in nature easily accessible—administrative procedure. A major difference between a judge and civil registrar is, of course, that the latter has no discretionary power: the civil registrar is only allowed to apply the law and cannot judge. The administrative procedure became even more accessible in 2017 when the medical conditions to change one's registered sex into the inner perceived gender identity were abolished.
- *From medical requirements to self-determination.* A major advancement was the abolishment of the medical and 'social' requirements to change one's registered sex. Until 1 January 2018 (i.e. the date on which the Gender Recognition Act entered into force) irrevocable sterilization and sex reassignment surgery were mandatory requirements in order to change the registered sex.[3] From this date and onwards, only requirements related to the self-determination of the person concerned (e.g. two written declarations reflecting the inner conviction) are necessary.
- *From a binary to a non-binary or*[4] *fluid conception of gender.* The Acts of 2007 and 2017 were based on a binary conception of gender: a person is either male or female. An intervention by the Constitutional Court in 2019 was needed to secure the rights of non-binary or gender fluid persons. The 2017 Gender Recognition Act was partially deemed unconstitutional by judgment no 99/2019.[5]

---

[1]Act (federal level) 10 May 2007 on transsexualism, *Belgian Gazette* (hereinafter: *BG*) 11 July 2007, p. 37823.

[2]Act (federal level) 25 June 2017 reforming the regulations concerning trans persons regarding the mention and amendment of the registration of sex in civil certificates and the consequences thereof, *BG* 10 July 2017, p. 71456.

[3]The 'social' requisite, i.e. the completion of a real-life test (a period of time during which the person requesting a change of registered sex, lives (behavior wise, clothing wise etc.) full-time in their preferred gender role) was abolished in 2007.

[4]This 'or' is meant inclusive and not exclusive.

[5]The French text of this judgment is available online on https://www.const-court.be/public/f/2019/2019-099f.pdf. Translation in English is expected.

1 The Legal Regulation of Civil Status

The Belgian legal system is a civil law system based on a hierarchy of legal norms. The country's federal structure has introduced further complexities as certain areas of law fall under federal jurisdiction while others fall under that of Regions or Communities. If we acknowledge that issues pertaining to the civil status fall under the federal legislature's competence, the hierarchy of legal norms may be schematized by recalling that the top of the pyramid is made of directly enforceable international conventions and treaties followed by the Belgian Constitution and then successively, statutes, royal decrees and ministerial decrees. The observance to the hierarchy of norms is ensured by the Constitutional Court, a single specialized Court independent from the judicial, legal and executive branches of Government.

In the area here concerned, this Court has exclusive jurisdiction to rule on the compatibility of the law with the fundamental rights and liberties guaranteed by the Constitution—principles of equality and non-discrimination—combined with that enshrined by the European Convention of Human rights (ECHR).
Cases may be brought before the Court in the context of a petition for the annulment of a provision[6] or in the case of a reference for a preliminary ruling regarding a legal provision's compatibility with the Constitution. When it succeeds, the action for annulment leads to the retroactive total or partial annulment of the challenged provision, the ruling having an absolute *res judicata*.

When the Court rules over a reference for a preliminary ruling, the challenged legal provision continues to exist in the legal system. However, the judicial court that referred to the Court as well as any other court asked to rule in the same case shall comply to the Constitutional Court's answer.

Finally, in the case of important reforms, the Minister of Justice adopts ministerial circulars, with for sole objective to explain the scope of application of new provisions to civil registrars invested in their enforcement. These circulars lack binding force, but their content is crucial for practice, sometimes containing extra requirements.[7]

1.1 Sex as an Element of Civil Status: The Current Organization of the Civil Registry

The civil status represents the range of elements and qualities determining the individual's legal position in the family and society, distinguishing this individual

[6]See the Judgment of 19 June 2019 (no 99/2019), discussed below in Sect. 6 on Gender-neutral and/or third-sex.

[7]See Sect. 5 on the Legal Recognition of Sexual Identity. For the circular concerning the Gender Recognition Act, see footnote 37.

from the others concerning the possession and exercise of rights (art. 6, § 2 of the Belgian Civil Code, hereinafter "BCC").

It is the civil status of the individual that makes it possible to define their rights and obligations towards the state (*status civitatis*, e.g. nationality), in the family (*status familiae*, e.g. as child, spouse, registered partner) and as an individual (e.g. legal address, name and sex). Sex is an identifying element of an individual, i.e. an element of their civil status and an element of distinctiveness which appears in the mandatory information of the birth certificate (art. 44, 1° BCC).

The civil registrar who drafts the birth certificate inscribes this element on the grounds of a medical certificate based on the morphological components revealed on the day of birth. If the registered sex is unclear or ambiguous on the day of birth—as is the case with intersex persons—the sex must be proven, based on a medical certificate, within a time-window of three months after the day of birth (art. 48 BCC).

The sexual identity of an individual nowadays encompasses the morphological gender (i.e. as it appears externally), the gonadic gender (presence of testicles or ovaries), the genetic gender, the hormonal gender, the psychological gender (as oneself perceives it), and the sociological gender (as perceived by others).

Although these components may diverge, the morphological component has precedent for the purpose of drafting the birth certificate considering its certainty, as opposed to the gonadic and hormonal components which are not visible and to the psychological and sociological components that will only develop over time.[8]

The person's civil status and its resulting effects are of interest to the person but also to all of society, that needs to be able to refer to it with certainty.[9] Consequently, the rules organizing the civil status are set by law (i.e. statutory provisions) and of public policy and, hence, not subject to one's contractual autonomy. This character of public policy explains the three main characteristics of the civil status being its inalienability, its imprescriptibility and its indivisibility. Imprescriptibility (or absence of statutory limitation) means that neither time nor use or absence of use shall entail the acquisition or loss of one's civil status. Indivisibility means that the civil status of a person has an *erga omnes* recognition (i.e. towards everyone).

Inalienability is a more complex notion. Traditionally, it implies that the civil status is imposed by law and that people may not disregard it: contracts, settlements or waivers that could have for purpose or effect to modify or amend the civil status imposed to a person by law shall be deemed as null and void by operation of law.[10]

However, inalienability does not mean immutability: certain elements may be modified or evolve over time depending on external circumstances (e.g. aging entailing going from minority to the age of majority), or on legal or personal acts performed by the person (marriage, divorce, fatherhood...), these acts express the concerned person's will which is however not completely autonomous as it requires

[8]Leleu (2016), p. 106; Branlard (1993), p. 454.

[9]Van Gysel (1996), p. 438; Court of Cassation 26 September 1980, *Pasicrisie belge* (hereinafter: *Pas.*) 1981, I, 94; Court of Appeal Mons 25 October 1990, *Pas.* 1991, II, 47.

[10]De Page (1990), p. 85.

the respect of substantive and formal conditions set by law.[11] This issue of the inalienability of the civil status lies at the center of the legal debate about transgenderism.[12] The certainty that must characterize the civil status explains why both its proving and certification are strictly regulated.

This proof shall be brought by civil status certificates (birth, marriage, death, child recognition certificates. . .) or by a court ruling over the matter (divorce, adoption. . .) (art. 23 BCC).[13] Civil status records are official certificates drafted by civil servants invested for this purpose—named civil status registrars.[14] The purpose of the civil registry is to officially register the events that constitute the civil status of a person (art. 6, § 1 BCC). Since 31 March 2019 these certificates are registered in dematerialized form in a national database called the "DABS/BAEC"[15] (liberal translation: Database for the Registration of Civil Status Certificates) (art. 14 BCC). All rules regarding the drafting and conservation of civil status records pertain to public policy: neither the parties nor the invested civils servants shall disregard them (art. 14 *et seq.* BCC). Consequently, an error unveiled after the drafting of the certificate may be corrected only by a judicial procedure towards the certificate's rectification (art. 35 BCC). So-called "material errors", i.e. typological errors and errors regarding time and date (art. 34 BCC), can be rectified by the civil status registrar himself (art. 33 BCC).

The civil status' organization involves three types of operations:

- Drafting certificates (art. 6 BCC);
- Rectification of certificates, i.e. changing an existing civil status certificate as a consequence of a rectification procedure (see above) or of the operative provisions of a Court ruling (e.g. a divorce) (art. 31 BCC);
- Modification of existing certificates, i.e. linking a newly drafted civil status certificate to an already drafted one in cases where the former is likely to modify the contents of the latter certificate.

Changes to the civil status authorized by law and operated while abiding to the substantive and formal rules set forth by the law are recorded within the civil status register by applying three operations.

As a result, the change of the registered sex into the inner perceived gender identity on the basis of the Gender Recognition Act, as amended by the Act of 18 June 2018, implies the drafting of a Gender Registration Certificate, its enactment within the civil status' register (the DABS/BAEC) and linking it to the certificates of the person concerned (art. 135/1, § 5 BCC). If the civil status registrar refuses to draft

[11]Massager and Van Gysel (1995), p. 191.

[12]See Sect. 1.2.

[13]Exceptionally, a person's apparent status (i.e. in French: "possession d'état", or descriptive: factual behavior) can suffice as means of proof.

[14]In certain circumstances, diplomatic personnel or consular agents stationed overseas may draft civil status documents related to Belgian citizens living abroad.

[15]"DABS" is the Dutch and "BAEC" is the French abbreviation of the same database.

the Gender Registration Certificate, a judicial remedy is available. If the competent Family Court grants the request for modification of gender registration, the civil status registrar shall draft the Gender Registration Certificate, shall transcript the court rulings' operative provisions in the register and shall link the certificate to the certificates of the concerned person and of their direct descendants it modifies (art. 1385*quater* and 1385*decies* of the Belgian Judicial Code, hereinafter: "BJC").

1.2 History and Evolution of Gender Registration

The history of the law applicable to change one's registered sex, which is registered in the birth certificate, into the inner perceived gender identity goes hand in hand with the history of the rule of inalienability of the civil status. The difficulties faced by trans persons to gain legal recognition of their gender identity, when it differs from the sex assigned at birth, stem from the way our legal system conceives the civil status, i.e. the elements allowing for the identifying of a person both individually and in their interactions with others. These elements, amongst which the sex, constitute the personal status, the regulation of which is of public policy considering its importance for the organization of society. From this public policy nature results the inalienability, i.e. an interdiction to modify the civil status by the sole will outside of legal conditions and proceedings.

The first civil status certificate of any person, which is the birth certificate, states the sex of the child: article 44, 1° BCC refers to the factual criteria of the biological and morphological nature allowing for the binary classification "male or female". "Gender identity" (which is the sense of oneself as male, female, something in between or genderless) cannot be defined at birth and is a concept that was completely ignored during the drafting of Napoleon's Civil Code.[16]

Transgenderism, especially, raises the issue of the perceived contradiction between the "sex" as stated in the civil status records and the personal experience of belonging to the other "gender", to both genders or not belonging to a gender at all.

The issue is all the more complex when we take into account that the manifestations of transgenderism are multiple, ranging from the adoption of a different sexual appearance without hormonal or surgical treatment to the decision to change secondary sexual characteristics through hormonal treatment, or, surgical

---

[16]The ambiguity resulting from the confusion between 'sex' and 'gender' still exists in the 2017 Gender Recognition Act, which refers to "gender" in its title but maintains the notion "sex" in the birth certificate. The explanatory memorandum of the Act also confuses the words 'transgenderism' and 'transsexuality' (*Parl.Doc.*, Chamber of Representatives (henceforth: 'Chamber') 2016-17, no 54-2403/1, p. 25 et 26).

interventions in order to provide for a morphological appearance in accordance with the perceived gender identity.[17]

At first, the law was confronted with this problem from the point of view of transsexuality alone, i.e. of the hypothesis of a complete and definitive sexual conversion by means of hormonal and surgical treatment. The persons concerned attempted at first to gain the recognition of their identity through petitions for the rectification of their birth certificate, i.e. a remedy which did not aim at the substantive law—i.e. the civil status by itself—but only the proof thereof. These legal actions were dismissed as they supposed a presumption that a material error was committed at the time of drafting of the certificate. Such error did not exist as the reference to the sex on the birth certificate is based upon the biological sex at the time of drafting of the birth certificate: hormonal and surgical interventions used by transsexuals, according to the first court rulings, were not indicative of a pre-existing condition erroneously mentioned in the birth certificate but were creating a new ex post civil status. There were hence no grounds for rectification in the absence of error nor grounds for proceedings aiming at assessing the change of the civil status, as such change would violate the civil status' inalienability principle which is of public policy.[18]

Gradually, under the influence of scientific data concluding that gender identity may be determined by elements others than those related to anatomy, biology and genetics, an evolution towards the recognition of the gender identity of transsexuals has taken form. This evolution would lead to the admissibility of proceedings both for the rectification of civil status records as for actions regarding the civil status itself.[19]

For the action related to the civil status records, the jurisprudence would indeed consider that the birth certificate as a legal title, cannot be more immutable that the situation it has the purpose to assess: being evidence of a person's civil status, the record is to be modified from the moment the status itself changes. The notion of 'error' was hence construed more broadly, i.e. without being restricted to the day the certificate was drafted to assess these characteristics.

[17]More complex issues arise for intersexual persons, *i.e.* those who present morphologic ambiguity. Those issues are not addressed in the Gender Recognition Act.

[18]See, in particular: Court of Appeal Brussels 7 May 1974, *Revue du notariat belge* (hereinafter: *RNB*) 1975, p. 137; the first proceedings are that of the rectification of an error on the birth certificate. In the case *Van Oosterwijck v. Belgium* of 6 November 1980, the European Court of Human Rights dismisses the claimant on the grounds of the absence of use of all the national remedies, while highlighting in its *obiter dicta* that the claims of transsexuals are related to the civil status and not to the rectification of the birth certificate. On these grounds, the claimant had to file a new petition to change his civil status.

[19]This confusion between proceedings for the rectification of civil status documents and civil status actions illustrates the difficulties faced by the courts to understand the shapes of transgenderism. Certain court rulings were so confused as to the point of stating they were asked to rule about an "action in the terms of an action for the rectification of the civil status (e.g. Court of Appeal Liège 22 April 1998, *Revue régionale de droit* (hereinafter: *RRD*) 1998, p. 303).

When a person acted by means of a civil status action, the courts bypassed the hurdle of the inalienability of the civil status by considering that the change of gender was not a fact that depended on the person's will or freedom, but the result of a constraint or even that of a "compelling force", which allowed for distinguishing between inalienability and immutability.[20]

At this stage in time, the judicial recognition of one's gender identity was possible but required proof (often with the help of a medical expertise) of a complete and irreversible sexual conversion as well as proof of the necessity of the judicial recognition. This approach was heavily criticized.

On the one hand, it can only be applied to 'transsexuals', i.e. to persons who, facing contradictions with their gender identities, are led to resort to hormonal and surgical treatments intended to make their bodies correspond to their gender identity. Transgenderism, however, manifests itself in different ways and does not necessarily entail the wish of an anatomic conversion nor does it imply that hormonal or surgical interventions are, medically speaking, possible (e.g. due to the high age of the person involved). On the other hand, the constraint of judicial proceedings and of an expertise violates the fundamental rights to privacy and intimacy, and one's control over their own body. To partially address these criticisms, the Transsexuality Act of 10 May 2007 introduced two new provisions in the Belgian Civil Code, articles 62*bis* and 62*ter*, which transfers the competence to modify the registered sex on the birth certificate from the courts to the civil status registrars.

The gender registration was allowed if three declarations are handed over to the civil status registrar. These declarations were:

(1) a declaration from the person concerned containing "the inner constant and irreversible conviction to be part of the opposite sex",[21]
(2) a declaration from a psychiatrist assessing this conviction, and

---

[20]Court of First Instance Brussels 7 December 1988, *Journal des tribunaux* (hereinafter: *JT*) 1989, p. 93; Court of First Instance Arlon 12 October 2001, *Revue trimestrielle de droit familial* (hereinafter: *RTDF*) 2004, p. 569; Court of First Instance Liège 22 April 1998, *RTDF* 1999, p. 92; Court of First Instance Liège 15 December 2003, *Revue de Jurisprudence de Liège, Mons et Bruxelles* (hereinafter: *JLMB*) 2004, p. 1210; Court of First Instance Dendermonde 3 October 2003, *Nieuw Juridisch Weekblad* (hereinafter: *NJW*) 2004, p. 19; Until 1 June 2003 (i.e. the date at which a same-sex marriage became legal) a change of gender of a married person would automatically lead to the dissolution of that marriage: Court of Appeal Antwerp 27 January 1999, *Echtscheidingsjournaal* (hereinafter: *EJ*) 1999, p. 50; *RTDF* 1999, p. 89; *Rechtskundig Weekblad* (hereinafter: *RW*) 1999–2000, p. 257, annotated by Verschelden, G.; Court of Appeal Antwerp 7 March 2001, *EJ* 2001, p. 56, annotated by Vanlede, K.; Court of Appeal Antwerp 27 June 2003, *NJW* 2004, p. 17.

[21]This wording highlights the fact that the Belgian legislature persists in a binary conception of gender which explains the irrevocable gender choice, see Simon (2016), p. 521.

(3) a declaration by a surgeon that the sexual reassignment therapy that was possible taking into account "the full extent of what is possible and justified from a medical standpoint" was performed[22] and, finally,
(4) that the person involved is unable to conceive children.

The civil status registrar then proceeded to a formal check of the legal conditions, without assessing the opportunity of the requested changes of the registered sex, followed by drafting a certificate mentioning the new gender (i.e. a Gender Registration Certificate[23]), which was to be registered in the civil status records and mentioned in the margin of the birth certificate.[24]

Changing a person's registered sex into the inner perceived gender identity did not change their parenthood with children born *before* the conversion. There was no legal provision regarding the parenthood of children born *after* the conversion, a situation which has not been considered by the legislature since the modification of the transsexuals' birth certificate entails a sterilization. This explanation, however, was insufficient and did not answer the question what happens if a transsexual (who was prevented from natural reproduction) resorts to a cryopreservation of gametes before the conversion for the purpose of an ex post artificial insemination or an in vitro conception.

The Transsexuality Act of 10 May 2007 solely and expressly refers, in its title, to 'transsexuality' leaving out of the legal framework trans persons advocating a lived intimate and personal identity that does not imply hormonal and surgical interventions modifying their morphology, either because such interventions are not desired, or because they are medically not possible. This Act also leaves out intersexed persons, i.e. persons who present morphological ambiguities. In such case, the child's gender is arbitrarily decided by the parents—generally in accordance with the child's pediatrician—according to an evaluation of their chances to flourish with or without subsequent hormonal and/or surgical interventions. In the event of a wrongful choice, a judicial procedure to rectify the error remains necessary.

The diversion of transsexuality may be perceived as progress but it is only an apparent one if we consider that the involved persons were subject to psychiatric evaluation and sterilization measures undermining the right to a private and family life, and in particular the right to parenthood.[25] Whatever (at least superficial) progress it implied, the Transsexuality Act of 10 May 2007 rapidly faced criticism

[22]Court of First Instance Antwerp 3 April 2009, *Rechtskundig Weekblad* 2009-10, p. 630; this third condition seems to introduce some humanity in the sexual conversion requirements but that humanity is immediately stripped away by the fourth condition.

[23]Not to be confused with a Gender Registration Certificate which does not describes one's morphological features (i.e. 'sex') but contains a person's inner perceived gender identity.

[24]Before the modernization of the civil registry by the Act of 18 June 2018, changes to an existing record were made by mentioning in its margin the record that changed its contents.

[25]The psychiatric evaluation requirement shows that the legislature regarded (with emphasis on the past tense of the verb) trans persons as persons suffering from a mental illness; the sterilization requirement reflected (with emphasis on the past tense of the verb) the legislature's concern not to expose children to parents 'suffering' from gender incongruence or gender dysphoria.

as the requirements of psychiatric evaluation and sterilization were deemed a violation of international soft law.[26] The sterilization requirement was later condemned by the European Court of Human Rights as it violated article 8 of the European Convention of Human Rights.[27]

Under the pressure of civil society and international law, the rules applicable to transgenderism were amended by the Act of 25 June 2017 "reforming the rules applicable to trans persons concerning the mention of a modification of the recording of the sex in civil status records and the legal effects of such a modification".[28] This act will hereinafter be named the "Gender Recognition Act".

Although this Act does not change the inaccurate use of the words 'sex' and 'gender', it is a major step forward: the conditions of psychiatric evaluation, sterilization and sex confirmation therapy are discarded in favor of a regime that is based, to some extent, on the personal autonomy of the persons involved (i.e. their wishes regarding their registered gender) and the new procedure of gender registration is no longer limited to transsexual persons.

2 The Belgian Specific Legal and Informative Framework

There are three different types of regulation for trans persons in Belgium: a recent federal Act, integrated in the Belgian Civil and Judicial Code (A), an explanatory Circular by the Minister of Justice (B) and an information brochure, dispersed by Royal Decree (C). An overview of all the applicable rules will be provided at the end of this subchapter.

2.1 The Gender Recognition Act of 25 June 2017 as Amended by the Act of 18 June 2018

On June 25, 2017, the King promulgated the Act Reforming the regulations concerning trans persons regarding the mention and amendment of the registration

[26]See especially: the Yogyakarta Principles on the enforcement of human rights international law in the fields of sexual orientation and gender identity, March 2007 and November 2017. https://yogyakartaprinciples.org. Accessed 1 July 2020. See also Resolution 2048 (2015) of the Parliamentary Assembly on discrimination against transgender people in Europe, 22 April 2015. Https://assembly.coe.int/nw/xml/XRef/Xref-DocDetails-en.asp?FileID=21736&lang=en. Accessed 1 July 2020; Recommendation of the Committee of Ministers to the Members States on the measures aiming to fight discrimination based on sexual orientation or gender identity, 31 March 2010. Https://search.coe.int/cm/Pages/result_details.aspx?ObjectID=09000016805cf40a. Accessed 1 July 2020.

[27]ECHR 10 March 2015, Y.Y. v. Turkey; ECHR 6 April 2017, A.P., Garçon and Nicot v. France.

[28]*BG*10 July 2017.

of sex in civil certificates and the consequences thereof[29] (hereinafter: "Gender Recognition Act"). The Belgian Gazette (henceforth: BG)[30] published this Act on 10 July 2017[31] and it entered into force on 1 January 2018, i.e. the first day of the sixth month after the announcement (in the absence of a Royal Decree establishing an earlier date).[32] This postponement of entry into force was to allow the actors in the field, in particular the civil status registrars, to prepare for the application of the new regulation.[33]

This Act was later amended by the Act of 18 June 2018 modernizing the civil registry,[34] which entered into force on 31 March 2019.[35] The existing provisions in the BCC regarding trans persons were moved because it was deemed illogical to place them amongst the provisions dealing with the different civil status certificates (now found in the articles 53 and 135/1-135/2 BCC). The content of the provisions was amended due to the modernization of the Belgian civil registry (i.e. introduction of the DABS/BAEC). A new civil status certificate, named "Certificate of Return to the Initial Sex" was created (art. 66 BCC) and the accessibility of civil records modified due to the change of the gender registration was limited (art. 78 BCC).[36]

---

[29]In French: "Loi du 25 juin 2017 réformant des régimes relatifs aux personnes transgenres en ce qui concerne la mention d'une modification de l'enregistrement du sexe dans les actes de l'état civil et ses effets". In Dutch: "Wet van 25 juni 2017 tot hervorming van de regelingen inzake transgenders wat de vermelding van een aanpassing van de registratie van het geslacht in de akten van de burgerlijke stand en de gevolgen hiervan betreft". All preparatory documents are available online in French and Dutch, see www.dekamer.be (documents, session 54, file no. 2403). This act was analyzed from six perspectives, i.e. sociology and human rights (Motmans & Cannoot), civil law (Verschelden), civil procedure (De Waele), child and youth psychiatry (Dhondt) and private international law (Verhellen) in Motmans and Verschelden (2020), 225 pages (written in Dutch).

[30]Belgium's official journal publishing legislation, decrees and official notices.

[31]Http://www.ejustice.just.fgov.be/eli/loi/2017/06/25/2017012964/justel. Accessed 1 July 2020.

[32]Art. 15 Gender Recognition Act.

[33]Explanatory Memorandum to the bill, *Parl.Doc.* Chamber 2016-17, n° 54-2403/1, p. 32. For example, a change had to be made to the software used by the civil registrars for editing their documents.

[34]In French: "Loi du 18 juin 2018 portant dispositions diverses en matière de droit civil et des dispositions en vue de promouvoir des formes alternatives de résolutions des litiges". In Dutch: "Wet van 18 juni 2018 houdende diverse bepalingen inzake burgerlijk recht en beplaingen met het oog op de bevordering van alternatieve vormen van geschillenbeslechting". All preparatory documents are available online in French and Dutch, see www.dekamer.be (documents, session 54, file n° 2919).

[35]Art. 118 Act 18 June 2018 as amended by art. 186 Act 21 December 2018 containing diverse provisions concerning the Department of Justice, *BG* 31 December 2018.

[36]Explanatory Memorandum to the bill, *Parl.Doc.* Chamber 2017-18, n° 54-2919/1, p. 139.

2.2 *Circular of 15 December 2017*

The Minister of Justice explained the scope of the new Act to civil status registrars in a circular, dated 15 December 2017,[37] which replaces[38] the circular explaining the previous Transsexuality Act.[39] It concerns an explanation, which has no force of law, but contains important clarifications that must guide the practice, without prejudice to the authority of courts and tribunals to interpret the law.[40] Annexes to this circular provide the citizens with five models: a model of the first[41] and second[42] Gender Registration Declaration, a model of an information sheet with reference to the information brochure and an acknowledgment that may serve as evidence that the civil status registrar has received the first declaration,[43] a model of declaration of a psychiatrist (specialized in children and adolescents) about the discernment of a minor aged 16 or older[44] and a model of declaration of honor regarding the change of first name.[45]

2.3 *Information Brochure by Royal Decree of 17 February 2019*

To inform trans persons, a Royal Decree[46] has spread an information brochure in laymen's terms.[47] This initial brochure was later revoked and replaced by the Royal Decree of 17 February 2019 in order to align it with changes introduced by the Act 18 June 2018.[48] The civil status registrar will make this information brochure

[37]Circular of 15 December 2017 explaining the Gender Recognition Act (hereinafter: Circular 15 December 2017), *BG* 29 December 2017, pp. 116785-116809. Http://www.ejustice.just.fgov.be/eli/loi/2017/06/25/2017012964/moniteur. Accessed 1 July 2020.

[38]Circular 15 December 2017, *BG* 29 December 2017, p. 116785 (preface *in fine*).

[39]Circular 1 February 2008 concerning the Transsexuality Act, *BG* 20 February 2008, p. 10758.

[40]Circular 15 December 2017, *BG* 29 December 2017, p. 116785.

[41]Annex n° 1 to Circular 15 December 2017, *BG* 29 December 2017, p. 116805.

[42]Annex n° 2 to Circular 15 December 2017, *BG* 29 December 2017, p. 116806.

[43]Annex n° 3 to Circular 15 December 2017, *BG* 29 December 2017, p. 116807.

[44]Annex n° 4 to Circular 15 December 2017, *BG* 29 December 2017, p. 116808.

[45]Annex n° 5 to Circular 15 December 2017, *BG* 29 December 2017, p. 116809.

[46]Royal Decree 17 December 2017 establishing the information brochure referred to in article 62*bis*, § 3, last subsection Civil Code, *BG* 29 December 2017, pp. 116869–116894, see, 17 Decembre 2017. - Arrêté royal établissant le modèle de brochure d'information visé à l'article 62bis, § 3, dernier alinéa du Code civil. http://www.ejustice.just.fgov.be/eli/arrete/2017/12/17/2017014307/moniteur. Accessed 1 July 2020.

[47]Annex n° 1 to the Royal Decree of 17 December 2017.

[48]The brochure can be found as an annex to the Royal Decree 17 February 2019 establishing the information brochure referred to in article 135/1, § 3, last subsection of the Belgian Civil Code, *BG* 1 March 2019, pp. 21186-21256. Http://www.ejustice.just.fgov.be/cgi_loi/loi_a.pl?N=&=&sql=

available to the person who wishes to register his or her gender identity. The official will hand over a copy of the brochure at the time of the initial declaration; the brochure is also available online.

This substantial brochure not only elaborates—in an understandable language and in a direct style—on the administrative gender registration procedure at the civil registry but also on the various legal and administrative consequences (such as identity documents, family ties and legacies, social security, mobility, housing, study certificates, employment, banks and insurances and existing convictions). At the end, the brochure guides the person concerned to the information and possible support of specialized organizations via their websites, for questions about other aspects. There is an explicit reference to the Institute for the Equality of Women and Men (IEWM) for complaints about unequal treatment because of gender identity, gender expression or gender reassignment.

2.4 *Overview of All Belgian Rules Applicable to Trans Persons*

The Belgian rules[49] specifically regarding trans persons can be found in:

- Title IV/1 *"Modification of sex registration"* of Book I of the Belgian Civil Code[50] with Article 135/1 BCC (former article 62*bis* BCC): the gender registration procedure via the civil status registrar; Article 135/2 BCC (former article 62*bis*/1 BCC): transgender affiliation law;

The new regime is explained in the Circular of 15 December 2017 concerning the Gender Recognition Act;[51]

- Chapter 3 *"Change of surname and first name"* of Title VIII/1 of Book I of the Belgian Civil Code, with Article 370/3, § 4 BCC: Conditions to change one's first name; Article 370/4, § 2, third subsection BCC: limitation of the fee due, in order to change one's first name, to 10% of the amount demanded by the municipality;

The last changes with regard to trans persons are explained in the Circular of 11 July 2018 concerning the Act of 18 June 2018.[52]

(text+contains+(%27%27))&rech=1&language=nl&tri=dd+AS+RANK&numero=1&table_name=wet&cn=2019021705&caller=image_a1&fromtab=wet&la=N&pdf_page=54&pdf_file=http://www.ejustice.just.fgov.be/mopdf/2019/03/01_1.pdf. Accessed 1 July 2020.

[49] All these references are liberal translations of the Dutch and French names.

[50] In French: https://www.ejustice.just.fgov.be/cgi_loi/change_lg.pl?language=fr&la=F&cn=1804032130&table_name=loi. Accessed 1 July 2020.

[51] In French: http://www.ejustice.just.fgov.be/eli/loi/2017/06/25/2017012964/moniteur. Accessed 1 July 2020.

[52] In French: http://www.ejustice.just.fgov.be/cgi_loi/change_lg.pl?language=fr&la=F&cn=2018071103&table_name=loi. Accessed 1 July 2020.

- Section 5 *"Excerpts and copies of civil status certificates"* of Chapter 1 of Title II of Book I of the Belgian Civil Code, with Article 29, § 1, third subsection BCC: limitation of the persons who are entitled to copy of the certificates modified in accordance with article 135/1 BCC (i.e. modified as a result of a change in registered sex) or article 1385*quaterdecies*, § 3 BJC (i.e. the judicial procedure to return, in exceptional cases to the initial registered sex[53]);
- Section 5 *"Gender Registration Certificate"* of Chapter II of Title II of Book I of the Belgian Civil Code, with Article 53 BCC (former article 62*ter* BCC): information included in a Gender Registration Certificate;
- Section 13 *"Adoption Rectification Certificate, Certificate of Return to the Initial Sex and Certificate of Annulment of Gender Registration"* of Chapter II of Title II of Book I of the Belgian Civil Code, with Article 66 BCC: information included in a Certificate of Return to the Initial Sex;
- Section 3 *"Access to the DABS/BAEC"* of Chapter III, of Title II of Book I of the Belgian Civil Code, with Article 78, third subsection BCC: limitation of the accessibility of the DABS/BAEC;
- Chapter XXV *"Judicial appeal concerning the change of a person's sex"* of Book IV of Part IV of the Belgian Judicial Code,[54] with The articles 1385 *duodecies-quaterdecies* BJC: judicial procedure before the Family Court concerning a refused gender registration or a return to the initial sex;
- Section 1*bis* "Adaptation of sex" of Chapter II of the Belgian *Private International Law* Code[55] (hereinafter: PILC), with Article 35*bis* PILC: international jurisdiction; Article 35*ter* WIPR: applicable law.[56]
- *Transitional provisions* can be found in The articles 12 till 14 of the Gender Recognition Act of 25 June 2017;[57]

Lastly, there is the official *information brochure*: *"Changing one's first or surname and gender registration via the civil registry"*.[58]

---

[53]This procedure is in fact rendered useless due to the recent judgment of the Belgian Constitutional Court.

[54]In French: http://www.ejustice.just.fgov.be/cgi_loi/change_lg.pl?language=fr&la=F&cn=1967101004&table_name=loi. Accessed 1 July 2020.

[55]In French text:http://www.ejustice.just.fgov.be/cgi_loi/change_lg.pl?language=fr&la=F&cn=2004071631&table_name=loi Accessed 1 July 2020.

[56]In French text:http://www.ejustice.just.fgov.be/cgi_loi/change_lg.pl?language=fr&la=F&cn=2004071631&table_name=loi. Accessed 1 July 2020.

[57]In French: http://www.ejustice.just.fgov.be/cgi_loi/change_lg.pl?language=fr&la=F&cn=2017062503&table_name=loi. Accessed 1 July 2020.

[58]In French: http://www.ejustice.just.fgov.be/cgi_loi/loi_a.pl?=&sql=(text+contains+(%27%27))&rech=1&language=fr&tri=dd+AS+RANK&numero=1&table_name=loi&F=&cn=2019021705&caller=image_a1&fromtab=loi&la=F&pdf_page=55&pdf_file=http://www.ejustice.just.fgov.be/mopdf/2019/03/01_1.pdf. Accessed 1 July 2020.

3 Terminology and Definitions

Although there is no specific provision with a legal definition of a trans person, the Gender Recognition Act of 25 June 2017 describes the scope of the new Act *ratione personae* as a person "having the conviction that the gender mentioned on the birth certificate does not correspond to the inner perceived gender identity".[59]

It is important to notice that the title of the previous Act was called '*Act of 10 May 2007 on* ***transsexuality***', whereas the title of the new Act refers to '*the reform of* ***transgender*** *regulations* (. . .)'(emphasis added). The Belgian legislature has clearly opted for this broader (umbrella) term.

3.1 Discrimination Protections for Gender Identity and Sexual Orientation

At the federal level, Belgium adopted three anti-discrimination laws in 2007: the General Anti-Discrimination Act, the Racial Equality Act, and the Gender Act.

People who feel discriminated because of their gender identity can invoke the Gender Act.[60] The Gender *Act of 10 May 2007 against discrimination between women and men* prohibits discrimination based on sex. It states that for the application of this act, any direct discrimination on the grounds of gender reassignment is the same as a direct discrimination on the grounds of sex (article 4, § 2). The Gender Act was amended in 2014, and the new subsection (article 4, § 3) explicitly mentions 'gender identity' and 'gender expression'. This made 'gender identity' an autonomous ground of prohibited discrimination. Before this amendment, only 'change of gender' was protected by law.[61] The body with jurisdiction is the Institute for the Equality of Women and Men (IEWM).[62] The IEWM has jurisdiction to rule on all complaints relating to discrimination based on gender, including transgenderism. Furthermore, in the information brochure there is an explicit reference to this institution.

---

[59] Art. 135/1, § 1 BCC.

[60] Act 10 May 2017 aiming at fighting against discrimination between women and men, *BG* 30 May 2007, see http://www.ejustice.just.fgov.be/cgi_loi/change_lg.pl?language=fr&la=F&cn=2007051036&table_name=loi. Accessed 1 July 2020.

[61] Report of FRA (European Union Agency for Fundamental Rights). 2015 Update. Protection against discrimination on grounds of sexual orientation, gender identity and sex characteristics in the EU Comparative legal analysis. Http://fra.europa.eu/sites/default/files/fra_uploads/protection_against_discrimination_legal_update_2015.pdf. Accessed 1 July 2020.

[62] Website of the IEWM: http://igvm-iefh.belgium.be/fr/activites/transgenre.

People who feel discriminated because of their sexual orientation can invoke the General Anti-Discrimination Act.[63] The *Anti-Discrimination Act of 10 May 2007* forbids discrimination on the basis of age, sexual orientation, civil status, birth, wealth, faith or personal belief, political orientation, syndical orientation, language, current or future health status, handicap, physical or genetic disorder, or social origin. The body with jurisdiction is UNIA, an independent institution that combats discrimination and promotes equal opportunities.[64] UNIA combats homophobia and, more broadly, all expressions of discrimination, rejection, exclusion, hate or violence, based on sexual orientation.[65]

Because of Belgium's federalist structure, the Regions and Communities have developed their own Acts on anti-discrimination, all of which contain provisions forbidding discrimination on the grounds contained in all three of the 2007 federal Acts. At the regional level, in Flanders/the Flemish Community, the main legislation of reference is the *Flemish Framework Decree on Equal Opportunities and Equal Treatment Policy* (2008),[66] while in the French-speaking Community, equal opportunities policies are governed by the *Decree on the Fight against Certain Forms of Discrimination* (2008).[67] Likewise, the Brussels-Capital Region adopted an ordinance that bans discrimination in employment, civil service, and social housing.[68] Earlier, the Walloon Parliament adopted a similar *Decree concerning the fight against certain forms of discrimination*.[69]

[63]Act 10 May 2007 aiming at fighting against certain forms of discrimination, *BG* 30 May 2007, http://www.ejustice.just.fgov.be/cgi_loi/change_lg.pl?language=fr&la=F&cn=2007051035&table_name=loi. Accessed 1 July 2020.

[64]Website of UNIA, https://www.unia.be/en/about-unia. Accessed 1 July 2020.

[65]Website of UNIA, grounds of discrimination, https://www.unia.be/en/grounds-of-discrimination/sexual-orientation. Accessed 1 July 2020.

[66]Decree of the Flemish Parliament of 10 July 2008 on Equal Opportunities and Equal Treatment Policy, *BG* 23 September 2008, http://www.ejustice.just.fgov.be/cgi_loi/change_lg.pl?language=fr&la=F&cn=2008071056&table_name=loi. Accessed 1 July 2020.

[67]Decree of the Flemish Parliament of 12 December 2008 on the Fight against Certain Forms of Discrimination, http://www.gallilex.cfwb.be/document/pdf/33730_002.pdf. Accessed 1 July 2020.

[68]Ordinance of 5 October 2017 concerning the fight against certain forms of discrimination and for equal treatment, *BG* 19 October 2017, http://www.ejustice.just.fgov.be/cgi/article_body.pl?language=fr&caller=summary&pub_date=17-10-19&numac=2017031347. Accessed 1 July 2020.

[69]Decree of the Walloon Parliament of 6 November 2008 concerning the fight against certain forms of discrimination, *BG* 19 December 2008, http://www.ejustice.just.fgov.be/cgi_loi/change_lg.pl?language=fr&la=F&cn=2008110649&table_name=loi. Accessed 1 July 2020.

4 The Legal Regulation of Name

The Belgian government drafted the new regulation concerning trans persons after years of ample consultation of all actors in the field. At the end of the legislative process, the bill was evaluated in two (unpublished) written advisory opinions of legal scholars.[70] On April 25, 2017, there was a hearing in the Commission for Justice of the Chamber of Representatives with three representative LGBT and transgender organizations, the Child Gender Team of Ghent University Hospital, the Equality Law Clinic of the Université libre de Bruxelles and the Institute for the Equality of Women and Men.[71] A consensus was reached on how to regulate the first name. The preparatory documents show no opposition. Especially the simplification of the procedure and the flexible rules for changing the given names from the age of twelve years were applauded, as well as the fact that a minor can decide to change his first name again, a second time, in a rather simple way, in case his sex registration was never executed.

One aspect of the rules related to name changes of trans persons was annulled by the Constitutional Court on 19 June 2019.[72]

4.1 *Requisites and Procedures: Declaration of Honor*

Any person, who has the conviction that the sex mentioned in his birth certificate does not match his inner perceived gender identity, adds to his request to change his/her first name a declaration of honor (art. 370/3, § 4, first subsection, first sentence BCC). From 1 August 2018 and onwards, this request has to be addressed to the competent civil status registrar (art. 370/3, § 3 BCC).[73] Now that medical conditions are no longer required in order to register one's gender identity in the registers of civil status, it follows that the conditions for trans persons to have their first name changed—at reduced rates—also had to be eased.[74] A declaration from a psychiatrist, endocrinologist, *etc.* are therefore no longer required for a request for a change of one's first name.[75]

[70]Prof. Jehanne Sosson (Catholic University of Louvain-la-Neuve) and Prof. Gerd Verschelden (Ghent University).

[71]The report of this hearing is available, see *Parl.Doc.* Chamber 2016-17, no. 54-2403/4, pp. 33–60.

[72]See Sect. 4.4.

[73]Until recently (i.e. before 1 August 2018) the competent authority was the *Federal Public Service (FPS) of Justice*.

[74]Explanatory Memorandum to the bill, *Parl.Doc.* Chamber 2016-17, n° 54-2403/1, pp. 13 *j*° 29.

[75]Old art. 2 of the Act of 15 May 1987 on Names and First Names.

4.2 Chosen First Name in Accordance with the Registered Gender

The chosen first name must be in accordance with the conviction of the trans person that the sex assigned at birth does not correspond to the gender identity (art. 370/3, § 4, first subsection, second sentence BCC). For example, a transwoman cannot get a new first name that is almost exclusively associated with a man (e.g. Adam, Bart, Henri, Mark, . . .) and a transman cannot choose a new first name that in practice is only given to women (e.g. Eva, Els, Marie, Helena, . . .). Such a change of first name would also be inadmissible on the grounds of the general procedure because the requested first name in that hypothesis could lead to confusion and/or could be detrimental to the applicant (see art. 370/2 BCC). Gender-neutral first names (e.g. Kris, Robin, Eden, Alex, . . .) are, of course, possible.[76]

4.3 Special Rules for Minors Aged 12 and Older: Parental Assistance

From the age of 12, the non-emancipated minor (i.e. the child remains subject to parental authority) is allowed to request a change of his/her first name, on the condition that he is assisted[77] by his parents or his legal guardian (art. 370/3, § 4, second subsection BCC).[78] The legislature acknowledges that minors can experience gender nonconformity at a young age and sees a simple procedure for first name change as a first important step towards a possible change of the registration of the registered sex (at the age of 16, see Sect. 5.3).[79]

The assistance regime for the first name change is the same as the assistance regime applicable to the change in registered sex for minors aged 16 and older. In the event that a parent or legal representative refuses to assist the non-emancipated minor, the minor may request the Family Court to authorize him to perform this legal act with the assistance of an ad hoc guardian (art. 370/3, § 4, third subsection BCC). The explanatory memorandum confirmed that the minor can personally request an authorization from the Family Court.[80]

---

[76]Explanatory Memorandum to the bill, *Parl.Doc.* Chamber 2016-17, n° 54-2403/1, p. 29. The Minister of Justice stated that it speaks for itself that “mixed” first names will be taken into account, see Parliamentary Committee for Justice report, *Parl.Doc.* 2016-17, n° 54-2403/4, p. 18.

[77]I.e. both parents and child need to appear before the civil registrar and need to agree to the name change; meaning that the parents have a veto right but cannot change their child’s first without the approval of that child.

[78]The two previous conditions are, of course, also applicable to minors aged 12 and older.

[79]Explanatory Memorandum to the bill, *Parl.Doc.* Chamber 2016-17, n° 54-2403/1, p. 30.

[80]Explanatory Memorandum to the bill, *Parl.Doc.* Chamber 2016-17, n° 54-2403/1, p. 14.

4.4 *The Unconstitutionality of the Impossibility to Change the First Name More Than Once at the Reduced Rate*

In its judgment of 19 June 2019, the Belgian Constitutional Court declared unconstitutional the in principle irrevocable nature of the change—at the reduced rate—of sex registration in the birth certificate as well as the fact that a first name change can only be requested once by trans persons, because it discriminates persons with a fluid gender identity.[81] The legal framework regarding the amount of changes of the first name will be briefly explained in order to fully understand what was deemed contrary to the principle of equality and non-discrimination.

The legal framework as in force before the 2019 judgment was as follows. A trans person has the *right* to request a first name change (art. 370/4, § 2, third subsection BCC). In principle, a change of first name can only be requested once—at the reduced rate of 10% of the communal rate (art. 370/4, § 2, fourth subsection BCC)—on the grounds that the applicant has the conviction that the sex assigned at birth does not correspond to his inner perceived gender identity (art. 370/3, § 3, first subsection, third sentence BCC). Afterwards, the normal procedure for change of first name—at the normal rate[82]—is still possible, as it is open to everyone.

For adults, the rule that a change of the first name can be requested only once for reasons related to transgenderism, only knows one exception. A second change of first name at reduced rate is possible if the Family Court allowed the return to the initial registered sex (art. 370/3, § 4, first subsection, third sentence read in conjunction with art. 370/4, § 2, fourth subsection BCC).

A non-emancipated minor aged 12 and older whose first name has already been changed because of reasons related to transgenderism, may request for a second change for the same reason, insofar as he did not proceed to change the registration of his/her registered sex in accordance with article 135/1 BCC (art. 370/3, § 4, fourth subsection BCC).

Considering the different age requirements for a change of first name (12 years) and the gender registration procedure (16 years) the legislature has, after a remark from the Council of State,[83] given the non-emancipated transgender minor the possibility to change his first name for a second time until his 18th birthday at the reduced rate of 10% of the communal rate. After the age of majority, a second (and next) change of first name is still possible, but then at the normal rate of euros.[84]

[81] See more details in Sect. 6 on Gender-neutral and/or third-sex.

[82] Based on art. 170, § 4 of the Belgian Constitution. This rate differs vastly among the different communities. In the larger cities (e.g. Ghent, Antwerp, Leuven, Mechelen) the first name can be changed for free. In smaller communities, it can be up to hundreds of euros (e.g. Meulebeke: 250 euros).

[83] Advice of the Council of State n° 60.690/2, *Parl.Doc.* Chamber 2016-17, n° 54-2403/1, p. 62 (point 2 of the remarks about art. 10 of the bill).

[84] Explanatory Memorandum to the bill, *Parl.Doc.* Chamber 2016-17, n° 54-2403/1, p. 30.

Together with the in principle irrevocable nature of the adaptation of sex registration, the Belgian Constitutional Court annulled the one-time first name change for trans persons.[85] As a consequence, trans persons are, nowadays, able to change their name as many times as needed at the reduced rate of 10% of the communal rate, without having to appeal to a judge and without having to prove exceptional circumstances.

5 The Legal Regulation of Sexual Identity

The Gender Recognition Act of 25 June 2017 was almost unanimously approved in the Belgian Federal Parliament. 117 votes were in favor, there were, however, six abstentions amongst the Flemish nationalist parties, four from the 'Nieuw-Vlaamse Alliantie' and two from 'Vlaams Belang'.[86] The two major points of discussion were (1) the obligation for minors between 16 and 18 to submit a declaration from the child psychiatrist and (2) the discretionary powers of the Public Prosecutor and the civil status registrar (details in this section).

The greatest merit is that the new Act decouples the legal aspect of transgenderism from the medical aspects and translates the right to self-determination into reality. The new Act is intended to offer all individuals maximum opportunities for self-development, without having to comply with excessive requirements. All political parties recognize that an important step is taken in favor of the recognition and inclusion of trans persons.[87]

During the hearing in the Chamber of Representatives, LGTB organizations criticized the fact that the rights of persons with multiple sex characteristics ('intersex'), non-binary and gender fluid persons are not (as such) addressed in the new Act (see also below, Sect. 6 on Gender-neutral and/or third-sex and Intersex Persons).

5.1 Persons Allowed to Bring Their Registered Sex in Accordance with Their Gender Identity

Every Belgian adult or Belgian emancipated minor or foreigner registered in the population register (i.e. a sub-register of the national register), who has the

[85]Technically, the Court annulled the words "if the change of first name was permitted by the Family Court" in article 2, third subsection of the Act of 15 May 1987 on Names and First Names, as replaced by article 11 of the Gender Recognition Act 2017 (but abolished by the Act of 18 June 2018). The corresponding content in the current legislation is to be found in article 370/3, § 4, subsection 1 BCC. This provision is not annulled.

[86]Acts Chamber 2016-17, 25 May 2017, CRIV 54 PLEN 170, p. 58.

[87]Acts Chamber 2016-17, 25 May 2017, CRIV 54 PLEN 170, pp. 36–51. Https://www.dekamer.be/doc/PCRI/pdf/54/ip170.pdf. Accessed 1 July 2020.

conviction that the sex mentioned in his birth certificate does not correspond with his inner perceived gender identity, can make a declaration of this conviction before the civil status registrar (art. 135/1, § 1 BCC).

Foreigners can only make a declaration if they are registered in the population register or, according to the circular, of the foreigners register.[88] The foreigners registered in the waiting register cannot make a declaration. This requirement of registration in the population registers for foreign nationals was motivated by the fact that close ties with Belgium are required for the declaration.[89]

From the age of 16,[90] the non-emancipated minor with discernment[91] can change his or her registered sex (art. 135/1, § 10, first subsection BCC). The government has acknowledged that children can already realize at an early age that the sex mentioned in their birth certificate does not match their gender identity. Medical practice in Belgium was taken into account when determining the age limit for the change of sex registration. First, puberty inhibitors and starting from the age of 16 cross-sex hormones (after at least 1 year of follow-up by a multidisciplinary pediatric gender team) are administered; the request to change the registration of the registered sex from 16 years and onwards was considered the next logical step.[92] For the registration by a minor, the legislature has imposed two additional conditions: the handing over of a declaration from a child and adolescent psychiatrist and the mandatory assistance from his parents, his legal representative or an *ad hoc* guardian (art. 135/1, § 10, first subsection BCC).[93]

5.2 *Procedure at the Civil Registry*

The procedure to change one's registered sex registration is divided into two parts: the first part consists of the registration of the declarations that express the will to change the registration of one's registered sex, the second part consists in the drawing-up of the Gender Registration Certificate.

At the registration, the person concerned submits to the civil status registrar a declaration signed by him, stating:

- that he/she has been convinced for a long time that the gender mentioned in his birth certificate does not correspond to his inner perceived gender identity; and
- that he/she wishes the administrative and legal consequences of a change of the sex registration in his birth certificate (art. 135/1, § 3, first subsection BCC).

[88]Circular 15 December 2017, *BG* 29 December 2017, p. 116786.

[89]Circular 15 December 2017, *BG* 29 December 2017, p. 116786.

[90]Remarkable difference vis-à-vis the age required for the change of one's first name.

[91]I.e. having the ability to distinguish right from wrong, having the ability to foresee consequences and to reason.

[92]Explanatory Memorandum to the bill, *Parl.Doc.* Chamber 2016-17, n° 54-2403/1, pp. 10 and 16.

[93]See more details *infra* Sect. 5.3.

This declaration and its legally determined content are expressions of an informed consent approach: the legislature set these requirements in order to prevent the person concerned from acting lightheartedly, without being properly informed about the important consequences of the principally irrevocable nature of the gender registration.[94]

A model of the declaration is available as an annex to the circular.[95] The person concerned can print it out and bring a signed copy to the registrar. If the person concerned does not have the declaration with him, the civil status registrar supplies him or her with a copy of the declaration.[96]

Although the declaration states that the person concerned has been convinced for "a long time" that his birth sex does not correspond to his inner perceived gender identity, it is not up to the civil status registrar to check the duration of that conviction. The registrar is only allowed to check whether the declaration contains these words.[97]

The person concerned must appear in person at the time of the registration. The circular clarifies that the registration is not possible by (registered) letter or by proxy, because the civil status registrar must at the same time also hand over the additional information to the person concerned.[98]

5.3 Minors Aged 16 and Older

Additional conditions exist for the declaration by minors aged 16 and older, including submitting a declaration of a child and adolescent psychiatrist and the assistance by the parents, the legal guardian or an ad hoc guardian.

5.3.1 Declaration of a Child and Adolescent Psychiatrist

The Gender Recognition bill initially required the intervention of a child and adolescent psychiatrist, in the capacity of treating physician, who had to confirm that the person concerned has the permanent conviction that the gender as stated in his birth certificate does not correspond to his inner perceived gender identity.[99] The explanatory memorandum clarified that the intervention of the psychiatrist is not intended to make a diagnosis, but is only aimed at confirming the deliberate and

---

[94]Explanatory Memorandum to the bill, *Parl.Doc.* Chamber 2016-17, n° 54-2403/1, pp. 17–18.

[95]Annex n° 1 to Circular 15 December 2017, *BG* 29 December 2017, p. 116805.

[96]Circular 15 December 2017, *BG* 29 December 2017, p. 116787.

[97]Circular 15 December 2017, *BG* 29 December 2017, p. 116787.

[98]Circular 15 December 2017, *BG* 29 December 2017, p. 116787.

[99]Proposed art. 62*bis*, § 11, first subsection Civil Code, as included in art. 3 of the bill, see *Parl.Doc.* Chamber 2016-17, n° 54-2403/1, p. 68.

unpressured will of the minor. According to the explanatory memorandum, it had to be a psychiatrist who had followed the minor for a long time.[100]

In view of the bill's ratio—i.e. to "demedicalize" the gender registration procedure and requirements—members of Parliament were of the opinion that non-emancipated minors, with sufficient discernment, could sufficiently realize themselves that their sex does not correspond to their gender identity and could also make their own assessment of the (legal) consequences that a gender registration entails. An amendment submitted by the majority was accepted,[101] aiming to maintain the intervention of the child and adolescent psychiatrist "in order to ascertain whether the minor in question has sufficient discernment to make the declaration and to assess its consequences".[102]

The Gender Recognition Act stipulates that the non-emancipated minor with discernment can make a declaration from the age of sixteen, provided that a declaration from a child and adolescent psychiatrist is handed over at the declaration, confirming that the person concerned has sufficient discernment to have the permanent conviction that the sex mentioned in his birth certificate does not correspond with his inner perceived gender identity (art. 135/1, § 10, first subsection BCC).

The circular clarifies that the child and adolescent psychiatrist only checks whether the minor is able to make this decision consciously and independently.[103]

Members of Parliament from the opposition tried, through even more far-reaching amendments, to eliminate psychiatrist's intervention, but none of these amendments were adopted, either in the Parliamentary Committee of Justice[104] or in the plenary session of the Chamber of Representatives.[105]

For example, the French-speaking Socialist Party and Christian-democratic Party wished that any medical intervention would disappear and any Belgian aged 16 or older could register his or her gender identity by means of a declaration of honor.[106] The Flemish Socialists pointed out that the gender registration of minors is a step in a

[100]Explanatory Memorandum to the bill, *Parl.Doc.* Chamber 2016-17, n° 54-2403/1, p. 17.

[101]Report of the Parliamentary Committee for Justice, *Parl.Doc.* Chamber 2016-17, n° 54-2403/4, pp. 24 and 26.

[102]Justification to Amendment n° 2 (Van Hoof *et al.*), *Parl.Doc.* Chamber 2016-17, n° 54-2403/2, p. 3.

[103]Circular 15 December 2017, *BG* 29 December 2017, p. 116788.

[104]Report of the Parliamentary Committee for Justice, *Parl.Doc.* Chamber 2016-17, n° 54-2403/4, p. 26.

[105]Acts Chamber 2016-17, 25 May 2017, CRIV 54 PLEN 170, pp. 52 *j*° 56–58. Https://www.dekamer.be/doc/PCRI/pdf/54/ip170.pdf. Accessed 1 July 2020.

[106]Justification to Amendment n° 6 (Winckel, Lalieux and Brotcorne), *Parl.Doc.* Chamber 2016-17, n° 54-2403/2, p. 7 (rejected in committee with 13 to 3 votes). See also Amendment n° 20 (Winckel and Lalieux), *Parl.Doc.* Chamber 2016-17, n° 54-2403/ 7, p. 3 (rejected in plenary by 78 votes against 40 and 6 abstentions).

long-term development that requires assistance from the parents or legal representative (and that this assistance as such could suffice as an additional condition).[107] The French-speaking Green parties were opposed to the parental assistance requirement and were in favor of establishing (in abstracto) the full legal capacity of a minor older than 16 to change his registered sex.[108]

From the latter fractions, the idea was also suggested that if the declaration of an external expert (about the discernment) stayed as a condition, every expert should be allowed to draw up this declaration, not just a child and adolescent psychiatrist, but also a (different) treating physician (including the general practitioner) or a psychologist.[109]

The question arises whether the opinion of the child and adolescent psychiatrist—who attests that the minor has the required discernment—is binding on the civil status registrar. That was certainly not the intention of the government, since the explanatory memorandum to the bill not only emphasizes that the registrar of civil status must check whether the legal conditions are fulfilled (mentioning the psychiatrist's declaration, the parents' assistance and the conditions that also apply to adults), but also specifically states that this official must judge the discernment of the minor.[110]

5.3.2 Assistance by the Parents, Legal Guardian or an Ad Hoc Guardian

At the registration, the person concerned is assisted by his parents or his legal guardian (art. 135/1, § 10, first subsection *in fine* BCC). If they refuse (meaning: in case a single parent or the legal representative refuses) to assist the non-emancipated minor, the minor may request the Family Court to authorize him to perform this act with the assistance of an ad-hoc guardian (art. 135/1, § 10, second subsection BCC). If the court appoints the guardian *ad hoc*, he or she will act on behalf of both parents.[111]

---

[107]Justification to Amendment n° 9 (Jiroflée and Lambrecht), *Parl.Doc.* Chamber 2016-17, n°. 54-2403/2, p. 10 (rejected in committee with 10 to 6 votes). See also Amendment n° 19 (Jiroflée and Lambrecht), *Parl.Doc.* Chamber 2016-17, n° 54-2403/ 7, p. 2 (rejected in plenary by 83 votes against 40 and 1 abstentions).

[108]Amendment n° 10 (Hellings and Gerkens), *Parl.Doc.* Chamber 2016-17, n° 54-2403/3, pp. 2–3 (rejected in committee by 10 votes against 4 and 2 abstentions) and Amendment n° 17 (Hellings and Van Hecke), *Parl.Doc.* Chamber 2016-17, n° 54-2403/ 6, pp. 2–3 (rejected in plenary by 83 votes against 40 and 1 abstention).

[109]Amendment n° 13 (Hellings), *Parl.Doc.* Chamber 2016-17, n° 54-2403/3, p. 7 (withdrawn in committee), amendment n° 16 (Hellings and Jiroflée), *Parl.Doc.* Chamber 2016-17, n° 54-2403/3, p. 10 (rejected in committee with 10 votes against 3 and 3 abstentions) and Amendment n° 17 (Hellings and Van Hecke), *Parl.Doc.* Chamber 2016-17, n° 54-2403/6, p. 4 (rejected in plenary by 83 votes against 40 and 1 abstention).

[110]Explanatory Memorandum to the bill, *Parl.Doc.* Chamber 2016-17, n° 54-2403/1, p. 17.

[111]Circular 15 December 2017, *BG* 29 December 2017, p. 116788.

From the plural form in the legal text ("parents") it can already be deduced that the law requires assistance from *both parents* and therefore both have to agree with the registration, for a minor who has an established (original or adoptive[112]) lineage with two parents exercising parental responsibilities. In this area, the new rules are stricter than the previous provisions, where assistance from one parent was sufficient. The Minister of Justice confirmed this interpretation during the discussions in the Chamber of Representatives: if one parent wants to assist the minor and the other does not, the Family Court will decide.[113]

In case both parents of the minor have died, if they are legally unknown or in the lasting impossibility to exercise parental responsibilities, or if they are legally incompetent, the minor is under guardianship (art. 389, first subsection BCC) and will have to obtain the assistance of his guardian, in his capacity as *legal representative*.

The *assistance* means that the person(s) providing assistance *act(s) together with*[114] the minor for the civil status registrar. The minor therefore acts personally, however not alone and independently. After all, the essence of the legal assistance is that the parents or the legal representative are aware of this fundamental legal act with regard to the person's civil status, and consequently complete this fundamental legal act.[115]

Each of the parents and/or legal guardians may appear separately with the minor before the (same) civil registrar, when they are unable to appear at the same time. In this way, according to the circular, both parents provide the legally required assistance (at two different times).[116]

The same circular clarifies that the parents or the legal representative can also provide this assistance through a special and authenticated letter of attorney. Personal appearance of the assistance provider(s) is therefore not required, but a general or private letter of attorney is not sufficient.

5.4 Role of the Civil Status Registrar

The role of the civil status registrar ~~main~~ comprises a/ Informing the person concerned about the remainder of the procedure and its (legal) consequences and

[112]Circular 15 December 2017, *BG* 29 December 2017, p. 116787.

[113]Report of the Parliamentary Committee for Justice, *Parl.Doc.* Chamber 2016-17, n° 54-2403/4, p. 25, *in fine*, at the request of MP Sonja Becq (CD&V).

[114]I.e. both parents and child need to appear before the civil registrar and need to agree to the name change; meaning that the parents have a veto right but cannot change their child's first without the approval of that child.

[115]Circ. 15 December 2017, *BG* 29 December 2017, p. 116787.

[116]Circ. 15 December 2017, *BG* 29 December 2017, p. 116787 *in fine*.

b/ Taking note of the declaration and issuing an acknowledgement of receipt to the person concerned.

The civil status registrar:

- informs about the further course of the procedure, its administrative and legal consequences; and
- provides the information brochure, drawn-up by Royal Decree, as well as the contact details of transgender organizations (art. 135/1, § 3, second subsection *j*° fifth subsection BCC).

The obligation to point out the principally irrevocable nature of the gender registration was annulled by the Belgian Constitutional Court in its recent judgment of 19 June 2019.[117]

According to the circular, the civil status registrar can simply emphasize here that the procedure has not yet been completed. The registrar informs the person concerned that, between three and six months after the exchange of the receipt, he has to make another declaration for the civil status registrar so that the gender can be registered and the registered sex can be changed.

On request, the civil status registrar may state that the waiting period between the first and second declaration is intended to ask for the advice of the Public Prosecutor and for the person concerned to inform himself about the concrete consequences of a gender registration. The civil status registrar refers to the information brochure provided for more information about the procedure and its consequences.

The registrar clarifies that the brochure contains all the practical consequences of the gender registration, and also announces that he or she can address additional questions to the transgender organizations, whose contact details are on the website of the FPS of Justice and the Institute for the Equality of Women and Men.

The registrar clearly communicates (on paper) to the person concerned where the information brochure is available (the website of the FPS of Justice, possibly also the website of the municipality, ...). The official provides the information sheet to the person concerned. If the person concerned requests him to do so, the registrar shall provide a physical copy of the brochure. As far as the person concerned asks more questions, the civil status registrar can refer to the contact details of the transgender organizations that are available on the website of the FPS of Justice and the IEWM. If the registrar of the civil registry wishes to provide additional oral explanations ~~at the counter~~, this has to be done with respect for the involved person's privacy.[118]

The registrar takes note of the declaration and issues an acknowledgement of receipt to the person concerned (art. 135/1, § 3, third subsection BCC). The receipt and information sheet are—integrated in one document—spread as an annex to the circular.[119] Taking note of the declaration means that the registrar receives the declaration and provides a receipt to the person concerned. The registrar does not

[117]See more details in Sect. 6 on Gender-neutral and/or third-sex.

[118]Circular 15 December 2017, *BG* 29 December 2017, p. 116789.

[119]Annex n° 3 to Circular 15 December 2017, *BG* 29 December 2017, p. 116789.

draw up a provisional document of civil status (on a separate sheet), as was previously the case. The declaration is not included in the civil status registers; it is included in the file.[120] The receipt shall indicate the first and last day on which the person concerned could make the second declaration.[121]

5.5 Mandatory Notification to and Binding Negative Opinion from the Public Prosecutor

The civil status registrar who takes note of the declaration must inform the Public Prosecutor at the Court of First Instance within three days. The Public Prosecutor will immediately give an acknowledgement of receipt (art. 135/1, § 3, fourth subsection BCC). The government considers the communication to the Public Prosecutor as a means of protection against (identity) fraud or problematic declarations (e.g. of persons wanted by the court).[122]

The Public Prosecutor may, within three months from the date of the acknowledgement of receipt, give a negative opinion due to an infringement of public order (art. 135/1, § 4, first subsection BCC). The opinion of the Public Prosecutor is only binding when it is negative (see Sect. 5.10).[123]

5.6 Territorial Competence of the Civil Status Registrar

The registration is made before the civil status registrar of the municipality where the person is registered in the population register (art. 135/1, § 2, first subsection BCC). This provision applies to both Belgian nationals and foreigners registered in the population registers.

A Belgian national who is not registered in the population register shall make the declaration before the civil status registrar of his birthplace. If he was not born in Belgium, he makes the declaration before the civil status registrar in Brussels (art. 135/1, § 2, second subsection BCC).

At the moment of registration, the Belgian citizen who is not registered in the population registers gives the civil status registrar the address on which he can be informed of a (potential) refusal to draw up the Gender Registration Certificate (art. 135/1, § 2, second subsection BCC). The civil registry officer will have to ensure that the person making the declaration gives his or her address.[124]

[120]Circular 15 December 2017, *BG* 29 December 2017, p. 116787.

[121]Circular15 December 2017, *BG* 29 December 2017, p. 116787.

[122]Explanatory Memorandum to the bill, *Parl.Doc.* Chamber 2016-17, n° 54-2403/1, p. 18.

[123]Explanatory Memorandum to the bill, *Parl.Doc.* Chamber 2016-17, n° 54-2403/1, p. 9.

[124]Circular 15 December 2017, *BG* 29 December 2017, p. 116787.

5.7 *Drawing up of the Gender Registration Certificate After a Second Written Declaration of the Person Concerned and After the Expiration of a Waiting Period*

5.7.1 Waiting Period of a Minimum of Three and a Maximum of Six Months

Not earlier than three months after and at the latest six months after the date of the acknowledgement of receipt, the person concerned appears a second time for the civil status registrar for whom the initial declaration was made (art. 135/1, § 5, first subsection BCC).

The legislature opted for a reflection period (in line with the Danish model[125]) to ensure that the person concerned was sufficiently informed about all legal, social and psychological consequences of the gender registration.[126] The goal was to be able to have a certain period of reflection about the information obtained.[127] If the second appearance occurs later than six-months after the initial declaration, the person concerned must make a new declaration and restart the procedure (including the waiting period).[128]

5.8 *Second Written Declaration*

The person concerned submits to the civil status registrar (of the place where the first declaration was made[129]) a signed declaration stating that he:

- is still convinced that the sex assigned in his birth certificate does not correspond to his inner perceived gender identity;
- is aware of the administrative and legal consequences of the adaptation of gender registration (art. 135/1, § 5, second subsection BCC).

The statement from the person concerned that he or she is aware of the irrevocable nature of the change of registered sex (art. 135/1, § 5, 3° BCC)[130] was ruled

[125]Although the regulation in Denmark is stricter: in that legal system, a reflection period of 6 months must have been completed before the first application can be renewed and the gender reassignment can be implemented.

[126]Explanatory Memorandum to the bill, *Parl.Doc.* Chamber 2016-17, n° 54-2403/1, p. 9.

[127]Explanatory Memorandum to the bill, *Parl.Doc.* Chamber 2016-17, n° 54-2403/1, p. 18.

[128]Circular 15 December 2017, *BG* 29 December 2017, p. 116789.

[129]This is also the case when the place of residence of the person concerned has changed between the first and the second declaration; see Circular 15 December 2017, *BG* 29 December 2017, p. 116789.

[130]Which was a part of the second declaration.

unconstitutional by the Belgian Constitutional Court in its recent judgment of 19 June 2019.[131]

A model of this second declaration is included as an annex to the circular[132] and is also available on the website of the FPS of Justice and the IEWM. The person concerned can print the declaration and bring a signed copy to the registrar. If the person concerned does not have the declaration with him, the civil status registrar supplies him or her with a copy of the declaration.

In the Gender Recognition *Bill*, the government had opted for a system where, at the time of the second appearance, in addition to the handing over of the second written declaration, a so-called 'certificate of awareness' of at least 14 days and at most 1 year old and issued by a transgender organization recognized by Royal Decree, had to be submitted.[133] This certificate would confirm that the person concerned was fully informed of the importance of the decision.[134]

During the hearing in the Chamber of Representatives, however, not a single transgender organization was in favor of this system because not every trans person feels the need to go to a transgender organization and a legally required consultation could be too high a threshold. An amendment to omit the mandatory submission of an 'awareness certificate' was unanimously adopted.[135]

5.8.1 Personal Appearance

It must be assumed that the person concerned must also appear in person at the second appearance for the registrar of civil status. At the time of the second declaration, the non-emancipated minor does not need assistance from the parents or the legal representative, nor a (second) declaration from a child and adolescent psychiatrist. The parental assistance requisite (art. 135/1, § 10, last sentence BCC) only applies, according to the circular, to the first appearance before the civil registrar.[136]

---

[131] See more details in Sect. 6.2.

[132] See Annex n° 2 to Circular 15 December 2017, *BG* 29 December 2017, p. 116806.

[133] Proposed art. 62*bis*, § 5, third-seventh subsection BCC, as included in art. 3 of the bill, see *Parl. Doc.* Chamber 2016-17, n° 54-2403/1, pp. 66–67.

[134] Explanatory Memorandum to the bill, *Parl.Doc.* Chamber 2016-17, n° 54-2403/1, pp. 19–20.

[135] Amendment n° 1 (Van Hoof *c.s.*), *Parl.Doc.* Chamber 2016-17, n° 54-2403/2, p. 2 *j*° Report of the Parliamentary Committee for Justice, *Parl.Doc.* Chamber 2016-17, no. 54-2403/4, pp. 20 and 26.

[136] Circular 15 December 2017, *BG* 29 December 2017, p. 116790.

5.8.2 Role of the Civil Status Registrar

According to the circular, the civil status registrar, at the second appearance, only has to check whether the formal conditions for the change of the registration of the registered sex have been met. More specifically, he must therefore check, before drafting the certificate, whether:

- the registration was done correctly, in particular whether the first declaration of the person concerned was received as provided for in article 135/1, § 3 BCC and (with respect to the non-emancipated minor) article 135/1, § 10 BCC;
- the second appearance took place before the same civil status registrar who received the first declaration;
- the person concerned has made a second declaration in which he or she confirms the first declaration and the fact that he or she is aware and wishes its legal consequences;
- the second appearance occurred at least three and not later than six months after the date of the acknowledgment of receipt of the first declaration;
- no negative opinion was given by the Public Prosecutor (if this is the case, the drawing up of the certificate must be refused);
- all general conditions have been met to draw up a valid civil status certificate;[137]
- the person concerned has not been declared incapable to express his or her will and is able to express his or her at that moment in time.

As soon as the second declaration has been received, the civil status registrar will in principle immediately proceed to draw up the Gender Registration Certificate (except in case of a negative opinion from the Public Prosecutor, see Sect. 5.10).

5.9 *The Gender Registration Certificate*

In the absence of a negative opinion from the Public Prosecutor, the civil status registrar can draw up the Gender Registration Certificate (art. 135/1, § 5, third subsection BCC). The Public Prosecutor can, within three months from the date of the acknowledgement of receipt—i.e. the acknowledgement that was handed over to the person concerned and not the acknowledgement given by the Public Prosecutor to the civil registrar—issue a negative opinion due to reasons of public order (art. 135/1, § 4, first subsection BCC).

The circular states that the possibility for the Public Prosecutor to issue a negative opinion is very limited because the basis of the Gender Recognition Act of 25 June 2017 is self-determination. A negative opinion is only possible if the request to change one's registered sex infringes public order. This may be in the case of fraud, e.g. when a person tries to escape his/her creditors or uses a false identity. The mere

[137]Circular 15 December 2017, *BG* 29 December 2017, p. 116790.

fact of having a criminal record, without further justification, cannot be a reason for negative advice.[138]

In the absence of negative opinion or in the event a notice was sent that no negative opinion will be issued at the end of the three-month period, the opinion is assumed to be positive (art. 135/1, § 5, third subsection BCC). Only a negative opinion of the Public Prosecutor is binding.[139]

The Gender Registration Certificate contains the following information:

- the name;
- the first name(s);
- the place of birth;
- the date of birth; and
- the new gender of the person concerned (art. 53 BCC).

The Gender Registration Certificate is registered in the DABS/BAEC (art. 14, second subsection BCC). The civil status registrar links the Gender Registration Certificate to the civil status certificates in which the sex of the person concerned is mentioned (art. 135/1, § 5, third subsection BCC).

5.10 Refusal to Draw Up the Gender Registration Certificate

The civil status registrar must refuse to draw up the Gender Registration Certificate in the event of negative opinion of the Public Prosecutor (art. 135/1, § 5, fourth subsection BCC). The civil status registrar cannot refuse to draw up the certificate because of a personal reason or conviction.[140] He cannot perform any opportunity check.[141]

In the absence of negative opinion, the civil status registrar can only refuse in exceptional cases. It remains the responsibility of the civil status registrar to check whether all conditions have been met to draw up a valid certificate. That will not be the case if, for example, the person is clearly unable to express his will as a result of his condition, e.g. due to alcohol intoxication.[142]

During the discussion in the Chamber Committee for Justice, the Minister clarified that the final decision lies indeed with the civil status registrar, except in the case of a negative opinion from the Public Prosecutor, in which case he must take a negative decision (against which judicial appeal is possible). If no opinion is given, this opinion is deemed to be positive, but this does not oblige the civil status registrar

[138]Circular 15 December 2017, *BG* 29 December 2017, p. 116789.

[139]Explanatory Memorandum to the bill, *Parl.Doc.* Chamber 2016-17, n° 54-2403/1, p. 9.

[140]Explanatory Memorandum to the bill, *Parl.Doc.* Chamber 2016-17, n° 54-2403/1, p. 20.

[141]Circular 15 December 2017, *BG* 29 December 2017, p. 116791.

[142]Explanatory Memorandum to the bill, *Parl.Doc.* Chamber 2016-17, n° 54-2403/1, p. 21; Circ. 15 December 2017, *BG* 29 December 2017, p. 116791.

to make a positive decision. In that case, he has discretionary authority, which is, however, limited to a marginal check of extreme cases relating to public order or the mental state of the person concerned. The Minister pointed out that no subjective right is automatically granted; the official is obliged and authorized to judge whether the legal conditions have been met.[143]

An amendment aimed at explicitly mentioning in the text of the law that the civil status registrar has no powers of appreciation[144] was rejected, both in the Committee for Justice[145] and in the Chamber's plenary session.[146]

The civil status registrar who refuses to draw up a Gender Registration Certificate, immediately informs the person concerned of his well-reasoned decision and, if applicable, the negative opinion of the Public Prosecutor[147] (art. 135/1, § 6 BCC). The Minister of Justice stated in his circular that it is appropriate to make this notification by registered letter with receipt confirmation or by direct handover that is confirmed by a receipt of acknowledgement.[148]

The person concerned can lodge an appeal against the refusal by the civil status registrar at the Family Court within 60 days starting from his notification of his decision, according to article 1385*duodecies* of the Judicial Code (art. 135/1, § 7 BCC).

5.11 Successive Changes of the Registered Gender

As mentioned before, changing one's registered sex as to bring it in accordance with the inner perceived gender identity has, in principle, an irrevocable nature. In exceptional cases, however, a person can return to his or her initial sex by means of judicial procedure. Although this irrevocable nature was later ruled unconstitutional (see Sect. 6.2) we will first explain the rules regarding the irrevocability of a gender change that were applicable before the judgment of 19 June 2019 of the Belgian Constitutional Court.

143 Report of the Parliamentary Committee for Justice, *Parl.Doc.* Chamber 2016-17, n° 54-2403/4, pp. 21 *j*° 23.

144 Amendment n° 7 (Winckel, Lalieux and Brotcorne), *Parl.Doc.* Chamber 2016-17, n° 54-2403/2, p. 8 and the identical amendment n° 21 (Winckel and Lalieux), *Parl.Doc.* Chamber 2016-17, n° 54-2403/7, p. 4.

145 Report of the Committee for Justice, *Parl.Doc.* Chamber 2016-17, n° 54-2403/4, pp. 20 and 26 (10 to 6 votes).

146 Acts Chamber 2016-17, 25 May 2017, CRIV 54 PLEN 170, pp. 56-57, https://www.dekamer.be/doc/PCRI/pdf/54/ip170.pdf.

147 The legal obligation to transmit the negative opinion of the Public Prosecutor was added because of a remark by the Council of State; see Advice n° 60.690/2, *Parl.Doc.* Chamber 2016-17, n° 54-2403/1, p. 59 (point 6 of the comments about article 3 of the preliminary draft).

148 Circular 15 December 2017, *BG* 29 December 2017, p. 116789.

Changing from the registered sex to the chosen gender identity is in principle an irrevocable process (art. 135/1, § 9 BCC). The in principal irrevocable nature of the gender registration constitutes, according to the Minister of Justice, evidence that the authorities really have confidence in the person concerned.[149] The irrevocability must of course also be seen as prevention against lighthearted changes.[150]

The legislature deliberately introduced a judicial return procedure with strict and harsh conditions as a guarantee against fraud[151] and to prevent multiple and ill-considered requests to change one's registered sex. After all, the registered sex concerns the person's civil status, which remains in principle inalienable. Comparative research[152] has shown that countries with a flexible registration procedure have a strict return procedure.[153]

5.12 Prerequisite for a Return to the Initial Registered Sex: Proof of Exceptional Circumstances

If proof of exceptional circumstances is provided, the Family Court may allow a return to the initial registered sex (art. 135/1, § 9, second subsection BCC). The legislative preparatory works cite two examples of exceptional circumstances:

- *transphobia:* if the person concerned proves that he or she is the victim of transphobia, in particular that he or she cannot deal with the social reaction after the (legal) change;
- *error:* if the person concerned has been mentally or physically less happy since the transition than before and his welfare has therefore deteriorated.[154]

The information brochure—which has, strictly speaking, no binding force but is nevertheless drawn up by the Belgian Government—states that exceptional circumstances are proven *when a person's gender identity no longer corresponds with his or her chosen registered gender.*[155]

---

[149]Report of the Committee for Justice, *Parl.Doc.* Chamber 2016-17, n° 54-2403/4, p. 17.

[150]Explanatory Memorandum to the bill, *Parl.Doc.* Chamber 2016-17, n° 54-2403/1, pp. 17–18.

[151]Explanatory Memorandum to the bill, *Parl.Doc.* Chamber 2016-17, n° 54-2403/1, p. 9.

[152]P. Borghs, *De medische criteria in de wet betreffende de transseksualiteit.* This comparative study (in Dutch) commissioned by the IEWM, completed in October 2013. Https://www.ilga-europe.org/sites/default/files/transseksualiteit_medische_criteria_tcm336-2371871.pdf. Accessed 1 July 2020.

[153]Explanatory Memorandum to the bill, *Parl.Doc.* Chamber 2016-17, n° 54-2403/1, p. 22 (see on page 30, n° 72 of the study mentioned in the previous footnote as to the example of Argentina).

[154]Explanatory Memorandum to the bill, *Parl.Doc.* Chamber 2016-17, n° 54-2403/1, pp. 22-23; Circular 15 December 2017, *BG* 29 December 2017, p. 116792.

[155]P. 21 of the information brochure, which can be found as an annex to the Royal Decree 17 February 2019 establishing the information brochure referred to in article 135/1, § 3, last subsection BCC, *BG* 1 March 2019, pp. 21186-21256. Http://www.ejustice.just.fgov.be/cgi_loi/

The burden of proof regarding the presence of exceptional circumstances lies with the person requesting the return (*Actori probatio incumbit*). It falls within the Family Court's discretionary power to assess the exceptional character of the supplied facts. It should also be kept in mind that, as a general rule, exceptions should be interpreted restrictively (*Exceptio est strictissisimae interpretationis*). However, the exceptional circumstances envisaged by the legislature himself will commonly occur, which may indicate that the legislature nevertheless has given a broad margin of appreciation to the Family Court.

Although the law does not list who can initiate the procedure to return to the initial registered sex, it must be assumed that every adult or emancipated minor, referred to in article 135/1, § 1 BCC, whose sex registration was changed, is entitled to do so. It was also clearly the intention of the legislature to allow non-emancipated minors aged 16 and older to change their registered sex to their gender identity. His exceptional legal capacity to register his inner perceived gender identity (with the assistance of his parents or legal representative)[156] and his legal capacity to request, in the absence of such assistance, the Family Court for the judicial authorization to carry out this act himself (with the assistance of an ad hoc guardian[157] appointed by the Family Court), also implies the right of the non-emancipated minor, who has reached the full age of 16, to request a procedure to return to his or her initial registered sex, subject to parental assistance, pursuant to article 135/1, § 9 BCC.[158]

Article 135/1, § 9 BCC explicitly states that the Family Court is the court competent to receive these requests. According to article 628, 24° BJC, the territorially competent Family Court is the one of the place where the Gender Registration Certificate was drawn up.[159] As a result there is a durable connection with the municipality where the trans person us registered in the population register (art. 135/1, § 2, first subsection BCC). The request to return to the initial registered sex must be reported to the Public Prosecutor under penalty of nullity (art. 764, 17° BJC).

5.13 Consequences of the Return to the Initial Registered Sex

If proof of exceptional circumstances has been accepted by the Family Court, then the judgment allowing to return to the initial registered sex will, after the period to

loi_a.pl?N=&=&sql=(text+contains+(%27%27))&rech=1&language=nl&tri=dd+AS+RANK&numero=1&table_name=wet&cn=2019021705&caller=image_a1&fromtab=wet&la=N&pdf_page=54&pdf_file=http://www.ejustice.just.fgov.be/mopdf/2019/03/01_1.pdf. Accessed 1 July 2020.

[156] Art. 135/1, § 10, first subsection BCC.

[157] Art. 135/1, § 10, second subsection BCC.

[158] Explanatory Memorandum to the bill, *Parl.Doc.* Chamber 2016-17, n° 54-2403/1, p. 17.

[159] Explanatory Memorandum to the bill, *Parl.Doc.* Chamber 2016-17, n° 54-2403/1, pp. 9 *j*° 27.

appeal against this judicial decision has expired, be sent to the civil registrar who drafted the Gender Registration Certificate. That civil registrar will have to draw up a Certificate of Return to the Initial Sex (art. 135/1, § 9, fourth subsection BCC).

The person asking the return will belong to his initial registered sex as from the day on which the Certificate of Return to the Initial Sex was drawn up (art. 135/1, § 9, third subsection BCC).

The rules establishing affiliation, applicable to the initial registered sex, are again applicable to children born after the day on which the Certificate of Return to the Initial Sex was drawn up (art. 135/1, § 9, last subsection BCC).[160]

5.14 Annulment of the Irrevocable Nature of the Change of Sex Registration

In its judgment of 19 June 2019,[161] the Belgian Constitutional Court ruled the irrevocable nature of the gender registration unconstitutional due to an infringement of the principle of equality and non-discrimination.

In its (English) press-release the Court stated as follows:

> The Court does not consider it reasonably justified that persons with a fluid gender identity, contrary to persons with a non-fluid binary gender identity, are required to accept a sex registration that does not correspond to their inner perceived gender identity. Neither is it reasonably justified that they are subjected to an exceptional procedure before the Family Court if they wish to change the sex registration in their birth certificate more than once.(...)
>
> The Court therefore annuls the provisions that make the sex registration in the birth certificate in principle irrevocable.[162]

Although this judgment has made it possible to change one's registered gender as many times as needed, making it possible for persons with gender fluidity to bring their registered gender in accordance with their perceived gender identity, equality will only be truly attained when a third gender option is created or when gender/sex is no longer a relevant legal criterion.[163]

---

[160] See more on Trans Parents in Sect. 10.

[161] For in-depth explanation of the Court's reasoning see Sect. 6.2.

[162] The English press-release can be consulted via: https://www.const-court.be/public/e/2019/2019-099e-info.pdf. Accessed 1 July 2020.

[163] See more details *infra*.

6 Gender Neutral and/or "Third Sex"

In Belgian law, a person can only be male or female. There is, to date, no third or gender-neutral option (for intersex persons, see Sect. 12). The Belgian Senate confronted two different federal Ministers with the topic, once in 2011 and once in 2013. The first written question (2011) from senator Anciaux[164] was about the possibility of a third sex category X on the identity card. The reply of the Minister of Home Affairs in July 2012 simply says that "the legislature assumes that everyone has one sex at birth: male or female". The second question (2013) asked by senator De Gucht[165] was about not registering the gender at birth, if this is not clear at birth, but to make the choice at a later age, as with the German regulation. The answer from the Minister of Justice was as follows:

> Extending the current law by analogy with the new German regulations would require a *radical change to our current legal system,* in which both the medical, psychological, ethical, social and legal aspects of this problem must be thoroughly investigated and in which we must carefully check and determine what the legal consequences are of such non-registration of the sex or the registration of a 'neutral gender'.(emphasis added)[166]

6.1 The Absence of Gender-Neutral or Third-Sex in the Gender Recognition Act

The rights of intersex, non-binary and gender fluid persons are not (as such) addressed in the Gender Recognition Act. Although some of these persons can undoubtedly benefit from the liberalized way to alter their sex registration in the civil status registers, it remains a switch from male to female or from female to male. The Belgian system remains binary.

During the hearing on 25 April 2017 in the Chamber of Representatives[167] the binary view of sex/gender in the new draft was denounced by several transgender associations.[168] The associations believed that the new Act could be problematic for intersex, non-binary and gender fluid persons.[169] Several members of the Committee for Justice acknowledged that the bill does not meet the needs of persons with gender

---

[164] *Q&A* Senate 2011-12, 23 December 2011, n° 5-4837 http://www.senate.be/www/?MIval=/Vragen/SVPrintNLFR&LEG=5&NR=4837&LANG=fr. Accessed 1 July 2020.

[165] *Q&A* Senate 2013-14, 22 November 2013, n° 5-10438 http://www.senate.be/www/?MIval=/Vragen/SVPrint&LEG=5&NR=10438&LANG=nl. Accessed 1 July 2020.

[166] *Q&A* Senate 2013-14, 22 November 2013, n° 5-10438 http://www.senate.be/www/?MIval=/Vragen/SVPrint&LEG=5&NR=10438&LANG=nl. Accessed 1 July 2020.

[167] Annex to the bill, *Parl.Doc.* Chamber 2016-17, n° 54-2403/4, pp. 33-60, http://www.dekamer.be/FLWB/PDF/54/2403/54K2403004.pdf. Accessed 1 July 2020.

[168] *Inter alia:* vzw Çavaria, vzw Arc-en-Ciel, Rainbowhouse Brussels, Equality Law Clinique.

[169] Annex to the bill, *Parl.Doc.* Chamber 2016-17, n° 54-2403/4, pp. 33-50 and 55-60, http://www.dekamer.be/FLWB/PDF/54/2403/54K2403004.pdf. Accessed 1 July 2020.

fluidity and intersex characteristics, but they emphasized that this is a step in an entire process, and that one cannot solve everything at once. Some members believe that they should, in the near future, have a discussion, to check whether sex/gender assignment on an identity document is necessary at all. Others suggested that a third sex marker could maybe provide a solution for intersex, non-binary and gender fluid persons. The MP's underline that, in any case, they must continue working with what is on the table, since this bill would cause an important change in mentality among the population.[170] The Minister of Justice developed the argument 'grasp all, lose all' or, as the Minister said, "the enemy of the good is the better. It is important to make progress gradually. It was wise not to abolish the reference to gender in legislation, although this abolition will be enforced one day. Time will come to take further steps".[171]

One week after its entry into force, LGBTQ-rights organizations 'Çavaria', 'Genres pluriels' and 'Rainbowhouse' challenged the Gender Recognition Act before the Constitutional Court,[172] arguing that the new Act—which they hailed as a victory—was not far-reaching enough. These organizations state that the binary choice (male or female) together with the irrevocable nature of the gender registration are discriminatory for non-binary and gender fluid persons.[173]

6.2 *The Binary and Irrevocability of Gender Held Unconstitutional*

The Belgian Constitutional Court, in its judgment of 19 June 2019,[174] has held the Gender Recognition Act unconstitutional both because of the binary system of gender registration and the, in principle, irrevocable nature of the change of sex registration. Regarding the *binary system of gender registration*, the reasoning of the Court, in light of the compatibility of that system with the principle of equality and non-discrimination, is as follows:[175]

---

[170] Annex to the bill, *Parl.Doc.* Chamber 2016-17, n° 54-2403/4, pp. 50-54, http://www.dekamer.be/FLWB/PDF/54/2403/54K2403004.pdf. Accessed 1 July 2020.

[171] *Parl.Doc.* Chamber 2016-17, n° 54-2403/4, p. 17.

[172] Request for partial annulment of Gender Recognition Act, case n°. 6813 on the case list of the Belgian Constitutional Court (see Notice, *BG* 2 February 2018, p. 8072).

[173] çavaria vzw. Https://cavaria.be/nieuws/cavaria-naar-grondwettelijk-hof-voor-optimalisering-transgenderwet (in Dutch). Accessed 1 July 2020.

[174] Constitutional Court 19 June 2019, no 99/2019, *Rechtskundig Weekblad* 2019-20, p. 1016, note Fonteyn, F. *Tijdschrift voor Jeugd en Kinderrechten* 2019, p. 276, note D'Espallier, A. *Tijdschrift voor Familierecht* 2020, p. 14, note Cannoot, P. These three annotations are written in Dutch. The French edition of this judgment is available online on: https://www.const-court.be/public/f/2019/2019-099f.pdf. Accessed 1 July 2020. Translation in English is expected.

[175] The reasoning of the Court is abridged and was freely translated (in a prosaic manner) to provide a better understanding by those not familiar with the Belgian legal system.

- a difference in treatment does not necessarily imply a breach of the principle of equality (para. B.6.2. of the judgment);
- the difference in treatment of persons with and without a binary gender is based on an objective criterion (para. B.6.4. of the judgment);
- the aim of the Gender Recognition Act was to maximize the opportunities of each individual to develop one's personality and the legislature explicitly stated in the preparatory works of the Gender Recognition Bill that each person is unique and has equal rights. Thus, the legislature seems to have regarded the principle of self-determination as the basis for the change in registered gender (para. B.6.5. of the judgment);
- in light of the previous remarks, no reasonable explanation exists to justify why only persons with a binary gender identity (i.e. a person who perceives him- or herself as male or female) and not persons with a non-binary gender identity (i.e. genderqueer) are able to bring their registered sex into conformity with their gender identity (para. B.6.5. of the judgment);
- it follows that the Gender Recognition Act, by restricting the possibility to change one's gender to persons with a binary gender, violates the principle of equality in conjunction with the right to self-determination (i.e. the principle of autonomy) (para. B.6.6 of the judgment);
- it is up to the legislature to remedy this unconstitutionality (para. B.7.1. and following of the judgment).[176]

Regarding the *irrevocable nature of the change* of the registered sex in the birth certificate to the perceived gender identity, the reasoning of the Court, in light of the compatibility of that irrevocable nature with the principle of equality and non-discrimination and the right to respect for private and family life, is as follows:[177]

- the legislature had different motives to restrict the possibility to change one's registered gender identity. Amongst those are (1) the wish to minimize (identity-) fraud (e.g. becoming untraceable to government authorities or creditors), (2) the wish to protect the person concerned from lighthearted changes of his registered gender and (3) the wish to safeguard the inalienability of the civil status[178] (para. B.8.3. of the judgment);
- these reasons, however, are insufficient to reasonably justify the distinction made between persons with a fluid gender identity:
- regarding the prevention and/or limitation of fraud: the Court fails to see why the safeguards that were put into place to combat fraud (i.e. mandatory and binding advice by the public prosecutor) during the first procedure to change one's

[176]See also *infra* Sect. 8.

[177]The reasoning of the Court is abridged and was freely translated (in a prosaic manner) to provide a better understanding by those not familiar with the Belgian legal system.

[178]See *supra* Sect. 1 on the Legal Regulation of Civil Status.

registered sex would not work in a second procedure (para. B.8.4. of the judgment);

- regarding the prevention of lighthearted changes: yet again the Court fails to see why the information duties that are put in place during the first procedure would not suffice in a second procedure (para. B.8.5. of the judgment);
- regarding the inalienability of the civil status: the Government cannot invoke the inalienability of the civil status because the Gender Recognition Act itself is the cause of the civil status becoming, to some extent, 'available' (para. B.8.6. of the judgment);
- the possibility of a judicial appeal to change the registered gender for a second time cannot justify the distinction made, because that procedure is far more complex than a simple declaration made before the civil registrar, that procedure can only be used in case of 'exceptional circumstances' (e.g. the person concerned is a victim of transphobia) whereas in case of a person with a fluid gender identity no such exceptional circumstance may exist, and that procedure only allows to return to the initial sex (para. B.8.7. of the judgment);
- in light of the previous remarks, it has become clear that the Gender Recognition Act by not allowing persons with a fluid gender identity to bring their registered sex in accordance with their inner perceived gender identity and subjecting them to a special judicial procedure to change and already changed registered sex, is contrary to the principle of equality and non-discrimination (para. B.8.8.-B.8.9. of the judgment);
- the following provisions are annulled:[179]
  - the obligatory mentioning of the irrevocable nature of the change of the gender registration by the civil registrar at the moment of the first declaration (well-defined words in the former article 62*bis*, § 3, second subsection BCC, i.e. the current article 135/1, § 3, second subsection BCC);
  - the declaration from the person concerned that he or she is aware of the irrevocable nature of the change of registered sex (the former article 62*bis*, § 5, second subsection, 3° BCC, i.e. the current article 135/1, § 5, second subsection 3° BCC);
  - the compulsory judicial procedure to return to the initial registered sex (the former article 62*bis*, § 10 BCC, i.e. the current article 135/1, § 9 BCC);[180]
  - the impossibility to change one's first name (at a reduced rate) after an initial change that followed a change in the registration of the registered sex unless the Family Court had allowed a return to the initial sex (well-defined words in

[179] A Constitutional Court judgment has effect starting from the day of publication (art. 9, § 1 Act 6 January 1989 concerning the Constitutional Court, *BG* 7 January 1989). The judgment was published in the three official languages—Dutch, French and German—in the *Belgian Gazette* (Belgisch Staatsblad / Moniteur belge) on 21 January 2020.

[180] This unconstitutionality renders article 1385*duodecies*, § 1, 1° BJC (i.e. the article concerning the competence of the Family Court for actions concerning the return to the initial sex) *de facto* useless.

the former article 2, third subsection of the Act of 15 May 1987 on Names and First Names, i.e. the current article 370/3, § 4 BCC).

7 Access to Treatment

The Gender Recognition Act undoubtedly constitutes progress in the recognition of trans persons' rights, but does not resolve the issue of their access and right to the reimbursement of their medical expenses. Regarding this topic, the obstacles are numerous:

- Difficulties in the search for information about the different steps of the "treatment of gender confirmation".
- A Belgian survey reveals that trans persons take a long time to become aware of their gender identity and reach out for help.[181]
- Information websites are not always qualitative and not all concerned persons are aware of the website www.transgenderinfo.be that has conceived, in consultation with the Gender Team of the Ghent University Hospital, a medical "care path" based upon the recommendations of WPATH (World Professional Association of Transgender Health).[182]
- The same survey denounces a barrier in the search for psychologic or medical care due to long delays in accessing transgender care qualified teams, the fear of moral judgment from medical staff and the (too) heavy financial burden of medical services.

The high cost of medical care (consultation, hormones, surgical interventions...) and the lack of transparency regarding their reimbursement by insurance companies and the National Institute for Disease and Invalidity Insurance (*l'Institut national d'assurance maladie-invalidité* (INAMI)) constitute a very important obstacle.

The Federal Minister of Health declared in 2017 that funding will be allocated to the Gender Team of Ghent University Hospital in order to provide better support to "diagnosed" persons. This announcement sets up a monopoly to the benefit of one medical facility which is contrary to the legislature's intent to suppress all medical conditions (including the diagnosis of gender dysphoria).[183] By doing so, one can fear an infringement of the patients' right to freely choose their practitioner and an infringement of the principle of equal reimbursement to all, regardless of whether or not they follow the program of a particular hospital. Furthermore, the reimbursement

[181] Www.infotransgenre.be; Motmans (2009).

[182] Standards of Care for the Health of Transsexual, Transgender and Gender Nonconforming People.

[183] Roelstraete, M. 2017. Nouvelle loi transgenre: de la stérilisation à l'autodétermination. *Journal du droit des jeunes* (hereinafter: *JDJ*), n° 367, 18.

of the costs must not only cover hormonal, surgical and medical interventions but also medical acts that are still gender-connoted; we think, for instance, of the reimbursement of childbirth costs of a transgender male born female.

8 The Current Discussion

The Gender Recognition Act 2017 which allows trans persons to obtain the recognition of their gender identity is an important reform—i.e. removal of the psychiatric evaluation and sterilization requirements—that brings the Belgian legislation in line with international human rights obligations. However, stereotypes are persistent and the legislature, obsessed with the trying to prevent any lighthearted changes, still acts upon the image of trans persons not being in the full possession of their capacities and that the State should protect them from their own choices. NGO's have repeatedly highlighted that this fear as well as the fear concerning repeated gender changes, are illusions and unveil, in the absence of a scientific basis, the legislature's ignorance about the experience of trans persons.

In such context, protecting trans persons should consist in granting them an immediate and unconditional possibility to bring their registered sex in accordance with their gender identity rather than in protecting them from the allegedly unanticipated and unexpected effects of such a change in legal status.

Finally, it is clear that the Gender Recognition Act, as amended by the Act the of 18 June 2018 does not regulate the issues related to access of medical treatment and related to the reimbursement of medical costs, nor the situation of minors under the age of 16 as well as the situation regarding intersex~~ed~~ persons.[184]

In its judgment of 19 June 2019, the Belgian Constitutional Court has held unconstitutional the impossibility of persons with a non-binary gender identity to change their registered sex, as mentioned in their birth certificate, into the gender that corresponds with their inner perceived gender identity because it discriminates persons with a non-binary gender identity from (transgender) persons with a binary gender identity.

Contrary to other judgments in which the Constitutional Court has held a provision unconstitutional whilst providing a constitution-proof interpretation of that provision, the Court has left it to the (federal) legislature to either introduce a third gender option or to eliminate sex or gender identity as legal criterion. Which option the legislature will choose and when the unconstitutionality will be resolved remains unclear since the Constitutional Court has not set a deadline to resolve this issue. It is to be expected that the preferable option will be discussed in Belgian legal doctrine.

---

[184]Bribosia et al. (2018), p. 266.

9 The Relationships Between Gay & Lesbian and Trans Legal Advancements Under Belgian Law

9.1 Partnerships and Marriage

The Act of 23 November 1998 introducing registered partnership[185] inserted a Title V*bis*, 'Legal cohabitation' in Book III of the Belgian Civil Code, which entered into force on 1 January 2000. The legislature defines legal cohabitation as "the state of cohabitation of two persons who have made a declaration in accordance with article 1476" (art. 1475, § 1 BCC). This definition shows that legal cohabitation is limited to two persons. However, being in a relationship (either affectionate or sexual) is not a requirement to make a declaration of legal cohabitation. The nature of the relationship between the two legally cohabiting partners can be very diverse: it can be a sexually affective relationship, but also mere friends or relatives can fall within the scope of a legal cohabitation.

In 1998, the intention of the legislature was to create a kind of "mini-marriage" for same-sex couples. Nowadays (i.e. after adding legal provisions regarding inheritance rights between registered partners in 2007) legal cohabitation is as attractive as marriage, for all kinds of couples.

The Act of 13 February 2003 regarding same-sex marriages,[186] which entered into force on 1 June 2003, made it possible for same-sex couples to marry. Marriage is gender neutral in Belgium. Article 143, first subsection of the Belgian Civil Code states: "A marriage can be entered into by two persons of different or the same sex."

9.2 Adoption and Co-maternity

Since the Act of 18 May 2006[187] a same-sex couple can adopt a child and adoption became possible by the spouse or the legally or factually cohabiting partner of the

[185] Act 23 November 1998 introducing the legal cohabitation, *BG* 12 January 1999, p. 786. The current legal provisions regarding legal cohabitation or legal partnership can be found in article 1475 and following BCC. In French: Http://www.ejustice.just.fgov.be/cgi_loi/change_lg.pl?language=fr&la=F&cn=1804032133&table_name=loi. Accessed 1 July 2020.

[186] Act 13 February 2003 on opening the marriage for persons of the same sex and to amend a number of provisions of the Civil Code, *BG* 28 February 2003, p. 9880. Belgium followed the example of the Netherlands, where same-sex couples have been able to marry since 1 April 2001 and thus became the second country in the world to legalize same-sex marriage. The current legal provisions regarding marriage can be found in article 143 and following BCC. In French: Http://www.ejustice.just.fgov.be/cgi_loi/change_lg.pl?language=fr&la=F&cn=1804032130&table_name=loi. Accessed 1 July 2020.

[187] Act 18 May 2006 amending a number of provisions of the Civil Code, in order to enable adoption by persons of the same sex, *BG* 20 June 2006, p. 31128. The current legal provisions regarding adoption can be found in article 343 and following BCC.

same sex as the child's original parent (art. 343, § 1, b) BCC). The conditions are identical as for adoption by persons of unequal gender.

The Act of 5 May 2014[188] created a new chapter: 'Establishment of co-maternity' (chapter II/1), under Title VII 'Affiliation' of Book I of the Belgian Civil Code. This chapter is located after the chapter regulating the establishment of maternity (chapter I) and paternity (chapter II). This new chapter II/1, which is very similar and directly inspired by the rules regarding the establishment of paternity, contains a presumption of co-maternity within marriage (art. 325/2 BCC), allows for voluntary recognition by the co-mother (art. 325/4 BCC) and enables Family Courts, under certain conditions, to judicial establishment of co-maternity, even contrary to the will of the co-mother, the mother or the child involved (art. 325/8 BCC).

The introduction of co-maternity marks the end of the singular character of affiliation (meaning non-adoptive parentage): since 1 January 2015 a child can have a legal bond based on affiliation with two women (not yet with two men; co-paternity does not exist in Belgium outside of adoption). The 'two-sided' nature of original affiliation has been preserved: the determination of co-maternity is only possible in cases were the child involved does not have a legal father (art. 325/1 BCC); existing co-maternity also prevents the establishment of extra-marital paternity (art. 319 and 322, first subsection BCC).

9.2.1 Right to Privacy of Trans Persons

In Belgium, persons who changed their registered sex into their gender identity do not receive a new birth certificate, nor (if applicable) a new marriage certificate and new birth certificates for children already born. Instead, the Gender Registration Certificate is linked with the existing certificates.[189]

When excerpts (i.e. summaries of the current data regarding one's civil status[190]) or copies (i.e. the original certificate with an overview of the changes made[191]) of the certificates are requested or the DABS/BAEC is consulted, the privacy of the person concerned could be jeopardized. The Gender Recognition Act, as amended by the Act of 18 June 2018, secured the right to privacy of trans persons, by severely restricting the persons who are entitled to a copy of an excerpt from or can consult

[188] Act 5 May 2014 regulating the establishment of the parentage of the co-mother, *BG* 7 July 2014, p. 51703. This Act was amended by the Act of 18 December 2014 (*BG* 23 December 2014, p. 104985) which came into operation on 1 January 2015 and provides clarity by means of a circular of 22 December 2014 (*BG* 29 December 2014, p. 106488). The current legal provisions regarding co-maternity can be found in article 325/1 *et seq.* BCC.

[189] Motmans, J. 2010. *Being Transgender in Belgium.* Institute for the equality of women and men, p. 55. Http://igvm-iefh.belgium.be/sites/default/files/downloads/34%20-%20Transgender_ENG.pdf. Accessed 1 July 2020.

[190] Art. 28, § 2 BCC.

[191] Art. 28, § 2 BCC.

the DABS/BAEC directly regarding civil status records on which a change in registered sex is visible.[192]

Anyone can request an excerpt or a copy of the following civil status records:

(1) a death certificate over 50 years old;
(2) a marriage certificate over 75 years old; and
(3) other certificates (e.g. birth certificates, a Gender Registration Certificate etc.) over 100 years old (art. 29, § 1, first subsection BCC).

This rule is subject to two exceptions:

(1) The person concerned in the certificate, his or her spouse or legal partner, his or her legal guardian, his or her ascendants and descendants, his or her heirs and their notary[193] or lawyer are entitled to a copy or an excerpt of a certificate regardless of when the certificate was drafted (art. 29, § 1, second subsection BCC);
(2) A *copy*[194] of the certificates *modified in accordance with article 135/1 BCC* (i.e. modified as a result of gender registration) or article 1385*quaterdecies*, § 3 BJC (i.e. the judicial procedure to return, in exceptional cases to the initial registered sex)[195] can only be handed out to the person concerned, his or her legal guardian, his or her heirs, their notary and lawyer (art. 29, § 1, third subsection BCC). This exception supersedes the previous exception.

Civil status records are not only accessible by print-outs but can be consulted directly by a number of persons (e.g. judges, the civil status registrar, notaries, Public Prosecutors etc.). The access to the civil status certificates which are modified in accordance with article 135/1 BCC (i.e. modified as a result of gender registration) or article 1385*quaterdecies*, § 3, BJC (i.e. the judicial procedure to return, in exceptional cases to the initial registered sex),[196] however, is, as is the case with the availability of copies of the same certificates (see above), restricted to judges, court clerks, officials working at the National service for changing surnames, the National Central Authority for adoptions and the Federal Central Authority of the Civil Register, notaries and Public Prosecutors *but only if and to the extent that* the consultation of these certificates are necessary for reasons regarding the civil status of the person concerned (art. 78, last subsection BCC).

[192]Circular 15 December 2017, *BG* 29 December 2017 and Explanatory Memorandum to the bill, *Parl.Doc.* Chamber 2016-17, n° 54-2403/1, pp. 15–16.

[193]The word ‘notary’ refers to the European civil law concept and not to the Anglo-American concept.

[194]This second exception does not apply to excerpts.

[195]This procedure is rendered useless due to the judgment of the Belgian Constitutional Court of 19 June 2019 (see Sect. 6.2).

[196]This procedure is rendered useless due to the judgment of the Belgian Constitutional Court of 19 June 2019 (see Sect. 6.2).

10 Trans Parents

It should be noted that the Belgian legislature has also provided specific affiliation rules for trans persons and their children. The Gender Recognition Act, as amended by the Act of 18 June 2018, does not change the parentage of children born before the gender registration of one (or both) their legal parents (art. 135/2, § 1 BCC). This rule stems from the wish to guarantee the stability of someone's parentage and to respect the non-retroactive character of the legal consequences of a Gender Registration Certificate.[197] As a consequence, a transgender parent can be, for instance, the legal father of one child and the legal co-mother of another child.

The issue of the parentage of a trans person's children born after the drawing-up of a Gender Registration Certificate has become more complex as a result of the suppression of the sterilization requirement and, therefore, due to the possibility to become a parent both based on sex prior to the change of civil status and based on the newly registered gender.

Article 135/2, § 2 BCC solves this issue by taking into consideration the date of birth of the child rather than that of its conception and by assimilating the child conceived and born (naturally or by medically assisted procreation) after the change with the child conceived before the change in registered sex but born after it.[198]

The Gender Recognition Act differentiates between three hypotheses for children born after the gender registration of their parent(s):

(1) *Female to Male.* The first hypothesis is that of the child born to a woman who has changed her registered sex to male (art. 135/2, § 2, first subsection 1 BCC). In that case, the maternity rules are applicable[199] because maternity is based on the maxim *Mater semper certa est*—i.e. the legal mother is the person giving birth to the child (art. 312, § 1 BCC). That basic principle cannot be modified without reconstruction of the entire affiliation law.

The paternity of the other parent (either male or female) can be established by applying non-transgender or transgender affiliation law. This could result in a child having two males as parents without having to take recourse to adoption.

[197] But also from the notion still present in the Belgian legal framework—despite the legal reforms and the adoption of co-maternity—of a "naturalistic" parenthood, that is to say necessarily binary or bisexual.

[198] Advice of the Council of State n° 60.690 of 16 January 2017, *Parl.Doc.* Chamber 2016-17, n° 54-2403/1, p. 60; taking into account the date of conception would have led to situations impossible to manage in the event of a conception before the change but of a birth after it or even in the case of a conception after the change and of a birth after a Family Court ruling over the termination of the effects of the change under exceptional circumstances.

[199] The Gender Recognition Act applies the whole of Chapter I of Title VII of Book I of the BCC to this first hypothesis that is to say the three possible successive modes of the establishment of maternity (also voluntary recognition and judicial establishment).

(2) *Conceiving Male to Female.* The second hypothesis is that of a child *conceived naturally or by means of medically assisted procreation* by a man who has changed his registered sex to female, who does not carry the child herself and the child is born after the change of the registered sex (art. 135/2, § 2, second subsection BCC).[200]

   a. In that case, the paternity rules apply *mutatis mutandis.*
   b. A transgender woman cannot be the legal mother of the child as she is not the one giving birth to it. The provisions concerning co-maternity cannot be applied because a trans woman can conceive child naturally.[201]
   c. However, since this parent is considered female as of the date of birth of the child, she will not be mentioned as the 'father', but as the 'co-mother' of the child (art. 135/2, § 2, third subsection BCC).

(3) *Other scenarios.* The third hypothesis covers the "other cases" within which the parentage of the child of the trans person is based on the latter's new gender (art. 135/2, § 2, fourth subsection BCC). For instance:

   a. a transgender male (female to male) who conceives a child with a woman by means of medically assisted procreation shall be the father;
   b. a transgender woman (male to female) who gives birth—hypothesis of a uterus transplant—shall be the mother.

Finally, the transitional provisions of the Gender Recognition Act, as amended by the Act of 18 June 2018, apply article 135/2 BCC to children born after the Act's entry into force but also to children born before this date and for which no parentage *by means of adoption* has yet been created towards the trans person who conceived the child or gave their consent for its conception by medically assisted procreation.[202]

It should be noted that the provisions relating to the parentage of trans persons' children are indicative of a fundamental evolution in affiliation law which abandons the "naturalistic" vision of parentage that led to a binary and bisexual vision of affiliation law, between paternity and maternal parentage.

This movement already observed in the context of the opening of adoption to same-sex couples and in the organization of co-maternity is hereby pursued.

---

[200] E.g. a transgender female, who has the reproductive parts that are typically associated with a 'male' and conceives a child with another woman.

[201] Explanatory Memorandum to the bill, *Parl.Doc* Chamber 2016-17, n° 54-2403/1, p. 24.

[202] Hypothesis of a transgender woman (born male) conceiving a child before conversion and having changed her registered sex before childbirth, or that of a transgender woman (born male) having cryopreserved her sperm and conceiving a child with a woman after the registry of her new gender.

11 Stakes in Sex

Sex, sexual identity, sexual orientation and gender constitute criteria that cannot be used to create differences in the rights granted to people, subject to being sanctioned under the interdiction of discrimination (art. 10 and 11 of the Belgian Constitution). In Belgian family law, these criteria are no longer useful for marriage nor for adoption: indeed, the Act of 13 February 2003 has removed the difference of sexes as a substantial condition for marriage and the Act of 18 May 2006 has made (intra-familial) adoption possible for same-sex couples.

The organization of the civil status and more particularly that of the provisions relating to the birth certificate (art. 42 *et seq.* BCC), however, remain characterized by a binary vision of one's sexual identity, without any reference to "gender". This terminology is not neutral and reveals the relationship still maintained by substantive law with an identity conceived as biologically determined rather than socially and culturally constructed.

In the law of affiliation (which is a part of the BCC), the reference to sex remains the bedrock to the law that subjects parentage to a division between maternity and paternity for everything related to "natural" procreation, i.e. non-medically assisted.

This binary and dual-sex vision is being challenged and is evolving:

- The Gender Recognition Act organizes the parentage of a trans person's children by abandoning its "naturalistic" vision. Although the law of affiliation is in fact constructed around the biological reproductive possibilities of a person, the legislature has nevertheless chosen, in principle and subject to some exceptions, to apply the rules concerning paternity on a person changing his registered sex as a female to the male gender and vice versa. It remains to be seen how the legislature will, as a consequence of the judgment of the Constitutional Court (see above), reconstruct or abolish the current specific affiliation rules applied to trans persons.
- The same applies to the parentage of children born out of the parental project of two women: the Act of 5 May 2014 allows co-maternity.
- The male couple realizing its parental project by resorting to surrogacy is treated differently than co-maternity. Only one of these two men can be the father based on affiliation while his partner will have to establish his parentage by means of adoption. Adoption by both male partners is also possible.

Bills trying to establish a legal framework for surrogacy have been submitted to Parliament and could lead, if approved, to co-paternity.

12 Intersex Persons

In Belgium, a strictly binary interpretation is given to 'sex' or 'gender': a person is male or female. Sex registration reflects binarity as a normative assumption.[203] Consequently, it is obligatory—but not always possible—to assign a sex to intersex newborns.[204]

According to the current Belgian birth registration legislation, every birth must be declared to the civil status registrar within fifteen days after delivery (art. 43, § 1 BCC). The civil status registrar draws up the birth certificate, without any delay (art. 43, § 4 BCC) and specifies, among other things, the sex of the child (art. 43, § 4 BCC). The sex is determined by a health care provider, usually on the basis of a superficial check of the genitals at birth.[205]

Since the Act of 15 May 2007,[206] the Belgian Civil Code does allow a specific delay in registering the sex of intersex newborns. For children whose sex is unclear, the indication of sex may be indicated by the father or mother or by both parents within a period of (at the latest) three months, if medical proof is provided (art. 48 BCC). The three-month period is motivated in parliament as the period necessary to carry out the medical examinations and to determine the (binary) sex of the child.[207] If, afterwards, it appears that the gender identity of an intersex person is not in accordance with the sex assigned at birth, the person concerned can submit a claim for the correction of the birth certificate at the Family Court. He or she can do this either by himself or through the parents/guardian pursuant to article 35 BCC, based on a (major) mistake as ground for judicial correction. The civil status registrar cannot correct this mistake on the ground of a (minor) "material mishit" (*cf.* art. 33-34 BCC; see also above the section on the Legal Regulation of Civil Status).

Another—simpler and more obvious—option for intersex persons is to invoke the Gender Recognition Act of 25 June 2017, as amended by the Act of 18 June 2018. All persons experiencing incongruity between the assigned sex and their gender identity can make use of the new Act.

Belgian anti-discrimination legislation also protects intersex persons. In the recent legislative changes, 'gender identity' and 'gender expression' were introduced as prohibited grounds of discrimination under 'gender'. This recent addition was meant to "include the group of trans persons (such as intersex)" in the protection

---

[203] Cannoot (2017), pp. 41–42.

[204] European Union Agency for Fundamental Rights. 2015. *The fundamental rights situation of intersex people.* Http://fra.europa.eu/sites/default/files/fra_uploads/protection_against_discrimination_legal_update_2015.pdf. Accessed 1 July 2020.

[205] Cannoot, P. *l.c.*

[206] Act 15 May 2007 amending article 57 of the Civil Code, concerning the mention of the sex of children whose sex is unclear, *BG* 12 July 2017, p. 38054.

[207] Explanatory Memorandum to the bill, *Parl.Doc.* Chamber 2006-07, n° 51-1242/1, p. 3.

of the Gender Act.[208] Legal doctrine has argued for an additional explicitly prohibited ground of discrimination on 'sex characteristics'.[209]

13 Conclusion

Belgian law is progressive and very advantageous for trans persons. At first, it was case law of the lower courts that prompted the legislature to enact the 2007 Transsexuality Act. Subsequently, international incentives compelled the Belgian federal parliament to found the 2017 Gender Recognition Act on the principles of autonomy and self-determination. And finally, it was up to the Constitutional Court to eliminate the binary system of sex/gender registration in order to secure the rights of genderqueer and gender fluid persons in Belgium. Not all Belgian legal scholars are positive to the ever-growing importance of the right to self-determination.[210]

The Belgian experience can probably be helpful for the many legal systems evolving in the same direction. May this chapter encourage their legislatures to avoid ostrich-like policy that arbitrarily excludes non-binary and gender fluid persons.

References

Branlard JP (1993) Le sexe et l'état des personnes. Aspects historique, sociologique et juridique. Paris, L.G.D.J., p 454

Bribosia E, Gallus N, Rorive I (2018) Une nouvelle loi pour les personnes transgenres en Belgique. JT 6724:266

Cannoot P (2017) Let it be: Het recht op persoonlijke autonomie van personen met intersekse/DSD. Tijdschrift voor Seksuologie, 41–42

De Page H (1990) Traité élémentaire de droit civil belge, tome II, vol. 1, 4 ed. par Masson, P.P. Bruxelles, Bruylant, p 85

Leleu YH (2016) Droit des personnes et des familles. Coll. Fac. dr. Liège 3rd edn. Larcier, Brussels, p 106

Massager N, Van Gysel ACh (1995) Les limites de l'autonomie de la volonté en droit des personnes. In: L'ordre public, concept et applications. Bruxelles, Bruylant, p 191

Motmans J (2009) Être transgenre en Belgique. Un aperçu de la situation sociale et juridique des personnes transgenres. Institut pour l'égalité des femmes et des hommes, Bruxelles

[208]Explanatory Memorandum to the bill, *Parl.Doc.* Chamber 2013-14, n° 53-3483/1, pp. 3 and 5.

[209]Cannoot, P. *l.c.*

[210]One author points out that people can and may decide how they feel and what they experience, but in his opinion that does not change the fact that we cannot decide, to a certain extent, what or who we are. Rules allowing a change of the registered sex may not deny the biological reality, see Renchon (2018), p. 273, n° 85: "[L]'être humain n'est pas en mesure de décider par lui-même qui **est**. Ce n'est pas parce qu'une femme se sent homme et souhaite être reconnue comme un homme qu'elle **est** pour autant un homme." (Emphasis in the original).

Motmans J, Verschelden G (eds) (2020) De rechtspositie van transgender personen in België. Een multidisciplinaire analyse na de wetten van 25 juni 2017 en 18 juni 2018 [The Legal Status of Transgender Persons in Belgium: a Multidisciplinary Analysis after the Acts of 25 June 2017 and 18 June 2018], Antwerp-Cambridge, p 225

Renchon JL (2018) Le nouveau régime juridique de changement de sexe. RTDF 2:273

Simon C (2016) Au-delà du binaire: penser le genre, la loi et le droit des personnes transgenres en Belgique. Can J Women Law 28(3):521

Van Gysel ACh (1996) Les personnes – Examen de jurisprudence (1991–1996). Revue critique de jurisprudence belge (hereinafter: RCJB), p 438

The Civil Status of Trans Persons in England

Peter Dunne

Abstract This chapter addresses the legal status of trans persons in England. The chapter considers English trans-focused laws against the background of their historical and contemporary context. The mechanics and consequences of trans-oriented laws in England (statute, policy and case law) are presented. The merits of existing law and potential future reforms are analysed. By exploring the myriad intersections of law and trans identities, this chapter presents a clear, detailed insight into the status of trans communities in modern English law.

This chapter considers the civil status of trans persons in England. It identifies the broader legal context in which English trans-focused laws operate, against the background of both the historical development of, as well as the current framework for, trans affirmation. The chapter focuses on explaining the mechanics and consequences of trans-oriented laws in England—providing detailed analysis of statute, policy and case law, along with commentary where appropriate on the merits of existing laws and the potential for future reforms. In doing so, the chapter draws upon numerous sources, including government consultations, parliamentary inquiries and the growing 'gender-critical' movement within English social debates. This is not an exhaustive account of legal rights for trans communities in England, and many legal matters—which directly impact upon trans lives in this jurisdiction—fall outside the scope of discussion. Yet, by exploring the myriad intersections of law and trans identities, the chapter hopes to present a clear, detailed insight into to the status of trans communities in contemporary English law.

P. Dunne (✉)
University of Bristol, Bristol, UK
e-mail: pd17653@Bristol.ac.uk

I. C. Jaramillo, L. Carlson (eds.), *Trans Rights and Wrongs*, Ius Comparatum - Global Studies in Comparative Law 54,
https://doi.org/10.1007/978-3-030-68494-5_12

1 Legal Sex in English Law

'Sex' is a legal status in English law. All children, who are born in England, must have their birth registered within 42 days.[1] Registration involves providing prescribed information to the General Registration Office, including the "name, surname and *sex* of the baby" (emphasis added).[2] While, as in other jurisdictions, the importance of sex status in English law has waned[3], it remains relevant in a number of key areas. Under s. 4 of the Equality Act 2010 (2010 Act)—England's primary non-discrimination framework—'sex' is a protected characteristic. According to s. 11 of the 2010 Act, for "the protected characteristic of sex", referring to a person "who has a particular protected characteristic" means referring to "a man or to a woman."[4] Similarly, references "to persons who share a protected characteristic" means referring to "persons of the same sex."[5]

In English law, both different-sex and same-sex couples can contract a civil marriage.[6] Since 2019[7], both can also form a civil partnership (following the UK Supreme Court judgment in *R (On the Application of Steinfeld and Keidan v Secretary of State for International Development*[8]). While Church of England officials can solemnise marital unions between male and female couples, the Marriage (Same-Sex Couples) Act 2013 prohibits solemnisation where there are spouses with the same legal sex.[9] Under the Matrimonial Causes Act 1973, spouses have a right to divorce where their husband or wife commits adultery and they find it intolerable to live with him or her.[10] However, in English law, adultery requires that there be sexual relations with an *opposite* sex individual.[11] So, for example, a male spouse, whose wife has an affair with another woman, could not rely upon the 'adultery' ground (even if sexual conduct with a man would have sufficed).

As discussed in greater detail below, legal sex also intersects with the imposition of criminal liability. Under s. 1(1)(a)-(c) of the Sexual Offences Act 2003, a person

---

[1] 'Register a Birth' (*UK Government Website, No Date Available*) https://www.gov.uk/register-birth/overview. Accessed 16 July 2017.

[2] *Ibid.*

[3] See e.g., the position of women in terms of property ownership prior to the Married Women's Property Act 1882; the right of women to vote prior to (and after) The Representation of the People Act 1918.

[4] Equality Act 2010, s. 11(a).

[5] *Ibid.*, s. 11(b).

[6] See: Marriage (Same-Sex Couples) Act 2013, s. 1(1).

[7] The Civil Partnership (Opposite Sex Couples) Regulations 2019.

[8] *R (On the Application of Steinfeld and Keidan v Secretary of State for International Development)*, [2018] UKSC 32.

[9] Marriage (Same-Sex Couples) Act 2013, s. 4(1)(5).

[10] Matrimonial Cause Act 1973, s. 1(2)(a).

[11] 'Get a Divorce' (*UK Government Website, No Date Available*) https://www.gov.uk/divorce/grounds-for-divorce. Accessed 16 July 2017.

commits an offence if *he* "intentionally penetrates the vagina, anus or mouth of another person...with *his* penis"[12] [emphasis added] where the other persons does not consent and the perpetrator does not reasonably believe that there is consent." Section 1(1) therefore is specifically directed towards *male* perpetrators.

When the birth of a child is recorded in the register of live-births, a short 'birth certificate' is issued to the individual who makes registration.[13] There are two types of birth certificates: (a) the 'full certificate' (which gives all the recorded details in the register of births);[14] (b) a 'short certificate' (which provides a person's full name, date of birth, place of birth and legal sex).[15] There are different procedures for correcting a birth certificate depending upon whether the requested amendment is minor or more serious (e.g. change of name, etc.).[16] The latter corrections must be made at the General Register Office,[17] and the requestor may be required to provide a statutory declaration.[18] Although individuals in England may obtain other identification documents with sex markers (e.g. drivers licence, passport, etc.), it is the birth certificate which is determinative for the purposes of legal sex. The historical movement for gender recognition in England was motivated in large part by the fact that, without amended birth certificates, a person's self-identified gender could not be fully acknowledged by the State.[19]

2 The Regulation of Trans Identities in England

English law provides partial regulation for the status of trans identities. Under the Gender Recognition Act 2004, binary trans adults may be formally acknowledged in their self-identified gender. Similarly, the 2010 Act offers non-discrimination protections for those individuals whose identity falls within the "gender reassignment" protected characteristic. The road towards gender recognition in England was a decades-long movement.[20] It involved both national advocacy campaigns and European-level litigation, and the legal and policy impact has extended across the Common Law world.

---

[12]Sexual Offences Act 2003, s. 1(1)(a).

[13]'Register a Birth—3. Birth Certificates' (*UK Government Website, No Date Available*) https://www.gov.uk/register-birth/birth-certificates. Accessed 16 Jul 2017.

[14]*Ibid.*

[15]*Ibid.*

[16]'Correct a Birth Registration—1. What Corrections can be Made' (*UK Government Website, No Date Available*) https://www.gov.uk/correct-birth-registration. Accessed 17 July 2017.

[17]*Ibid.*

[18]*Ibid.*

[19]See e.g. *Sheffield and Horsham v United Kingdom* (1999) 27 EHRR 163.

[20]See generally: Sharpe (2009), p. 241; Sandland and Ralph (2005), p. 43; Ellis (2004), p. 467.

The seminal judgment was delivered by Ormrod J, for the English High Court, in *Corbett v Corbett (otherwise Ashley) (No1).*[21] The judge was required to adjudicate an action for nullity brought by Arthur Corbett against April Ashley. The primary questions were: (a) whether Ashley, a trans woman who had submitted to gender affirmation surgery, was a legal woman for the purposes of the Matrimonial Causes Act 1965; and (b) whether she had the capacity to enter into a valid, different-sex marriage with a legal male. Justice Ormrod concluded that Ashley was not a woman for the purposes of English marriage law.[22] Although she had medically transitioned, the judge held that men and women have different (and immutable) biological configurations, which establish their sex status.[23] As Ashley was unable to definitively modify her sex characteristics, she could not be a legal woman and, therefore, could not contract a martial union with a male person (the first same-sex marriages were not held in England until 2014). Although *Corbett* concerned only the narrow question of legal sex for the purposes of marriage law (Ormrod J declined to "determine the 'legal sex' of the respondent *at large*" [emphasis added][24]), the judgment was subsequently adopted as the definitive statement on trans recognition rights in England.

In *R v Tan*, for example, the Court of Appeal applied the *Corbett* reasoning to conclude that a trans woman could be convicted of living off the earnings of prostitution, a crime which only men could commit.[25] Despite the fact that she had physically transitioned, English law considered that the defendant would always have a male legal sex.[26] In *Bellinger v Bellinger*, Lord Nicholls, delivering judgment in the House of Lords, observed that the "present state of English law regarding the sex of transsexual people is represented by the well-known decision of Ormrod J in *Corbett v Corbett*."[27] Beyond England, *Corbett* had a stark impact across the Common Law world, encouraging numerous national courts to deny legal affirmation to trans litigants.[28]

Faced with a reticent domestic judiciary and an unresponsive national parliament, many trans persons began to petition the European Court of Human Rights (ECtHR) for relief. Their primary claim was that failing to formally acknowledge gender was a disproportionate interference with private life under art. 8 ECHR. Starting with *Rees v United Kingdom*[29] in 1986, the ECtHR reviewed the Convention-compatibility of England's gender recognition vacuum four times in 13 years (*Cossey v United*

---

[21][1971] 2 All ER 33.

[22]*Ibid.*, 50.

[23]*Ibid.*, 48.

[24]*Ibid.*

[25][1983] QB 1053, 1063—1064.

[26]*Ibid.*

[27][2003] 2 UKHL 21, [11].

[28]*Lim Ying v Hiok Kian Ming Eric* [1991] SGHC 135; *W v Registrar of Marriage*, High Court of the Hong Kong Special Administrative Region, HCAL 120/2009 (5 October 2010).

[29][1987] 9 EHRR 56.

Kingdom;[30] *X, Y and Z v United Kingdom*;[31] *Sheffield and Horsham v United Kingdom*[32]). On each occasion, the Strasbourg judges concluded that withholding an amended birth certificate fell within the United Kingdom's margin of appreciation. However, as the case law developed, and individual judges engaged in sharper dissents,[33] the Court noted that legal trans affirmation was an area that "needs to be kept under permanent review by Contracting States."[34] Pressure on the United Kingdom only intensified when, in 1992, the ECtHR held that France's absolute failure (in the UK, it was at least possible to obtain alternative documents, such as a passport, with correct gender markers) to affirm trans identities violated art. 8 ECHR.[35]

In *Goodwin v United Kingdom* (2002), the Grand Chamber of the ECtHR finally concluded that the UK's total prohibition on gender recognition violated arts. 8 and 12 of the European Convention (failure to issue an amended birth certificate meant that Christine Goodwin could not marry her male partner).[36] While the Court acknowledged that there was not yet a "[c]ommon European approach" to trans identities[37], it nevertheless emphasised the "clear and uncontested evidence of a continuing international trend in favour not only of increased social acceptance of transsexuals but of legal recognition of the new sexual identity of post-operative transsexuals."[38] Although the Court did not prescribe any form of legal recognition (i.e. the precise conditions of access) which the UK must adopt,[39] it concluded that absolutely withholding an amended birth certificate was incompatible with guarantees of private life and marriage.

Taking account of the *Goodwin* jurisprudence, the House of Lords issued a Declaration of Incompatibility in *Bellinger v Bellinger*, inviting Parliament to introduce reform.[40] The Department of Constitutional Affairs published a Draft Gender Recognition Bill in July 2003, which was considered by the House of Lords and House of Commons Joint Committee on Human Rights in November 2003.[41] The Gender Recognition Act 2004 (2004 Act) received Royal Assent on 1 July 2004, and came into effect on 4 April 2005.

---

[30] [1991] 13 EHRR 622.

[31] [1997] 24 EHRR 143.

[32] [1999] 27 EHRR 163.

[33] See e.g. *ibid.*, [1]–[10] (per Judge Van Dijk).

[34] *Ibid.*, [60].

[35] [1993] 16 EHRR 1.

[36] [2002] 35 EHRR 18, [93] and [104].

[37] *Ibid.*, [85].

[38] *Ibid.*

[39] *Ibid.*, [85].

[40] [2003] 2 UKHL 21, [11].

[41] House of Lords and House of Commons Joint Committee on Human Rights (2003).

Prior to the 2004 Act, trans individuals were already protected under England's equality frameworks. In *P v S and Cornwall Country Council*,[42] the Court of Justice of the European Union found that "the scope of the [employment equality] directive cannot be confined simply to discrimination based on the fact that a person is of one or other sex" but also extends to "discrimination arising…from the gender reassignment."[43] This statement has now also been enshrined in the recitals to the 2006 Equal Treatment Directive.[44] In response to the *P v S* decision, the Government introduced the Sex Discrimination (Gender Reassignment) Regulations 1999 (1999 Regulations). Section 2(1) of the 1999 Regulations inserted a new provision in the Sex Discrimination Act 1975 (s. 2A), which prohibited discrimination on the basis that a person "intends to undergo, is undergoing or has undergone gender reassignment."

Under the present law, trans-focused protections are consolidated into the 2010 Act. Section 7(1) of the 2010 Act provides that individuals have "the protected characteristic of gender reassignment" if they are "proposing to undergo…undergoing or [have] undergone a process (or part of a process) for the purpose of reassigning" their "sex by changing physiological or other attributes of sex." A person commits direct discrimination if, because another individual has a gender reassignment characteristic, the person treats that individual less favourably.[45]

The express inclusion of trans identities within England's equality frameworks (as opposed to tying trans identities to 'sex' protections) is a positive development. During the Transgender Equality Inquiry[46] (Trans Equality Inquiry)—conducted by the Commons Select Committee on Women and Equalities (the Committee) in 2015—James Morton, former Scottish Trans Manager at the Transgender Scottish Alliance, stated that "pulling the trans protected characteristic out from underneath the sex discrimination protected characteristic was really, really helpful."[47] Naming trans experiences in the 2010 Act increases trans visibility, and ensures that both employees and service users, as well as employers and service providers, understand and respect the scope of trans non-discrimination guarantees.[48]

Yet, the 2010 equality structures are not without critique. The specific language of 'gender reassignment', while mirroring EU law terminology, suggests both a medical and binary gender model. Although s. 7 of the 2010 Act might have been intended to embrace even persons who do not medically transition (this is expressly

[42]Case C-13/94 [1996] 2 CMLR 247.

[43]*Ibid.*, [20].

[44]See: Directive 2006/54, Preamble, [3].

[45]Equality Act 2010, s. 13(1).

[46]'Transgender Equality Inquiry' (*UK Parliament Website, No Date Available*) https://www.parliament.uk/business/committees/committees-a-z/commons-select/women-and-equalities-committee/inquiries/parliament-2015/transgender-equality/. Accessed 17 July 2017. ***

[47]Commons Select Committee on Women and Equalities (2016), p. 24.

[48]*Ibid.*

suggested by the Explanatory Notes[49]), there remains, for many trans individuals, a fear that 'gender reassignment' requires past, present or future physical interventions.[50] Within a contemporary trans context, the language of 'reassignment' is overwhelmingly associated with medical pathways.

It is also unclear whether the 2010 Act extends to non-binary persons.[51] Employers cannot disfavour trans men and trans women, but are there obligations in relation to identities which fall outside 'man'/'woman' norms? Expert evidence presented to the Trans Equality Inquiry raised the prospect that non-binary claimants are protected only to the extent that their discrimination arises from a perception that they have the 'gender reassignment' characteristic.[52] In response, the Women and Equalities Committee has recommended that Parliament introduce "gender identity" in place of gender reassignment. In the recent case of *Taylor v Jaguar Land Rover*, the Employment Tribunal concluded that s. 7 of the 2010 Act does cover gender fluid and non-binary identities, although a definitive statement on this from the superior courts in England remains outstanding.[53]

Schedule 3, Part 7, s. 28 of the 2010 Act provides that there is no discrimination if an individual disfavours persons with a gender reassignment characteristic in "the provision of separate services for persons of each sex",[54] "the provision of separate services differently for persons of each sex"[55] and "the provision of a service only to persons of one sex."[56] As a result of the Schedule 3 Exception, providers can remove trans individuals from sex-segregated services where exclusion is a proportionate means of achieving a legitimate aim.[57]

A similar result is achieved under Schedule 23, s. 3 of the 2010 Act. There is no discrimination if a person disfavours trans individuals in accessing communal accommodations or "benefit[s], facilit[ies] or service[s] linked to the accommodation."[58] Schedule 23 defines 'communal accommodation' as "residential accommodation[s] which [include] dormitories or other shared sleeping accommodation which for reasons of privacy should be used only by persons of the same sex."[59] Accommodation providers must consider reasonable alterations to the facility,[60] the

[49]Equality Act 2010, Explanatory Notes, [43].

[50]Commons Select Committee on Women and Equalities (2016), p. 24.

[51]*Ibid.*, 24–26.

[52]*Ibid.*, 24.

[53] For the recommendation of the Women and Equalities Committee, see: ibid, 27. *Taylor v Jaguar Land Rover* (Case No: 1304471/2018).

[54]Equality Act 2010, Sch. 3, Pt 3(28)(2)(a).

[55]*Ibid.*, Sch 3, Pt 3(28)(2)(b).

[56]*Ibid.*, Sch 3, Pt 3(28)(2)(c).

[57]*Ibid.*, Sch 3, Pt 3(28)(1).

[58]Sch 23(3)(1)(b).

[59]*Ibid.*, Sch 23(3)(5).

[60]*Ibid.*, Sch 23(3)(3)(a).

provision of additional space[61] and the extent to which the service is used by only one sex.[62]

The Schedule 3 and 23 exceptions were introduced because of a fear that vulnerable populations, such as female victims of intimate partner violence, would not access important services (e.g. counselling, etc.) if trans women were also present.[63] During the Trans Equality Inquiry, these concerns were reiterated by a number of organisations, which work with women. Their argument is not that trans women should be denied non-discrimination protections, but rather that an appropriate balance must be struck between the various interests concerned.[64]

On the other hand, many contributors criticised these trans-focused exceptions.[65] The seemingly open-ended wording of the 2010 Act would, depending on the circumstances, allow providers to exclude *any* trans individual from their service or communal accommodation.[66] In their current form, the Schedules 3 and 23 Exceptions are only limited by the requirement for a legitimate aim (a term which, even itself, is not clearly defined) and proportionality. Therefore, it is possible that providers could refuse services to trans persons who have undergone a full medical transition or who have even obtained a Gender Recognition Certificate ("GRC"—a certificate which is issued where a person obtains legal gender recognition under the 2004 Act).[67] In its concluding recommendations for the Trans Equality Inquiry, the Women and Equalities Committee suggests that the 2010 Act should "be amended so that the…single-sex/separate services provision shall not apply in relation to discrimination against a person whose acquired gender has been recognised under the Gender Recognition Act 2004."[68] However, throughout 2020, the question of single-sex spaces has become a particularly sensitive topic within wider UK politics. In April 2020, the Minister for Women and Equalities, when appearing before the Women and Equalities Committee and discussing ways in which the Government Equalities Office might reform the 2004 Act, stated that any amendments would ensure the "protection of single-sex spaces."[69] While the Minister's comments can be critiqued as legitimising historic tropes about trans rights being a general threat to cisgender women, her statement does suggest that, rather than extending access to

[61] *Ibid.*, Sch 23(3)(3)(a).

[62] *Ibid.*, Sch 23(3)(3)(b).

[63] Commons Select Committee on Women and Equalities (2016), pp. 27–28. See: Equality Act 2010, Explanatory Notes, [740].

[64] *Ibid.*

[65] *Ibid.*, 27–30.

[66] *Ibid.*, 29.

[67] For a fuller explanation of the relationship between the Gender Recognition Act 2004 and the Equality Act 2010, see generally: Sharpe (2020), p. 539.

[68] Commons Select Committee on Women and Equalities (2016), p. 32.

[69] "Minister for Women and Equalities Liz Truss sets out priorities to Women and Equalities Select Committee", (22 April 2020), *Government Equalities Office Website,* https://www.gov.uk/government/speeches/minister-for-women-and-equalities-liz-truss-sets-out-priorities-to-women-and-equalities-select-committee. Accessed 8 June 2020.

preferred services and accommodations, any Government reform will either maintain, or possibly partially repeal, the current status quo in the Schedules to the 2010 Act.[70]

Under the existing rules, trans individuals in the United Kingdom can obtain passports, with an accurate gender marker, even if they do not have a GRC. Trans persons can apply for an amended passport where they have: a "Gender Recognition Certificate" (GRC) or "a new birth or adoption certificate showing [their] acquired gender" *or* "a letter from [their] doctor or medical consultant confirming [their] change of gender is likely to be permanent."[71] Thus, while a GRC can facilitate passport amendments, it is not an absolute requirement.

The protected categories of either "intersex" or "sex characteristics" are not included within the 2010 Act. Unlike the trans population, persons who experience intersex (and who confront discrimination because of that variance) do not have a specific right of action. Although intersex fell outside the scope of the Trans Equality Inquiry, the Women and Equalities Committee did observe that "intersex people face a number of difficult equalities issues" and encouraged the Government to "consider how best to address the needs of intersex children and adults."[72] In January 2019, the UK Government Equalities Office called for evidence "to provide everyone in the United Kingdom, especially people with variations in sex characteristics, with an opportunity to engage with Government and to tell us in detail about their experiences and what they think Government could or should be doing to improve their lives."[73]

Access to legal gender recognition and involuntary gender 'normalising' surgeries are a particular concern. Many intersex individuals are assigned a birth-sex with which they never have had a connection. Like their trans peers, these people would benefit from formally amending their legal gender. Yet, as English law currently requires a diagnosis of gender dysphoria[74] (see below), which intersex populations often do not experience (intersex persons may never have lived in or been distressed by their birth-assigned sex), intersex narratives may be excluded from the 2004 Act.[75] In addition, there is currently no legal framework which explicitly prohibits

---

[70]See Dunne, Peter. 2020. Equality for All? LGBTI Rights and the Future Priorities of the Government Equalities Office. *European Human Rights Law Review* (forthcoming).

[71]'Change Your Name or Personal Details on Your Passport—4. Gender Change' (*UK Government Website, No Date Available*) https://www.gov.uk/changing-passport-information/gender. Accessed 17 July 2017.

[72]Commons Select Committee on Women and Equalities (2016), p. 5.

[73]'Variations in Sex Characteristics Call for Evidence' (*Government Equalities Office, 17 January 2019)* https://www.gov.uk/government/consultations/variations-in-sex-characteristics-call-for-evidence. Accessed 10 July 2019.

[74]Gender Recognition Act 2004, s. 2(1)(a).

[75]Tanya Ni Mhuirthile, Tanya Ni, and Ryan, Fergus. 2013. Ni Mhuirthile and Ryan on the Legal Recognition of Gender Bill 2013. *Human Rights in Ireland Website*. Http://humanrights.ie/gender-sexuality-and-the-law/ni-mhuirthile-ryan-on-the-legal-recognition-of-gender-bill-2013/. Accessed 17 July 2017.

non-therapeutic intersex surgeries. In July 2016, the UN Committee on the Rights of the Child called upon the United Kingdom to "[e]nsure that no one is subjected to unnecessary medical or surgical treatment during infancy or childhood, guarantee bodily integrity, autonomy and self-determination to children concerned and provide families with intersex children with adequate counselling and support."[76]

3 Name Change

Trans individuals in England can access legal recognition of their self-identified name. Under the English common law, persons have the right to change their name without undertaking a formal legal procedure (provided there is no fraudulent or criminal intent).[77] It suffices that the individual begins to consistently use his or her name in daily life. However, in many circumstances, a person may choose to complete an official amendment process. This will particularly be the case if the individual wishes to subsequently alter state-issued identity documents, such as a passport or drivers licence, and formal evidence of a name-change is required by the governing state institution.[78]

Individuals may formally amend their legal name by 'deed poll'.[79] This is a "legal document that proves a change of name."[80] In England, there are two ways to obtain a deed poll. First, individuals can make their own document by drawing up a prescribed statement (relinquishing the old name and adopting the new name), which is witnessed by two other persons.[81] Second, if an organisation, with whom the individual is interacting, requires official registration of a name change, the deed poll can be enrolled at the Royal Courts of Justice.[82]

Before entering the gender recognition process, many trans individuals will obtain a formal name change (although this is not specifically required by the 2004 Act). Under s. 2(1)(b) of the 2004 Act, an applicant can only access a GRC where he or she "has lived in the acquired gender throughout the period of two years

[76] UN Committee on the Rights of the Child. 2016. Concluding observations on the fifth periodic report of the United Kingdom of Great Britain and Northern Ireland. UN Doc No. CRC/C/GBR/CO/5, [47(c)].

[77] Commons Select Committee on Women and Equalities (2016), p. 59.

[78] 'Change Your Name by Deed Poll—1. Overview' (*UK Government Website, No Date Available*) https://www.gov.uk/change-name-deed-poll/overview. Accessed 17 July 2017.

[79] *Ibid.*

[80] *Ibid.*

[81] 'Change Your Name by Deed Poll—2. Make Your Own Deed Poll' (*UK Government Website, No Date Available*) https://www.gov.uk/change-name-deed-poll/make-an-adult-deed-poll. Accessed 17 July 2017.

[82] 'Change Your Name by Deed Poll – 3. Enrol A Deed Poll with the Courts' (*UK Government Website, No Date Available*) https://www.gov.uk/change-name-deed-poll/enrol-a-deed-poll-with-the-courts. Accessed 17 July 2017.

ending with the date on which the application is made" (the 'Real Life Experience' (RLE) requirement). In submitting proof of this 'real life experience', it is helpful for applicants to show both a name-change deed poll and other formal documents (e.g. passport, driver's licence, etc.), which acknowledge an 'acquired' name that is congruent with the applicant's self-identified gender.[83] In providing advice to individuals who are entering the gender recognition system, the UK Government states that proof of RLE must "be in [the applicant's] acquired name."[84] Indeed, applicants should also submit "copies of any official documents that show [their] birth name has changed to [their] name."[85] While persons under the age of majority (18 years old) are excluded from the 2004 Act,[86] it is possible to obtain a name change for trans children.[87] This requires either: (a) (usually) the agreement of all persons who have parental responsibility for the young person; (b) a court order.[88] The minor's new name must be enrolled at the Royal Courts of Justice. In *In re W, F, C and D (minors)(Name changes disclosing gender reassignment and other)*, Master McCloud sought to enhance the privacy protection of young people who amend their name by enrolling a public Deed Poll.[89]

4 Legal Gender Recognition

The formal rules for obtaining legal gender recognition are set out in the Gender Recognition Act 2004. In England, applying to be acknowledged in one's self-identified gender (referred to as 'acquired gender' under the 2004 Act) involves petitioning a Gender Recognition Panel[90] for the grant of a Gender Recognition Certificate.[91] The Lord Chancellor (with the consent of specified individuals[92]) appoints persons who are eligible to sit on the Gender Recognition Panels.[93] Each panel must include "at least one legal member"[94] and "at least one medical

[83] 'Apply for A Gender Recognition Certificate – Documents You Must Provide' (*UK Government Website, No Date Available*) https://www.gov.uk/apply-gender-recognition-certificate/documents-you-must-provide. Accessed 17 July 2017.

[84] *Ibid.*

[85] *Ibid.*

[86] Gender Recognition Act 2004, s. 1(1).

[87] 'Change Your Name by Deed Poll—4. Change a Child's Name' (*UK Government Website, No Available Date*) https://www.gov.uk/change-name-deed-poll/change-a-childs-name. Accessed 17 July 2017.

[88] *Ibid.*

[89] *[2020] EWHC 279 (QB), 2020 WL 00710769*

[90] See generally: Gender Recognition Act 2004, Sch. 1.

[91] Gender Recognition Act 2004, s(1)(1)-(3).

[92] *Ibid.*, Sch. 1(1A).

[93] *Ibid.*, Sch. 1(1).

[94] *Ibid.*, Sch. 4(2(a).

member."[95] It is the Gender Recognition Panels that decide whether to issue a GRC. Where a panel is satisfied that an applicant meets the relevant application criteria (see below), it "must grant the application"[96] and "issue a gender recognition certificate."[97] Section 8(1) of the 2004 Act provides for a right to "appeal to the High Court (or Family Court)…on a point of law against a decision by the Panel to reject [an] application."

Under the standard application process, individuals will apply for a GRC on the basis of "living in"[98] their "acquired gender".[99] Section 1(1)(b) also envisages requests where a person has "changed gender under the law of a country or territory outside the United Kingdom."

Where an individual applies by reason of "living in" the acquired gender, there are a number of qualifying conditions, which must be satisfied. Applicants must be at least 18 years old (i.e. minors are absolutely excluded from gender recognition in England).[100] Second, they must show that they have or have had gender dysphoria (i.e. the diagnosis requirement).[101] This condition can be satisfied by either: "a report made by a registered medical practitioner practising in the field of gender dysphoria and a report made by another registered medical practitioner" or "a report made by a registered psychologist practising in that field and a report made by a registered medical practitioner."[102] Third, as noted above, there is a requirement for proof that applicants have been living in their acquired gender for at least two continuous years prior to the request.[103] This condition, often imposed as part of a medical transition pathway,[104] is (supposedly) to ensure that trans persons can sufficiently understand and function in the reality of their acquired gender before undertaking formal recognition. Finally, the applicant must "[intend] to continue to live in the acquired gender until death"[105] (i.e. gender recognition is intended to be permanent).

---

[95] *Ibid.*, Sch. 4(2)(b).

[96] *Ibid.*, s. 2(1).

[97] *Ibid.*, s. 4(1).

[98] *Ibid.*, s. 1(a).

[99] *Ibid.*, s. 1(2) of the 2004 Act provides that "[i]n this Act 'the acquired gender', in relation to a person by whom an application under subsection (1) is or has been made, means— (a) in the case of an application under paragraph (a) of that subsection, the gender in which the person is living, or (b)in the case of an application under paragraph (b) of that subsection, the gender to which the person has changed under the law of the country or territory concerned."

[100] *Ibid.*, s. 1(1).

[101] *Ibid.*, s. 2(1)(a).

[102] *Ibid.*, ss. 3(1)(a)-(b).

[103] *Ibid.*, s. 2(1)(b).

[104] World Professional Association for Transgender Health. 2012. *Standards of Care for the Health of Transgender, Transsexual and Gender Nonconforming People (Version VII).* WPATH 59 – 60. Https://s3.amazonaws.com/amo_hub_content/Association140/files/Standards%20of%20Care%20V7%20-%202011%20WPATH%20(2)(1).pdf. Accessed 24 May 2017.

[105] *Ibid.*, s. 2(1)(c).

When originally introduced, the 2004 Act was a landmark statute.[106] Within a legal environment where gender recognition had always been tied to medical interventions, the 2004 Act adopted a progressive stance in omitting compulsory surgery and sterilisation.[107] Instead, England's laws began the movement away from expressly medicalising trans identities. The 2004 Act suggests that legal gender should reflect experiences of identity rather than the presence (and acceptability) of specific body parts.

Yet, as the 2015 Trans Equality Inquiry illustrated, the 2004 Act remains problematic in many respects.[108] The total exclusion of minors places an intolerable burden on trans youth in England. It effectively denies the existence of trans children and, at least symbolically, reinforces the social marginalisation of this vulnerable group. In defence of the status quo, politicians and healthcare specialists have pointed to the complexity of young trans experiences.[109] There is a risk, it is argued, that recognising minors would be premature, inappropriate and potentially emotionally harmful. However, while best practice for younger children (i.e. pre-puberty) remains contentious, and while medical interventions for children have been curtailed in England by a recent High Court judgment ('*Bell*'),[110] there is growing evidence of the benefits of supervised affirmation processes for minors.[111] Apart from *Bell*, there have been few cases to come before the English courts addressing the issue of gender identity in youth. In *Re J (A Child)*,[112] the Court was not convinced that the young person concerned, who was assigned male at birth, actually identified as female. Rather, the Court believed that the child had been improperly influenced by the mother, whose contact with the child was thus limited. Conversely, in *Lancashire County Council v TP*, the Court affirmed the decision to support early social transition.[113]

The diagnosis requirement is another area of English law which has inspired critique. This has taken the form of symbolic objections to obtaining a 'gender dysphoria' diagnosis, as well as arguments that having to access healthcare specialists limits enjoyment of gender recognition rights. For many trans persons, the diagnosis requirement is both unnecessary and humiliating.[114] Like the imposition of gender panels (which adjudicate applications), diagnosis suggests that trans

---

[106]Sharpe (2004), p. 37; Dunne (2015), pp. 530–531.

[107]Cowan (2005), p. 76.

[108]Commons Select Committee on Women and Equalities (2016), p. 11.

[109]*Ibid.*, 18–19.

[110]*R(Bell and A) v Tavistock and Portman NHS Trust [2020] EWHC 3274(Admin).*

[111]Susset (2014), p. 117; Gray et al. (2012), pp. 21–22; Vance Jr et al. (2014), p. 1187; Alegria (2016), p. 524; Bonifacio and Rosenthal (2015), p. 1005. See generally: de Vries et al. (2014), p. 696; Olson et al. (2016).

[112][2016] EWHC 2430 (Fam).

[113][2019] EWFC 30.

[114]Commons Select Committee on Women and Equalities (2016), pp. 12–13.

individuals are incapable of understanding their own gender and that they need supervision to filter out inappropriate applications.[115] Requiring healthcare interventions—even without physically altering trans bodies—pathologises non-cisgender narratives.[116] It legitimises perceptions that experiencing a trans identity is inevitably a mental health concern.[117] The diagnosis is deeply disempowering. Ignoring trans agency, it (along with the gender panels) prefers the external judgment of third-party actors over individual trans realities.

In addition to the negative symbolism of diagnosis, there are practical difficulties which it creates. During the Trans Equality Inquiry, the Women and Equalities Committee identified numerous failings in the public provision of healthcare services (see below).[118] Trans individuals in England often confront a medical system which is under-resourced and under-trained to accommodate their unique needs.[119] In such circumstances, it is not difficult to foresee that many applicants—particularly those who experience intersecting marginalisation, such as poverty and disability—will not (and may never) be in a position to obtain the necessary medical documentation.

Indeed, even for trans persons who can access NHS gender treatment centres, securing a 'dysphoria' diagnosis implies that they must be distressed by their gender identity. For those who embrace their trans experiences, and who want gender recognition as an affirmation rather than a cure, there remains a question mark as to whether medical professionals can (and should) provide the necessary support.[120] While the diagnosis requirement was undoubtedly introduced to safeguard applicants, it can act as an insurmountable obstacle for many people who would benefit from formal acknowledgement.

There are also objections to the 'real life experience' test imposed under s. 2(1)(b) of the 2004 Act. While, as with the diagnosis requirement, this is (at least nominally) a safeguard against flippant or ill-considered applicants, it may work practical disadvantages. Proving that a person has "lived in the acquired gender" means that individuals must express (on documentation, such passports, payslips or utility bills) an identity for two years, without the protection and guarantees of a congruent legal sex.[121] There is a continuous risk that, without legal recognition, the trans history of an individual will be revealed. This increases the potential that people may experience discrimination and violence. While it is perhaps not unreasonable that law-makers would want evidence that (before recognition) applicants can live conformably in their acquired gender, one must not underestimate the dangers of publicly manifesting an identity, which conflicts with official sex status.

---

[115] *Ibid.*, 13.

[116] Sharpe (2004), p. 38.

[117] *Ibid.*

[118] House of Commons Select Committee on Women and Equalities (2016), pp. 35–55.

[119] *Ibid.*, 43 and 49.

[120] Sandland (2005), p. 50.

[121] Commons Select Committee on Women and Equalities (2016), p. 13.

Under the 2004 Act, as originally enacted, a person seeking legal gender recognition was obliged to submit a statutory declaration relating to marital status.[122] Where an applicant was in an existing marriage, he or she could only be issued with an Interim Gender Recognition Certificate. According to Schedule 2 of the 2004 Act, the issue of an interim certificate creates a new ground for annulment,[123] after which the applicant would be entitled to access a full GRC. An individual who wished to retain a legal relationship with his or her spouse could thereafter register a civil partnership, which were also introduced in 2004 (Civil Partnership Act 2004). The official justification for the 'annulment requirement' was the existing prohibition on equal marriage rights.[124] Although civil partnerships were opened to same-sex couples in 2004, England did not permit same-sex marriages until the Marriage (Same-Sex Couples) Act 2013 (2013 Act). During that period, there was a perception that allowing spouses to remain married after they had legally transitioned would create a loophole in England's marriage laws and undermine the State's commitment to traditional marriage.[125]

In England, the introduction of same-sex marriage significantly reduced concerns regarding the relationship status of trans individuals. Schedule 5 of the 2013 Act permits applicants for recognition to remain in an existing marriage where the non-transitioning spouse consents to conversion from a heterosexual union into a same-sex marriage.[126] According to s. 4(3A) of the 2004 Act, "[i]f a Gender Recognition Panel issues a full gender recognition certificate" to an applicant who is in an existing marriage, "the Panel must give the applicant's spouse notice of the issue of the certificate." Section 11A(2) of the 2004 Act ensures that "[t]he continuity of the...marriage is not affected by the relevant change in gender."

Schedule 5 is intended to protect the integrity of trans families, while ensuring that an applicant's spouse is not forced into a legal institution to which he or she may morally object. While broadly welcome as a movement away from forced annulments, Schedule 5 can be criticised for (a) stigmatising same-sex marriages, by legitimising the moral prejudice of spouses,[127] and (b) allowing a third party—the spouse—to dictate the process by which an applicant can obtain gender recognition. Where a spouse withholds consent, the applicant can only obtain an interim certificate, which in accordance with Schedule 2 of the 2004 Act, can be used to apply for an annulment. There is evidence that cisgender spouses may manipulate or abuse the consent requirement to "ridicule, deny and disempower" applicants.[128] While, in

---

[122]Gilmore (2015), pp. 195–196. Section 3(6)(a) of the 2004 Act still requires applicants to state whether or not they are married.

[123]Gender Recognition Act 2004, Sch. 2, Part 1, ss. 1 and 2.

[124]Sandland (2005), p. 57.

[125]Sharpe (2004), p. 37; Dunne (2015), pp. 533–534.

[126]Marriage (Same-Sex Couples) Act 2013, Sch. 5, Part 1, s. 2. See: Gender Recognition Act 2004, s. 3(6B).

[127]Commons Select Committee on Women and Equalities (2016), pp. 15–16.

[128]*Ibid.*, 15.

2016, the Women and Equalities Committee did not recommend removal of the consent requirement, it did encourage the Government to remain "informed about the extent" to which "the spousal-consent provision [may lead to]. . .married trans people [being] victimised by spouses with malicious intent."[129] Consistent with its general policy not to make substantive changes to the Gender Recognition Act 2004, the current Johnson government, in September 2020, proposed to leave the spousal consent requirement in place.[130]

Under s. 22(1) of the 2004 Act, it is an offence for certain individuals, who have "acquired protected information ['information which relates to a person who has made an application' for a GRC] in an official capacity" to disclose that information. Exceptions to the s. 22 rule include disclosures which do not identify individuals,[131] disclosures with consent,[132] disclosures through an order of a court or tribunal,[133] disclosures for the "purpose of instituting, or otherwise for the purposes of, proceedings before a court or tribunal",[134] disclosures for the purposes of social security or pensions systems,[135] and disclosures to prevent or investigate crime.[136]

Despite the existence of s. 22(1), there is evidence that inappropriate disclosures are routinely being made, particularly as part of litigation processes.[137] In some circumstances, individuals will raise the other party's trans history in order "to create, deliberately, a negative view of [that party]."[138] The President of the Family Division of the English High Court has advised that "[d]isclosure should not [be] permitted in those cases where it is unnecessary and irrelevant to the issues."[139] Similarly, the Women and Equalities Committee has recommended that the Ministry of Justice "work with the courts to tackle the issue of trans people being inappropriately 'outed' in court proceedings."[140] In its 2015-2016 inquiry into transgender equality in the UK, the Committee discussed concerns that, despite anecdotal

---

[129] *Ibid.*, 17.

[130] 'Government responds to Gender Recognition Act consultation' (Gov.uk, 22 September 2020) https://www.gov.uk/government/news/government-responds-to-gender-recognition-act-consultation. Accessed 31 March 2021.

[131] *Ibid.*, s. 22(4)(a).

[132] *Ibid.*, s. 22(4)(b).

[133] *Ibid.*, s. 22(4)(d).

[134] *Ibid.*, s. 22(4)(e).

[135] *Ibid.*, s. 22(4)(h).

[136] *Ibid.*, s. 22(4)(f).

[137] Commons Select Committee on Women and Equalities (2016), pp. 20–21.

[138] *Ibid.*, 20.

[139] Sir James Munby, 'Gender Recognition Act 2004: Protected Information relating to a person who has acquired a Gender Recognition Certificate' (*Courts and Tribunals Judiciary Website*, 11 March 2014) https://www.judiciary.gov.uk/announcements/gender-recognition-act-2004-protected-information-relating-to-a-person-who-has-acquired-a-gender-recognition-certificate/. Accessed 18 July 2017.

[140] Commons Select Committee on Women and Equalities (2016), p. 22.

evidence of numerous unlawful disclosures, "[n]ot a single prosecution has yet been brought for breach of Section 22."[141]

Moving forward, a central question is whether Parliament will adopt a model of self-declaration for legal gender recognition. While the 2004 Act inspired legislative change in other European jurisdictions, such as Spain[142] and Portugal,[143] it has now been superseded by countries, such as Denmark, Malta, Belgium, Iceland, Luxembourg, Ireland and even Portugal itself, which acknowledge gender on the basis of self-determination.[144] During the Trans Equality Inquiry, the Committee on Women and Equalities recommended "proposals to update the Gender Recognition Act, in line with the principles of gender self-declaration that have been developed in other jurisdictions."[145]

In the intervening years, however, the question of self-identification reforms for the 2004 Act has created deep political polarisations. Despite broad support within LGBT+ communities, self-declaration has been strongly critiqued by gender-critical feminists.[146] This latter group argue that, if persons can access gender recognition through the mere act of self-identification, there will be increased risks of abusive applications and that the very concept of legal sex (which has continued importance for women's equality movements) will be rendered meaningless. While concerns about abuse have not be realised in other self-ID jurisdictions, and while some claims within the gender critical movement appear to misconstrue existing UK law, broader concerns about potential unintended consequences of self-declaration reforms have led to uncertainty as to when (and if) parliament will reform the 2004 Act. In September 2020, responding to a lenghty public consultation on the 2004 Act, the Minister for Women and Equalities, Liz Truss, announced that the Government did not intend to make substantive changes to the current process for accessing a Gender Recognition Certificate in England.

5 Non-binary Recognition

English law does not currently provide non-binary gender recognition. Under s. 9 (1) of the 2004 Act, obtaining a GRC means that a "if the acquired gender is the male gender, the person's sex becomes that of a man and, if it is the female gender, the

[141] *Ibid.*, 21.

[142] Act 3/2007 of March 15 BOE No. 65.

[143] Law No. 7/2011 of 15th March 2010.

[144] Gender Recognition Act 2015 (Ireland). See generally: Munkholm (2015), p. 167.

[145] *Ibid.*, 14.

[146] Kathleen Stock, "Why Self-Identification Should not Legally Make You a Woman" *The Conversation,* October 1, 2018,. Accessed March 29, 2020, https://theconversation.com/why-self-identification-should-not-legally-make-you-a-woman-103372; 'Shifting Sands: Six Legal Views on the Transgender Debate' (*Guardian,* 19 October 2018) https://www.theguardian.com/society/2018/oct/19/gender-recognition-act-reforms-six-legal-views-transgender-debate 30 June 2020.

person's sex becomes that of a woman..." The 2004 Act does not acknowledge genders outside the man-woman dichotomy. In *R (On the Application of Christie Elan- Cane) v Secretary of State for the Home Department*, the High Court, in an opinion which was recently upheld by the Court of Appeal, and which will be heard by the UK Supreme Court in 2021,[147] concluded that withholding an 'X' passport (note: the litigation did not concern legal gender recognition) from the applicant did not violate art. 8 ECHR.[148] The Court observed that, while the decision to withhold a non-binary passport did engage the applicant's Convention rights, the judgment of whether and how to provide alternative gender options remained, at present, within the Government's margin of discretion.[149]

During the Trans Equality Inquiry, the Women and Equalities Committee recommended the introduction of "an option to record gender as 'X' on a passport."[150] This proposal was subsequently endorsed by the national LGBT rights organisation, Stonewall.[151] The Committee also called upon the Government to "[move] towards 'non-gendering' official records as a general principle and only recording gender where it is a relevant piece of information."[152]

6 Consequences of Legal Gender Recognition

Under s. 9(1) of the 2004 Act, where an applicant obtains a Gender Recognition Certificate, his or her gender "becomes for all purposes the acquired gender." Section 9(1) establishes the general consequences of legal recognition but is qualified by both further sub-sections and by subsequent provisions in the statute. According to s. 9(2) of the 2004 Act, although a GRC "*does* operate for the interpretation of enactments passed, and instruments and other documents made, before the certificate is issued", it "*does not* affect things done, or events occurring, before the certificate is issued" [emphases added]. Similarly, under s. 9(3), the general right to recognition set out in s. 9(1) is "subject to provision made by this Act or any other enactment or any subordinate legislation." Section 12 of the 2004 Act provides that "[t]he fact that a person's gender has become the acquired gender under this Act does not affect the status of the person as the father or mother of a

---

[147] *R (on the application of Elan Cane) v Secretary of State for the Home Department; Human Rights Watch intervening* [2020] EWCA Civ 363.

[148] *R (On the Application of Christie Elan-Cane) v Secretary of State for the Home Department* [2018] EWHC 1530 (Admin).

[149] For an overview of the reasoning at first instance and on appeal, see: Peter Dunne, "Travelling Beyond the Binary: No Right to Unspecified Passports under the European Convention on Human Rights" (2020) 79(2) Cambridge Law Journal 240.

[150] Commons Select Committee on Women and Equalities (2016), p. 63.

[151] Stonewall (2017), p. 33.

[152] Commons Select Committee on Women and Equalities (2016), p. 63.

child." An individual, who is affirmed in his self-identified male identity, does not automatically lose or escape his rights and obligations as the legal mother of a child. In its recent judgment, *R (Alfred McConnell) v The Registrar General for England and Wales and others,* the Court of Appeal confirmed that a trans man, who gave birth to his own son, had to be registered as a "mother" even though he had already obtained a male Gender Recognition Certificate.[153]

Under s. 15 of the 2004 Act, "[t]he fact that a person's gender has become the acquired gender under this Act does not affect the disposal or devolution of property under a will or other instrument made before the appointed day." A trans woman will not lose her succession entitlements because she no longer has a male legal gender. Similarly, being formally acknowledged in an acquired gender affects neither "the descent of any peerage or dignity or title of honour"[154] nor the "devolution of any property limited. . .by a will or other instrument to devolve" save where "an intention that it should do so is expressed in the will or other instrument."[155]

Trustees and personal representatives have no "duty, by virtue of the law relating to trusts or the administration of estates, to enquire, before conveying or distributing any property, whether a full gender recognition certificate has been issued to any person or revoked."[156] In consequence, such officers are "not liable to any person by reason of a conveyance or distribution of the property made without regard to whether a full gender recognition certificate has been issued" so long as "the trustee or personal representative has not received notice of the fact before the conveyance or distribution."[157]

As noted above, certain crimes in English law are gender-specific. They can only be committed by or against legal men or legal women. Under s. 20(1) of the 2004 Act, the fact that a person (who commits such a crime) has obtained a GRC is not a defence to the commission or attempted commission of the offence. This is a welcome assurance that gender recognition cannot become a loophole for criminal actors. However, prosecutors must also be sensitive to the fact that the provision may require the (implicit) disaffirmation of a trans man's acquired gender. Where prosecuting an offence, committed against a trans man, which (nominally) can only be perpetrated against legal women, state actors must take all appropriate measures to avoid additional and unnecessary distress for the survivor.

Under s. 195(2) of the 2010 Act, it does not constitute unlawful discrimination "relating to gender reassignment" to do "anything in relation to the participation of a transsexual person as a competitor in a gender-affected activity if it is necessary to do so to secure in relation to the activity—(a) fair competition, or (b) the safety of competitors." Section 195(3) of the 2010 Act defines a gender-affected activity as a "sport, game or other activity of a competitive nature in circumstances in which the physical strength, stamina or physique of average persons of one sex would put them

[153] [2020] EWCA Civ 559.

[154] Gender Recognition Act 2004, s. 16(a).

[155] *Ibid.*, s. 16(b).

[156] *Ibid.*, s. 17(1).

[157] *Ibid.*, s. 17(2).

at a disadvantage compared to average persons of the other sex as competitors in events involving the activity." The s. 195 exception is intended to ensure that, where a trans individual (irrespective of whether they have a GRC[158]) would create an unsafe or unfair competition environment, regulating organisations can withhold the right to compete.

In recent times, much of the opposition to self-identification reforms in England for the Gender Recognition Act 2004 have centred around potential consequences for fairness within sex-segregated sports.[159] In particular, there is concern that, if it becomes easier for trans women to obtain a GRC, this will increase participation by women who have (what society perceives to be) 'male' bodies, disadvantaging cisgender women and girls. However, as s. 195(2)-(4) of the 2010 Act illustrates, the mere fact that an individual has a GRC does not automatically guarantee access to sporting competitions/activities in accordance with legal gender. If there is potential for unsafe or unfair competition, sports organisations have a legal right to exclude entry. Therefore, making it easier to obtain a GRC does not make it easier to get into women's sport events. Furthermore, debates around a potential influx of 'male' bodies in women's sport as a result of gender recognition reform ignore the fact that, since 2005, individuals in the United Kingdom have been accessing GRCs without any requirement for physical intervention. If the de-medicalisation of the 2004 Act creates threats to women's sport, surely those threats would have been realised in the 15 years since GRCs were available?

7 Intersections of LGB and T Rights in England

The year, 2017, marked the fiftieth anniversary of the partial decriminalisation of private, consensual sexual intercourse between two legal males in England.[160] In the half-century since 1967, lesbian, gay and bisexual people have (with some notable exceptions[161]) progressively gained increased rights under English law.[162]

---

[158]The s. 195 exception applies to a "transsexual person". Such an individual is defined, in s. 7(3) of the 2010 Act, as "a person who has a particular protected characteristic" of gender reassignment. As gender reassignment applies to a person who "is proposing to undergo, is undergoing or has undergone a process (or part of a process) for the purpose of reassigning the person's sex by changing physiological or other attributes of sex", it includes individuals who have a GRC. As such, if participation of a trans woman, who has obtained a GRC, would create unfair competition or undermine the safety of competitors, she can be lawfully excluded from women-only sports even though she is legally acknowledged as being a woman.

[159]See e.g. Sean Ingle, 'Sports stars weigh in on row over transgender athletes' (*Guardian,* 3 March 2019) https://www.theguardian.com/society/2019/mar/03/sports-stars-weigh-in-on-row-over-trans gender-athletes.
Accessed 10 July 2019.

[160]Sexual Offences Act 1967, s. 1.

[161]See e.g. Local Government Act 1988, s. 28.

[162]'Rainbow Europe Index 2020' (*ILGA-Europe Website*, 14 May 2020) https://www.ilga-europe.org/sites/default/files/Attachments/ilgaeurope-rainbowindex-2020-interactive.pdf. Accessed 30 June 2020.

In 2004, Parliament enacted the Civil Partnership Act, which, for the first time, extended formal legal recognition to same-sex couples. Parliament had already introduced a right to same-sex adoption two years previously under the Adoption and Children Act 2002 (2002 Act). According to s. 49 of the 2002 Act, "[a]n application for an adoption order may be made by ... a couple." Section 144 (4) defined "couple" to include "two people (whether of different sexes or the same sex) living as partners in an enduring family relationship." The Marriage (Same-Sex Couples) Act 2013 now permits two persons, with the same legal sex, to contract a marriage in England. The 2013 Act has also impacted legal gender recognition, creating a spousal consent requirement in favour of the prior annulment provisions.

Under s. 4 of the 2010 Act, "sexual orientation" is a protected characteristic. In *Bull v Hall*,[163] the UK Supreme Court ruled against the proprietors of a hotel, who had (for religious reasons) refused a double room to civil partners. A majority of the Court held that the hoteliers committed direct discrimination. In UK law, there was no material difference between marriage and civil partnerships.[164] The hoteliers had, therefore, unlawfully based their decision on the couple's sexual orientation. Even if the hoteliers only engaged in indirect discrimination, there was no justification because permitting "someone to discriminate on the ground that he did not believe that persons of homosexual orientation should be treated equally with persons of heterosexual orientation" creates a "class of people who [are] exempt from the discrimination legislation."[165]

It is hard to accurately judge the current intersections of LGB and T rights in England. Without doubt, recognition of the former population (both social and legal) preceded gender identity rights (the exception being the 1999 Regulations which were enacted prior to sexual orientation protections within UK law). While decriminalisation occurred in 1967, it was not until 2005 that trans people could first obtain GRCs. Some gay, lesbian and bisexual rights groups were slow to embrace trans equality movements, with Stonewall being the most high-profile example.[166] Even today, trans communities enjoy narrower and less inclusive guarantees under the 2010 Act. While the broad characteristic, "sexual orientation", suggests numerous experiences of sexuality, there is at least doubt that non-binary persons are protected within a "gender reassignment" framework. The report of the Women and Equalities Committee in 2016, detailing the findings and recommendations of the Trans Equality Inquiry, is a stark reminder of the challenges, which trans

---

[163] [2013] UKSC 73.

[164] [2013] UKSC 73, [26].

[165] [2013] UKSC 73, [37].

[166] Aisha Gani, 'Stonewall to start campaigning for trans equality' (*The Guardian*, 16 February 2015) http://www.theguardian.com/uk-news/2015/feb/16/stonewall-start-campaigning-trans-equality. Accessed 24 March 2016.

populations in England continue to face—challenges which have only been magnified by toxic social and political debates on trans rights in 2020 and 2021.[167]

References

Alegria CA (2016) Gender nonconforming and transgender children/youth: family, community, and implications for practice. J Am Assoc Nurse Practition 28(10):521

Bonifacio HJ, Rosenthal SM (2015) Gender variance and dysphoria in children and adolescents. Paediatric Clin North Am 62(4):1001

Commons Select Committee on Women and Equalities (2016) Transgender equality. The Stationary Office Limited, London, p 63

Cowan S (2005) "Gender is no substitute for sex": a comparative human rights analysis of the legal regulation of sexual identity. Feminist Legal Stud 13(1):67

de Vries A et al (2014) Young adult psychological outcome after puberty suppression and gender reassignment. Paediatrics 134(4):696

Dunne P (2015) Ten years of gender recognition in the United Kingdom: Still a "Model for Reform"? Public Law 530:530–531

Ellis E (2004) The gender recognition bill 2013. Public Law:467

Gilmore S (2015) The legal status of transsexual and transgender persons in England and Wales. In: Scherpe JM (ed) The legal status of transsexual and transgender persons. Intersentia, Cambridge, pp 195–196

Gray S, Carter A, Levitt H (2012) A critical review of assumptions about gender variant children in psychological research. J Gay Lesbian Mental Health 16(1):4

House of Lords and House of Commons Joint Committee on Human Rights (2003) Draft gender recognition bill – nineteenth report of session 2002 – 03: vol 1 report. The Stationary Office Limited, London

Munkholm NV (2015) The legal status of transsexual and transgender persons in Denmark. In: Scherpe JM (ed) The legal status of transsexual and transgender persons. Intersentia, Cambridge, p 167

Olson KR et al (2016) Mental health of transgender children who are supported in their identities. Paediatrics 137(3):e20153223

Sandland R (2005) Feminism and the gender recognition Act 2004. Feminist Legal Stud 13(1):43

Sharpe A (2004) A critique of the gender recognition Act 2004. Bioethical Inquiry 4:33

Sharpe A (2009) Gender recognition in the UK: a great leap forward. Soc Legal Stud 18(2):241

Sharpe A (2020) Will gender self-declaration undermine women's rights and lead to an increase in harms? Modern Law Rev 83(3):539

Stonewall (2017) A vision for change: acceptance without exception for trans people. Stonewall, Auroville, p 33

Susset F (2014) Between a rock and a hard place: the experience of parents of gender-nonconforming boys. In: Meyer EJ, Pullen Sansfaçon A (eds) Supporting transgender and gender creative youth: schools, families and communities in action. Peter Lang, Bern, p 113

Vance S Jr, Ehrensaft D, Rosenthal S (2014) Psychological and medical care of gender nonconforming youth. Paediatrics 134(6):1184

[167]Commons Select Committee on Women and Equalities (2016).

Trans Rights in Germany

Theresa Anna Richarz and Anne Sanders

Abstract This chapter provides an introduction to the development and current discussion of the legal status of trans persons in Germany. The development of the law on inter persons is also briefly discussed in order to provide a complete picture of the German legal development, from a heteronormative legal framework to one that is increasingly flexible with respect to gender identities—occasional backlashes included.

The following chapter provides an introduction to the development and current discussion of the legal status of trans persons in Germany. The development of the law on inter persons is also briefly discussed in order to provide a complete picture of the German legal development, from a heteronormative legal framework to one that is increasingly flexible with respect to gender identities—occasional backlashes included.

Distinguishing between sex as a biological feature and gender as a social process seems outdated as categorizing one's bodily features as "male", another's as "female" and a third one's as "inter" is also the result of social negotiation processes. German law though makes this distinction referring at times to physical features and sometimes to gender identity. The German language does not distinguish between sex and gender, but uses the word *Geschlecht* for both. Consequently, it is often difficult to accurately translate German legislation and jurisprudence in this regard. Furthermore, it often remains unclear even for German readers whether the law (written law and especially jurisprudence) refers to sex or gender. In the course of this chapter we will show that the Federal Constitutional Court and the Federal Court of Justice refer to both in different ways, revealing different concepts of gender determinants.

T. A. Richarz (✉)
Institute for Social and Organizational Pedagogy, Hildesheim University, Hildesheim, Germany
e-mail: richarz@uni-hildesheim.de

A. Sanders (✉)
Bielefeld University, Faculty of Law, Bielefeld, Germany
e-mail: anne.sanders@uni-bielefeld.de

I. C. Jaramillo, L. Carlson (eds.), *Trans Rights and Wrongs*, Ius Comparatum - Global Studies in Comparative Law 54,
https://doi.org/10.1007/978-3-030-68494-5_13

Germany was one of the first countries in Europe, already in 1980, to implement a specific law addressing the legal status of trans[1] persons. The law provided different legal solutions for changing legal name and legal gender (the "small" and "big" solution). However, as a "child of its time", the law transported a pathologizing understanding of transgenderism and put the transition of a person from one legal gender to the other under strict state control. Trans persons were "sanitized"[2] by fitting them into the narrow frame of a binary, heteronormative system of gender.

No legislative reforms were pursued after 1980. However, the Federal Constitutional Court emerged as an engine for the development of trans rights in Germany. The court increasingly promoted a legal approach to transgenderism protecting the individual gender identity of trans persons based on constitutional law. Due to the jurisprudence of the Federal Constitutional Court, a change of a legal name and of a legal gender now have the same requirements. The substantial remaining legal obstacles in acquiring either are proof of living "according to the other gender" for more than 3 years and the requirement of two expert opinions that have to be paid for privately.

Despite the jurisprudence of the Federal Constitutional Court, legislative reform has been both long demanded and overdue. The requirement of two expert opinions for a change of legal name or gender is heavily criticised by trans activists. Inter, non-binary and trans movements have joined in campaigning for a self-determined gender marker and whether legal gender registration should be banned altogether. Another important aspect under discussion is the legal recognition of trans parents.

1 The Legal Development Concerning Trans Persons up to 1980

The first legislation concerning trans persons was introduced after a 1978 judgment by the Federal Constitutional Court. Before that, the law did not allow a change of legal gender. Homosexual persons were attacked and prosecuted during the time of rule of the National Socialist Party between 1933 and 1945. However, the situation of trans persons varied. While some were attacked as homosexuals, others were allowed to undergo genital adjusting surgery and live with names indicating the gender with which they identified just as in the Weimar Republic.[3]

[1]The adjective "trans" here is used to refer to persons whose gender differs from the one they were assigned at birth. The adjective "inter" refers to persons whose bodies were read as differing from standardized "male" and "female" bodily characteristics.

[2]Adamietz (2011), p. 157 f.

[3]See Fels, E. 2014. Einmahnung der Transgender-Geschichte im Nationalsozialismus. Paper presented at Fachkonferenz—Gedenken neu gedacht—Wien gedenkt vergessener Opfer; Zeithistorische, gesellschaftliche, queere und künstlerische Dimensionen des Gedenkens an homosexuelle und transgender NS-Opfer, Wiener Antidiskriminierungsstelle, Wien, 28–29 October 2014. http://eva.transgender.at/Loc/Docs/TGuNS.pdf. Accessed 24 June 2019.

Acceptance for trans persons and research grew in the 1960 and 1970s.[4] Trans persons who had undergone hormonal treatments and operations asked to have their legal gender changed. When the civil registry offices refused their requests, they went to court. The courts denied their claims, arguing that hormonal treatments and operations did not change the gender of a person.[5] A few scholars in the 1960s informed lawyers about the research of psychologists and medical researchers; the article of *Nevinny-Stickel* and *Hammerstein*" is a good example of this.[6] They argued that transgenderism was a normal variation of human life and could not be treated or changed. Rather, courts should help trans persons to legally adopt the gender with which they identified.

After this increased focus in research, by the 1970s the need for legal regulation had also been realised on the political level. By a unanimous vote, the federal parliament (Bundestag) requested in October 1976[7] that the federal government prepare a proposal as to regulating the situation of trans persons. Accordingly, a draft act was submitted that provided for trans persons changing their legal gender if certain requirements had been met, including a gender adjusting operation of the genitalia (the "big solution"). The draft act also provided that a trans person could change their first name according to the identified gender (the "small solution"). Before the draft law came into effect, however, the Federal Constitutional Court handed down its important decision of 11 October 1978.[8]

1.1 The 1978 Decision of the Federal Constitutional Court

The Federal Constitutional Court's decision begins by summarising the current research concerning trans persons.[9] The Court differentiates between homosexual persons, inter- and trans persons. The latter, as current research indicated, would feel "trapped in the wrong body". Consequently, trans persons were depicted as working systematically towards adjusting their bodies and outward appearance to the gender they identified with, sometimes even using self-mutilation and castration. The Court stated that any attempts to "cure" a trans person's identification with the other gender by hormonal treatments or psychological therapy could not succeed.[10] Rather, the Court held that a person had the constitutional right under articles 2 (1) in

[4]For interdisciplinary insights on the concepts of gender and transsexuality prior to, and during the legislative process leading to the Transexual Act see de Silva (2018).

[5]See a list of decisions in BT-Drs. 8/2947, p. 8.

[6]Nevinny-Stickel and Hammerstein (1967), p. 663.

[7]StenBer. S. 17 818 B (stenographic reports of the debates in the German federal parliament).

[8]BVerfGE 49, 286. See Federal Constitutional Court (2013).

[9]BVerfGE 49, 286, 287 f.; see for an extensive discussion of the case law of the Federal Constitutional Court: Adamietz (2011), pp. 124–150.

[10]BVerfGE 49, 286, 301.

conjunction with Article 1 (1) of the Basic Law to have his or her legal gender adjusted to the gender the person identified with. At least in situations where the transgenderism of the person seemed "irrevocable" and the person had undergone an operation to change his or her physical appearance (especially of the genitalia), the Constitution demanded that a trans person could change their legal gender even before parliament had put such a right into law.

Article 2 (1) of the Basic Law, to which the Court referred, provides that every person has the right to express his or her personality. Article 1 (1) of the Basic Law declares human dignity to be inviolable. The two articles in conjunction form the basis of the "general personality right" *(Allgemeines Persönlichkeitsrecht)*. This right protects privacy and allows every person to decide what information shall be available about them. It also concerns data protection, the right of everybody including celebrities to be left alone by the press and to keep personal secrets.[11] With this decision of 11 October 1978, the" Court held that the "general personality right" also protected a person's right to legally belong to the gender this person belonged to physically and psychologically.[12] The traditional assumption that gender was an unchangeable certainty tied to a person's genitalia, the court held, had become more and more questionable.[13]

1.2 The Introduction of the TSG

After this 1978 decision by the Federal Constitutional Court, the *Gesetz über die Änderung der Vornamen und die Feststellung der Geschlechtszugehörigkeit* (Transsexuellengesetz—hereafter TSG)" of 10.9.1980[14] was enacted and came into effect. The statute's title literary translates as "Law on the change of first names and the assessment of the affiliation to a gender" (Transsexual-law).

The drafting of the TSG took into consideration comparative legal research as to the different legal approaches that had already been developed by that time in other countries.[15] Only Sweden already existed a legal act (1972) that allowed the change of the legal gender. In some other countries, a change of the first name was possible, or even the change of the legal gender was allowed without specific legal regulation.[16]

Even though adressing the legal status of trans persons was considered progressive at the time the TSG pathologized transgenderism and put a person's transition under strict governmental observation and control. The TSG contained sections

[11]See for an introduction: Jarass and Pieroth (2014). Art. 2 Rn 36.

[12]According to Grünberger (2008), p. 84, the "birth of a human right".

[13]BVerfGE 49, 286, 299.

[14]BGBl. 1980 I S. 1654, see for the official reasons for the draft: BT-Drucks 8/2947.

[15]BT-Drucks 8/2947, pp. 10–11.

[16]See for references BT-Drucks 8/2947, pp. 10-11.

regulating almost every part of the private life of trans persons, such as marriage and the parent-child-relation. The law allowed a change of simply the first name ("small solution") or a change of the legal gender ("big solution") according to certain prerequisites.

Sections 1–7 of the TSG provide the prerequisite and procedural rules according to which a trans person can change her name. In the original version, section 1 read (in a translation by the authors):

> (1) the first name of a person shall be changed according to an application, if
>
> 1. due to a transsexual imprint this person does not feel that he or she belongs to the gender stated in the birth registry, but to another gender and this person has felt the urge to live due to this conviction for at least 3 years.
> 2. there is a high probability that this feeling of belonging to the other sex will not change in the future and
> 3. the person is
>
>   a) German according to the Basic Law
>   b) is without citizenship of any country or a homeless foreigner who has his/her residence in Germany
>   c) has been granted asylum or has a right to remain in Germany as a refugee
>   d) is a foreigner who has
>
>   aa) an unlimited right of residence, or
>   ba) a right of residence which can be renewed and who has taken his or her permanent residence in Germany.
>
> (2) In the application, the first name shall be indicated which the applicant wants to bear in the future.[17]

Section 8 TSG read in the original version (in a translation by the authors):

> (1) Upon application of a person, who - due to a transsexual imprint - does not identify with the gender registered upon birth but with the other gender and who has lived for 3 years with the urge to live according to this conception, a court shall state that this person shall be perceived as belonging to the other gender if the person

[17]§ 1 Voraussetzungen:

(1) Die Vornamen einer Person sind auf ihren Antrag vom Gericht zu ändern, wenn; 1. sie sich auf Grund ihrer transsexuellen Prägung nicht mehr dem in ihrem Geburtseintrag angegebenen Geschlecht, sondern dem anderen Geschlecht als zugehorig empfindet und seit mindestens drei Jahren unter dem Zwang steht, ihren Vorstellungen entsprechend zu leben, 2. mit hoher Wahrscheinlichkeit anzunehmen ist, dass sich ihr Zugehörigkeitsempfinden zum anderen Geschlecht nicht mehr ändern wird, und; 3. sie; a) Deutscher im Sinne des Grundgesetzes ist, b) als Staatenloser oder heimatloser Ausländer ihren gewöhnlichen Aufenthalt im Inland hat, c)als Asylberechtigter oder ausländischer Flüchtling ihren Wohnsitz im Inland hat oder, d)als Ausländer, dessen Heimatrecht keine diesem Gesetz vergleichbare Regelung kennt, aa)ein unbefristetes Aufenthaltsrecht besitzt oder; bb)eine verlängerbare Aufenthaltserlaubnis besitzt und sich dauerhaft rechtmäßig im Inland aufhält. (2) In dem Antrag sind die Vornamen anzugeben, die der Antragsteller künftig führen will. Version of 20.7.2007 (BGBl. I S. 1566). English translation by the authors.

1. fulfils the preconditions of § 1 (1) Nr. 1-3,
2. is unmarried.
3. is permanently unable to reproduce*
4. has undergone surgery of the sexual characteristics which have achieved a considerable alignment with the appearance of the other gender. *

(2) If the applicant has not changed his or her name according to § 1, the name he or she wants to bear in the future shall be stated in the application.

These original legislative versions were changed considerably by a line of decisions of the Federal Constitutional Court as discussed below.

2 Changing First Names: The "Small Solution"

As names are a daily piece of evidence of a person's gender, the possibility to change one's name according to one's gender identity is very important for trans persons. However, in Germany, a name is part of a person's status and cannot be changed at will. As the name is part of a personal status it is registered at birth. Traditionally, a person's first name had to clearly indicate the person's gender. Only in 2009 the Federal Constitutional Court loosened this condition somewhat, so that parents can now choose names more freely. The name can be gender neutral but has to allow the child to develop his or her personality and individuality by identifying the name with his or her gender. Therefore, a name that does not allow a child at all to "reconcile" the name with his or her gender cannot be given.[18] The name does not have to be on an official list of names. However, the name may not ridicule or humiliate a child.

Once registered, a first name can be changed if there was a mistake in the registration (section 45 PStG). Otherwise, a change of names—be it a change of the first name or family name—requires an "important reason" according to sections 3 and 11 *Namensänderungsgesetz* (Change of Names Act). Moreover, the TSG provides rules on the change of a trans person's first name.

2.1 Legally Changing Names for Trans Persons

In the official reasons given for the draft TSG, no extensive justification was given for the introduction of the small solution. It was explained, however, that the change of the first name allowed the applicant to quickly lead a "new" life aligned with their gender role.[19] Another argument was that the "small solution" made it possible to try out the "new" identity without having to fulfil the irreversible step of a genital-

[18]BVerfG NJW 2009, 663.
[19]BT-Drucks 8/2947, S. 12.

altering operation and sterilization.[20] Part of this argument was the understanding that transgenderism is potentially reversible.

The decision about changing the name is made by the District Court (*Amtsgericht*) (section 2 TSG). Section 4 TSG regulates the judicial procedure: The applicant will be heard personally.[21] Moreover, the court can only grant the application, if two experts, who based on their training and experience are sufficiently familiar with the "problems of transsexualism",[22] have independently given their opinion on the case and confirmed, that the 3-year waiting period is fulfilled and have given the prognosis that the gender identification of the applicant is permanent. Today, experts are usually psychologists. This does not mean, however, that the court can only grant the application if the two experts agree that the preconditions of section 1 have been met.[23] If the experts do not agree, the court must ask them to further explain their findings or maybe even request a third opinion.[24] And even if the experts do not confirm the trans "imprint" of the applicant, the court still can grant the name change if the judge is convinced that the application is well founded.[25]

Nonetheless the requirement of these opinions places a heavy burden on trans people. Activists criticize the expert opinions as arbitrary and often based on stereotypical perceptions of gender and transgenderism, e.g., trans persons claim that they feel pushed to perform stereotypical gender roles according to their "new" gender during the examinations.[26] The necessity to present intimate information about one's upbringing, relationships and sex life is seen as an obstacle on the way to

[20]BGBl. 1980 I p.

[21]Also at the appeal level: KG, decision of 20.5.2008 – Case No. 1 W 62/08, Praxis der Freiwilligen Gerichtsbarkeit (FGPrax) 2008, 200.

[22]§ 4 Gerichtliches Verfahren: (1) Auf das gerichtliche Verfahren sind die Vorschriften des Gesetz über das Verfahren in Familiensachen und in den Angelegenheiten der freiwilligen Gerichtsbarkeit anzuwenden, soweit in diesem Gesetz nichts anderes bestimmt ist. (2) Das Gericht hört den Antragsteller persönlich an. (3) Das Gericht darf einem Antrag nach § 1 nur stattgeben, nachdem es die Gutachten von zwei Sachverständigen eingeholt hat, die auf Grund ihrer Ausbildung und ihrer beruflichen Erfahrung mit den besonderen Problemen des Transsexualismus ausreichend vertraut sind. 2 Die Sachverständigen müssen unabhängig voneinander tätig werden; in ihren Gutachten haben sie auch dazu Stellung zu nehmen, ob sich nach den Erkenntnissen der medizinischen Wissenschaft das Zugehörigkeitsempfinden des Antragstellers mit hoher Wahrscheinlichkeit nicht mehr ändern wird. (Version of 20.7.2007 (BGBl. I S. 1566), English translation by the author.) (4) 1Gegen die Entscheidung, durch die einem Antrag nach § 1 stattgegeben wird, steht den Beteiligten die sofortige Beschwerde zu. 2Die Entscheidung wird erst mit der Rechtskraft wirksam.

[23]OLG Schleswig, StAZ 2003, 270; KG FGPrax 2008, 200.

[24]Augstein, M. S. 2012. Transsexuellengesetz. Nomos, Baden-Baden Augstein. § 4 Rn. 5.

[25]Kammergericht Berlin, Beschluss v. 20.05.2008,—1 W 62/08—, FGPrax 2008, 200.

[26]See testimonials by Arcuri, E., Govrin, J. 2018. Es ist nicht Willkür. Es ist das System. In: Der Spiegel, 25th October 2018. Hamburg. http://www.spiegel.de/kultur/gesellschaft/geschlechtliche-selbstbestimmung-es-ist-nicht-willkuer-es-ist-das-system-a-1234909.html. Accessed 24 June 2019. See also for extensive descriptions, Adamietz and Bager (2016), p. 100 ff. https://www.bmfsfj.de/blob/114064/460f9e28e5456f6cf2ebdb73a966f0c4/imag-band-7-regelungs%2D%2Dund-

legal recognition and reinforces the pathologization of being trans. Furthermore, the examinations are expensive and time-consuming whilst they almost entirely result in the confirmation of the trans persons request to change their gender. It is argued that it should be the trans persons rather than an expert's opinion which should be decisive to determine the gender they identify with.[27] This was also a central claim of the interviewed trans persons in *Adamietz/Bagers* paper on the needs for legal reforms in Germany.[28] The requirement of two expert opinions was challenged by an individual claim before the Federal Constitutional Court in 2017, but the "Court" refused to admit and decide the constitutional complaint. The Court explained that the requirement of an expert opinion was not based on a pathologization of transgenderism but a legitimate procedural means to ascertain the stability of the gender identification.[29]

Once the application is granted and the name changed accordingly, no enquiries may be made into the previous name (section 5 (1) TSG). Recently, however, the Federal Court of Justice has decided that previous entrances in a commercial register, where the trans person was registered as the director of a company, cannot be changed retrospectively.[30]

In the birth certificate of the children of the trans person born or adopted before the change of name, the trans person's previous name will be kept (section 5 (3) TSG).[31] The trans person's former spouse, parents, children or grandchildren have to use the new name only in official documents (section 5 (2) TSG). Another important exception establishes section 7 TSG: If within a time frame of 300 days after the name change decision a child of the applicant is born, the name change will be reversed. This rule is yet another manifestation of the heteronormative understanding prevalent when the TSG was established: Procreation as the pinnacle of gender manifestation.

Section 6 TSG provides that the change of name is to be revoked upon an application of the trans person saying that they identify again with the gender registered at birth. Such cases are very rare, however. Ten years after the TSG came into power, only five cases had been reported where trans persons revoked the change of their names.[32]

---

reformbedarf-fuer-transgeschlechtliche-menschen%2D%2D-band-7-data.pdf. Accessed 24 June 2019.

[27]Bundesweiter Arbeitskreis TSG-Reform. 2012. Forderungspapier zur Reform des Transsexuellenrechts. http://www.tsgreform.de/wp-content/uploads/2012/06/Forderungspapier_AK-TSG-Reform_1.6.201211.pdf. Accessed 24 June 2019.

[28]Adamietz and Bager (2016), p. 100 ff.

[29]BVerfG, NJW 2018, 222.

[30]BGH, NJW 2015, 2116.

[31]Plett (2015), p. 56, claims that this rule is unconstitutional, for more detail see below.

[32]Augstein (2012), § 6 Rn. 1.

There is no rule that sets a limit to the change of names. However, it would probably be more difficult to convince the court and experts to agree with the application a second or third time.

2.2 *Important Decisions of the Federal Constitutional Court*

As already pointed out, the influence of the Federal Constitutional Court on the development of the law regarding trans persons cannot be overestimated. The TSG as it now stands is a result of the different decisions handed down by the Court.

Initially, the law required that a trans person to be allowed to change his or her name had to be 25 years of age. In a 1993 decision,[33] the Court held this age limit to be unconstitutional. In a chamber decision of three judges, the court held in 1996[34] that after a trans person had changed their first name, the personality rights of this person required that they had to be addressed in person and in writing by public authorities according to the persons identified rather than legal gender. This shows, that even before the adjustment of the legal gender, the Federal Constitutional Court respects the gender with which the trans person identifies.

Moreover, the initial version of the law stated that a trans person had to forfeit their new name if they got married. The law assumed that a trans person who got married identified with their former legal gender again. In a 2005 decision, the Court held this provision to be unconstitutional.[35] In 2006,[36] the first senate held that the right to a name change under the TSG could not be refused to trans persons without a German citizenship if the law of their home country did not offer this option to them. In both these decisions, the Court considered research stating that not all trans persons felt a heterosexual orientation.[37] Moreover, the Court held, that mandatory surgery as to genitalia was not the right way for many trans persons to express their identity. While the "small solution" had first been introduced as means to provide some relief for a trans person before an operation could be obtained, the Court took up research by the German Society for Research on Sexuality *(Deutsche Gesellschaft für Sexualforschung)* which stated that remaining in the "small solution" could be a permanent solution for some trans persons. About 20–30% remained in the "small solution" permanently.[38] These reasons were also brought forward in the 2011 decision of the Court that held that a prerequisite of a complete operation to change one's legal gender was unconstitutional.[39]

[33]BVerfGE 88, 87.
[34]BVerfG NJW 1997, 1632.
[35]BVerfGE 115, 1.
[36]BVerfGE 116, 243.
[37]BVerfGE 115, 1, 4 ff.
[38]Becker et al. (2001), pp. 258–268; cited by BVerfGE 115, 1, 4 ff.
[39]BVerfGE 128, 109, 115.

3 Changing Legal Gender, the "Big Solution"

The "big solution" describes the change of legal gender. Gender is a category of legal status, which is defined in section 1 (1) s 1 *Personenstandsgesetz* (PStG) as the "position of a person within the legal system resulting from all family law characteristics, including the name". According to section 1 (1) s 2 PStG, status contains data about birth, marriage, civil partnership and death as well as related facts regarding family law, including the name.[40] A person's gender is part of his or her civil status and is registered at birth (section 21 (1) Nr. 3 PStG) together with the child's name, the date, hour and minute of its birth, the parents' names. What gender is though, is not legally defined. The time of registration (right after birth) shows that rather a person's sex and not their gender is registered.

The 1794 General State Law for the Prussian States acknowledged a third gender marker called "hermaphrodite", which could be used by self-declaration. The Law on the certification of civil status and marriage from 1875 and the PStG from 1937 did only state *that*, but not *which* legal gender should be registered. Apparently, it seemed too obvious that it could only be either male or female to name the categories explicitly. Only in 2010, perhaps as a reaction to the emerging activism of inter persons and their claim to be correctly registered, did an administrative order appear which clarified that the legal gender to be registered could only be male or female.[41] If in doubt, a doctor's opinion was consulted.[42] Since 2013, the gender of the child was to be left open in the registry if it was not possible to assign it to the male or female marker. Trans persons did not have the option to invoke the new law. Due to the legal reform following a Federal Constitutional Court decision on the "third option",[43] from 1 January 2019 onwards persons who are "medically diagnosed with a variation of their gender development" can choose between leaving the gender marker open or using the male, female or "diverse" one. After various trans persons used the vague definition as a gateway for a legal gender change without having to wait for 3 years and acquiring two expert opinions, the Federal Court of Justice decided in April 2020 that this law is not applicable on trans persons and directed them once again at the TSG.[44] An individual complaint of a non-binary person who seeked a "diverse"-genderentry, is now pending at the Federal Constitutional Court (for more details see below).

[40]Dethloff and Gössl (2014), p. 137.

[41]Administrative Rule, March 29th 2010, § 21.4.3 PStG-VwV.

[42]German Institute for Human Rights (2017), p. 18. https://www.bmfsfj.de/bmfsfj/service/publikationen/gutachten%2D%2Dgeschlechtervielfalt-im-recht%2D%2Dstatus-quo-und-entwicklung-von-regelungsmodellen-zur-anerkennung-und-zum-schutz-von-geschlechtervielfalt/114072. Accessed 24 June 2019.

[43]BVerfG, BVerfGE 147, 1.

[44]BGH, NJW 2020, 1955.

The law of civil status is extensively regulated in the *Personenstandsgesetz* (civil status law, PStG). The law was last reformed in 2007[45] and last amended 17 July 2017;[46] and 1 January 2019.[47] The civil registry office (*Standesamt*) is responsible for keeping the register on marriages, civil partnerships, births and deaths (section 3 PStG). The personal data registered by the civil registry office are used by other authorities, e.g., the residence registry, the federal office of statistics, the family court, the social security office or the authority which issues passports.[48] Therefore, the registered personal data are of fundamental importance for every person in Germany. Legal gender is shown on a persons's birth certificate and passport, but not on the identification card (i.d.). Either one can be used for identification.

After the registration, a person's gender can be changed if there was a mistake in writing in the registration (section 47 (1) s. 1 PStG) or if the registration was based on mistaken or incomplete information (section 47 (1) s. 2 PStG). This possibility does not allow, however, to change a person's gender marker because the person's gender identity is different from the registered gender.

3.1 Legally Changing Gender

Just as with the introduction of the opportunity to change one's name, the current state of the law regarding the change of legal gender has been heavily influenced by the case law of the Federal Constitutional Court. Initially, a trans person could only change their legal gender if they were over 25 years of age, unmarried, had undergone surgery of the genitalia to "adjust" them to those of the gender identified with and were permanently infertile. In relation to the precondition of the operation, the 1979 official reasons of the draft law argued[49] that it was unacceptable that a man who could still "act as a man" could marry another man. At that time, there was still criminal punishment for consensual sex between a man over 18 years of age and a man under 18 years of age (section 175 Criminal Code).[50] The official draft of the TSG explained that an operation was necessary to prevent that a person who was by law a woman could be guilty of an offence under section 175 of the Criminal Code.

Section 9 TSG refers to the procedure used for the change of names. If a minor submits the application, no separate decision of the family court is necessary. In practice, a minor will need the consent of their parents, though they can submit the

[45]BGBl 2007 I. S. 122.

[46]BGBl. 2017 I. S. 2522.

[47]BGBl. 2018 I, S. 2635.

[48]Dethloff and Gössl (2014), p. 137. See also Gössl (2016), pp. 1122–1128.

[49]BT-Drucks 8/2947 S. 12.

[50]Until 1969, consensual then "sodomy" could be punished with a prison sentence. After that, there were milder sanctions, especially aimed at "protecting" young men, until the different treatment of homosexual and heterosexual male sex was abolished in 1994.

application themselves when 14 years old.[51] Section 9 TSG also refers to section 6 TSG. This means that even after a change of the legal gender, a trans person can submit an application to adopt their prior gender again. No other preconditions must be met, in particular. Even before the decision of the TSG, no operation of the genitals was required in this case. Just as with the change of the first name, no maximum numbers of changes of the legal gender are prescribed. However, cases where trans persons wanted to reverse changing their legal gender are extremely rare. In the decade after the TSG came into effect, only one trans person had taken this opportunity.[52] Studies indicate that the rate is below 1% of trans persons undoing their name and/or legal gender change.[53]

According to section 10 TSG, after the decision, the rights and duties of the trans person will be determined by the new gender unless the TSG prescribes otherwise. One important exception is the legal relationship between the trans person and their children, which will continue to be determined by the previous legal gender of the trans person (section 11 s. 1 TSG). The situation is different however, if the child was adopted after the trans person changed his or her legal gender (section 11 s. 2 TSG). The trans person's rights to retirement benefits or a pension are not affected by the change of the legal gender (section 12 s.1 TSG).

Since the legal recognition of both the new name and gender take a minimum of 3 years in Germany, daily life without the adequate papers holds potential for discrimination. The German Association fir Transidentity and Intersexuality (*Deutsche Gesellschaft für Transidentität und Intersexualität e.V.)* helps out by offering an additional identity card (*Ergänzungsausweis*) which correctly labels the trans person's gender and name and explains, why so far it is not matching the person's official documents.[54]

3.2 Access to Hormonal Treatments and Gender Confirmation Surgery

The German health care system provides both hormonal treatments and gender confirmation surgeries. There are no legal requirements for receiving hormonal treatment or surgery. As explained below, no treatment of any kind is a legal requirement to change a name or even legal gender anymore. Such treatments will be invoked only when individuals requests them.

---

[51] See OLG Brandenburg, NZFam 2017, 720.

[52] Augstein (2012), § 6 para. 1.

[53] Becker et al. (2001), pp. 258, 264.

[54] Deutsche Gesellschaft für Transidentität und Intersexualität e.V. (n.d.). Deutsche Gesellschaft für Transidentität und Intersexualität e.V. (n.d.) Der neue Ergänzungsausweis der dgti. https://www.dgti.org/ergaenzungsausweis#wozu. Accessed 24 June 2019.

However, in order to have the cost of hormonal treatment and surgery covered by health insurance, a trans person has to submit proof that such a treatment is necessary to preserve or restore physical or mental health. At this point, an expert opinion by a specialised doctor and/or psychiatrist is needed. Cost coverage for certain measures is still under discussion.[55]

Trans persons object against the necessity to perceive their transgenderism as an illness. In line with the World Health Organization's decision from May 2018 to ban transgenderism from the list of mental illnesses, they demand that costs of treatments should be borne by health insurance in any case.[56] It means a challenge to the current system of health insurance to get a treatment financially covered without a medical diagnosis.

3.3 *Important Decisions of the Federal Constitutional Court*

Section 8 TSG allows a change of legal gender. This section was introduced with four preconditions (see above). However, the decisions of the Federal Constitutional Court have declared all preconditions except one to be unconstitutional. The only remaining precondition, that "the person has felt the compulsion to live due to this conviction for at least three years" is the one which must be fulfilled also for a name change. So far (spring 2021), the responsible ministries (the Federal Ministry of the Interior and the Ministry of Law and Consumer Protection) could not agree on a draft law with new preconditions to be voted on by the German Parliament. This means that since 2011, when the most recent decision of the Federal Constitutional Court was handed down, the preconditions for the change of name (so called "small solution") and the change of the legal gender (so called "big solution") are the same.

This development of the TSG under the case law of the Federal Constitutional Court began with a 1982 decision. The Court then declared that it was unconstitutional that a young trans person who had undergone surgery had to wait until his or her 25th birthday to change his or her legal gender.[57] Since the legislator had only restricted the legal gender change, but not access to genital altering surgery, the age requirement could not be constitutionally justified. While this decisions allowed young trans persons to change legal gender earlier, sanitization might also be part of this argument: If a person already had the outer appearance of a certain gender, their legal gender marker should follow their physical appearance.

[55]See for example epilation for removing facial hair: LSG Nordrhein-Westfalia, decision of May 8th 2014 - L 16 KR 453/12; On the payment of an operation to improve the result of a previous mastectomy (which at the time was paid for by health insurance): LSG Hessen, decision of April 24th 2014—L 8 KR 27/12.

[56]Bundesweiter Arbeitskreis TSG-Reform (2012).

[57]BVerfGE 60, 123 (Ger.).

In a 2008 decision,[58] the Court ruled on the preconditions to changing legal gender (the "big solution"). The TSG required that a person who changed their legal gender could not be married in order to prevent same gender marriages. The trans person in question argued that she and her wife did not want to divorce and that her fundamental right of the protection of marriage (article 6 BL) was violated. The law could not force her to choose between either adopting the legal gender she identified with or the life partner to whom she still felt bound by marriage. The Court agreed and declared the precondition that a person needed to be unmarried to change their legal gender unconstitutional.

The most recent significant decision concerning trans persons was handed down in 2011.[59] In this case, a lesbian trans woman wanted to form a civil partnership with her girlfriend. However, since she had not changed her legal gender but just her first name, the civil registry office only offered her marriage. The trans woman argued that forming a marriage was meant for partners of different gender, the law would not accept theirs as a same gender union. Being married meant that her transgenderism would be made known to the world, because only a trans woman could marry another woman. She was too old to undergo the invasive surgery required for the change of legal gender. The court held that the legislator had been free to differentiate between civil partnership and marriage by referring to the legal gender rather than sexual orientation. However, the prerequisite that the legal gender could only be changed after enduring a potentially dangerous operation was unconstitutional. The legislator could possibly demand certain measures to align the outward appearance with the possibility to make exceptions for medical reasons, for example that someone was too old to undergo the operation without serious health risks. Yet the legislator had demanded the operation without an exception. This judgment demonstrates how much the Federal Constitutional Court now values gender self-determination—the applicant could have concluded a marriage, who at that time, still differed positively in some ways from a civil partnership, but her identification and will to have her lesbian partnership officially registered was decisive.

The effects of the Court's 2008 and 2011 judgments is that of a list of four preconditions, only one, the same as for a change of the name, remains in force. The other three were declared unconstitutional. Since 2011, no new preconditions have been introduced nor has the TSG been changed/substituted altogether.

Since 2019 the new section 45b PStG allows persons which present a "variation of gender development" to change their gender marker to either "male", "female", "diverse" or have no entry at all. The new law appeared to offer a less discriminating procedure of legal gender change for trans persons as well, until the Federal Court of Justice declared it to be inapplicable for trans persons.[60] Now yet again the Federal

[58]BVerfGE 121,175.

[59]BVerfGE 128, 109.

[60]BGH, NJW 2020, 1955.

Constitutional Court has to decide on the fundamental rights of trans persons – in the pending case on the question, if the TSG has been replaced by section 45b PStG.[61]

4 Family Law and Parenthood

Ever since the Federal Constitutional Court's 2011 decision, a person who is legally registered as male can bear a child and a legal woman inseminate another person with her sperm. Thus, trans persons no longer have to choose between legal recognition of their gender and having children. However, German parent-child law was not reformed. It distinguishes between two gendered parental roles, motherhood and fatherhood. The former is a manifestation of the traditional principle "mater semper certa est"; section 1591 of the Federal Family Code defines that the "mother of a child is the woman *who gave birth* to it," whereas according to section 1592 the "father of a child is the man *who is married* to the mother of the child at the date of the birth or *who has acknowledged* paternity or whose paternity has been *judicially established* [...]."

So far, two cases concerning the registration of trans parents have reached the highest German Court for the interpretation of civil law, the Federal Court of Justice. Both cases were decided by this Court in 2017.[62] In the first case, a trans man became pregnant after a change of legal gender. In line with his legal gender marker he was seeking legal recognition as the father of the child. The civil registry office registered the man as the "mother" of the child with his former female names in the birth registry as well as in the birth certificates of the child. A second case of a trans woman, who inseminated her life partner with her cryopreserved sperm and was seeking the legal status as mother of the child, was decided shortly after. Authorities registered her as the father of the child with her former male name.

Section 11 TSG states that "The decision that the applicant is registered with the opposite gender, *leaves* the legal relationship [...] between the applicant and his children unaffected. [...]." The legal wording of the paragraph refers to an already established parent-child-relationship, which remains unaffected by the transition of the parent. When the TSG was established, it contradicted the predominant understanding of gender that a person which identified themselves as male wanted to bear a child. Permanent infertility was a prerequisite for the legal gender change. Still, already the explanatory memorandum of the TSG considered the possibility of a trans person becoming a parent *after* their legal gender change and declared section

[61]As clearly argued in the expert opinion by Mangold, A. K., Markwald, M., Röhner, C. 2019. Rechtsgutachten zum Verständnis von „Varianten der Geschlechtsentwicklung" in § 45b Personenstandsgesetz, https://eufbox.uni-flensburg.de/index.php/s/WwkHJkHaEaHpkQk#pdfviewer. Accessed 17 July 2020.

[62]BGH, NJW 2017, 3379; BGH, NJW 2018, 471.

11 TSG to be applicable.[63] In the Federal Constitutional Court's 2011 judgment, this interpretation was reaffirmed.[64]

4.1 Current Case Law

It is one of the core principles of the TSG that from the decision as to belonging to the other gender onwards, all legal rights and duties apply according to the new gender. Hence, section 11 TSG constitutes an exception to this rule. The registration as a parent with the old gender and name reverses the former decision to be fully recognized according to the new gender and constitutes a constant threat of an outing for trans persons in a gender-based especially vulnerable area of life.[65]

The Federal Court of Justice confirmed the authorities' decisions. It justified its assessment in two ways: firstly, by emphasizing the best interest of the child and secondly by alerting of "far reaching consequences for the legal order". Registering trans parents according to their legal gender endangered the child's right to know its descent. The Court went even further, creating a new right: the "explicitly protected right of the child to have the specific biological contribution of its parents to its procreation reflected by law".[66]

Firstly, the right of a child to know its descent is nationally and internationally recognized; yet it does not necessarily result in the legal parenthood of the biological/genetically parent. German law recognises this for example when a mother's husband becomes the legal father of a child. A biological father may only challenge the husband's paternity if there is no social relationship between the legal father and the child. The assumption that the law must mirror the "specific biological contribution of a parent to the procreation of a child" attributes weighty meaning to kinship law. It has to be scrutinized critically, if this is really the purpose of kinship law and if so, how far the state's responsibility to record private family history should go. This case however shows that the birth certificate as an important piece of evidence for the legitimacy of the parent-child relation in daily life is not the right archive for storing this kind of private information.[67] With the establishment of the sperm donor's registry act in 2017,[68] the legislator has shown that information about the biological and genetical descent and legal parenthood can be kept separate.

Secondly, the Court claimed that the child needed to be protected against an outing of the transgenderism of its parent. This can benevolently be seen as illogical: a male person with a male name will have to explain himself constantly if he is

[63]BT-Drucks 8/2947, p. 23.

[64]BVerfG, BVerfGE 128, 109, para. 77.

[65]For further details see Richarz (2019).

[66]BGH, NJW 2017, 3379.

[67]Adamietz and Bager (2016), p. 55.

[68]BGBl. I, p. 2513.

registered in the birth certificate of the child as "mother" with a different name. In this situation, a (forced) outing is far more likely. Beneath the Court's argument though lays the outdated understanding of transgenderism as a possibly reversible life choice. Full recognition in daily life is hindered this way and trans parents have to explain themselves constantly. By this, they are pushed back into their old identity.

Eventually the Federal Court of Justice argued that: "German kinship law is – like most legal systems worldwide – characterized by connecting the specific biological contribution of a parent to reproduction with their gender by assigning the role of the birth giver to a female and the role of the impregnator to a male". The Court goes on to state that "finally, the connection between reproductive function and gender is undoubtedly based on biology". The challenge as to assessing whether the Federal Court of Justice refers to sex or to gender highlights the fact that the Federal Court of Justice and the Federal Constitutional Court have a different concept of "Geschlecht". Here, the Federal Court of Justice strictly connects biological features to a certain gender, thus addressing the sex of the trans parents. But the trans applicants referred to their registered gender. The Federal Court of Justice contradicts not only modern knowledge on gender, but also the Federal Constitutional Court's decisions from 2011[69] and 2017.[70] The connection between the biological contribution to reproduction to a certain sex/gender makes a correct registration of trans parents impossible.

The Federal Constitutional Court refused to admit an individual complaint of a trans father in June 2018.[71] The case is now pending at the European Court of Human Rights.

4.2 Possible Solutions

In the course of the Federal Constitutional Court's jurisprudence, the importance of bodies as an indicator for a person's gender is decreasing and individual gender self-determination is gaining ground. At the same time, we experience a general trend to biologize legal parenthood. This can be seen as a reaction to the break-up of traditional family models and the questions that arise from this: Who are the parents of a child?[72] The biologization of legal parenthood resonates with a heteronormative understanding of family bonds and establishes a biologist understanding of gender. Trans persons which were already legally recognized with their new gender, are pushed back into their old gender role once they become parents. The Federal

[69]BVerfG, BVerfGE 128, 109.

[70]BVerfG, BVerfGE 147, 1.

[71]BverfG, non-acceptance decision without justification of May 15th 2018, 1 BvR 2831/17.

[72]See in detail: Baker (2008), p. 649. Chicago. https://scholarship.kentlaw.iit.edu/fac_schol/49. Accessed 24 June 2019. Baker (2008).

Constitutional Court held in 2013 that there are no constitutional reasons against the legal establishment of same-gender parenthood.[73] A person's gender thus does not need to be a factor in assigning legal parenthood at all. Despite the arguments of the Federal Court of Justice, this cannot be justified by the child's interests. First, the interest of the child to know its biologic origin can—as pointed out already—be secured in a way that is less revealing for the trans parent. Second, if the court should have argued upon the assumption that trans parents are unfit to be parents anyways, the registration of the trans father as legal mother and vice versa does not change anything about their role in their child's life. It is just a fact that the child will grow up with a trans parent and it would be much easier for both child and parent if they had not to explain the parent's gender identity every time kindergartens and schools request a birth certificate. Their right to family life can be seen as infringed.

In the judgment as to the "third gender marker", the Federal Constitutional Court formulated the State's obligation to "protect persons from being disfavoured that belong to groups structurally prone to being discriminated against" and carved out the essential meaning of gender identity in our society.[74] Following this ruling, it can be said that parenthood makes the ones who do not confirm to the heteronormative, cis-gendered norm especially vulnerable. Thus, there is a legal obligation to protect trans parents from being forcefully outed by law and complicating their lived parenthood.

Since the courts have denied this protection to trans parents and their children, the ball is in the field of the legislator. At the very least, a provision should be introduced which allows the legal registration of trans parents according to their gender. But the legislator could take a bolder step: A gender neutral parent-child law, as presented e.g. by the German Institute for Human Rights in 2017, is an uncomplicated way to ensure the protection of trans and inter persons and at the same time protecting the child's rights.[75] Parental rights and duties have been (almost) gender-neutral for quite some time now. Instead of "mother" and "father", legal terminology could refer to the "birthing parent" or "first parent" and "second parent".

5 Sex and Gender: What's Law Got to Do With It?

Parent-child law is one of the last remaining gendered areas in law;[76] others are anti-discrimination law and affirmative action. The gender of a person played a role for deciding if a couple can conclude a Civil Partnership or marriage. Only married

[73]BVerfG, BVerfGE 133, 59 para. 1.

[74]BVerfG, BVerfGE 147, 1, para. 59.

[75]See German Institute for Human Rights (2017) Bundesverfassungsgericht (2017) Jahresstatistik 2016. http://www.bundesverfassungsgericht.de/DE/Verfahren/Jahresstatistiken/2016/statistik_2016_node.html. Accessed 24 June 2019, p. 33, 55 ff, 58; see also Adamietz and Bager (2016), p. 55.

[76]See Dutta (2015), pp. 207–222 Dutta (2015), p. 208.

couples could adopt children jointly, civil partners can only adopt their partners child. After the introduction of same gender marriage in 2017,[77] however, this distinction loses its importance.

Article 3 (3) and (2) of the Basic Law, the German Constitution, guarantees that men and women are equal and that discrimination because of a person's gender is unconstitutional. The General Equal Treatment Act *(Allgemeines Gleichbehandlungsgesetz, AGG),* introduced in 2006,[78] also forbids in section 1 discrimination based on a person's gender and gender identity. It is applicable in relation to the selection of employees and their working conditions and promotion, career counselling, social and health services, as well as access to publicly offered goods and services, especially housing. A person's gender plays a role in affirmative action, i.e. rules which aim at having more women in leading positions at University and on the boards of companies. Health insurance regulations also differ between genders.

It is possible to find workable solutions for those areas of law. The German Institute for Human Rights indicated precisely which areas of law required change[79] and discussions about post-categorial anti-discrimination law are happening in various legal systems.

6 The Rights of Inter Persons

The struggle for legal recognition of inter persons has highlighted how the system of gender registration works. Already in the 1990s, inter activists in Germany brought the binary gender registration system to the courts.[80] Since 2013, the sex of the child was to be left open in the registry if it was not possible to assign it to the male or female marker. The campaign "third option" supported the individual complaint of Vanja, an inter activists, for a third gender marker.[81] On 10 October 2017, the First Senate of the Federal Constitutional Court held that the legislator was indeed required to introduce the possibility to register under a third gender in the birth register or to abandon the registration of a person's sex/gender all together.[82] Article 2 (1) in conjunction with Article 1 (1) of the Basic Law, the "general personality right" *(Allgemeines Persönlichkeitsrecht)* protected a person's gender identity, the

[77]BGBl. I 2017, 2787.

[78]BGBl. 2006 I 1897.

[79]German Institute for Human Rights (2017), p. 18.

[80]LG München I, decision of June 30th, 2003 – 16T 19449/02 = NJW-RR 2003, 1590; AG München, decision of September 13th, 2001 – 722 UR III 302/00 = NJW – RR 2001, 1586.

[81]The Federal Court of Justice had denied this request, see BGH, NJW 2016, 2885 = FamRZ 2016, 1580 with a casenote by Sieberichs. Sieberichs (2016), p. 2887.

[82]BVerfG, BVerfGE 147, 1.

Federal Constitutional Court held.[83] The law of personal status infringed this right by demanding that a person who did not identify as male or female was nonetheless required to be registered this way or to have no legal gender marker at all.[84] The option to leave the gender marker open did not provide an adequate solution as long as gender is still a category of personal status. It forces the inter person to identify as a “nothing” or gives the impression that a registration had been forgotten by mistake.[85] According to the Federal Constitutional Court, there was no justification for this infringement.[86] Administrative difficulties could be handled and thus did not provide a justification for not introducing a third gender marker. Moreover, the registration of people as belonging to one of three different genders did not introduce more legal uncertainty. Rather, the registration of persons under one of three options provided as much clarity as under two options and leaving registration open as a third option. While there could indeed be difficulties on how to apply laws differentiating just between a male and female on persons registered as belonging to a third gender, such difficulties would also arise under a law differentiating between male, female and persons, where the legal gender had been left open.[87]

Apart from the general personality right, the Federal Constitutional Court furthermore held, that the law was unconstitutional because of sex discrimination, forbidden under Article 3 (3) of the Basic Law.[88] The Court stated that “persons who identify as neither female nor male are particularly vulnerable in a society primarily organised according to binary gender patterns” and so embedded the individual’s complaint in a structural context. The statements about the meaning of sex/gender can be applied to the legal status of trans persons.

The Federal Constitutional Court gave the legislator until 31 December 2018 to introduce a third gender into legislation or to abandon the registration of gender in the birth registry completely.[89]

The Ministry of Interior presented a legal reform[90] that was criticized heavily by various interest groups as the bare minimum.[91] It contains the implementation of a

[83]BVerfG, BVerfGE 147, 1, para 37–40.

[84]BVerfG, BVerfGE 147, 1, para 41–48.

[85]BVerfG, BVerfGE 147, 1, para 43; see also Brachthäuser and Richarz (2014).

[86]BVerfG, BVerfGE 147, 1, para 49–55.

[87]BVerfG, BVerfGE 147, 1, para 54.

[88]BVerfG, BVerfGE 147, 1, para 56–64.

[89]BVerfG, BVerfGE 147, 1, para 65.

[90]BGBl I. 2018 I. p. 2635.

[91]See Verein Intersexuelle Menschen e.V. 2018, Gemeinsame Stellungnahme von Intersexuelle Menschen e.V., den LandesverbÄnden und den angeschlossenen Selbsthilfegruppen zum Referentenentwurf: Referentenentwurf des Bundesministeriums des Innern, für Bau und Heimat VII1- 20103/7#6. http://www.im-ev.de/pdf/2018_07_16_Stellungnahme_IMeV_Referentenentwurf_Aenderung_PStG.pdf. Accessed 12 July 2019; Bundesvereinigung Trans*. 2018. Stellungnahme der Bundesvereinigung Trans* zum Entwurf eines Gesetzes zur Änderung der in das Geburten- register einzutragenden Angaben (Stand vom 5. Juni 2018). https://www.bv-trans.de/wp-content/uploads/2018/08/StellungnahmeBVTGeburt. Accessed 12 July 2019;

new gender marker category (in the original draft first named "other", then "further", then, after harsh criticism, changed to "diverse"). The draft did not further discuss the option to abolish legal gender registration all together. The third gender marker is only open to those "medically diagnosed" as inter. A self-identification is not sufficient. Against the high hopes after the revolutionary decision of the Federal Constitutional Court in 2017, the legal change means just another special law for a small group of people and does not cease to pathologize inter persons. The law was adopted at the end of 2018 and came into force on 1 January 2019.

The law demands that a person shows a "variation of gender development"—a term which even though it refers to the findings of a medical conference on intersexuality in 2005,[92] can hardly be defined—neither medically nor legally. Thus trans persons with trans-friendly doctors used the procedure to change their registered gender without the need of waiting 3 years and obtaining two expensive expert opinions.[93] However, the Ministry of the Interior reacted quickly and sent out an order in March 2019 to all civil registry offices in Germany, that only inter persons are to be registered under the new law.[94]

Mangold, Markwald and Röhner argue in a joint legal opinion that—following the Federal Constitutional Court's statements on the nature of legal "Geschlecht" and the States' respective protective mandate—section 45b PStG must be applicable to trans persons.[95] Nonetheless, the Federal Court of Justice in April 2020 distinguished yet again between medically proven "intersexuality" (sex) and "merely felt intersexuality"—a term the court developed—for a non-binary person's gender identity (gender), directing the latter to the TSG procedure.[96] A constitutional complaint is now pending at the Federal Constitutional Court.

Deutscher Juristinnenbund. 2018. Stellungnahme zum Referentenentwurf des Bundesministeriums des Innern, für Bau und Heimat: Entwurf eines Gesetzes zur Änderung der in das Geburtenregister einzutragenden Angaben (Stand: 5. Juni 2018). https://www.djb.de/verein/Kom-u-AS/K2/st18-11/. Accessed 24 June 2019; eneintrag_BVT.pdf. Accessed 12 July 2019.

[92]Lee et al. (2006), pp. e488–500. http://pediatrics.aappublications.org/cgi/reprint/118/2/e488. Accessed 12 July 2019.

[93]See Löffler, J. 2019. Das Transsexuellengesetz ist so schlecht, dass trans Personen jetzt ein Gesetz nutzen, das gar nicht für sie gedacht war. Buzzfeed. https://www.buzzfeed.com/de/julianeloeffler/transsexuellengesetz-intersex-lgbt-dritte-option. Accessed 12 July 2019, with the title "The TSG is so bad, that trans persons are now using a law that wasn't even meant for them."

[94]See https://pstg45b.de/anwendungshinweise-des-bmi-an-die-innenministerien-senatsverwaltungen-fuer-inneres-der-laender-bmi-am-10-04-19/. Accessed 25 July 2020.

[95]Mangold/Markwald/Röhner (2019).

[96]BGH, NJW 2020, 1955.

7 Quo vadis Trans Rights?

Today, it is widely argued that the TSG is seriously outdated. [97] Political statements as to the intent to change the TSG have been made for a decade.[98] In the 18th legislative period, between 2013 and 2017, an "interministrial working group on trans- and intersexuality" was formed between the Federal Ministries of Justice and Family which commissioned two legal opinions on the legal statuses of both groups. The expert opinion "Needs for legal regulations and reforms for transgender people" by Adamietz and Bager addressed the outdated approach to transgenderism in the TSG and presented possible legal reforms.[99] In 2017, the Federal Council issued a resolution to reform the TSG.[100]

Finally in May 2019, a joint draft by the Federal Ministry of the Interior and the Ministry of Justice and Consumer Protection was published, the *"Gesetz zur Neuregelung der Änderung des Geschlechtseintrags"*, law on the reform of a change of the legal gender marker, which aims at addressing inter and trans persons together in one act.[101] It was argued that after years of a political standstill, the draft was presented now also because trans persons were using the procedure for a legal gender change according to section 45b PStG.

According to the draft, trans persons can change their legal gender to the marker male, female, diverse or even choose to leave the marker open. This has to be seen as a big progress in the promotion of trans rights, since it affirms that trans persons do not necessarily identify themselves within a binary spectrum. The possibility not choose to a gender at all opens the gateway for reform discussions towards a gender-neutral law. It is important to note though, while inter persons, who present a medical confirmation of their "gender variation", according to the draft shall change their legal gender at the civil registry office, the decision whether or not trans applicants may change name and legal gender will still be made by courts.

The draft does not require any change of the applicant's physical appearance and abandoned the necessity of two expert opinions." However, the draft law demands

[97] See Adamietz and Bager (2016); Güldenring (2013), pp. 160–174; Grünberger (2008), p. 84.

[98] Already in 2009 the conservative-liberal government promised a reform, see CDU, CSU, FDP. 2009. Wachstum. Bildung. Zusammenhalt. Koalitionsvertrag zwischen CDU, CSU und FDP. 17. Legislaturperiode p. 108; 2013 the conservative-social government promised to take "the special situation of trans and intersexual persons into focus", CDU, CSU, SPD. 2013. Deutschlands Zukunft gestalten. Koalitionsvertrag zwischen CDU, CSU und SPD. 18. Legislaturperiode p. 74; in 2018, it was only stated that "we condemn homo- and transhostility and work against any discrimination", see CDU, CSU, SPD. 2018. Ein neuer Aufbruch für Europa Eine neue Dynamik für Deutschland Ein neuer Zusammenhalt für unser Land. Koalitionsvertrag zwischen CDU, CSU und SPD. 19. Legislaturperiode.p. 21.

[99] Adamietz and Bager (2016).

[100] Federal Council, Resolution of June 02nd 2017, BR-Drs. 362/17.

[101] Bundesinnenministerium und Bundesjustizministerium, Entwurf eines Gesetzes zur Neuregelung der Änderung des Geschlechtseintrags, 08.05.2019 Bundesinnenministerium und Bundesjustizministerium (2019).

proof of "competent counselling" which the applicant will not have to pay for. Furthermore, the draft does not include a solution for trans parents who want to be registered according to their gender identity in their children's birth certificate but rather confirms the current law.

The draft was heavily criticised by inter and trans activists.[102] Since inter and trans persons would be directed to different formal procedures, it was criticised for attempting to separate the respective interests. While providing a counselling certificate was easier and cheaper than two costly expert opinions, the draft law did not improve but rather worsened the position of trans persons, they argued. Courts and medical staff continue to hold a "gate way" position for a person's legal transition. Furthermore, a new draft section demands that the applicant's spouse is to be heard in the court procedure. Yet again it is not trans persons who are trusted to make a decision about their own personal gender identity. Moreover, avoiding the pressing need to provide regulation for trans parents and their children was a serious omission. It is hoped that a solution will be found in the drafting process of a new law of parentage which is under discussion now.

The reform process now is on a standstill. Meanwhile, in May 2020, the opposition's Green party presented a so called *"Selbstbestimmungsgesetz"* (Selfdetermination-law), which aims (amongst other rules) at the applicability of section 45b PStG to *all* persons according to their self-declaration, banning genital altering operations on inter children, registering trans parents according to their gender and securing the ban of unwanted disclosure.[103] This umbrella law combines the legal reforms which trans and inter activists have been demanding for decades; since the draft was presented by the opposition, however, it remains doubtful, if it becomes effective.

Some inter, trans and non-binary activists though have joined in demanding the banishment of the gender marker altogether, working instead towards a

---

[102]The two ministries set a time frame of merely 48 h to comment on the draft. Despite this, several associations, politicians and other activists reacted, see e.g. TransInterQueer (TrIQ) e. V. 2019. Stellungnahme von zum Referentenentwurf eines Gesetzes zur Neuregelung der Änderung des Geschlechtseintrags v. 08.05.2019. http://www.transinterqueer.org/wp-content/uploads/TrIQ-Stellungnahme-Referentenentwurf-v.-08_05_2019.pdf. Accessed 12 July 2019; Trans*Recht e.V. 2019. Stellungnahme von Trans* Recht e.V. im Rahmen der VerbÄndebeteiligung zum gemeinsamen Referentenentwurf des BMI und des BMJV "Entwurf eines Gesetzes zur Neuregelung der Änderung des Geschlechtseintrags". https://trans-recht.de/wordpress/wp-content/uploads/2019/05/2019-05_Stellungnahme_Trans-Recht_Final.pdf. Accessed 12 July 20; Bundesverband Trans*. 2019. Stellungnahme der Bundesvereinigung Trans* (BVT*) e.V. zum Referentenentwurf eines Gesetzes zur Neuregelung der Änderung des Geschlechtseintrages von BMJV und BMI vom 8. Mai 2019. https://www.bv-trans.de/wp-content/uploads/2019/05/BVT-Stellungnahme-Referentenentwurf-BMIBMJV-10-05-2019-1.pdf. Accessed 12 July 2019.

[103]Bündnis 90/Die Grünen. 2019. Entwurf eines Gesetzes zur Aufhebung des Transsexuellengesetzes und Einführung des Selbstbestimmungsgesetzes (SelbstBestG), Drucksache 19/19755.

gender-neutral law.[104] The meaning of gender in law is shrinking; the most important remaining areas are those of anti-discrimination law and affirmative action. Imaging such systems genderneutral stimulates fruitful discussions about their purpose: The state's mandate concerning gender is steadily shifting from normative standards to protection against gender-based discrimination and it is about time, that this shift is realized for trans rights in Germany as well.

References

Adamietz L (2011) Geschlecht als Erwartung. Nomos Verlagsgesellschaft, Baden-Baden, p 157 f

Adamietz L, Bager K (2016) Gutachten: Regelungs- und Reformbedarf für transgeschlechtliche Menschen. In: Senioren, Frauen und Jugend (ed) Bundesministerium für Familie. Begleitmaterial zur Interministeriellen Arbeitsgruppe Inter- & Transsexualität, Berlin, p 100 ff, Band 7

Augstein MS (2012) Transsexuellengesetz. Nomos, Baden-Baden

Baker K (2008) Bionormativity and the construction of parenthood. Ga Law Rev 42:649

Becker S, Berner W, Dannecker M, Richter-Appelt H (2001) Stellungnahme zur Anfrage des Bundesministeriums des Innern (V 5a-133 115-1/1) vom 11. Dezember 2000 zur Revision des Transsexuellengesetzes. Zeitschrift für Sexualforschung 2001:258–268

Brachthäuser F, Richarz T (2014) Das Nicht-Geschlecht: Die rechtliche Stellung intergeschlechtlicher Menschen. Forum Recht 2014:41–44

de Silva A (2018) Negotiating the borders of the gender regime. Developments and debates on Trans(sexuality) in the Federal Republic of Germany. Transcript, Berlin

Dethloff N, Gössl S (2014) Country Report for Germany. In: van den Brink M, Tigchelaar J (eds) M/V en verder. WODC, The Hague, pp 137–147

Dutta A (2015) The legal status of transsexual and transgender persons in Germany. In: Scherpe J (ed) The legal status of transsexual and transgender persons. Intersentia, Cambridge, pp 207–222

Federal Constitutional Court (ed) (2013) Family-related decisions 1957–2010. Decisions of the Bundesverfassungsgericht - Federal Constitutional Court - Federal Republic of Germany, vol 5. Nomos, Baden-Baden

German Institute for Human Rights (2017) Gutachten: Geschlechtervielfalt im Recht. Status quo und Entwicklung von Regelungsmodellen zur Anerkennung und zum Schutz von Geschlechtervielfalt. In: Senioren, Frauen und Jugend (ed) Bundesministerium für Familie. Begleitmaterial zur Interministeriellen Arbeitsgruppe Inter- & TranssexualitÄt, Berlin, p 18, Band 8

Gössl SL (2016) Intersexuelle Menschen und ihre personenstandsrechtliche Erfassung. NZFam 2016:1122–1128

Grünberger M (2008) Die Reform des Transsexuellengesetzes: Großer Wurf oder kleine Schritte? In: Groß D, Neuschaefer-Rube C, Steinmetzer J (eds) Transsexualität und Intersexualität.

[104]See Baars, G. 2018. New German Intersex Law: Third Gender but not as we want it. In: VerfBlog 24th August 2018. https://verfassungsblog.de/new-german-intersex-law-third-gender-but-not-as-we-want-it/. doi: 10.17176/20180824-121837-0. Accessed 25 July 2020. For reform proposals, see Völzmann, B. 2019. Postgender! Für ein Recht ohne Geschlecht, VerfBlog, 11.10.2018, https://verfassungsblog.de/postgender-fuer-ein-recht-ohne-geschlecht/. Accessed 12 July 2019; German Institute for Human Rights (2017).

Medizinische, ethische, soziale und juristische Aspekte. Medizinisch Wissenschaftliche Verlagsgesellschaft, Berlin, pp 81–111
Güldenring A-K (2013) Zur "Psychodiagnostik von Geschlechtsidentität" im Rahmen des Transsexuellengesetzes. Zeitschrift für Sexualforschung 2013:160–174
Jarass, Pieroth (eds) (2014) Grundgesetz, 13th edn. Beck, München
Lee PA, Houk CP et al (2006) Consensus statement on management of intersex disorders. Pediatrics 118(2):e488–e500
Nevinny-Stickel J, Hammerstein J (1967) Medizinisch-juristische Aspekte der menschlichen Transsexualität. NJW 1967:663–666
Plett K (2015) Diskriminierungspotentiale gegenüber trans- und intergeschlechtlichen Menschen im deutschen Recht. Senatsverwaltung für Arbeit, Integration und Frauen, Berlin, p 56
Richarz T (2019) Rechtliche Elternschaft jenseits der Geschlechternorm. RDJB 2019:53–75
Sieberichs W (2016) Casenote to BGH decision of June 22nd 2016 – XII ZB 52/15. FamRZ 2016:2887

The Protection of Trans Rights in Israel

Ido Katri

Abstract This chapter traces the development of the status and legal rights of trans persons under Israeli law, which in certain ways has been dependent upon, influenced as well as limited by Israeli statehood.

The status of trans persons under Israeli law has changed dramatically for better and for worse in the past decade. In one of the first collective actions in 2008, a group of trans persons interrupted a medical conference entitled "Transsexuality and Unclear Genitalia". The group, wearing neon green attire, the color that would become identified with local trans activism, and bearing the slogan "nothing about us without us", demanded to be included in the discussions determining their access to health care. Quickly following that action, organized trans activism sprung quickly, with different trans organizations being founded in the past 10 years,[1] and trans activism becoming a focal point for all major LGBT organizations. The Israeli media has a variety of trans representation, from reality TV to in depth documentaries, and public support seems to be on the rise. At the same time, lived realties suggest that local trans communities suffer from disparate exposure to premature death, especially among racialized trans women. Local trans communities have lost three of their leaders since 2015, May Peleg,[2] Dan Veg Baizawi[3] and Maya Hadad,[4] all young racialized trans women.

[1]Project Gila For Trans Empowerment (2011), Maavarim (2014) and Transwomen Israel (2018).

[2]Zeveloff, Naomi. 2015. Transgender Activist May Peleg Wins Fight for Cremation—After Her Own Suicide *The Forward*. Https://forward.com/news/325306/may-peleg-transgender-suicide-cremation-battle/. Accessed 16 April 2020.

[3]Dekel, Yanar. 2016. Transgender Activist Found Dead. *Times of Israel- The Blogs*. Http://blogs.timesofisrael.com/transgender-activist-found-dead/. Accessed 16 April 2020.

[4]Family of trailblazing Israeli trans model Maya Haddad refuse to be a part of her funeral. *PinkNews - Gay news, reviews and comment from the world's most read lesbian, gay, bisexual, and trans*

I. Katri (✉)
Tel Aviv University, Tel Aviv, Israel

I. C. Jaramillo, L. Carlson (eds.), *Trans Rights and Wrongs*, Ius Comparatum - Global Studies in Comparative Law 54,
https://doi.org/10.1007/978-3-030-68494-5_14

Gender-nonconformity has a longer history in the state currently called Israel. Individual acts of activism have been occurring for years. Notably, Ms. Nora Grinberg, a long time trans advocate, was the head of the Aguda, the Israeli LGBT task force, already by 2003.[5] Ms. Gila Goldstein and her crew of transwomen sex workers have been involved in local Gay and Lesbian liberation from its beginning in the 1970s, and have used their own monies to fund early activism and support community members in need.[6] Even prior to that we know of at least one pioneering transwoman, Ms. Rina Natan, who led and won a public battle in order to get access to genital-related surgery in the late 1940s and early 1950s.[7] Mr. Karl M. Bear, who in 1907 was one of the first female-assigned persons to undergo a "sex change" with the help of Dr. Magnus Hirschfeld, emigrated to Palestine from Nazi Germany in 1938 and died near Tel- Aviv in 1956.[8]

While these historical figures are all Jews, gender-nonconformity was abundant in the region before and despite Zionism.[9] Organized Palestinian queer activism has been going on since the early 2000s, focusing not only the needs and aspirations of local communities, but also on the effects of the Israeli regime on local communities and the ways in which the Israeli government is using LGBT rights to justify its colonial practices.[10]

As noted, the last decade has seen great turmoil with respect to trans rights. Community-based advocates have worked tirelessly to the de-pathologize trans persons and to loosen the grip of medical institution on the lives of gender nonconforming persons. Advocates have demanded the revision of protocols regrading access to gender affirmative health care, reclassifying sex on the public registrar and the conditions of incarceration of trans persons. Advocates have started working directly with social services providers, education institutions, homeless and youth shelters. In all these arenas, the trans advocates have pushed forward the move from a pathologizing model to one based on gender self-identification and autonomy, a move away from understating needs in terms of medical classification to a centering on the voices and experiences of gender nonconforming persons themselves. This heightened activity has rendered a once invisible community into a political force. However, this work has been going on under a highly conservative

---

news service (2020), https://www.pinknews.co.uk/2020/01/23/maya-haddad-israel-trans-woman-death-model-beauty-pageant-liaoz-levy/. Accessed 17 April 2020.

[5]Engelstein and Rachamimov (2019), p. 155.

[6]*Ibid.* at 147–155.

[7]*Ibid.* at 144–147.

[8]Savran and Rachamimov (2015), pp. 22–33.

[9]See, for instance, Massad, Joseph A. 2008. Desiring arabs 1 & 2. However Massad's own critique would suggest that the use of the term gender-nonconformity is misplaced in the Middle Eastern context, as it is a post-modern Western concept. Others have critiqued Massad for ignoring the affective experiences of non-normative sexual and gender experiences in the service of discursive purity, see for instance: Georgis, Dina. 2013. *The better story: Queer affects from the Middle East* 5.

[10]*Ten Years of alQaws: Looking Back, Pressing Ahead, 8–10* (2017), http://www.alqaws.org/ckfinder/userfiles/files/10_Year_Report_EN.pdf. Accessed 2 July 2020.

neo-liberal authoritative colonial regime in which legislative change is almost impossible to achieve, and the majority of the government deliberately ignores trans issues. The Israeli government policies toward non-citizens under its control, almost solely Palestinians, has heightened impact on trans persons. Yet, as in other parts of the world, with the rise of trans visibility, local communities have seen an increase in anti-trans attitudes and the little achievement that has been secured with respect to healthcare and sex reclassification hang on a very thin thread.

1 The Legal Regulation of Civil Status

A bit of background as to the Israeli legal system is necessary to better understand the legal treatment of civil and personal status, as well as the more specific regulations concerning the rights of trans persons. The Israeli legal system[11] is a mixed legal system,[12] combining elements of civil and common law jurisdictions.[13] Civil law elements include, but are not limited to, bone fide principle, codification and the judicial power to complete gaps (lacunas) in legislation.[14] Common law elements include, but are not limited to, the principal of legal precedent, rules of interpretation[15] and the pyramidal structure of the judiciary system with a fifteen-member supreme court on top.[16] The judiciary is bestowed with the power to create new

[11]The State of Israel is officially a parliamentary democracy. The parliament and legislative power, the Knesset, is elected in a general election. By law, elections are held every 4 years. However, in practice the Israeli parliament rarely makes it to full term and in most cases, elections are held once every 3.5 years. As of 2014, the election threshold stands at 3.25%. This threshold was designed to curtail Palestinians' representation in the Knesset, since, historically, most of their political parties fell short of reaching this threshold. Therefore they, prior to the 2015 general elections, the joint list, a political alliance of the four Palestinian dominated parties, was formed and is now the third biggest party in the Knesset.

[12]Aeyal Gross has noted that the selective application of international legal standards in the West bank and Gaza is designed to provide maximum control to the military government. The same can be said for the selective import of common and civil law characteristics into the Israeli law. That is to say that they are designed to provide maximum control to the judiciary over the law and its application. This contributes to the phenomena referred to as legalization of politics and public administration (see Menachem. 2011. *Mautner, Law and the culture of Israel* 7).

[13]Barak (1992), p. 209.

[14]Either by using analogy and in the absence of a legal analogy by in light of the principles of freedom, justice, equity and peace of the Jewish heritage (see Section 1 of the Foundation of the law act, 5740-1980).

[15]Mainly the prevailing status of purposive interpretation, i.e., within the context of the law's purpose. Purposive interpretation looks at both, subjective purpose as was intended by the historical legislator and objective purpose reflecting the core societal values (see Barak, Aharon. 2001. *Some Reflections on the Israeli Legal System and Its Judiciary* and Barak, Aharon, *supra* note 18 at 210.

[16]*Ibid.* at 203.

norms vis-à-vis both legal precedent and by the power to fill in lacunas by referring to general principles of the legal system.[17] The Supreme court of Israel can also sit as the High Court of Justice in any matter which it deems necessary to "provide relief for the sake of justice."[18] Major legal issues regarding trans[19] rights have been filed as High Court of Justice (HCJ) petition.[20] Significant legal achievement in the realm of trans rights in recent years has come through precedential setting decisions characterized by purposive interpretations. Israeli law does not have a single-document written constitution. Instead, it is an uncodified constitutional system, based in legal precedents and provisions of the Basic Laws.[21] Basic Laws enjoys the highest normative status, achieved by applying purposive judicial interpretation.[22] Lower in the normative status are Knesset legislations, considered principal legislation, and below them is the delegated legislation, enacted by the functions of the executive power. Many regulations regarding the status of trans persons are found in

---

[17]*Ibid.* at 211.

[18]Section 15(c) of the Basic Law: The Judiciary. This is because the HCJ (the Supreme Court) has vast powers, including the power to grant orders to "the State, to local authorities, to their officials, and to other bodies and persons holding public office under the law, to act or refrain from acting". http://knesset.gov.il/laws/special/eng/BasicLawTheJudiciary.pdf. Accessed 2 July 2020.

[19]In this report, I am using the thermology offered by the general Reporter on the "Conditions of the recognition of the civil status of transsexual and transgender people" for the XXth International Congress of Comparative Law at Fukuoka, Japan in July 2018 as follows: "*trans* persons (by opposition to *cisgender* persons) are those persons whose gender identity doesn't correspond to that assigned to them at their birth. Further, since sexual identity is not the same as sexual orientation, trans persons can be asexual, straight, gay or lesbian. Finally, since the transitioning processes of trans persons do not follow the same path—as they depend on each person individual experience in a given social context—, we use trans as the umbrella term that includes others such as *transsexual*, *transgender*, *transvestite*, *drag*, etc." However, as trans and others relating 'umbrella' terms such as transgender have been also criticized for limiting the range of possible identification and experience of gender diversity, I also use the term gender diversity to denote more broadly persons and communities whose gendered experience and performance deviate from the accepted norms femininity or masculinity. For instance, butch lesbian also suffer for gender-based harassment and exclusion in sex segregated spaces, yet they do not identity as trans, see Davis, Heath Fogg, *Beyond Trans: Does Gender Matter*? Other gender-diverse persons do not adhere to current terminology, for instance among indigenous peoples in North America exist more than 500 words to describe gender/sexual diversity (See Ochrym 2017, 26.4.2017).

[20]For instance, HCJ 6035/14 *Ronit Liran-Shaked v. the Ministry of Interior* (27.12.2015) dealing with sex designations amendments.

[21]Over the years, the Knesset have legislated 14 basic laws which were intended, upon their completion, to form the future constitution of the state. This was articulated in a political compromise (known as the Harari Compromise), struck in June of 1950 after the Knesset (functioning as the constituent assembly), reached an impasse in its efforts to pass a constitution, The Basic Laws that have been enacted are the following: Basic Law: The Knesset (1958); Israel Lands (1960); The President (1964); The Government (1968,1992,2001); The State Economy (1975); The military (1976); Jerusalem, the Capital of Israel (1980); The Judiciary (1984); The State Comptroller (1988); Human Dignity and Freedom (1992); Freedom of Occupation (1992, 1994); State Budget for the Years 2009–2016 (Special Orders) (Temporary Order); Referendum (2014); State Budget for the Years 2017–2018 (Special Orders) (Temporary Order).

[22]Barak, Aharon. 2001. *Some Reflections on the Israeli Legal System and Its Judiciary* 210.

delegated legislation, including protocols on change of name and sex designation in the public registrar, protocols on accessing public funded health care and prison placement.

Under Israeli law exist coinciding court systems.[23] These include a secularist legal system which includes a general court, as well as traffic, family- and labor-specific courts; religion-specific legal systems in charge of significant aspects of one's civil status which are classified as "matters of personal status";[24] and a military legal system in charge of both the army and the Palestinian protected population under Israeli control. All systems have different, even if sometimes overlapping, jurisdictional reaches over different parts of the population, territory or subject matter.

The Israeli public registrar documents the following information about citizens and residents of the state: name (including previous names), parental names, date and place of birth; sex (male or female); national affiliation (Jewish, Arab, etc.); religion (Jewish, Muslim, etc.); marital status (single, married, divorced or widower); children's names, birthdates and citizenship status (Israeli, Jordanian, etc.).[25] Israel also effectively controls the Palestinian public registrar,[26] any changes to which must be recorded by Israel to be valid. The laws and regulations reviewed in this report refer to the Israeli registrar, and I have no knowledge of parallel protocols for the Palestinian one. Seemingly, the limited civil status amendments possibilities, available for gender-nonconforming persons who have status in Israel, do not apply to those under Israeli control.

According to the Public Registrar Act, 5725-1965, a change or corrections to any of this information, except for names, will only be recorded based on a public certificate. According to the Names Act, 5716-1956, which precedes the Public Registrar Act, a declaration is enough to facilitate a name change (given or middle or surname). The population, immigration and borders authority (PIBA) is the unit of the Ministry of Interior in charge of the public registrar. At its discretion, it publishes and enforces protocols which regulates changes and corrects specific data on the public registrar (protocol on changing names, protocol on changing sex designation, etc.) *De facto* these protocols govern access to changes in the public registrar, which is considered, *prima facie*, proof of its accuracy. As will be further elaborated, while the protocol governing name change allows a quick and efficient change for gender-nonconforming persons, the protocol governing changes or amendments to sex designation places an enormous burden on the applicants, limiting access to proper identification documents.

[23]Barak, Aharon, *supra* note 18 at 198.

[24]Blecher-Prigat, Ayelet. 2015. Same-Sex Relationships and Israeli Law. In *Same Sex Couples-Comparative Insights on Marriage and Cohabitation*, 131–161, 132. http://link.springer.com/chapter/10.1007/978-94-017-9774-0_6. Accessed 2 July 2020.

[25]Section 2 to the Public Registrar Act, 5725-1965.

[26]Gisha | *Separating land, separating people*. http://gisha.org/publication/4379. Accessed 17 July 2017.

Sex is assigned at birth by a medical practitioner, usually based on the newborn's visible genitals,[27] newborns with coherent vaginas are declared as female and newborns with coherent penises are declared male. This classification is documented on the live birth notification, issued by the hospital or, when the birth is not in an institution, by the parents.[28] The registrar officials, at their discretion and based on the notification of a live birth, issue a birth certificate and document it in the public registrar. With respect to sex designation, the protocol governing this procedure only states that the registrar official should "mark X in the appropriate box for male/ female". Sex designations appear on most[29] public documents, notably on the identification document which is required to be carried at all times by the law.[30]

2 Matters of Personal Status

Israeli family law is a "split jurisdiction", where significant aspect of the law defined as "matters of personal status" are under the control of the respective "personal law".[31] That is, under Israeli law, different sex partners of the same religion must marry and divorce in their respective religious courts,[32] because the acts of marriage and of divorce are personal status matters.[33] Given the conservative law applied in those courts, it is reasonable to assume that none of these respective courts recognize any sort of gender-nonconformity as they do not recognize same-sex unions. Until now only rabbinical courts have faced such questions. Yet, as all religious court stickily apply *orthodox* religious law there is no reason to assume that they would recognize gender nonconformity or same-sex unions. On the other hand, because the respective 'personal laws' do not recognize sex reclassification amendments, marital

[27]Unless the visible genitals or other medical information suggest that the newborn cannot be easily classified into one of the binary sex categories of female and male (see, Mor, Sagit, Sudai, Mayeen & Shai, Or. 2016. This Law Which Is Not One: On Intersex People in Israeli Law. In *The Rights of the LGBT Community in Israel: Law, Sexual Orientation and Gender Identity*).

[28]Their declaration is not enough and should be accompanied by a document provided by the medical practitioner who delivered the baby. If no such function exists, a certificate from the doctor who has monitored the pregnancy is necessary; if this is not possible, then a genetic testing of the parents and the baby is required. See Section B3 of PIBA Protocol No. 2.2.001 "Procedures for Registration of In-state Birth" [Hebrew] https://www.gov.il/BlobFolder/policy/birth_registry_in_israel_procedure/he/2.2.0001.pdf. Accessed 2 July 2020.

[29]The Israeli driver license does not have a sex designation and is thus a prefer identification document by many gender-diverse persons.

[30]Section 2 of the Identity Card Carrying and Displaying Act, 5742-1992.

[31]Blecher-Prigat, *supra* note 27 at 135.

[32]There exists a rabbinical (Jewish) court system, Sharia (Muslim) court system, Druz court system as well as 10 recognized religious communities: Greek Orthodox, Latin Catholic, Armenian Orthodox, Armenian Catholic, Syriac Catholic, Chaldean Catholic, Melkite Greek Catholic, Maronite, Syriac Orthodox and Evangelical Episcopalian communities.

[33]Blecher-Prigat, *supra* note 27 at 133.

status is not affected by changes to sex designations; which means that those who reclassify their sex are not required to divorce. In other words, for better or worst marriages and divorces of trans persons are not recognized in Israel.

In practice, only the rabbinical courts system, which constitutes the majority of religious courts, has taken a clear position on these matters. Rabbinical courts do not recognize the possibility for sex reclassification. In at least two cases, rabbinical courts annulled a marriage when it discovered that the groom was assigned female at birth, arguing that according to Halachic law, same-sex marriage is prohibited.[34] In another case, a trans woman was refused the right to give a 'Gett' (Jewish divorce) to her ex-partner because this is a male privilege, and she is a woman.[35]

Funerals and burials are also governed by 'personal law'. Outside the public religious system, very limited private secular burial is available. Religious officials managing burials can prefer the family's will over that of the deceased and their community, leading to some gender nonconforming persons being buried under their birth-designated identities.[36]

In 2015, May Peleg, an ex-orthodox transwoman and a leader in trans communities, committed suicide. She had prepared for the possibility that her mother would ask to bury her under her birth name and according to orthodox laws. Peleg have made all arrangements for a secular cremation ceremony, which is by itself prohibited in Jewish tradition, and she expressed her last wishes explicitly in a will that was left with her attorney. Peleg's mother objected her will and appealed to the district court, which sided with the deceased. The mother appealed the decision to the Supreme court, arguing that non-Jewish burial is contradictory to the best interests of the deceased's children.[37] The Supreme court again sided with Peleg, finding that a duty to respect the wishes of the deceased is a part of the right to the autonomy enshrined in the Basic Law: Human Dignity and Liberty.[38] This is, however, a notable exception. In the absence of an explicit will and trustees that would ensure its implementation following their deaths, gender-nonconforming persons are still subjected to the will of their birth families.

---

[34] ואז הרבי גילה: החתן בכלל נולד כאישה, Mako (2015), http://www.mako.co.il/pride-weekend/Article-36a888569f29e41006.htm. Accessed 17 July 2017.

[35] הטרנסג' נדרית סירבה לתת גט: "אני לא גברקובי נחשוני, , " Ynet, March 16, 2017, http://www.ynet.co.il/articles/0,7340,L-4936568,00.html. Accessed 2 July 2020.

[36] הטרנסג'נדרית הראשונה של תל אביב נקברה כגבראיתי בלומנטל0, Ynet, June 2, 2017, http://www.ynet.co.il/articles/0,7340,L-4918469,00.html. Accessed 2 July 2020.

[37] Although the deceased's ex wife and legal guardian of those children refused to join the procedure or have her children join.

[38] CA 7918/15 *Plonit v. Gal Friedman and others* (24.11.2015).

3 Specific Regulations for Trans Persons in Legislation

Israeli law has only one piece of legislation referring to the rights of trans persons. Since 2013, section 5(A) of the Students Rights Act, 5761-2000, prohibits discrimination of K-12 students on a variety of bases, including ‘gender identity’. The commentary to the 2013 amendment of the law states that its purpose is to prevent discrimination based on the incongruence of sex and gender. The law itself lacks such a clarification. Beyond that, the Israeli legal system has yet to internalize any international legal standards with respect to gender nonconformity, and the most substantive legal achievements, so far, have been secured through the courts.

The Supreme Court ruling in CA 5833/12, *Plonit v. the State of Israel* (12.9.2013) is considered a milestone in recognizing a constitutional right for autonomy and equality for gender nonconforming persons.[39] This was an appeal of a district court decision which found a young transman, ploni(t),[40] and two other cisgender men guilty of armed robbery. The three had appealed their sentence, asking for it to be reduced. Ploni(t)’s appeal was grounded in the fact that he was to be incarcerated in administrative segregation, due to a policy of the Israeli Correction Service (ICS) of housing gender nonconforming prisoners in segregation and isolation, that would be further discussed later with respect to the criminal law. Ploni(t)’s appeal was partially accepted, and his sentenced was reduced.

The majority opinion agreed to reduced Ploni(t)’s sentence because, unlike other prisoners who are kept in segregation and isolation, the reason for which Ploni (t) would be kept under these conditions is rooted in the “core of his inner world” and not in external actions or facts. Yet, the importance of this decision comes from Justice Salim Jubran’s dicta, which has been by now widely-cited by lower courts as a legal precedent. The dicta grants, for the first time in Israeli law, a substantive meaning to trans persons’ right to autonomy. Jubran writes:

> The right for equality of transgender persons, much like the constitutional right for equality of members of the gay and lesbian community, is a constitutionally protected right in accordance with the Basic Law of Human Dignity and Freedom. Therefore, the transgender inmate has the right to be incarcerated in same condition as other inmates, as much as possible. The protection of the right for equality does not apply only to those who completed the process of gender reassignment. The social and legal difficulties facing a transgender individual do not depend on the level of completion of the physiological process of sexual reassignment. Non-recognition of one’s gender identity, as he himself sees it, is a harm to equality.[41]

This short paragraph explicitly enshrines gender-nonconforming persons’ right for equality, a right that was not previously acknowledged and declared by the Israeli

---

[39]The court actually talks about transgender, but here also I have used a more inclusive term.

[40]In Hebrew, ‘Plonit’ means ‘Jane Doe’, while ‘Ploni’ means ‘John Doe’, even though the High Court of Justice recognized Ploni(t) is a trans man, the Court continued to refer to him in female pronouns and to call him Plonit. I use the term ploni(t) to designated that offensive incoherence.

[41]5833/12, *Plonit v. the State of Israel*, *supra* note 371, para 5 Justice Jubran.

legal system. This right is not exclusive to those who have accessed gender affirmative medical care, thus alluding to a right for gender-self-identification, or at least to a right of autonomy over their bodies for gender-nonconforming persons. In other words, this right place the responsibility on others, such as state officials or private actors, to respect the way people exprience and express gender.[42]

4 Particular Regulations for Trans Persons in Labor Law

At least 84% of gender-diverse persons living in Israel struggle with underemployment.[43] Two-thirds of those who are employed have suffered from discrimination, either in job-seeking, the hiring process or on the job.[44] Nonetheless, only a handful of lawsuits have been filed over the years, due to a lack of financial resources, legal knowledge, and a general distrust of the law, among other reasons.[45] The relevant legislation, the Equal Opportunities in Employment Act 5748-1988, does not include a specific protected category designated for gender-nonconforming persons such as gender identity or gender expression. However, in 2015, new judicial legislation entered Israeli Labor Law, recognizing that the prohibition to discriminate on the basis gender nonconformity is included within the prohibition to discriminate on the basis of sex.

The recognition of a prohibition to discriminate on the basis of gender identity is a result of the litigation of a labor discrimination case concerning a trans woman, Ms. Marina Meshal. The National Labor Court, in the case of NA 23372-06-14 *Center for Educational Technology (CET) v. Marina Meshel* (2.6.2015), has stated that gender identity is included in the prohibition to discriminate on the basis of sex and sexual orientation found in section 2 of the Equal Opportunity Act (EOE). As the National Labor Court holds a precedential-making power over the regional labor courts and is considered the interpretative authority with respect to labor law, this decision is a judicial legislation. The court did not go further in explaining what discrimination on the basis of 'gender identity' actually is.

However, this decision resulated from an appeal of a regional labor court decision, LDJ 791-06-13 *Marina Meshel v. CET* (13.5.2014), which employed an extensive purposive interpretation to section 2 of the EOE act. According to the

---

[42]Katri (2014), p. 26.

[43]Kupfe, Hana. 2016. *Discrimination Experiences in Employees from The LGBT Community in the Israeli Job Market (2015)* 30 12. http://economy.gov.il/Research/Documents/Lahatab2015.pdf. Accessed 8 March 2017.

[44]According to a 2016 survey published by the state's Equal Employment Opportunity Commission. Note that this survey did not touch upon the high rate of the sex workers among gender-diverse communities, who often end up in sex work because of inability to get other adequately paying jobs alongside limited access and long waiting times for universal gender affirmative health care (for further reading see, Katri and Yona (2017)).

[45]Katri (2016).

head of the judicial panel in the case, Justice Itzkuvitch, the prohibition to discriminate on the basis of sex includes 'gender identity' because "the term sex is not limited to ones biological sex but also their gender identity and to deviations from the accepted norms of correlation between sex and gender."[46] Justice Itzkuvitch continues to argue that the protected category of sex should be read as 'sex plus', and includes "any fact, characteristic or neutral feature" in addition to 'sex'. With respect to trans persons, this can refer to gender transition, a gender identity that differ than the one usually associated with one's birth assigned sex and even "the very deviation from the accepted categories of 'women' and 'men', however it is manifested."[47]

5 The Legal Regulation of Names

Two legal aspects are integral for trans persons formal legal recognition, changing names and sex reclassification. According to the Names Act 5716-1956, an adult is allowed to change their name by submitting a written notice to the Minister of Interior. Parents of minors, until the age of 10, are given the authority to change the minor's names, provided that the minor, as much as possible, was given a chance to voice their position and feelings in the matter. After the age of ten, the minor must voice their consent directly to the registrar official. A minor can change their name with the permission of their parents, and, if the parents refuse, the minor can appeal to a family court.

The procedures for changing names in the public registrar are regulated through protocol no. 2.10.0001 of the Population and Immigration Authority (PIBA). According to protocol, an adult need to fill in a "notice of name changing." The notice requires that the applicant provide detailed reasons for the application. Section C27 of the protocol, referring to section 16 of the Names Act, authorizes the registrar officials to determine that the application does not harm or mislead the public or offend it. Prior to 2004, trans person's applications to change their names in

[46]LDJ 791-06-13 *Marina Meshel v. CET* (13.5.2014), par 8.

[47]It should be noted that Justice Itzkuvitzh was in dissent. Yet, the disagreement between her and the two other members of the judicial panel, who are not jurist but employers' and employees' representatives, regarded the question of employee-employer relations and not the interpretation of section 2 to the law. Moreover, the higher court decision clearly states that the lower court decision is canceled and that it would not give its opinion on either the question of employee-employer relations or that of discrimination according to section 2 of the law. Yet, the higher court does state that gender identity is included in the prohibition to discriminate on the basis of sex and sexual orientation, and the parties were not disagreeing on these matters. That is, the substantive part of Justice Itzkuvitch decision was not rejected by either parties or the National Court, which reinforced her principal finding and elevated them to a status of judicial legislation. In the absence of further elaboration by the National Court, only Justice Itzkuvitch reasoning remains. In fact, the state in her preliminary response to a High Court of Justice appeal about transmen's reproductive rights have cited Itzkuvitzh decision as the precedent (see HCJ 8391/16 *Yonatan Maraton Marom and others v. The Minister of Interior and others* (preliminary response by the respondents, 6.7.17).

accordance with their felt or expressed identity were at times denied on these grounds and they were asked to provide proof of having undergone surgery. However, following appeals from trans advocates, namely that of Ms. Nora Grinberg to the Minister of Interior,[48] the protocol was amended to accommodate the needs of trans persons. Accordingly, section C30 of the protocol now clarifies that an application for changing a name from a masculine to a feminine name or vice versa should be approved without requiring further explanation or a proof of surgery. Currently, changing a name to reflect one's felt or expressed sex/gender identity is done quickly and without any unnecessary inquires.

Changing a name for a minor might be a more complicated issue and is regulated through a separate protocol no. 2.10.007. The least complicated scenario for a minor is one in which both parents agree to the change. Yet, if only one parent agrees and the other does not or if neither agree, then an application to the family court must be submitted, and the court's approval must be sought. This protocol does not make special reference to changing a name from a feminine to masculine or vice versa, but it can be assumed that the relevant section permitting that would be applied also with respect to minors.

Both for minors and adults, according to the Names Act and its regulating protocols, a change of name is only permitted once every 7 years, unless a special approval have been sought from the minister. Protocol 2.10.0001 states an application to change a name within the 7-year period should include detailed reasons and a declaration that the applicant commits to not change their name again within the next 7 years. There seems to be no other limitation a to how often one can change one's name.

One significant obstacle with respect to a name change is the administrative practice of recording the previous name on the annex of the Identity Card and in brackets next to the new name on Passports. The previous name is automatically deleted after 7 years. This administrative practice is rooted in section 2(A)(1) of the Public Registrar Regulation (Identification Document Registrations), 5750-1990. Moreover, section 19 of the Names Act provides that name changes would be recorded on a public designated public register that would be open to the public. These regulations expose trans persons to harm and discrimination because they can 'out' them as trans by revealing their previous names, since names tend to be gender-distinct. Some trans persons have managed to exempt themselves from these requirements by appealing in writing to the minister, but this practice is not regulated under any protocol.

---

[48] At the time, the Minister of Interior was Mr. Avrahm Poraz of the liberal-secular party, Shinuy.

6 The Legal Regulation of Sex Classifcations

The Israeli public registrar only allows for binary sex designations (female or male; no third options exist). Sex and gender are understood as an all-encompassing binary system that is not regulated but merely documented through the act of registration. Paradoxically this position of alleged 'neutrality' in documenting 'natural facts' is achieved through intense policing of the access to proper identification documents, to changing sex designations.

In recent years, the regulation on changing sex designation under Israeli law has went through many trumoils. As noted above, according to the Public Registrar Act 5725-1965, a change or amendment to the personal data recorded on the public registrar can only be made based on a public certificate. The question of what counts as public certificate has been at the center of the ongoing debates with respect to sex designations.

According to the protocol that was in place prior to 2014, applicants were asked to provide proof that they had undergone a "sex change". Over the years, this regulation was applied in a variable way, changing from case to case based on how the official handling the application perceived the applicant. Though the protocol referred to a "medical approval of surgery", the population, immigration and borders authority (PIBA) officials on the most part did not inquire as to what constituted a sex change but have asked applicants to provide a letter from a doctor declaring that they have undergone "irreversible sex change". Over the years the protocol was applied in a gradually straitlaced-manner, with a growing tendency to demand more and more proof of actual genital-related surgery.[49]

In September 2014, three trans women and the Israeli LGBT Task Force, the Aguda, petitioned the High Court of Justice against the Minister of Interior.[50] The petition demanded the removal of the requirement to undergo surgery as implied in the protocol.[51] The petition argued that the idea that genitals should (and do) correlate to gender identity is wrong, outdated and unfounded. They have also argued that this requirement dramatically contradicts the right for autonomy, privacy, body integrity, parenthood and equality. With respect to legal demand for a

[49]There are different possible explanations for what has caused this: The growing numbers of applications; a backlash to the rise of local trans political movements; the strengthening of authoritarian forces in Israeli politics; the continuous role of conservative politicians over the Ministry of Interior and more. At least in part, the harshening of the application of the regulation can be attributed to the fact that transmen have begun giving birth and asking to be registered as fathers of their babies.

[50]HCJ 6035/14 *Ronit Liran-Shaked v. the Ministry of Interior* (27.12.2015).

[51]Statement of Claims in HCJ 6035/14 *Ronit Liran-Shaked v. the Ministry of Interior* (8.9.2014).

'public certificate', the petitioners argued that a declaration before a public notary is a sufficient certificate.[52]

In response to the petition, the state officially agreed to abolish the surgical requirement in the protocol. In its place, a new protocol was introduced which included three routes to changing one's sex designation:[53]

a) Based on a certificate that 'sex change' surgery has been performed, provided by the state appointed public committee for accessing gender affirmative care,[54] in addition to a certificate from a doctor that attests that a 'sex change' has been completed.
b) Based on a certificate that 'sex change' surgery has been performed privetly, provided by the surgeon performing the surgery, in addition to a certificate from another doctor that attests that a 'sex change' has been completed.
c) Based on certificate provided by the state appointed public committee for approving 'sex reclassification without surgery', also known as the medical committee on sex designations.

This new protocol made a few significant changes simultaneously. First, it designated the state-appointed medical committee for accessing gender affirmative care as the sole authority that can provide a public certificate, albeit only a small part of gender non-conforming persons use its service. As will be further elaborated, this is because of its long waiting times, pathologizing practice and varying quality of results.

The second major change was to establish a new committee—the medical committee on sex designations—authorized to provide a public certificate for persons who do not undergo surgery. It should be noted that this is still de facto a smaller version of the same medical committee, consisting of a psychologist, psychiatrist and endocrinologist, and therefore still applies pathologizing standards of assessment. As of 2020, the directive requires that an applicant provide proof of living in the acquired gender for a period of at least 6 months. The committee is also authorized to condition its approval on consent to hormone replacement therapy.

Since its introduction, community advocates have made efforts to reform the new protocol on sex reclassification, arguing that it continues to harm autonomy, privacy,

---

[52] *Ibid*. According to section 29(2) of the Evidence Ordinance [New Version], 5731-197, a public certificate can be provided by the following: government minister, municipal authority, court, tribunal, any other institution who has judicial or quasi-judicial authority, public notary or any other official body of Israel.

[53] The protocol also included a route to 'amend' the sex designation. On a principal level this section could apply to gender-diverse persons who feel that their birth assignment to begin with was wrong. Yet, in order to amend a sex designation, one is required to provide a declarative ruling from the family court, which is an even more completed process.

[54] This is a state-appointed medical committee working within a public hospital, whose job is to asses and approve state-funded access to sex/gender affirmation medical technologies. Obviously only gender-diverse persons requesting access to such technologies need the committee's approval. According to the protocol governing the work of the committee, genital-related surgery should only be done under its supervision. Private surgery is prohibited.

bodily integrity, parenthood and equality. Even within the new protocol, the applicant needs to apply for an approval of a medical authority instead of relying on their self-identification. The protocol still gives priority to genital surgery, while it does not provide any 'medical free' route for sex reclassification.

Shortly after the implementation of the new protocol on changing sex designation, it has become harder to do so. If in the past, non-genital surgeries have been sufficient, after the implementation PIBA started demanding more and more proof that actual genital surgery had been performed, reducing access to proper identification documents. In August 2016, the Ministry of Justice held a meeting with the Ministry of Health and Interior in order to reinstate the option of persons who underwent any kind of gender affirmative surgeries to apply for sex reclassification. In that meeting, it was agreed that general physicians could provide a certificate stating that the applicant has undergone a 'sex change' without making reference to completion (or lack thereof), and that document should be a sufficient public certificate if it have been validated by the State Appointed Medical Commitee. A standard form was published by the Ministry of Health. This discussion was not made public.

On 8 March 2017, in a hearing of the state control committee on the status of trans persons, the representative of the Ministry of Health presented a unified form that allow 'any doctor' to attest that their patient have underwent 'sex surgery' and is should be considered as either male or female.[55] Trans advocates quickly followed up with a demand for clarification and asked whether someone who did not have genital surgery can ask their doctor to fill out this form on their behalf, and whether that would suffice as a public certificate. The representatives of the Ministries of Justice, Health and Interior all said in no uncertain terms that it did. The state has presented a new route to changing sex designation, allowing any doctor to provide a public certificate based on their professional judgment.

Subsequently, the state control committee issued a press release celebrating the achievement. By the next morning, applications, based on the form introduced in the meeting, were being submitted to public registrar officials across the country. However, the officials refused to accept the applications, rejecting all of them and issuing their own press release claiming there had been a 'misunderstanding'.[56]

A coalition of trans advocates have appealed to the Ministry of Justice, pointing to grave breaches of human rights and proper administration processes. In May 2017, a first of its kind meeting was held between advocates and the Deputy Attorney General of Israel in charge of the legislation and administrative law, Adv. Dina Zilber. Following this meeting, the Ministry of Justice held a series of cross-governmental meetings in order to advance access to proper identification documents.

---

[55] Hearing on the Status of Transgender Communities. 2017.

[56] Yaron, Lee. 2017. Minister Apologizes for Miscommunication but Maintains Israel's Policy Opposing LGBT Adoption. *Haaretz*, July 17, 2017. http://www.haaretz.com/israel-news/1.801749. Accessed 2 July 2020.

In early 2018, the Deputy Attorney General published a new directive allowing for sex reclassification for those who underwent privately-funded gender affirmative surgery of any kind. This route for reclassification is the least pathologizing and is done based on proving documents without the need to appear before a medical committee. In February 2020 the Deputy Attorney General Zilber , publicized a letter introducing new standards for sex reclassification that do not require any bodily modifications (albeit including a process that is still controlled by a state-appointed medical committee). The letter concludes with the shared notion (of trans advocates and the Ministry of Justice) "the right to realize gender identity is at the heart of the human right to liberty and autonomy". Further, in 2020 Deputy Attorney General Zilber spearheaded an inter-governmental committee on trans rights. The intermediate report of the committee published in 2021 suggest that the public trustee would also provide public certificates for sex reclassification through a document based process. The suggested process would include a statement of self-identification by the applicant and a statement by medical practitioner affirming the applicant statement. This model has yet to be implemented and the inter-governmental committee has yet to be rectified.

However, these more progressive paradigms do not seem to be shared by other branches of the government such as PIBA. Seemingly the PIBA considers gender-nonconforming applications as inherently at risk of being dishonest. In PIBA's eyes, the fact that trans persons can use their body to reproduce after they have had surgery is evidence that they are not 'real' men or women. The State seemingly moves away from gender self-determination, believing its legitimacy to police gender/sex categories. This position is most apparent when considering how it has dealt with transmen who have given birth to their genetically-related child.

7 Parenting and Sex Designations

In 2012, Yuval Topper, a trans man, was the first legal male, under Israeli law, to give birth to a child. Years before the birth, Topper had reclassified his sex designation based on a letter provided by the surgeon who had performed his chest-related surgery. When Topper asked to register his child, who was genetically-related to both his parents, PIBA refused to do so, claiming that there is no classification in their system for a male-birthing parent, just for female.[57]

Only after threatening to go to court, the PIBA reluctantly agreed to a settlement according to which Topper's sex would be change back from M to F only for the purpose of registering the child and then immediately changed back from F to M. A few years later, when Topper gave birth to a second child, the story was repeated.

[57] "המקור": אבא מתל אביב מתכונן בהתרגשות ללידה השנייה פרי בטנו", http://news.nana10.co.il/Article/?ArticleID=1046828. Accessed 4 August 2017.

Yet this time because it was a home birth, PIBA even refused to recognize that the baby existed. Topper was treated as if he deceived the system. He recorded a public registrar official arguing that he should ‘pick sides’, since he is either a man or a person who gives birth, and the two positions just cannot reside in the same person. Again, and only after the story broke in the media and legal threats have been made, the same settlement was reached. Topper’s sex designation has been changed twice more, in total five times. [58]

In 2016 another trans man, Yonatan Maraton, gave birth to his genetically-related child in a public Israeli hospital. Like Topper, Maraton also had changed his sex designation years before based on a letter from the surgeon who performed chest-related surgery on him.[59] While the hospital staff provided Maraton with a live birth notification, they refused to register Maraton’s partner as the second parent on that notification, for no apparent reason besides their general sense of administrative gender dysphoria.[60] Later on, the PIBA official at the hospital refused to provide the couple with a birth certificate, claiming again that they cannot register that baby because it has no mother. PIBA refused to register the baby as a citizen at all.[61]

Maraton, who was familiar with the Topper case, agreed to have his sex designation changed back and forth in order to facilitate registration of the baby. PIBA stalled for months, inviting the family for a questioning about how the baby was conceived, asking for ultrasound pictures, among other things. PIBA refused to make a decision, leaving the newborn undocumented, even in the face of legal action threats. When Maraton was finally contacted by PIBA, they told him that they agreed that he should change his sex again from M to F in order to register the baby. Yet, in order to change back from F to M, Yonatan would have to reapply for changing of his sex designation. What had changed in the meantime, between the time Maraton changed his sex designation to the time he gave birth to his child, were the protocols on amending sex designation. If, in the past, the letter Maraton used was a sufficient public certificate, now Maraton would have to either have genital surgery or agree for a 2-year assessment of his gender. Maraton refused and PIBA continued to stall.

Finally, when threatened with a legal petition, PIBA changed Maraton’s sex from M to F without informing him, and they registered the baby. Therefore, he was registered as the baby’s mother and the father’s slot was left empty. Only later when Maraton approached PIBA again was he notified of these developments. PIBA

---

[58] ההיריון היה תקופה מורכבת, אבל הייתי ממוקד מטרה, Ynet, http://www.yediot.co.il/articles/0,7340,L-4763706,00.html. Accessed 4 August 2017.

[59] Section 20 to Statement of Claims in HCJ 8391/16 *Yonatan Maraton Marom and others v. The Minister of Interior and others.*

[60] *Ibid.*, section 24.

[61] Lior, Ilan. 2017. After Court Battle, Israeli Transgender Man, Male Partner Are Both Registered as Child’s Fathers. *Haaretz*, April 4, 2017, http://www.haaretz.com/israel-news/.premium-1.781413. Accessed 2 July 2020.

refused to re-designate Maraton as male or to register his partner as the parent.[62] The couple, alongside a coalition of LGBT organizations, appealed to the High Court of Justice against the Minister of Interior and PIBA.[63] They asked the court to register both parents on the public registrar; to withdraw the 'forced change' from male to female in the public registrar of Maraton; and to set a policy wherein the public registrar official would register newborns and their parents based simply on the notification of lived birth, without discriminating between 'cisgender mothers' and 'transgender fathers'. During the legal procedures, the state agreed to register Maraton's partner as a parent and to change Maraton's sex designation back to male, based on the same documents he had provided originally.[64]

On the question of policy, the state and the petitioners were heavily divided. The solution offered by the state was that trans men who have changed their sex designation to male and become pregnant should apply to the state's sex designation approval committee to determine whether or not the pregnancy had resulted in a 'gender change'. The state argued that pregnancy is a significant event that requires reconsideration of the data recorded on the public registrar. The public registrar official is authorized by law to inquire about and change the public registrar if they find that data recorded on the registrar is contradictory to a public certificate.[65] In other words, the pregnancy of a transman makes his male sex designation less valid.

The state-appointed medical committee itself was asked to give its opinion on the question of whether a person who gives birth can be considered a man.[66] The committee's official opinion found that gender is a subjective and internal feeling, instead of hormones, secondary sex characteristics, sex organs or how the person uses those organs. The committee continues to explain that according to the international medical standards there is no justification to demand genital surgery as a prerequisite for recognition that a 'sex change' has been completed. They found that after a trans man changes his sex designation, it should not be reversed, even if that person is menstruating.[67] That is, the same medical officials that are supposed to decide on a case-by-case basis whether pregnant trans men are still to be registered as male have clearly stated that pregnancy or genital surgery has nothing to do with how one identifies and what sex designation they should have.[68] As of this writing,

[62]Section 64-67 to Statement of Claims in HCJ 8391/16 *Yonatan Maraton Marom and others v. The Minister of Interior and others.*

[63]HCJ 8391/16 *Yonatan Maraton Marom and others v. The Minister of Interior and others.*

[64]State's Update Statement in HCJ 8391/16 *Yonatan Maraton Marom and others v. The Minister of Interior and others* (6.7.2017).

[65]Section 26 of the State's Update Statement in HCJ 8391/16 *Yonatan Maraton Marom and others v. The Minister of Interior and others* (6.7.2017).

[66]*Ibid.*, Section 30 the State's Update Statement in HCJ 8391/16 *Yonatan Maraton Marom and others v. The Minister of Interior and others* (6.7.2017).

[67]Appendix 4 to the State's Update Statement in HCJ 8391/16 *Yonatan Maraton Marom and others v. The Minister of Interior and others* (6.7.2017).

[68]State's Update Statement in HCJ 8391/16 *Yonatan Maraton Marom and others v. The Minister of Interior and others* (6.7.2017).

April 2020, another petition challenging this protocol still stands before the Israeli Supreme Court.

What can be learned from the state's response in these affairs? Foremost, perhaps, that in the eyes of the state there exists binary 'biological' positions, F or M, out of which binary gender Man or Woman, and all the binary social position associated with those gender, mothers and fathers, naturally flow. In this context, the public registrar merely documents these pre-legal facts captured at the moment of birth assignment. Gender nonconformity is only understood as a move from one binary position to the other, achieved through modifications to the body. A public certificate that justifies a change of sex designation is one that attests to the stability and irreversibility of gender transition. Appeals to stability of gender itself, such as to the idea that only mother gives births, render one's sex designation less valid and in need of assessment.

Little research has been done about the status of gender-nonconforming parents under Israeli law, specifically those who have transitioned after their children have been born. An alarming picture arises from the little research that does exist. In different cases, including the case of the deceased May Peleg discussed above, when a trans parent separates from a non-trans parent, social services and the court tend to find that it is in the child's best interest to not have contact or to have minimal contact with the trans parent.[69] In at least one documented case, a child had been removed from the home solely because the parent were trans.[70] In general, it seems that when the parents are together or at least in agreement on issues of custody and upbringing, social services tend to respect the family arrangements.

8 Access to Medical Treatment

The Israeli health system provides publicly-funded access to sex/gender affirmative technologies for trans persons. Some technologies, such as hormone replacement therapy, are easier to access than others, such as genital surgery, and the scope of coverage appears to be increasingly challenged as the demand grows. Israel has a universal health care system, and its insurance coverage changes from time to time. Alongside the universal health care, private insurance also exists, filling the gaps in the public system. As trans health care was provided by the state prior to the legislation of the Universal Healthcare Act, 5754-1994, it became part of the universal coverage. However, the question of what medical technologies are considered a vital part of "sex change" has never been officially decided and thus tend to vary.

[69]Stoler, Michal & Uad, Hadil. 2014. *The Interactions of Social Services with Transgender People* 19. https://goo.gl/3PQU5G. Accessed 2 July 2020.

[70]Case on file with the writer.

Following cases of medical malpractice by doctors who have performed private genital surgeries, in 1986 the Ministry of Health published Health Administration Directive no.39/86 whose subject was "a) Sex change for TRANSSEXUALS b) Repairing defects in state of HERMAPHRODITISM". The directive is an internal protocol that is binding for all medical professionals and public health officials.[71] The directive sets rules for performing surgeries. It states that 'transsexuals' are those who qualify the criteria set by the accepted professional standards of the time. It required that surgeries would take place in a public hospital, and that the hospital that performing such surgeries should instate a committee composed of the following: psychiatrist, plastic surgeon, clinical psychologist, urologist and endocrinologist. The directive mandated hormone replacement therapy and a 2-year 'real life test' period prior to accessing surgery. However, the exact nature of the surgeries provided is not detailed.

Based on Directive 39/86, only one public hospital formed such a public committee. Thus this hospital was given the monopoly over the access to surgeries. Over the years, doctors (including one on the committee) have continued to privately perform non-genital-related surgeries for trans patients, while both kinds of surgeries were also provided by the committee. The long waiting time at the committee and its outdated pathologizing standards of care, which were outdated when instated in 1986, have pushed toward the committee only those who cannot pay for surgery privately.

Following separate campaigns of both the intersex and trans movements, both directives have been revised in recent years. Trans advocates have consistently demanded that the surgeries committee should be disbanded and that non-pathologizing standards based on informed consent should be adopted. In 2014, the Minister of Health published Health Administration Directive 16/2014, of which the primary subject is 'sex-change surgeries'. The new directive is framed in more inclusive terms, using the term transgender and self-describing its purpose as to update the directive with respect to the needs of gender-nonconforming persons. However, the directive did not disband the committee but rather gave the existing committee a state appointment.

The new directive did provide some major improvements. The applicant is now asked to be under only one year of assessing their "proven experience in the desired gender identity." A community representative was added to the committee. The applicants now have a right to bring someone to accompany them and receive a written and reasoned reply in case of rejection. The committee has also drafted (but not yet published) an internal protocol governing its assessment procedure.[72]

The new directive, as well as personnel changes within the committee, has brought about a rise in applicants. However, the waiting time after approval (the 1-year assessment period) is still 1–2 years. Only certain surgeries are available

---

[71] Mor, Sagit, Sudai, Maayan and Shai, Or, *supra* note 20 at 126.126 סודאי ומור..

[72] Health Administration Directive 16/2014 https://www.health.gov.il/hozer/mr16_2014.pdfvu. Accessed 2 July 2020.

through the committee—namely chest-related surgeries and genital surgeries for women. Surgeries are currently performed only twice a month.[73]

Up until recently, female feminization surgeries could also be accessed through the committee. However, the inclusion of this surgeries is being challenged by insurance companies, arguing they were never part of the universal health care. Trans plaintiffs took the insurers to court and the insuring companies had to withdraw their position before the case reached a decision. Various private non-genital surgeries are also available. A reference letter from a mental health professional is required in many private clinics, although it is not required officially. Some private insurance covers some of these procedures within the country and abroad, but the range of coverage seems to differ significantly from case to case.

The regulation of hormonal replacement therapy (HRT) is much more flexible. It can be administered by any doctor.[74] Yet, many doctors refuse to prescribe HRT and instead send their patients to an external endocrinologist. All doctors require that the patient provide a reference letter from a mental health professional prior to prescribing hormones. Purchasing of hormones can be a challenging task for those who do not have access to proper identification documents, i.e. those who have not changed their sex designation in the public registrar.[75] According to the marking on the drugs, feminine associated hormones are not to be distributed to males and vice versa. If a male designated person wishes to purchase such hormones, they need to provide special permit issued by the prescribing doctor, usually an endocrinologist.

To conclude, although a variety of medical technologies can be accessed under Israeli law, some form of pathologization is always involved, whether it is a 1-year or 2-year assessment of "proven experience in the desired gender identity," or by demanding a reference letter from a mental health professional. The trans movement continual demands for the adoption a simple model of informed consent, already existing in the Patient Rights Act, 5767-1994, have yet to be answered. Instead, gender-nonconforming persons are treated as a group who are unable to give informed consent, resonating with the pathologizing notion that gender diversity is a mental illness.

---

[73]Hearing on the Status of Transgender Communities at The Knesset State Control Committee. 2017.

[74]מעברים - ארגון למען הקהילה הטרנסיתמעברים - ארגון למען הקהילה הטרנסית | טיפול הורמונלי, https://www.maavarim.org/hormone-therapy (last visited Aug 4, 2017).

[75]Which is anyway not an available option for those who are just starting hormone replacement therapy.

9 Intersex Persons

Israeli law has yet to recognize and protect the legal status of intersex persons.[76] They are absent from Israeli legislation, judiciary rulings and have only recently entered the legal scholarship.[77] For many years, the only reference to their existence was in two paragraphs hidden in the Ministry of Health directive 39/86, of which the main purpose was the regulation of genital-related surgery for gender-diverse persons. The directive refers to 'Hermaphroditism', stating that the sole purpose of performing surgeries in that context is to "amplify and enhance the genetic sex" with respect to secondary sex characteristics. These surgeries would not be approved based on a psychiatric evaluation but based on genetic differentiations. That is, the directive makes a clear distinction between intersex and gender-diverse persons—the former subjected to immediate 'genetic' evaluation, while the latter are subjected to a long 'psychiatric' evaluation. As Mor, Sudai and Shay have shown, the directive reflects the 'medical approach,' according to which surgery should be performed on intersexed babies as soon as possible in order to assign them to a binary sex category.[78] Under the directive, surgery was routinely performed on intersex babies, children and adults.

The legal approach dramatically changed when in March 2017, the Minister of Health published a new extensive directive on diagnosing and treating persons with a difference in sex development, some of whom identify as intersex.[79] The directive was drafted in collaboration with advocates, scholars, social workers and government officials and introduces ethical and human rights standards.[80] The directive establishes a designated medical center that would both specialize in relevant medical treatment and provide support to patient and their families.[81] According to the directive, medical interventions would in principal be provided only in the presence of a medical need, and for the purposes of saving lives, avoiding emotional or physical harm, and preventing sexual dysfunctions or irreversible disability.[82] Notably, the directive states that Intersex/Disorders of Sex Development (DSD) conditions which do not pose a threat to the patient's life, physical and emotional wellbeing, do not necessitate medical intervention.[83]

[76]"Intersex" is a general term used for a variety of conditions in which a person is born with a reproductive or sexual anatomy that does not seem to fit the typical definitions of female or male." (see What is intersex? | Intersex Society of North America. http://www.isna.org/faq/what_is_intersex. Accessed 3 August 2017).

[77]Mor et al. (2013), p. 93.

[78]*Ibid.* at 109.

[79]Sudai, Maayan. 2017. Changing ethical and legal norms in the management of differences of sex development. *Lancet Diabetes Endocrinol.* http://www.sciencedirect.com/science/article/pii/S2213858717300438. Accessed 2 July 2020.

[80]*Ibid.*

[81]*Ibid.*

[82]Section 4.3.1 of the Health Administration Directive No 10/2017.

[83]Section 4.7.1 of the Health Administration Directive No 10/2017.

The directive leaves most of the decision-making power in the hands of the parents. However, it does try to accommodate the autonomy of minors. Surgeries on minors would only be performed after the patients themselves have given their informed consent, unless there is an actual urgent threat to the patient's health or well-being. A non-urgent irreversible surgical procedure on minors will only take place after the psychosocial team has guaranteed that the procedure is coherent with the patient's understanding of themselves and their expressed will. Parents are still allowed to refuse informing the minor of their condition, though this decision would be evaluated by a multidisciplinary committee. At the latest, when the patient turns 18, the medical diagnosis would be disclosed to them, unless an ethics committee have decided otherwise.[84]

The directive differentiates between social gender assignment and surgical sex assignment, and it makes it clear that the former does not necessitate the latter.[85] In anticipation of the many conflicts that can arise, As Sudai offers the following analysis:

> [The directive] contains many conflict resolution mechanisms for disagreements between stakeholders, including parents, medical staff, and patients, as well as procedural checks and balances to solidify certainty in irreversible decisions made by patients and their families.[86]

It also provides that when DSD is diagnosed prenatally, information would be given to the parents and they would be directed to the specialized medical center, in an attempt to prevent parents from terminating the pregnancy.

The above is only a partial review of the directive, which is nineteen pages and details the diagnosis, treatment and support needed for those with DSD/intersex and their parents. It covers a range of issues from prenatal until adulthood, such as privacy and confidentiality, the presence of a medical student at examination of patients, photographing of patient or their body parts, informed consent including that of minors and the mentally challenged, psychosocial counseling and treatment, consideration for choosing gender identity and considerations for gender assignment. The directive reflects the balancing of the social and medical approaches to treating DSD/intersex conditions[87] and answers many of the demands made by DSD/intersex advocates. How the directive will be implemented is unclear at this early stage. Whether or not DSD/intersex needs would be further recognized and protected by Israeli law—for instance, with respect to sex designations—remains to be seen.

---

[84] Section 4.5.4.3 of the Health Administration Directive No 10/2017.

[85] Section 4.6.1 of the Health Administration Directive No 10/2017.

[86] Sudai, *supra* note 85.

[87] *Ibd.*

10 Criminal Law

As in many other jurisdictions around the world, gender-nonconforming persons under Israeli law are disproportionally criminalized. The high rate of under employment and the limited access to universal affirmative health care, discussed above, are two of the major factors leading gender- nonconforming persons, especially racialized women, to make their living in criminalized activities, notably in sex work. Although sex work is not illegal in Israel, sex workers are criminalized in many other ways.[88] A recent review of criminal decisions, where the defendant self-identified or was identified by the system as gender-nonconforming, showed that many charges involved threats to bodily integrity or non-aggravated assault in a sex work context.[89]

A major interaction of gender nonconformity and the criminal law is found in frualdent identity offences. In 2003, Hen Alkobi was charged with indecent assault, attempting rape by deception and false impersonation under sections 348(a) and 345 (a)(2) of the Israeli Penal Code, which prohibits "sexual acts if consent to them was obtained by deception regarding the perpetrator's identity".[90] Alkobi, a trans man, had intimate relations with younger cisgender women.

Alkobi pleaded guilty in a plea deal. In its judgment, the court found that while one can "look like a male and act like a male and have female sexual organ and vice versa", they would not be charged with impersonation. However, in the case of 'intimate relations', one "should expose to the other party that fact that s/he is male or female in the narrow and socially-accepted way."[91]

In 2009, another indictment was made against a person who was assigned female at birth and had intimate relations with other females while presenting as a man.[92] The defendant was charged with "indecently assaulting the female minor with the latter's consent, when that consent had been obtained by deception regarding the perpetrator's identity, and with the offense of statutory rape of a minor with consent."[93] In a partial plea bargain, the defendant admitted to the terms of the indictment and was convicted of them.[94]

The Israeli Correction Service claims that they make case-by-case determinations regarding prison placement of gender-nonconforming persons. However, almost all

---

[88] Katri, Ido and Yona, Lihi. *Supra* note 49.

[89] *Ibid.*

[90] Gross, Aeyal. 2009. *Gender Outlaws Before the Law: The Courts of the Borderlands.* https://papers.ssrn.com/sol3/papers.cfm?abstract_id=1537534. Accessed 2 July 2020.

[91] CrimC (Hi) 389/02 *Israel v. Alkobi*, [2003] IsrDC 3341(3) para. 13.

[92] Verdict, CrimC (Kfar Saba) 2372/07 *State of Israel v. Jane Doe* (2007) (unpublished) (Isr.); Sentencing Judgment, CrimC (Kfar Saba) 2372/07 *State of Israel v. Jane Doe* (Jan. 28, 2009) (unpublished) (Isr.).

[93] Gross, *supra* note 96 at 8.

[94] *Ibid.* at 8.

gender-nonconforming persons spent part or all their time incarcerated in segregation and isolation, whether they had been sentenced or simply detained.[95,]

The ICS policy regarding "prisoners whose sexual identity is unclear", uncovered in the hearings of Ploni(t), differentiatse between gender-nonconforming prisoners whose "sexual identity" is "conclusive" and those whose "sexual identity" is "not conclusive". Only those whose identity is conclusive would be housed in a prison in accordance with their "visible identity". From the parts of the policy that were exposed in court, it seems that conclusive identity includes "surgery" (apparently genital-related surgery). Those whose identity is not conclusive are to be placed in administrative segregation.

In practice, this policy was applied inconsistently.[96] The decision on where (male or female prison) and how (with the general population or in segregation) was left at the discretion of the police and prison official on site. In almost all cases, persons who are classified as trans by the system were placed for part or all of their incarceration in segregation and isolation. There is very limited information regarding those who have been arrested but not sentenced. In response to a freedom of information act request, the ICS would only be willing to acknowledge that between January 2015 and January 2017, 28 gender-diverse persons were kept for short or long periods of time in the ICS facilities.[97]

In July 2017, Dorin Bilia petitioned to the High Court of Justice asking for a review of the ICS policies regarding gender-nonconforming incarcerated persons.[98] Bilia was arrested following conflict with her neighbor and ended up spending an entire week in administrative segregation in a men's facility. The petition asked for the abolition of the policy, for a court order prohibiting placement of gender-nonconforming prisoners and detainees in segregation and isolation and for an order declaring that insofar as ICS cannot guarantee the safety of gender-diverse persons in its facility, alternatives to incarceration should be implemented. During the deliberations in the case, the ICS published a new protocol prohibiting the usage of administrative segregation solely because a prisoner is gender non-conforming. The new protocol continues to distinguish between those who 'completed' their gender affirmation process and those who have not. With respect to the latter the protocol state that they should be assessed based on their appearance, self-identification, and the 'stage of gender transition their at'. Since this policy was implemented trans women, even if they had reclassified their sex, have still been housed in segregation and isolation for long periods. Given the extreme gender segregation of prisoners, the ICS struggles with implementing its new protocol.[99]

[95]Katri, Ido and Yona, Lihi, *supra* note 49.

[96]Katri, Ido and Yona, Lihi, *supra* note 49.

[97]Freedom of Information Act, 5758, 1998.

[98]HCJ 5480/17 *Billia and others v. ICS and others.*

[99]For a detailed account of the reform and its limitations see Yona and Katri (2019), p. 201.

11 Current Discussions

As part of the global rise of trans rights, the legal status of gender-nonconformity under Israeli law is highly unstable. As discussed, while many advancements have been achieved over the years, the status of trans issues tends to fluctuate, with respect to both access to proper identification documents and affirmative healthcare, as well as other issues. The current political reality in the country does allow for pro-trans legislation. Yet, there are more individual public officials than ever, including Knesset members and senior government officials, who are committed to advancing the recognition and protection of gender non-conforming persons. There has been far greater dialogue between the government and advocates than ever before.

Inter-governmental debates are taking place on the regulations for changing sex designation.[100] On the judicial front, two major issues currently are before the court, parental recognition and state funding for gender affirmative care, including in prison. Both legal battles try to promote the autonomy of gender non-conforming persons over their self-expressions and identifications, regardless of access to affirmative medical care. On both issues, the state seems to be insisting on the signification of genitals and retroactive capabilities in recognizing and protecting gender non-conformity.

The Israeli Goverment is invested in portraying itself as pro-LGBT allegedly in contrast with other political forces in the region, especially the Palestinians. Yet, in reality, it controls major avenues of rights assertion for gender non-conforming persons living in the West bank, Gaza and East Jerusalem, vis-à-vis its control over the Palestinian public registrar and freedom of movement within and between these spaces. Moreover, the status of gender non-conforming citizens of Israel is no better, in many accounts, than that of gender non-conforming persons in the region. The state provides very limited and pathologizing healthcare, criminalizes marginalized trans persons, regularly incarcerates them in administrative segregation and imposes obstacles to gender non-conforming parenthood. It is worth noting that unlike its government, public attitudes in Israeli society seem to be becoming more accepting of gender non conformity and trans communities are becoming more organized and influential.

12 Gays and Lesbians and Trans

Historically the gay and lesbian legal movements ignored trans issues, despite the fact that trans persons, specifically trans women, have played a significant role in the history of gay liberation in the Israeli context.[101] While gays and lesbians have

[100]Letter from the Ministry of Justice to the Author from 10.7.2017.

[101]See for example, Shapari, Avner. 2013. Pioneering Pride: The Unsung Heroes of Israel's LGBT Community. *Haaretz*, June 6, 2013. http://www.haaretz.com/israel-news/.premium-1.528204.

secured recognition and protection through legislation and litigation at an astonishing pace starting from the late 1980s,[102] the movement tended to only represent gender normative persons. Gay and lesbian advocates have successfully campaigned for the inclusion of sexual orientation within legislation. Yet, these campaigns have failed to promote the inclusion of gender identity or expression within the law. The first mention of gender identity in legislation appeared in a 2013 amendment to the Students Rights Act, 5761- 2000, mentioned above. Strategic litigation led by gay and lesbian activists has focused on the recognition of same-sex unions and their families,[103] overlooking the specific gender non-conforming vulnerabilities related those exact issues.

In recent years, with the rise of trans political and legal movement and the founding of three gender non-conforming organizations, gay and lesbian advocates have increased their cooperation with trans advocates. Major gay and lesbian organizations, such as the Aguda, the Israeli LGBT task force, now regularly join strategic litigation as well as provide the most extensive legal aid to trans persons. Yet, it does seem that gender non-conforming issues are still secondary on the gay and lesbian legal agenda. For instance, the publication of the state's position that gay and lesbian families should not be allowed to adopt[104] has brought about a wave of public uproar, while the prevailing phenomenon of trans parents being found 'unfit' by social services and having their children taken away remains largely undiscussed by the public, the media and gay and lesbian advocates.[105]

Accessed 2 July 2020.; Gila Goldstein, Italian-born Israeli actress, Died at 69, Dead Obituary (2017), https://deadobituary.com/gila-goldstein-italian-born-israeli-actress-died-at-69/. Accessed 4 August 2017.

[102] Harel (1999), p. 443.

[103] At first glance, same-sex marriages are not recognized by the Israeli law; however, in practice, same-sex couples can register as married, or alternately have their common-law partnership recognized. As noted, under Israeli law, marriage and divorce are "matters of personal status" and are controlled by one's "personal law" (See Blecher-Prigat, *supra* note 27 at 133.). There is no civil marriage under Israeli law, and those who do not belong to any religion or to any recognized religious community, or belong to different communities, or are of the same sex cannot marry in Israel. Many choose to get married abroad and register their marriage based on the foreign certificate (see *Id.* at 138.). In 2006, the High Court of Justice applied the practice of registering foreign marriage certificates to same-sex couples, forcing the registrar official to record such marriages, without deciding on their validity (see HCJ 3045/05 *Ben-Ari v. Ministry of the Interior*, 61(3) P.D. 537 (2006). Official translation can be found on the Israeli Supreme Court's web-site:

http://elyon1.court.gov.il/files_eng/05/450/030/a09/05030450.a09.htm). Accessed 2 July 2020.

At the same time, the Israeli law developed the institution of common law partners as an alternative to civil marriage, which was lacking. The law does recognize same-sex common law partners and gives them an almost identical status to heterosexual common law partnership, see *ibid.* at 6.4.2.

[104] Yaron, *supra* note 62.

[105] Stoler, Michal and Uad, Hadil, *supra* note 75 at 19.

13 Stakes in Sex

Sex designation is used throughout Israeli law and in many governmental regulations. In addition to the laws and regulations discussed above, the main sites of these differentiated regulations are the following: The income tax provides a credit point to all women based on the public registrar; the Retirement Age Act, 5674-2004 sets different retirement ages for men and women; there exists a gender specific employment law, The Equal Wage for Men and Women Act, 5767-1996, which is meant to promote equality and prevent discrimination "between the sexes" with respect to wage other remuneration; The Women's Labor Act, 5714-1954, protects "the working woman", including household workers, pregnant women, postnatal women, women going through fertility treatments, residents of shelters for battered women and more; the act authorizes the Minister of Labor to limit or prohibit women's employment, if s/he finds that a certain line of work or working conditions to be harmful to women's health; there is a compulsory military service in Israel which is 32 months for men and 24 months for women;[106] there are more avenues available to women for avoiding the draft, including exemption for religious reasons and exemption for consciences reasons, available only for women;[107] adoption and certain fertility-related options are only available to cisgender couples, that is defined as requesting a relationship between a person who have been assigned female and a person who have been assigned male.

Looking at this list of laws and regulations, it is noticeable that Israeli law holds a traditional view of women, offering them gendered-specific protection. It goes without saying that in all these cases, the law understands the category of woman to correlate to the birth assignment as female and the category of man to correlate with the birth assignment as male, in fact in these laws the category of sex, that is female or male, and gender, men and women, are used interchangeably.

Often when trans advocates demand the end of birth assignment of sex, their arguments are countered with an alleged fear that persons who are assigned male at birth would change their sex to enjoy the benefits provided to women. The Israeli state employs a hands-on approach to policing gender by the juxtaposing of multiple gender-specific regulations and laws with strict access to sex-reclassification and pathlogized access to gender-affirmative health care. If the gender non-conforming demands for justice are to be taken seriously, it would entail a review of the necessity

[106]Sections 15-16 of the Compulsory Defense Service Act, 5746- 1986. Notably, the Israeli army is one of the most advanced militaries in its treatment of gender diversity. Trans persons can serve in their preferred gender identity, and can also undergo the transition during their military service, including having surgeries funded by the army. In 2016, a genderqueer person named Eden Lee Katri refused to enlist in the army on political grounds. She was sent to a male military prison contrary to her demand to be held in a women facility. When she appealed this decision, she was discharged from military service for 'mental health'-related reasons, again contrary to her demand to be discharged as a political objector.

[107]Note that significant portions of the population, mainly major communities of Palestinians citizens of Israel, are not even drafted into the army.

of sex/gender specific laws and regulations and of birth assignments to beginwith. Sex/gender self-identification legal models could include a ban on birth assignment for the reason that it creates distinct legal statuses—female and male, and finding alternative ways to distribute public resources and life chaces that do not differintiate between citizenship status in realtion to reproductive realted bodily configurations.

References

Barak A (1992) Shitat Ha'Mishpat Be'Yisrael: Masorta ve Tarbuta. Ha'Praklit 40:197–217
Engelstein G, Rachamimov I (2019) Crossing borders and demolishing boundaries: the connected history of the Israeli transgender community 1953–1986. J Mod Jew Stud 18:142–159
Harel A (1999) The rise and fall of the Israeli gay legal revolution. Colum Human Rights Rev 31:443
Katri I (2014) Between conservatism and radicalism- the Israeli Supreme Court on gender variance. Ha-Mishpat Bareshet 26:26
Katri I (2016) You scare the costumers: mechanism of gender policing in anti-discrimination law. In: Gross A, Ziv A, Yosef R (eds) An other sex- Israeli queer theory. Resling Publishing House, Tel Aviv
Katri I, Yona L (2017) Prison within a prison- gender variant experiences of incarceration. In: Harel A (ed) Law, society and culture. Tel Aviv University Press, Tel Aviv-Yafo
Mor S, Sudai M, Shai O (2013) From absence to presence: a critique of intersex surgeries. Mishpatim Hebr Univ Law Rev 44:89–157
Ochrym N (2017) Resilience, representation and colonialism: 2 spirit and indigenous sexualities. Bonham Centre for Sexual Diversity at the University of Toronto, Toronto
Savran A, Rachamimov I (2015) In the folds of a skirt: the many lives of Karl M. Baer. Zmanim 131:22–33
Yona L, Katri I (2019) The limits of transgender incarceration reform. Yale J Law Fem 31:201

Part IV
Self- determination in the Registration of Sex

Argentina, Trans Persons and the Development of a Human Rights Discourse

Laura Saldivia Menajovsky

Abstract This chapter analyzes the juridical and political context in which the 2012 Gender Identity Act was enacted in Argentina.

The 1983 return to democracy in Argentina after seven bloody years of military dictatorship can be identified as a starting point for conceptualizing the genealogy of the legal regulation of sexual identity. This was a time of high expectations, particularly in those sectors of society where greater rights were being sought. From this restoration, democracy was treated as inseparably conjoined with human rights. This conception of democracy was alien to the political discourse of democracy prior to the dictatorship, and would become the rhetoric used to obtain the recognition of the rights of marginalized groups. The importance of the human rights discourse that consolidated during Argentina's transition to democracy was fundamental in imbuing the right to gender identity with substance.

1 The Initial Legal Breakthroughs

Paradoxically, despite the liberalization regarding sexual discourse and practice, the LGBT community continued to experience stigmatization and discrimination. They encountered limitations with regards to access to resources and rights fundamental for their well-being (marriage, adoption, fertility treatments, legal name changes, gender reassignment medical procedures, etc.) and often faced criminal charges. Agents of public security backed by the judicial system often subjected LGBT persons to detention for the purposes of verifying identity or based on presumed offenses or infractions. At this point of time, legislation in Argentina, such as

L. Saldivia Menajovsky (✉)
Universidad de Palermo, Universidad Nacional de General Sarmiento, CABA, Provincia de Buenos Aires, Argentina
e-mail: laurasaldivia@yahoo.com

I. C. Jaramillo, L. Carlson (eds.), *Trans Rights and Wrongs*, Ius Comparatum - Global Studies in Comparative Law 54,
https://doi.org/10.1007/978-3-030-68494-5_15

municipal codes for offenses and infractions, still penalized "homosexuality and transvestism;" such norms were used to legitimize state violence as directed towards trans persons. Against this background, LGBT organizations realized the advantages that could be reaped by coordinating their demands with those of other social groups. The principal bridge for this collective approach was the repressive deployment of police forces against homosexuals, usually consisting of raids and perfunctory detentions under the pretext of checking for criminal antecedents (particularly violations of the municipal police edicts). The dynamics of this repression, despite the restoration of democracy, were connected to the continued presence of the dictatorship's repressive apparatus. In this way, the LGBT organizations sought to join their campaign with those of the human rights movement and groups representing feminists, lesbians, transvestites, transsexuals, university students and victims of police brutality.[1] Furthermore, and of significance, those organizations resolved to present the demands of the various sexual minorities as an inseparable part of a project to democratize Argentine society in which human rights were to be primary.[2]

During the 1990's, when the AIDs epidemic was raging and the need to stop it long established and accepted at the political and social levels, transvestites and transsexuals mobilized to make their demands heard. The first transvestite group to organize was the Association of Argentine Transvestites (ATA) in 1991. Shortly after, because of internal differences regarding whether prostitution should be lawful, the ATA split into two different organizations: The Organization of Transvestites and Transsexuals of the Argentine Republic (OTTRA) and the Association for the Fight for Transvestite and Transsexual Identity (ALITT). What stands out most about the organization of the trans movement is the collectivization of issues, converting them into action.

The notion of "gender identity" enters the lexicon of the campaign during this period. Although the transvestite organizations were supported by the gay associations at the very outset, the relations between the two groups were not always calm at the beginning. It took time for gays and lesbofeminists to fully recognize the transvestite movement, a period during which it was necessary for them to overcome their rejection of transvestism.[3] Over the decade, the transvestites gradually managed to impose their identity and presence within the movement for sexual diversity, an accomplishment that "facilitated the creation of a new political scenario."[4] A circumstance leading to agreement was the fact that these groups had two adversaries in common: the police and the Catholic Church.

[1]See Bellucci and Palmeiro (2013) and Bellucci (2010), p. 20.

[2]*Ibid.*

[3]Fernández (2004), pp. 120, 121. An inflection point for the LGBT collective occurred in 1999 during the 8th GLTT & B Pride March in which points of agreement and contact begin to be seen among the various groups representing sexual diversity.

[4]*Ibid.*, 143.

The re-establishment of the first Constitution of the City of Buenos Aires[5] in 1996 provided an opportunity to initiate public discussions related to the rights of sexual minorities. The new Constitution specifically included sexual orientation as an unlawful criterion for discrimination. Gay and trans organizations supported this amendment, even though the antidiscrimination guarantee did not extend to the trans community.[6] Another key issue were the police edicts (or municipal codes for misdemeanors and minor offenses) in the city of Buenos Aires and other provinces that criminalized prostitution, homosexuality, and dressing as someone of a different sex.[7] At the beginning of the 1990s, the LGBT launched a campaign against this type of municipal legislation, an issue that served as a catalyst for the organization and mobilization of transvestites and transsexuals.[8] At the time, the themes and spaces around which political power with the LGBT organizations was being disputed involved the position that each organization took with respect prostitution-sexual work[9] and the inclusion or exclusion of transvestites and transsexuals in the gay pride parades. The trans organizations actively participated in political discussions, thus gaining political visibility. This also gave them occasion to meet other actors with whom ties were established that later would become important in the struggle for the right to gender identity, groups such as the feminists, traditional human rights organizations (the Peace and Justice Service, Center for Legal and Social Studies (CELS), the Mothers of the Plaza de Mayo, among others) and organizations for women in prostitution.[10]

The City of Buenos Aires exercised its autonomous power in 1998 to replace the police edicts, which dated back to 1946 and were enforced by the Federal Police, by a new code of misdemeanors and infractions establishing the duties and rights of the city's inhabitants. Sex work was decriminalized in the new code. The complete decriminalization of sex work did not, however, last long. Four months after the new

---

[5]The reform of the National Constitution in 1994 established the autonomy of this locality (Article 125), which is why it had to produce its own constitutional text.

[6]Berkins (2003), p. 130.

[7]See "Informe sobre códigos contravencionales y de faltas de las provincias de la República Argentina y la Ciudad Autónoma de Buenos Aires" ('*Report on the misdemeanor and violation codes of the provinces of Argentina and the Autonomous City of Buenos Aires*') concerning discrimination against and repression of gay, lesbian, bisexual and transindividuals that was published by the Argentine Federation.

[8]See Sabsay (2011) (where the process of criminalization and discrimination is portrayed in the context of decriminalized sex work and public exposure of transsexual women and transvestites in the City of Buenos Aires); Fernández (2004), note 22; and Berkins (2003).

[9]There is no consensus within the Argentine feminist movement on the stance to be taken regarding the exercise of prostitution by women and transvestites. Some feminists consider these women and transvestites as voluntary sex workers, and others see them as forced into prostitution. The demand common to both perspectives is that they be considered rights holders and included as full citizens of the community. See Berkins and Korol (comp.) (2007).

[10]Berkins (2003), p. 130. Josefina Fernández says that, by the end of 1990, among the human rights organizations that supported the LGBT community was the organization HIJOS y Madres de Plaza de Mayo. Fernández (2004), p. 131.

municipal code was implemented, the decriminalization of prostitution was amended and limited to the "offer and solicitation of sexual services in public spaces." Sex work was once again prohibited in 1999, and in 2004, a reform created an official red zone in which sex work was tolerated, demonstrating the limits and challenges for the rights of trans persons as sought by different organizations representing the trans community (such as the ATA, ALITT, and OTTRA).

The four month period of decriminalization represented a significant event in that it made possible "the political articulation of new demands concerning sexual rights and citizenship, opening a space for debate that could not be closed afterwards."[11] The decriminalization of street-based sex work, which affected both women and transvestite prostitutes, and the parallel decriminalization of trans identities, were key in the destabilization and renegotiation of the normative mechanisms that regulate the relation between sexuality and citizenship.[12] Alongside the discussions spurred by the reform of the municipal misdemeanor code that conferred visibility to transvestites, organizations for sexual diversity also undertook action to alter stereotypes and promote positive images of sexual diversity. These actions were part of or can be best understood as what was known as "the politics of visibility"—that is, a set of strategies for the criticism and creation of new social patterns of "representation, interpretation, and communication."

2 The Convergence of the LGBT Movement with the Human Rights Discourse

The timeline above was closely intertwined with the development of the human rights discourse aimed at dealing with the human rights atrocities perpetuated during the dictatorship. One of the most pressing issues for human rights organizations concerned identifying and finding the children seized under the dictatorship.

As part of the repressive policies under that government, newborns of women who gave birth while detained were seized. The mothers were kept alive in clandestine detention centers until they gave birth so that their babies could be taken. Once the babies were delivered, the mothers were generally assassinated and false documents were concocted to hide the babies' true identity. The babies were then given to couples who in most cases were to greater or lesser degree complicit in the assassination of the infants' biological parents and the suppression of the children's identity. Sometimes the babies were registered as if the couple that had appropriated them were the biological parents and sometimes adoption papers were forged.

The biological origins (understood in terms of who their biological parents were, that is, from whom the babies were kidnapped) of these children were hidden; birthdates were often altered and birth certificates falsified; in sum, the possibility

---

[11] See Sabsay (2011), p. 60.

[12] Ibid. See Fernández (2004) and Berkins (2003).

of the formation of a personal identity that incorporated biological origins was negated and the truth about these origins erased. For these children, who are now adults, learning that their historical and biological origins were not what they had been told was a strong blow to the personal identity they had been constructing over the course of their lives. This seizure of babies during the dictatorship underscored the importance of knowing biological and historical origins for personal identity. Suppression of that knowledge was an atrocious violation of human rights and a crucial part of the dictatorship's design to exterminate its enemies. These reasons were why the right to personal identity attained its status as a human right.

The central role of the right to identity in the development of human rights provided a platform on which the right to gender identity would later be based. While the history of babies seized from their biological parents by the authorities under the dictatorship is centered in part on personal identity with regards biological origin, which can be verified using certain scientific technologies, the personal identity of trans individuals is centered on the part of identity related to gender, the veracity of which can only be verified/determined in terms of self-perception. Hence the movement for the rights of trans persons defined gender identity on a human rights basis, just as was done for the right to identity of the children appropriated, to move the discussion away from the definitions provided, for example, by the psychiatric literature on gender identity.

It is vital to understand how deeply engraved in the Argentine psyche the story of seized babies and the political and legal responses articulated to deal with this crime is. Only after understanding this facet of Argentina's political history, is it possible to appreciate why the deprivation of identity so vehemently triggers a need for a response. It is precisely this understanding of the reach and consequences that the deprivation of personal identity has for a human being, an understanding with which the trans movement can relate their own experiences, that explains why Argentina is the first country in the world to regulate the right to gender identity in a way that respects trans identities—by refusing to consider them abnormal.

The right to gender identity grew out of this conceptual framework by adopting its lexicon to promote the recognition of the rights claims of trans persons, using the right to identity as the starting point from which the possibility of guaranteeing other rights (housing, health, education, access to justice, etc.) would derive. By adopting the human rights discourse and adapting it to the claims of the trans community, the trans movement facilitated the reception of those demands by the public, as the human rights discourse had become widespread and internalized among legislators, judges, civil servants, academics, and human rights activists. Furthermore, that some of the most well-known human rights organizations such as the Mothers of the Plaza de Mayo backed the demands of the "movement" commanded respect for and dignified them. The shift to democracy was also accompanied by liberalization in attitudes and practices involving sexuality, which made possible the spread of positive images of sexual diversity.

In summary, recognition of the rights of sexual minorities in Argentina was obtained following a very intense and complex deliberative and democratic process. During this process, a wide range of actors had the opportunity to express their positions, actors that not only included groups in favor of recognizing those rights, but also detractors, such as the Catholic Church. With the enactment of the statute number 26.618 about egalitarian marriage (2010) and statute number 26.743 about the right to gender identity (2012), hereinafter referred to as the Gender Identity Act, such deliberative process reached its peak.

3 The Role of the Judiciary in Creating and Protecting LGTB Rights

The French Revolution's codification idealism, which privileged the legislative branch's role in creating a complete and coherent set of rules, strongly influenced Argentina's legal system. According to this Civil Law Tradition, the law is presumed to be clear, precise, and infallible, and therefore, the courts must 'only' technically apply it. Thus, the—intended—role of the judiciary consists in enforcing the law created by the legislative branch without any kind of interpretation by the courts. A result of this approach is that judicial decisions are not considered a real source of law as only legislative enactments, where the sovereign is represented, are validly recognized. For this reason, judicial decisions are not binding on future cases, as this practice would constitute judicial legislation—this being antithetical to the Civil Law Tradition.

However, the continental tradition of law is not the only influence on the Argentine institutional design. The U.S. federal constitution has also had an impact, with the Argentine Carta Magna setting forth a government of three branches, legislative, executive, and judicial, each functioning independently and providing checks and balances on one another. Moreover, the Argentine Constitution provides for a government that is guided by the principles of federalism. However, this is a weaker form of federalism than that of the United States; the Argentine states can dictate their procedural norms but not those of "de fondo" (substantive). These lasts norms can only be sanction by Congress. And as in the famous "Marbury" U.S. case, the Argentine Supreme Court also makes itself the ultimate interpreter of the meaning of the Constitution, in this fashion adopting the institution of judicial review.

Consequently, while the U.S. constitutional framework strongly influenced the Argentine Constitution, Argentina's legal system is also deeply rooted in the continental Civil Law tradition. Inferentially, there seems to be an ongoing tension between the Supreme Court's right to declare laws unconstitutional and the legislative primacy at the Civil Law Tradition. This Continental Tradition has largely influenced the Argentine judicial system. The decisions of courts in principle do not have *stare decises*, as judges do not decide what the law is; only the representatives of the people can do it.

This scenario has, however, been altered by the 1994 constitutional reform. Article 43 of the Constitution grants the ombudsman and those associations which promote rights of public interest the standing to be a party in any summary proceeding against any form of discrimination and about rights protecting the environment, competition, users and consumers, as well as the public interest. This provision has created a sort of stare decisis effect as to those judgments where the ombudsman and any organization promoting the public interest are involved. With respect to international human rights law, the Supreme Court has asserted that, as a result of the constitutional amendment of 1994, the decisions by the Inter-American Court on Human Rights and the Inter-American Commission on Human Rights must serve as interpretative guides for the resolution of cases in which the American Convention on Human Rights is relevant.

The Argentine Supreme Court has dealt with sexual minority rights in two cases: *CHA* (Argentine Homosexual Community, 1991)[13] and *ALITT* (Fight for Transvestite-Transsexual Identity' Association, 2006).[14] Both names refer to the organizations involved in the lawsuits. In each case, which were separated by a span of fifteen years, the administrative regulatory authority in charge of conferring legal personality to civil associations, the Inspección General de Justicia (Inspector General for Justice, or IGJ), rejected the petitions from the organizations. The reason given by the IGJ was that the associations did not fulfill the common good requirement mandated by the Argentine Civil Code. In both cases the plaintiffs filed appeals at the National Civil Court of Appeals, which agreed with the IGJ's opinions. Finally, both cases reached the Supreme Court but with different outcomes based on conflicting meanings of common good. In the first, the 1991 *CHA* case, the Supreme Court upheld the General Justice Inspector and Appellate Court decisions. In contrast, in the second case in 2006, *ALITT*, the Court decided to reverse its prior ruling, arguing that the denial of legal recognition to an association whose main goal is fighting discrimination against sexual minorities is unconstitutional as it violates human rights treaties signed and ratified by the Argentine State.

The IGJ refused to confer legal recognition to the CHA on the grounds that the goals of the association "do not respond to the idea of common good as an expression of general or public interest"—a requirement established by the Civil Code that all civic organizations must fulfill for state recognition as an entity with legal standing.[15] Moreover, the IGJ claimed that, according to the National Academy of Medicine, "homosexuality is treated as a deviation from the normal sexual instinct" and that "it hinders the formation of new families, and thus goes against it."[16]

This administrative denial prompted the CHA to appeal on the grounds that the rejection of its petition violated its right of association and freedom of speech guaranteed by Article 14 and the equal protection clause of Article 16 of the National

[13]Case *CHA*, CSJN Fallos 314:1531 (1991). The case was decided 7-2 with each Justice writing a separate opinion.

[14]Case *ALITT*, CSJN Fallos 329:5266 (2006), decided unanimously.

[15]Resolution IGJ 1005, December 7, 1989.

[16]Id.

Constitution, as well as analogous provisions of international human rights treaties ratified by Argentina and integrated into the Constitution. The CHA also argued that the concept of common good embraces an individual's right to fully develop the potentialities for the fulfillment of their perfection. The Civil Appellate Chamber agreed with the IGJ that homosexuality was a psychological anomaly affecting morality and good manners as well as the foundation of family as an institution.[17] The Court of Appeals added that, in addition to the objectives of the CHA's mission statement—fighting discrimination against homosexuality, the CHA also pursued another objective unrelated to common good, that of the "public defense of homosexuality in itself, and promotion of its social acceptance." Because of the Appellate Court's negative ruling, the CHA went to the Supreme Court, which, in 1991, by a majority of seven judges to two, confirmed the Appellate Court's decision.

The majority of the Supreme Court (with each judge writing a separate opinion) in the *CHA* case agreed with the Appellate Court, holding the decision constitutional. The Court wrote that if it were to accept CHA's definition of common good, the majority still failed to see how promoting homosexuality furthered an individual's pursuit of the fulfillment of their perfection.[18] According to the reasoning in some of the opinions of the majority, if homosexuality were morally disdained by most Argentine society, the law outlawing it would be justified. In the end, despite the decision of the Supreme Court to uphold the denial of the IGJ and Court of Appeals, the CHA was granted legal recognition by other means. Under pressure from various international organizations, then-President Carlos Menem ordered the General Inspector to retract its decision and grant legal capacity to CHA on January 15, 1992.[19]

Another association seeking legal status to defend the rights of sexual minorities almost fifteen years later was also denied state recognition by the IGJ. In *ALITT*, first the General Inspector and then the Appellate Court used arguments similar to those elaborated in the *CHA* case. In April 2003, ALITT applied for recognition of its legal standing to the IGJ. This petition had as one of its main aims the struggle for legal and social recognition of transvestites as an identity in its own right, and sought to promote the perception of transvestites and transsexuals as citizens endowed with full rights. In its petition, ALITT claimed that the "common good" involved articulating and balancing various interests honored by society, among which was the acknowledgement of existing diversity, and their existence in harmony, provided their objectives are lawful and do not interfere with the freedom or diversity of third parties. Moreover, ALITT's presentation proposed conceiving of common good from the point of view of concrete cultural, social and historical conditions, considering the evolution of society reflected in the law that has gradually admitted that the

[17] National Civil Appellate Chamber, Courtroom I, "Comunidad Homosexual Argentina", July 12, 1990.

[18] CHA, CSJN Fallos 314:1538.

[19] See the account of this story in Verbitsky (2006), pp. 310–319.

struggle for diversity has characterized the second half of the twentieth century in a special way.

The IGJ adopted a position contrary to that argued by ALITT, considering that the aims of the association ran contrary to the requirements of common good as framed in the civil code. According to the General Inspector, the aims of ALITT "[did] not offer a valuable framework for the development of cohabitation, thus merging the spiritual and cultural heritage of the community, an essential condition if an association seeks to obtain the legal recognition of the State."[20] This rejection led ALITT to file a petition at the Civil National Appellate Chamber, which confirmed the IGJ's decision.[21] The main argument against legal recognition of ALITT was that it is not sufficient to simply possess a lawful objective for such recognition, but that a legal association must also prove its social worth. In other words, according to the Appellate tribunal, the association's purpose should not only be helpful to its members but to society as a whole.

ALITT appealed the decision to the Supreme Court. On this occasion, fifteen years since CHA, the high court—whose composition had changed since then—unanimously decided not only to fully recognize the validity of the association's statutory objectives, but also criticized the notion of common good expressed in the previous judicial decisions. Similarly, the Supreme Court considered that the denial of state recognition to ALITT was an unjustifiable and discriminatory initiative, and stated that its right of association should be respected in the name of human dignity. In this regard, the Court qualified the instrumental character of the right of association as an essentially useful means to secure and foster the freedoms of speech and dignity of humankind.[22]

The Court recognized that people belonging to the sexual minorities represented by ALITT "not only endure social discrimination but have also been victimized in serious ways, suffering abuse, harassment, rape, bullying, even murder. As a result of prejudice and discrimination that deprives them of work, these people are practically condemned to marginality, a fact that is aggravated in a number of cases for people from poorer classes, with ominous consequences for their health and quality of life, noted by the high levels of mortality, all of which has been verified and registered in field work."[23]

Much had transpired during the fifteen years between *CHA* and *ALITT*. One of the demands that benefited from the favorable context generated by the case was partner pension benefit for gay couples. Two years after *ALITT*, the Executive intervened to order the National Social Security Administration (ANSES) to recognize the right of

---

[20]Resolution IGJ 001142, September 16, 2003: 3, 7.

[21]*ALITT*, National Civil Appellate Chamber, Courtroom K, April, 2004.

[22]*ALITT*, par. 11.

[23]Ibid., par. 17.

homosexuals to receive the pensions of their partners.[24] A relevant factor to consider here is that the *ALITT* and gay pension cases took place prior to Congress passing the laws on marriage equality and the right to gender identity, and both judgments served as precursors for those laws. In this regard, the campaign strategy of the movement for the marriage equality bill primarily concentrated on lobbying legislators and filing lawsuits when administrative authorities refused to perform homosexual marriages.[25] This strategy eventually proved successful and the marriage equality law was passed in 2010, paving the way for the statute regulating the right to gender identity referred to here as the Gender Identity Law. Argentina was the first country in Latin America to recognize the right of people of the same sex to marry with the right to adoption and the tenth country in the world.

Just as in the case of marriage equality, the fight for the right to gender identity played out both in the courts through individual cases where authorizations for name changes and gender reassignment medical care was sought, or in which the constitutionality of police edicts was questioned, and in Congress where lobbying efforts were concentrated. With a clear strategic objective, the sexual minority organizations formulated their struggle for the passing of both laws using a discourse that centered on and exalted the right to equality and non-discrimination.

The fight for the rights of sexual minorities had previously primarily focused on the violation to personal autonomy comprised of restrictions on marriage, adoptions, and sex change procedures. With this change in how demands were framed, the LGBT movement was able to show that the main reason for refusing to extend the right to marry to people of the same sex was based on the opinion that these people were considered inferior and second-class in comparison with heterosexuals. This also increased awareness of the extreme level of marginalization of the trans community and how this situation was driven by the predominance of heterosexuality and gender binarism which served as devices of oppression. The imposition of heterosexuality and gender binarism as the only valid lifestyles subjected people who diverge from them to revulsion and subordination, making their lives precarious. By invoking this strategy of centering the argumentation on the structural facets of the right to non-discrimination, the LGBT movement disputed and expanded the boundaries of citizenship and the limits of what the State and society considered legitimate and normal. The result was that a large majority of legislators and other relevant actors ceased speaking in terms of pathology and criminalization and focused instead on the protection of rights that were being denied to sexual minorities.

---

[24]Resolution ANSES 671, 2008 declares that cohabiting members of the same sex are included as relatives with a right to pension after the pensioner's death, an invalid's retirement benefits, or current member of Régimen Previsional Público or Régimen de Capitalización.

[25]For an account of the process that led to the passing of the law on egalitarian marriage, see Hiller (2010).

4 Data on the Structural Inequality of Trans Population

To comprehend the extent of the structural vulnerability to which gender variant personas are subjected in Argentina, we need go no further than the minimal data that exists on the rates of mortality, violence, health, education, housing, and other metrics, for this group of people. The absence of information collected by state agencies is telling.

In the little data available, one study needs to be highlighted: "La Revolución de las Mariposas. A diez años de la Gesta del Nombre Propio" (*The Butterflies Revolution. 10 years from the Feat of the Own Name*).[26] The report contains empirical data that reveals the grim economic and social circumstances that these people face in the City. The survey reveals data from 202 persons from Autonomous City of Buenos Aires, 169 male-to-female trans persons and 33 female-to-male trans persons. A relevant factor is that 92.2% of male-to-female trans persons were said to self-perceived as women since 13 years of age or before, but most of them socially assumed it between the ages of 14 and 18 years.[27] There is similar data regarding female-to-male trans persons, but 58% of trans men socially assumed their self-perceived identity after the age of 19 years.

With respect to employment, 70% of trans women surveyed indicated that their principal source of income was prostitution. Only 9% were in the formal labor market, 15% in the informal and precarious labor market and 3.6% made their livings through benefits from different public policies. On the other hand, 85% of trans men were in employment, 48.5% in the informal labor market, 36.4% in the formal market and the others made their livings from family support.[28] The urgency in the right to employment is made evident by the data revealing the age when trans women started to earn their living from prostitution, 30% started between the ages of 11 and 13 years, 46% between the ages of 14 and 18 years and 24.3% after 19 years of age.[29]

With regards to the right to education, 24.3% of the trans women responding completed secondary school (20.8% in 2005); 10.1% were involved in incomplete vocational or university educations (8.7% in 2005); and only 5.9% completed vocational or university (4.6% in 2005).[30] As to trans men, 72.8% completed secondary school. In 2005, the primary reason for the absence of any study was discrimination, whereas in 2016, the reason now proffered is lack of funding.[31]

[26]Ministry of Public Defense of the Autonomuos City of Buenos Aires. *La Revolucion de las Mariposas. A 10 anos de la Gesta del Nombre Propio*. Coord: Programa de Género y Diversidad Sexual and Bachillerato Popular TransMocha Celis. (Buenos Aires: March 2017). The study is an update of Berkins and Fernández (2005).

[27]*Ibid:* 37.

[28]*Ibid:* 47.

[29]*Ibid:* 60.

[30]*Ibid:* 87.

[31]*Ibid:* 91-91.

In terms of the right to adequate housing, the precarious conditions in which transvestite, transsexual, and transgender persons live is demonstrated in the survey by the fact that 65.1% of trans women lived in hotels, pensions or apartments "taken" (63.7% in 2005), only 5.9% of those surveyed stated that they owned a residence (8.8% in 2005).[32] In the case of trans men, 84.8% lived in a residence (owned or rented). After the enactment of the Gender Identity Act, only 21.2% of trans women and 25.9% of trans men noticed an improvement regarding access to an adequate housing since 2012, 47.4% of trans women and 44.4% of trans men did not notice any change after the Act was passed, and 31.4% and 29.6% observed that access got worse.[33]

Taking into account the Mandatory Medical Program, there is an increase in numbers—although not a significant one—of access to treatments in health institutions.[34] As to regular health controls, 87.6% of trans women (57.8% in 2005) and 75.8% trans men interviewed mentioned undergoing them; those trans women who did not have these health controls (12.4%) explained that it was because of the discrimination and the mistreatment they received in health institutions.[35] Of those interviewed, 61.5% considered that the behavior by the medical community was improved after the enactment of the Gender Identity Act, 32.5% pointed out that it was the same behavior and 3.6% observed that it was worse.[36]

Regarding the degree to which this group of people is prone to early death due to preventable illnesses and violence, the report puts at 194 the number of transvestite, transsexual, and transgender people who died in the last five years, according data provided by the interviewees. The primary cause of death was HIV/AIDS (63.9%). The second was murder (14.7%). Other causes were cirrhosis or overdose (4.2%), medical problems with silicones (3.1%), suicide (2.6%), cancer (2.1%), transport accident (1.6%), syphilis (1%) and causes unknown (6.8%). In terms of age, 82.8% were dead before the age of 40 years.[37]

Here it should be mentioned that 74.6% of trans women suffered some kind of violence (91.9% in 2005): 84.6% admitted to having been subjected to insults and mocking, 66.9% robberies, 63.9% physical assaults, 25.4% sexual abuse and 6.5% related to domestic violence, harassment or psychological violence.[38] Furthermore, 73% of trans men interviewed admitted to having been subjected to violence, mostly through insults and mocking (90.9%).[39] After the Gender Identity Act, 39% of trans women admitted to be victim of violence in 2016, 35.2% between 2012 and 2015,

---

[32] *Ibid:* 103.

[33] *Ibid:* 111–113.

[34] *Ibid:* 172.

[35] *Ibid:* 71–73.

[36] *Ibid:* 72.

[37] *Ibid:* 159.

[38] *Ibid:* 128.

[39] *Ibid:* 131.

22% before 2012. In this sense, only 22.6% of trans men interviewed referred to being a victim of violence prior to 2012.[40]

The National Observatory of LGTBI Hate Crimes, created by the LGBTI Ombudsman Office of the Autonomous City of Buenos Aires with support of the LGBT Argentinean Federation (Federacion Argentina LGBT) and the National Ombudsman Office, issued a report regarding LGBTI hate crimes with 2016 as the period of study (from January 2016 to December 2016). The National Observatory registered 31 hate crimes in 2016, 77.4% against trans women, 13% against lesbians and 9.6% against gays. Those 31 hate crimes can be categorized as 42% murders and 58% physical violence. Out of the total number of trans persons murdered, 92,.% was trans women and 7.7% lesbians. With regards those who produces violence against LGBTI community, 66.6% were private citizens and 33.4% members of the security forces. As to locality, 25,.% took place in Buenos Aires, 19.35% in the Autonomous City of Buenos Aires, 16.13% Salta, 9.67% Santa Fe, 9.67% Cordoba and 19.35% in other provinces.[41]

5 The Legal Regulation of Sexual Identity

This section takes up the regulation of the civil statute before the gender identity act was passed and how this was modified by its enactment. The gender identity conceptual framework under the Gender Identity Act is explicitly addressed, being praised for its structural power to question and dismantle the binary model of sexuality.

5.1 Registration, Identification, and Name

To understand the extraordinary changes concerning gender identity prompted by the Gender Identity Act, the legal structure regulating the civil statute of people prior to the Act must be explained. This structure involves several legal regulations connected to gender identity that are separate but also interdependent: the national registry, the national identification system and the regulation of the name.

The national registry is responsible for recording acts and occurrences that give rise to, alter, or modify civil status and personal capacity (birth, marriage, disability, and death, and so on) and for issuing the respective certificates. Its organization corresponds to each province and the Autonomous City of Buenos Aires. Gender and sex for this system are essential pieces of information, as name, surname, and

[40] *Ibid:* 131.

[41] See: http://www.defensoria.org.ar/wp-content/uploads/2017/03/Observatorio-Nacional-de-Cr%C3%ADmenes-de-Odio-LGBT.pdf.

sex are required in birth records (Article 36 of Law 26.413). Moreover, for the "Medical Certification of Birth" to be valid, the sex of the newborn must be stated. At such an early phase of life, biological criteria hold sway in differentiating between the sexes of newborns.

The second system consists of the national repository for identifying individuals that is responsible for issuing national identity cards (DNI) each of which bears a permanent, exclusive, and unchangeable record of identification and involves the use of fingerprinting technology (in accordance with Law 17.671). In this system, the gender or sex of individuals does not normatively comprise an obligatory field for documented identification. The identification record is compiled from the moment of birth and in it are gathered all personal life occurrences of significant importance that accumulate over and reflect the activity of the distinct phases of life (Article 7). Since both at birth and on the occasion of the life events sex is considered relevant information, it ends up in the record.

The third regulation consisted of the statute about the use of names by individuals (Law 18.248) that contained specific dispositions that have had a direct effect on the binary construction of gender identity. Article 15 of this law established the procedure for name changes, a procedure subjected to severe restriction by requiring judicial resolution and just motives—without specifying which 'just' motives are worthy of consideration. These restrictions were responsible for what is commonly known in Spanish as the principle of the *inmutabilidad del nombre*—'name immutability' or the practical impossibility of changing one's name—a policy whose purpose is to protect the function that names have in identifying individuals, whether for monitoring legal relations between people or for facilitating the operation of various collective institutions necessary for community life. Basically, names had become the basis for a method of civil policing that sought control over the identification of individuals. Justification for the practice was found in the guarantee it represents for third parties; that is, to ensure certainty in identifying others. In practice, this regulation has meant that the alleged interest in changing one's name had to be deemed more important than the public interests that provided the basis for the general rule prohibiting name changes. The interest of a trans person to change gender was not deemed sufficient. This normative has been modified by Article 69 of the recently passed Civil Code that considers gender identity as a just motive for name changes without requiring judicial intervention.

Another aspect of the name statute that was in fact modified is Article 3, paragraph 1 that established that new names were required to reflect the sex one was assigned at birth; that is, one could not choose a name that led to ambiguity with regards the sex of the person who adopted it. As seen below, the Gender Identity Act has destabilized that which for a long time was considered to be a man or woman. Therefore, the ambiguity that the name system searched to erase is now at the core of the alteration that the Gender Identity Act provokes in the name's *status quo*. It now has to be harmonized with the gender identity right that, as we will see, is deeply transforming it.

5.2 *Judicial Intervention*

Prior to the Gender Identity Act, the Court's approval, both for changing one's gender on the registry and documents and to access surgery and medical treatment for gender modification, was granted only after an exhaustive verification of life history of the person soliciting the change. This violated the principle of self-determination with regards to the free choice of life that the person desired to lead, and also the respect, in terms of human dignity, that such a decision deserves from the rest of society. Submitting the decision for judicial approval represented an invasion of the State into the sphere of privacy, an invasion which was intensified when, for deciding whether to approve the change, the person was subjected to intense, meticulous scrutiny covering the most intimate aspects of their life. An examination of cases in which judges had to make pronouncements regarding the validity of the gender demanded reveals the level of scrutiny and state interference in the lives of trans persons.

In the early years, these cases were largely individual initiatives; that is, cases brought by concerned individuals who neither were activists nor had organizational support. Only a few years prior to the Gender Identity Act did cases pursued by activists begin to be seen, cases invoking litigation as a new tool in the rights struggle. For example, there was a cluster of cases in which modifications of name and gender in the registries and documents were ordered because the person had already modified—in another country—their body via feminizing genitoplasty to conform to the gender with which they identified. The person had hence, by the changes operated on the body, been transformed into a "true" woman.[42]

Many of the cases in which the result could seem to be a triumph, since authorizations for name and sex changes were obtained, involved questionable processes. Beyond the final grant of authorization, which of course had a fundamental impact on the life of the person who solicited the change, the process through which the favorable decisions were reached remained nonetheless stigmatizing, inasmuch as requiring prior "scientific" verification of the pathology and suffering of the person in question. Nor do these verifications leave any possibility for recourse to gender change for motives such as pleasure, desire, or well-being. Furthermore, in all decisions of this type, connections are drawn—with egregious consequences—between gender identity and the stereotypical ways gender is lived out (masculine men and feminine women), sexuality (grounded in heterosexual orientation), and corporal morphology.

[42]These cases include: "J., L. J.," National Civil Appellate Chamber, Sala F, November 14, 2006; "S. S., E. A.," National Civil Appellate Chamber, Sala B, July 11, 2007; "C., H. C.," Supreme Court of Buenos Aires, March 3, 2007, "MSE," CCiv. y Com., Rosario, sala IV Integrada, February 15, 2008; "T.M.G.," Neuquén Family, Child, and Adolescent Court No. 4, October 7, 2008; "S. D. A." C/GCBA s/ amparo," Administrative Appeal Court of First Instance N° 13, Autonomous City of Buenos Aires, December 29, 2010.

Two years before the Gender Identity Act was passed, the first case evidencing progress with regards to the procedures employed for accommodating requests was decided, a case that opened the door for the hope that a non-pathological model of diverse gender identity was possible. In the *Trinidad Florencia* case, authorization for a name and gender change on identification documents of a trans individual was granted without treating the person's condition in pathological terms.[43] The deciding judge observed in reflection: "We realize that, on the basis of predominant 'normalizing' paradigms, genuine institutional violence has, without interruption, been inflicted by Argentine society, violence that has certainly had great emotional impact on psyches, on souls, and on the rights of people who feel and want to live, who want to lead their lives as they wish in full enjoyment of the rights they possess as human beings, who want respect and the protection of the State."[44]

Two norms played a great deal in the judicial approach towards the regulation of the sex changes. Article 19 Paragraph 4 of Law 17.132 on medical practice regulated gender reassignment by prohibiting medical professionals from carrying out surgical interventions that modify "the patient's sex." The exception allowed was for such interventions subsequent to court approval. Furthermore, Article 20 of the same statute prohibited interventions that would result in the sterilization of the patient. As seen, when judges authorized surgery and other medical treatments, these treatments were for people whose bodies reflected without any doubt the characteristics of the gender to which they claimed to belong, or to people who were in the process of attaining that level of concordance. Other legal norms that created the conditions for the way judges approached demands for gender-sex change were Articles 90 and 91 of the Penal Code in the chapter on injury. These articles established punishments for people responsible for damaging the health, awareness, organs, or members of a person. This was another regulation that dissuaded many doctors from performing such surgeries and relevant medical treatments.

As shown, the requirement of judicial authorization was one of the greatest obstacles impeding people from exercising their right to self-perceived gender identity as well as the rights that depend on it. This restrictive regulatory regime for personal identity described was modified by the Gender Identity Act.

5.3 *The Right to Gender Identity*

The Gender Identity Act, Law 26.743, putting into place the statutory regulations relating to the right to gender identity, was unanimously passed by the National Congress in May 2012. It constitutes an extraordinary advance for the human rights of trans persons. It defines gender identity as:

---

[43] Caso *Trinidad Florencia, c. GCBA s/amparo*, Juzgado Contencioso Administrativo y Tributario de la Ciudad de Buenos Aires, N. 4, November 19, 2010.

[44] Liberatori (2012), p. 114.

> [T]he internal, individual experience of gender just as each person feels it, which may or may not correspond to the sex assigned at birth, and including the personal experience of one's body. It may involve modifying corporal appearance or function through pharmacological, surgical, or other means, if the modification is made by free choice. Other expressions of gender, such as dress, speech, and manners, are also included (Article 2).

In adopting this definition, the Argentine law carries out a concrete normative application of the definition provided by the Yogyakarta Principles on the Application of Human Rights Law in relation to Sexual Orientation and Gender Identity published in 2006.

The Gender Identity enacts the idea that people have the right to develop and accommodate their identity according to their own perception and experience of gender means depriving "medical/scientific authorities" of their prerogative to decide whether a given expression and experience of gender is an affliction requiring diagnosis and treatment. It has also removed from judges the power to validate, or not, the pathology (and cure) advanced by health "experts" and officials. Neither the possibility to change one's name in official registries and on identification cards nor access to gender modification surgery and treatments depends any longer upon judicial consent as granted based on medical reports, but rather only requires the decision of the person in requesting the modification.

The formulation adopted by the Gender Identity Act separates the sex assigned at birth, which is marked in the registry and subsequently on identification documents under the person's name, from gender identity, and establishes a subordinate relationship between them, superimposing self-perceived gender identity over sex and the identificatory practices that follow birth. In so doing, the definition formulated by the Gender Identity Act effectuates a conceptual excision, splitting gender from a person's physical attributes. This has substantial effects, as it starkly departs from medical classifications of gender centered on biological appearance and sexual equipment—for example, the presence, absence, or size of the penis.

The Gender Identity Act contains a provision that empowers those who do not fit in either of the sex/gender fields or who wish to move from one to the other, or who wish to be both, to demand respect from society for the gender identity they adopt when that identity means using a first name that differs from the one inscribed on their national identification document. The Gender Identity Act stipulates that "upon its request alone, the first name adopted must be used for reference, registry, files, calling and any other administrative task or service, in the private sphere as well as the public (Article 12)." This is to be respected immediately after the request is communicated or manifested by any person, adult or minor, without any need to present any documentation to verify it. In this way, people who are dissatisfied with the binary labeling that the Gender Identity Act still preserves can take advantage of the great flexibility offered by this provision.

In addition to depathologizing the determination of one's gender identity, the Gender Identity Act makes no pretense of establishing gender identity once and for all. This is because the Act does not assume that the credentials for authenticating gender identity are available from the very moment it must be registered. Accordingly, for such authentication, the Act considers the dynamic rather than static nature of gender identity, as it may be modified without any other procedural prerequisite than the individual's expressed volition.

The judicial authorization required by the Act in those cases where a person wishes to modify their gender identity more than once (Article 8) is justified by concern for fraudulent use of the law and public policies that could be made by changing one's name. The Act was not designed as an isolated, unique instance of legislative action but rather as the central axis for a set of public policies addressing issues of gender identity, such as indemnization, employment subsidies, affirmative action policies, and other benefits meant to reverse the situation of vulnerability of trans individuals.[45]

In this sense, those participating in the formulation of the legislative bill felt it necessary to prevent people from exploiting the law by changing the gender on their identification documents in order to benefit from these policies, by requiring judicial authorization if a person decides to change their gender a second time[46] To obtain that authorization, the person must explain the reasons for the new change such that the absent of fraud is corroborated—the character of the authorization is not to approve or disapprove gender identity but rather to verify that the gender change is not being sought for the purpose of committing a criminal offense. Proof of this lies in the fact that the transformation of gender binarism carried out by the Gender Identity Act establishes no place to turn to out of regret or to undo decisions, since its point of departure is no longer binarism but rather another place that is in consonance with self-perceived gender identity.

The development of technology making possible to identify individuals regardless of gender is largely responsible for the successful implementation of the model for gender identification discussed here. One argument that has traditionally been used against allowing name changes on identification documents refers to the importance of unmistakable, and therefore immutable, identification for ensuring public security against threats such as terrorism or crime in general. New technologies of identification have now made this type of argument irrelevant. In this respect, an important aspect of the context surrounding the sanction of the Gender Identity Act is the parallel decision by the executive branch to establish by executive decree the Federal System of Biometric Identification for Security (SIBIOS).[47]

SIBIOS consists of a new, centralized, nationwide identification service that enables security agencies to cross check information using biometric and other data gathered. In addition to the biometric identifiers, the service contains a digital image, civil status, blood type, and other basic information that is collected from

[45]According to an interview with Marcelo Sunstein, an activist with the Argentine Homosexual Community (CHA). He was Secretary of this organization from 2000 until 2010 and one of the greatest forces behind the legislative bill for the right to gender identity that was eventually passed by Congress.

[46]*Ibid.*

[47]Executive Decree 1766, November 7, 2011, "Créase el Sistema Federal de Identificación Biométrica para la Seguridad", available at http://www.infoleg.gob.ar/infolegInternet/anexos/185000-189999/189382/norma.htm.

birth over the course of one's life. The system was not only designed for the federal police as other security forces and organizations, such as Migrations Management, border police, and national gendarmery, have full access, and its information is also made available to provincial police forces and entities through an agreement with the national state. The timing of the approval of this federal system of identification opened the path for the approval of the law on the right to gender identity by effectively refuting the arguments based on the necessity of immutable identification documents for national security.

The Gender Identity Act also stipulates that gender identity "may involve modifying corporal appearance or function through pharmacological, surgical, or other means, as long as the modification is made by free choice" and that "other expressions of gender, such as dress, speech, and manners, are also included" in the right (Article 2). It is important to emphasize, however, that gender identity and the consequent registries and documentation of it do not depend on genital reassignment nor any of the customary medical practices or interventions associated with it, as "in no case shall accredited surgical intervention for total or partial genital reassignment be required, nor shall it be necessary to accredit hormone therapy or other psychological or medical treatment" (Article 4).

Access to total or partial gender modification or hormonal treatments for corporal adjustments of people over eighteen years of age does not require judicial or administrative authorization.[48] For both, access to integrated hormonal treatment and total or partial gender modification surgery, all that is necessary is the informed consent of the person alone (Article 11), and, moreover, informed consent is the only condition taken under consideration when granting access to corporal modification technology. Dejudicialization and the importance given to informed consent are two central aspects of the Gender Identity Act.

Dejudicializing access to gender identity is along with the depathologizing of atypical gender identity is another of the pioneering facets of the Gender Identity Act. Judges no longer hold the power to laboriously examine the body and life history of a person requesting gender modification for the determination of whether the alleged gender is genuine or not, a process involving invasion of the person privacy/intimacy. Another advantage of dejudicialization is the elimination of unnecessary delays in bureaucratic procedures and of the stress produced by the legal uncertainty of the person requesting recognition of a new gender knowing that each judge interprets the matter differently and that many take considerable time to reach any decision. Removing delays also reduces the costs occasioned by the need to go to court.

The Gender Identity Act does this as it does not adopt an essentialist posture towards gender, meaning that it is not necessary to obtain expert opinion, or psychiatric evaluations, or even witnesses before access to some form of medical treatment is granted. Medical intervention or treatment is understood as a right, not

[48]Regarding persons underage, the Gender Identity Act mandates that whenever surgical intervention is required—with or without the consent of the legal guardians—a judge must intervene.

as some sort of corollary for a supposedly authentic gender identity that is determined by actors (doctors, teachers, parents, society at large) other than the person in question, a shift that represents a new relationship between medical science and individuals.

This relationship, however, does not emerge at birth, when gender binarity is still imposed on newborns—often literally by means of surgical mutilation. This is the case for many babies who demonstrate varying conditions of intersexuality. In this respect, although the Gender Identity Act contemplates a new relationship between people and medicalization and surgical intervention, and in fact posits a revolutionary relationship with regards the level of depathologization it advances, for the moment it has not been incorporated into the registry system for newborns, not even with regards the mutilating surgical interventions that the scheme entails. The topic of legal regulation and prohibition of gender modification surgery on newborns remains pending.

As was previously mentioned, a revolutionary aspect of the law consists of the free provision of medical surgery and treatments necessary to complete the desired gender change by healthcare providers, be they state-run, private, or part of the subsystem of social assistance (Article 11). For this purpose, the Gender Identity Act stipulates that these health services be included in the Mandatory Medical Program (PMO) (Article 11). This program consists of a basic set of healthcare services of which beneficiaries can avail themselves. The public healthcare system must offer the PMO and cover the obligatory services detailed in the program without exception, regardless of preexisting conditions, and without preliminary tests for admission.

Here it should be remembered that the law does not remove the necessity of obtaining a medical referral or prescription in order to access the necessary treatments and surgeries. The referral consists of a valid motive to carry out a given medical procedure or surgery, to administer a certain drug, or to perform a test. These referrals are usually regulated and authorized by professional colleges or state or international health organizations. Medical authorities thus still retain an enormous power in terms of the diagnosis and medical referrals they provide that grant people access to the modifications that are needed to adjust their gender to their self-perception. That is why a current battleground for LGBT movements around the world concerns the classifications in psychiatric and medical manuals used for categorizing pathologies (the DSM and ICD already mentioned). Those gender identities diverging from the gender imposed at birth and not reflecting sexual/gender binarity are considered disorders or diseases in these manuals. Individuals are questioning why these pathologizing diagnoses should be a necessary condition for access to the right to gender identity and the rights that derive from it.

The Gender Identity Act guarantees trans individuals access to medical science in a manner that must consider their needs. The Act states that total and partial treatments and surgeries to modify the body in concordance with the gender identity experienced is a criterion that must be prioritized. In other words, the Act gives doctors a parameter for such a prioritization in their triage. The technology for modifying the gender of a person's body already exists; the question is by who and how the decision over the necessity of the modification is decided. Previously, the person who made the decision was solely the doctor in accordance with the existing global medical classifications; today the patient is included and must be given prevalence. Regarding how the decision is made, the person involved must be consulted—it is no longer solely in the hands of the doctor. The Gender Identity Act entered the world of medicine and requires doctors to respect the human rights of trans individuals, that they change the way they had been doing things. This includes providing the medical treatments and procedures of gender change listed in the PMO, which contains all the basic healthcare services that the State and medical suppliers must cover free of charge.

The right to health is in Argentina is another field that is being conquered by human rights. This was largely driven by the campaign to provide medicine for HIV/AIDS. This conquest displaced perspectives focused on the economic calculation of what could or could not be done according to the availability or unavailability of resources. Human rights dictate that medicine, surgery, and other medical treatments must be provided to victims of HIV/AIDS, cancer, diabetes, and so on, regardless of whether certain economic calculations represent an obstacle for their provision. If the money or resources do not exist, they must be found, for the obligations imposed by human rights cannot be countered by arguments favoring economic calculations. This understanding of the right to health has not, granted, prevented a serious deficit in the access to basic healthcare from occurring, or in the specific medical treatments and set of healthcare services offered by social security and prepaid insurance policies. Still, the fact that the Argentine legal system understands the right to health in terms of human rights has allowed such arguments to be used in courts and before the authorities that control the healthcare system (the Superintendent of Health Insurers of the Nation), resulting in important victories against the State and medical insurers.

The unanimous passing of the Gender Identity Act by Congress represents an auspicious start in the effort to depathologize and decriminalize diverse gender identities so that this population can cease to fall victim to grave human rights abuses and discrimination in Argentina. Specifically, it dismantles the rigid binary legal regulations that presuppose the existence of only two kinds of bodies—man and woman—, which are defined in clear, definitive manner for life. The Act finally legitimizes the trans experience—not only in terms of the needs and histories of the people but of the people themselves. This has begun the process of disarming, retracting, and discrediting laws and state actions that stigmatized people of atypical gender identities and sexual orientations as sick or unwell. According to data provided by the National Interior Ministry, the number of gender changes in the National Registry between the entry into force of the Gender Identity Act, Law No. 26.743 (May 2012) and June 25, 2014, amounted to 3099 changes to the feminine gender and 461 to the masculine gender, totaling 3560 modifications all in all.[49] The total number of gender changes in the National Registry has increased to 7451 as of November 2016.[50] Furthermore 10 children under the age of 12 years changed their gender in the Registry between the entry into force of the Act and March 2016.[51]

6 Resistances and Advances to the Gender Identity Act

The Gender Identity Act is not only emancipatory for trans persons because of its judicial, administrative, and medical depathologization of gender, it is also especially so because it covers the right to gender identity of children.

6.1 Children's Right to Gender Identity

Article 5 stipulates the procedure for name and gender change that must be followed by persons underage, that is, children and teenagers:

> [T]he request for rectification of sex in the registry, for changes of the first name, and of the photograph must be effectuated by legal representatives of the minor and with the expressed consent of the minor, taking into account the principles of progressive capacity and the best interest of the child in accordance with the Convention on the Rights of the Child and Law 26,601 on the Comprehensive Protection of the Rights of Children and Adolescents. Therefore, the person below the age of majority must be accompanied by a children's lawyer as stipulated in Article 27 of the Law 26,601.

That most notable here is that the Act incorporates the idea of the progressive capacity of children, an idea whose concrete application is fundamental for the recognition of children's right to gender identity. This idea implies that a young person's decision must be respected to the degree that the conditions of informed consent are met. In this regard, Article 12 of the Act concerning children establishes that:

> The gender identity adopted by persons, and especially by children and adolescents, who use a first name different from the one inscribed on their national identification documents, must be respected. At their request and without any other prerequisite, the first name adopted must be used for citation, in registries and files, for the purposes of calling the person or in any other interaction or service, both public and private.

---

[49]Information available at http://www.cha.org.ar/a-4-anos-de-la-ley-de-matrimonio-igualitario-se-superarian-las-10-000-parejas/. This website also provides the details available for same-sex marriages performed in the City and Province of Buenos Aires.

[50]See https://www.clarin.com/sociedad/trans-cambiaron-DNI-trabajos-formales_0_Bynug2wq.html.

[51]See http://www.perfil.com/sociedad/diez-chicos-trans-menores-de-12-anos-ya-tienen-su-dni-con-cambio-de-genero-0306-0053.phtml.

This requires compliance from the moment any person, whether adult or minor, manifestly expresses the desire to be addressed according to their will, without the need to present corroborating documentation.

Concerning the access of minors to total and partial surgical interventions and/or integrated hormonal treatment to adjust the body, including genitalia, to one's self-perceived gender identity, the Gender Identity Act establishes that, in addition to the informed consent stipulated in Article 5 (pertaining to the change of identity on identification documents), the following procedure:

> [M]ust conform with the judicial authority of each jurisdiction, which must safeguard the principles of progressive capacity and the best interest of the child in accordance with the stipulations of the Convention on the Rights of the Child and Law 26,061 on the integral protection of children and adolescents. The judicial authority must pronounce itself in a term no longer than sixty (60) days from the time the request for conformity is submitted (Article 11).

At this point some caution is warranted with regards to the different kinds of decisions that a minor can adopt regarding their gender identity.[52] It is one thing to change the gender indicated on identification documents, whereas it is quite another to change the gender reflected by the body inasmuch as such a decision is irreversible. In the case of changing gender identity on identification documents, it is subsequently possible for a minor to change it back to the original gender indicated. The same is true in the case of hormonal treatments.

The law gives prominence to the autonomy of children and adolescents, establishing their importance in making decisions relating to their bodies. These means that judges, as well as public officials, doctors, therapists and other health professionals involved have to adapt their practices to the right that children and adolescents have to be the only person in charge of making decisions in this realm.[53] In neighborhoods, parks, public restrooms, schools, hospitals, etc., trans children are exposed to an infinite number of violent and discriminatory situations.[54] These are the prelude to the many human rights violations that will be present throughout their lives. Recognizing the right to gender identity for underage individuals is slowly transforming the social perception of trans childhood and adolescence, and starting to form a basis for a substantive respect for their rights. According to data from the National Registry of Individuals, the entity in charge of registration and

[52]In turn, articule 11 must be read in light of the reform to article 26 of the Civil and Comercial Code that was approved three years after the Gender Identity Act entered into force. This article establishes that adolescentes from 13 to 16 years of age have the right to decide on medical interventions that do not compromiso their health.

[53]For a critique of judicial reactions to statutory changes see my article: Laura Saldivia Menajovsky, "Tomándose la Desjudicialización en Serio: Comentario a una Decisión Judicial sobre el Derecho a la Identidad de Género de una Adolescente Trans", Revista Jurídica de Palermo, Año 16, Nro. 1, Mayo 2018.

[54]For an analysis of the current situation of trans children in Argentina see: Asociación Civil Infancias Libres, "Informe sobre la situación actual de las experiencias de niñeces trans", Julio 2019.

identification of all physical persons living in Argentina and Argentineans living in other places, since the adoption of the law on gender identity and to 20 April 2018, 83 new documents were issued to underage individuals as a result of changes in the sex originally registered.[55] To March 2016, only 10 were under 12 years of age.[56] In 2019, in the Province of Santa Fe, five persons under 12 years of age changed their gender in their documents and forty other individuals in this age range are receiving counseling from provincial authorities.[57] Positive media coverage of several of these cases has increased the positive perception of this issue.[58]

6.2 Registering Gender

Another scenario where the meaning of gender has been disputed concerns registration. At the end of 2018 there was an unprecented decision by registration officials: the Civil Registry of Mendoza produced a birth certificate without writing down the person's gender. In the subsequent two years, roughly ten more individuals have been registered in this way.[59]

In March 2020, a judge in the city of Buenos Aires granted an individual's petition to be identified as "travesti" in his national identity document (DNI).[60] She additionally ordered the rectification of the birth certification of the petitioner to include "travesti femininity" in the field reserved for sex and noted that "the Civil registry must note that, in the future, to guarantee and recognize the self determined gender identity of each person, petitions such as the one being studied here will be directed to the administrative authority, which shall provide a multiplicity of gender markers as options for indivuals".[61] This decision was appealed by the National

---

[55] See https://chequeado.com/el-explicador/casi-100-ninos-ninas-y-adolescentes-trans-cambiaron-su-identidad-de-genero-en-sus-dnis/.

[56] "Diez chicos trans menores de 12 años ya tienen su DNI con cambio de género", Diario Perfil, 6 de marzo 2016, https://www.perfil.com/noticias/sociedad/diez-chicos-trans-menores-de-12-anos-ya-tienen-su-dni-con-cambio-de-genero-20160306-0053.phtml.

[57] "Cinco santafecinos menores de 12 años ya cambiaron su identidad en el DNI", Diario El Litoral, 20 de mayo 2019, https://www.ellitoral.com/index.php/id_um/197295-cinco-santafesinos-menores-de-12-anos-ya-cambiaron-su-identidad-de-genero-en-el-dni-infancias-trans-area-metropolitana.html.

[58] See the story of Luana, the first trans child to obtain the recognition of her gender in her oficial documentation, in my book *Subordinaciones Invertidas*, capítulo V. See also the experiencies of Facha and Maria, respectively: "Un niño de 10 años cambió de género y ahora se llama Facha", Diario Infobae, 29 de octubre 2014, http://www.infobae.com/2014/10/29/1605058-un-nino-10-anos-cambio-genero-y-ahora-se-llama-facha/. Neuquén: tiene 5 años y es la primera nena trans en obtener una nueva identidad, Diario Infobae, 25 de junio, 2017, http://www.infobae.com/sociedad/2017/06/25/neuquen-tiene-5-anos-y-es-la-primera-nena-trans-en-obtener-una-nueva-identidad/.

[59] Eleonora Lamm kindly offered this information on September 3, 2019.

[60] Caso "Bertolini, Lara María", Juzgado Nacional en lo Civil 7, 1 de Marzo de 2019.

[61] *Ibid.*

Registry of Persons arguing that the Gender Identity Act does not transcend the male-female binary. The lawyers acting on behalf of the institution explained that sex and gender are "different concepts" and that while "self-perceived" genders might be multiple, sex remains dichotomic as there are only two possible sexes: woman and man. They added that the birth certificate, as well as the DNI, are meant to register sex and not gender.

The province of Santa Fe is another place where the meaning of self-determined gender for official documentation has been extended. On 11 July 2019, the local Civil Registry ordered the creation of a birth certificate with the expression "self-perceived" in the sex field. Six more petitions in the same direction are awaiting resolution.[62]

6.3 Medical Treatments

It has been more difficult to guarantee access to gender-confirming surgeries and hormonal treatments without an order from a judicial or administrative authority, regardless of the clear wording of article 11 of the Gender Identity Law.[63] The two major obstacles are the long waiting lists in public hospitals and the refusal of private insurers to recognize the claims as included in the portfolio of mandatory services. For example, in the Gutiérrez de La Plata Hospital there are 150 persons on the waiting list to date (2020). The estimate nationwide is that there are 800 persons waiting for an intervention.[64] The case of Lhuanna Diaz, on the other hand, exemplifies the ordeal of getting treatment through private coverage. In 2018, she requested a neovaginoplasty from her health insurance company. The request was denied on two grounds: she did not have a certificate from a psychologist regarding a proper diagnosis, and her plan did not include the surgery. She went before a judge to petition for the surgery and finally got a positive resolution on appeal on August 2019.[65] This last decision simply followed a clear precedent on the duty of private

[62]"Una partida de nacimiento definirá a un santafecino como "autopercibido"", Diario El Litoral, 12 de julio de 2019, https://www.ellitoral.com/index.php/id_um/201865-una-partida-de-nacimiento-definira-a-un-santafesino-como-autopercibido-por-primera-vez-en-la-historia-area-metropolitana.html.

[63]"Salud trans: cuáles son los hospitales públicos que realizan cirugías de reafirmación de género", Diario Infobae, 13 de marzo de 2019, https://www.infobae.com/salud/2018/03/13/salud-trans-cuales-son-los-hospitales-publicos-que-realizan-cirugias-de-reafirmacion-de-genero/.

[64]*Ibid.*

[65]"Pidió hacerse una vagina y la mandaron al psicólogo: ahora la Justicia le dio la razón", Diario Infobae, 29 de agosto de 2019, https://www.infobae.com/sociedad/2019/08/29/pidio-hacerse-una-vagina-y-la-mandaron-al-psicologo-ahora-la-justicia-le-dio-la-razon/.

insurers to include all gender confirming surgeries and feminizing treatments in the basic coverage.[66]

6.4 Other Fields Recognizing the Non-binary Character of Gender

The disruption of the gender binary as introduced by the Gender Identity Act is noticeable in other fields as well. In the domains of criminal law,[67] housing,[68] and employment,[69] arguments concerning the human rights of trans persons have been used to fight structural discrimination and vulnerability in their lives.

In criminal law, the case of the murder of the travestite and human rights activist Diana Sacayán, has been framed by the prosecution as one of a "travesticide", that is, a hate crime against a travestite.[70] The National Sex Education Program has been changed to include igualitarian marriage and gender identity in the curricula. In 2020, the census will include a question on gender in addition to the question about sex. Among the options available for gender identity the following are included: woman, man, trans woman, trans man, other or ignored.[71] Schools, universities,

[66]Juzgado en lo Civil y Comercial N° 6 de Rosario, "X, Sandy c/ IAPOS s/ Recurso de Amparo – CUIJ N° 21-02862082-6" septiembre del 2016; Superior Tribunal de Justicia de la Provincia de Río Negro, "E., A.C./ U.P.C.N. s/ Amparo (c) s/ Apelación" (Expte. N° 29845/18-STJ), julio 2018; Juzgado en lo Civil y Comercial Federal N° 10 de la Ciudad de Buenos Aires "Puccini, C. M. V. c/ Obra Social de la Unión de Personal Civil de la Nación y otro s/Amparo de Salud (Expte. 10037/ 2017), mayo 2018; Sala I de la Cámara de Apelaciones del Fuero Contencioso Administrativo y Tributario, "F., T. (R.F.) c/ Obra Social de la Ciudad de Buenos Aires (OBSBA) s/ Amparo de Salud- Medicamentos y Tratamientos" EXP 12330/2018-0, abril del 2019, Juzgado N° 11 en lo Contencioso Administrativo y Tributario de la Ciudad Autónoma de Buenos Aires "P., M. c/ Obra Buenos Aires (OBSBA) s/ amparo - salud - medicamentos y tratamientos" Expte. N° EXP 2748/ 2019-0, agosto del 2019. Agradezco mucho a Anabella Calvo por haberme facilitado esta información.

[67]"Dictamen reconoce "vulnerabilidad estructural" a cinco mujeres trans acusadas de vender droga", La Izquierda Diario, 17 de abril 2019, https://www.laizquierdadiario.com/Fallo-reconoce-vulnerabilidad-estructural-a-cinco-mujeres-trans-acusadas-de-vender-droga.

[68]"La casa propia, más cerca", Diario Página 12, 3 de mayo 2019, https://www.pagina12.com.ar/190776-la-casa-propia-mas-cerca.

[69]"Mapa del cupo laboral travesti-trans en Argentina", Agencia Presentes, 1 de mayo de 2019, http://agenciapresentes.org/2019/05/01/1m-mapa-del-cupo-laboral-travesti-trans-en-argentina/.

[70]See Diana Maffia y Alba Rueda, "El concepto de travesticidio/transfemicidio y su inscripción en el pedido de justicia por Diana Sacayán", en Diana Maffia, Patricia Gómez y Aluminé Moreno (comp.), *Miradas Feministas sobre los Derechos*, Editorial Jusbaires, 2019.

[71]"¿Mujer, varón, trans, o ignorado? La identidad de género llegó al censo", Diario La Nación 3 de septiembre https://www.lanacion.com.ar/sociedad/identidad-de-genero-la-novedad-clave-del-censo-nacional-que-se-hara-en-2020-nid2283970.

museums and libraries have led the way in the transformation of public restroom and inclusive language use.[72]

Welfare programs have also been challenged to adapt their categories following the adoption of the Gender Identity Act. The case of a trans man pregnant with his trans woman partner raised the question of the possibility of including either of them as beneficiary of the subsidy for pregnant women (ANSES). Finally, Maximiliano was included as the beneficiary of the subsidy, after an initial refusal to include either of them.[73]

Sports regulations have been another example of resistance to the Gender Identity Act. In sports, the cases of Jessica, Mia, Victoria and other trans women reveal the obstacles in the implementation of the Gender Identity Act.[74] Most of these trans women have been playing hockey since their childhood. In order to play in different tournaments, they asked to be registered at the Hockey Province's Leagues as women. The province authorities argued at the Argentinean Hockey Confederation sporting advantage and the lack of specific regulations relating trans persons. The mediation of judicial authorities was needed in some of these cases, as in the Jessica's case (2016) where the district judge of Rawson (Province of Chubut) decided that the province league could not forbid Jessica's registration and mandated that she should be allowed to play.[75] This situation has been changed by the Circular Letter N° 33-2017 (April 2017) of the Argentinean Hockey Confederation which allows trans women to play hockey by adopting guidelines developed in the consensus meeting about "change of gender and hyperandrogenism" of the International Olympic Committee (November 2015).[76]

These examples demonstrate that the supposed point of reference for the gender of individuals that implies classification as man or woman is blurred in practice by gender realities and practices that exceed that classification and that are now legitimated and backed by the Gender Identity Act. As shown above, there are challenges about the effective enforcement of the Act throughout Argentina. The Gender Identity Act provides a baseline for further discussion and a legitimizing

[72]The Museum of Contemporary Art of Buenos Aires (MACBA), for example, has posted a sign in all restrooms stating: "Self-perceived Gender Restroom" Then follows an explanation: "Restrooms in the Museum are not separated as to gender; they are to be freely used by individuals of any self perceived gender. In order to promote inclusive experiences for visitors, artists, and employees, MACBA embraces the internal and individual experience of desire, the body, and gender. We respect the way in which each individual expresses and perceives herself" (T.). In the introduction to my book *Subordinaciones Invertidas, op.cit.,* I register the discusion that I had in 2016 with the University's publishing house regarding inclusive language. Following an initial resistance, the publlisher accepted the use of inclusive language througout the book.

[73]See Soledad Vallejos, "Un Embarazo Trans, Protegido", *Diario Página 12*, 2/6/2015.

[74]See https://www.clarin.com/sociedad/jugadoras-piden-permitan-jugar-hockey_0_Sk0hsihi.html and http://www.telam.com.ar/notas/201609/162858-deportistas-trans-denunciaron-en-diputados-problemas-para-jugar-en-las-ligas-provinciales.html.

[75]See https://www.clarin.com/sociedad/razon-jugadora-hockey-vuelve-jugar_0_SycbfIjo.html.

[76]See http://www.cahockey.org.ar/circulares/view/447.

framework to promote and reinforce the effective recognition of the legal and political visibility achieved over the past two decades.[77]

7 Has the Gender Identity Act Improved the Conditions of Trans Life?

The Gender Identity Act provides a legal model for trans rights that is realistic in the local context and establishes basic conditions to implementing the self-determination of gender. It has been the starting point of multiple actions, both legal and social, that no longer tie up gender to a person's sex at birth.

The law did not come into existence in a total legal and social vacuum but rather inserts itself in a context where the rights of LGBT persons have been increasingly recognized (egalitarian marriage, pensions for surviving gay spouses, rules on non-discrimination for sexual orientation and gender identity, the Supreme Court's decision in the ALITT case, etc.). All these events created a scenario that made it possible to legally speak of non-binary genders.

The trans movement has been good at linking the trans experience to the human rights framework that is idiosyncratic to the way in which Argentineans think of the consequences of military dictatorship. One of those consequences, the stealing of babies that were born in prisons and their identities, led to a strong articulation of the right to personal identity as a human right. This right was adopted as frame for the demands regarding the recognition of the rights of non-binary persons. By incorporating the human rights discourse and by adapating it to its own cause, the LGBT movement facilitated the acceptance of trans claims by the general public and also by public officials who were deeply committed to the language of human rights.

The fight for the recognition of the right to gender identity reveals the close connection between the State, in its multiplicity of actors and institutional diversity,

[77]Other initiatives surrending the right to gender identity are been discussed at local level. For example Law No 14.783 of the Province of Buenos Aires (2015), also called "Ley de Cupo Laboral Trans" ("TransLabor Quota Law"), aimed at the introduction of a 1% quota for transpersons in the public employment of the province. This law is for the compensation for trans's rights violations. It has been regulated last December, see https://agenciapresentes.org/2019/12/05/tras-4-anos-se-reglamento-la-ley-de-cupo-laboral-travesti-trans-en-provincia-de-buenos-aires/. This is a state statute so its enforcement would only be effective in Buenos Aires territory. Some other municipalities have passed ordinances setting a "translabor quota" in the public employment, such is the case of 13 municipalities around the country (See: http://www.cadena3.com/contenido/2017/05/30/El-municipio-de-Rio-Grande-aprobo-el-cupo-laboral-trans-184759.asp). The Municipality of Rio Grande in the Province of Tierra del Fuego passed the Ordinance 22 (May 2017) establishing a quota of 0.5% of transpersons. In other case, the Municipality of Rosario in the Province of Santa Fe passed the Ordinance 9.543 (May 2016) setting a quota of 5 transpersons incorporated per year, the goal is 10 transpersons incorporated for 2017, and there was 62 transpersons registered until March 2017 (http://www.lavoz.com.ar/ciudadanos/la-municipalidad-de-rosario-abre-el-primer-cupo-laboral-trans-del-pais).

and society. Without a doubt, the activism of the LGBT movement not only has led to the recognition of rights that had previously been denied, but also has impacted the construction of the State as it forces it to renounce its traditional fear of sexual and gender diversity. Of course, this change in the State does not happen at once and with all intensity in every one of its parts; to the contrary, in its heterogeneous existence, the State still contains discourses that deny the rights of LGBT persons and gives them the legitimacy of formality. The change however, seems stoppable as more laws are enacted and the LGBT movement continues to press for more.

Not only the State but society is affected by law. In turn, many societal actions—related to public restrooms, inclusive language and the media—end up streghtening and molding the Gender Identity Act.

References

Bellucci M (2010) Orgullo. Carlos Jáuregui, una biografía política. Emecé, Buenos Aires, p 20

Bellucci M, Palmeiro C (2013) Lo queer en las pampas criollas, argentinas y vernáculas. In: Fernandez AM, Peres WS (eds) La Diferencia Desquiciada. Géneros y Diversidades Sexuales. Editorial Biblios, Buenos Aires

Berkins (2003) Un itinerario político del travestismo. In: Maffía D (ed) Sexualidades migrantes. Género y transgénero. Feminaria Editora, Buenos Aires, p 130

Berkins L, Fernández J (eds) (2005) La gesta del nombre propio. Informe sobre la situación de la comunidad travesti en la Argentina. Ediciones Madres de Plaza de Mayo, Buenos Aires

Berkins L, Korol C (comp.) (2007) Diálogo Prostitución/Trabajo Sexual: Las protagonistas hablan, Feminaria Editora, Buenos Aires

Fernández J (2004) Cuerpos Desobedientes. Travestismo e identidad de género. Edhasa, Buenos Aires, pp 120, 121

Hiller R (2010) Matrimonio igualitario y espacio público en Argentina. In: Aldao M, Clérico L (eds) Matrimonio Igualitario. Perspectivas sociales, políticas y jurídicas. Eudeba, Buenos Aires

Liberatori H (2012) A propósito de los casos de identidad autopercibida. In: Von Opiela C (Coord) Derecho a la Identidad de Género Ley 26.743. La Ley, Buenos Aires, p 114

Sabsay L (2011) Fronteras Sexuales. Espacio urbano, cuerpos y ciudadanía. Editorial Paidós, Buenos Aires

Verbitsky H (2006) Hacer la Corte. Editorial Sudamericana and Página 12, Buenos Aires, pp 310–319

La reconnaissance des droits des personnes trans au Canada

Michelle Giroux et Louise Langevin

Résumé Le texte vise à présenter et à expliquer les règles juridiques mises en place au Canada, tant sur le plan national, que provincial ou territorial, pour reconnaitre les droits des personnes trans. Nous abordons la question de la reconnaissance de leurs droits fondamentaux, les changements en droit de la famille et à l'état civil, l'accès aux traitements médicaux et les droits des personnes intersexes. Les revendications des personnes trans ne sont pas pour autant terminées. Le prochain débat risque de se trouver dans la remise en question complète du sexe, comme critère de distinction dans les lois, dans les politiques, de même que comme élément d'identification de la personne, dans les documents officiels, et en matière de filiation.

Abstract This text presents and explains the legal norms in Canada (on the federal, provincial and territorial levels) recognizing the rights of trans people. We deal with the protection of their fundamental rights, the amendments in family law and in the act of birth and official documents, the health care and the rights of intersex persons. The next challenge lies in the relevance of sex as a criteria in laws, policies, and as an identification element of the person in official documents and in parentage laws.

M. Giroux (✉)
Faculté de droit, Université d'Ottawa, Ottawa, ON, Canada
e-mail: m.giroux@uottawa.ca

L. Langevin
Faculté de droit, Université Laval, Québec, QC, Canada
e-mail: louise.langevin@fd.ulaval.ca

I. C. Jaramillo, L. Carlson (eds.), *Trans Rights and Wrongs*, Ius Comparatum - Global Studies in Comparative Law 54,
https://doi.org/10.1007/978-3-030-68494-5_16

1 Introduction

Bien que les statistiques varient, une partie de la population est trans.[1] Cette population est vulnérable à la discrimination. Ces dernières années, on a vu les militant-e-s trans au Canada s'organiser et revendiquer des changements pour enrayer les discriminations envers ces personnes et leur permettre de vivre plus librement et avec plus de dignité leur identité. Ces revendications identitaires s'inscrivent dans la foulée de celles qu'ont défendues avant eux ou elles, les femmes et les personnes homosexuelles. Ces revendications somme toute assez bien organisées ont donné lieu à des changements législatifs, qui n'auraient pu voir le jour sans la coordination de la communauté trans, jumelée à une ouverture sociale et politique à la diversité des sexes, des genres, des sexualités et des familles. Ainsi, depuis le début du nouveau millénaire, les nombreuses transformations sociales en ces domaines se sont transposées dans la loi. Il ne se passe pas une semaine sans que la problématique du genre ne se retrouve dans les médias. Pensons notamment aux personnes trans qui ont été refusées et réadmises dans l'armée américaine, mais acceptées dans l'armée canadienne[2] ou à l'annonce que le passeport canadien peut désormais comporter une mention neutre, en lieu et place du sexe.[3] Évidemment, on ne peut affirmer que la discrimination envers les personnes trans est chose du passé, mais au moins, des mécanismes juridiques et une plus grande tolérance sociétale leur rendent la vie plus facile.

Dans ce domaine, la terminologie évolue avec les réalités, toujours en mouvance. Dans le présent texte, nous utilisons l'expression personnes trans pour désigner les personnes dont l'identité de genre ne correspond pas au sexe qui leur a été assigné à la naissance. Ces personnes peuvent avoir subi une transition médicale ou non. Nous

---

[1]Selon Gary J Gates, « How many people are lesbian, gay, bisexual, and transgender », The Williams Institute on Sexual Orientation and Gender Identity, Law and Public Policy at UCLA School of Law, avril 2011, il s'agit approximativement de 0,3 % de la population. Pour la Fédération des commissions scolaires du Québec, cela représente « environ 2 500 enfants d'âge scolaire » au Québec, voir http : //www.fcsq.qc.ca/commission-scolaires/statistiques/. Ces deux références sont citées dans Barreau du Québec, *Mémoire du Barreau du Québec. Projet de loi n° 103 – Loi visant à renforcer la lutte contre la transphobie et à améliorer notamment la situation des mineurs transgenres,* présenté à la Commission des relations avec les citoyens, 8 juin 2016, à la p. 4, disponible en ligne : https://www.barreau.qc.ca/pdf/medias/positions/2016/20160608-memoire-pl-103.pdf. Jean-Sébastien Sauvé avance que « [l]'intersexualité impliquerait environ 4 % de la population ». Voir *Aux confins du « M » et du « F ». Une généalogie critique de ce sexe que l'on catégorise aux fins de l'état civil québécois*, thèse de doctorat en droit, Université de Montréal, 2016, p 13, note 46.

[2]Voir Lee Berthiaume, « Militaires transgenres: le Canada prend le chemin inverse de Trump », La Presse canadienne, **(26 juillet 2017), en ligne :** https://www.lapresse.ca/actualites/national/201707/26/01-5119499-militaires-transgenres-le-canada-prend-le-chemin-inverse-de-trump.php.

[3]Voir Immigration et Citoyenneté Canada, « Choisissez ou mettez à jour l'identifiant de genre sur votre passeport ou document de voyage » (dernière modification le 11 juillet 2019), en ligne : https://www.canada.ca/fr/immigration-refugies-citoyennete/services/passeports-canadiens/changer-sexe.html.

employons l'expression personnes intersexes pour désigner les personnes qui sont nées avec un sexe biologique indéterminé.[4] Le terme cisgenre est utilisé pour désigner une personne dont le sexe indiqué à l'acte de naissance correspond à celui auquel elle s'identifie.[5] Quant au terme non-binaire, il désigne une personne qui ne s'identifie pas exclusivement au sexe masculin ou féminin. Nous référons également à l'acronyme LGBTQ qui désigne les personnes qui ne sont pas strictement hétérosexuelles, étant entendu que cette expression regroupe les lesbiennes (L), les gais (G), les bisexuel-le-s (B), les trans (T) et les queer (Q).[6] Si on ajoute les personnes intersexes (I), on utilise plutôt l'acronyme LGBTQI ou LGBTQ+. Les autochtones revendiquent le terme « bi-spirituel » pour désigner le statut valorisé dans cette culture des personnes qui peuvent être identifiées comme incarnant à la fois les spiritualités masculine et féminine.[7]

Dans les lignes qui suivent, nous nous attardons à expliquer et définir les règles juridiques mises en place au Canada, tant sur le plan national, que provincial ou territorial. Nous abordons la question de la reconnaissance de leurs droits fondamentaux, les changements en droit de la famille et à l'état civil, l'accès aux traitements médicaux et les droits des personnes intersexes.

---

[4]Pour des distinctions intéressantes, voir Michel Dorais, « Repenser le sexe, le genre et l'orientation sexuelle » (2015) 40:3 Santé mentale au Québec 37. Sur les difficultés à établir le sexe biologique, voir notamment Sauvé, *supra* note 1 aux pp 3 et s.

[5]Cisgenre (« cisgender » en anglais), « qui vient du préfixe latin [« cis »] signifiant du « même côté » ... « désigne une personne dont le ressenti de l'identité personnelle correspond au sexe et au genre qui lui ont été assignés à la naissance ». Son contraire est « transgenre ». Le terme « cisgenre » a fait son entrée dans le *Grand dictionnaire terminologique* de l'Office québécois de la langue française en 2018. Voir Laure Bereni et al, *Introduction aux études sur le genre*, 2e éd, Bruxelles, de Boeck, 2012, p 50. Voir aussi Ontario, Commission des droits de la personne, *Politique sur la prévention de la discrimination fondée sur l'identité sexuelle et l'expression de l'identité sexuelle*, Toronto, Ontario, 2014.

[6]En Ontario, le préambule de la *Loi modifiant la Loi sur l'éducation en ce qui a trait à l'intimidation et à d'autres questions,* 2012 LO 17/*An Act to amend the Education Act with respect to bullying and other matters*, 2012 SO 17, est intéressant sur le plan terminologique. Il emploie l'expression « LGBTTIQ (lesbian, gay, bisexual, transgender, transsexual, two-spirited, intersex, queer and questioning) people », traduite en français par l'expression « les personnes LGBTTBIQ (lesbiennes, gaies, bisexuelles, transgenres, transsexuelles, bispirituelles, intersexuées, queer et en questionnement) ». À comparer : le terme « queer » est aussi traduit par « allosexuel » : voir des conseils de voyage du gouvernement canadien « Lesbiennes, gais, bisexuels, transgenres, *allosexuels* et bispirituels du Canada à l'étranger » (dernière modification le 11 juillet 2019) (nous soulignons), en ligne : https://voyage.gc.ca/voyager/sante-securite/lgbt-voyage; « Lesbian, gay, bisexual, transgender, queer and two-spirit Canadians abroad », en ligne : https://travel.gc.ca/travelling/health-safety/lgbt-travel?_ga=2.243415361.533771413.1499440179-1221505983.1499440179.

[7]Voir à cet effet : http://www.btb.termiumplus.gc.ca/tpv2alpha/alphafra.html?lang=fra&i=1&srchtxt=BI+SPIRITUEL&index=alt&codom2nd_wet=1#resultrecs.Voir aussi Val Napoleon, « Raven's Garden : A Discussion about Aboriginal Sexual Orientation and Transgender Issues » (2002) 17 Can J L & Soc 149.

2 La reconnaissance des droits fondamentaux des personnes trans

Au Canada, les lois protégeant les droits fondamentaux reconnaissent maintenant explicitement l'identité de genre et l'expression de genre comme motifs illicites de discrimination.[8] C'est le cas de toutes les lois provinciales et territoriales sur les droits de la personne,[9] ainsi que la loi fédérale sur les droits de la personne.[10] Il ne s'agit pas d'un nouveau motif à proprement dit, puisque le motif illicite du sexe a été interprété très largement par les tribunaux pour inclure la discrimination vécue par les personnes trans.[11] Quant à la *Charte canadienne,*[12] l'identité de genre et

---

[8]Les auteurs ne partagent pas tous la même opinion sur la pertinence de cet ajout aux chartes. Comparez : Jean-Sébastien Sauvé, « L'interdiction de discriminer les personnes trans* dans la Charte des droits et libertés de la personne. Pour son amélioration par l'ajout de l'« identité de genre » et de l'« expression de genre » à la liste des motifs de distinction illicites » (2015) 23 Enfances Familles Générations 108; Lane R Mandis, « Human Rights, Transsexed Bodies and Health Care in Canada: What Counts as Legal Protection? » (2011) 26 R Can Dr & Soc 509; Florence Ashley, « Don't be so hateful: The insufficiency of anti-discrimination and hate crime laws in improving trans well-being » (2018) 68:1 U of T L J 1.

[9]Territoires du Nord-Ouest : *Loi sur les droits de la personne*, LTN-O 2002, c 18, Préambule et art 5 (1); Manitoba : *Code des droits de la personne*, CPLM c H175, art 9 (2) g); Ontario *: Code des droits de la personne*, LRO 1990, c H.19, art 1, 2, 3, 5, 6, 7 (1) et 7 (2) ; Nouvelle-Écosse *: Human Rights Act*, RSNS 1989, c 214, art 5 (1); Île du Prince-Édouard : *Human Rights Act*, RSPEI 1988, c H-12, préambule et art 2 d) et 10; Terre-Neuve-et-Labrador : *Human Rights Act*, 2010, SNL 2010, c H-13.1 : Préambule et art 9 (1); Colombie-Britannique : *Human Rights Code*, RSBC 1996, c 210: art 7 (1), 8 (1) b), 9 c), 10 (1) b), 11, 13 (1) b) et 14 c); Alberta : *Alberta Human Rights Act*, RSA 2000, c A-25.5, préambule et art 3 (1) b), 4 b), 5 b), 7 b), 8 a) et b) et 9 c); Saskatchewan: *The Saskatchewan Human Rights Code*, SS 1979, c S-24.1, art 2 (1) m.01 (xv); Québec : *Charte des droits et libertés de la personne*, RLRQ, c C-12 [*Charte québécoise*], art 10 ; Nouveau-Brunswick : *Loi sur les droits de la personne*, LRN-B 2011, c 171, art 2.1 (modifiée par LN-B 2017 c 63) ; Yukon : *Loi sur les droits de la personne*, LRY 2002, c 116, art 7 (modifiée par LY 2017, ch 4); Nunavut : *Loi modifiant la loi sur les droits de la personne*, LNun 2017, c 8, *Loi sur les droits de la personne*, LNun 2003, c 12, art 7. Notons que l'orientation sexuelle fait déjà partie de la liste des motifs illicites de discrimination de ces lois.

[10]*Loi modifiant la Loi canadienne sur les droits de la personne et le Code criminel,* LC 2017 c 13. Voir Julian Walker, *Résumé législatif du projet de loi C-16 : Loi modifiant la Loi canadienne sur les droits de la personne et le Code criminel*, Division des affaires juridiques et sociales, Ottawa, Bibliothèque du parlement, le 21 octobre 2016. Depuis 2005, de nombreux projets de loi sur le même sujet ont été déposés. Sur l'historique de l'adoption de cette loi, voir Brenda Cossman, « Gender Identity, Gender Pronouns, and Freedom of Expression: Bill C-16 and the Traction of Specious Legal Claims » (2018) 68 U of T L J 37.

[11]Voir *Québec (Commission des droits de la personne et des droits de la jeunesse) c Maison des jeunes*, 1998 CanLII 28 (QCTDP). En Colombie-Britannique : *Vancouver Rape Relief Society c Nixon*, 2005 BCCA 601 (CACB). En Ontario, au même effet : *Forrester v Peel Regional Police Services Board*, 2006 HRTO 13 (CanLII); *Hogan v Ontario (Health and Long-Term Care)*, 2006 HRTO 32 (CanLII); *Finan v Cosmetic Surgicentre (Toronto)*, 2008 HRTO 47 (CanLII); *MacDonald v Downtown Health Club for Women*, 2009 HRTO 1043 (CanLII).

[12]*Charte canadienne des droits et libertés,* partie I de la *Loi constitutionnelle de 1982*, constituant l'annexe B de la *Loi de 1982 sur le Canada (R-U)*, 1982, c 11 [*Charte canadienne*].

l'expression de genre ne sont pas nommées dans les motifs illicites de discrimination à l'article 15 (1). Il est cependant vraisemblable que ce motif puisse être considéré comme analogue et être inclus dans la liste, comme l'ont déjà fait les tribunaux inférieurs.[13]

Ces lois ne donnent pas de définition de ces termes,[14] tout comme pour les autres motifs de discrimination illicites, laissant aux tribunaux la tâche de les définir.

Toutes les personnes possédant une identité de genre qui se manifeste par une expression de genre, on peut se demander si ce motif discriminatoire ne vise que les personnes trans, fluides, non binaires et exclut les personnes cisgenres (les personnes gaies et lesbiennes étant déjà incluses sous le motif illicite d'orientation sexuelle). Les motifs illicites de sexe et d'identité de genre sont-ils interchangeables? L'intention législative était de nommer de façon officielle la discrimination que vivent les personnes trans et de l'enrayer. Dans la tâche de définir la portée de ce motif, certains tribunaux ont refusé d'y inclure le cas d'un homme cisgenre à qui l'employeur avait imposé de se couper la barbe pour des raisons de sécurité et qui plaidait discrimination basée sur son expression de genre.[15] Dans une affaire d'expulsion violente d'un bar d'un homme trans pour avoir utilisé les toilettes des hommes, le juge conclut que la discrimination fondée sur l'identité de genre est à l'œuvre. Il ne définit pas ce concept, mais est convaincu qu'il s'agit bien d'identité de genre en raison des qualificatifs utilisés par les gardiens de sécurité du bar pour insulter la personne trans.[16] On peut penser que ce motif exclut les personnes cisgenres, mais inclut les personnes trans qui ont ou non subi une transition

---

[13]Par exemple, *Québec (Commission des droits de la personne et des droits de la jeunesse) c Maison des jeunes*, *supra* note 11. L'orientation sexuelle ne figurait pas parmi les motifs de discrimination illicites énumérés de l'article 15 (1) de la *Charte canadienne*. Les tribunaux ont décidé que l'orientation sexuelle faisait partie des motifs de discrimination illicites analogues, s'ajoutant ainsi aux motifs de discrimination illicites énumérés. Voir *Egan c Canada*, [1995] 2 RCS 513.

[14]Pour des définitions des termes sexe, identité de genre, expression de genre, transphobie et cisnormativité, voir *Center for Gender Advocacy* c. *Attorney general of Quebec*, 2021 QCCS 191, porté en appel, sur le seul point des éléments de preuve à faire valoir pour le mineur de 14 ans et plus, voir *infra* note 137, Ontario, Commission des droits de la personne, *Politique sur la prévention de la discrimination fondée sur l'identité sexuelle et l'expression de l'identité sexuelle*, Toronto, Ontario, 2014.

[15]Les employés de la fonderie devaient porter un masque pour des raisons de sécurité. La moustache était tolérée, mais pas la barbe. Sans justifier ou expliquer sa position, le tribunal considère qu'un homme cisgenre ne peut soulever le motif de discrimination illicite d'identité de genre. Le syndicat de cet employé avait déjà plaidé sans succès au cours des années que la politique « sans barbe » de l'employeur équivalait à de la discrimination fondée sur le sexe, puisque les femmes n'assumaient pas l'obligation de se faire la barbe quotidiennement. Cet argument avait été rejeté. *Browne v Sudbury Integrated Nickel Operations*, 2016 HRTO 62.

[16]*Lewis v Sugar Daddys Nightclub*, 2016 HRTO 347 au para 49. Dans cette affaire, le plaignant se définit comme un « transgender neutral questioning transgender male ».

médicale,[17] les personnes non binaires, polygenres,[18] les personnes trans qui ont ou non demandé une modification de la mention du sexe et du prénom au registre de l'état civil.

Quant au motif de l'expression de genre, contrairement à l'identité de genre qui est issue du vocabulaire psychiatrique, elle a été formulée par les chercheur-e-s sur la théorie du genre dans les années 1990.[19] Ce motif illicite, qui vise les comportements et l'apparence, comme les choix vestimentaires, la coiffure, le port de maquillage, le langage corporel et la voix,[20] pourrait-il servir dans un cas où un employeur impose à une employée un code vestimentaire sexualisé?[21] Selon une décision, le motif illicite de l'expression de genre, qui est plus large et plus souple que l'identité de genre, semble être réservé aux personnes trans.[22]

---

[17]Voir *Vanderputten v Seydaco Packaging Corp,* 2012 HRTO 1977. L'employeur ne peut exiger une transition médicale pour permettre à l'employée trans d'utiliser les toilettes pour femmes.

[18]Voir *T A v Ontario (Transportation)*, 2016 HRTO 17 (CanLII). Le demandeur se qualifie de personne « pan-gender » (polygenre, qui inclut tous les genres à la fois). Il demande que les documents officiels de l'Ontario retirent la mention du sexe. (Nous n'avons trouvé aucune décision sur le fond.) Michel Dorais donne la définition suivante : « [L]es personnes non conformistes ou créatives sur le plan du genre, sans doute les plus nombreuses, ne sont pas forcément trans. Par leur façon néanmoins de transgresser, sciemment ou pas, et de diverses façons, les normes et les stéréotypes de genre, elles rappellent qu'il existe une infinie variété dans l'expression possible du masculin et du féminin, ou de l'androgynie, chez un être humain ». *Supra* note 4 à la p 45.

[19]Sur l'origine de ce terme, voir Kyle Kirkup, « The Origins of Gender Identity and Gender Expression in Anglo-American Legal Discourse » (2018) 68 U of T L J 80. Voir la définition qu'en donne la Commission ontarienne des droits de la personne : « Expression de l'identité sexuelle (ou expression de genre) : Manière dont une personne exprime ou présente ouvertement son sexe. Cela peut inclure ses comportements et son apparence, comme ses choix vestimentaires, sa coiffure, le port de maquillage, son langage corporel et sa voix. De plus, l'expression de l'identité sexuelle inclut couramment le choix d'un nom et d'un pronom pour se définir. Ces attributs déterminent comment l'identité sexuelle sera perçue par autrui. Toutes les personnes, quelle que soit leur identité sexuelle, ont une expression de l'identité sexuelle pouvant prendre une variété de formes. Chez les personnes trans, le choix d'un nom et d'un pronom adaptés et l'apparence vestimentaire sont des façons courantes d'exprimer son identité sexuelle. Certaines personnes trans prennent aussi des moyens médicaux pour assurer la correspondance entre leur corps et leur identité sexuelle. En français, le terme « expression de genre » tend à s'installer en remplacement du terme « expression de l'identité sexuelle ». La présente politique utilise le terme « expression de l'identité sexuelle » étant donné qu'il s'agit du terme figurant dans le *Code des droits de la personne* de l'Ontario. La CODP reconnaît toutefois la valeur synonymique du terme « expression de genre ».» *Politique sur la prévention de la discrimination fondée sur l'identité sexuelle et l'expression de l'identité sexuelle*, *supra* note 14, Annexe B : Glossaire des termes associés à l'identité sexuelle et à l'expression de l'identité sexuelle, à la p 64.

[20]Voir par exemple *Sojourner c Conseil de la justice administrative*, 2014 QCCS 5071.

[21]Voir Commission ontarienne des droits de la personne, *Position de la CODP sur les codes vestimentaires sexualisés et fondés sur le sexe*, Toronto, Ontario (sans date).

[22]Voir *Barksey v Four Corners Medical Walk In Clinic/Northwood Medical Clinics Inc*, 2016 HRTO 1116 aux para 36 et 37. Le demandeur plaide qu'il a été victime de discrimination basée sur son handicap et sur son expression de genre (un homme qui parle fort) parce que la clinique médicale a refusé de lui remettre son dossier et de lui permettre d'enregistrer les conversations avec le personnel de la clinique. Il aurait alors élevé la voix et aurait été expulsé de la clinique. L'argument de la discrimination fondée sur l'expression de genre est rejeté par le tribunal.

Les employeurs, les locateurs et les personnes qui dispensent des services au grand public (par exemple, des restaurateurs, des tenanciers de bars, des centres sportifs) sont soumis à une obligation d'accommodement raisonnable: ils doivent tenter d'accommoder de façon satisfaisante les personnes trans qui subissent de la discrimination, sans contrainte excessive pour l'auteur de la discrimination.[23] Par exemple, le code vestimentaire en milieu de travail doit être flexible et permettre aux personnes trans de s'habiller selon le genre auquel elles s'identifient, tout en respectant des mesures de sécurité, s'il y a lieu. Les personnes trans doivent avoir accès à des vestiaires et des toilettes selon le genre auquel elles s'identifient.[24]

Les tribunaux ont reconnu de la discrimination fondée sur l'identité de genre en matière de logement,[25] d'accès à des lieux publics (toilettes),[26] d'emploi,[27] dans les rapports entre la police et les personnes trans[28] et dans les rapports entre un juge administratif et une personne trans.[29]

Dans le domaine de l'immigration, le Canada a accordé le statut de réfugié à des personnes trans dont la sécurité était menacée dans leur pays d'origine.[30] Les autorités de l'immigration ne peuvent exiger une transition médicale pour modifier la mention du sexe sur un certificat de citoyenneté.[31]

Depuis l'automne 2016, des voyageurs étrangers détenant des passeports sans mention de sexe peuvent choisir leur sexe dans la demande d'autorisation de voyage électronique (dont la mention « non spécifié »).[32] Le gouvernement fédéral a

[23]Sur les fondements de l'accommodement raisonnable en droit du travail, voir *Colombie-Britannique (Public Service Employee Relations Commission) c BCGSEU (Meiorin)*, [1999] 3 RCS 3.

[24]Voir Sarah-Maude Lefebvre, « Les élèves transgenres dans le vestiaire de leur choix », Journal de Montréal, (21 mars 2016). En ligne : https://www.journaldemontreal.com/2016/03/21/les-eleves-transgenres-dans-le-vestiaire-de-leur-choix. En Ontario, les entraineurs de hockey devront suivre une formation sur l'identité de genre. (19 juillet 2017). En ligne : https://ici.radio-canada.ca/nouvelle/1045954/formations-obligatoires-identite-de-genre-hockey-ontario.

[25]*Voir McMahon v Wilkinson*, 2015 HRTO 1019 (CanLII).

[26]*Voir Lewis v Sugar Daddys Nightclub*, *supra* note 16; *Sheridan v Sanctuary Investments Ltd (c.o.b. B.J.'s Lounge)*, [1999] BCHRTD no 43.

[27]Voir entre autres *Vanderputten v Seydaco Packaging Corp, supra* note 17*; Montreuil c Canada (Les Forces canadiennes)*, 2006 TCDP 54 (CanLII); G Bauer et al, « We've Got Work to Do: Workplace Discrimination and Employment Challenges for Trans People in Ontario, » Trans PULSE e-Bulletin 2(1), May 30, 2011; Marie Geoffroy et Line Chamberland, « Discrimination des minorités sexuelles et de genre au travail : quelles implications pour la santé mentale ? » (2015) 40:3 Santé mentale au Québec 145; *Québec (Commission des droits de la personne et des droits de la jeunesse) c Maison des jeunes, supra* note 11.

[28]*Voir Sojourner c Conseil de la justice administrative, supra* note 20.

[29]*Voir Dawson v Vancouver Police Board (no 2)*, 2015 BCHRT 54.

[30]Voir entre autres *X (Re)*, 2011 CanLII 67655 (CA CISR); *X (Re)*, 2013 CanLII 73865 (CA CISR).

[31]*Voir Chédor v Canada (Citizenship and Immigration)*, 2016 FC 1205 (CanLII) (une femme trans n'ayant pas subi la transition médicale).

[32]Voir le formulaire pour faire une demande d'AVE : http://www.cic.gc.ca/francais/visiter/ave-commencer.asp.

annoncé en 2017 que la mention X peut être ajoutée sur les documents officiels canadiens, tels que les passeports[33]. Dans le système fédéral canadien, il va sans dire que cette règle uniforme à certains égards, pour les passeports, ne peut avoir un impact direct et uniforme sur l'état civil d'une personne, qui est de compétence provinciale ou territoriale. Cela dépend du droit applicable en matière d'état civil. L'Ontario et l'Alberta permettent l'indication d'un sexe neutre sur les documents officiels.[34]

Enfin, la protection contre la propagande haineuse s'étend maintenant au groupe identifiable par l'identité et l'expression de genre.[35]

Afin de combattre entre autres l'homophobie, la transphobie et l'intimidation envers les étudiant-e-s trans à l'école, des lois provinciales prévoient des mesures pour contrer cette situation.[36] Les écoles sont soumises à l'obligation d'accommodement envers les étudiant-e-s trans et doivent adopter des plans d'action pour enrayer toute forme de discrimination.

Les droits des prisonnier-ère-s trans dans les prisons fédérales appellent des commentaires. Les Services correctionnels du Canada ont changé leur politique au sujet des prisonnier-ère-s trans.[37] Ceux-ci et celles-ci sont placés dans les établissements en fonction de leur identité de genre et non de leurs organes

[33]Voir Immigration et Citoyenneté Canada, en ligne : https://www.canada.ca/fr/immigration-refugies-citoyennete/services/passeports-canadiens/changer-sexe.html.

[34]Voir ci-dessous notre développement sur la mention du sexe au registre de l'état civil.

[35]*Loi modifiant la Loi canadienne sur les droits de la personne et le Code criminel, supra* note 10, art 318 (4) C cr.

[36]Voir en Ontario : *Loi sur l'éducation*, LRO 1990, c E.2 (version du 30 mai 2017), art 1, définition d'intimidation (bullying); motif de l'identité sexuelle et de l'expression de l'identité sexuelle; art 300 et s pour des mesures pour contrer l'intimidation entre élèves. Le même genre de loi existe au Manitoba : *The Public Schools Amendment Act (Safe and Inclusive Schools)/Loi modifiant la Loi sur les écoles publiques (milieux scolaires favorisant la sécurité et l'inclusivité)*, 2012 bill 18, 2013, 2e Sess, 40e Lég, Manitoba, 2012 [Bill 18]. Voir Joshua David Michael Shaw, « The Queer Child Deserves Protection: Bill 18 and the Justifiable Infringement of Denominational Schools' Freedom of Religion » (2015) 38 Man L J 331. Au Québec : *Loi visant à prévenir et à combattre l'intimidation et la violence à l'école*, LQ 2012, c 19 modifiant la *Loi sur l'instruction publique*, RLRQ, c I-13.3, art 75.1, 63.1. Voir Line Chamberland et al, « Les violences homophobes et leurs impacts sur la persévérance scolaire des adolescents au Québec » (2013) 8 Recherches & Éducations 99; M-P Petit et al, « Jeunes de minorités sexuelles victimes d'homophobie en milieu scolaire : quels facteurs de protection? » (2011) 30 (2) J of Community Mental Health/R can de santé mentale communautaire 13.

[37]Kathleen Harris, «Trudeau promises to house trans inmates based on gender identity, 'Trans rights are human rights,' PM says, but pledge runs counter to new prison policy », (12 janvier 2017); Kathleen Harris, CBC News, « Correctional Service flip-flops on transgender inmate placement policy, Reversal comes day after Trudeau promise; equality rights for incarcerated trans Canadians », Jan 13th 2017; voir Services correctionnels du Canada, Lignes directrices, dysphorie sexuelle, en ligne : http://www.csc-scc.gc.ca/politiques-et-lois/800-5-gl-fra.shtml. L'Ontario et la Colombie-Britannique ont adopté des politiques identiques pour les prisons de compétence provinciale.

génitaux.[38] Afin d'obtenir une transition médicale, une personne incarcérée doit avoir vécu dans le genre auquel elle s'identifie pour 12 mois consécutifs et avec la recommandation d'un médecin.[39] Elle n'a pas besoin de prouver, comme c'était le cas auparavant, qu'elle a vécu sous ce genre dans la communauté avant son incarcération.

Les Services correctionnels du Canada doivent assumer les coûts de la transition médicale. Ils déterminent sans délai l'échéancier pour la transition médicale en prenant en compte la date de libération de la personne. Les services du médecin qui avait déjà traité la personne trans avant son incarcération sont retenus. La direction de l'établissement doit s'assurer que le personnel qui a des contacts réguliers avec les personnes trans incarcérées possède les connaissances nécessaires pour répondre efficacement à leurs besoins. Les personnes trans incarcérées peuvent porter des vêtements selon le genre auquel elles s'identifient.

3 Le droit de la famille

Dans le domaine du droit de la famille, les changements législatifs pour reconnaitre la diversité des familles ont été amorcés par des actions devant les tribunaux. Les demandeurs et demanderesses ont fait valoir leur droit à l'égalité protégé par la *Charte canadienne.*[40] Les législateurs ont ensuite modifié leur droit.[41] Nous examinons les questions de conjugalité et parentalité, d'accès à la procréation assistée (PA) et de détermination de la filiation, dans la mesure où elles intéressent les membres de la communauté LGBTQ+. Tant au Québec que dans les provinces ou territoires de common law, le droit de la famille se transforme pour reconnaitre la diversité des familles.

---

[38]Selon une décision antérieure, une femme trans n'ayant pas subi une transition médicale devait être placée dans une prison pour hommes afin de protéger les femmes (cisgenres) dans les prisons. *Kavanagh v Canada Attorney General*, 2001 CHRD no 21. Voir Allison Smith, « Stories of Os: transgender women, monstrous bodies, and the Canadian prison system » (2014) 23 Dal J Leg Stud 149. Voir aussi *Lovado v BC (Ministry of Public Safety & Solicitor General)*, 2017 BCHRT 115. Au sujet des fouilles à nu de prisonnier-ère-s trans, voir Kyle Kirkup, « Indocile Bodies: Gender Identity and Strip Searches in Canadian Criminal Law » (2009) 24 Can J L & Soc 107.

[39]Voir Kathleen Harris, CBC News, « Correctional Service flip-flops on transgender inmate placement policy, Reversal comes day after Trudeau promise; equality rights for incarcerated trans Canadians », *supra* note 37. Voir la politique, en ligne, *supra* note 37.

[40]*Supra* note 12.

[41]Voir notamment Michel Morin, « La longue marche vers l'égalité des conjoints de même sexe » dans Pierre-Claude Lafond et Brigitte Lefebvre, dir, *L'union civile. Nouveaux modèles de conjugalité et de parentalité au 21e siècle. Actes du colloque du Groupe de réflexion en droit privé*, Cowansville, Yvon Blais, 2002, 63 aux para 75 à 81.

3.1 La conjugalité et la parentalité

Depuis 2005, la loi fédérale sur le mariage, qui prévoit les conditions de fond du mariage, permet le mariage civil entre personnes de même sexe[42]. Toutes les provinces ou territoires au Canada reconnaissent le mariage civil pour les couples de même sexe.[43] Au Québec, une autre forme d'union, l'union civile, est instituée dès 2002.[44] N'ayant pas compétence sur les conditions de fond du mariage, le Québec adopte l'union civile, calquée sur le mariage, mais ouverte aux conjoint-e-s de même sexe, pour les accommoder dans l'attente de l'action du gouvernement fédéral, qui adopte le mariage pour tous en 2005.[45] Cette forme de conjugalité est peu utilisée aujourd'hui.[46]

Les conjoint-e-s de fait de même sexe sont reconnus dans les lois à caractère social et fiscal. Dans toutes les provinces, sauf au Québec,[47] en cas de rupture

---

[42]*Loi sur le mariage civil*, LC 2005, c 33, art 2 et 4. Avant la modification de 2005, les tribunaux dans neuf provinces avaient déjà reconnu la légalité du mariage entre personnes de même sexe. Voir aussi *Renvoi relatif au mariage entre personnes de même sexe*, [2004] 3 RCS 698 et *Loi d'harmonisation n° 1 du droit fédéral avec le droit civil*, LC 2004, c 4. Sur la reconnaissance du mariage de conjoints de même sexe au Canada, voir Robert Leckey et Nicholas Bala, « Les trente premières années de la charte canadienne en droit de la famille » (2012) 42 RDUS 409 aux pp 419 et s. Pour un historique de l'évolution des droits des personnes LGBT au Canada entre 1993 et 2003, voir John Fisher, « Outlaws or In-laws? Successes and Challenges in the Struggle for LGBT Equality » (2003-2004) 49 R D McGill 1183; Michelle Giroux, « Le mariage homosexuel : perspective québéco-canadienne » dans Susana Navas Navarro, dir, *Matrimonio homosexual y adopcion. Perspectiva nacional e internacional*, coll Juridica General. Jornadas, 2006, Madrid, Editorial Reus, aux pp 17-44.

[43]Québec : Code civil du Québec (CcQ), RLRQ c CCQ-1991, art 365 et *Loi d'interprétation*, RLRQ c I-16: définition de conjoint; Ontario : *Loi sur le mariage*, LRO 1990, c M.3 : on utilise l'expression neutre « personne »; Nouveau- Brunswick : *Loi sur le mariage*, LRN-B 2011, c 188, art 2 (1); Manitoba : *Loi sur le mariage*, CPLM c M50, art 29 ; Terre-Neuve et Labrador : *Marriage Act*, SNL 2009, c M-1.02, art 2 : (l); Ile-du-Prince Édouard : *Marriage* Act, RSPEI 1988, c M-3; Alberta : *Marriage Act*, RSA 2000, c M-5, art 22 (1); Saskatchewan : *Loi de 1995 sur le mariage*, LS 1995, c M-4.1 : on utilise l'expression neutre « parties » ou « personnes »; Yukon : *Loi sur le mariage*, LRY 2002, c 146, art 44; Territoires du Nord-Ouest : *Marriage Act*, LTN-O 2017, c 2, art 1; Nunavut : *Loi sur le mariage*, LRTN-O (Nu) 1988, c M-4 : on utilise l'expression neutre « les parties », art 1 (f); Nouvelle-Écosse : *Solemnization of Marriage Ac*t, RSNS 1989, c 436 : on utilise l'expression neutre « persons »; art 10 (1), 22 (2), 45 (1); Colombie-Britannique : *Marriage Act*, RSBC 1996, c 282 : on utilise l'expression neutre « parties ».

[44]*Loi instituant l'union civile et établissant de nouvelles règles de filiation*, LQ 2002, c 6.

[45]*Supra* note 42.

[46]« En moyenne, les unions civiles représentent seulement 1% des unions légalisées chaque année (en additionnant les mariages et les unions civiles). Bien que cette part soit plus élevée parmi les unions de conjoints de même sexe (4 % en 2016), ces derniers préfèrent aussi largement le mariage à l'union civile. » Anne Binette Charbonneau, « Les mariages au Québec en 2016 », n° 57, Institut de la statistique du Québec, Québec, juillet 2017.

[47]*A c Québec (Procureur général)*, 2013 CSC 5. Dans ce jugement serré (5 juges contre 4), le plus haut tribunal du pays a refusé d'invalider l'article 585 CcQ au motif qu'il était discriminatoire en traitant différemment les couples mariés et non mariés lors de la rupture. Au total, cinq juges ont

conjugale, le conjoint de fait économiquement vulnérable pourra obtenir une pension alimentaire de l'autre conjoint-e, selon ses besoins et la capacité de payer de son ex-conjoint-e. Partout au pays, les conjoint-e-s de même sexe peuvent adopter des enfants.[48] Les tribunaux ont décidé que le fait d'être un parent trans n'affecte en rien ses capacités parentales ou ses droits de garde; le seul critère qui prévaut en cette matière est celui de l'intérêt de l'enfant.[49]

3.2 L'accès à la procréation assistée (PA)

Selon leur situation particulière, des personnes trans infertiles (qui ont subi une transition médicale et qui ont été stérilisées) ou des couples de même sexe (dont un des membres est trans) auront parfois besoin d'accéder aux technologies de procréation assistée, aux gamètes et aux services de mère porteuse[50] pour concevoir des enfants. Il va sans dire que d'autres n'en auront pas besoin, par exemple un couple d'hommes dont l'un est trans, sans avoir été par ailleurs stérilisé, pourrait avoir un enfant sans l'aide de la procréation assistée. Néanmoins, la communauté LGBTQ+ rencontre parfois des difficultés d'accès à ces services, qui sont pensés pour des couples cisgenres et hétérosexuels, ce qui équivaut à de la discrimination selon certains auteurs.[51]

---

considéré qu'il y avait discrimination au sens de l'article 15 de la *Charte canadienne*, *supra* note 12, mais pour la juge en chef McLachlin, cette discrimination se justifie dans une société libre et démocratique en vertu de l'article 1. La positionde la juge en chef a permis de maintenir la validité des articles du Code civil du Québec qui reconnaissent seulement les couples mariés en cas de rupture conjugale. Voir Robert Leckey, « Strange Bedfellows » (2014) 64:5 U of T L J 641.

[48]Au Canada généralement, voir Lori E Ross et al, « Policy, Practice, and Personal Narratives: Experiences of LGBTQ People with Adoption in Ontario, Canada » (2009) 12 Adoption Quarterly 272; Lori E Ross et al, « Policy and Practice Regarding Adoption by Sexual and Gender Minority People in Ontario » (2009) 35-4 Canadian Public Policy 451.

[49]En Ontario, voir entre autres *Ghidoni v Ghidoni*, 1995 CanLII 1018 (BCSC); *Forrester v Saliba*, 2000 CanLII 28722 (Ont Ct J); *Boyce v Boyce*, 2004 CanLII 1602 (Ont Ct J). LGBTQ Parenting Network, *Transgender Parents and Ontario Family Law: parenting through transition, together or apart*, Toronto, 2014. Au Québec, voir entre autres *C (V) (D) c H (E), sub nom Droit de la famille – 133870*, 23 mai 2013, Cour supérieure; *Droit de la famille — 151902*, 2015 QCCS 3615. Émilie Biland et al, «Quelles expériences du droit et de la justice pour les parents LGBTQ+ qui se séparent?», Collection Débats et enjeux (9), Québec : Partenariat derecherche Séparation parentale, recomposition familiale, en ligne: https://arucfamille.ulaval.ca/wp-content/uploads/2021/03/124943_Debats_et_enjeux-1.pdf

[50]Aucun terme n'est neutre. Nous utilisons le terme « mère porteuse » plutôt que « femme porteuse » ou autres. C'est le terme utilisé dans la *Loi sur la procréation assistée*, LC 2004, c 2. La loi ontarienne utilise le terme substitut (« surrogate » dans la version en anglais) pour désigner la femme qui porte l'enfant, art 10, *Loi portant réforme du droit de l'enfance*, LRO 1990, c C.12.

[51]Aucun tribunal canadien ne s'est encore prononcé sur cette question. Certains auteurs considèrent qu'il s'agit de discrimination. Voir Stu Marvel et al, « Listening to LGBTQ People on Assisted Human Reproduction: Access to Reproductive, Material, Services and Facilities » dans Trudo

Au Canada, seule la pratique de la maternité de substitution à titre gratuit est permise par la loi fédérale sur la procréation assistée.[52] Toute forme de rémunération est interdite. Selon un nouveau règlement,[53] seules les catégories de dépenses de la mère porteuse prévues peuvent être remboursées par le parent ou les parents intentionnels sur présentation des reçus. Il s'agit de dépenses de base en lien avec la grossesse et l'accouchement. Cependant, la mesure dans laquelle une convention de mère porteuse est juridiquement contraignante varie d'une province ou d'un territoire à l'autre. Par exemple, le droit québécois prévoit expressément la nullité absolue de telles ententes (art 541 CcQ). Cependant, les tribunaux permettent l'aménagement de la filiation de l'enfant, malgré la nullité de la convention, au nom de l'intérêt supérieur de l'enfant, ce que nous verrons plus bas. En Ontario,[54] en Colombie-Britannique[55] et en Alberta,[56] la convention de préconception est imposée par la loi mais elle est inexécutoire, et la mère porteuse peut décider de garder l'enfant. Cependant, la convention peut être utilisée comme preuve de l'intention à l'égard de la filiation de l'enfant. Dans l'éventualité où la mère porteuse refuse de renoncer à ses droits de filiation (elle dispose de sept jours pour le faire), toute partie à la convention peut saisir le tribunal pour obtenir une déclaration de filiation à l'égard de l'enfant.[57]

Les couples de même sexe trans ne pouvant avoir d'enfant naturellement peuvent éprouver des difficultés à trouver des femmes qui veulent devenir mère porteuse.[58]

Lemmens et al, dir, *Regulating Creation, The Law, Ethics, and Policy of Assisted Human Reproduction*, Toronto, University of Toronto Press, 2017, p 325; Green Datejie et al, « Meeting the Assisted Human Reproduction Needs of Lesbian, Gay, Bisexual, Trans and Queer (LGBTQ) People in Canada : A Fact Sheet for AHR Services Providers », Sherbourne Health Center, Ontario, 2012.

[52] *Loi sur la procréation assistée*, *supra* note 50, art 6 et 12 (art 12 en vigueur le 10 juin 2020). Voir Susan G Drummond, « Fruitful Diversity: Revisiting the Enforceability of Gestational Carriage Contracts » dans Trudo Lemmens et al, dir, *Regulating Creation: the Law, Ethics, and Policy of Assisted Human Reproduction*, Toronto, University of Toronto Press, 2017, p 274.

[53] *Règlement sur le remboursement relatif à la procréation assistée*, DORS/2019-195, *La Gazette du Canada*, Partie II, volume 153, numéro 13, 10 juin 2019 (en vigueur le 10 juin 2020).

[54] *Loi portant réforme du droit de l'enfance*, *supra* note 50, art 10 (9); *Loi de 2016 sur l'égalité de toutes les familles (modifiant des lois en ce qui concerne la filiation et les enregistrements connexes)*, LO 2016 c 23, en vigueur le 1er janvier 2017.

[55] *Family Law Act*, SBC 2011, c 25, art 29 (6).

[56] *Family Law Act*, SA 2003, c F-4, art 8.2 (8), modifiée en 2010.

[57] *Loi portant réforme du droit de l'enfance, supra* note 50, art 10 (6).

[58] Il faut ajouter que le financement associé à la procréation assistée varie d'une province ou d'un territoire à l'autre. L'Ontario a à l'heure actuelle le régime le plus généreux, incluant la possibilité de remboursement dans le cas du recours à une mère porteuse. Sur les coûts couverts par le programme ontarien, voir en ligne : https://www.ontario.ca/page/get-fertility-treatments. Au Québec, le régime public d'assurance-maladie assurait, entre autres, le remboursement de trois cycles stimulés de FIV. Comme le programme était vite devenu très populaire et en conséquence coûteux, d'autant que les conditions d'accès étaient définies très largement, le gouvernement a décidé en 2015 de revoir l'admissibilité et la gratuité des services de PA. Voir *Projet de loi 20, Loi édictant la Loi favorisant l'accès aux services de médecine de famille et de médecine spécialisée et modifiant diverses*

Plusieurs personnes se tournent vers les États-Unis ou d'autres pays pour faire affaire avec des mères porteuses. Le même problème se produit avec l'accès aux ovules et au sperme. Puisque seul le don d'ovules et de sperme est permis au Canada (l'achat directement auprès de la fournisseuse est criminalisé), et que les banques de sperme et d'ovules ne répondent pas à la demande,[59] cette situation force de nombreuses personnes infertiles à les obtenir aux États-Unis ou ailleurs.

Selon le *Règlement sur la sécurité des spermatozoïdes et des ovules*[60], des hommes qui ont eu entre autres des activités sexuelles avec d'autres hommes ne peuvent être donneurs de sperme, sous réserve du programme d'accès spécial.[61] Donc, certaines femmes trans ne peuvent donner leur sperme à des amies lesbiennes qui veulent utiliser les services de cliniques de fertilité.[62]

dispositions législatives en matière de procréation assistée, RLRQ 2015, c 25. Le régime public ne couvrait alors plus que les services d'insémination artificielle ; les personnes ayant recours à la FIV ne bénéficiaient dorénavant que d'un crédit d'impôt. Voir ministère des Finances du Québec, Modification à la liste des frais admissibles à une aide fiscale pour le traitement de l'infertilité et à la suite de la sanction du projet de loi n° 20 (Bulletin d'information n°2015-6), 2015, en ligne : http://www.finances.gouv.qc.ca/documents/bulletins/fr/BULFR_2015-6-f-b.pdf. Depuis mars 2021, un nouveau programme étatique permet le remboursement d'un cycle de FIV par couple ou personne, en excluant, sous toutes réserves, les mères porteuses. *Loi modifiant diverses dispositions en matière de procréation assistée*, LQ 2021, c 2.

[59]Selon des études, 95 % du sperme serait acheté aux États-Unis. Voir Marvel et al, « Listening to LGBTQ People on Assisted Human Reproduction: Access to Reproductive, Material, Services and Facilities », *supra* note 51 à la p 329; Jocelyn Downie et Françoise Baylis, « Transnational Trade in Human Eggs : Law, Policy and (In)action in Canada » (2013) 41 J L Medecine & Ethics 224; Marc-André Sabourin, « Le sperme et l'ovule ne sont pas égaux au Canada », L'Actualité, 10 mars 2016; Françoise Baylis et Jocelyn Downie, « Achieving National Self Sufficiency in Human Eggs for Third Party Reproduction in Canada » (2014) 7:2 International Journal of Feminist Approaches to Bioethics 164; Susan G Drummond et Sara R Cohen, « Eloquent (In)action: Enforcement and Prosecutorial Restraint in the Transnational Trade in Human Eggs as Deep Ambivalence about the Law » (2014) 26:2 CJWL 206.

[60]*Règlement sur la sécurité des spermatozoïdes et des ovules*, DORS/2019-192, Gazette du Canada, Partie II, volume 153, numéro 13 (10 juin 2019). Voir Stu Marvel, « Tony Danza Is My Sperm Donor? : Queer Kinship and the Impact of Canadian Regulations around Sperm Donation » (2013) 25 CJWL 221; Fiona Kelly, « One of these Families is not like the Others : The Legal Response to Non-normative Queer Parenting in Canada » (2013) 51 Alta L Rev 1.

[61]Le *Règlement sur la sécurité des spermatozoïdes et des ovules, ibid,* exige que tous les donneurs de spermatozoïdes et d'ovules, y compris les hommes ayant eu des relations sexuelles avec d'autres hommes, soient soumis à une évaluation ayant pour but de déterminer les facteurs de risque de transmission de maladies infectieuses et génétiques. L'exclusion des hommes ayant eu des relations sexuelles avec d'autres hommes concerne les donneurs soumis au processus régulier. Voir en ligne : https://www.canada.ca/fr/sante-canada/services/medicaments-produits-sante/produits-biologiques-radiopharmaceutiques-therapies-genetiques/information-demandes-presentations/lignes-directrices/programme-acces-special-sperm/guide-sperme-donneur-admissible-autorisation-acces-special.html.

[62]Voir Fiona Kelly, « An Alternative Conception: The Legality of Home Insemination under Canada's *Assisted Human Reproduction Act* » (2010) 26:1 CJFL 149.

3.3 La détermination de la filiation

La détermination de la filiation peut causer certains problèmes surtout pour le parent qui n'a pas fourni ses gamètes, entre autres en cas de recours aux services d'une mère porteuse. Certaines provinces canadiennes ont modifié leur droit de la famille pour refléter les nouvelles réalités sociales.

Les personnes trans seules ou en couple peuvent avoir accès à la PA pour être parents (avec un don de gamètes ou d'embryons, ou par mère porteuse). La question de la filiation se pose pour la personne qui n'a pas fourni ses gamètes. Ainsi, un couple formé d'un homme trans et d'une autre femme qui désire concevoir un enfant aura besoin d'un don de sperme. Si elles font affaire avec un donneur connu (un ami), celui-ci pourra, selon la province ou le territoire où la procréation a lieu, demander à être reconnu comme le père légal de l'enfant, même si une entente entre les parties prévoit le contraire. Selon cette alternative, la conjointe ou le conjoint qui n'a pas fourni ses gamètes ne sera pas reconnu dans le cas où la loi limite le nombre de parents à deux, comme au Québec.[63]

La question de la filiation se pose aussi pour la personne trans qui a fourni ses gamètes pour concevoir un enfant, par exemple, un homme trans qui aurait fait congeler ses ovules avant la transition médicale. Dans certains cas, la filiation de cette personne pourrait ne pas être reconnue si la mère porteuse garde l'enfant et que son mari est considéré comme le père légal de l'enfant par le jeu des présomptions.

Quelques provinces de common law ont adopté des législations pour régler la filiation par PA.[64] Par exemple, en Ontario, avant l'adoption de la loi entrée en vigueur en 2017, la *Loi de 2016 sur l'égalité de toutes les familles,*[65] les parents qui faisaient appel à un don de gamètes pour concevoir un enfant devaient toujours

[63]CcQ, art 538.2. Par ailleurs, les tribunaux québécois se sont prononcés dans le cadre d'un scénario de pluriparentalité où trois adultes jouent un rôle parental, mais où deux mères étaient inscrites à l'acte de naissance de l'enfant conçu avec don par insémination artificielle faite à la maison (Il n'est pas clair si l'enfant a été concu par relation sexuelle. Le tribunal ne détermine pas de quelle façon la conception de l'enfant s'est faite. Le géniteur a demandé à être reconnu comme le père légal. La décision de première instance avait rompu le lien de filiation entre l'enfant et la mère non biologique ayant subi une transition médicale. Sous la plume du juge Kasirer, la Cour d'appel a infirmé cette décision et a maintenu le lien de filiation maternelle par procréation assistée entre l'homme trans (autre mère à l'état civil) et l'enfant. L'article 538.2 CcQ permettant au donneur par relation sexuelle de réclamer sa paternité au détriment de la mère non biologique (l'homme trans) dans l'année de la naissance de l'enfant n'était pas applicable, l'enfant étant âgé de plus d'un an. Voir *Droit de la famille – 18968,* 2018 QCCS 1900, infirmé en appel par *Droit de la famille – 191677*, 2019 QCCA 1386. Les deux instances reconnaissent toutefois que le droit québécois ne permet pas la pluriparenté. Le demandeur ne désirait pas la reconnaissance de la pluriparentalité.

[64]C'est notamment le cas de Terre-Neuve, *Vital Statistics Act*, SNL 2009, c V-6.01, de la Nouvelle-Écosse, *Birth Registration Regulation*, NS Reg 390/2007 (*Vital Statistics Act*, RSNS 1989, c 494), de la Colombie-Britannique, *Family Law Act*, *supra* note 55, de l'Alberta, *Family Law Act*, *supra* note 56 et tout récemment l'Ontario, *Loi de 2016 sur l'égalité de toutes les familles (modifiant des lois en ce qui concerne la filiation et les enregistrements connexes), supra* note 54.

[65]*Loi de 2016 sur l'égalité de toutes les familles (modifiant des lois en ce qui concerne la filiation et les enregistrements connexes), ibid.*

s'adresser au tribunal pour obtenir une déclaration de filiation à la suite de la naissance de leur enfant, car aucune disposition législative n'empêchait le géniteur d'établir un lien de filiation avec l'enfant conçu à la suite de son don de gamètes. Avant l'adoption de cette loi, la Cour d'appel de l'Ontario a rendu la première décision au Canada reconnaissant la pluriparenté[66]. En l'occurrence, il y avait trois parents : le père (le géniteur, un donneur de sperme connu), la mère ayant donné naissance et une autre mère (la conjointe de la mère ayant donné naissance avec laquelle elle avait conclu le projet parental). Aujourd'hui, l'article 9 de la *Loi portant réforme du droit de l'enfance* leur permettrait de faire reconnaître cette pluriparenté sans s'adresser au tribunal, sous réserve d'avoir préparé une convention à cet effet avant la conception.[67]

Une décision de l'Alberta illustre les difficultés de parents homosexuels n'ayant pas eu recours à leurs gamètes (parents intentionnels) à faire reconnaitre leur filiation.[68] La saga judiciaire, qui a duré six ans, a débuté en 2007 par une demande de droit d'accès à l'enfant par le père homosexuel n'ayant pas utilisé ses gamètes pour concevoir l'enfant. Dans cette affaire, un couple de lesbiennes et un couple de gais se sont entendus pour concevoir, à l'aide d'une mère porteuse, deux enfants qui vivront dans les deux familles (un enfant par famille). Le couple gai se sépare alors que l'enfant est âgé de trois ans. L'ex-conjoint du père de l'enfant n'a plus de contact avec celui-ci (la mère porteuse et le père ayant fourni ses gamètes y faisant obstacle), même s'il en avait pris soin pendant trois ans. La loi de l'Alberta ne reconnaissait pas le lien de filiation du conjoint du père n'ayant pas fourni ses gamètes (comme il le fait pour les couples lesbiens et hétérosexuels mariés ou pas).

Le tribunal a déclaré cette loi invalide au sens de l'article 15 (1) de la *Charte canadienne*, parce que discriminatoire à l'égard des couples gais[69] et de plus, elle ne respectait pas l'intérêt supérieur de l'enfant. Le tribunal a utilisé son pouvoir discrétionnaire *parens patriae* pour reconnaitre un droit d'accès au père demandeur. Même le père génétique des deux enfants n'était pas reconnu comme le parent au sens de la loi, parce qu'il n'était pas le conjoint de la mère. Puisque la loi ne permettait pas de reconnaitre plus de deux parents, la mère (chez qui l'enfant n'avait pas habité) et le père non génétique (qui n'avait pas eu de contact pendant six ans

---

[66]Voir *AA c BB*, 2007 ONCA 2 (appel à la Cour suprême refusée, 2007 3 SRC 124) : Comme la loi de l'Ontario ne permettait pas à un enfant d'avoir plus de deux parents, le tribunal a utilisé sa compétence *parens patriae* pour ce faire. Sur cette décision, voir Nicole Laviolette, « Dad, Mom-and Mom: The Ontario Court of Appeal's Decision in *A.A. v B.B.* » (2007) 86:3 Can Bar Rev 665; Elaine Craig, « Converging Feminist and Queer Legal Theories : Family Feuds and Family Ties » (2010) 28 Windsor Y B Access Just 209.

[67]*Loi portant réforme du droit de l'enfance, supra* note 50. Voir Robert Leckey, « One Parent, Three Parents: Judges and Ontario's All Families Are Equal Act, 2016 » (2019) 33:3 International Journal of Law, Policy and the Family 298.

[68]*DWH c DJR*, 2011 ABQB 608, 2013 ABCA 240 : Sur cette décision, voir Kelly, « One of these Families is not like the Others : The Legal Response to Non-normative Queer Parenting in Canada », *supra* note 60.

[69]Une décision de l'Alberta avait reconnu le droit de deux femmes d'être mères : *Fraess v Alberta (Minister of Justice and Attorney General)*, 2005 ABQB 889.

avec l'enfant) ont été reconnus comme parents légaux de l'enfant. Le père génétique, chez qui l'enfant habitait, n'a pas été reconnu comme parent légal, mais comme donneur de sperme. À la suite de cette décision, la *Family Law Act* de l'Alberta a été modifiée pour permettre aux couples gais qui signent une entente avec une mère porteuse d'être reconnus comme les deux pères légaux,[70] si celle-ci accepte de renoncer à son droit de filiation. La loi albertaine ne reconnait pas plus de deux parents.

Comme l'affirme une auteure, les parents hétérosexuels (dont un n'a pas fourni ses gamètes) n'ont pas eu à se battre devant les tribunaux pour faire reconnaitre leur droit, car ils profitent d'une présomption de paternité. Par exemple, le mari ou le conjoint de la mère qui a eu recours à un don de sperme est le père légal de l'enfant.[71]

3.3.1 Le nouveau droit de la famille: La Colombie-Britannique et l'Ontario

La Colombie-Britannique et l'Ontario sont les deux provinces canadiennes à avoir réformé leur droit de la famille le plus récemment, respectivement en 2013[72] et en 2017,[73] en mettant de côté le modèle traditionnel de deux parents génétiques. Ces provinces possèdent les régimes parentaux les plus ouverts à toute forme de réalités familiales au pays. Nous décrivons les règles en matière de filiation qui sont d'un intérêt pour les personnes trans. Nous renvoyons les lecteurs à un tableau analytique du droit de la filiation dans toutes les provinces canadiennes.[74]

En Colombie-Britannique, les parties, future mère porteuse et futurs parents intentionnels, doivent rédiger un contrat avant la conception de l'enfant.[75] Ce contrat

[70] *Family Law Act*, *supra* note 56, art 8.1 (3).

[71] Voir Kelly, « One of these Families is not like the Others : The Legal Response to Non-normative Queer Parenting in Canada », *supra* note 60 à la p 19.

[72] *Family Law Act, supra* note 55.

[73] *Loi de 2016 sur l'égalité de toutes les familles (modifiant des lois en ce qui concerne la filiation et les enregistrements connexes), supra* note 54. La partie 3 porte sur la filiation. Voir Dave Snow, « Litigating Parentage : Equality Rights, LGBTQ Mobilization and Ontario's All Families Are Equal Act » (2017) 32 :3 Can J L & Soc 329; Stefanie Carsley, « Reconceiving Quebec's Laws on Surrogate Motherhood » (2018) 96 Rev B Can 120 aux pp 150 et s.

[74] Voir Carol Rogerson, « Determining Parentage in Cases Involving Assisted Reproduction: An Urgent Need for Provincial Legislative Action » dans Trudo Lemmens et al, dir, *Regulating Creation, The Law, Ethics, and Policy of Assisted Human Reproduction*, Toronto, University of Toronto Press, 2017, p 91. Il faut noter que ce tableau n'est pas à jour en ce qui concerne l'Ontario, tel que déjà mentionné depuis l'adoption du nouveau droit de la famille le 1er janvier 2017. Voir également Rapport du Comité consultatif sur le droit de la famille, Alain Roy, prés, *Pour un droit de la famille adapté aux nouvelles réalités conjugales et familiales*, Québec, Ministère de la Justice du Québec, 2015, Annexe III, pour le droit applicable à la maternité de substitution dans les provinces canadiennes.

[75] *Family Law Act*, *supra* note 55, art 29 (2) (en vigueur mars 2013). Voir Carsley, « Reconceiving Quebec's Laws on Surrogate Motherhood », *supra* note 73. En matière de filiation, le nouveau droit

prévoit, entre autres, que la future mère porteuse, qui peut avoir ou non fourni le matériel génétique,[76] sera la mère de l'enfant conçu grâce à la procréation assistée, mais après la naissance de l'enfant, si elle consent par écrit, elle remettra l'enfant aux parents intentionnels, renoncera à ses droits sur l'enfant et ne sera pas considérée comme le parent légal de l'enfant.[77] Un délai de 30 jours est prévu pour remettre l'enfant. Les parents intentionnels, qui peuvent être de même sexe ou de sexes différents (il peut aussi s'agir d'un seul parent), sont présumés être les parents légaux de l'enfant, qu'ils aient fourni ou non le matériel génétique.[78] Les parties n'ont pas l'obligation d'obtenir des avis juridiques indépendants avant la signature du contrat de préconception. Si les parties n'ont pas rédigé de contrat de préconception, la procédure judiciaire d'adoption s'applique.

En cas de conflit, le contrat entre les parties ne lie pas la mère porteuse, qui peut toujours changer d'avis et garder l'enfant.[79] Son consentement à agir comme mère porteuse n'équivaut pas à son consentement à renoncer à ses droits parentaux. Le contrat peut cependant servir de preuve de l'intention des parties au sujet de la filiation de l'enfant. Un tribunal prendra une décision sur la filiation de l'enfant, selon son intérêt supérieur.

Les parents intentionnels ne peuvent pas changer d'avis.[80] La loi prévoit qu'ils seront les parents légaux. Si la mère porteuse et les parents intentionnels refusent l'enfant, ce dernier sera pris en charge par les autorités, mais les parents intentionnels demeurent les parents légaux et sont tenus des obligations qui en découlent.[81]

Les parents de l'enfant (les parents intentionnels) doivent dans les trente jours de la naissance de l'enfant compléter et remettre au registraire général les renseignements nécessaires sur le formulaire prescrit.[82] Le transfert de filiation par voie administrative a été préféré à un processus judiciaire.[83] Il n'est donc pas

---

de la Colombie-Britannique reprend en grande partie la *Loi uniforme de 2010 sur le statut de l'enfant* de la Conférence pour l'harmonisation des lois au Canada. En ligne : http://www.ulcc.ca/fr/lois-uniformes-nouvelle-structure/lois-uniformes-courantes/655-lois-uniformes-courantes/statut-de-l-enfant-1/1414-loi-uniforme-de-2010-sur-le-statut-de-l-enfant.

[76] *Family Law Act*, *ibid* art 20 (1).

[77] *Ibid* art 29 (2) b).

[78] *Ibid.*

[79] *Ibid* art 29 (6).

[80] *Ibid* art 29 (3) (a) et (b) (i)).

[81] Selon l'analyse de Drummond, « Fruitful Diversity: Revisiting the Enforceability of Gestational Carriage Contracts», *supra* note 52 à la p 290.

[82] *Vital Statistics Act*, RSBC 1996, c 479, art 3 (1.1).

[83] Pour les cas de PA interprovinciale : *DD (Re),* 2016 BCSC 22. Les requérants sont un couple homosexuel du Québec. L'ovule provient de la sœur de l'un d'eux et le sperme est celui de l'autre conjoint. Les ovules ont été prélevés dans une clinique au Connecticut en 2011, puis fertilisés et cryopréservés jusqu'en 2015, alors que le couple signe un « surrogacy agreement » avec une mère porteuse canadienne. Celle-ci se fait implanter l'un des embryons en Colombie-Britannique. Le certificat de naissance identifie les deux hommes comme les parents, mais un avocat du Québec recommande aux deux hommes d'obtenir un avis de la cour afin que soit reconnue leur filiation au Québec. La Cour conclut que le « surrogacy agreement » respecte les exigences de l'article 29 du

nécessaire de présenter une requête devant le tribunal pour faire corriger les registres de l'état civil.

Selon la volonté des parties, la mère porteuse ou le donneur de sperme peut être un des parents légaux, avec les parents intentionnels. Dans ce cas, l'article sur la pluriparentalité s'applique, qui reconnait la possibilité de trois parents.[84]

En Ontario, la loi apporte des changements majeurs à la détermination de la filiation. C'est l'intention et non plus la biologie qui devient son principal fondement.[85] La femme qui accouche, selon l'application de la maxime de droit romain *mater semper certa est,* est la mère de l'enfant, sous réserve d'une exception en cas de recours à une mère porteuse.[86] Tout comme en Colombie-Britannique, une série de présomptions s'applique pour déterminer qui est l'autre parent biologique de l'enfant en cas de relation sexuelle.[87]Ces présomptions peuvent parfois mener à des réponses contradictoires et peuvent être repoussées dans ce cas.[88]

Par ailleurs, si une convention a été conclue par écrit entre les parties avant la conception selon laquelle la personne fournira son sperme, sans être partie au projet parental, alors elle ne sera pas le parent légal de l'enfant.[89] Sans avoir recours au tribunal, la filiation de l'enfant pourra être établie. Cette convention peut inclure au

Family Law Act de la Colombie-Britannique. Le juge précise également que la voie administrative a déjà établi la filiation, mais qu'un avis de la cour est nécessaire pour que cette filiation soit reconnue dans la province d'origine des parents et que l'article 31 de la *Family Law Act* permet au tribunal de dissiper une incertitude. Le juge déclare les deux requérants parents légaux de l'enfant.

[84]*Family Law Act, supra* note 55, art 27. Voir Fiona Kelly, « Multiple-Parent Families Under British Columbia's New Family Law Act: A Challenge to the Supremacy of the Nuclear Family or a Method by which to Preserve Biological Ties and Opposite-Sex Parenting? » (2014) 47 UBC L Rev 565. Voir le tableau portant sur la Colombie-Britannique dans Rogerson, « Determining Parenthood in Cases Involving Assisted Reproduction : An Urgent Need for Provincial Legislative Action», *supra* note 74 aux pp 100 et s; voir note 53 de ce texte. Pour un enfant avec trois parents en Colombie-Britannique, voir Abigale Subdhan, « Vancouver baby becomes first person to have three parents named on birth certificate in B.C. », National Post,10 février 2014.

[85]*Loi portant réforme du droit de l'enfance, supra* note 50, art 4 à 13.

[86]*Ibid* art 6 et 10

[87]*Ibid* art 7.

[88]*Ibid* art 7 (3). Sur la règle applicable aux conflits de présomptions, l'article 7 (3) de la loi ontarienne est clair : on repousse l'application des présomptions lorsqu'elles permettent d'établir la filiation à l'égard de plus d'une personne. Les présomptions en common law et en droit civil ne jouent pas exactement le même rôle; elles constituent une preuve réfutable de la filiation, alors que la présomption de paternité en droit civil est très difficile à repousser et constitue la façon de prouver la paternité. Le droit civil québécois se situe en quelque sorte entre la common law et le droit civil classique. Depuis la réforme de 1980 du droit de la famille, l'acte de naissance est une preuve de la filiation hiérarchiquement supérieure à la présomption légale de filiation ; il peut contredire la présomption de paternité ; il prime (art 523 CcQ).

[89]*Ibid* art 7 (4), comme exception à l'article 9 (2) qui lui permet d'être parent autrement. Voir Leckey, « One Parent, Three Parents: Judges and Ontario's All Families Are Equal Act », *supra* note 67.

maximum quatre parties. Avec l'autorisation du tribunal, plus de quatre parents pourraient être reconnus. [90]

Cette situation prévaut aussi en cas de recours à une mère porteuse,[91] mais l'enfant doit être conçu par procréation médicalement assistée et non par relation sexuelle. La mère porteuse et les parents d'intention doivent avoir également reçu, préalablement à la signature de la convention, un avis juridique indépendant.[92] Enfin, la mère porteuse (la loi la nomme « substitut ») doit consentir à remettre l'enfant aux parents d'intention dans les sept jours de la naissance de l'enfant.[93] Dans l'éventualité où la mère porteuse ne donne pas ce consentement, toute partie à la convention peut saisir le tribunal pour obtenir une déclaration de filiation à l'égard de l'enfant.[94] C'est l'intérêt de l'enfant qui dictera la décision du tribunal.[95]

Dans les provinces n'ayant pas de législation (Ontario jusqu'en 2017, Saskatchewan et Nouveau-Brunswick), des déclarations de parenté ont été émises par le tribunal au nom de l'intérêt de l'enfant à l'égard de parents d'intention.[96]

3.3.2 Le droit québécois: besoin de réforme

Quant au Québec, l'article 541 CcQ prévoit la nullité des conventions avec une mère porteuse, peu importe qu'il s'agisse d'une convention de gestation ou de procréation, à titre gratuit ou non. Parce qu'il les considère comme contraires, notamment, au principe de non-commercialisation du corps humain, à l'indisponibilité de l'état des personnes de même qu'à l'intérêt supérieur de l'enfant *a priori* ou *in abstracto*, depuis 1994, le législateur a édicté expressément dans le Code civil la nullité absolue de ces conventions. Ainsi, toute personne ayant recours à cette technique le fait à ses propres risques. Dans l'éventualité d'un conflit concernant la convention, celle-ci n'est pas susceptible d'exécution. Cela a un impact sur l'établissement de la filiation de l'enfant. Pour la déterminer, plusieurs possibilités existent selon le scénario en jeu, mais dans tous les cas, on utilise d'abord les règles de la filiation par le sang pour déterminer la filiation de l'enfant ainsi conçu. En effet, conformément à la maxime de droit romain *mater semper certa est*, la femme qui accouche est la mère de

---

[90] *Loi portant réforme du droit de l'enfance, ibid* art 9 (2) a).

[91] *Ibid* art 10.

[92] *Ibid* art 10 (2).

[93] *Ibid* art 10 (4).

[94] *Ibid* art 10 (6).

[95] *Ibid* art 10 (8).

[96] Voir notamment Karen Busby, « Of Surrogate Mother Born : Parentage Determinations in Canada and Elsewhere » (2013) 25 CJWL 284. Voir aussi Rapport du Comité consultatif sur le droit de la famille, *supra* note 74 aux pp 166-186, 507.

l'enfant, peu importe si elle a fourni ou non ses gamètes.[97] Si elle est mariée ou unie civilement, la présomption de paternité trouvera application à l'égard de son conjoint ou de sa conjointe.[98] Par ailleurs, l'un des parents d'intention, qui est généralement le parent biologique, pourra déclarer son lien de filiation à l'égard de l'enfant au directeur de l'état civil. Comme on l'a brièvement évoqué, la présomption de paternité en cas de mariage ou d'union civile, cède le pas à la déclaration de naissance si celle-ci est faite par l'un des parents d'intention.

Puis, pour éventuellement régler la filiation de l'enfant ainsi conçu, l'adoption est utilisée, quoique ce mécanisme n'ait pas été conçu pour ce type de scénario. Ainsi, par consentement spécial à l'adoption du parent inscrit à l'acte de naissance[99] et de la mère porteuse, le processus d'adoption par la mère d'intention (ou le co-père) pourra dès lors être enclenché par le mécanisme qui permet l'adoption intrafamiliale.[100]

C'est la Cour d'appel du Québec qui a dû trancher la question de l'établissement de la filiation de l'enfant conçu à la suite d'une convention de mère porteuse. Celle-ci a autorisé l'adoption de l'enfant du conjoint, par l'autre parent non biologique, au nom de l'intérêt de l'enfant, mettant ainsi fin au débat jurisprudentiel de droit interne qui hésitait, en première instance en Cour du Québec, entre ordre public et intérêt de l'enfant. Comme la Cour ne peut qu'interpréter le droit applicable, l'article 541 CcQ n'a toujours pas été modifié et cela peut paraître contradictoire. Bien qu'aucune proposition de modification législative n'ait été déposée à ce jour, une réforme est

---

[97]CcQ, art 111. Certains remettent en cause ce principe, c'est le cas de Marie-France Bureau et Édith Guilhermont, « Maternité, gestation et liberté : réflexions sur la prohibition de la gestation pour autrui en droit québécois » (2011) 4 R droit et santé de McGill 43 aux pp 65 et s, ainsi que d'Anne-Marie Savard, « L'établissement de la filiation à la suite du recours à la gestation pour autrui : l'adoption par consentement spécial est-il le moyen approprié en droit québécois » dans Christelle Landheer-Cieslack et Louise Langevin, dir, *La personne humaine, entre autonomie et vulnérabilité. Mélanges en l'honneur d'Édith Deleury,* Montréal, Éditions Yvon Blais, 2015 à la p 589.

[98]Conformément à l'article 525 CcQ.

[99]CcQ, art 555. Toutes les décisions publiées et accessibles au Québec qui portent sur la maternité de substitution sont des requêtes en matière d'adoption ou des demandes de correction au registre de l'état civil. Comme le contrat entre la mère porteuse et les futurs parents d'intention est inexécutoire, il n'est pas possible de savoir s'il y a eu des conflits entre les parties.

[100]Pour plus de détails sur l'établissement de la filiation de l'enfant ainsi conçu, voir Michelle Giroux, « Le recours controversé à l'adoption pour établir la filiation de l'enfant né d'une mère porteuse: entre ordre public contractuel et intérêt de l'enfant » (2011) 70 Rev du B 509 aux pp 521-524. Sur les difficultés de ce mécanisme d'adoption, voir Isabel Côté et Jean-Sébastien Sauvé, « Homopaternité, gestation pour autrui : no man's land? » (2016) 46 RGD 27.

requise et en effet demandée, tant par les auteur-e-s de doctrine[101] et certaines institutions[102] que par le Comité consultatif sur le droit de la famille.[103]

L'étude comparée du droit de la famille à travers le Canada montre bien que certaines provinces ont réformé leur droit et que d'autres possèdent une législation en décalage avec les nouvelles formes de famille. Devant l'inaction de certains législateurs provinciaux ou territoriaux à adapter le droit de la famille, de nombreuses personnes membres de minorités sexuelles ont intenté des actions en justice contre les gouvernements pour faire reconnaitre leur filiation légale, comme en Ontario avant la réforme recente.[104] Plusieurs demandent des réformes en profondeur du droit de la famille et une certaine uniformité entre les provinces.[105]

4 L'encadrement juridique du changement de la mention du sexe/genre et du prénom à l'état civil

Ici aussi, la façon de réglementer la question varie d'une province ou territoire à l'autre. Généralement, les lois provinciales portant sur les statistiques de l'état civil (les *Vital Statistics Acts*) connaissent un processus de réforme afin de faciliter les changements de la mention du sexe sans exiger de traitement médical ou de

[101]Voir notamment Louise Langevin, « La Cour d'appel du Québec et la maternité de substitution dans la décision Adoption – 1445 ; quelques lumières sur les zones d'ombres et les conséquences d'une solution *la moins insatisfaisante* » (2015) 49 RJT 451; Mireille D-Castelli, « L'évolution des fondements du droit de la filiation : dichotomie entre valorisation croissante du lien biologique et prééminence de la volonté » dans Christelle Landheer-Cieslak et Louise Langevin, dir, *La personne humaine, entre autonomie et vulnérabilité. Mélanges en l'honneur d'Édith Deleury*, *supra* note 97 à la p 107; Savard, « L'établissement de la filiation à la suite d'une gestation pour autrui : le recours à l'adoption par consentement spécial en droit québécois constitue-t-il le moyen le plus approprié ? », *supra* note 97 à la p 589.

[102]Voir les prises de position en faveur d'une réforme de la part du Conseil du statut de la femme, *Avis, Mères porteuse : réflexions sur des enjeux actuels,* Québec, 2016 et Commissaire à la santé et au bien-être, *Avis détaillé sur les activités de procréation assistée*, Québec, 2014, aux pp 24-25, 30, en ligne : http://www.csbe.gouv.qc.ca/fileadmin/www/2014/Procreation_assistee/CSBE_PA_detaille_2014.pdf.

[103]Rapport du Comité consultatif sur le droit de la famille, *supra* note 74 aux pp 166-189 et 231.

[104]*AA c BB*, *supra* note 66.

[105]Au Québec, voir notamment Comité consultatif sur le droit de la famille, *supra* note 74 . Dans le reste du Canada, voir Rogerson, « Determining Parentage in Cases Involving Assisted Reproduction : An Urgent Need for Provincial Legislative Action », *supra* note 74 à la p 91; Susan Boyd, « Gendering Legal Parenthood : Bio-genetic Ties, Intentionality, and Responsibility » (2007) 25 Wind Year Book Access to Justice 63; Wanda Weigers, « Assisted Conception and Equality of Familial Status in Parentage Law » (2012-13) 28 CJFL147; Fiona Kelly, « Equal Parents, Equal Children: Reforming Canada's Parentage Laws to Recognize the Completeness of Women-led Families » (2013) 64 UNB L J 253. De plus, la conférence pour l'harmonisation des lois au Canada propose un modèle législatif pour favoriser l'harmonisation à travers le Canada, *Loi uniforme sur le statut de l'enfant* (2010), Conférence pour l'harmonisation des lois au Canada, *supra* note 75.

transition médicale, ainsi que le changement du prénom.[106] Le Québec ne fait pas bande à part, mais les changements adoptés se trouvent incorporés dans le Code civil, plutôt que dans les lois sur les statistiques de l'état civil, comme dans le reste du Canada. En droit comparé, c'est une différence digne de mention entre les systèmes de common law et de droit civil. Dans certains cas, sur certains documents officiels, la mention du sexe a disparu ou il est possible de choisir une option plus neutre que le sexe masculin ou féminin, le « x » par exemple. Plusieurs de ces changements législatifs sont le résultat d'actions intentées devant les tribunaux par des militant-e-s. Nous nous attardons à l'étude des lois adoptées dans différentes provinces canadiennes.

4.1 La *Loi sur les statistiques de l'état civil* en Ontario

À la suite du jugement *XY v Ontario (Government and Consumers services),*[107]qui a décidé que l'exigence d'une transition médicale afin d'obtenir une modification de la mention du sexe au registre de l'état civil était discriminatoire à l'égard des personnes trans, le Bureau du registraire général de l'Ontario n'exige plus une telle transition. Outre une déclaration solennelle de la personne adulte faisant la demande de changement de désignation du sexe figurant sur l'enregistrement et au certificat de naissance, elle doit aussi fournir une corroboration, par exemple une lettre d'un médecin ou d'un psychologue, praticien et autorisé à pratiquer au Canada.[108] L'enfant de moins de 17 ans doit donner son consentement, en plus de

[106]Toutes les provinces permettent le changement de la mention du sexe sans exiger la transition médicale. Ontario : La *Loi sur les statistiques de l'état civil*, LRO 1990, c V.4, art 36, telle que modifiée à la suite de *XY v Ontario (Government and Consumers services),* 2012 HRTO 726. Colombie-Britannique : *Vital Statistics Act*, RSBC 1996, *supra* note 64, art 27. Alberta : *Vital Statistics Act*, SA 2007, c V-4.1 art 30. Manitoba : *Loi sur les statistiques de l'état civil*, CPLM c V60, art 25; Terre-Neuve et Labrador : *Vital Statistics Act*, 2009, SNL 2009, c V-6.01, art 26; Île-du-Prince-Édouard : *Vital Statistics Act*, RSPEI 1988, c V-4.1, art 12; Saskatchewan : *Loi de 2009 sur les services de l'état civil*, LS 2009, c V-7.21, art 31 (2); Yukon : *Loi sur les statistiques de l'état civil*, LRY 2002, c 225, art 12 (1). Nunavut : *Loi sur les statistiques de l'état civil*, LRY 2002, c 225, art 12 (1); Nouvelle-Écosse : *Vital Statistics Act*, RSNS 1989, c 494, art 25 (1); Québec: *Loi modifiant le Code civil en matière d'état civil, de successions et de publicité des droits*, LQ (2013), c 35, art 3 à 5 et 38, modifications intégrées dans le CcQ, notamment à l'art 71 al 2. Nouveau-Brunswick : *Loi sur les statistiques de l'état civil*, LN-B 1979, c V-3 art 34 (1); Territoires du Nord-Ouest : *Loi sur les statistiques de l'état civil*, LTN-O 2011, c 34, art 41 (2).

[107]*Ibid*. Pour une analyse de la décision, voir Jena McGill et Kyle Kirkup, « Locating the Trans Legal Subject in Canadian Law: *XY v Ontario* » (2013) 33 Windsor Rev Legal & Soc Issues 96.

[108]Pour les autres preuves à fournir, voir Bureau du registraire général de l'Ontario en ligne : https://www.ontario.ca/fr/page/changer-la-designation-de-votre-sexe-sur-votre-enregistrement-de-naissance-et-votre-certificat-de. La *Loi sur les statistiques de l'état civil*, *supra* 106 (à jour le 20 juillet 2019) : il semble que cette loi (art 36, exigence de la chirurgie de réassignation de sexe) n'ait pas été modifiée après le jugement *XY v Ontario (Government and Consumers services)*, *supra* note 106. Pour une critique de l'exigence de corroboration, voir McGill et Kirkup, *ibid*.

celui de ses parents. Il doit aussi fournir une lettre d'un médecin ou d'un psychologue qui atteste de la volonté de la personne de changer la mention du sexe.

Cette modification n'a pas d'effet rétroactif. Ainsi ni les actes de mariage antérieurs au changement, ni les actes de naissance des enfants déjà nés de cette personne ne seront modifiés.

Quant au changement de prénom ou de nom pour un adulte en Ontario, le demandeur doit indiquer le motif du changement. L'avis de changement de nom ne sera pas publié dans la *Gazette de l'Ontario* si la personne trans, adulte ou enfant, en fait la demande.[109] Les enfants entre 12 ans et 16 ans doivent donner leur consentement écrit.[110].

Depuis le 13 juin 2017, la carte Santé de l'Ontario, donnant accès à des soins de santé fournis par l'État, ne comporte plus de mention du sexe de la personne.[111] Depuis le début de 2017, les titulaires d'un permis de conduire en Ontario qui ne s'identifient pas comme homme ou femme ont la possibilité d'inscrire un « X » comme identifiant de genre.[112]

Les changements se situent parfois auprès des institutions non étatiques. Par exemple, l'Université de Toronto a adopté une politique qui permet aux étudiant-e-s de changer leur nom et la désignation de leur sexe dans les dossiers scolaires, listes d'étudiants des cours et bases de données d'étudiants en ligne, en en faisant la demande par écrit au registraire de leur collège. L'étudiant-e qui soumet une telle demande doit établir l'authenticité de son identité.[113] D'autres universités ailleurs au Canada ont suivi le pas à divers degrés.[114]

---

[109] *Loi sur le changement de nom*, RRO 1990, c C-7, *Règlement 6, Dispositions générales, Dispense de l'obligation de publier un avis de changement de nom*, art 6 (1).

[110] En ligne : http://www.forms.ssb.gov.on.ca/mbs/ssb/forms/ssbforms.nsf/GetFileAttach/007-11156F~6/$File/11156F.pdf.

[111] En ligne : https://news.ontario.ca/mgs/fr/2016/06/le-genre-sur-la-carte-sante-et-le-permis-de-conduire.html#:~:text=Une%20carte%20Sant%C3%A9%20de%201,de%20la%20personne%20est%20valide.&text=Pour%20obtenir%20une%20carte%20Sant%C3%A9,n'importe%20quel%20centre%20ServiceOntario.

[112] *Id.*

[113] *University of Toronto's Statement Concerning Changes of Student Personal Information in Official Academic Records (approuvé le 16 avril 2009)*, en ligne : University of Toronto *http://sgdo.utoronto.ca/resources/resources-for-trans-people-u-of-t/*.

[114] Des toilettes non genrées sont présentes dans les universités québécoises, voir Jennifer Graham, « Les toilettes non 'genrées' en hausse », La presse canadienne, 10 décembre 2016. En ligne : https://www.lesoleil.com/actualite/les-toilettes-non-genrees-en-hausse-bd94c4a45e595b4e8c1b56bcd961b8f9.

4.2 La *Loi sur les statistiques de l'état civil* en Colombie-Britannique

La loi de la Colombie-Britannique n'exige plus une transition médicale pour modifier la désignation de sexe sur le certificat de naissance.[115] Une procédure administrative prévoit que la personne, adulte[116] ou mineure (avec le consentement des parents),[117] dépose une demande de modification de la désignation du genre ainsi qu'une confirmation par un médecin ou un psychologue appuyant la demande. Dans le cas de l'enfant de moins de 19 ans, les parents doivent consentir.

En 2017, une poursuite a été déposée par Kori Doty, une personne non binaire, contre le registraire général de l'état civil de la province pour que le certificat de naissance de son enfant ne mentionne aucun genre.[118] Le registraire a voulu émettre un certificat de naissance, mais le document doit indiquer le sexe, comme la loi le lui impose. L'enfant n'a pas reçu son certificat de naissance, mais a obtenu une carte d'assurance-maladie non genrée avec la mention « U » (pour « unspecified »).[119]

La procédure de changement du prénom est assez simple et n'exige pas de justifier les motifs du changement de prénom ou de nom de famille pour un adulte. Les enfants entre 12 et 18 ans doivent expliquer les motifs de leur changement de nom dans une lettre écrite à la main.[120]

Le registraire général peut utiliser sa discrétion pour ne pas publier l'avis de changement de prénom ou de nom dans la Gazette officielle.[121]

---

[115] *Vital Statistics Act*, *supra* note 64, art 27.

[116] Application For Change of Gender Designation (Adult) – Changing BC Birth Certificate. En ligne : https://www2.gov.bc.ca/gov/content/life-events/birth-adoption/births/birth-certificates/change-of-gender-designation-on-birth-certificates.

[117] Instructions for the Application For Change of Gender Designation (Minor). En ligne : http://www2.gov.bc.ca/assets/gov/health/forms/vital-statistics/vsa509c_fill.pdf.

[118] Cette personne non binaire fait partie d'une coalition en Colombie-Britannique, *The Gender Free ID Coalition*, qui a déposé huit plaintes à la Commission des droits de la personne de la province pour faire enlever la mention du sexe sur l'acte de naissance. En ligne : http://gender-freeidcoalition.ca/. Voir aussi Raymond Desmarteau, « Terre-Neuve-et-Labrador : un tribunal se penchera sur les certificats de naissance non binaires », RCInet, (28 juillet 2017) en ligne : https://ici.radio-canada.ca/nouvelle/1047778/certificat-naissance-neutre-terre-neuve-labrador-activiste-transgenre.

[119] Audrey Ruel-Manseau, « Un bébé « sans genre » en Colombie-Britannique », *La Presse* (4 juillet 2017) en ligne : https://www.lapresse.ca/actualites/national/201707/03/01-5113030-un-bebe-sans-genre-en-colombie-britannique.php.

[120] Application for Change of Name Under the Provisions of the British Columbia Name Act. En ligne : http://www2.gov.bc.ca/assets/gov/health/forms/vital-statistics/vsa529.pdf

[121] *Name Act*, RSBC 1996, c 328, art 12 (3) b.

4.3 La *Loi sur les statistiques de l'état civil* en Alberta

En Alberta, la *Vital Statistics Act*,[122] qui exigeait une transition médicale pour permettre une modification de la mention du sexe au registre de l'état civil, a été modifiée à la suite d'une décision la déclarant discriminatoire.[123] Une lettre par un médecin, un psychologue, un infirmier ou un travailleur social appuyant la demande est nécessaire.[124] Le mineur entre 12 et 18 ans doit donner son consentement, lorsque le parent fait la demande. La demande de changement de sexe ne sera pas publicisée.[125] Aucune raison pour un tel changement n'est exigée.

Depuis août 2017, l'Alberta permet de choisir un X pour la mention du sexe sur les documents officiels comme les certificats de naissance.[126]

4.4 Le changement de nom et de sexe au Québec

En droit civil québécois, à l'instar des autres systèmes de droit civil, le sexe constitue généralement un élément servant à l'identification ou à l'individualisation des personnes sur le plan de l'état civil. Ainsi, le sexe est une mention obligatoire sur l'acte de naissance d'une personne.[127] Cette façon de faire a été remise en question. Le 28 janvier 2021, la Cour supérieure a néanmoins maintenu la mention du sexe à l'acte de naissance, car elle considère que la question de l'identité de genre ne se manifeste que vers l'âge de trois ou quatre chez l'enfant et qu'il peut par la suite

[122]*Vital Statistics and Life Events Modernization Act*, SA 2016, c 26 modifie l'article 30 du *Vital Statistics Act*, *supra* note 106. Voir aussi art 16.1, *Vital Statistics Information Regulation*, Alta Reg 3/2012.

[123]*CF v Alberta (Vital Statistics)*, 2014 ABQB 237. La demanderesse trans avait obtenu un changement de prénom mais pas de sexe sur son certificat de naissance, parce qu'elle n'avait pas subi une transition médicale. La loi est déclarée invalide.

[124]*Vital Statistics Information Regulation*, *supra* note 122, art 16.3.

[125]*Vital Statistics Act*, *supra* note 106, art 26 (2) c).

[126]*Vital Statistics Act*, *supra* note 106, art 29.1 (1). Part 3.1 : « 29.1(1) In this Part, "non-binary identifier" means an identifier that signifies non-binary gender and that may be used instead of the sex identifiers "M" and "F", (2) A non-binary identifier may be used on vital event records in accordance with the regulations ». Voir Emma Graney, « Changes to Alberta vital statistics adds a third gender marker », 8 nov 2016, en ligne : http://edmontonjournal.com/news/local-news/changes-to-alberta-vital-statistics-add-a-third-gender-marker.

[127]Voir notamment les articles 111 et 115 CcQ, qui prévoient que sexe de l'enfant qui vient de naître doit être indiqué, d'une part sur le constat de naissance dressé par l'accoucheur et d'autre part, sur la déclaration de naissance, effectuée par les père et mère. Une fois l'acte de naissance confectionné, des ententes administratives entre les ministères permettent l'utilisation de ces données pour dresser d'autres documents importants, dont la carte d'assurance-maladie du Québec, qui contient également la mention du sexe. Pour plus de détails sur l'utilisation du sexe sur les différentes cartes d'identité, voir Dominique Goubau, *Le droit des personnes physiques*, avec la collaboration d'Anne-Marie Savard, 6e éd, Montréal, Yvon Blais, 2019 au para 234.

demander une modification de la mention du genre et prénom dans les documents officiels. Selon la lettre du Code civil et à notre connaissance, aucun accommodement n'est permis lorsqu'il y a indétermination du sexe à la naissance comme chez les personnes intersexes.[128] Les seules catégories possibles étant binaires, soit masculin, soit féminin, aucune autre mention faisant état de l'indétermination n'est envisagée, sous réserve des modifications qui seront apportées suite au jugement de la Cour supérieure qui a suspendu la validité constitutionnelle de plusieurs articles du CcQ jusqu'au 31 décembre 2021 et qui autorise une personne d'obtenir un certificat d'état civil sans mention de sexe.[129]

En revanche, le droit québécois a subi des ajustements importants depuis 2013, mais ces changements sont effectifs depuis 2016.[130] Le droit québécois n'exige plus « que la personne ait subi quelque traitement médical ou intervention chirurgicale que ce soit »[131] pour obtenir un changement de la mention de sexe sur son acte de naissance, accompagné ou non d'un changement de prénom lorsqu'elle ne

[128]Au Québec, le délai est de 30 jours pour assigner le sexe à l'enfant (art 113 CcQ) Une déclaration de naissance transmise après ce délai entraîne le paiement des frais exigibles. Le directeur de l'état civil refuse d'émettre un acte de naissance s'il ne possède pas le sexe de l'enfant puisque la loi lui impose d'indiquer le sexe de l'enfant. L'article 115 CcQ impose aux père et mère d'indiquer le sexe de l'enfant. Si l'enfant ne possède pas d'acte de naissance, il ne pourra avoir accès aux autres services de l'État, tels des soins de santé et l'accès à l'école.

[129]Voir *Center for Gender Advocacy* c. *Attorney general of Quebec*, *supra* note 14, notamment les par 338-344. Veuillez noter que ce texte a été soumis pour publication bien avant cette décision, mais nous avons tout de même tenu à l'incorporer lors de la relecture des épreuves, avec les limitations que cela comporte. De plus en plus, les recherches et les revendications des personnes impliquées démontrent que le sexe n'est pas toujours facilement identifiable. Il ne peut toujours être considéré comme une vérité de la nature, biologique ou chromosomique, sans même entrer dans les ambiguïtés plus sociales qui peuvent s'ajouter. Voir Ilana Löwy, « Intersexe et transsexualités : les technologies de la médecine et la séparation du sexe biologique du sexe social » (2003) 34 Cahiers du genre 91. Selon des études, il y aurait entre 1 % et 2 % des naissances qui seraient intersexes. Voir l'étude citée par Joëlle Wiels, « La détermination génétique du sexe : une affaire compliquée » dans Évelyne Peyre et Joëlle Wiels, dir, *Mon corps a-t-il un sexe? Sur le genre, dialogues entre biologies et sciences sociales*, Paris, La découverte, 2015 à la p 57; Anne Fausto Sterling, « The Five Sexes : Why Male and Female are Not Enough », The Sciences, March/April 1993, p 20. Voir aussi Sauvé, *supra* note 1.

[130]*Loi modifiant le Code civil en matière d'état civil, de successions et de publicité des droits*, LQ (2013), c 35, art 3 à 5 et 38. Bien qu'adopté en 2013, ces changements ne sont entrés en vigueur que lors de l'adoption du *Règlement modifiant le Règlement relatif au changement de nom et d'autres qualités de l'état civil,* GO II, 16 septembre 2015, 147e année, no 37, p 3238. En plus du CcQ, le *Règlement relatif au changement de nom et d'autres qualités de l'état civil*, RLRQ r 4, a été modifié par le même changement terminologique. Certains groupes avaient décrié le délai qui s'est écoulé entre l'adoption de la loi et celle du règlement permettant son entrée en vigueur et ajoutant les conditions applicables à ce changement. La réforme a été complétée par l'adoption de la *Loi visant à renforcer la lutte contre la transphobie et à améliorer notamment la situation des mineurs transgenres,* LQ 2016 c 19. Cette loi a ajouté à ses articles 8 et 9 les articles 71.1 et 73.1 au CcQ. De même, à son article 11, elle a modifié l'article 10 de la *Charte québécoise*, *supra* note 9, en ajoutant « l'identité ou l'expression de genre » aux autres motifs de discrimination prévus à cet article, après le « sexe ».

[131]CcQ, art 71 al 2 (avant la modification de 2013).

correspond pas à son « identité de genre ».[132] On a ainsi donné plus d'importance à l'autonomie de la personne pour déterminer à quel genre elle s'identifie. Cette demande peut être faite par voie administrative devant l'officier de l'état civil, qui au Québec est le directeur de l'état civil[133].

À la suite des modifications additionnelles apportées par la *Loi visant à renforcer la lutte contre la transphobie et à améliorer notamment la situation des mineurs transgenres,* adoptée le 10 juin 2016, non seulement la personne majeure peut bénéficier d'un changement de la mention de sexe, accompagné ou non d'un changement de prénom,[134] mais dorénavant, la personne mineure également. L'article 71.1 CcQ permet donc au mineur de 14 ans et plus de faire seul cette demande « ou par son tuteur avec son consentement » et pour le mineur de moins de 14 ans, c'est son tuteur qui doit faire la demande.[135]

En ce qui a trait aux conditions devant être satisfaites pour obtenir une telle demande, elles varient selon l'âge de la personne qui en fait la demande. Une déclaration sous serment doit accompagner la demande et inclure les détails prévus à l'article 23.1 du *Règlement relatif au changement de nom,*[136] notamment « que la mention du sexe qu'il demande est celle qui correspond le mieux à son identité de genre, qu'il assume et a l'intention de continuer à assumer cette identité de genre, que sa démarche est faite de façon volontaire ». La personne majeure doit fournir aussi « une déclaration sous serment d'une personne majeure qui atteste connaître le demandeur depuis au moins un an et qui confirme que le demandeur reconnaît le sérieux de sa demande ». La demande présentée par le tuteur pour l'enfant mineur doit au surplus attester une série de détails similaires à ce qui doit l'être par la personne majeure ou mineure de 14 ans et plus et fournir une lettre d'un professionnel de la santé « qui déclare avoir évalué ou suivi l'enfant et qui est d'avis que le changement de cette mention est approprié. » L'exigence d'une telle lettre a été déclarée inconstitutionnelle par la Cour supérieure du Québec en janvier

[132]*Ibid* art 71 al 1. Avant cette réforme, les nombreux litiges impliquant Micheline Montreuil ont démontré qu'aucun accommodement n'était possible sans avoir réalisé avec succès la transition médicale. Voir *Montreuil c Québec (Procureur général),* [2001] RDF 452 (CS), *Montreuil c Directeur de l'état civil,* [1999] RJQ 2819 (CA) (demande d'autorisation d'appel en Cour suprême du Canada rejetée) et *Montreuil c Société de l'assurance automobile du Québec,* JE 98-1988 (CS).

[133]CcQ, art 72.

[134]Le changement du nom de famille n'est pas possible. *Règlement relatif au changement de nom, supra* note 130, art 24.

[135]Dans ce cas, le code précise que « le changement de la mention de sexe n'est pas accordé, à moins d'un motif impérieux, si l'autre tuteur n'a pas été avisé de la demande ou s'il s'y oppose ». En cas d'opposition de l'autre tuteur, l'article 73.1 prévoit que l'autre tuteur peut « saisir le tribunal avant qu'une demande pour obtenir un tel changement ne soit présentée au directeur de l'état civil ». La cour supérieure n'a pas invalidé l'objection parentale, car selon la preuve présentée au procès, elle ne fait pas obstacle au changement demandé par la personne mineure, *Center for Gender Avocacy* c. *Procureur général du Québec, supra* note 14, par. 309.

[136]*Règlement relatif au changement de nom, supra* note 130.

dernier, ce que consteste le Procureur général en appel pour les mineurs de 14 ans et plus.[137]

S'il ne s'agit pas d'une première demande de changement de la mention du sexe à l'acte de naissance, l'article 23.3 du *Règlement relatif au changement de nom*[138] prévoit en outre que la personne faisant la demande fournisse une lettre d'un professionnel de la santé attestant qu'il a « évalué ou suivi » cette personne et qu'il « est d'avis que le changement de cette mention est approprié ».

Le mariage entre personnes de même sexe étant permis depuis 2005 au Canada, le divorce n'est plus requis lorsque la personne trans s'était mariée avant de procéder à un changement de sexe, puisque le mariage entre personnes de même sexe est permis. Le divorce pourra être demandé seulement si ce changement entraine l'échec du mariage au sens de l'article 8 de la *Loi sur le divorce*.[139]

De plus, comme on l'a déjà mentionné auparavant, la personne trans pourra adopter un enfant.[140] Le fait d'être un parent trans n'influe pas sur ses capacités parentales ou sur ses droits de garde; le seul critère qui prévaut en cette matière est celui de l'intérêt de l'enfant.[141] Enfin, le lien de filiation entre le parent trans et son enfant n'est jamais modifié par le changement de sexe.[142]

En adoptant ces changements permettant au mineur de modifier la mention de sexe à l'état civil, le Québec assure un plus grand respect des droits de l'enfant et du principe de l'intérêt supérieur de ce dernier, tel que reconnu dans la *Convention relative aux droits de l'enfant*.[143] Le Québec rejoint ainsi d'autres provinces canadiennes (l'Alberta, la Colombie-Britannique, l'Ontario et la Nouvelle-Écosse).[144]

Ces modifications apportées au droit civil québécois ne sont pas les dernières. En effet, on s'interroge de plus en plus sur la pertinence de la mention de sexe à l'état

---

[137] *Ibid* art 23.2 al 2. La déclaration d'invalidité est cependant suspendue jusqu'au 31 décembre 2021 pour donner le temps au législateur d'apporter des modifications en ce sens, voir *Center for Gender Advocacy* c. *Attorney general of Quebec*, *supra* note 14.

[138] *Ibid*.

[139] *Loi sur le divorce*, LRC 1985, c D-3.4.

[140] Voir notamment Alain Roy, *Le droit de l'adoption au Québec*, 2e éd, (coll Bleue) Montréal, Wilson & Lafleur, 2006 au para 20; Jean Pineau et Marie Pratte, *La famille*, Montréal, Thémis, 2006 au para 443; Pierre-Claude Lafond et Brigitte Lefebvre, dir, *L'union civile. Nouveaux modèles de conjugalité et de parentalité au 21e siècle. Actes du colloque du Groupe de réflexion en droit privé*, Cowansville, Yvon Blais, 2002 aux pp 305 et s.

[141] CcQ, art 33; *Droit de la famille – 133870*, 2013 QCCS 6825. Voir aussi Goubau, *supra* note 127 au para 308. Voir aussi Emilie Biland et al., *supra* note 49.

[142] Voir *J. . .M. . ., et JE. . .M. . ., et Le Directeur de l'état civil*, Cour supérieure du Québec, dossier no : 405-04-002669-045, 16 juin 2004 (J Dubois).

[143] *Convention relative aux droits de l'enfant,* RT Can 1992, no 3, Res. A.G. 44/25 Annexe, signée par le Canada le 28 mai 1990, ratifiée le 13 décembre 1991 et entrée en vigueur le 12 janvier 1992. Le gouvernement du Québec s'est engagé, par décret, à en assurer le respect (Décret 1676-91, (1992) 124 GO II, 51).

[144] Pour plus de détails, voir l'Annexe 1 dans Barreau du Québec, *Mémoire du Barreau du Québec. Projet de loi n° 103 – Loi visant à renforcer la lutte contre la transphobie et à améliorer notamment la situation des mineurs transgenres*, *supra* note 1.

civil.[145] Le recours intenté en 2014 par le Centre de lutte contre l'oppression des genres (Centre for Gender Advocacy) et d'autres qui demandait à la Cour supérieure du Québec d'invalider plusieurs articles du Code civil, exigeant la mention du sexe sur les actes de l'état civil, a été accueilli en partie.[146] Les requérants allèguaient notamment, comme on l'a vu, que la désignation du sexe, mais aussi que celle de « père » ou « mère » à l'acte de naissance devraient être optionnelles et non obligatoires. Dans ce dernier cas, on suggère que le terme « parent » devrait pouvoir être choisi et que le changement de la mention de sexe pour le parent d'un enfant devrait produire des effets sur l'acte de naissance de son enfant. La Cour supérieure leur a donné raison en suspendant, jusqu'au 31 décembre 2021, l'invalidité des articles 111, 115 et 116 CcQ. Les articles 71 et 146 CcQ subissent le même sort pour mettre fin à la discrimination à l'égard des personnes non-binaires. On remet également en question la condition d'être citoyen canadien pour obtenir un changement de la mention de sexe et cette exigeance est invalidée par la Cour supérieure. Les articles 59 et 71, al.3 CcQ sont ainsi immédiatement modifiés . Ces changements demandés et accueillis en partie reposent sur le fait que le droit actuel porte atteinte aux droits à la vie, à l'intégrité et à la sécurité de la personne ainsi qu'à la vie privée et à l'égalité et à la dignité garantis par les Chartes québécoise et canadienne.[147]

---

[145]Voir Laurence Brunet, « Ordre social contre ordre « naturel » : la mention du sexe sur l'état civil des personnes intersexes » (2016) 64 Neuropsychiatrie de l'enfant et de l'adolescence 255; Marie-Xavière Catto, « La mention du sexe à l'état civil » dans Stéphanie Hennette-Vauchez, Marc Pichard et Diane Roman, dir, *La loi et le genre, études critiques de droit français*, Paris, CNRS Éditions, 2014 à la p 29; Elsa Fondimare, « Le genre, un concept utile pour repenser le droit de la non-discrimination » (2014) 5 La Revue des droits de l'Homme 1; Daniel Borillo, « Le sexe et le droit : De la logique binaire des genres et la matrice hétérosexuelle de la loi » (2011) Jurisprudence revue critique 263; Sylvio Normand, « État civil et identité élective » dans Christelle Landheer-Cieslak et Louise Langevin, dir, *supra* note 97, *à* la p 491; Dorian Needham, « A categorical Imperative? Questionning the need for sexual classification in Quebec » (2011) 52 Cahiers de droit 71; Danièle Lochak, « Dualité de sexe et dualité de genre dans les normes juridiques » dans Pierre Noreau et Louise Rolland, dir, *Mélanges Andrée Lajoie*, Montréal, Thémis, 2008, p 659; Marcela Iacub, « Aspects juridiques actuels en France et en Europe » dans Haute Autorité de Santé, *Situation actuelle et perspectives d'évolution de la prise en charge médicale du transsexualisme en France*, 2009.

[146]*Voir Center for Gender Advocacy* c. *Procureur général du Québec*, *supra* note 14. Deux autres jugements ont été rendus dans cette cause. Le 17 décembre 2015, la Cour supérieure a reconnu le statut d'intervenant à ÉGALE Canada, à la Coalition LGBT et à Gender Creative Kids Canada, *Centre for Gender Advocacy* c *Québec (Attorney General),* 2015 QCCS 6026 et le 21 octobre (rectifié le 25 octobre), la Cour rejetait une demande présentée par le Procureur général du Québec de communication de documents, les données brutes d'une recherche faite par un expert dont le rapport est déposé au dossier, *Centre de lutte contre l'oppression des genres (Centre for Gender Advocacy) c Québec (Procureure générale)*, 2016 QCCS 5161.

[147]*Charte québécoise*, *supra* note 9, art 1, 4, 5 et 10 et *Charte canadienne*, *supra* note 12, art 7 et 15.

4.5 L'accès aux traitements médicaux

Bien que la question soit très complexe et encore pas complètement bien saisie par le monde médical, la transsexualité et l'intersexualité requièrent parfois des traitements médicaux, tant concernant la santé physique que psychologique. Par ailleurs, les transitions médicales et la médicalisation de cette problématique sont remises en question par certains et à d'autres moments, ces traitements sont considérés comme nécessaires pour la santé d'une personne aux prises avec des enjeux d'identité de genre. Une personne peut avoir une anomalie physique qui a été corrigée, mais pas toujours dans le sens désiré par elle. Parfois une personne peut ne pas s'identifier au sexe qui lui a été assigné à la naissance.[148] Quand des traitements médicaux ou transitions médicales sont requis, la question du remboursement des frais qui y sont associés se pose.

Quelques explications sont nécessaires pour comprendre le financement du régime d'assurance-santé universel du Canada. Le gouvernement fédéral peut intervenir par son pouvoir de dépenser en matière de santé par la *Loi canadienne sur la santé*.[149] En retour d'une aide financière aux provinces et aux territoires,[150] la *Loi canadienne sur la santé* leur impose d'offrir les services de santé nécessaires et d'offrir un accès égal à ces services à tous et toutes les habitant-e-s de chaque province ou territoire.[151]

La surfacturation et les frais modérateurs (le paiement des services de santé nécessaires) exigés aux patient-e-s (habitant-e-s de la province) ne sont pas permis.[152] Pour obtenir le financement fédéral, les provinces et territoires doivent fournir gratuitement à leurs citoyen-ne-s les services hospitaliers, les services en cabinets (médecins), et les soins de chirurgie dentaire en centre hospitalier. Les provinces et territoires peuvent offrir un nombre de services de santé additionnels, incluant les médicaments, les résidences pour personnes âgées et les soins à domicile pour personnes âgées (services complémentaires de santé).[153] Les soins de santé fournis dans le cadre des régimes de santé varient donc selon la province ou le

---

[148]Voir Goubau, *supra* note 127 aux para 292 et s, et plus particulièrement au para 294; Sauvé, *supra* note 1 aux pp 88 et s et 163 et s.

[149]Voir *Loi canadienne sur la santé,* LRC 1985 c-6. Sur le partage des compétences en matière de santé au Canada, voir William Lahey, « Medicare and the Law : Contours of an Evolving Relationship » dans Jocelyn Downie et al, dir, *Canadian Health Law and Policy*, 4e éd, Markham, LexisNexis Canada, 2011, ch 1, p 1; Alana Klein, « Jurisdiction in Canadian Health Law » dans Jocelyn Downie et al, dir, *Canadian Health Law and Policy*, 5e éd, Markham, LexisNexis Canada, 2017, p 29.

[150]*Loi canadienne sur la santé*, *ibid* art 5.

[151]Les cinq conditions suivantes doivent être respectées : la gestion publique, l'intégralité, l'universalité, la transférabilité, l'accessibilité. *Loi canadienne sur la santé, ibid* art 7 à 12,

[152]*Loi canadienne sur la santé, ibid* art 18 et 19.

[153]Voir Howard A Palley et Pierre-Gerlier Forest, « Canadian Fiscal Federalism, Regionalization, and the Development of Quebec's Health Care Delivery System » (2004) 20: 2 New Global Development: Journal of International and Comparative Social Welfare 8.

territoire.[154] Ceci explique que certaines provinces peuvent refuser de couvrir certains coûts découlant d'une transition médicale.[155]

Au Québec, par exemple, c'est le ministère de la Santé et non la Régie de l'Assurance maladie du Québec qui rembourse les dépenses associées à la procédure médicale de réassignation du sexe, conformément à une entente administrative entre un centre hospitalier et à l'époque, une agence de services de santé et de services sociaux.[156] Alors que les frais de la transition médicale sont remboursés, parce que requis par l'état de santé de la personne, d'autres frais accessoires ne le sont pas nécessairement. Ainsi, dans la décision *M F c Régie de l'Assurance-maladie du Québec*, le tribunal administratif du Québec a refusé le remboursement des frais de rhinoplastie pour féminiser le visage de la requérante que celle-ci juge trop masculin, au motif que ce soin n'est pas lié à un trouble fonctionnel et est donc purement esthétique et non requis par l'état de santé de la requérante.[157]

Comme le démontre une étude menée auprès de personnes trans en Ontario et portant sur leur accessibilité aux soins de santé, ces dernières vivent différents problèmes comme des refus de soins, des difficultés à accéder aux soins, un manque d'information sur les questions trans, un manque de formation du personnel soignant sur ces questions, et des interactions difficiles ou inconfortables, même discriminatoires, avec le personnel soignant.[158] Une autre étude démontre que, comparativement aux personnes non trans, les personnes trans en Ontario n'obtiennent pas les services de santé auxquels ils et elles ont droit.[159] De

[154] *Loi constitutionnelle de 1867,* 30 & 31 Victoria, c 3, art 92 (7).

[155] L'Association professionnelle canadienne pour la santé des personnes transgenres (CPATH) fournit un tableau sur les coûts de l'opération couverts par les provinces. En ligne : http://www.cpath.ca/wp-content/uploads/2016/02/Publicly-Funded-Transition-Related-Medical-Care-in-Canada_poster8x11_EN.pdf. Le Nouveau-Brunswick rembourse maintenant les coûts de l'opération de réassignation de sexe. La Presse canadienne, « Le gouvernement du Nouveau-Brunswick améliorera les services de santé pour les transgenres », (3 juin 2016) en ligne : http://journalmetro.com/actualites/national/974189/n-b-operations-de-confirmation-de-genre-couvertes/. Voir *Brodeur v Ontario (Health and Long-Term Care)*, 2013 HRTO 1229: Les demanderesses, femmes transgenres, considèrent que la non-couverture par le régime d'assurance-santé de l'Ontario des traitements d'épilation au laser du visage et de la thérapie pour la voix est discriminatoire à leur égard. Selon le juge, il ne s'agit pas de soins de santé nécessaires et il n'y a pas de discrimination envers les demanderesses. Il ne s'agit pas de services offerts aux autres assuré-e-s de la province. Notons que le traitement d'épilation au laser du visage et de thérapie pour la voix ne sont couverts par aucun régime d'assurance-santé au Canada.

[156] *Entente relative à la mise en place d'un guichet administratif pour les transsexuels,* citée dans la décision *M F c Régie de l'Assurance-maladie du Québec,* 2015 QCTAQ 11782.

[157] *M F c Régie de l'Assurance-maladie du Québec, ibid* aux para 22 et 35.

[158] Voir Greta R Bauer et al, «"I don't think this is theoretical; this is our lives": how erasure impacts health care for transgender people » (2009) 20(5) J Assoc Nurses AIDS Care 348.

[159] Voir Rachel Giblon et Greta R Bauer, « Health care availability, quality, and unmet need: a comparison of transgender and cisgender residents of Ontario, Canada » (2017) 17 BMC Health Services Research 283.

nombreuses études ont été menées sur les questions de santé concernant les personnes trans en Ontario.[160]

Pour obtenir une transition médicale au Centre métropolitain de chirurgie plastique de Montréal (Québec),[161] la personne doit fournir : deux lettres d'un psychiatre, d'un psychologue ou d'un sexologue qui a traité le patient pour au moins six mois et une autre lettre d'évaluation d'un de ces spécialistes. Il doit aussi fournir une lettre d'un médecin (endocrinologue ou médecin de famille) qui prescrit le traitement hormonal et une lettre d'un médecin de famille indiquant que la personne est en bonne santé.[162]

5 Les droits des personnes intersexes

Au Canada comme ailleurs, les personnes intersexes contestent la médicalisation et revendiquent une dépathologisation de leur situation.[163] De plus en plus d'études remettent en question la pertinence d'une chirurgie normative chez les enfants

[160]Ces études sont disponibles sur le site de Trans Pulse Ontario : AI Scheim et al, « Drug use among transgender people in Ontario, Canada: Disparities and associations with social exclusion » (2017) 72 Addictive Behaviors 151; AI Scheim et al, « Heavy episodic drinking among transgender persons: Disparities and predictors » (2016) 167 Drug and Alcohol Dependence 156; AI Scheim et al, « HIV-related sexual risk among transgender men who are gay, bisexual, or have sex with men » (2017) 74 (4) Immune Defic Syndr 89; G R Bauer et al, « Factors impacting transgender patients' discomfort with their family physicians: a respondent driven sampling study » (2015) PLoS ONE 2015; 10(12): e0145046; G R Bauer et al, « Intervenable factors associated with suicide risk in transgender persons: a respondent driven sampling study in Ontario, Canada » (2015) 15 BMC Public Health 525; G R Bauer et R Hammond, « Toward a broader conceptualization of trans women's sexual health » (2015) 24(1) The Canadian Journal of Human Sexuality 1.

[161]« Au Centre métropolitain de chirurgie (CMC) de Montréal, la seule clinique spécialisée en chirurgie de réassignation de sexe au Canada, près de 500 personnes ont eu recours au bistouri l'an dernier seulement, et plus de 8300 depuis la création de la clinique en 1990. Au cours des cinq dernières années, pas moins de 1888 femmes trans s'y sont présentées pour transformer leur sexe en un organe pleinement féminin, et 264 hommes trans pour obtenir un sexe masculin. Les trois chirurgiens y ont procédé autant à des mastectomies chez des adolescentes de 16 ans en transition que chez un homme de 78 ans ayant attendu le décès de sa conjointe pour vivre pleinement sa réelle identité de genre.» Voir Pauline Gravel, « Changer de genre sans changer de sexe. La chirurgie pour faire la paix avec son corps », Le Devoir, 23 mars 2019. En ligne: https://www.ledevoir.com/societe/550516/changer-de-genre-sans-changer-de-sexe.

[162]Action santé travesti(e)s et transsexuel(le)s du québec (ASTT(e)Q), *Je m'engage : Un manuel pour les professionnels de la santé et des services sociaux qui travaillent avec des personnes trans,* référence en ligne publiée le 12 mars 2014: http://enfantstransgenres.ca/ressources/je-mengage-un-manuel-pour-les-professionnels-de-la-sante-et-des-services-sociaux-qui-travaillent-avec-des-personnes-trans/.

[163]Pour des écrits au Canada, voir Janik Bastien Charlebois, « Femmes intersexes: sujet politique extrême du féminisme » (2014) 27 Recherches féministes 237; André Wilcox et al, « L'enfant intersexué: dysphorie entre le modèle médical et l'intérêt supérieur de l'enfant » (2015) 142 Intervention 65. Voir aussi G Davis et E Murphy, « Intersex Bodies as states of Exception: An Empirical

intersexués en santé.[164] Les personnes intersexes demandent que le droit à l'intégrité physique des enfants intersexués soit respecté: il ne faut pas leur imposer une chirurgie normative pour corriger une « erreur de la nature ».[165] Les enfants intersexués ont le droit de choisir. Les parents doivent être pleinement informés des conséquences de l'opération corrective sur leur enfant.

Les personnes intersexes majeures ou mineures sont protégées contre la discrimination fondée sur l'identité ou l'expression de genre par les chartes canadienne et québécoise ainsi que par les lois provinciales sur les droits de la personne.[166] Dans les écoles, les autorités doivent s'assurer que les enfants intersexués, comme tout autre enfant membre d'une minorité sexuelle, ne sont pas victimes de discrimination et jouissent d'accommodement raisonnable (par exemple, accès aux toilettes et vestiaires selon le sexe auquel ils et elles s'identifient).

Des personnes intersexes ayant subi une transition médicale en bas âge peuvent vouloir corriger la mention du sexe au registre de l'état civil. La même procédure administrative que pour les personnes trans s'applique alors.

En Ontario, pour la confection du certificat de naissance, les parents d'un enfant dont le sexe n'est pas déterminé ne sont pas obligés d'indiquer un prénom aux fins du certificat de naissance.[167]

6 Conclusion

Nous avons fait état des revendications des personnes trans qui ont mené à des changements importants dans les différentes législations, tant sur le plan fédéral que provincial ou territorial, partout au Canada. Les revendications des personnes trans

---

Explanation for Unnecessary Modification » (2013) 25 Feminist Formations 129. L'Association médicale canadienne défend la position selon laquelle les adolescent-e-s et les personnes adultes ont le droit de choisir leur propre identité de genre; Resolutions adopted by general council (Confirmed) 147th Annual Meeting of the Canadian Medical Association Aug 18-20, 2014 – Ottawa, ON.

[164]Wilcox, *ibid*; Davis et Murphy, *ibid*.

[165]Ces chirurgies sont considérées comme des abus médicaux selon les experts qui ont rédigé les Principes de Jogjakarta. Le consentement de l'enfant doit être libre et éclairé. Voir Principe 18, « Protection contre les abus médicaux, Principes sur l'application de la législation internationale des droits humains en matière d'orientation sexuelle et d'identité de genre (Principes de Jogjakarta) », 2007. Pour une discussion sur cette remise en question et son impact sur le droit, voir Brunet « Ordre social contre ordre « naturel » : la mention du sexe sur l'état civil des personnes intersexes », *supra* note 145.

[166]*Supra* note 10.

[167]*Statistiques de l'état civil (Loi sur les)*, *supra* note 106, art 10 (2). À notre connaissance, rien de semblable n'existe au Québec ni dans les autres provinces canadiennes, où il faut absolument choisir un des deux sexes (féminin ou masculin) pour dresser le certificat de naissance, CcQ, art 115. Il semble que le seul pays européen à offrir l'option d'un sexe indéterminé pour le registre de l'état civil soit l'Allemagne : Gabrielle Houbre, « Un « sexe indéterminé » ? : l'identité civile des hermaphrodites entre droit et médecine au XIXe siècle » (2014) Revue d'histoire du XIXe siècle 48.

ne sont pas pour autant terminées. Le prochain débat risque de se trouver dans la remise en question complète du sexe, comme critère de distinction dans les lois, dans les politiques, de même que comme élément d'identification de la personne, dans les documents officiels, mais aussi le sexe partout où il se trouve, comme en matière de filiation également. Tel était l'objectif de la demande en jugement déclaratoire du Centre de lutte contre l'oppression des genres (Centre for Gender Advocacy) qui a contesté le caractère discriminatoire de plusieurs articles du Code civil qui reproduisent la binarité sexuelle.[168] On a démédicalisé les corps et désexualisé le mariage. Certaines provinces comme l'Ontario ne recourent plus au sexe pour l'établissement de la filiation. Il est fort à parier que le sexe mais également le genre plus globalement disparaitra progressivement des législations au Canada et dans le monde à l'avenir.

[168] *Supra* note 14.

Gender Identity, Human Dignity and Self-Determination in Chile

Fabiola Lathrop

Abstract This chapter explains the legal regulation of sexual identity in Chile and presents a critical view of recent statutory changes oriented to safeguard the rights of transpersons but actually defective in providing certainty for the exercise of such rights.

In Chile, it has been possible to build recognition at the level of a fundamental right of the right to gender identity based on the open catalogue of rights established in the Political Constitution of the Republic and various international treaties incorporated via Article 5, paragraph 2, of the Constitution. Consequently, recognition of the right to gender identity emanates from the right to identity, enshrined in the various international instruments signed by Chile, and from the protection of human dignity and the free development of the personality, complemented by the principle that imposes on Chile the duty to generate conditions conducive to the self-determination of the individual.

On the statutory level, the right to gender identity is recognized by Law No. 21,120 of 28 November 2018. Its enactment filled an enormous gap in the national law through the regulation of both the content of the right to gender identity, its definition, its exercise and by the procedures it establishes. Despite the positive results of the enactment of legislation that formally recognizes the right to gender identity, threats to the dignity of individuals can be found in its provisions, through the violation of the principle of self-determination and non-pathologization by requesting that petitioners between 14 and 18 years of age provide proof of mental health, or through the violation of the right to family life, as it still is the duty of the judge to end any marriage when approving a request made by a person with a valid

The author acknowledges the assistance of Francisco Galli and Diego Cuadra.

F. Lathrop (✉)
Civil Law, Facultad de Derecho, Universidad de Chile (Santiago de Chile), Santiago, RM, Chile
e-mail: flathrop@derecho.uchile.cl

I. C. Jaramillo, L. Carlson (eds.), *Trans Rights and Wrongs*, Ius Comparatum - Global Studies in Comparative Law 54,
https://doi.org/10.1007/978-3-030-68494-5_17

marriage bond. The statute has not yet entered into force, so no data is available as to its reception at the judicial level, its application and even at the doctrinal level, it is still not yet possible to find comments on the law.

In effect, until the new law enters into force, in the absence of a special regulation, the recognition of the right to gender identity must be built, on one hand, on the basis of constitutional provisions that protect the right to dignity, identity and psychological integrity and the incorporation of the various international treaties signed by Chile and, on the other hand, its exercise on the basis of the provisions of Law No. 17,344 that authorizes the change of name and, together with a correct hermeneutic of the legislation in force, of sex. Faced with the lack of specific regulation in force, each time a petitioner wishes to change their name and sex on a birth certificates to reflect his or her gender identity, recourse must be had to the provisions established by Law No. 17,344 authorizes name changes. The object of this law is too far removed from the protection of the recognition and correct exercise of the right to gender identity. Consequently, in the application of the law, various criteria are observed that often are dependent on the internal convictions of the judge, erroneous understandings about gender and even incorrect interpretations as to the legal texts in force, which lead to absurd decisions that access the change of name but not the registered sex, thus leaving name and sex discordant in the identification records. All this subjects those interested in adapting their identification documents to their gender identity to a patent violation of their dignity and privacy.

This creates a situation of legal uncertainty that undermines the formal recognition and exercise of the right to gender identity, leaving applicants in a complete state of violation of their dignity and privacy. On the other hand, despite the situation existing in the country's various courts of justice, initiatives are being taken by certain ministries and state administrative bodies to protect the right to gender identity through incentives to use language that recognizes gender and its various components.

1 The Regulation of Civil Status in Chile

Civil status is regulated in the Civil Code, defined in Article 304, as the "quality of an individual insofar as it enables him to exercise certain rights and to contract certain civil obligations." This concept has been criticized by scholars as it fails to define what is to be construed by the "quality" that enables a person to exercise and contract, respectively, certain rights and obligations.[1] The majority position follows the interpretation of Manuel Somarriva,[2] who in 1946 defined it as the permanent place of a person in society, which depends mainly on family relations and which empowers the person to exercise certain rights and to contract certain obligations.

[1] Ruz Lártiga (2011), p. 523.

[2] Somarriva Undurraga (1946), p. 485.

The sources of civil status are filiation, marriage, the death of a spouse (which leads to the status of widow or widower) and judicial rulings (which establishes in some cases the status of legally separated or divorced). From this perspective, the law recognizes the following civil statuses: child, father or mother, married, legally separated, divorced and widowed.[3]

In addition, Law No. 20,830 of April 21, 2015 on Civil Unions established the status of civil partner, conferred at the time the union is performed. Furthermore, No. Law No. 4,808 of February 10, 1930, on the Office of Vital Records makes mention in two articles of the civil status of "single", first in regulating the registration of marriages (Article 39 numeral 3) and again in the context of the registration of religious marriage (Article 40 bis numeral 5). Sex, furthermore, is not a category recognized as an element of civil status, but rather as a fundamental prerequisite for the valid recording of a birth.

The determination and proof of civil status are regulated in Title XVII of the Book 1 of the Civil Code. The primary means of evidence thereof is the records kept by the Vital Records and Identification Service or Civil Registry (SRCEI). Article 305 of the Civil Code provides that:

- The civil status of married, legally separated, divorced, or widowed, and of father, mother or child, shall be verified vis-a-vis third parties and shall be proven by means of the corresponding records of marriage, death, and birth or baptism.
- The civil status of father, mother or child will also be verified or proven by the corresponding registration or sub-registration in the act of acknowledgment or of the judicial resolution that establishes filiation.
- Age and death may be verified or proven by means of the corresponding birth or baptism and death records.

Article 309 establishes alternative means of proving civil status:

- The absence of a marriage record may be supplemented by other authentic documents, by statements of witnesses who have witnessed the marriage and, failing this evidence, by the conspicuous possession of that marital status.
- Filiation, in the absence of a birth record or sub-registration, may only be verified or proved by the authentic instruments through which it has been legally determined. In the absence of these, the status of father, mother or child must be proven in the corresponding filiation proceeding in the manner and means set forth in Title VIII.

The creation of, or changes to, civil status depend on the applicable legal hypothesis. Thus, the law sets forth the rules for filiation in Title VII of Book 1 of the Civil Code, assigning the status of father, mother and child based on either natural birth or adoption. In the case of natural birth, the law recognizes the categories of in-wedlock and out-of-wedlock affiliation. In general, we can say that kinship is determined either through certain hypotheses or legal presumptions,

[3]Ruz, Gonzalo, *Explicaciones...*, *op. cit.*, p. 253.

by a final and enforceable judicial decision handed down in a filiation proceeding, or by the act of acknowledgment by the father, mother or both, especially in the case of out-of-wedlock filiation.

The civil status of married is acquired through a marriage performed in keeping with the provisions of the Civil Code, Title IV, Book 1 and Law No. 19,947, dated May 17, 2004, which introduced substantive changes to existing legislation. In any case, such weddings may only be performed between a bride and groom of different sexes. Legal separation and divorce are also regulated in that same legislation. Divorce may be unilateral or bilateral, but in any case is to meet certain requirements. In contrast to *de facto* separation, legal separation—as the name implies—involves the formal recognition by the courts that the spouses are no longer together. The primary effect of legal separation, in accordance with Article 34 of Law No. 19,947, consists of the cessation of the existing asset management regime between the spouses and, additionally, pursuant to Article 33 thereto, the suspension of certain conjugal rights and obligations such as cohabitation and fidelity, insofar as they are incompatible with the newly-acquired status of "separated". Lastly, the status of widow or widower is acquired when the death of the spouse occurs. The death is required to be recorded with the Office of Vital Records.

2 Specific Regulations for Trans Persons

There is a constitutional duty of the Chilean State to recognize and protect the right to gender identity. Based on the Constitution, the right to *gender identity* must be construed as recognized as a fundamental right in Chile's legal system. This is because the Constitution acknowledges a broad catalog of fundamental rights, composed of those rights explicitly recognized in Article 19, as well as those set forth in international treaties and conventions which, as we have seen, are incorporated into domestic law in accordance with Article 5, paragraph 2, of the Constitution. The right to *gender identity* is included among that broad catalog in two different places within the Constitution: first, as a fundamental right enshrined in international treaties signed and ratified by Chile and, second, as an implicit right inherent to the Constitution itself.

In terms of the former, as we know, the right to *gender identity* is specifically recognized by the Convention on the Rights of the Child (CRC) and the American Convention on Human Rights (ACHR). Both instruments have been signed and ratified by Chile. The CRC was ratified on January 26, 1990 and incorporated into domestic legislation by means of Decree 830 of September 27, 1990. For its part, The ACHR was ratified on October 8, 1990 and incorporated at the internal level by means of Decree No. 873 on January 5, 1991. In that context, based on the international treaties ratified by Chile, the Constitutional Court[4] has recognized the existence of the right to identity as one among the catalog of fundamental rights protected by the Constitution: "It should be recognized that the various international instruments, ratified by Chile and in force, cited by the petitioning judge in support of his argument, enshrine the right to personal identity, thus generating the obligation of State agencies to respect and promote them pursuant to the provisions of Article 5, paragraph 2 of the Charter."[5]

Furthermore, the recognition and the implicit protection of the right to *gender identity* within the Constitution stems directly from the protection of human dignity and freedom to develop personal rights contained in Article 1, paragraph 1 of the Constitution, that is, in the context of the chapter on the Institutional Foundations of the legal order. The Constitution recognizes that people are born free and equal in dignity and rights. On that basis, the Constitution sets forth the State's obligation to create a legal framework that protects human dignity, including the creation of opportunities for individual autonomy. In addition, Article 1, paragraph 3, enshrines the principle of the State being at the service of human beings. Among other aspects, this means that the State is required to foster and contribute to the creation of such social conditions that will allow each and every one of the members of the national community to attain their greatest possible spiritual and material fulfillment. Thus, this provision reinforces the duty of the State to create conditions that facilitate an individual's self-determination. The right to *gender identity* should be construed in this framework.

The Constitutional Court has reaffirmed the existence of an implicit protection of the right to identity within the Charter:

> Although the Constitution of Chile does not recognize the right to identity per se, this shall not impede this Court from providing adequate protection thereof, precisely because of the close relationship [between identity and] human dignity and because [the right to identity] is expressly protected in several international treaties ratified by Chile and in force in our country (Judgment 834, recital 22); TENTH: That, from this perspective, the recognition of the right to personal identity -as it emanates from human dignity- means the possibility for every individual to be himself and not another. This translates into a person's right to be registered immediately after birth, to have a name from that moment on and, to the extent possible, to know his parents and to be cared for by them. Although this understanding the right to personal identity stems from Article 7 of the Convention on the Rights of the Child, such recognition and protection should not be limited to underage minors. That is because

---

[4]Since the 2005 constitutional reform, Chile's Constitutional Court has been solely responsible for overseeing the legality of legislation: "Thus, since 2006 the Constitutional Court has served as the guardian of the regulations, principles and values enshrined in the Constitution, insofar as its previous role in the *a priori* examination of pending legislation has, since the 2005 reform, been supplemented by a transcendental and crucial a posteriori oversight of the regulations in force. This is effected by means of appeals based on the inapplicability of existing laws [on the grounds of unconstitutionality], which translates in concrete terms into the oversight of legal tenants, as well as the control of constitutionality, with the powers to order the offending provision removed from Chile's legal system." (emphasis added) *See* Colombo Campbell, Juan, "La historia explica el presente y el presente el futuro. Tribunal Constitucional, Memoria 2007 – 2008," p. 10.

[5]Chile's Constitutional Court, rol 1.340-2009, September 29, 2009, considerando 9.

> the right to personal identity is a highly personal one, inherent to every person, regardless of age, sex or social status. The close link between the right to personal identity and human dignity is undeniable, since dignity is only affirmed when the person enjoys the security of knowing his or her origin and, on that basis, can aspire to the social recognition he or she deserves. From this point of view, the right to personal identity enjoys a status similar to that of the right to nationality which a person shall not be denied.

Additionally, it should be noted that the notion of human dignity which gives rise to the recognition of *gender identity*, is closely linked to the right to freedom, that is, the power of each person to develop their own individualism autonomously. This right is also implicitly recognized in Article 1 of Chile's Constitution, as cited above, as acknowledged by the Constitutional Court: "*FIFTY-ONE: That the fact that the Legislature selected the final option described does not refute that the unfettered development of a person's individuality is an expression of the dignity of every person, which is emphatically affirmed in Article 1, Paragraph 1 of the Basic Charter.*"[6] (Emphasis added)

3 Reception of the Right to Gender Identity at the Legal Level

The right to gender identity is formally recognized and regulated in Law No. 21,120 "Recognizes and protects the right to gender identity" of 28 November 2018, which, as will be seen below, despite being a law of the Republic, has not yet entered into force. With the eventual enactment of this law, despite this period of legal vacancy, an enormous gap will be filled in Chilean legislation, incorporating for the first time the right to gender identity into positive legal language, recognizing the different components of gender, guaranteeing its recognition and protection, and regulating the necessary procedures to access the rectification of birth records and name change insofar as these are not in accordance with the gender identity of the interested party. Prior to the date mentioned above, the right to gender identity was treated indirectly based on the general regulations contained in Law No. 4,808, referred above, Law No. 17,334 of 22 September 1970, which authorizes the change of first or surnames in indicated cases; as well as in Law No. 20,609 of 24 July 2012, which establishes measures against discrimination.

Thus, the right to gender identity initially was not addressed by any comprehensive perspective in the legislation; it was not expressly regulated at any legal level, neither as a fundamental right nor as a right of personality, nor were there any regulations to deal with rights collisions that might occur with respect to third parties from the exercise of the right to gender identity. On the other hand, there was no legal language recognizing the different components of gender and, more broadly, sexuality. Without prejudice to the foregoing, certain ministries and state

[6] Chile's Constitutional Court, rol 1.683-2010, January 4, 2011, considerando 51.

administrative bodies made progress in safeguarding and protecting gender identity, including within the policies developed the incentive to use a language that recognized gender and its various components. We will in the following review the areas of education and healthcare.

3.1 Gender Identity in the Field of Education

The Ministry and the Superintendence of Education have issued guidance on *gender identity* in the field of education, including the use of language that respects, protects and is compatible with individual identity. These instruments include the following:

(a) Ministry of Education. Document "Training in sexuality, affectivity and gender", published in June 2013: Contains a section with a glossary of terms associated with gender and sexuality and differentiates between the concepts of biological sex and gender.[7]
(b) Ministry of Education. Plan entitled "Education for Gender Equality. 2015–2018 Plan", published in January 2017: Contains a paragraph entitled "Categories of Gender" that defines the different components of sexuality.[8]
(c) Ministry of Education. Document entitled "Guidelines for the inclusion of lesbian, gay, bisexual, trans and intersex people in the Chilean educational system", published in April 2017: Contains a paragraph entitled "Sexual and gender diversity: basic definitions"[9] which defines the concepts of sex, gender, sexual orientation, gender identity, gender expressions, LGTBI, heterosexual, homosexual, lesbian, gay, bisexual, trans and intersex.
(d) Superintendence of Education. Circular 0768, issued in April 2017 and addressed to Chilean school managers and principals: it explains the meaning and scope of the provisions regulating the rights of male, female and trans students in the field of education. The memorandum expressly defines, in a special paragraph, the concepts of gender identity, gender expression and trans.[10]
(e) Ministry of Education. Website www.convivenciaescolar.cl: Contains a special section entitled "Sexuality, Affectivity and Gender" which describes the

[7]http://portales.mineduc.cl/usuarios/convivencia_escolar/doc/201307221719000.PDF_formacion_sexualidad.pdf [last accessed 23-06-2017].

[8]http://www.mineduc.cl/wp-content/uploads/sites/19/2017/01/CartillaUEG.pdf [last accessed 23-06-2017].

[9]http://portales.mineduc.cl/usuarios/convivencia_escolar/File/2017/LGBTI_27_04_2017.pdf [last accessed 23-06-2017].

[10]https://www.supereduc.cl/wp-content/uploads/2017/04/ORD-N%C2%BA0768-DERECHOS-DE-NI%C3%91AS-NI%C3%91OS-Y-ESTUDIANTES-TRANS-EN-EL-%C3%81MBITO-DE-LA-EDUCACI%C3%93N-A-SOSTENEDORES.pdf [last accessed 23-06-2017].

legislation and materials on each of these subjects in the context of education;[11] contains a section dedicated to the difference between biological sex and gender.

3.2 Gender Identity in the Field of Health Care

In the area of health care, we also find instruments that recognize and protect the right to *gender identity* and foster the use of appropriate language that respects that identity:

(a) Ministry of Health. Circular 34 of September 13, 2011, which provides instructions "on the care of trans persons and the strengthening of Hospital strategy for diverse sexuality persons at public health care facilities": Measures to facilitate timely access of trans persons to health care; Contains a variety of definitions on *gender identity* and the difference with biological sex.[12]
(b) Ministry of Health. Circular 21 of June 14, 2012, that "Reiterates Instructions on care of trans persons in the public health care system":[13] Supplements and expands on Circular 34; particularly, in terms of language, the circular improves the definitions contained in Circular 34, by eliminating references to the mismatch between gender and biological sex as an identity disorder.
(c) Ministry of Health. Document "Clinical Pathway for the Physiological Alignment of People with Inconsistencies between Physical Sex and Gender Identity", dated 2010:[14] it refers to the recommended interventions and flow charts for working with trans persons, from initial contact with the health care system to sex change.
(d) Ministry of Health Document. "Practical Guide on Counseling in Sexual and Reproductive Health for Adolescents, Orientation for Primary Care Teams (2016),"[15] adopted on February 5, 2016: addresses the notions of trans genderism and explicitly states that the inconsistency between physical sex and gender is not a mental illness. Additionally, the Guide contains a glossary of terms which addresses the notions of sexuality and the different components of gender.
(e) Talcahuano Health Service. Document "Protocol for Care and Referral of Trans Patients",[16] approved on December 12, 2015: with the objective of standardizing

[11] [Last accessed 23-06-2017].

[12] www.movilh.cl/documentacion/trans/Circular-Salud-Trans.pdf [last accessed 23-06-2017].

[13] www.movilh.cl/documentacion/CIRCULAR21MINSAL.pdf [last accessed 23-06-2017].

[14] www.minsal.cl/portal/url/item/d126e58ba4cb53f5e040010165017912.pdf [last accessed 23-06-2017].

[15] http://web.minsal.cl/wp-content/uploads/2015/09/CONSEJERIA-EN-SALUD-SEXUAL-Y-REPRODUCTIVA-PARA-ADOLESCENTES-2016.pdf [last accessed 23-06-2017].

[16] www.sstalcahuano.cl/file/diversidad/Resolucion_y_Protocolo_Trans.pdf [last accessed 23-06-2017].

the admission procedure for trans persons into secondary care at the public health care network in the city of Talcahuano. The document contains, among other items, a glossary of terms on sexuality and gender.

(f) Carlos Van Buren Hospital. Document "Protocol for the Care of Transgender Polyclinic Patients: Gender Identity":[17] The primary objective was to establish a mental health practice that reflected the principles of de-pathologization of *gender identity*; contains definitions on *gender identity* and expressions associated with trans genderism.

3.3 Gender Identity and the Medical Examiner's Medical Service

Finally, the Medical Examiner's Medical Service, a government agency operating under the purview of the Ministry of Justice and Human Rights, issued Circular 1297/2012 on November 9, 2012 which provides instructions on "Compliance with the Technical Expert Guidance on Forensic Sexology for Cases of Trans and Intersex Persons."[18] It states that sexological examinations must be carried out within the framework of respect for the dignity of the examinee, adding that "physical exams shall not be invasive to the human body, unless specifically court-ordered. In the latter case, the protocol for information and informed consent applicable to all other court-ordered exams shall be implemented. The examinee shall be informed of the right to refuse such examination. The order further adds that the name the examinee uses socially, or that the person prefers, shall be used in all interactions.

3.4 Law No. 20,609 of July 24, 2012 Establishes Measures Against Discrimination

This body of law provides grounds for action against arbitrary discrimination and allows for relief in the form of termination of the discriminatory act or omission. The competent Court is empowered to order any measures as may be necessary toward that end. In the context of the definition of arbitrary discrimination, Article 2 of Law No. 20,609 expressly identifies *gender identity* as an area where there is a propensity for concern, and list gender identity as a "suspect class." Additionally, Article 17 of Law No. 20,609 amended the Criminal Code to include the gender identity of the victim as a motivation in the commission of a crime as an aggravating factor.

---

[17] http://www.senado.cl/appsenado/index.php?mo=tramitacion&ac=getDocto&iddocto=2650&tipodoc=docto_comision [last accessed 23-06-2017].

[18] www.fundacionrenaciendo.org/images/PROTOCOLOSML.pdf [last accessed 23-06-2017].

That said, Law No. 20,609 is wholly insufficient to protect the right to *gender identity* of individuals, given that it regulates the defense of *gender identity*, that is, an individual's right not to suffer undue interference in the exercise of *gender identity*. As such, this legislation does not recognize nor does it protect the active phase of the right to *gender identity*:

> [T]his is a matter for which Law 20,609, which establishes measures against discrimination, is not sufficient. In fact, although they are often treated unfairly and discriminated against by the health services or the courts; in school when they are children or adolescents; at work; or even when performing an act apparently as simple as crossing the border of the country or voting in an electoral process -which will undoubtedly lead in many cases to situations addressed in Law 20,609- the truth is that the most heartfelt demand for equality of certain individuals transsexual or trans persons - is to ensure that Chilean law- and society and its actors, political or otherwise- abandon the laws, practices and general lack of uniformity that occurs when they seek to adapt their legally-registered identity to the reality they live and feel and which, moreover, leads to the violation of other rights such as privacy, honor, freedom of expression, or physical and mental integrity.[19]

In addition, Law No. 20,609 fails to comply with international standards on discrimination. Iván Díaz García explains that there is a discrepancy between the concept of discrimination contained in the law and the one expressed in International Human Rights Law and constitutional law:

> The law states that discrimination exists when there is a difference in treatment for which there is no admissible justification and that, in addition, when a fundamental right is violated. However, from the point of view of international law and constitutional rights, a conduct may be discriminatory even if other fundamental rights are not affected. Thus, the law establishes a requirement beyond the scope of constitutional and international regulations to qualify certain behaviors as discriminatory.[20]

The law contains also inadequate regulation of this "suspect class": "The law uses the indeterminate expression "specifically" to associate such class with the presence of discriminatory conduct. This generates an acute problem of interpretation which deprives such classes of their role, in particular, in international law, to raise an alert to discrimination when the difference in treatment is based on one of these categories."[21]

Finally, the formula contemplated in the law for resolving conflicts between non-discrimination and fundamental and other constitutional rights is in breach of the standards set forth in international law: "The law establishes a relationship of unconditioned precedence to the detriment of the former. This solution is directly opposed to the way in which international law and constitutional law resolve such

---

[19]Gauché Marchetti, Ximena, "La necesidad de una ley de identidad de género en Chile", 2013, (online) http://www.elmostrador.cl/noticias/opinion/2013/05/18/la-necesidad-de-una-ley-de-identidad-de-genero-para-chile/ [last accessed 23-06-2017].

[20]Díaz García (2013), p. 667.

[21]*Ibid.*

collisions, since they are based on criteria of reasonableness, objectivity and proportionality."[22]

4 Legal Regulations Concerning Names and Sexual Identity

Until 2018, there was no law specifically regulating the exercise of the right to gender identity in Chile; the possibility that trans persons could adapt the name and sex consigned in the birth records to their gender identity was not expressly enshrined. Consequently, for both purposes, trans persons should be subject to the general name change procedure established in Laws No. 4,808 and No. 17,344, referred to above.

4.1 Object and Procedure for Name Changes

Article 1 of Law No. 4,808 seeks to regulate the Office of Vital Records and its various inscriptions and certificates, particularly birth, marriage and death, as well as the registration of other acts and contracts relating to the civil status of persons. These regulations are supplemented by Law No. 19,477 of October 19, 1996 which establishes the organic law for the Vital Records and Identification Service.

Article 31 of Law No. 4,808 provides for the content of records of birth, establishing therein the name and surname of the newborn. In addition, that legislation requires that records of birth contain the names, surnames, nationality, profession or trade, and address of the parents, or those of the father or mother that recognizes or has recognized the newborn. In that context, Article 31, subparagraph 3, bans the use of names that are extravagant, ridiculous, unbecoming, sexually ambiguous or contrary to the proper use of language. These restrictions were incorporated through Law No. 17,344. For purposes of monitoring compliance with this restriction, Vital Records officials are empowered to oppose the registration of a name. In such a case, at the insistence of the petitioner, the information is forwarded to the corresponding Court, which is required to rule on whether the name is subject to the ban in the shortest possible time following a hearing with the parties. Said hearing is expressly barred from taking the form of a trial. Another requirement of Article 31 related to the right to *gender identity* is the designation of the sex of the newborn on the record of birth. Pursuant to Article 33 of Law No. 4,808, the date of birth and both sex and name are essential prerequisites and no registration can be done in their absence.

Although Law No. 17,344 regulates the procedure for a change of name, it does not specifically contemplate the recording a change of sex on records held by the

[22] *Ibid.*

Office of Vital Records. Article 1 of Law No. 17,344 authorizes a change in name or surname, or both at the same time, in the following cases:

(a) When one or the other is ridiculous, laughable or morally or materially degrading;
(b) When the applicant has been known for more than 5 years, on plausible grounds, with names or surnames, or both, other than his own, and;
(c) In cases of out-of-wedlock filiation or in which the filiation is not determined, a surname may be added when the person has been registered with just one, or one of those recorded at birth may be changed, when both were identical.[23]

The request for a change of name may be filed by adults or by a legal guardian of the child or adolescent. In the case of a child or adolescent lacking a legal guardian, or should such legal representative be unable or refuse to authorize the underage minor to request the change or deletion of the names or surnames pursuant to Law No. 17,344, the judge will rule, after a hearing with the child, at the request of any blood relative, child advocate or *sua sponte.*

From the above it is clear that the petition cannot be filed by the child directly, but only by their legal guardians. Only in case of opposition, or when the guardian is unable to authorize the child, may the judge resolve the request of at his or her own initiative. The petition must necessary be processed by a court of law. Reaffirming the foregoing, Article 17 of Law No. 4,808, prescribes in paragraph 1 that birth records may not be altered or modified except by an enforceable judicial ruling.

As set forth in Article 817 of the Code of Civil Procedure, those proceedings are, in principle, non-contentious. An excerpt of the petition must be published to allow affected third parties to file a motion of opposition. The excerpt shall necessarily contain the individualization of the petitioner and the indication of the names and surnames that the applicant intends to use instead of those duly recorded. In other words, the procedure is not confidential. Following the publication of the petition, third parties enjoy a period of 30 days to file grounds for opposition to the change. If the request is unopposed, the petition is processed in keeping with the procedures applicable in non-contentious cases; if opposed, the procedure is deemed contentious. The evidence of the grounds on which the petition is based shall be presented in the form of a brief, defined in Article 818 of the Code of Civil Procedure as "evidence of any nature, introduced without prior service of process or intervention of a contradictory party and without prior indication of a discovery period." Such evidence notwithstanding, the SRCEI shall always be heard in these proceedings, be they contentious or voluntary.

The only specific cause for the automatic rejection of the petition is if the applicant is currently on trial or has been convicted of a felony or other offense carrying a sentence of incarceration, unless more than 10 years have elapsed since the date of the final judgment and the sentence has been served. Compliance with

[23]In Chile, an individual's last name is normally recorded with both the both patronymic and the matronymic.

this requirement is to be effected by means of the corresponding certificate the SRCEI is required to present during the proceeding. A judgment in favor of the petitioner will contain an order to the Office of Vital Records to perform a new registration. Pursuant to Article 4 of Law No. 17,344, once the birth record has been legally modified, the individual changing his or her name or surnames may in the future only use those new names for all acts and activities. The malicious use of the prior name(s) is punishable in the terms set forth in Article 5.

4.2 Application of the Regulations on Name Change

The rulings of the Civil Courts of Santiago on petitions for name and gender changes to birth records filed by trans persons between 2005 and 2009 were researched in 2012 by Claudia Llanquilef and Luis Barrientos—students at the University of Chile School of Law—under the guidance of Professor Lorena Lorca, in the context of an undergraduate thesis.[24] The investigation showed:

> [T]that between 2005 and 2009, 19 petitions for modifications to transgender birth records were processed. Of those, in 18 cases the request was for a change of both sex and name; in the remaining case, only a name change was requested. Of these 19 cases, a final, enforceable ruling was handed down in only 14 cases. The case load seems to have risen over the years, with just one final judgment in 2005; two in 2006 and 2007, respectively; five in 2008; and, six in 2009. In the same period, in five cases an unfavorable judgment was issued in the first instance, that is, the petition was rejected. Only one of those cases was appealed. In that case, the Court overturned the lower court's order in part and ordered the office of Vital Records to perform the name change. The Appellate Court did not, however, order a change in sex, ergo it remained the same.[25]

Professor Lorena Lorca stressed that the most frequent argument of the Courts in denying the requests for a change of name and sex submitted by trans persons between 2005 and 2009 was a legal void that kept them from resolving the case. In addition, applicants were required to have undergone sex reassignment surgery as an added criterion to for the petitions to be granted.[26] In fact, at that time, the general rule was that courts required both a report and expert examination by the Medical Examiner's Service to substantiate gender dysphoria and the existence of successful sex reassignment surgery.[27]

---

[24]Refers to: Barrientos Walls and Llanquilef Candia (2012).

[25]Lorca Muñoz, Lorena, "La defensa de las personas transexuales en Chile para obtener el reconocimiento de su identidad de género". VII Conferencia Internacional de Educación en Derechos Humanos, 2016, (online) http://ihrec2016.org/wp-content/uploads/2016/12/Ponencia-conferencia-internacional-EDH-de-Lorena-Lorca-Muñoz.docx [last accessed 09-06-2017].

[26]*Ibid.*

[27]Centro de Derechos Humanos, Universidad Diego Portales, *Informe Anual sobre derechos humanos en Chile*, Capítulo 9, Diversidad Sexual y Derechos Humanos, 2009, (online) http://www.derechoshumanos.udp.cl/derechoshumanos/images/InformeAnual/2009/Cap%2009%20Diversidad%20sexual%20y%20ddhh.pdf [last accessed 26-01-2017].

Furthermore, co-author Adriana Palavecino also emphasizes that paragraph 3 of Article 31—referred to above—was initially interpreted at the jurisprudential level as a basis for refusing name change petitions when the name did not match the registration.[28] It is worth repeating that paragraph 3 of Article 31 of Law No. 4,808 on the Vital Records and Identification Service notes that newborns may not be given names that are extravagant, ridiculous, unbecoming, sexually ambiguous or contrary to the proper use of language.

One example of the difficulties is the judgment issued by the 16th Civil Court of Santiago, case number V-9-2009, dated October 30, 2009, which concluded:

> 6). That Law 17,344 authorizes the change of name and surnames in the circumstances mentioned above, but nothing says about sex change. On the other hand, the law on Office of Vital Records, in Article 31, provides that 'newborn may not be given a sexually ambiguous name';
>
> 7). That it is not within the purview of the Office of Vital Records to alter the birth record when the anatomical characteristics of the child born have been established according the certification thereto of the competent medical professional or practitioner present at the delivery and, as in the instant case, has not varied over time, the petition set forth on page 8 hereto must be denied.[29]

Along the same lines, we find a judgment from the 22nd Civil Court of Santiago dated November 28, 2008, case number V-87-2007: "TEN: That notwithstanding the contents of justification 9 above, pursuant to current legislation containing a prescriptive list of qualifying grounds which entitle an interested party to petition for a change in birth records, such cause is not foreseen in the legal system."[30]

Next, in relation to the requirement for sex reassignment surgery, the judgment issued by the 22nd Civil Court of Santiago expressly relied on report from the Office of Vital Records recommending against the name change on the grounds that:

> Notwithstanding the witness evidence presented on page 21 hereto which attests to the presence of the circumstances that fall within the confines of the aforementioned Article 1 (a) of Law 17,344, that is, moral impairment by the use of the proper names 'J.E.', this Service deems that it would not be legally appropriate to accede to the request unless the 'sex' section of the inscription were to be changed first from 'male' to 'female'. Such a change would necessitate that the petitioner undergo a surgical procedure, lest the name he seeks to register on the record of birth become ambiguous in terms of identifying the sex currently assigned to him. Were the petition to be granted absent said surgery, the identification of the individual would be compromised insofar as the national identity card would contain inconsistent data in stating the sex as 'female' and the name 'J.E.R.E.', which is precisely what is regulated in Article 31 of Law 4,808, which requires a correlation between the sex and the name of the individual registered.[31]

Based on the SRCEI's opinion, the court concluded that it was not possible to grant the name change because the applicant had not had sex reassignment surgery:

[28]Cfr. Palavecino Cáceres (2012), p. 97.

[29]Barrientos, Luis y Llanquilef, Claudia, *Jurisprudencia...*, *op. cit.*, pp. 280–281.

[30]Barrientos, Luis y Llanquilef, Claudia, *Jurisprudencia...*, *op. cit.*, pp. 291–293.

[31]*Ibid.*

"ELEVEN: That, furthermore, in the instant case, it is not just a change in the praenomen, but also an effort to secure a court-ordered change to the sex of the applicant, which is impracticable until the corresponding surgery is medically performed [after which], once the physical aspect has been resolved, the court may apply existing current legislation."[32] As we can see from the cases cited above, the judgments were based on the lack of regulations on sex change and on the requirement of prior sex reassignment surgery.

Similarly, a ruling of the 4th Civil Court of Santiago in case V-91-2007, dated December 31, 2008, is also based on the requirement for sex reassignment surgery. Alleging the existence of a regulatory void, the finding quotes paragraph 3 of Article 31 in refusing the petitioner's request for a change of name:[33]

> In the absence of evidence of a sex change through surgical intervention, which would have a direct impact on the records of the petitioner, the solution to the case in question is not expressly regulated in our legislation, insofar as a change in registered sex is lawful only in the case of individuals who have undergone surgery for that purpose (...). Wherefore, in keeping with the above, the request by the petitioner for a change of name is unlawful, as stated in the reports presented.
>
> This includes the report issued by the Medical Examiner's Office stating that although the petitioner appears at first blush to be a female, the external and internal genitalia are male and, therefore, it is essential to complete the standard and plastic surgery to form a neovagina to record a change of sex.
>
> The same issue is addressed by the Office of Vital Records in its report, noting that despite the lack of regulations on a change of sex, the judge must rule, but only in the case of persons who have undergone surgery, which is absent in the instant case.
>
> Wherefore, granting the request for a change of name would also be against the law, insofar as recording the birth of Alison R. M. as male would be ambiguous.

As is evident from these rulings, both the Court and the SRCEI in its their reports, required that sex reassignment surgery be performed as a prerequisite to a change of name and sex. In the absence of such surgery, moreover, the Court concluded that the change of name would lead to ambiguity regarding the male sex set forth on the petitioner's birth record.

Nonetheless, at the appellate level, the same Article 31 was interpreted very differently in the context of name change, but not sex change. Thus, the Court of Appeals of Santiago, in case number 2,541-2009, in a ruling dated June 25, 2009, granted the change of name in accordance with Article 31: "8. Whereas the granting of the option for the requested change of name allows, furthermore, compliance with the goals of Article 31 of the Law on the Office of Vital Records, that is to avoid imposing upon an individual a name that may be ambiguous with respect to sex, which in this specific case had occurred as a consequence of the petitioner's transsexual status, unveiled during adolescence and accepted by the petitioner

[32] *Ibid.*

[33] Barrientos, Luis y Llanquilef, Claudia, *Jurisprudencia..., op. cit.*, p. 252.

more than a decade ago, according to the expert report contained on page 55 of these proceedings."[34]

That is, the court of second instance associated sex with the *gender identity* of the petitioner, concluding that denying the request for a change of name would result in ambiguity in the records at Office of Vital Records pertaining to the petitioner's *gender identity*. Nevertheless, the same court maintained the requirement of sex reassignment surgery for the purpose of granting the sex change:

> 9. That, however, to authorize the change of sex in the respective records of birth, it seems reasonable to require that the petitioner first undergo surgery to align the external genitalia to the petitioner's lifestyle gender. In fact, although the decision on the name change presupposes an admission that the psychological component of sexuality is decisive for the purposes of defining a true identity in that area, it is equally true that the presence of external genitalia different from that of the lifestyle gender constitutes an element of uncertainty that must be prevented, even though it is highly unlikely that the petitioner would want to return to live in the manner of his original sex. That approach considers, inter alia, aspects such as procreation and the difficulties that could arise in the event the petitioner should become a father, insofar as they would have a profound impact on the rights of a third party.[35]

In 2009, the reports issued by the SRCEI in the framework of procedures for a change of name and sex required sex reassignment surgery as a prerequisite. That position was adopted by the courts:

> In sum, notwithstanding the arguments of the 'strict registration function', and of a 'dearth of regulations' which returned the matter to the consideration of the Judiciary, neither of which in fact constitute real arguments for accepting or rejecting the petitions under study, the trend at the Office of Vital Records is to report favorably on the rectification of birth records in those cases in which the petitioner has undergone surgery to conform his or her body to the desired sex and, in those cases in which there is no such intervention, suggests that such adjustment is a prerequisite to the change requested.[36]

Subsequent to 2009, there was evidence of a jurisprudential advance, particularly in the line of excluding the need to accredit a sexual reassignment operation, as well as the practice of a series of medical examinations. However, the criteria continued to lack total uniformity: "Fortunately, civil courts have been evaluating their rulings on transsexuality. If a few years ago it was indispensable for a change of name and sex registration to be granted that the trans person had undergone a series of surgical interventions to align the body, including sterilization, such plastics are no longer required nor are expert physical or psychological examinations required to be produced by the Medical Examiner's Office."[37]

This progress in precedent was largely due to the outstanding research by Professor Lorena Lorca and her students at the Legal Clinic of the Law School at the University of Chile. In a review of rulings handed down in between November 2009 and May 2014, conducted in the context of an undergraduate thesis by students

---

[34] *Ibid.*

[35] *Ibid.*

[36] Barrientos, Luis y Llanquilef, Claudia, *Jurisprudencia..., op. cit.*, p. 191.

[37] Álvarez Rubio et al. (2015), p. 383.

Jorge Pacheco Silva Martínez and Eduardo Silva Jerez, under the guidance of Professor Lorena Lorca, to their credit, we see that a final, enforceable ruling in favor of the petitioner was handed down in all 24 of the cases handled by the clinic.[38]

That precedent reflects progress in the arguments given by the courts for accepting the requests for a change of name and of sex by trans persons. Key among them is the recognition and protection of the fundamental rights of the petitioners. Similarly, such authority also expressly recognizes the identity rights of petitioners and avoids pathologizing *gender identity*.[39] As an example of these judgments, Professor Lorena Lorca[40] cites the following:

(a) The name of a person must be consistent with their sex, a matter that cannot be reduced to visual examination of the genitals at birth as, obviously, the sexuality of human beings is much more complex and an examination limited to genitalia cannot be construed as conclusive (Judgment of August 31, 2010 issued by the 7th Civil Court of Santiago, Case Number V-178-2009).
(b) The petitioner bases her request on her interpretation of the Political Constitution of the Republic, International Treaties and of Article 31 of Law 4,808 itself. Insofar as it is salient to analyze these regulations as a single, organic whole—given that their final purpose is the dignity and protection of individuals in all their dimensions, not only physical, but also psychological—this Court is obligated to review the request for a change of name and sex at the Office of Vital Records within the context of a reality beyond the scope of the legal realm and that affects petitioners in their daily lives in unimaginable ways that include moral and material impairment, [a situation that] this Court is obligated to rectify within the means available to it. (Judgment of March 18, 2013 issued by the 22nd Civil Court of Santiago, Case Number V-7-2012).
(c) It is evident to this court that a name, as an attribute of personality and essential component of a person's identity which determines his or her relationship with society and distinguishes him or her from others, [in the instant case] cannot be associated with a male, as such an allocation would prevent the petitioner from developing her true personality (. . .) That the need to resolve the issue presented to this court stems, at the end of the day, from an understanding of the fundamental right to personal development which is associated with a primary concept, which is the basis of all other principles and rights that the Political Constitution enshrines, that is, the dignity of the person. (Judgment of June 25, 2009, Case Number 2541-09 handed down by the Court of Appeals of Santiago).
(d) That the pertinent part of Article 19 of the Political Constitution of the Republic, guarantees to all persons, among others, the right to life and physical and psychological integrity; respect and protection of private life, honor of the

[38]Pacheco Martínez and Silva Jerez (2015).

[39]Lorca, Lorena, "La defensa...", *op. cit.*

[40]*Ibid.*

person and family, all of which are essential rights to human dignity and the provisions authorizing the rectification of a birth certificate are grounded in those rules of constitutional authority. (Judgment dated October 22, 2012 issued by the 25th Civil Court of Santiago, Case Number V-174-2010).

(e) That the spirit and foundation for the regulations that authorize a change in the birth record, and other documents, are contained in such constitutional precepts, insofar as they correspond to administrative actions that have been self-imposed by the social order to which we ascribe, but that, in and of themselves, may not cause harm to the human person. (Judgment dated August 26, 2011 issued by the 17th Civil Court of Santiago, Case Number V-115-2010). (Highlighted as per the original)

Moreover, a ruling issued by the 7th Civil Court of Santiago in case number V53-2016, dated August 22, 2016, is particularly germane, given that in a watershed decision, the change of name and sex registration of a 5-year old trans girl was granted. The ruling states that:

> [T]he name of a person must be consistent with their sex, a matter that cannot be reduced to visual examination of the genitals at birth as, obviously, the sexuality of human beings is much more complex and requires additional information as to the identity of the individual, and an examination limited to genitalia cannot be construed as definitive (. . .); adding that (. . .) of the analysis of the facts presented by the petitioners and of the results of the reports filed in this case, it can only be concluded that the request for rectification of the child's birth records must be granted (. . .) for the purpose of safeguarding the integrity and dignity of the person, ensuring a legal and social identity in keeping with the child's gender identity that allows [the child] to develop in fullness and in harmony with said identity.

Notwithstanding these advances, this trend is not absolute:

> For the purposes of this paper, we analyzed forty cases in which a final judgment had been issued. In 33 cases, the petition for change of name and sex was accepted; one of them noted that surgical interventions are a complementary element to the case and not a requirement for the petition to be granted (First Civil Court of Rancagua, August 16, 2011, Case Number 419-2010). Moreover, only four rejected the petition, and three granted it partially (for example, authorizing a name change only).[41] (Emphasis added)

Fernando Muñoz León found similar results in his research[42] through 2015. He reviewed 86 petitions for sex change within the previous 5 years, noting that some 80.2% of such petitions had been granted. Muñoz suggests that the fact that the change of sex was not granted when filed in conjunction with a name change petition in 19.8% of cases is because that the creative application of existing regulations is insufficient. The author points out that the partial rejection or acceptance of the application is due to an absence of complete sex reassignment. Furthermore, he notes that, in certain cases, the argument regarding the existence of a regulatory void continued to be used, and in others, the court relied on a purely biological conception of sexuality.

---

[41] Espejo Yaksic y Lathrop Gómez (2015), p. 395, footnote n° 4.

[42] Cfr. Muñoz León (2015), pp. 1018–1019.

As an example of the dearth of regulations, the author cites a judgment issued by the 26th Civil Court of Santiago dated May 25, 2011: "The mere examination of the case file makes it clear that the petitioner is a male (...) and since there is no provision of law in our legal system that allows the court to rule on the change of sex for an individual who at birth was in fact registered as a male, the court must dismiss the case initiated."[43]

In another publication, the author highlights cases in which the request for sex change is denied because of a binary conception of *gender,* based exclusively on biological sex, thus denying the possibility of adjusting *gender* on birth records when such documents do not coincide with said biological sex.[44] This is done both implicitly and explicitly, with the courts alleging the lack of express regulations that formally recognize the right to *gender identity*. This is the case of the following ruling cited by the author, issued by the 26th Civil Court of Santiago on October 16, 2015:

> The fact is that the male or female sex is determined by certain biological and non-psychological characteristics, in such a fashion that if male sex organs are present one is a male and, consequently, a female if a woman's sexual organs are present. And the above, which may be self-evident, in the case of the corresponding registration in the Office of Vital Records, is of the greatest importance, since if a woman, with vagina, ovaries, fallopian tubes and a uterus becomes by judicial decision in man, rectifying the corresponding record, it is possible that in the future she will become pregnant and give birth, giving rise to the curious situation that someone who the legal order treats as a man is at the same time a mother, with all the legal conundrums that such a situation would entail, resulting in confusion that must be avoided.

Given the variable reasoning of Chilean courts with respect to the treatment of requests for rectification of birth records, including registered sex, it is necessary to review a sentence issued by the Supreme Court on November 27, 2018, one day before the enactment of Law No. 21,120 and perhaps imbued with the discussion that was presented at the time, where a name change and registered sex is accessed.

On cassation, after the Court of Appeal upheld a decision authorizing the change of name, but not of sex—which led to the applicant bearing a name corresponding to male and female registered sex—based mainly on the fact that the applicant had children and had lived for quite some time as a woman for her age, the Supreme Court points out that the contested ruling:

> [N]ot only errs in considering that maintaining at one point in life a gender condition different from the one it holds today, and having had offspring, makes it impossible for it to seek the legal adjustments of name and sex registry change according to the situation of transsexualism accredited at present. Furthermore, forcing a person to continue living a sexual identity different from the real one or a situation as irregular as the combination between a male name and a female registered sex is thus contradictory with human nature and generates a serious affectation of the psychic integrity, autonomy and dignity of the person.

---

[43] *Ibid.*

[44] Cfr. Muñoz León (2016), p. 176.

Referring to the absence of a law specifically regulating the situation, the Court points out that "even when our legal system does not expressly regulate this specific situation, the interpretation of the regulations in force leads to maintaining -as was said-, reasonably, that it is not possible to rectify the name of a person without it corresponding to the sex indicated therein, otherwise the norm of article 31, paragraph 2, of the Civil Registry would be violated." It then goes on pointing out that "the interpretation of national laws, as our jurisprudence has repeatedly pointed out, must be carried out in the light of constitutional and legal principles, beginning with the right to identity and dignity of persons who are in close contact, which is why the former belongs to all persons without discrimination" and concluding that "[i]n this type of special situation is where the face of gender identity must prevail, precisely as an essential axis in self-recognition as a singular person and in front of society."

In sum, it is possible to argue that the regulatory gap that existed in terms of the formal recognition of the right to gender identity was detrimental to its due exercise; there was legal uncertainty, lack of jurisprudential uniformity and, what is more serious, unacceptable judicial impositions, particularly with regard to demands that insisted on considering the discordance between biological sex and gender adopted by each individual as a pathology or disease.

Moreover, none of the grounds established in Law No. 17,344 for authorizing a name change duly safeguard the exercise of the right to gender identity. Nor are they based on the self-determination of the petitioner's gender identity, but on certain factual hypotheses that, in the abstract and beforehand, allow the configuration of the application for a name change, which must be accredited by the applicant, since the object of the law in question is alien to the protection of the right to gender identity, and only because of the circumstances of a normative gap should the procedure established by it be used.

The Annual Report on Human Rights in Chile for 2015, prepared by the Center for Human Rights of the School of Law of University Diego Portales reinforces this conclusion: "The problem with the current state of affairs, described in the previous paragraph, is that each judge, because there is no normative body that recognizes the right to gender identity, rules according to his or her own convictions about transsexuality, regardless of the parameters and standards that exist in the international human rights system."[45]

Furthermore, one issue that we observed with respect to the old legislation is that the change of sex recorded in the Office of Vital Records is not expressly regulated, but must be processed in along with the name change pursuant to the general regulations set forth in Law No. 17,344. However, a mere change in name, as a general rule, does not resolve the underlying discrepancy in the *gender identity* of the individual or their identification in the Vital Records and Identification Service.[46] Lastly, the procedure established in Law No. 17,344 must be applied by the courts, including public notice of the request. Such an obligation is incompatible with

[45] Álvarez, Juan José; Del Pino, Sebastián; Vial, Tomás; *et al,* "Derechos...", *op. cit,* p. 382.

[46] Cfr. Palavecino, Adriana, "El derecho...", *op. cit.,* pp. 97 and 101.

respect for the right to *gender identity*, since such identity is part of the dignity, privacy and intimate sphere of the petitioner.

5 Gender-Neutral and/or "Third-Sex"

Chile does not currently allow for gender-neutral forms of notation in the records of the Vital Records and Identification Service. As noted above, the indication of biological sex is a fundamental prerequisite for the issuance of a birth record and certificate. There is no specific procedure to enable that sex to be modified to reflect the petitioner's *gender identity*. The means of securing such a change is through the procedure established by Law No. 17,344, which regulates, in general terms, the procedure to be used to modify a name. From this perspective, the existing authority on sex change is primarily associated with the *gender identity* of the applicant -fundamentally trans persons- and is requested in conjunction with a petition for a change of name.[47]

There is, therefore no, legal guidance from the courts on how a request for a change to a gender-neutral designation would be received. Nonetheless, given that the courts continue to relate gender to biological sex, it would appear that the approval of an application for recognition of a *gender identity* that is not aligned with the conceptions of male or female sex, would be highly unlikely to succeed.

6 Access to Medical Treatment

In June 2010, the Ministry of Health issued a document entitled "Clinical Pathway for the Physiological Alignment of People with a Disparity between Physical Sex and Gender Identity"[48] which seeks to facilitate access to health care for individuals grappling with a difference between their biological sex and their *gender identity*. The document described the disparity as a health problem, characterizing it as: "The ongoing feeling of disassociation between physical sex and gender identity that causes significant discomfort, stress or impairment in any area of the individual's personal life; adding that this definition reflects a description of the issue of disparity as noted, plus an element of minimal affectation that translates into harm to the state of health." The target population the document addresses is all individuals over age 18 who suffer from the aforementioned health issue.

The standard of care was set based on the recommendations of the World Professional Association for Transgender Health (WPATH), which seeks, according

[47]See, for example, Pacheco, Jorge and Silva, Eduardo, *Análisis...*, *op cit.*

[48]www.minsal.cl/portal/url/item/d126e58ba4cb53f5e04001016501 7912.pdf [last accessed 23-06-2017].

to this document, to "achieve a lasting feeling of comfort with personal gender identity to maximize psychological well-being and the feeling of self-satisfaction."[49] The Pathway contains three types of interventions:

Mental Health Interventions:
• Initial evaluation • Psychotherapy (may include Real Life Experience) • Counseling and Follow-up (may include Real Life Experience) • Confirmation of eligibility and preparedness
Hormone Alignment
• Prescription and control of feminization / masculinization therapy
Surgical Alignment:
• Pectoral reshaping • Hysterectomy and Ophorectomy (Female to Male Alignment) • Orquidectomy • Sex reassignment • Facial feminization • Other procedures

The initial evaluation set forth in the document entails a review of any pathological conditions; including:

(a) Ruling out a diagnosis of related psychiatric disorders that may be disserved by physiological alignment;
(b) Ruling out the presence of a diagnosis of psychiatric comorbidity (e.g. depressive disorder, anxiety, use and abuse of alcohol or drugs, etc.).

The document also allows for the use of the parameters contained in DSM-IV or version 10 of the International Classification of Diseases (ICD-10) on gender identity even though these parameters have been criticized precisely because of their tendency to pathologize. Although it should be noted that the document seeks to overcome this shortcoming with the express caveat that: "The use of DSM-IV or ICD-10 diagnostic criteria does not authorize the stigmatization or deprivation of rights of affected persons. The classification in these manuals (DSM-IV and ICD-10) of people who manifest a feeling of disparity between physical sex and gender identity has been strongly questioned as it is associated with the stigmatization of the condition."

To determine eligibility and preparedness for hormone therapy, the document refers to the criteria set forth by the WPATH, with some adjustments:

Eligibility
– Age 18 or older. – Demonstrated understanding of what hormones can and cannot do and their risks. – In addition: (a) Three months documented real-life experience prior to initiation of hormone management;

(continued)

[49] *Ibid.*, p. 3.

Eligibility
or (b) A period of psychotherapy specified by the mental health professional after the evaluation (usually no less than 3 months).[50]

Preparedness
– The person has consolidated his or her gender identity during the process of Real Life Experience or psychotherapy. – The person has shown progress in handling other identified problems (substance abuse, psychosis, suicidal tendencies) and improved or maintained stable mental health. – The patient is likely to follow hormone therapy in a responsible manner.

That said, it must be noted that there is no plan in place for financing or implementing the program at the national level. This has led to a number of operational problems at care centers specially designated for assisting trans persons in making the physical shift in from their biological sex to their *gender identity*.[51] Given the lack of a National Plan provided by the Ministry of Health, the care of trans persons operates within the general framework of the public health system regulated pursuant to DFL 1 of the Ministry of Health, published on April 24, 2006, which sets forth the consolidated, coordinated and systematized text of Decree Law No. 2,763 of 1979 and of Laws No. 18,933 and No. 18,469.

The National Health Fund (FONASA)[52] is regulated in Chapter III of Book 1 of the DFL, specifically from Article 49 on. The regulations state that, among other functions, FONASA is responsible for financing, in whole or in part, the services granted to beneficiaries of the Public Health Regime defined in Book II of the DFL, independent of the mode of care, in keeping with the health policies and priorities for the country defined by the Ministry of Health and the provisions of the Health Benefits Regime of Book II of the DFL. This financing is composed of contributions, direct payments, agreements or other mechanisms established by administrative resolution. FONASA is also responsible for collecting, managing and distributing resources allocated to public health, as set forth in Article 55 of the DFL. FONASA offers, fundamentally, two options or modes of care.

[50]It should be noted that psychotherapy does not seek to correct the discrepancy between biological sex and *gender identity*, but rather to:

- Alleviate the stress, discomfort and conflicts associated with the discrepancy between gender identity and sex, which could threaten a stable lifestyle.
- Work and develop concerns and conflicts related to gender identity.
- Work and support the grappling with physiological alignment.

[51]See press note: Herrera, Lilith, "Policlínico Identidad de Género de Valparaíso: las irregularidades que afectan su funcionamiento", (online) http://www.laizquierdadiario.cl/Policlinico-Identidad-de-Genero-de-Valparaiso-las-irregularidades-que-afectan-su-funcionamiento [last accessed 23-06-17].

[52]Fonasa is Chile's public health insurance program. Private insurance is available through Isapres (see below).

First, pursuant to Article 141 of the DFL, the standard procedure is for care to be provided to beneficiaries through the regular and experimental public health networks using the physical and human resources available to them, in addition to any agreements with other public institutions or private providers that the Ministry or FONASA may have in place. This is called the "institutional" mode. The amount a beneficiary has to pay for services in this context will depend on the person's income-based classification group.

Second, Article 143 of the DFL allows beneficiaries the freedom to choose a public or private sector provider or facility. This is called the "free choice" mode. The cost to the beneficiary will depend on the accreditation of the provider or the facility and their co-pay agreement with FONASA. In this context, a study entitled "Health Care System Coverage and the Right to Align Appearance to Gender Identity" published on July 24, 2016 in the framework of the gender identity bill, concluded that: "Sex reassignment surgery should not be considered cosmetic, but rather a procedure that allows an individual to adopt the gender identity with which that person most identifies. Nonetheless, current coverage of these benefits is made at the health care level rather than ensuring full resolution and, as such, the cost to FONASA affiliates will depend on the type of care they choose (institutional or free choice)."[53] It was also found that: "According to information provided by FONASA, despite the Clinical Pathway, the existing coverage for sex change is at the level of health care rather than comprehensive resolution. Thus, the fees for services and procedures involved in certain aspects of the problem, are not exclusive benefits in the context of a change of sex." Lastly, the study showed that the total cost of the surgeries required to adjust biological sex to *gender identity*, in keeping with the Clinical Pathway, amounts to US$ 13,068 in the Level 3 Free Choice mode.

7 The Gender Identity Legislative Bill

On May 7, 2013, the bill of reference was submitted to the Senate of the Republic by motion of the Honourable Senators Lily Pérez San Martín and Ximena Rincón and Messrs. Camilo Escalona, Ricardo Lagos Weber and Juan Pablo Letelier, and was studied by the Human Rights, Nationality and Citizenship Committee to which they belong. The bill sought to:

> [E]stablish an effective and adequate regulation, in accordance with constitutional and international provisions on equality, non-discrimination, the right to identity and general protection of human dignity, and fundamental rights and freedoms, in order to grant a change in the registration with regard to the sex and name of an individual with the Vital Records and Identification Service, in those cases in which said registration does not correspond or is not consistent with the true gender identity of the petitioner.

[53]Aguayo Ormeño et al. (2016).

As can be seen from the foregoing, the project sought to bridge the existing normative gap by formally recognizing the right to gender identity in Chile, particularly by regulating access to change of registration in the records kept by the Office of Vital Records relating to sex and name, when it does not conform to the applicant's gender identity. The original text of the project was written by the Association "Organizando Trans Diversidades" (OTD), with the support of the Iguales Foundation, and the active participation of the academic from the University of Concepción Ximena Gauché.[54]

The academic Gauché explained the purpose of the project in the following sense: "What the project does is to create a judicial procedure so that people, once in a lifetime, request a correction to their birth record and the adjustments of their name to the gender they live and feel, in the understanding the root cause of the problem of transsexual people face in our country is that their gender identity does not match the assigned gender on record".[55] The definition adopted by the bill about gender identity corresponds to that contained in the Yogyakarta Principles. As the authors Valentina Verbal and Sebastián del Río[56] note, the adoption of this conception of gender identity implies the de-pathologization of requests to rectify name and sex items registered in the Office of Vital Records, exempting applicants from requirements associated with medical reports and treatment, particularly the requirement to undergo a sexual reassignment operation.

The bill was widely debated, with more than three hundred indications submitted during its 4 years it has been in Congress. As an example of the divergences that arose in the processing of this bill, it is possible to point out that a series of groupings for and against the formal recognition of gender identity participated in it. Among the former, they stand out: Iguales Foundation, Humanas Corporation, Renaciendo Foundation, Organizando Trans Diversidades OTD Chile, Movement of Homosexual Integration and Liberation (MOVILH in spanish), Afrodita syndicate, Acción Gay Valparaíso, Opción Corporation, "Daniel Zamudio" Foundation, "Sin Odio" Foundation, and Fuerza Trans.

On the other hand, there are, among others: NGO Padres Objetores Chile, "ISFEM" Research, Training and Study on Women, Red por la Vida, Soñando Chile Foundation, NGO Comunidad y Justicia, Advocates Chile, Jaime Guzmán Foundation, Christian Lawyers of Chile Foundation, "Acción Familia", "Movimiento Unidos por la Vida de la Familia", Ideapaís, Education, Orientation and Familiar Mediation "Familia Viva" Corporation. These groups were joined by several professionals from different disciplines, who spoke in support or rejection of the formal recognition of the right to gender identity. One of the most discussed

[54]Cfr. Fundación Iguales, "Incidencia Política, ley de identidad de género", (online) https://www.iguales.cl/incidencia-politica/ley-de-identidad-de-genero/ [last accessed 10-02-2017].

[55]Fundación Iguales, "Abogada de la U. de concepción lidera proyecto de ley sobre identidad de género", 2013, (online) https://www.iguales.cl/abogada-de-la-u-de-concepcion-lidera-proyecto-de-ley-sobre-identidad-de-genero/ [last accessed 10-02-2017].

[56]Del Pino Rubio and Verbal Stockmeyer (2016), pp. 187–188.

issues regarding the project was the inclusion of indications to expressly recognize and regulate the right to gender identity of children and adolescents, excluding this possibility in the Session of January 18, 2017 developed by the Human Rights Commission of the Senate.[57]

8 Law No. 21,120 Recognizing and Protecting the Right to Gender Identity

Finally, and after more than 5 years of legislative processing, on November 28, 2018, Law No. 21,120 "recognizes and protects the right to gender identity" was enacted complying with the publication process in the Official Gazette of the Republic of Chile, necessary for its entry into force under Article 7 of the Civil Code, on December 10 of the same year.

However, the law has a transitory article (third transitory article) that prevents the law from coming into force one hundred and twenty days after the last publication of the regulations referred to in Article 26 of the law. One depends on the Ministry of Social Development, also subscribed by the Ministry of Health, which attends to gender transition accompaniment programs, and the other depends on the Ministry of Justice for requirements and accreditation for name and sex change. Due to the above, despite being a law of the republic, it has not yet entered into force.

[57]This perspective contrasts with the reality of living conditions of children and adolescents in Chile. In this regard, in Observatorio de Derechos Humanos–Chile (Andrés Rivera Duarte), International Gay and Lesbian Human Rights Commission (IGLHRC), "Situation of Trans and Intersex Children in Chile, Submitted to the United Nations Committee on the Rights of the Child on the Occasion of Its Pre-sessional Working Group Meeting to Consider Chile's joint Fourth and Fifth Periodic Report, 2015, we see the following: "A study by the United Nations Education Scientific and Cultural Organization (UNESCO) placed Chile as the Latin American country with the highest rate of reported homophobic bullying among LGBTI students (68 percent of LGBTI students report to have suffered some kind of bullying). Another study, by the Organization of Economic Cooperation and Development (OCED) marks Chile as the second country, after South Korea, with the fastest growing rate of suicides among children, generally." (p. 3). Further on, this report indicates that: "In 2014, the Chilean government created the National Children's Council by Supreme Decree 21, with a view to advancing towards a more comprehensive fulfillment of state obligations on children's human rights at the national level. On December 30, 2014, this Council circulated an invitation to civil society organizations working on sexual diversity, for them to participate in a January 2015 meeting on this topic, considering that the National Policy on Childhood and Adolescence is due to be launched in March 2015. It is paramount that this new policy appropriately reflects the needs and rights of LGBTI children in Chile." (p. 4).

9 The Content and Object of Law No. 21,120

Law No. 21,120 regulates the content of the right to gender identity, the definition of gender identity, its exercise, requirements for such exercise, procedures and the effects of the rectification provided for in the law, structured in seven titles, 29 articles and 3 transitory articles. Article 1 of the Act, unlike the original bill, defines the right to gender identity as "the right of any person whose gender identity does not coincide with its sex and registered name to request the rectification thereof". Then, regarding what will be understood as gender identity, it states that it is "the personal and internal conviction of being a man or a woman, as the person perceives itself, which may or may not correspond to the sex and name verified in the birth registration certificate". This definition, although slightly different from the one given in the original Project, accounts for the same aspects and objectives, that is, the fact that it is an internal experience and the need to de-pathologize requests for rectification.

Its purpose, as stated in Article 2, is "to regulate the procedures for accessing the rectification of a person's birth certificate with regard to sex and name, before the respective administrative or judicial body, when such certificate does not correspond or is not congruent with their gender identity". However, a strictly procedural character can be appreciated in the delimitation of its object, the law, from an integral perspective and reflecting the spirit that motivated the parliamentary motion to legislate on the subject, introduces into the national legal system and language for the first time together with the right to gender identity, a series of specific guarantees and principles derived from its enjoyment and exercise.

Thus, as a specific guarantee derived from gender identity, Article 3 states that "[e]veryone has the right to be recognized and identified in accordance with its gender identity, once the rectification regulated by this law has been made, in public or private instruments that accredit his or her identity with respect to the name and sex".

As guarantees associated with the enjoyment and exercise of the right to gender identity (Article 4), it is stated that everyone has the right to: (a) the recognition and protection of gender identity and expression, which must be understood, according to the law itself, as the external manifestation of the person's gender, that is, ways of speaking, dressing, behavior, among others; (b) to be recognized and identified according to their gender identity and expression in public or private instruments that accredit their identity; and (c) to the free development of their person, according to their gender identity and expression, allowing for the greatest possible spiritual and material fulfillment -thus reproducing the constitutional mandate contained in the third paragraph of Article 1 that establishes the principle of the State's servitude[58]—and indicating that it will not be a condition for this recognition that they have undergone treatments or interventions that modify their appearance.

[58]Article 1 paragraph 3 of the Constitution reads that the State is at the service of the individual and its goal is to promote common welfare. To this effect, it must contribute to the creation of the social

With regard to principles relating to the right to gender identity, Article 5 recognizes the following, among others, the:

(a) *Principle of non-pathologization*, by virtue of which the recognition and protection of gender identity entitles trans persons not to be treated as sick;
(b) *Principle of arbitrary non-discrimination*, which obliges State organs to guarantee that in the exercise of the right to gender identity no person may be affected by distinctions, exclusions or restrictions that lack reasonable justification;
(c) *Principle of confidentiality*, which establishes the right of every person to have the confidentiality of data considered sensitive protected in procedures regulated by law;
(d) *Principle of dignity in treatment* that obliges the State to respect the inherent dignity of persons by treating them kindly and respectfully at all times and in all circumstances;
(e) *Principle of the best interests of the child* that obliges the State to ensure to all children the maximum satisfaction in the exercise and full and effective enjoyment of their rights and guarantee in the terms of Article 3 of the Convention on the Rights of the Child; and
(f) *Principle of progressive autonomy* that allows all children to exercise their rights on their own, in accordance with their evolving capacities, age and maturity.

10 The Procedure for Rectification of Sex and Registry Name

Every request for rectification of sex and registry name must contain the first name or names with which the interested person intends to replace those that appear in his birth records, as well as the request to rectify the documents with which the person was identified before the Office of Vital Records and Identification Service. However, allows the possibility of requesting only the rectification of the registered sex if the first names are not equivocal with respect to their new sex, which can only be understood possible for those who have already obtained a ruling authorizing the change of name, but not sex, under Law No. 17,344. If the request is made by foreigners, they must prove their definitive stay in Chile, and may only rectify their sex and name for the purposes of issuing Chilean documents. Linked to the principle of confidentiality established in Article 5(c) is that the procedures dealt with by the law will have the character of reserved with respect to third parties and all the information linked to them will be considered as sensitive data.

The Act regulates two types of procedures for the rectification of names and sex. One of an administrative nature, when the request is made by a person of legal age

---

conditions which permit each and every one of the members of the national community to achieve the greatest possible spiritual and material fulfillment, with full respect for the rights and guarantees established by this Constitution.

without a current marital relationship, and another of a judicial nature for requests made by persons over 14 years of age, but under 18 years of age, and those made by persons with a current marriage bond in force.

11 The Administrative Procedure

This procedure is regulated between articles nine to eleven of the act and will be applicable each time the petition is made by an adult without a valid marriage bond. By means of this procedure it can the applicant for up to two times (unlike the original project that only contemplated one opportunity) obtain the rectification of sex and name with which it appears individualized in its birth records. Any Office of Vital Records, regardless of the applicant's domicile or residence, shall be competent to take cognizance of the application.

Once the application has been received, the officer of the Office of Vital Records, must verify the identity of the applicant either through its current identity card or, if necessary, from its fingerprint. The officer will also verify that the applicant has no valid marriage bond in force and in the case the applicant is a foreigner, it must verify that it has accredited his permanent stay in Chile. The officer shall, within a short period of time, summon the applicant and two competent witnesses to a special hearing, where they will declare under oath that the former is aware of the legal effects of granting its application.

Finally, and within a maximum period of 45 days from the presentation of the application, the National Director of the Office of Civil Records must issue the corresponding order of the Office, which may accept, reject in a justified manner or declare it inadmissible because it has been made by a person, even though it is of legal age, who has an undisclosed marriage bond. In this case, the Office of Vital Records must inform the applicant of the judicial procedures established by law. The request will only be rejected because the applicant has not proved his/her identity, or the statement of the applicant and competent witnesses has not been verified.

12 Judicial Procedure: Requests for Rectification of Persons Over 14 and Under 18

This is regulated in paragraph 1° of Title V of Law No. 21,120 from Articles 12 to 17, being applicable whenever the application is made by a person older than 14 years but under 18. As can be seen, and as mention above, the possibility is excluded for children under 14 years of age to request the rectification of their birth records to match their gender identity through procedures regulated in the same law. It should be noted that this possibility was not included in the law after the necessary quorum was not reached in the Joint Commission of the National Congress. The court with jurisdiction in family matters of the applicant's domicile shall be competent to take cognizance of the application.

The application must be submitted through their legal representatives or one of them, at the election of the eldest of 14 and under 18, if he has more than one. The request must be well-founded and clearly and precisely state the factual and legal background on which it is based, with express indication of the specific petitions that are submitted to the court's decision. It must also include the reasons why, in the applicant's opinion, the application is beneficial to the person over 14 and under 18 years of age.

This application may be accompanied by any relevant background information, especially those that consider the psychosocial and family context of the minor and his or her family group. In addition, the reports referred in Article 17 may be accompanied, namely, a psychological or psychosocial report stating that the child over 14 and under 18 and his or her family environment have been professionally accompanied for at least 1 year prior to the application and a psychological or psychosocial report ruling out the decisive influence of third parties such as the father, mother or the one who in charge of minor's personal care on the will expressed by the child as to its gender identity.

Once the application has been received and in compliance with the requirements set out above, the judge will admit it for processing and will summon the eldest of 14 and youngest of 18, together with the applicants, to a preliminary hearing within a period of 15 days. Eventually, and in the same resolution that cites the preliminary hearing and for the same day of it, the judge shall summon the person who is over 14 and under 18 years and the parent or legal representative who has not acceded to the application.

In the hearing, the judge will have an active role in informing the minor of 14 and over 18 and the applicant(s) about the characteristics of the rectification and its legal consequences.

A minor over 14 and under 18 years of age is to have the right to be heard at all stages of the proceedings, and the judge shall consider its opinions, considering its age and degree of maturity. In this way, the minor will be able to express his willingness to change his sex and register names, as well as the names with which it intends to replace those appearing in his birth certificate. To this end, the court must ensure that any action taken by the minor is carried out in an environment that ensures its physical and mental health and in conditions that guarantee its voluntary, private and safe participation.

Immediately after the preliminary hearing, the court will hold the preparatory hearing with the parties in attendance. Certain persons may be summoned *ex officio* or at the request of a party to testify about the factual background presented in the application. At this time, the psychological or psychosocial reports listed above must necessarily be accompanied if they were not accompanied by the presentation of the application. This contravenes the principle of self-determination and non-pathologization that should govern the exercise of the right to gender identity and pathologizes it by introducing as a requirement that the applicant submit evidence regarding his or her state of mental health. In this hearing, the judge may order the performance of one or more diligences the judge deems necessary for the correct resolution of the case, which in no case may be physical examinations of minors under 14 and under 18. Without prejudice to this, and with the agreement of the parties, the judge may immediately hold the trial hearing. At the trial hearing, those who have been summoned shall be heard and the evidence admitted by the court shall be taken.

The final judgment must be well founded and must state the fact that the eldest of 14 and the youngest of 18 have been heard, as well as the reasons that the court has considered for deciding in accordance with or against that opinion. The judge must, have the reports of the proceedings before him or her. If the application is denied, the remedies relating to family disputes shall apply. If the application is accepted, the court shall order the Office of Vital Records to rectify the birth certificate. The Office will proceed only by virtue of a final sentence and only once the corresponding rectifications and sub-registrations have been made, the new identity documents will be issued.

13 Judicial Procedure: Applications Made by Persons in a Valid Marriage

The applicable procedure is regulated in Paragraph 2 of Title IV of the law in Articles 18 and 19. The court with jurisdiction in family matters corresponding to the domicile of either of the spouses, at the applicant's choice, shall be competent to hear applications made by persons with a valid marriage bond, whether they are of legal age. The applicable procedure is the same as that for applications made by persons aged over 14 and under 18 years of age. If the application is accepted, in the same sentence, the judge will declare the termination of the marriage by virtue of the grounds of numeral 5 of Article 42 of the Civil Marriage Law, which states: "The marriage ends: (. . .) By final sentence that accepts the request for rectification of sex and name by reason of gender identity". In Chile, because of Article 102 of the Civil Code, marriage between two persons of the same sex is prohibited. Thus, for all legal purposes, the appearing parties shall be deemed to be divorced.

This requirement violates the right to family life, since it is fully possible and perfectly legitimate for the applicant's consort to want to remain united by that bond (however, the modification of the other's gender identity)[59] and against the principle of continuity of family relations, unfoundedly limiting the exercise of the right to gender identity. By virtue of the termination of the marriage the spouses shall be entitled to claim financial compensation in accordance with the general rules of the Civil Marriage Act and the Family Courts Act.[60]

[59]Cfr. Espejo, Nicolás and Lathrop, Fabiola, "Identidad. . .", *op. cit.*, pp. 393–418.

[60]Articles 61 to 66 of the Law of Civil Marriage No. 19,947 and Law of Family Courts No. 19,968.

14 Rectification of Birth Certificates, New IDs and the Effects of Rectification

Once the request for rectification has been accepted and the judgment is enforceable, the Office of Vital Records must carry out the relevant amendments and sub-registrations, after which the new identification documents may be issued. The interested party will be summoned to attend any Vital Records office for the new documents to be issued. For all legal purposes, these will replace the previous identity documents. Once the previous dispositions and subscriptions have been made, the person must be recognized and identified according to its gender identity. Any instrument with which the person appears in public registers must match that identity.

The effects of the rectification of the birth record will be enforceable against third parties from the time the entry is made in accordance with the Organic Rules of the Vital Records Office. In no case will the rectification affect the ownership of the rights and patrimonial obligations that could correspond to the person prior to the registration of the change, nor will it affect the relations of family law in all its orders and degrees, which will remain unchanged. Likewise, it will not affect the guarantees, rights and health benefits that could correspond to the person prior to the registration of the change.

15 Gays & Lesbians and Trans

On October 22, 2015, Law No. 20,830 was published on Civil Union Agreements, creating legislation that allows same-sex partners recognition as a couple. This agreement grants the civil status of "civil partner" which is recognized as a founding element of the family, establishing the rights and obligations of a personal and patrimonial nature very similar to those of marriage. The entry into force of this legislation has occurred prior to the regulation and protection of the right to *gender identity*. The other relevant progress, prior to the enactment of a *gender identity* law, was the inclusion of *gender identity* and *sexual orientation* as suspect classes within the law that establishes measures against discrimination, Law 20,609, as noted above.

16 Stakes in Sex

In the World Bank biennial report entitled "Women, Business and the Law 2016"[61] Chile was listed 42 out of 173 in the ranking of countries with gender-based legal differences in the economy with 8 such differences. These relate mainly to the system of marital property in which in Chile's community property regime, the husband administers the assets. This is just one of three options available to couples when they marry. The other two are partial community property (known as "shared profits") and complete separation of assets.

The community property system is regulated in Title XXII of Book Four of the Civil Code. This regime distinguishes between the property shared by the spouses and the property of each of them as individuals. As noted, the husband is responsible for managing the couple's joint assets, his own property and that of his wife, in accordance with Article 1749 of the Civil Code. In addition, Article 150 of the Civil Code grants women control over the money they make working outside the home and allows them to waive the benefits of the community property system and withdraw the full amount of those personal assets upon the termination of the community property arrangement.

Other differences at the civil level have to do with legal standing. The law identifies two impediments to standing based on age: prepubescence (Absolute incapacity) and minor adult status (Relative incapacity). Pursuant to Article 26 of the Civil Code, a female who has not yet reached the age of 12 is considered prepubescent, whereas for males that age stands at 14 years of age. An adult is an individual who is no longer prepubescent.

In the workplace there are also differences, particularly in terms of the parental benefits derived from pregnancy and birth, as well as the type of work that can be performed by men and women. The first of these matters is regulated by law 20,545 of the Ministry of Labor and Social Security, dated October 17, 2011, which amended the regulations on maternity protection to incorporate postnatal leave for the father as well. Those regulations afford the woman protection from the date of conception of the child until the age of 1 year and 84 days. Such protection extends to entitling the woman to return to an equivalent job following mandatory pre-natal leave of 42 days prior to the birth and post-natal leave of 84 days following the birth. The father, for his part, enjoys automatic post-natal leave of 5 days.

Following the standard post-natal leave, the mother may opt for up to 18 additional weeks of full or part-time leave or share up to 12 weeks of that with the father. If the leave is full-time, the mother may transfer to the father only 6 of the 12 weeks. If the leave is part-time, she may transfer up to 12 weeks to the father. In addition, the law grants female workers with children under the age of two special leave of one hour a day to feed them.

---

[61]Cfr. Grupo Del Banco Mundial, *Women, Business and the Law 2016: Getting to Equal. Banco Mundial*, Washington, DC, 2015, (online) http://wbl.worldbank.org/~/media/WBG/WBL/Documents/Reports/2016/Women-Business-and-the-Law-2016.pdf [last accessed on 23-06-17].

On the topic of what work women may perform, pursuant to Article 203 of the Labor Code, women may not carry out work that may be detrimental to their health during pregnancy and must be transferred to other work that is not detrimental to their health. No reduction in pay is permitted. Other differences between men and women are observed in pensions, with the retirement age standing at 65 for men and 60 for women.

Finally, in the area of access to health care, within the private system administered by the so-called ISAPREs, the law expressly permits a distinction to be made in the pricing of health insurance plans based on sex and age. In practice, this results in higher insurance costs for women than men.[62]

17 Intersex Persons

There is no specific regulation on intersexuality in Chile, nor is there a bill pending in Congress to regulate it. In the context of existing regulations, two Circulars issued by the Ministry of Health stand out and reflect a dichotomy in the Government's approach to intersexuality which, in turn, leads to legal uncertainty for intersex persons.

The first of these Circulars is number 18, dated December 22, 2015.[63] The document orders an end to "unnecessary normalization" treatments of intersex boys and girls, including the use of irreversible surgeries until they are old enough to decide about their own bodies. It is further added that the assignment of sex in birth records must be made according to "best expectations" and medical studies are required to be carried out in this regard.

As noted above, Article 31 of Law 4,808 requires the sex of the newborn to be recorded at the time of registration with the Office of Vital Records. That notation is a prerequisite and no record of birth may be performed without it, pursuant to Article 33 thereto. This is reinforced by means of the regulations contained in the Organic Law on the Vital Records and Identification Service issued through DFL 2,128, enacted on August 28, 1930. Articles 123, 124 and 307 prescribe the sex of the newborn as a prerequisite for the validity of the registration of birth. This sex refers to the biological sex and must necessarily be noted on the record of birth for the Office of Vital Records record it. Sex is determined by means of the record of birth signed by a medical professional. As noted above, there is currently no gender-neutral registration option for newborns. At present, babies can be listed in one of three categories: "male", "female" and, when there is uncertainty, "indeterminate".

[62]Cfr. Superintendencia de Salud, *Discriminación, equidad de género y reforma de salud en el Sistema Isapre*, 2008, (online) http://www.supersalud.gob.cl/documentacion/666/articles-4992_recurso_1.pdf [last accessed 23-06-17].

[63]https://oii.org.au/wp-content/uploads/2016/01/Circular-08-22.12.15-Instruye-Sobre-Ciertos-Aspectos-de-la-atencion-de-Salud-a-Ninos-y-Ninas-Intersex.pdf [last accessed 26-06-17].

According to statistics from the SRCEI, from 2006 to November 2015, of some 200,000 births recorded, only some 20 were listed as "indeterminate".[64]

Furthermore, Circular 18 orders each Public Health Service to create a working group composed of a variety of specialists associated with intersexuality and for the team to meet with the Ethics Committee at that location to determine appropriate actions. Their joint proposal is then submitted to the National Committee for review, until such a time as a protocol is defined by the Ministry of Health to regulate the care of intersex children. In the Circular, the Ministry commits to drafting such a protocol.

Finally, it is relevant to mention that the Circular in question makes express mention of the grounds upon which the Service's recommendations must be based, including a series of international instruments regarding the process of "normalization":

> The Inter-American Human Rights System has recognized these treatments as systematic violations of human rights (2013), pointing out that they may constitute torture (2015). The Universal Human Rights System has expressed concern about the specific situation of these persons in Chile through three treaty-review entities: the Human Rights Committee (2015), the Committee on Economic, Social and Cultural Rights (2015) and recently, the Committee on the Rights of the Child (2015). The primary recommendation made recently to Chile is to develop a protocol that guarantees the protection of the human rights of intersex persons - especially children and adolescents -and to ensure that they will not undergo such surgical interventions until they are old enough to decide on their own bodies (Committee on the Rights of the Child, 2015).

This implies recognition of the progressive autonomy of children as a cross-cutting principle of the Convention on the Rights of the Child, ratified by Chile in 1990. In this same vein, the Circular refers to the contents of a document entitled Sexual Health, Human Rights and the Law:[65]

> One of the main concerns for intersex people is that so-called sex normalization procedures are often carried out during infancy and childhood to alter their bodies, particularly sexual organs, to conform to gender norms, including repeated surgeries, hormonal interventions, and other procedures. As a result, these children may be subjected to unnecessary, often irreversible medical interventions which can have consequences on their physical and mental health for a lifetime, including the irreversible termination of all or a portion of their reproductive and sexual capacity. Medical procedures may be justified in cases where conditions pose a health risk or are considered life-threatening. Such procedures, however, are sometimes proposed on the basis of weak evidence, without discussing and considering alternative solutions.

Circular 18 was complemented by Circular 8, dated August 23, 2016,[66] which allows for "normalization" treatment under several hypotheses and, additionally, incorporates the pathologizing concept of Sexual Development Disorder (DDS) as

---

[64]https://www.registrocivil.cl/PortalOI/PDF/Banner_de_genero_Final.pdf [last accessed 23-06-2017].

[65]http://apps.who.int/iris/bitstream/10665/175556/1/9789241564984_eng.pdf [last accessed 26-06-17].

[66]https://brujulaintersexual.files.wordpress.com/2017/06/circular-7.pdf [last accessed 26-06-17].

official and pertinent language when informing patients about this condition. As such, the provisions of Circular 8 put those contained in Circular 18 in doubt, in part by noting: "The recommendation referring to abstaining from unnecessary genital surgery does not refer to pathologies in which there is a clearly defined sex, both genetically and/or somatically", and includes a series of examples of such "pathologies" (Article 2 of the Circular). Moreover, Articles 3 and 4 of Circular 8 completely ignore the principles of the CRC, particularly those of progressive autonomy, best interest and the right to be heard, establishing that decisions on any procedures will be adopted exclusively by the legal representatives of the child or adolescent in conjunction with the medical team. In addition, Article 6 allows for surgery to be performed in cases of medical urgency.

Lastly, at the end of the day, in practice, the decision on whether an infant will undergo surgery is left to the discretion of health care professionals, even though such surgery may be unnecessary and irreversible, and yet is performed to ensure that their bodies resemble "normal" male or female physiques.[67]

18 Conclusions

Recognition at the level of a fundamental right of the right to gender identity in Chile is based on the open catalogue of rights established in the Political Constitution of the Republic and the various international treaties signed by the country. Recognition of the right to gender identity consequently emanates from the right to identity, enshrined in the various international instruments signed by Chile, and from the protection of human dignity and the free development of the personality, complemented by the principle which imposes on it the duty to generate conditions conducive to the self-determination of the individual.

The right to gender identity is recognized at the statutory level by Law No. 21,120 of 28 November 2018, regulating both the content of the right to gender identity, its definition, its exercise and the procedures it establishes. The statute however has not yet entered into force, so there are no data as to its application and enforcement. Weaknesses however have been identified, including requesting that petitioners over 14 and under 18 years of age provide proof of mental health, or the requirement that marriage be terminated when granting requests for gender changes by person in a valid marriage.

Nevertheless, jurisprudential advances can be detected demonstrating a more nuanced understanding of the gender problem. These, however, are not absolute, so there is an urgency for new law entering into force as soon as possible in order to

[67]Observatorio De Derechos Humanos–Chile (Andrés Rivera Duarte), International Gay and Lesbian Human Rights Commission (IGLHRC), "Situation of…", *op. cit.*, p. 5: *"Medical professionals operate with discretion as to whether or not intersex infants will be subjected to unnecessary and irreversible surgery to visually resemble "normal" male or female bodies."*

put an end once and for all to the normative vacuum and the legal uncertainty to which all applicants for rectification are subjected.

References

Aguayo Ormeño I, Lampert Grassi MP, Meza-Lopehandía GM (2016) Derecho a adecuar la apariencia a la identidad de género y su cobertura en el sistema de salud. Asesoría Técnica Parlamentaria. Departamento de Estudios, Extensión y Publicaciones, (online) https://www.bcn.cl/asesoriasparlamentarias/categorias?id=1&pag=8&K=1&sort=fecha_desc [last accessed 23-06-2017]

Álvarez Rubio JJ, Del Pino Rubio S, Vial Solar T et al (2015) Derechos de la diversidad sexual 2015: avances y falencias. In: de Derechos Humanos C (ed) Informe Anual sobre derechos humanos en Chile. Universidad Diego Portales, p 383

Barrientos Walls L, Llanquilef Candia C (2012) Jurisprudencia de los tribunales civiles de Santiago sobre solicitudes de rectificación de partida de nacimiento en cuanto al nombre y en cuanto al sexo formuladas por personas transexuales durante los años 2005-2009. Universidad de Chile – Facultad de Derecho, Santiago, Chile, (online) http://www.repositorio.uchile.cl/handle/2250/112757> [last accessed 09-06-17]

Del Pino Rubio S, Verbal Stockmeyer V (2016) El proyecto de ley de identidad de género. Una aproximación a sus disposiciones y fundamentos. Liminales. Escritos sobre psicología y sociedad 7:187–188, (online) http://revistafacso.ucentral.cl/index.php/liminales/article/view/176 [last accessed 11-11-2016]

Díaz García I (2013) Ley chilena contra la discriminación: una evaluación desde los derechos internacional y constitucional. Revista Chilena de Derecho 40(2):667

Espejo Yaksic N, Lathrop Gómez F (2015) Identidad de Género, Relaciones Familiares y Derechos de Niños, Niñas y Adolescentes. Revista de Derecho de la Universidad Católica del Norte 22 (2):395

Muñoz León F (2015) El reconocimiento legal de la transexualidad en Chile mediante el procedimiento judicial de cambio de nombre: Un caso de complementariedad epistemológica entre medicina y derecho. Revista Médica de Chile 143(8):1018–1019

Muñoz León F (2016) Cisnormatividad y transnormatividad como ideologías que articulan el tratamiento jurídico de la condición trans. Revista Austral de Ciencias Sociales 30(2):176

Pacheco Martínez J, Silva Jerez E (2015) Análisis de la legislación, procedimiento y jurisprudencia de las rectificaciones de partida de nacimiento por cambio de nombre y sexo de personas transexuales. Universidad de Chile - Facultad de Derecho, Santiago, Chile, (online) <http://repositorio.uchile.cl/handle/2250/131900> [last accessed 09-06-2017]

Palavecino Cáceres A (2012) El derecho a la identidad de las personas transgéneros. In: Justicia, Género y Sexualidad: primer encuentro académico Santiago de Chile 2009. Universidad de Chile, Facultad de Derecho, Centro de Derechos Humanos, p 97

Ruz Lártiga G (2011) Explicaciones del Derecho Civil. Derecho de las personas en familia, Tomo V, AbeledoPerrot, Santiago de Chile, p 523

Somarriva Undurraga M (1946) Derecho de Familia. Nascimento, Santiago de Chile, p 485

The Story of the Recognition of Sexual Identity as a Source of Harm in Colombian Constitutional Law

Isabel C. Jaramillo

Abstract This chapter tells the story of the incremental change in legal rules regarding the protection of sexual identity by the Constitutional Court from 1993 to 2020. It starts by explaining the mechanisms for judicial intervention in the protection of rights, follows with an account of the creation of sexual identity as a protected category under Colombian law, and ends with a critical appraisal of the effect of these legal interventions. The author points out that the available information, which is very scarce, shows that the Court has been quite successful in changing patterns of discrimination and aggression towards trans persons in education and health, and even in housing and work environments.

In 1991, Colombia adopted a modern constitution including a generous amount of civil, political, economic and cultural rights, and a new Constitutional Court in charge of adjudicating matters of abstract constitutional control and concrete protection of rights.[1] This modern text, however, did not include sexual orientation or identity as categories for protection. The Constitutional Court has been the main actor in the production of a framework for the protection of choices regarding sexuality. This chapter tells the story of the incremental change in legal rules regarding the protection of sexual identity by the Constitutional Court from 1993 to 2020. It starts by explaining the mechanisms for judicial intervention in the protection of rights, follows with an account of the creation of sexual identity as a protected category under Colombian law, and ends with a critical appraisal of the effect of these legal interventions. I point out that the available information, which is very scarce, shows that the Court has been quite successful in changing patterns of discrimination and aggression towards trans persons in education and health, and

[1] A good general introduction to Colombian Constitutional law may be found in Cepeda and Landau (2017).

I. C. Jaramillo (✉)
Universidad de Los Andes, Bogota, Colombia
e-mail: ijaramil@uniandes.edu.co

I. C. Jaramillo, L. Carlson (eds.), *Trans Rights and Wrongs*, Ius Comparatum - Global Studies in Comparative Law 54,
https://doi.org/10.1007/978-3-030-68494-5_18

even in housing and work environments. These changes, though, are still not enough to significantly improve the daily lives of those trans persons mostly dedicated to sex work. As sex workers, they endure poverty and persecution, and have little access to social security, including the health system.

1 The Writ for Protection of Rights—*Tutela*—and the Colombian Constitutional Court

The 1991 Colombian Constitution introduced an expedited procedure to claim rights before judges as part of an institutional design that sought to solve considerable inequalities in access to justice.[2] *Tutelas*, according to article 86 of the Constitution, may be submitted to any judge in the Republic, do not require a lawyer, may be presented orally or in writing, do not demand intensive evidentiary work, may be in response to the actions of private persons as well as public officials, may be preventive or remedial in nature, and may even include requests for damages.[3] The Constitutional Court has added to this that children and adolescents are competent to file *tutelas* for the protection of their rights, even when this implies contradicting their parents.[4]

Tutelas are not submitted directly to the Constitutional Court. According to article 241 of the Constitution, this Court is in charge of the Constitutional review of all international treaties adopted by the country, organic and statutory laws approved by Congress, emergency decrees promulgated by the President in times of emergency; Constitutional claims against ordinary laws approved at any time by Congress, as long as they are still in force; and *tutelas* as discretionally selected to avoid an irreparable harm, or to develop or unify constitutional doctrine.[5] This selection process does not allow for the intervention of the parties to the case, and it generally proceeds without personal notification or further evidence collection. It does include

[2]On access to justice in Colombia during the eighties and nineties, see de Soussa Santos and Villegas (2001).

[3]On *tutelas* and how they have become a successful mechanism to close the gap between law in the books and law in action, see Merhof (2015), pp. 714–732.

[4]From very early on, the Court has insisted that when the Constitution established that *tutelas* could be filed by any person (article 86), it meant any human being, not only those which civil law recognized as capable to file suits. *See* Sentencia T-341 de 1993 (involving a thirteen year-old expelled from school for a four-day absence; the Court granted protection of her right to due process having established that the director of the school had not followed any procedure to adopt the decision). In Sentencia T-293 de 1994, the Court granted protection to two underage girls who sued their mother for intending to publish a book revealing details of their private life. The Court granted an injunction against the publication of the book.

[5]On the selection of *tutelas* for review by the Constitutional Court, see Isabel C. Jaramillo Sierra and Antonio Barreto Rozo, "El problema del procesamiento de información en la selección de tutelas por la Corte Constitucional, con especial atención al papel de las insistencias" in *Colombia Internacional*, No. 72 (2010) https://doi.org/10.7440/colombiaint72.2010.03.

an "insistence" mechanism that lets individuals, organizations and public authorities present their arguments about the relevance of the case or the severity of the harm derived from the decisions adopted by inferior judges. Insistence is restricted to Justices of the Constitutional Court, the office of the Ombudsperson and the office of the Solicitor General. These authorities, nonetheless, may be approached by any party interested in a case.[6] Existing data on *tutelas* does not allow any conclusions about the selection of cases involving trans and intersex issues; we cannot know whether the Court is aggressively selecting cases to develop constitutional doctrine on sexual identity, or is merely choosing cases that are representative of the situation of trans persons. Given the number of *tutela* cases that have been heard by the Court involving the rights of internally displaced individuals and litigation of health and social security rights, though, it is reasonable to assume that the cases involving trans persons have received special attention.[7]

Indeed, according to the data gathered by the Constitutional Court, 7,774,060 *tutelas* have been assigned a file number by the Secretary General of the Court, that is, about 250,000 per year for the last 28 years.[8] The number of *tutelas* filed by citizens before ordinary judges, though, has varied greatly: while from 1992 to 1994 a total of 57,809 *tutelas* were filed in the country, in 2006 there were 256,372 and in 2019 there were 620,242.[9] The number of decisions on *tutelas* by the Court has also varied but not in direct relation to the number of cases. In 1993 there were just about the same number of Court decisions on *tutelas* as in 2019 (394 and 398, respectively).[10] In 2000 and 2005 there were the most *tutela* decisions by the Court: 1340 and 1161, respectively.[11] Official data for 2019, in addition, shows what other studies have found: that most *tutela* cases seek the payment or rendering of a service already established in the law and recognized by an administrative authority.[12] Cases in which individuals seek to muster the force of the Constitution to transform practices not mandated by the law are very few and must actively be sought after by Justices in order to develop constitutional doctrine on the matter.[13] These are exactly the cases involving trans and intersex individuals: rare but important. As

[6] *Ibid.*

[7] The office of the Ombudsperson (Defensoría del Pueblo) has been gathering information on *tutelas* concerning the right to health. Data from 2015 showed that they were 24% of the total of *tutelas* presented by citizens in the country: https://www.defensoria.gov.co/es/nube/enlosmedios/5911/Cada-35-minutos-se-presenta-una-tutela-por-la-salud.htm (last visited may 19, 2020) The number of *tutelas* filed by internally displaced individuals has been tracked by the Special Unit for Victims: https://www.unidadvictimas.gov.co/es/institucional/defensoria-destaca-labor-de-la-unidad-para-las-victimas-en-disminucion-de-las-tutelas (last visited may 19, 2020).

[8] See statistical data on *tutela* in the web page of the Constitutional Court: https://www.corteconstitucional.gov.co/lacorte/estadisticas.php (last visited April 10, 2020).

[9] *Ibid.*

[10] *Ibid.*

[11] *Ibid.*

[12] *Ibid.*

[13] *Ibid.*

shown in this chapter, the Court has adopted fifteen decisions on trans persons and eight on intersex individuals. This is a negligible amount when compared to the total of 19,601 decisions adopted by the Court, but this is sufficient to substantially change the outlook of the legal framework governing these issues.[14]

The Constitutional Court has also been crucial to the transformation of the legal system via constitutional review. In its 28 years of existence, it has decided more than thirteen thousand cases under this modality of constitutional control. As mentioned above, constitutional review proceeds either automatically—in the case of international treaties, organic and statutory laws, and emergency decrees—or on demand—in the case of ordinary laws. Demands for the constitutional review of laws may be filed by any Colombian citizen at any time if they refer to a substantive issue, or within the year of their promulgation if they relate to a legislative procedural matter. Requests for constitutional review of ordinary laws are filed directly before the Constitutional Court, and the Court has to answer each petition individually. Although this openness to constitutional challenges has been crucial in the transformation of issues that Congress has addressed, the silence of legislators when it comes to sexual identity has rendered this mechanism quite useless.[15]

2 Sexual Identity as a Protected Category in Colombian Constitutional Law

On a case-by-case basis, the Constitutional Court has addressed most issues of sexual identity: name change, sex change, cross dressing, discrimination in educational facilities, gender modification surgeries, the draft, prisons, and access to medical treatments. Even if the decisions are few, they may be separated into two quite distinct periods. The first period, including decisions adopted from 1993 to 2007, was dominated by the framing of autonomy and found many reasons to delegate the protection of rights to other authorities. It was also important in this first stage that the Court did not clearly distinguish sexual orientation and sexual identity; rather, it spoke of a homosexual identity that included both sexual preference and the display of traits belonging to the other gender. Interestingly, during this period the Court was more prone to protect the expression of sexual identity than sexual preference, arguing in favor of restrictions based on public morality when it came to kisses or caresses among individuals of the same sex. The second group of decisions, from 2007 to 2020, still uses the framing of autonomy but highlights

[14] *Ibid.*

[15] The Colombian Constitutional Court famously struck down criminal legislation concerning the use of drugs and euthanasia in the nineties (C-221 de 1994 y C-239 de 1997) and reformed abortion law in 2006 (C-355 de 2006). It also reformed the law on marriage to authorize same sex marriage and same sex unions (C-577 de 2011, C-075 de 2007, C-029 de 2009). On the judicial reform of abortion law in Colombia, *see* Sierra and Sierra (2008). On the recognition of rights for same sex couples, *see* Albarracín (2011), pp. 7–34.

structural equality, and assumes the task of protecting rights even if other authorities should or could do more. Here, the distinction between sexual orientation and gender identity becomes the foundation for protection. It is also relevant that sexual preference gradually becomes recognized as related to the choice of partner and not only to the expression of self.

2.1 Homosexual Identity and the Right of Individuals to Freely Develop Their Personality: 1993–2008

The first decision on sexual identity was adopted by the Constitutional Court in 1993 (T-594 de 1993) and it involved the change of name before a notary public. The freedom to change names, as the Court explains, was introduced by legislation in 1988. The relevant legal rule established, and still does, that individuals may change their name once to "affix their personal identity" at will. The case studied by the Court involved a notary public that refused changing a masculine name for a feminine one, arguing that the claimant needed to go before a judge in order to change his name in this exact manner. The Court, in a chamber decision, determined that the Constitution protected the right of individuals to express their individuality through their name as part of their right to freely develop their personality (article 16 Colombian Constitution). It ordered the notary public to change the name as requested by the petitioner and informed the authority that supervises the work of notaries about its decision.[16]

A substantial group of decisions in the following years addressed the issue of school discipline and punishment for homosexual identity/acts. In half of these decisions the Court found in favor of the claimant, while in the other half it found that the institution had correctly applied existing bylaws and procedures. The first of these decisions was T-097 of 1994 and it involved a young man who had been expelled from the Police Academy for engaging in "homosexual acts" with a classmate. The Court established that there was no evidence for the charge of "homosexual acts", and that the sanction had been materially grounded on the assumption that the "homosexual traits" of the student were enough to find that he had engaged in "homosexual acts". Emphasizing that homosexuality was a choice protected by the Constitution as part of the right to freely develop personality, the Court explained that individuals could not be expelled from educational institutions, even those related to the armed forces, for merely their homosexuality. There should be evidence that the individual's actions produced harm to the institution. The Court ordered the readmission of the petitioner within the next 48 h. Similarly, in decision

[16]In the following year, T-504 de 1994, the Court studied a case involving the change of sex in the civil registry. It confirmed the established practice that only judges could order this type of corrections and only after verifying that the physiological and psychological conditions of the new sex were fulfilled.

T-101 de 1998, the Court protected the right of two high school students who voluntarily left the school for economic reasons and were denied reentrance for their "perverse identity". The Court explained that even if the school was managed by a religious community, it was public by nature and the religious beliefs of the authorities could not be imposed as law. It also reiterated that homosexual identity could not give rise to unequal treatment, and arguing that this measure protected the students from the harm that could come from their fellow students was discriminatory. The Court ordered the admission of the students.

The Court distinguished the cases in which students were expelled for their "identity" from cases in which they were expelled for their "acts". Thus, in decision T-569 de 1994, it established that a student that decided to not return to school for being constantly disciplined for his attire and was forced to engage counselling with the school psychologist, had willingly decided to disregard school bylaws and to withdraw from the educational system. The very fact that the *tutela* was presented by his mother, and not by the student himself, was regarded as evidence that he was not willing to follow rules that prevented him from wearing heels and make-up at school. In decision T-037 de 1995, the Court also upheld the expulsion of a student from the Police Academy as this decision was grounded on evidence that he had engaged in "homosexual acts" that were disruptive of school discipline.

The Court's position on the difference between homosexual identity and acts in the realm of education and the armed forces started to change in 1998, when decision C-481 de 1998 determined that legislation on disciplinary faults of public officials could not be interpreted to include sanctions for homosexual teachers, and that the protection of homosexual identity barred the state from attempting to punish homosexual acts if those acts were not harmful. The Court noted that:

> There is no justification for homosexuality to be a disciplinary fault for teachers . . . there is no evidence that these persons are more inclined to abuse others sexually, nor that their presence in the classroom affects the free development of their students. In addition, the law guarantees that teachers who harm their students will be punished, whether they are homosexuals or heterosexuals. Rules such as the one considered reflect old and deep prejudices against homosexuality, that prevent the development of a pluralist and tolerant democracy. (Decision C-481 de 1998, translation by the author)

In 2002, the Court found that a Catholic School that forced one of its students to be tested to determine whether she was a lesbian had violated her rights to intimacy and free development of her personality. In decision 435 of 2002, the Court established that no school could include in its internal bylaws homosexuality as a disciplinary fault and could not interrogate students as to their sexual inclinations or activities. The student, however, was not found to be deserving of readmission as her actions contravened quite a few other rules and were proven following due process.

In this same period, the Court used the difference between homosexual identity and acts to decide cases involving the media, public events and child custody. In the first of these decisions, T-539 de 1994, two different individuals claimed that the decision of the National Television Council to bar a commercial that showed a kiss between two men, violated the right to equality and free development of personality. The commercial had been commissioned by the Ministry of Health and it encouraged the use of condoms to prevent HIV. The Court found that there was no evidence of a discriminatory intention of the National Television Council or any of its members, that such intention should be addressed before administrative authorities, and that publicity oriented to gay men in matters concerning the prevention of HIV was misleading as it misrepresented this disease as solely a concern of that community. In decision T-268 de 2000, the Court found that it could not protect the rights of individuals affected by a Major's determination to not allow a parade sponsored by the National Gay Pageant. The Court pointed out that the Major's decision should be submitted to an administrative tribunal as there were no individual rights at stake but rather collective rights to the enjoyment of culture. Finally, in decision T-290 of 1995, the Court found that when the Family Welfare Institute separated a child from her trans mother for raising her in a negative environment (notwithstanding evidence that the child was healthy and presented no signs of any kind of abuse), the removal was not discriminating against her for her identity, but rather giving justified differential treatment for her choice of residence and line of work (she was a sex worker).

One last case to be included here is T-152 de 2007. In this case, the Court established that it was discrimination to treat individuals differently on the basis of their sexual orientation, referring here to their "homosexual identity", and established that this was a category meriting suspect scrutiny under the Colombian Constitution regardless of the fact that it is not explicitly mentioned in the equality clause of article 13. The Court, however, did not grant the protection demanded by the petitioner arguing that she had not provided evidence of discrimination. This despite the facts that she was a trans woman and provided a few witnesses that testified that she had been hired verbally, but not allowed entrance into the workplace the next day.

2.2 *Sexual Identity as a Suspect Category to be Actively Protected by the Court*

The Court first used the expression "sexual identity" with regards to trans persons in a 2008 case involving a change of name, T-1033 de 2008.[17] From a timid elaboration that allowed for orders to change names as many times as needed in the case of trans persons, the Court moved to an extensive understanding of gender identity that has brought about generous rules concerning the rights to identity, health, education and equality. The Court also changed its approach of deferral to administrative agencies and private parties for one of active intervention that includes ordering the enactment of regulations, adopting pedagogical campaigns, as well as hiring and admitting individuals without going through extensive evidence of harm.

[17]The Court has reiterated this rule in two more cases: T-977 de 2012 and T-086 de 2014.

With regards to identity, the Court changed its initial position dramatically as to the need of a judicial decision for a change in the civil registry to recognize that ordinary judicial proceedings are long and costly, and that the demand of "evidence" regarding the biological and psychological markers of sex is excessive for individuals who are intensely discriminated in society. Indeed, in decision T-918 of 2012, the Court studied the claim of an individual who was denied medical treatment for her condition as a trans woman. The petitioner not only demanded medical treatment (this part of the decision is revisited below), but also demanded that once surgery was complete, her sex was changed in the civil registry. The Court considered that the long time the plaintiff had invested in the process of changing her sex, she provided evidence of 3 years of hormonal treatment, and the fact that she had to use a judicial decision to obtain medical treatment for her condition, made the ordinary requirement of going before a judge to obtain an order for a change in the civil registry excessive. The Court consequently ordered the notary public in the city where the petitioner was registered to change her sex as soon as she could provide proof that the surgery—also ordered in the decision—had been performed.

Decision T-476 of 2014 went further in protecting lived gender identity, as opposed to certified identity, by ordering that the city of Bogotá hire a trans woman who was selected as an administrative assistant following proper proceedings, but later not hired for failing to produce proof of having served in the military. The Court declared that legislation concerning the duty of Colombian males to prove they served in the military to access employment was inapplicable to trans women, regardless at what age at which they started to make their decision evident, and of the formalization of such decision before public authorities. It was enough, the Court explained, that individuals present themselves as being women for the military to exclude them from the draft and for employers to be able to hire them.[18] The following year, in decision T-063 de 2015, the Court established that to change the sex marker in the civil registry, individuals need only make a public declaration regarding their intention. It recommended that the government enact regulations that would facilitate the implementation of this new rule, which resulted in Decree 1227 of 2015.[19]

Finally, in 2017, the Court adopted two decisions regarding the possibility of using the abbreviated procedure before public notaries by underage transsexuals. In T-498 de 2017, the Court studied the case of a 17 years-old trans man who asked Colombian authorities to change his documentation in order to alleviate the burden he would endure in the process of becoming a United States citizen. In this case, the

[18]This rule was reiterated in decision T-099 de 2015. The Court ordered the Ministry of Defense and relevant authorities in the military to create a protocol to exclude trans women from the draft and to include trans men. It also ordered the realization of pedagogical campaigns to sensitize members of the military towards gender identity issues.

[19]The decree established that for the public deed, individuals only needed to present their official documentation and make a public statement regarding their intention to change their sex, that sex could only be changed every ten years, that the deed should be ready in five working days and that the cost should be the same as that of similar deeds.

Court used the rationale developed for intersexual individuals and determined that it was excessive to ask trans minors to go through a judicial procedure to change their sex in documents, as well as it was excessive to prevent them from obtaining corrections altogether. In T-675 de 2017, the Court confronted the case of a 17 years-old trans woman who simply argued that she thought it was crucial to her development to have the possibility to change her sex in official documents. In this second case, the Court not only ordered the correction, but demanded that the entity in charge of supervising public notaries instruct them as to the conditions in which underage persons could change their sex. The Court determined that the following conditions should be considered by public notaries when confronted with a request for a change of sex: (1) age of the person bearing in mind that the closer the person is to reaching 18 years of age, the more her autonomy should be acknowledged; (2) the free and informed consent of the individual requesting the change; and (3) the existence of professional evaluations regarding the process.

As to the right to health, the Court has insisted that beyond the legal recognition of basic access to gender confirming surgeries (involving the suppression or creation of penises), trans persons have the right to comprehensive information regarding possible interventions, alternatives and consequences; and the right to request additional treatments, as long as they are considered essential to the affirmation of their identity and this conviction is supported by a medical doctor. These rights have been considered as within the reach of underage trans boys and girls.

In T-552 de 2013, the Court decided two cases of trans persons whose requests to the health system were denied. The first case involved the claim of a 45 years-old trans woman for gender reassignment surgeries she decided herself she needed as her insurer refused to allow her an appointment with a specialist, claiming that her plan did not cover the surgeries she had in mind. The Court found that the woman had never received proper medical advice about her options or about the coverage of her plan and the possibilities it offered. It clarified that only after proper evaluation of her situation could the insurer reject her claim. The second case involved a 17 years-old trans man that requested several gender affirming procedures that were denied him on the basis of age. The Court established that the principles introduced in decision SU-337 de 1999 regarding medical treatment of underage intersexuals should be used in cases concerning trans persons.[20] The Court reiterated that underage trans persons could be authorized to consent to interventions in their bodies bearing in mind how close they were to reaching 18 year of age, the importance or perceived

[20]In SU-337 de 1999, the Court decided the case of an eight-year-old intersexual whose parents insisted on having medically intervention. The doctors refused to proceed without a judicial order. The Court clarified that a judicial order was not necessary to make such decisions, but also established that in light of the importance of the intervention and its severity, the child should make the decision on his own. The Court insisted that there was no "urgency" in this case, and that it was more important that the child be fully and actively involved in the decision-making process than rushing the procedures.

urgency of the intervention, and the severity of the consequences of the intervention.[21]

The Court has not granted every request for gender affirming treatment, but it has established two basic principles for the health system to address when making such decisions. The first principle is that when deciding whether a medical treatment is to be included in the basic medical plan, the standard should not be that of a risk to life, but rather of a risk to health. Health, according to the Court, should be understood as the maximum state of welfare, both physical and mental. The second principle is that gender identity is related to the right to health not because it is a disease or an anomaly, but rather because absent interventions that can only be provided by the health system, the individual will not be able to reach the maximum state of welfare that the right to health involves. *Tutelas* on breast reduction and enlargement were granted, as well as those concerning counseling.[22] Decisions on other treatments were deferred to doctors.[23]

The Constitutional Court has also protected the right to education of trans persons, both by insisting that trans men should be allowed to use male uniforms, and trans women should be allowed to use female uniforms, and by establishing that educational institutions should actively seek to retain trans students by allowing extraordinary admissions and adopting special adjustment programs to guarantee their adaptation at the moment in which they enter the school.[24] In decision T-804 de 2014, the Court determined that the burden of proof in cases of access to education of trans persons was with educational institutions. In this case, a young trans woman claimed that she requested admission to a school but was not given any documents as "they did not accept people like him". The youth approached a human rights organization with her case and they instructed her as to how to present a claim. Information about the whereabouts of the individual were lost and never recovered. She never requested access to the school again. The school denied having rejected her. The Court argued that the severity of the exclusions faced by trans women warranted shifting the burden of proof to the institution and ordered an extraordinary admission process accompanied by efforts to reach out to the petitioner.

Crossdressing has been addressed also in the contexts of prisons and employment. In both cases, the Court found that it was enough for petitioners to start *tutela* proceedings for the directives to allow the changes demanded by individuals. Even if at the moment of the decision by the Court petitioners were no longer prevented from deciding how to appear before their inmates/colleagues, the Court ordered prisons/

[21]This position was reiterated in T-622 de 2014.

[22]Decisions T-876 of 2012 and T-771 of 2013.

[23]Decision T-876 of 2012.

[24]Decision T-552 de 2013 (on use of feminine uniforms by trans women), T-363 de 2016 (on the use of masculine uniforms by transmen) and T-804 de 2014 (on access to education).

employers to adopt protocols that would guarantee that the type of obstacles faced by claimants would be removed.[25]

One last case worth mentioning is T-314 of 2011. In this case, a trans woman argued that she was not allowed access to a concert because of her identity. Organizers claimed that her identity was not the reason to prevent her entrance since: (a) the event was especially geared to the LGBT community; (b) she had used drugs or alcohol and exhibited a behavior that could endanger other participants in the event. The Court explained that even if there was no evidence of discrimination, public authorities should develop a comprehensive policy on the rights of LGBTI individuals to ensure full knowledge and respect of these rights. It explicitly stated that the claimant had enough evidence from the environment as to her vulnerability to have misinterpreted the situation as one of discrimination, and that responsibility regarding the change in the context lied with public authorities.[26]

3 Trans Lives in the Context of Rights

It is quite difficult to trace the effect of the framework developed by the Constitutional Court because there is very little information available about the lives of trans persons in Colombia. As one of the leading LGBTI organizations in Colombia, *Colombia Diversa*, has pointed out, this is the result of years of intentional disregard of citizen's petitions and judicial orders concerning the production of information on LGBTI individuals and not merely the result of administrative inertia.[27] More than a decade of interaction with authorities in charge of registering violence in Colombia reveals the unwillingness of institutions to reply to legitimate calls for information and their indifference in underscoring the unequal impact of violence in Colombia.

Existing data, nonetheless, places Colombia as the second highest country with respect to LGBT violent deaths in the region.[28] As opposed to the tendencies in the region, where gay men and trans women are equally victims of hate murders, in Colombia the number of gay men murdered is double the number of trans women as victims.[29] That 40% of all LGBTI murders can be attributed to prejudice is relevant

[25]Decision T-062 de 2011 (about use of make up by a male convict) and T-143 de 2018 (about use of a masculine uniform by a trans man).

[26]This policy was adopted by the Ministry of the Interior in 2018: http://es.presidencia.gov.co/normativa/normativa/DECRETO%20762%20DEL%2007%20DE%20MAYO%20DE%202018.pdf (last visited April 2020).

[27]Colombia Diversa, Aunque intenten borrarnos. Informe de Derechos humanos de personas LGBT en Colombia 2018 (available at: https://colombiadiversa.org/colombiadiversa2016/wp-content/uploads/2020/03/Aunque-intenten-borrarnos.pdf) (last visited May 12, 2020).

[28]Comisión Interamericana de Derechos Humanos, Violencia contra Personas Gay, Lesbianas, Bisexuales, Trans e Intersex en América, OAS/Ser.L/V/II.rev.2 Doc. 36, nov. 2015 (available at: http://www.oas.org/es/cidh/informes/pdfs/violenciapersonaslgbti.pdf) (last visited May 12, 2020).

[29]*Ibid* and Colombia Diversa, *op cit.*

even as violent death is the second cause of death generally in Colombia, with intentional homicides still high as a percentage of violent deaths: 25 per 100,000 people.[30]

The most extensive information available about trans persons has been collected by the city of Bogotá for the design and implementation of its diversity policy.[31] The two surveys conducted to diagnose and evaluate the situation of LGBTI individuals living in the city and the impact of the policies adopted, reveal some patterns that might be positively, even if very loosely, connected to the framework developed by the Constitutional Court. First, the data shows a drastic reduction in discrimination in the education and health systems. According to 2014 data, while in 2010 more than 70% of trans persons included in the survey noted discrimination in education, in 2014 only 3.77% answered positively when inquired about discrimination.[32] Similarly, individuals included in the 2014 survey declared fewer aggressions on the part of doctors, nurses and administrative personnel: from 85% in 2010 to 21% in 2014.[33]

In contrast to this reduction, however, a second pattern emerges: trans persons identify more violations to their right to health in 2014 than they did in the past, in particular they point out that they have not received medical attention to conditions related to their sexual identity.[34] Although there are small decreases in the number of trans persons seeking treatments outside of the formal health system, and parallel increases in those that use the health system, it is crucial that trans persons still do not trust doctors with respect to medical affirmation procedures. Thirty-five percent of surveyed individuals in 2010 and 25% of surveyed individuals in 2014 declared to have intervened their bodies hormonally or surgically in informal settings: a friend recommended hormones (50% of all those that used hormones), an esthetician

[30] *See* Colombia Diversa, *op.cit.*; Statista, Number of Violent Deaths in Colombia in 2018, by cause (available at: https://www.statista.com/statistics/917122/number-violent-deaths-colombia-cause/); and UN Office on Drugs and Crime's International Homicide Statistics database, Intentional Homicides (per 100,000 people) Colombia available at: https://data.worldbank.org/indicator/VC.IHR.PSRC.P5?locations=CO&most_recent_value_desc=true.

[31] The city's first policy on LGBT rights was adopted in 2010; a second version was adopted in 2015, *see* Alcaldía Mayor de Bogotá, Balances y Perspectivas: política para la garantía de derechos de lesbianas, gays, bisexuales y transgeneristas y otras identidades de género y orientaciones sexuales en Bogotá, 2011 (available at: http://old.integracionsocial.gov.co/anexos/documentos/2014_politicas_publicas/politica_publica_lgbt_balances_y_perspectivas.pdf) Alcaldía Mayor de Bogotá, Política Pública para la Población LGBTI (available at: http://www.saludcapital.gov.co/Paginas2/PoliticaLGBTI.aspx).

[32] Alcaldía Mayor de Bogotá, Medicion de la línea de base para la garantía plena de derechos de las personas de los sectores LGBT, 2015 p. 219 (available at: http://www.sdp.gov.co/sites/default/files/medicion_linea_de_base_de_la_politica_publica_lgbt_0.pdf).

[33] *Ibid*, p. 227.

[34] This failure to transform health services is not particular to the trans population. Constitutional Court has attempted structural interventions with little success: Sentencia T-760 de 2008. On the right to health and the role of the Colombian Constitutional Court see: Yamin and Parra Vera (2010), pp. 101–129.

increased the size of the buttocks (6.6%), etc.[35] Their rates of affiliation to the health system are incredibly low, at 68%, while the national rate of affiliation is 94%, according to the Ministry of Health.[36] Trans persons in Bogotá also are poorer (75% are in the two lowest socio economic strata), less educated, and endure worse hosing conditions.[37]

The impact of measures regarding military service and documentation, on the other hand, is still not traceable in changes in occupation. The procedure introduced by Decree 1227 of 2015 for sex change does not seem to have been resisted by notaries in charge of the implementation: for the first 2 years, the cost has been a steady 12 dollars and the amount of individuals whose sex has been changed has been about one per day.[38] Nevertheless, about 70% of trans women and 50% of trans men surveyed are still sex workers.[39] As sex workers, they not only have fewer protections regarding their income and property, but also have trouble being recognized by the social security system. Sex work is not a crime in Colombia, and has not been a crime for a long time.[40] Sex workers, though, are more exposed to persecution by police for subverting the boundaries of zones of tolerance, and by social service workers when they dare to raise children.[41]

The Constitutional Court's approach to sex work has been mixed, to say the least. On the one hand, the Court has clearly endorsed zoning regulations that prevent sex workers from freely selling their services in cities.[42] The Court has also admonished that in most circumstances, sex work is performed in conditions of exploitation that render prostitutes victims of trafficking.[43] On the other hand, the Court has emphatically asserted that sex work is work and sex workers should be affiliated to social security as regular workers.[44] These tensions of recognition place trans persons in particularly vulnerable positions: while they cannot be incarcerated for their activities, they are not recognized as part of the "poorest of the poor" by the minimal

[35]Alcaldía Mayor de Bogotá, Medicion de la línea de base, p. 232.

[36]Alcaldía Mayor de Bogotá, Medicion de la línea de base, p. 224. Also, Ministerio de Salud, Indicador del comportamiento histórico de la afiliación al SGSSS (available at: https://www.minsalud.gov.co/proteccionsocial/Regimensubsidiado/Paginas/coberturas-del-regimen-subsidiado.aspx).

[37]Alcaldía Mayor de Bogotá, Medicion de la línea de base, pp. 212–214 and 235.

[38]El Tiempo, "Cada día una persona cambia el sexo en su documento" 18 de marzo de 2018 (available at: https://www.eltiempo.com/economia/sectores/solicitudes-de-cambio-de-sexo-en-la-cedula-en-colombia-195316) These clearly contrasts with the strong opposition of these same notaries to the formal recognition of same sex unions. Sarmiento (2009), pp. 57–96.

[39]Alcaldía Mayor de Bogotá, Medicion de la línea de base, pp. 243–244.

[40]See Martínez and Rodríguez (2002).

[41]Colombia Diversa, *op.cit.* See also Montoya (2012), pp. 143–161.

[42]*See* Sentencia SU 062 de 2019.

[43]Sentencia T- 629 of 2010 and T-073 of 2017.

[44]*Ibid.* On this contradictory approach to sex work, see Esteban Restrepo Saldarriaga, "La Constitución Sentimental. Prostitución, trabajo sexual y trata de personas en Colombia" en *Isonomía* no.48 México abr. 2018.

welfare provided by the state. Ciswomen prostitutes, in contrast, use their status as mothers to claim aid for families with small children.

In conclusion, legal reform to recognize and include trans persons in Colombia has been led by the Constitutional Court with little participation of other government authorities or even social mobilization. These changes introduced doctrinally seem to reduce discrimination and violence in areas such as education and health. But this framework can only go so far in protecting trans persons from the cruelty of poverty and invisibility.

References

Albarracín M (2011) Corte Constitucional y Movimientos Sociales: El Reconocimiento Judicial de los Derechos de las Parejas del Mismo Sexo en Colombia. Revista Sur 8(14):7–34

Cepeda MJ, Landau D (2017) Colombian constitutional law: leading cases. Oxford University Press, New York

de Soussa Santos B, Villegas MG (2001) El Caleidoscopio de las Justicias en Colombia, vol 2. Siglo del Hombre y Universidad de los Andes, Bogotá

Martínez A, Rodríguez P (eds) (2002) Placer, Dinero y Pecado, Historia de la Prostitución en Colombia. Aguilar, Bogotá

Merhof K (2015) Building a bridge between reality and the constitution: the establishment and development of the Colombian Constitutional Court. Int J Const Law 13(3):714–732. https://doi.org/10.1093/icon/mov043

Montoya V (2012) ¿Trabajadora Sexual o Víctima Perfecta? Límites en el acceso a la justicia. En Prisma Jurídico 11:143–161

Sarmiento JP (2009) Las uniones maritales de hecho entre las parejas del mismo sexo, una lucha inconclusa contra la discriminación. en Revista de Derecho 32:57–96. Available at: http://rcientificas.uninorte.edu.co/index.php/derecho/article/viewArticle/661

Sierra ICJ, Sierra TA (2008) Mujeres, Cortes y Medios. La reforma judicial del aborto en Colombia. Siglo del Hombre editores, Bogotá

Yamin A, Parra Vera O (2010) Judicial protection of the right to health in Colombia: from social demands to individual claims to public debates. Hast Int Comp Law Rev 33(2):101–129

The Civil Status of Trans Persons in Denmark

Ditlev Tamm and Ingrid Lund-Andersen

Abstract The legal recognition of trans persons has gradually taken place in Denmark in the last decades. The development has been peaceful, the tone of the debate mostly moderate and objective. In general, legal solutions have been pragmatic, placing Denmark today in the international lead as to the recognition of such rights. Changes as to the law of transgendered persons have been made through legislation and not by referring such issues as constitutional rights raised before the courts.

The recognition of trans persons as a group, who require specific regulations in the law, has gradually taken place in Denmark in the last decades. The development has been peaceful, the tone of the debate mostly moderate and objective. In general, legal solutions have been pragmatic, placing Denmark today in the international lead as to the recognition of such rights.

Changes as to the law of transgendered persons have been made through legislation and not by referring such issues as constitutional rights raised before the

D. Tamm (✉) · I. Lund-Andersen
University of Copenhagen, The Faculty of Law, Copenhagen, Denmark
e-mail: Ditlev.Tamm@jur.ku.dk

I. C. Jaramillo, L. Carlson (eds.), *Trans Rights and Wrongs*, Ius Comparatum - Global Studies in Comparative Law 54,
https://doi.org/10.1007/978-3-030-68494-5_19

courts.[1] An Act of Parliament from 1971 (amended 1987)[2] prohibits discrimination for various reasons—including sexual orientation—in commercial and public affairs. Additionally, an Act on Prohibition of Discrimination in the Labor Market,[3] which was implemented according to EU Directive 2000/78/EF, prohibits discrimination based on sexual orientation. The Danish Gender Equality Act prohibits both direct and indirect discrimination based on gender.[4] The board for complaints established by this act has decided cases on transgenderism. The complexity of the field is highlighted by a decision made in 2016 by the Danish Board of Equal Treatment to the effect that it was not a violation of the Equality Act that the complainant, legally a transwoman who had not undergone a physical sex reassignment, could not use the women's changing room.

Public services and public facilities thus still are not always updated or consistent with transgender rights to have their legal sex changed without surgery or changing their physical appearance. In the above-mentioned decision by the Equal Treatment Board (*Ligebehandlingsnævnet*), the transwoman, who had had her civil registration number changed and therefore legally had had a sex change, was not allowed to use the women's changing room in an indoor swimming-pool but was referred to the men's changing room or the handicap changing room. The Equal Treatment Board found that the consideration for the other women's modesty was sufficient reason to banish her from the women's changing room and therefore concluded that even

[1] As a constitutional monarchy, the current Danish (written) constitution stems from 1953 but still follows the model of the first modern constitution of 1849. No specific amendments have since been added to the constitution and gender issues do not form part of the catalogue of human rights in the constitution. The constitution is supplemented by the European Convention of Human Rights, which has been adopted as part of Danish law. Denmark is one of the few European countries that does not have a specific constitutional court. Judicial review, however, is part of the Danish legal system although there is no specific article in the constitution guaranteeing such review. Ordinary courts, however, may interpret the constitution under appeal to the Supreme Court. To the present date only in one case was a statute adopted by the Danish Parliament found to be unconstitutional by the Danish Supreme Court. The Danish judiciary has generally been hesitant as to using judicial review. In Denmark there is a high respect for the democratically-elected Parliament (one chamber known as the Folketing) and judges consider themselves as legal specialists and therefore are not likely to make what may be seen as political or semi-political decisions.

[2] *Bekendtgørelse af lov om forbud mod forskelsbehandling på grund af race m.v. (*Act no 289 of 9 June 1971 as changed by act no 357 of 3 June 1987: "§ 1. Den, som inden for erhvervsmæssig eller almennyttig virksomhed på grund af en persons race, hudfarve, nationale eller etniske oprindelse, tro eller seksuelle orientering nægter at betjene den pågældende på samme vilkår som andre, straffes med bøde, hæfte eller fængsel indtil 6 måneder. *Stk. 2.* På samme måde straffes den, som af nogen af de i stk. 1 nævnte grunde nægter at give en person adgang på samme vilkår som andre til sted, forestilling, udstilling, sammenkomst eller lignende, der er åben for almenheden."

[3] https://www.retsinformation.dk/forms/r0710.aspx?id=122522. Accessed 4 July 2020.

[4] https://www.retsinformation.dk/forms/r0710.aspx?id=160578 – Ligestillingsloven. Accessed 4 July 2020.

though there was an actual discrimination, this did not constitute a violation of the Equality Act.[5]

The Human Rights' catalogue of the Danish constitution is not framed in a way that provides much room for development by the courts. Since the European Convention of Human Rights was incorporated in Danish law in 1999, judgments of the ECtHR have been guiding for the Danish courts. The Danish Constitution is only amendable by referendum. The basic development of human rights, including the rights of trans persons, has not taken as a starting point any articles of the constitution but stems from legislation enacted by Parliament, and to a high degree, promoted by transgender organizations and influenced by the international developments and discussions in the field. Thus the rather radical changes in the status of trans persons which have been carried out in Denmark mostly in the last decade basically stem from parliamentary statutes which to a great majority (and sometimes across party lines) is positive as to improving the rights of trans persons. There is a tradition in Danish parliamentary life of aiming at compromises. Details as to legislation on trans issues have, however, been often intensely-debated and opinions have been divided as to how far and how quickly legislation should cover this issue.

1 Terminology and Legislation

In Denmark there are no particular regulations covering the rights of trans persons. There are, however, specific articles within certain acts or regulations that do refer to trans persons. The 2005 Danish Health Care Act (*Sundhedsloven*) thus expressly provides for the possibility of castration (still only for persons above the age of 18) with the purpose of sex change (below). See also about passport legislation and about name change below.

There is no specific norm as to the denomination or definition of trans persons or transgender. Words such as "*transseksuel*" are used as a general denomination for persons who feel that they are born in the wrong sex and wish to change sex or the word "*transkønnet*" as a more broad denomination of gender dysphoria. The word "*transvestit*" is also used for persons wearing the clothes of the opposite sex but evidently transvestitism is not prohibited nor subjected to any legislation. In the debate on transgender issues, Danish LBGT organisations have been politically very active and stress that the term "transsexual" can be misguiding as a person's gender identity has nothing to do with his/her sexual orientation[6] and prefer the term

[5] https://ast.dk/naevn/ligebehandlingsnaevnet/afgorelser-fra-ligebehandlingsnaevnet#?FreeTextSearch=kønsskifte&AdmMyndighedNavn=Ligebehandlingsnævnet. Accessed 4 July 2020.

[6] http://ordnet.dk/ddo/ordbog?aselect=transseksuel&query=transkønnethed. Accessed 4 July 2020.

"transgender". However, both terms are used and mostly perceived as having the same meaning.

According to the Danish Health Board's "Guidance on the Examination and Treatment of transgender",[7] a trans*sexual* is a person who has been given the diagnose "transsexual" (F64.0). The diagnosis is according to the WHO's ICD-10 classification a gender identity disorder, characterized by a desire to live and be recognized as belonging to the opposite sex, usually accompanied by a sense of discomfort or inadequacy with one's own anatomical gender characteristics, and desire for hormone treatment or surgical treatment to change these towards the preferred sex.[8] In Denmark this diagnosis as transsexual is *not* viewed as a diagnosis that indicates a somatic or psychiatric illness. By 1 January 2017, Denmark, as the first country in the world, removed transgender/transsexual from the list of mental illnesses. The only reason a transgender must still receive the diagnosis transsexual is so that the health care system can offer free sex modifying treatments, (see below).

2 Sex Change (SRS) and The Danish Sexological Clinic

Trans persons are and have been in Denmark for a long time allowed to change sex. There is no official limit as to how many times. Until 2014 a trans person in order to change gender should be officially declared transsexual *and* undergo a complete sex reassignment operation (hormonal treatment and castration).[9]

In Denmark medical care is free. The Danish public healthcare system provides both medical and surgical treatments for diagnosed transgendered persons. A pre-condition for sex modifying treatment is the submission to an "examination- and observation process" (*udrednings- og observationsforløb*) performed at The Sexological Clinic.[10] This clinic was founded in 1986 as a department of the nationwide *Rigshospitalet* in Copenhagen This process is carried out by a multidisciplinary team of experts within psychiatry, psychology, gynecology and plastic surgery with knowledge of transsexuality. The process involves a number of conversations with an assigned therapist, and a psychiatric/psychological evaluation conducted by a psychiatrist. It is a requirement that significant conditions (somatic,

[7]https://www.retsinformation.dk/Forms/R0710.aspx?id=167172 - Sundhedsstyrelsens vejledning. Accessed 4 July 2020.

[8]"Ved transseksuelle forstås personer, der har fået stillet diagnosen transseksualitet. Diagnosen transseksualitet (F64. 0) er i henhold til WHO's ICD-10 klassifikation en kønsidentitetsforstyrrelse, som er karakteriseret ved et ønske om at leve og blive anerkendt som medlem af det modsatte køn, sædvanligvis ledsaget af en følelse af ubehag eller utilstrækkelighed ved egne anatomiske kønskarakteristika og et ønske om hormonbehandling eller kirurgisk behandling, for at ændre disse i retning af det foretrukne køn…", see https://www.retsinformation.dk/Forms/R0710.aspx?id=167172 - pkt. 1. Accessed 4 July 2020.

[9]Holdgaard and Lemann Kristiansen (2004), p. 15.

[10]https://transfaq.info/sexologisk-klinik/. Accessed 4 July 2020.

psychiatric, social etc.) are not present that could speak against hormonal treatments. The process takes about six months,[11] the main purpose being to determine whether criteria for the diagnosis of transsexualism are sufficiently met. The overall requirement is a deep and persistent urge to change sex which has been in place for a certain time.[12] If the person has been diagnosed as transsexual by The Sexological Clinic, and is medically approved for medical and surgical treatment, the person is offered free treatment by the public healthcare service.[13] Individuals, who after an examination- and observation process are not diagnosed as transsexual by The Sexological Clinic[14] are not provided with any free gender confirming treatments. However, free supportive and advising counseling is being offered.[15]

Even though Denmark can be considered one of the most advanced countries regarding transgender rights, trans persons are still exposed to certain discriminations. The period of transition within the official system requiring an observation period by The consultation at the Sexological Clinic is often particularly mentioned as rather tough and embarrassing. The rather long terms in order to have a physical sex change and the waiting time for having official documents corresponding to the actual gender appearance also may cause embarrassing situations.[16]

Since 2014, trans persons under the age of 18 can get the same free hormonal treatments as those over 18 including suppressive hormonal treatment (stop hormones) which stop a child's development of gender characteristics. Requirements for such treatment are that the person in question[17] is over 12 years of age (and has reached Tanner Stage 2–4), has completed an examination- and observation process (just as persons over 18), has been diagnosed with "gender identity disorder of childhood" (F64.2), and is suitable for treatment with a persistent desire for this change and together with his/her parents (guardians), understand the consequences of the treatment and that both child and parents has given their informed consent. The psychiatric examination includes a thorough initial examination and assessment by a specialist in child- and adolescent psychiatry based on, inter alia, age of the patient, development, social function, family relationship, etc. with the main purpose

[11]https://transfaq.info/sexologisk-klinik/. Accessed 4 July 2020.

[12]https://www.retsinformation.dk/Forms/R0710.aspx?id=167172 - Sundhedstyrelsens vejledning. Accessed 4 July 2020.

[13]https://www.retsinformation.dk/Forms/R0710.aspx?id=167172. Accessed 4 July 2020. The socalled Center for Kønsidentitet (Centre for Gender Identity) since 1 February provides advice on issues related to gender dysphoria.

[14]http://justitsministeriet.dk/sites/default/files/media/Pressemeddelelser/pdf/2014/Rapport%20om%20juridisk%20kønsskifte.pdf, p. 8. Accessed 4 July 2020.

[15]https://www.retsinformation.dk/Forms/R0710.aspx?id=167172 pkt. 2.3.1. Accessed 4 July 2020.

[16]http://amnesty.dk/nyhedsliste/2016/danmark-kraenker-transkoennedes-rettigheder. Accessed 4 July 2020.

[17]https://www.retsinformation.dk/Forms/R0710.aspx?id=167172 - Pkt. 3.3. Accessed 4 July 2020.

of a diagnostic clarification.[18] For normal hormonal treatment (with opposite sex hormones) the same requirements must be met, however with the addition that the young adult/teenager[19] must be diagnosed as *transsexual,* is over 16 years old and has been living as the opposite sex for at least one year.

Gender confirmation when a person is diagnosed as transsexual, is partly carried out by castration. Requirements[20] include, that the person has turned 18,[21] will go through the 6 months' extermination- and observation process, has a persistent wish to undergo castration, understand the consequences of such surgery, has completed at least 12 months of continuous hormonal treatment, has targeted the desired sex, has had real life experience for a year and has had surgery approved by the Danish National Board of Health (*Sundhedsstyrelsen).*

The question whether SRS (Sex reassignment surgery) should be kept as a condition for sex change was raised already in 2006 by the Danish leftist party *Enhedslisten* (Unity List), which (together with party *Alternativet*) has been especially active in promoting trans rights. The party presented a motion for a resolution regarding the rights of trans persons to change the civil registration number without undergoing previously a complete sex reassignment.[22] The proposal was controversial, and it was opposed by other parties fearing abuse and the consequences of what was seen as a too easy way to have incorrect personal data introduced into the civil registration system. It was, accordingly, maintained that this possibility should only be open for trans persons who had completed a sex reassignment. The motion was after a heavy debate in Parliament rejected.

3 The 2014 Act Allowing Legal Sex Change

The general authority in Denmark as to civil status is the Det Centrale Personregister (*Central Personal Registry* or CPR), which keeps the basic personal data concerning citizens and residents with a Danish social security number. The CPR-administration is a section of the Ministry of Economy and the Interior. Sex is normally not included in civil status (which refers to status as married/unmarried, separated or divorced or widow/widower) but taken into consideration as a *legal* status.[23] In practice, citizens and residents are provided with a civil registration number (CPR-number) consisting

[18]https://www.retsinformation.dk/Forms/R0710.aspx?id=167172 pkt. 3.1- 3.2. Accessed 4 July 2020.

[19]https://www.retsinformation.dk/Forms/R0710.aspx?id=167172 - Pkt. 3.4. Accessed 4 July 2020.

[20]Sundhedsloven (The Health Act) section 104, 115 and 116, and https://www.retsinformation.dk/Forms/R0710.aspx?id=167172 pkt. 2.3.5.2. Accessed 4 July 2020.

[21]Castration cannot be performed on persons under 18 years of age, cf. above and The Health Act section 115 (3).

[22]http://www.ft.dk/samling/20061/beslutningsforslag/b142/beh1-90/forhandling.htm?startItem=-1#alleindlaeg - Beslutningsforslag nr. B 142 2006-07. Accessed 4 July 2020.

[23]Holdgaard and Lemann Kristiansen (2004), p. 15.

of 10 digits. The first 6 digits indicate date of birth and the last 4 constitute a sequence number which indicate sex as female last digits are even and male last digits are odd. A person who wishes to change his or her legal sex can today have the last number of the civil registration changed.

After a change of government in 2014, the "statement model" (*erklæringsmodel*) allowing a legal sex change by statement to the personal registration-authorities was accepted. Trans persons above the age of 18 were granted a right to change their legal sex without surgery or being diagnosed as transsexual.[24] In Parliament there still was an opposition as to not upholding the demand for surgery,[25] whereas others wanted at least to keep a request for a transsexual diagnosis. A diagnosis, thus it was maintained, ensures that the trans person in question is fully aware of her or his choice and prevents eventual misuse of the possibility for legal sex change.[26] In support of the bill it was argued that trans persons should be allowed a free choice regarding their own body and mind, and that the bill would improve equality.[27] The bill was adopted by the narrow majority of 58 out of a total of 111 votes.[28] The conditions according to the latest 2014 legislation are few, and in principle only the conditions mentioned above on civil status must be complied with. A requirement is that the trans person submit a statement that the wish for the legal sex change is based on an experience of belonging to the other sex. The person in question must be above 18. The submission of the application is followed by a six-month reflections period, where the person is to reflect on whether he/she really wishes to change their gender. The length of this period can be shortened.[29] After the reflection period is over, the trans person must reconfirm her or his application.[30] When this procedure is performed, the applicant has fulfilled the conditions for a legal sex change. The basic condition for the legal change of sex is thus that a person conceives him or herself as belonging to another sex, that a written statement is given in which the conception of

---

[24] http://www.ft.dk/samling/20131/lovforslag/l182/beh1-91/forhandling.htm?startItem=-1#alleindlaeg - L 182 2013-14: indlæg 2. Accessed 4 July 2020. The actual change was a new article in the Act on personal registration. I *§ 3* indsættes efter stk. 5 som nyt stykke:

»*Stk. 6.* Økonomi- og Indenrigsministeriet tildeler efter skriftlig ansøgning nyt personnummer til en person, som oplever sig som tilhørende det andet køn. Tildeling af nyt personnummer er betinget af, at den pågældende afgiver en skriftlig erklæring om, at ønsket om nyt personnummer er begrundet i en oplevelse af at tilhøre det andet køn, og at den pågældende efter en refleksionsperiode på 6 måneder fra ansøgningstidspunktet skriftligt bekræfter sin ansøgning. Det er endvidere en betingelse, at den pågældende på ansøgningstidspunktet er fyldt 18 år.«

Stk. 6 og 7 bliver herefter stk. 7 og 8.

[25] Indlæg 34 og 120 i lovforslag L 182 2013-14.

[26] http://www.ft.dk/samling/20131/lovforslag/l182/beh1-91/forhandling.htm?startItem=-1#alleindlaeg - L 182 2013-14: indlæg 2. Accessed 4 July 2020.

[27] See Indlæg 36 i lovforslag L 182 2013-14.

[28] http://www.ft.dk/samling/20131/lovforslag/l182/99/367/afstemning.htm#dok. Accessed 4 July 2020.

[29] https://transfaq.info/juridisk-konsskifte-cpr/. Accessed 4 July 2020.

[30] The Civil Registration Act, section 3 (6) - https://www.retsinformation.dk/Forms/R0710.aspx?id=163824. Accessed 4 July 2020.

belonging to another sex is expressed and that after 6 months of reflection the wish to change sex legally is confirmed.

Among the arguments for the legislative change was reference to Argentina, which country in the meantime has introduced a legal sex-change based on statement. The change that took place in 2014 reflects a growing influence from transgender-organizations alongside with a change of mind among Danish politicians with a desire to be open-minded as to transgender-issues. LGBT Denmark, a NGO fighting for transgender rights—which for many years had wanted such a right for transgender—hailed the new act but still fights for the same right to be given trans persons under the age of 18.[31] This issue is currently under debate, the present government is considering it, and the debate is to a high degree influenced by the fact that Norway has introduced such a right. There is a tradition of collaboration in family law within the Nordic countries. Even if the legislation in the Nordic countries does not always move at the same pace, changes carried out in family law in other Nordic countries are a strong argument. However, several voices in the current (summer 2019) Danish debate point to the issue of protecting immature youths from taking such vital decisions at too early an age.

On 31 March 2017, two leftist parties represented in Parliament, "The Unity List" and "The Alternative", submitted a proposal originating from the association LGBT Denmark[32] for a parliamentary resolution asking the Government to prepare a bill modifying the rules governing recognition of a person's legal sex in the Children's Act.[33] That which was being sought was the recognition of the gender of a parent in accordance with the legal gender. A person born as a man in a relationship with a pregnant woman who is *not* the child's biological father, can obtain recognition as the child's *legal* father by signing a responsibility-statement with the child's mother. That the same right should be granted to a trans person born as a woman but legally recognized as a man was accordingly stated by the High Court of Copenhagen already in November 2017 in a case in which a child was born after the trans person had changed his sex.

4 Names

Names in Danish law are regulated by a specific Act on Names. Any child has to be given a first name within six months after birth. Names are to correspond to sex and be included in a specific list of recognized names. The purpose for this legislation is

[31]http://lgbt.dk/?s=kønsskifte. Accessed 4 July 2020.

[32]http://lgbt.dk/wp-content/uploads/20170327_LGBTdk_BSM.pdf. Accessed 4 July 2020.

[33]http://www.folketingstidende.dk/RIpdf/samling/20161/beslutningsforslag/B119/20161_B119_som_fremsat.pdf - Beslutningsforslag nr. B 119 – 2016-17. Accessed 4 July 2020.: "Folketinget pålægger regeringen inden udgangen af 2017 at fremsætte forslag til lov om ændring af de relevante regler i børneloven og ændre praksis, således at forældres køn defineres ud fra det juridiske og dermed selvvalgte køn."

to ensure that the person who bears the name will not get a name that may become a nuisance to that person.[34]

In 2005 (and 2009) the Act on Names (*Navneloven)* was changed in order to give trans persons[35] the possibility of choosing a first name normally reserved for persons of the opposite sex. This was the first mention of "*transseksuel*" as a phenomenon in Danish legislation. Up to 2002, trans persons were only entitled to a change of their first name to make it consistent with their gender identity when the person in question had undergone a sex reassignment.[36] In 2002, The Ministry of Justice under certain conditions allowed trans persons a change of their first name to a name that exclusively belonged to the opposite sex without first undergoing a complete sex reassignment.[37] An essential condition was that the relevant person by the Sexological Clinic was recognized as a transsexual.[38] By April 2004, fifteen persons had obtained a name change according to this pilot scheme.[39] Since 2006 the prohibition of carrying a name that is not gender-correct, applied only for persons who had *not* been declared transsexual by the Sexological Clinic.[40] In 2009, the possibility to take a non-gender-correct name was extended to cover also persons who simply wished to be treated as transsexuals.[41]

When a trans person has changed their legal sex (has been given a new civil registration number), a first name must be chosen that is gender-correct in relation to the new gender.[42] If the person does not wish to change his/her legal sex, but only his/her first name so that the name is consistent with their gender identity, the person in question must apply for dispensation from the rule that first names must not denote the opposite sex. In determining whether a dispensation may be granted, normally two to three consultations are held with the person concerned.[43] There is no

[34]Holdgaard and Lemann Kristiansen (2004), p. 64.

[35]"[*P*]*ersoner, der er transseksuelle eller ganske må ligestilles hermed*".

[36]Holdgaard and Lemann Kristiansen (2004), pp. 66–67.

[37]Estrup and Aarø-Hansen (2006), pp. 18–19.

[38]Sexological Clinic is a treatment facility at the National Hospital of Denmark (Rigshospitalet) that offers free examination, concealing and treatment for persons with gender identity problems.

[39]http://www.statensnet.dk/betaenkninger/1401-1600/1446-2004/1446-2004_pdf/printversion_1446-2004.pdf - pkt. 3.3.1.2.3. Accessed 4 July 2020.

[40]See below. Estrup and Aarø-Hansen (2006), p. 354.

[41]https://www.retsinformation.dk/eli/ft/200812L00107 - Pt. 4.2. Accessed 4 July 2020.

[42]The Ministry of Justice decided that there should be some extension of the scope so that persons who themselves felt transgendered and full-time lived as such, even if they had not been declared transsexual by the Sexological Clinic, should have a right to choose a first name denoting the opposite sex. Sexological Clinic defined this particular group as persons who for a number of years regularly dressed up as the opposite sex, and after long deliberations had a basic need to permanently dress like and in general live as belonging to the opposite sex. Such individuals appear transgender, but could not by the Sexological Clinic be diagnosed as transgender or get a permission for a sex reassignment surgery, see http://justitsministeriet.dk/sites/default/files/media/Pressemeddelelser/pdf/2014/Rapport%20om%20juridisk%20kønsskifte.pdf, p. 23. Accessed 4 July 2020.

[43]Rapport fra Arbejdsgruppen om Juridisk kønsskifte. 2014, p. 24.

requirement for the applicant to go through any specific process or hormonal treatment. The Clinic will take into consideration whether the applicant lives full-time as the opposite sex and in relation to family, friends, work colleagues etc., presents her or himself as the desired sex, whether the person is seen as belonging to the other sex and has done so for some time.[44] In cases of doubt, an additional statement from the Medico-legal Council can be requested.[45] The individual can bring any decision concerning name changing before a higher administrative authority (*Statsforvaltningen*).[46]

5 Gender Neutrality

There is in Denmark no general legislation on gender neutrality or "third-sex".[47] In 2009 a new article was inserted in the Danish passport regulation (art. 5) allowing a person who had not had a sex change but was recognized by the Central Sexology Clinic to be transsexual or in a similar position to have his or her sex indicated by an X instead of a M or a F.[48] Since 2013, municipal authorities may allow (without any official recognition by medical authorities) an applicant to have a neutral X in the passport instead of a denomination of sex, when the applicant declares in writing that the wish is caused by the sensation of belonging to another sex.[49]

6 Civil Union, Same-Sex Marriage and Adoption

Denmark was the first country to allow civil unions (registration) of same-sex couples in 1989 by the "Act on Registered Partnership" (civil union) of 26 May 1989. Only in 2010, the Parliament went on with a motion requiring the Government to prepare an act permitting two persons of the same sex to marry on equal terms

---

[44] Rapport fra Arbejdsgruppen om Juridisk kønsskifte, 2014, pp. 24–25.

[45] https://www.retsinformation.dk/Forms/R0710.aspx?id=176085. Accessed 4 July 2020.

[46] http://www.statsforvaltningen.dk/site.aspx?p=9224. Accessed 4 July 2020.

[47] https://www.information.dk/indland/2015/09/danmark-moeder-kritik-operere-interkoennede-boern. Accessed 4 July 2020.

[48] "Rigspolitichefen kan tillade, at kønnet for en person, som ikke har gennemgået et kønsskifte, men som af Rigshospitalets Sexologiske Klinik vurderes at være transseksuel eller ganske ligestillet hermed, betegnes X."

[49] "Stk. 5: Kommunalbestyrelsen kan tillade, at kønnet betegnes X, hvis en pasansøger, der er fyldt 18 år, afgiver en skriftlig erklæring om, at ønsket om kønsbetegnelsen X er begrundet i en oplevelse af at tilhøre det andet køn, eller den pågældende dokumenterer tidligere at være blevet tildelt nyt personnummer efter § 3, stk. 6, i lov om Det Centrale Personregister."

with other couples.[50] This proposal, however, was not approved, but the same proposal two years later after a heavy debate in 2012 was accepted and led to a change of the Marriage Act to the effect that the same rules were to govern marriages between two persons of different sex and between two persons of the same sex.[51] This change[52] at that time was supported by a large majority in the Parliament. Only the Danish Popular Party (*Dansk Folkeparti*) voted against. Same-sex couples can thus be married by both a civil officer or by a minister of the Danish official Church (Folkekirken). There exists however a reservation which makes it possible for a minister of the church to refuse (for conscience reasons) to marry same-sex couples. This legislation (of course) also includes the right for persons who legally have changed their sex to get married on equal terms as anyone else without sex reassignment. It also made it possible for a married couple to stay in the same marriage, if one of the persons has undergone sex change so that both partners are the same sex.[53] This legislation was made before a right was established for trans persons to change sex without undergoing a complete sex reassignment. In 2015, the first transgender couple (two transwomen who both were born as men) was married in a Danish church.

There are no specific rules on a trans person's right to adopt. Trans persons can in principle adopt on same terms as non-trans persons. Since 2010 same-sex couples in civil unions can adopt children on the same terms as non-homosexual couples. Today married same-sex couples may adopt as well. As mentioned above, the parliamentary party "Unity List" in 2006 made a proposal for a motion regarding general rights for transgender,[54] which included the demand that approval for adoption could not be declined based on a person's gender or sexual orientation. Such a proposal was at that time rejected on the grounds that there was no need for legislation as current legislation did not discriminate on neither gender nor sexual orientation.[55] Accordingly, there is no specific legislation on trans- persons' right to adopt.

Acknowledgements The authors wish to thank Jane Hagelin Mindstrup for help with collecting the materials for this chapter. A substantive and very informative national account of Denmark by Natalie Videbæk Munkholm can be found in Scherpe, Jens M. (ed.). 2014. *The Legal Status of Transsexual and Transgender Persons.* Intersentia, pp. 147–181.

---

[50] http://www.folketingstidende.dk/RIpdf/samling/20091/beslutningsforslag/B122/20091_B122_som_fremsat.pdf - Beslutningsforslag nr. B 122 2009-10. Accessed 4 July 2020.

[51] The Marriage Act (Ægteskabsloven) section 1.

[52] http://www.ft.dk/samling/20111/lovforslag/l106/index.htm - Lovforslag 106 2011-12. Accessed 4 July 2020.

[53] http://www.ft.dk/samling/20091/beslutningsforslag/b122/bilag/1/796838.pdf. Accessed 4 July 2020.

[54] http://www.ft.dk/samling/20061/beslutningsforslag/B142/index.htm#dok - Beslutningsforslag nr. B 142 2006-07. Accessed 4 July 2020.

[55] http://www.ft.dk/samling/20061/beslutningsforslag/b142/beh1-90/forhandling.htm?startItem=-1#alleindlaeg - indlæg 1. Accessed 4 July 2020.

References

Estrup H, Aarø-Hansen N (2006) Navneloven med kommentarer (Name Act with commentaries). Jurist- og Økonomforbundets Forlag

Holdgaard M, Lemann Kristiansen B (2004) Kønsskifte – Juridisk set. Jurist- og Økonomforbundets Forlag

The Civil Status of Trans Persons in Greece

Anna-Maria Konsta

Abstract This chapter presents the relevant legislation and case-law concerning the recognition of the civil status of trans persons in Greece with reference to existing national, European and international standards of protection. More specifically, the recent Greek Gender Identity Law is presented and critically analyzed and proposals are made for possible legislative reforms. Even if there are still some unresolved issues that need to be addressed, Greece has undoubtedly moved forward in creating an institutional framework for the recognition of the civil status of trans persons, which may promote their visibility and acceptance by society.

This chapter presents the relevant legislation and case-law concerning the recognition of the civil status of trans persons in Greece with reference to existing national, European and international standards of protection. More specifically, the recent Greek Gender Identity Law is presented and critically analyzed and proposals are made for possible legislative reforms. Even if there are still some unresolved issues that need to be addressed, Greece has undoubtedly moved forward in creating an institutional framework for the recognition of the civil status of trans persons, which may promote their visibility and acceptance by society.

The Greek state even before joining the European Union (EU) in 1981 had established a legal framework regarding discrimination in a range of provisions starting with the Greek Constitution. Article 5 par. 2 of the Constitution states: "All persons living within the Greek territory shall enjoy full protection of their life, honour and liberty irrespective of nationality, race or language and of religious or political beliefs. Exceptions shall be permitted only in cases provided by international law".[1]

[1] All translations of Greek legal provisions here into English are the author's with the exception of the Greek Constitution which translation is taken from the official translation made by the Hellenic

A.-M. Konsta (✉)
Aristotle University of Thessaloniki, Thessaloniki, Greece
e-mail: akkonsta@law.auth.gr

I. C. Jaramillo, L. Carlson (eds.), *Trans Rights and Wrongs*, Ius Comparatum - Global Studies in Comparative Law 54,
https://doi.org/10.1007/978-3-030-68494-5_20

The Penal Code of Greece[2] states in article 79 that the "commission of a crime on the basis of national, racial or religious hatred or hatred on the grounds of a different sexual orientation constitutes an aggravating circumstance". Thus, hate crime is equated to an "aggravating circumstance" in the context of the commission of any crime and, it is not considered as a separate crime.

Sexual orientation was added as a ground following a 2008 amendment of the Penal Code, and another amendment of article 79 of the Penal Code (as amended by Article 66 of Law 4139/2013) added "gender identity" as a separate ground of discrimination. It was the first time in the history of the Greek legal system that trans persons were considered by law as a separate category. They formerly were seen as "non issue" under the Greek legal system, and it was unclear whether they should be covered by legislation prohibiting discrimination on the basis of sexual orientation or on the basis of sex.[3]

In September 2014, Law 4285/2014 on tackling certain forms and expressions of racism and xenophobia was passed by the legislature. The law also added "gender identity" along with "sexual orientation" to the protected grounds against hate speech and hate crimes. It also introduced an amendment to the older legislation, adding "gender identity" to the list of protected grounds in the provision concerning aggravating circumstances within the Greek Criminal Code. The amendment prohibits the suspension of sentence in cases where the motive of prejudice is proving an aggravating circumstance. Thus, the last paragraph of paragraph 3 of Article 79 of the Penal Code was deleted and replaced by Article 81A which incorporates racist crimes: "If the act is based on hatred on the basis of race, color, religion, birth, national or ethnic origin, sexual orientation, gender identity or disability, the lower limit of penalty shall be increased. . .".

Moreover, in December 2016, Law 4443/2016 was adopted which transposed two European Union Anti-Discrimination Directives 2000/43/EC and 2000/78/EC[4] into the Greek national legal order. Even though Directive 2000/78/EC only mentions "sexual orientation", and does not refer to gender identity as a ground of discrimination, the Greek legislator added next to "sexual orientation", "gender identity" and "sex characteristics" as separate grounds of discrimination in Article 1 of the Law.

Parliament, https://www.hellenicparliament.gr/UserFiles/f3c70a23-7696-49db-9148-f24dce6a27c8/001-156%20aggliko.pdf. Accessed 4 July 2020.

[2]Act of Parliament 1492/1950 as amended by Law 3719/2008.

[3]Hatzopoulos, Vassilis. 2010. Legal study on Homophobia and Discrimination on Grounds of Sexual Orientation and Gender Identity. In *Thematic study on Greece for the European Agency for Fundamental Rights (FRA)*, p. 5. Http://fra.europa.eu/sites/default/files/fra_uploads/1352-LGBT-2010_thematic-study_EL.pdf. Accessed 30 April 2019.

[4]EU Council Directive 2000/43/EC of 29 June 2000 implementing the principle of equal treatment between persons irrespective of racial or ethnic origin, *Official Journal L 180,* 19/07/2000 pp. 22–26, and EU Council Directive 2000/78/EC of 27 November 2000 establishing a general framework for equal treatment in employment and occupation, *Official Journal L 303,* 02/12/2000, pp. 16–22.

On 10 October 2017, a new Law 4491/2017 on the Legal Recognition of Gender Identity[5] (Gender Identity Law) was passed by the Greek Parliament with 171 votes in favour and 114 against amid fierce condemnation by the Greek Orthodox church and accusations that the law would "destroy human beings".[6] The new law only concerns an individual's civil status as regards gender identity, i.e., the relationship between the state and citizens as regards this specific element of registry, municipal, conscription and police identification. Therefore, it is legislation in the sphere of public law that mainly regulates the requirements for the change of gender in the civil registry. It is not a comprehensive legislation granting legal protection to individuals due to their gender identity, as such would require further provisions concerning equal treatment as they exist for other grounds of discrimination, such as sexual orientation, in Law 4443/2016, which has transposed into the Greek national order the two European Union non-discrimination Directives, 2000/43/EC and 2000/78/EC.

Furthermore, the Gender Identity Law also concerns relationships between private citizens, in that individuals must respect each other's changes in terms of gender and name. This respect not only concerns proper conduct, but also the official use of the altered name and gender data and relationships between private citizens. All legal acts (contracts, declarations of intent, etc.) must be harmonised with the official name following a change of gender identity. At the same time, this results in further limitations due to gender in the sphere of private law, where these are provided for in law, e.g. in family law. Therefore, a law concerning civil status as regards gender identity directly concerns public law and individual rights vis-à-vis the state, but also indirectly reflects on private law, classic civil law, personality law, contract law, etc.

1 The Legal Procedure Prior to the Gender Identity Law

The first public document in which an individual's gender is recorded is the registry act of birth. This act serves as the basis for all subsequent registrations, such as the municipal registry and the male registry (solely for men, as it is exclusively linked to conscription), as well as registrations that include police-issued identity cards, electoral rolls and the records of the educational system, taxation service and social welfare.

In order to change one's name and gender in the official documents of the Greek State, one first has to alter the relevant entry in one's registry act of birth. Alterations of registry acts are provided for in Law 344/1976, which provides for three main

[5] Law 4491/2017 published in the Official Journal 152/A/13-10-2017.

[6] Smith, Helena. 2017. Greece passes gender-change law opposed by Orthodox church. *The Guardian*, October 10. Https://www.theguardian.com/world/2017/oct/10/greece-passes-gender-change-law. Accessed 4 July 2020.

categories of corrections, of clerical errors, by mayoral order and of material changes.

1.1 Correction of Clerical Errors

This type of correction is a simple case that concerns spelling and other errors and is resolved by the registrar with or without an order issued by a public prosecutor. In such an event, interested parties must submit an application to the public prosecutor, who is to issue a court order to the registrar concerning the change. In the event of change of religion or cessation of its reproduction in copies of registry acts, a simple request submitted by the interest party to the registry suffices. The registrar records the change requested in the ledger of the registry act, but without deleting the original religion. All changes in particulars during an individual's life are recorded in the registry ledger and no previous states are deleted, but printed copies of registry acts only list the status of the individual's particulars valid at that particular time, without presenting the 'history' of changes. In other words, if individuals change their religion, the change will be recorded in the registry ledger, but the copy of the registry act they and any interested parties receive will only list the most recent religion (unless non-reproduction of religion has been requested, in which case no religion will be listed in copies, but these will remain in the history of changes of the registry ledger).

1.2 Change of Surname by Mayoral Order

It should be noted that a change in surname for specific reasons set out in a Ministerial decision, administrative practice and case-law may be carried out without a court judgment by virtue of a Mayoral order (following the Kallikratis reform—Law 3852/2010; prior to the enactment of that law, the competency belonged to Prefects).[7] However, this concerns just the surname, not the given name and gender. Therefore, there is no 'monopoly' as regards changes in registry data solely through judicial means.

[7]See the sole Article of Legislative Decree 2573/1953 (Gov. Gazette, Series I, No 241 'Change of surname and adoption of surname, father's name, mother's name', as amended by and in force following Article 9(9) of Law 2307/1994 (Gov. Gazette, Series I, No 113), in combination with the provisions of Article 282(1A) of Law 3851/2010 ('Kallikratis' Programme). Following Article 94 (6) of Law 3852/2010 that amended Article 75(2) of the Municipalities and Communities Code, the competency of adoption and change of surname was transferred to Municipalities.

1.3 Correction of Material Changes

The other case that concerns material changes to particulars, such as the given name and gender, takes place through judicial means: the interested parties, who must be represented by an authorised attorney, submit a request to the registry of the District Civil Court requesting that the court 'attest' that a change was effected to any of the particulars listed in the registry act. The District Civil Court must be that of the region of the registry where the birth was registered. It has been recently accepted that this may also be the District Civil Court of the individual's domicile, but this is not set out in law: judges have accepted this due to the flexibility of non-adversarial proceedings.

Judges, prior to the adoption of Law 4491/2017, used to try petitions for changes to full name and gender by applying a single article in practice, namely Article 13 of Law 344/1976, which stipulates that "the correction of a registry act requires a final court judgment" (i.e. a decision not contested by appeal), in combination with Article 14, which stipulates that the change may concern a "sex change".[8] The law provided the judges with no further instructions concerning the interpretation of the term "sex change". As a result, judges sought the meaning of this term in medical science and, of course, the relevant analysis for respect towards human rights. This is why their judgments frequently used Article 5(1) of the Constitution as a legal basis, which states that all persons have the right to develop freely their personality and to participate in the social, economic and political life of the country, insofar as they do not infringe the rights of others or violate the Constitution and the good usages.[9]

2 The Case-Law Prior to the Adoption of the Gender Identity Law

Until recently, "sex change" was understood by Greek courts to mean surgical operations for the reassignment of genitals (vaginoplasty, phalloplasty, clitoroplasty, etc.) and other body parts (breast removal or prosthesis) and hormone therapy for the occurrence of secondary sex characteristics (hair growth etc.), while the contribution of psychiatry was crucial in order to ascertain that individuals suffer from "gender dysphoria" and that there are no elements of psychopathology that would cause confusion as regards their gender.

This perception of judges of the Athens and Thessaloniki District Civil Courts changed in recent years. In judgments issued in 2016 and 2017, judges complied with international and European standards stating that change to identity particulars for reasons of legal recognition of gender identity should not require medical

[8]The term "gender reassignment" was never used by the Greek judges.

[9]The term "good usages" has been taken from the official translation of the Greek Constitution and it literally means "the accepted principles of morality".

operations. In fact, a European Commission report[10] found that compulsory sterilisation is contrary to articles of the International Covenant on Civil and Political Rights (ICCPR), ratified by Greece, that concern equality and the prohibition of discrimination. Thus, the first judgment of this category of judgments, namely Judgment No 418/2016 of the Athens District Civil Court, found that, under Article 8 of the European Convention of Human Rights (ECHR), which enshrines respect for private life, and Articles 2 and 26 ICCPR, removal of genitals is not required in order to certify "sex change" from female to male. Other judgments followed, the most important being Judgment No 1572/2016 of the Athens District Civil Court, which provides a definition for gender identity and accepts that hormone therapy is an excessive requirement.[11] In 2017, the first judgments were issued, under the same rationale, for the opposite direction: male to female, without the removal of genitals. These judgments are final and individuals they concern have completed the procedure and have been granted new police-issued identity cards.

Relevant cases of the Greek District Courts are more specifically discussed below.[12]

2.1 Case 418/2016 Athens District Civil Court

The first decision in a trans man (female to male) with mastectomy and hormone therapy, without removal of female genitalia. It has been ruled that compulsory sterilization constitutes a breach of the right to respect for private life (Article 8 ECHR) and the right to equal treatment and non-discrimination (Articles 2 and 26 ICCPR).

2.2 Case 1572/2016 Athens District Civil Court

The first decision, which includes a definition of "gender identity" ("individual and internal experience of gender that may not be in direct correspondence to the sex one is born with, and encompasses the personal sensation of the body and gender (i.e. gender expression which can be expressed in dressing, talking mode, behavioral patterns). This is a trans man (female to male) case without mastectomy, and without

---

[10]European Commission, Directorate-General for Justice and Consumers (2012).

[11]Galanou, Maria. 2017. Taftotita filu horis hirurgio kai horis ormones (Gender identity without surgery and without hormones). *T-Zine*. January 20. Http://t-zine.gr/taftotita-fylou-choris-chirourgio-ke-choris-ormones/. Accessed 4 July 2020.

[12]The list of the cases is translated in English from Greek from the E-lawyer blog of the attorney of most of these cases, Sotiropoulos, Vassileios. 2017. I taftotita filu sta elinika dikastiria (Gender identity in Greek courts). *E-Lawyer*, September 27. http://elawyer.blogspot.gr/2017/09/h.html. Accessed 4 July 2020.

genitals' removal. It was considered that even hormonal therapy is an excessive requirement. The individual's personality grew more towards the characteristics that belong to male individuals and the choices in both appearance and leisure interests were identical to those of males: "Moreover, [the person] feels attraction for persons of the female sex since adolescence, without wanting relationships as a homosexual, but as a male".[13]

2.3 *Case 1479E/2016 Thessaloniki District Civil Court*

The first decision of the Thessaloniki District Court for trans man (female to male): "As early as the age of 9, the way the applicant was living her gender did not correspond to her appearance, and the photos she presented showed that her choices from an early age (clothing, footwear, appearance, etc.) were attributable to a male person". The existence of official documents showing the applicant as a female causes a number of particularly serious difficulties, namely the difficulty of self-identification in various transactions with public services but also with other entities (such as tax administration, banks, post office). Also, the recourse to public health services (hospitals, health committees) is now a permanent focal point of psychological tension and anxiety for the individual, because the process of proving the correspondence between the real facts and those presented in the official documents is difficult and often psychologically detrimental for the person. Lastly, the failure to issue official identity documents (identity card, passport) is an insurmountable obstacle to migrating and relocating abroad for reasons related to better addressing certain health issues. The registration in the books of the Registry as a female seriously damages the individual's legitimate interests, and has serious implications for his transactions and affects his personality."

2.4 *Case 572/2017 Athens District Civil Court*

The first Greek judgment on behalf of a trans woman (male to female) who had only hormone therapy, without prosthetic breasts and without surgical procedures.

[13]Sotiropoulos, Vassileios. 2017. I taftotita filu sta elinika dikastiria (Gender identity in Greek courts). *E-Lawyer*, September 27. Http://elawyer.blogspot.gr/2017/09/h.html. Accessed 4 July 2020.

2.5 *Case 604/2017 Athens District Civil Court*

This is a case of a trans woman (male to female) who had only hormone therapy, without prosthetic breasts and without surgical procedures. From the age of 17 she had informed family members that the way in which she lived her gender did not correspond to her appearance. The photos she presented to the Court showed that her choices from an early age (clothing, footwear, appearance, etc.) corresponded to a female person.

2.6 *Case 281E/2017 Thessaloniki District Civil Court*

This case concerned a trans man (from female to male) which fully implemented the previous case-law as well as Article 2 of the International Covenant on Economic, Social and Cultural Rights (ICESCR). The Court accepted local jurisdiction because of the person's residence in Thessaloniki, despite the fact that the registry was issued at the Municipality of Chalkida. From the age of 12, his personality developed more towards the attributes of male persons. The existing mismatch between his appearance and his formal identification with the ID card poses a serious problem in his everyday life and may cause confusion in transactions, so the application is accepted and the new situation regarding gender and name must be portrayed in the registry.

2.7 *Case 146/2017 Maroussi District Civil Court*

This is a case of a trans male (male to male).The Court mentions for the first time as the legal basis for its decision on the change of the documents of the trans person the Charter of Fundamental Rights of the EU, and more specifically article 35 of the Charter concerning the right to health care.

2.8 *Case 1092E/2017 Thessaloniki District Civil Court*

This case concerns a trans man (female to male) case with mastectomy and hormone therapy.

2.9 Case 1147/2017 Thessaloniki District Civil Court

The first case of a trans woman (male to female) at the Thessaloniki District Court, with prosthetic breasts.

2.10 Case 1708/2017 Athens District Civil Court

A case of a trans man (female to male). The novelty of this decision is that it makes absolutely no reference to previous case law. The Court follows the stereotypical wording that sterilization is not a prerequisite for legal recognition of gender identity and no longer accompanies this interpretative conclusion with reference to previous case-law.

Other cases have been before the Greek District Civil Courts, such as the appeal before the Drama Single-Member Court of First Instance in a case which declared that compulsory male transplant surgery is against Article 3 ECHR (prohibition of torture). As well as the decision of the Drama District Court, which accepted the above in a case of a trans woman.

This new case-law by Greek courts is in conformity with the European Court of Human Rights (ECtHR) which found in the joint cases, *A.P., Garçon and Nicot v. France*,[14] that the condition of compulsory sterilizing surgery or treatment for legal gender recognition violated the right to respect for private life as embodied in Article 8 ECHR. In this case, however, the ECtHR denied that forced medical examinations ordered by the national Court (*E. Garcon v France*) or a mental health diagnosis (*A.P. v France*) contradict the Convention.

Nevertheless, with its judgment the ECtHR expanded human rights protection of trans persons in Europe. While it mostly affirmed its previous case law with regard to non-consensual sterilisation[15] and the compulsory requirement of sterility in order to have access to medical gender confirmation treatment,[16] the ECtHR held for the very first time that compulsory sterilisation for legal gender recognition violated Article 8 of the Convention. The judgment will therefore have as a result that the contracting states which have ratified the ECHR and recognised the jurisdiction of the ECtHR will be obliged to reform their legislation with regard to legal gender recognition, in order to remove the compulsory condition of sterility.

---

[14] ECtHR *A.P., Garçon and Nicot v. France* (Applications nos. 79885/12, 52471/13 and 52596/13), 6 April 2017.

[15] ECtHR *V.C. v. Slovakia* (Application no. 18968/07), 8 November 2011.

[16] ECtHR *Y.Y. v. Turkey* (Application no. 14793/08), 10 March 2015.

3 The Law 4491/2017 on the Legal Recognition of Gender Identity

On 10 October 2017 Law 4491/2017 on the Legal Recognition of Gender Identity (Gender Identity Law) was passed by the Greek Parliament. In the following section an article per article analysis of the Gender Identity Law is presented.[17]

3.1 Article 1 Gender Identity Law: Individual Rights

The first paragraph of the first article of the Gender Identity Law states that gender identity is a characteristic of personality, while the second paragraph states that individuals have the right of respect towards their sex characteristics. The definitions of gender identity and sex characteristics are provided in the subsequent Article 2. The wording of Article 1 is 'declarative': it does not set out legal consequences due to infringement. It is clear that the legislator tacitly refers to the protection of personality under civil law, clarifying that this meaning includes gender identity and sex characteristics pursuant to Article 57 Greek Civil Code: "Any person whose personality has been offended has the right to demand that the offense be lifted and not repeated in the future. Claims for damages under the provisions on torts are not excluded".

According to Article 59 of the same Code, in the cases of Articles 57 and 58, the court may, at the request of the respondent and having regard to the nature of the offense, also order the accused to make good the non-material damage inflicted and, in particular, to oblige him/herself to pay a sum of money, or produce a publication or whatever else is required by the circumstances. Thus, the above articles protect the personality and, by extension, the human dignity as an individual right guaranteed by Article 2 paragraph 1 of the Greek Constitution.[18]

3.2 Article 2 Gender Identity Law: Definitions

A definition of gender identity can be found in the Yogyakarta Principles on the Application of International Human Rights Law without discrimination due to sexual orientation and gender identity:[19]

[17]For the discussions held prior to the adoption of the Law 4491/2017, see Kounougeri-Manoledaki et al. (2017).

[18]As decided in case 1735/2009 of the Supreme Civil and Criminal Court of Greece (Areios Pagos).

[19]The Yogyakarta Principles, a non-binding set of international standards, apply international human rights standards to issues that affect the LGBTQI community. Developed by a group of experts, the Yogyakarta Principles have been used by the United Nations (UN) and other groups in

> Gender identity is understood to refer to each person's deeply felt internal and individual experience of gender, which may or may not correspond with the sex assigned at birth, including the personal sense of the body (which may involve, if freely chosen, modification of bodily appearance or function by medical, surgical or other means) and other expressions of gender, including dress, speech and mannerisms.[20]

Other definitions of gender identity have been given by the Council of Europe and its bodies, such as the Committee of Ministers that issued Recommendation number 5 in 2010 on measures to combat discrimination on grounds of sexual orientation or gender identity.[21] Therefore, Article 2 paragraph 1 of the new Greek law follows the previous definitions to some extent:

> Gender identity is the internal and personal way with which the person experiences its gender regardless of the sex assigned to it at birth according to its biological characteristics. Gender identity includes the personal sensation of the body, and the social and external expression of the gender which correspond to the will of the person. The personal sensation of the body may be connected to changes induced by freely chosen medical treatment or medical interventions.

However, legal recognition of gender identity should not be contingent on consistency between the new gender marker and the person's external appearance. Such requirement is grounded in stereotypical notions of gender and expectations; legal recognition of gender should not be contingent on conforming to gender stereotypes.[22]

Moreover, Article 2 paragraph 2 of the Gender Identity Law includes a similar definition of sex characteristics as provided for in the aforementioned international texts: "Sex characteristics are the chromosomal, genetic and anatomical features of the person, including primary characteristics, such as reproductive organs, and secondary features such as muscle mass, breast growth or hair growth".

One criticism concerning the definitions is the issue of recognition of other non-binary categories of gender identity and sex characteristics (non-binary, genderqueer) such as being agender or genderfluid. Furthermore, the possibility of

---

their effort to promote and protect the human rights of sexual minorities. The Principles affirm that "human beings of all sexual orientations and gender identities are entitled to the full enjoyment of all human rights" (principle 1). Each Principle identifies a particular right and then sets forth the duties and obligations states should satisfy to ensure that LGBTQI persons are able to exercise and enjoy that right. The Principles also offer recommendations concerning the realization LGBTQI persons' human rights to the UN, regional human rights organizations, national human rights institutions, and other relevant stakeholders.

[20]See https://yogyakartaprinciples.org/introduction/. Accessed 4 July 2020.

[21]Recommendation CM/Rec(2010)5 of the Committee of Ministers to member states on measures to combat discrimination on grounds of sexual orientation or gender identity, 31 March 2010. Moreover, the judgment in case No 1572/2016 of the Athens District Civil Court followed these definitions.

[22]See Amnesty International Public Statement "Greece: Draft law on legal recognition of gender identity must be strengthened so that trans persons enjoy human rights without discrimination, AI Index: EUR 25/6692/2017, 10 July 2017, https://www.amnesty.org/download/Documents/EUR2566922017ENGLISH.pdf. Accessed 4 July 2020.

not declaring any gender at the registry has not been recognised; this could take place through an amendment to Law 344/1976, which defines gender as one of the elements of civil status. Furthermore, the Greek Constitution adheres to the traditional gendered man—woman duality and uses it as a basis to set—ostensibly—discrete military obligations. The provision for a blank statement of gender or other non-binary identity requires the will of the legislator to re-determine the content of the Constitution in regard to the discrete obligations of the sexes. No such will has been reflected in the wording of the new Greek law. In any event, the obligation of respect towards sex characteristics also covers at least in terms of the protection of personality, non-binary gender identities.

However, in February 2018, the Maroussi District Civil Court ruled in favour of a non-binary person's request to have their male birth name, Jason, changed on Registry Office files to a gender-neutral one by adding the female name Antigone next to it.[23] However, while the Court did rule in favour of the person's request for displaying a gender-neutral name on their identity card, it decided against having their legal gender entry changed from male to "third gender", citing the "lack of a relevant institutional framework for individuals not classified in a distinct case of a non-dual gender identity (third gender entry)" in Greece, although Law 4491/2017 does state that "the person has the right to the recognition of its gender identity as an element of its personality".[24]

3.3 *Article 3 Gender Identity Law: Correction of Registered Gender—Requirements*

Article 3 of the Gender Identity Law establishes requirements for the correction of registered gender. The two requirements (legal capacity and celibacy) constitute additional obstacles to gender reassignment which were not previously provided by the law. The third—negative—requirement consisting of the fact that no examinations or medical operations and attestations are required, is an important step forward even in relation to the major steps taken by the recent Greek courts' case-law in this direction.

3.3.1 Legal capacity

The development of legal capacity in the Greek Civil Code (GCC) is as follows:

- Whosoever has completed the 18th year of age is capable of any transaction (full legal capacity, Article 127 GCC).

[23] Decision 67/2018 of the Maroussi District Civil Court.

[24] The plaintiff's lawyer announced that they will appeal part of the ruling to a higher court concerning the third gender marker on identity cards.

- Those incapable of transactions are (a) whosoever has not completed the 10th year of age; and (b) whosoever is under complete privative legal guardianship (complete legal incapacity, Article 128 GCC).
- The following have limited legal capacity: (a) minors who have completed the 10th year of age; (b) individuals under partial private legal guardianship; (c) individuals under concurrent legal guardianship, i.e. where the guardian does not fully substitute them but requires their contribution (Article 129 GCC). Minors who have completed the 10th year of age are capable of concluding transactions from which they solely draw legal benefits (Article 134 GCC). Minors who have completed the 14th year of age may freely dispose of their earnings from their personal labour or granted to them, to be used or disposed of freely (Article 135 GCC). Minors who have completed the 15th year of age may, with the consent of the persons charged with their care, conclude an employment contract as employees (Article 136 GCC). Married minors may engage *in propria persona* in any transaction necessary to maintain/improve their property or to meet the needs of their families (Article 137 GCC).
- The statement of intent is null and void if, at the time it was drafted, the individuals were not aware of their actions or were suffering from a psychological or mental disorder that decisively affected their intention (Article 131 GCC).

Statements submitted to the Registry do not constitute "transactions" under the Civil Code, therefore legal capacity was not required prior to the adoption of the 2017 Gender Identity Law for individuals wishing to proceed with correction of gender at Registries. It is self-evident that anyone appearing before a court to request anything must be suitably represented: minors are legally-represented by the individuals charged with parental custody, while individuals under legal guardianship who do not have full legal capacity are represented by their guardians before the court. Prior to the 2017 law, legal minors and those under legal guardianship were able to request that the court issue an attestation stating that their registry act of birth must be corrected as regards gender.

With the Gender Identity Law there are two exceptions to the rule of full legal capacity: First, it is possible for a person aged 17 or older, who is unmarried, and has acquired parental consent, to appear before a judge who would then assess the request for change of first and adjusted last names, and gender marker. Persons aged 15–16 year-olds may use a different procedure which involves assessment by a psycho-medical committee comprising a) a child psychiatrist, b) a psychiatrist, c) an endocrinologist, d) a pediatrician, e) a psychologist, f) a social worker, and g) a pediatrician acting as president, who all are specialized in this issue. Younger than 15 years-old individuals cannot anymore request a change of their gender in their identity cards with or without parental consent. The Gender Identity Law's added age requirements removed the ability individuals already had to be represented by the persons charged with their legal representation (parents, persons charged with parental custody, guardians).

Therefore, this 2017 law deprives a number of individuals entitled to respect towards their gender identity of the judicial pursuit of this respect, without any proportionality whatsoever. It is noted again that the law does not concern surgical procedures, as the change to gender data takes place without such operations. Therefore, the concerns regarding minors being subjected to non-reversible medical procedures that could justify the proscription of change to registry acts before the completion of 15 years of age do not apply. The proscription of changes to data before the age of 15 deprives individuals from claiming the legal (and, by extension, the social) respect of their gender identity and sex characteristics during particularly sensitive periods of their life, such as childhood and early adolescence. During these periods, trans persons suffer grave attacks (e.g. at school), a fact that necessitates state protection for the imposition of respect towards gender identity/sex characteristics even before individuals acquire legal capacity.

Furthermore, full legal capacity is not required for any other registry declaration. Even partial (and not full) legal capacity suffices to enter into marriage (civil partnerships require full legal capacity: when a right is envisaged for individuals who are not heterosexual or cis, the legal requirements suddenly increase). The procedure for correcting the data entered in a registry act is not a "transaction" that would require legal capacity.

However, in this manner, the Gender Identity Law falls short of the current level of protection of respect towards gender identity, infringing the assurance of application of Article 5 paragraph 1 of the Greek Constitution by common legislation, which states that "All persons shall have the right to develop freely their personality and to participate in the social, economic and political life of the country, insofar as they do not infringe the rights of others or violate the Constitution and the good usages".

Furthermore, through the legal capacity wording, the Gender Identity Law collaterally requires an additional medical certificate that attempts to obviate the third negative requirement: the psychiatric evaluation. Legal capacity does not only concern minors and those under guardians. Individuals may temporarily lose their legal capacity for other reasons, i.e., health reasons. Article 131 GCC clearly states that individuals have no legal capacity if they are not aware of their actions due to a mental disorder. Unfortunately, "gender dysphoria" and other related disorders are still found in medical protocols and official state categorisations even to this day. The practice to date is that psychiatrists attest that an individual has been examined and that no "other" psychopathological conditions (characteristically noting "transvestism") apply. They also attest that the individual's decision to live as their "desired" gender does not appear to have changed and under these circumstances the individuals in question live a life of quality and must continue in this manner, recommending the relevant registry changes. However, if this procedure is associated with legal capacity that an individual may lack due to a "mental disorder", then there is nothing to stop judges under non-adversarial proceedings (who, acting on the basis of the "investigative system", have the power to ascertain actual facts using any evidence, even if not adduced by the interested party) to request a medical certificate stating that the individual in question is not suffering from any "other" mental disorder.

In other words, while article 3 paragraph 4 stipulates that: "The correction of the registered gender does not require an attestation whereby the individual has been subjected to any prior medical procedure. Furthermore, no prior examination or medical treatment concerning their physical or mental health is required", if a judge has reservations concerning an adult's legal capacity, there is nothing prohibiting that judge from requesting a relevant medical evaluation in order to dissociate the issue of gender identity from the "other" disorders from which any judge may be concerned that the individual in question may be suffering. Through the above and due to Article 131 GCC, the legislator's requirement for full legal capacity may, in practice and collaterally, add a medical certificate that the Law explicitly aims to abolish.

Legal capacity as a requirement has nothing at all to do with human rights; it concerns the narrow field of private law transactions and not public law. Therefore, for all the above reasons, this requirement which was not required prior to the adoption of the legislation should not have been introduced into the new legislation. Furthermore, blanket age restrictions should have been removed giving access to minors, on the basis of their best interest, taking into account their evolving capacities and their right to be heard. Therefore, the age restrictions provided by the Gender Identity Law may be considered, under certain conditions, as violating Article 21 of the Charter of Fundamental Rights of the European Union, which embodies the principle of non-discrimination on grounds of age and Article 24 of the same Charter enshrining the rights of the child.

3.3.2 Celibacy

The Gender Identity Law introduces celibacy as an additional requirement in order for an individual to request the correction of a registry act. In other words, individuals must submit a "celibacy certificate" to the court in order to lawfully request a registry change (clearly meaning a family status certificate). This further exacerbates the existing bureaucracy.

This requirement did not exist prior to the adoption of the Gender Identity Law. On the basis of the previous legal framework, married individuals could also request the change of their gender particulars recorded in registry acts. The issue is linked to the validity of same-sex marriage: if a married individual proceeds with a registry change of his or her gender, this will result in an ongoing marriage between two individuals who will now be of the same sex.

The argument is that since Greek law does not allow for same-sex marriage, a procedure that could result in the married cohabitation of same-sex couples cannot be allowed. Proponents of this view believe that such individuals can continue living together by concluding a civil partnership, which is now possible in Greece after the adoption of the Law 4356/2015 which extended civil partnership rights to same-sex couples.

The criticism brought against this provision is that it violates Articles 8 and 12 ECHR, as it intervenes in the family life of individuals and does not allow them to marry before proceeding with the registry change. This criticism is not in line with the case-law of the ECtHR, which in its judgment in the case of *Hämäläinen v. Finland*[25] ruled by a majority opinion that the requirement of a change to marital status for the recognition of a trans person as a woman does not violate Article 8 (respect for private and family life) nor Article 12 (right to marry) ECHR. Therefore, as long as the ECtHR maintains this view, there is no issue of violation of the ECHR by the Greek Law.

The view that the marriage may "automatically" be converted into a civil partnership ignores the augmented contractual autonomy of the civil partnership (with the possibility of waiving alimony, or waiving reserved portions, etc.) in relation to the institutional 'package' that is marriage in Greece and from the provisions of which private will may not deviate. One cannot conceive of the automatic transition of an institution under mandatory provisions to an institution under supplementary provisions.

The celibacy requirement forces trans persons to choose between their rights to marry and to found a family and to respect for private and family life, and their right to recognition before the law. Because of the requirement of single status, persons who are married and seek recognition of their preferred gender will face an invidious and costly choice. They must either give up the legal protection acquired in their union, and the right of their partner and children to private and family life, or forego legal recognition of their preferred gender, a violation of their right to private life and to recognition before the law. Trans persons who choose to form a new legal union with their ex-spouse, who is legally the same gender as them, can only opt for civil partnerships, as Greek legislation does not include recognition of same-sex marriage. But, civil partnership in Greece stipulates a more limited set of rights than marriage: for instance, same-sex couples in civil partnerships cannot adopt children. However, the Greek Parliament adopted Law 4538/2018 in May 2018 allowing in Article 8 for same-sex couples in civil partnership to provide foster care to children but this right does not extend to adopting a child.

Moreover, serious concerns arise over the stipulation that the gender marker of trans persons cannot be corrected in the birth certificates of an offspring born prior to the legal recognition of a parent's gender. Such provision breaches the right to family life and privacy for both the children and their parents and is in contradiction with Resolution 2048 (2015) of the Council of Europe Parliamentary Assembly, which calls the member states to "remove any restrictions on the right of transgender people to remain in an existing marriage upon recognition of their gender; ensure that spouses or children do not lose certain rights".[26]

---

[25]ECtHR *Hämäläinen v. Finland (Application no. 37359/09)*, 16 July 2014.

[26]Parliamentary Assembly of the Council of Europe, Resolution 2048 (2015), 22 April 2015 at 6.2.3.

3.4 *Article 4 Gender Identity Law: Procedure*

Article 4 stipulates that: (a) the correction takes place through a trial where the special procedure of "non-adversarial proceedings" is applied according to Article 782 of the Greek Code of Civil Procedure; (b) a statement made in person by the interested party in court is required, which was not mandatory prior of the adoption of the Law, as individuals had the right to be represented by their authorised attorney; (c) the statement is made in a private office, and is not made publicly; (d) on the basis of the new registry act, the competent services proceed with the relevant corrections, making no reference to the fact that gender correction took place; and (e) the new registry act may henceforth be changed only once more under the same requirements.

However, this Article applies alongside numerous other provisions and laws and, therefore, its assessment requires the presence of all requirements concurrently applying in order to finally rule on whether it is a "transparent" and "simple" procedure, as required by Recommendation number 5 of 2010 of the Committee of Ministers of the Council of Europe.

3.4.1 Judgment Regarding Article 782 of the Code of Civil Procedure

There was no reason whatsoever to legislate anew that "the correction of the registered gender takes place by virtue of a court judgment issued in accordance with Article 782 of the Code of Civil Procedure". This is already envisaged by Article 782 of the Code of Civil Procedure itself, as well as Article 13 of Law 344/1976. Therefore, the first paragraph of Article 4 of the Gender Identity Law simply repeats what was already in force.

As previously noted, the ways in which registry particulars may change also include procedures where the judgment of the court is not compulsory:

a) correction of errors by the registrar with or without an order issued by the Public Prosecutor;
b) mayoral decision concerning a change to surname;
c) change of religion following an ordinary application submitted by the interested party.

For "unprecedented" events, a simple statement submitted to the registry by the interested person suffices (birth, death, marriage, adoption, civil partnership). Therefore, the courts should not necessarily have a 'monopoly'. In other countries, legislation permits gender change simply with a statement made by the interested party at the registry. In the case at hand, the legislation simply repeats what was already in force, removing medical procedures and examinations through Article 3, which courts had anyway already decided under the law previously in force.

Non-adversarial proceedings constitute a unique judicial procedure whereby the law requires an individual to ask the court to attest or permit a situation. Under non-adversarial proceedings, individuals must be accompanied by an authorised attorney. They are obligated to submit a petition drafted by their attorney and communicate it within a set period of time prior to the court date (at the discretion of the District Civil Court Judge, in gender entry change cases, judges have set a period between 15 and 3 days prior to the court date) to the Public Prosecutor via a court process server, whom interested parties must pay for the service of the petition to the Public Prosecutor.

The problem with non-adversarial proceedings is that the court judgment issued is not binding upon registrars. As odd as it may sound, a court judgment issued under non-adversarial proceedings has been found, in accordance with the settled case-law of the Greek Supreme Administrative Court (Council of State), to be non-binding on the Registry, but to be taken into account alongside other official information. Therefore, non-adversarial proceedings constitute a doubtful procedure when selected by the legislator to protect an individual right such as, in the case at hand, the legal recognition and respect towards gender identity under Article 8 ECHR. It can be anticipated that if the specific procedure of non-adversarial proceedings is implemented, court judgments could be considered "indicative" by Registrars, who may take it upon themselves to request additional information and, in particular, an attestation concerning legal capacity or even the medical certificates and medical acts already excluded by Article 3 of the Gender Identity Law, because the exclusion may be considered to concern the ruling of the court and not the subsequent use of the court judgment at the registry.

Furthermore, following the issuance of the judgment, since Law 344/1976 requires the judgment to be final in order for the correction to be entered, the process of service to the Public Prosecutor and lapse of the period during which the Public Prosecutor has the right to exercise legal remedies must be followed. So, the Gender Identity Law preserved in this case an unnecessary bureaucracy.

With these characteristics, the adjudication of requests under non-adversarial proceedings does not grant the legal certainty established in Recommendation 5 (2010) of the Committee of Ministers of the Council of Europe for a quick, simple and transparent process for the correction of documents, since the use of the court judgment by interested parties appearing at the registry is uncertain. Generally speaking, the problem of the judicial procedure is that it breaks down the correction into two major stages: the judicial stage and the administrative stage; there should be a single stage and it should not be up to the discretion of each registrar whether or not to apply the court judgment.

It would be simpler and safer to have a process whereby interested parties would directly submit a change application to the registry, as is the case for changes in religion, as well as any initial statement of a registry occurrence (birth, death, adoption, marriage, civil partnership). The request for a gender correction has many elements of the "rebirth" of an individual that would justify the enactment of a process of initial statement of gender reassignment as a new registry occurrence and not as a "correction" of the act of birth.

3.4.2 Statement Made in Person by the Interested Party

The requirement to make the statement in person was not envisaged prior to the adoption of the Gender Identity Law: citizens always have the right—in fact, more often than not, the obligation—to be represented by an authorised attorney. The obligation to appear accompanied by an attorney remains in the Gender Identity Law (as the process of issuance of a judgment under Article 782 of the Code of Civil Procedure is followed, which is part of non-adversarial proceedings where appearance accompanied by an attorney is compulsory). The added obligation for a statement made "in person" by the individual requesting gender correction in a registry act is an indication of distrust. This is an *a priori* legislated limitation of trans rights in order avoid circumvention. However, under what criteria will judges rule on whether the person making the statement in person is or is not transgender? Shall we abolish medical certificates and allow judges to replace the science of medicine? Is there something cryptic at play that judges must diagnose and which requires—for the first time in civil procedure—a statement made in person by the interested party?

The introduction of a statement made in person by interested parties in order to change the registry entry of their gender disregards the fact that transgender individuals very often face serious problems with appearing before a public authority, such as the court, even under terms of secrecy, as imposed by Article 4 of the Gender Identity Law.

Moreover, the legal issue is what the content of this "statement made in person" will be when a petition for the correction of a registry act has already been lodged before the court in order for the case to be tried. What is the actual reason for this "statement made in person" when the procedure is based on the petition?

The procedure previously in place was clearly more reliable: a witness appeared before the court and testified under oath that the interested party is transgender, that they use this or the other name in their social relations (in the "desired" gender), and that the correction of their registry act is necessary in order to allow them to live a dignified life. Witnesses testify under oath, therefore they are personally liable (even with criminal liability) for any perjury. Under the new procedure, this is abolished and a sworn testimony is downgraded to a simple statement made in person, with no consequences in the event that this statement made before the court is fraudulent.

In summary, through statements made in person, individuals are deprived of their right to be represented by an authorised attorney, whom they must hire in any event for the procedure in question. Furthermore, the judge "examines" whether they are transgender, and therefore, they are also deprived of the legally reliable process of sworn testimony by a witness, which grants the court additional certainty that what is testified is true, is abolished.

3.4.3 No Publicity

According to Article 93 paragraph 2 of the Greek Constitution: "The hearings of all courts shall be public, except when the court decides that publicity would be detrimental to the accepted principles of morality, or that special reasons call for the protection of the private or family life of the litigants". Furthermore, under paragraph 3 of the same Article of the Constitution: "Every court judgment must be specifically and thoroughly reasoned and must be pronounced in a public hearing".

These constitutional rules impose publicity as a rule for court hearings and the pronouncement of the court judgment, except in regard to the hearing itself. Under the system previously in force, trials concerning the correction of registry acts in terms of gender identity were public and the courts had the right to order the hearing to take place *in camera*. The Gender Identity Law has changed this. It is not the first time that non-adversarial proceedings take place with the submission of a file (e.g. approval of the establishment of a union). However, this does not involve the simple submission of a file, but requires a "statement made in person" by the interested party in a private office, without publicity.

The correction of a registry act in terms of gender is an affair that concerns one's private life. It is reasonable to expect interested parties to be discouraged from going forward with the process when they know that they must stand in a courtroom during a public hearing. Publicity is an inhibiting factor for the exercise of trans rights due to psychological reasons: the concern over potential humiliation.

However, publicity is guaranteed by the Constitution to ensure the proper functioning of Justice and to avoid misconduct on the part of judges. The secret examination of the interested party with the obligation of a "statement made in person" could foster an environment where judges ask unpleasant questions. It should be noted that under non-adversarial proceedings, judges have the discretion *ex officio* to request evidence and this can lead to highly unpleasant situations when the subject of the case is the attestation of "sex change", in combination with the abolition of medical attestations concerning the reassignment.

The constitutional rule of public hearings could have been preserved, with the court deciding on a case-by-case basis to hold hearings *in camera* in order to protect individuals provided that there was also no requirement of an "in person" statement. When trans individuals require secrecy, they can submit a relevant request. In any event, the court judgment is pronounced in a public hearing and the Gender Identity Law does not change this.

3.4.4 Correction by Other Competent Services

This provision of Article 4 (3), whereby other competent services are obligated to follow the "new" registry act of birth, should, in drafting terms, have been part of the subsequent Article 5 ("Effects of the correction of the recorded gender").

Furthermore, this is not a "new" registry act but a corrected registry act: there is a single registry act, i.e. the one initially drafted, to which changes (e.g. naming as regards the given name) and corrections are added. There is no "new" and "old" registry act. There is a new copy of the registry act issued after the correction.

The problem with this Article is that it does not set out precisely which the competent services are, under which procedure they will carry out corrections (*ex officio* or following an application submitted by the interested parties?) and when the relevant corrections must be completed, given that the public interest requires the absolute coordination of files containing the civil status information of citizens.

In practice, we know that the registry correction must follow the relevant deletion or entry in the male registry and the relevant correction in the municipal registry in order for the new identity card to be issued by a police precinct. At present, interested parties submit requests, producing not only the new copy of the registry act, but also the court judgment and the report concerning service to the Public Prosecutor's Office, and the certificate issued by the court registry in order for the relevant corrections to be completed—all this when a single document would suffice: the corrected registry act stating the reason for the correction.

Public services should not have to rely on actions taken by the interested parties themselves: once it has completed the correction, the registry should immediately and *ex officio* notify the male registry and the municipal registry (whether or not the latter belongs to the same Municipality) so that the procedure can immediately progress internally. The infrastructure and legal basis for internal communication via e-mail and fax (Law 2462/1998, Law 3979/2011) exists and individuals do not have to repeat the trial from the beginning or explain the same things over and over to each public service. Where their contribution is required (e.g. photograph and payment of a duty for the issuance of an identity card by a police precinct), it is obvious that they must appear in person, but as regards the male registry and the municipal registry, the process should be completed *ex officio*.

3.4.5 Change of Gender Particulars Only Up to Two Times

Article 4, paragraph 4 of the Gender Identity Law introduces another limitation not currently envisaged in legislation: "The new registry act may henceforth be changed once, under the same procedure and requirements". This wording is unfortunate: an individual may wish or be forced to change any other civil status information except gender (e.g. religion does not change "under the same procedure and requirements"), while the generality of this wording will not allow them to make further changes. More careful wording would be required in order to avoid such proscriptions. Furthermore, it is not easy to comprehend why the state would specifically allow two changes to the entry of gender and not only one or more.

3.5 Article 5 Gender Identity Law: Effects of the Correction of Recorded Gender

According to Article 5 paragraph 1 of the Gender Identity Law, "rights, obligations and all responsibilities of individuals prior to the gender correction shall remain in place". The wording is exceptionally unfortunate, as an individual transitioning from male to female had (initially as a man) a military service obligation and, on the basis of this provision, would continue to do so as a woman, even after having been deleted from male registries and conscription lists. Therefore, the provision should have been worded differently so as to add a reservation in regard to rights and obligations integrally linked to the gender initially recorded, so that no misplaced obligations arise.

The second paragraph of that same article stipulates that the correction of the recorded gender of a parent does not alter the registry act of birth of a child. In other words, while the parent's entry in the municipal registry will change and while the child's family share will include the correction of its parent's recorded gender, the child's registry act of birth will remain the same, contradicting the same child's family status certificate. It is understood that the purpose is not to create questions and problems for children, but the solution is not to create registry situations that contradict the municipal registry. The 'concealment' of the parent's corrected gender from the child's registry act constitutes intervention on the part of the legislator in the right of respect towards an individual's family life and distortion of their actual family status. It is an unreasonable attempt to preserve, obstinately against reality, the perception that children have a "mother and a father", when life itself has moved past it. As a result, this provision is contrary to Article 8 ECHR.

3.6 Article 6 Gender Identity Law: Secrecy

Article 6 of the Gender Identity Law repeats for no reason whatsoever the duty of professional secrecy that is binding, in any event, on registry employees and attorneys. However, it notes that the original registry act of birth of individuals, from which the gender correction that took place emerges, may be accessed solely by those individuals themselves and persons they have authorised, while access by third parties requires the permission of the Hellenic Data Protection Authority for access to sensitive personal data.

In drafting terms, the above provision presents the following issue: Article 8(2) of Law 344/1976 establishes the principle of publicity for registry ledgers, which are characterised as "public". Article 4(d) of the same Law establishes the registrars' obligation "to issue copies, excerpts and certificates from the acts contained in the ledgers or the public documents related to those found therein". The explanatory memorandum of that Law stresses that the publicity of registry ledgers means that "anyone may request copies, excerpts or certificates from the ledgers without having to justify any legal interest in doing so, and be notified if there is a registry occurrence, e.g. if a registry act of marriage of a specific individual has been drafted". As to these matters, the Supreme Administrative Court of Greece (Council of the State) has issued two opinions,[27] accepting that although registry acts concern the private or family life of third parties, due to the publicity of registry ledgers enacted by the special provision of Article 8(2) of Law 344/1976, copies, excerpts or certificates from registry ledgers must be issued to any applicant, without the latter having to invoke and prove any legal interest. The above provision, being special, was not adversely affected by the subsequent provisions of Article 5(3) of Law 2690/1999, which exempts documents that concern private or family life from the right of access to public documents, nor was it repealed or amended by the provisions concerning the protection of personal data of Law 2472/1997, which is also more recent (see Authority Decision No 19/2007). Subsequently, the Hellenic Data Protection Authority issued Decision 7/2015, which contained a different view:

> Whereas the above registry acts may contain sensitive personal data and, to wit, data concerning the religious beliefs of individuals (e.g. baptism, religious beliefs, etc.), it is necessary in such events to have previously secured the permission of the Authority which shall rule, on the basis of Article 7 of Law 2472/1997, on whether or not the sensitive data may be lawfully provided, with the additional requirement that the applicant third party is interested in being provided the sensitive data contained therein. Otherwise, in the event that the applicant is not interested in being provided with the subjects' sensitive data and in order to adequately apply the right of access under Article 8(2) of Law 344/1976, your service may grant the registry acts in question with redaction of the sensitive data and other additional information these acts may contain that could, even indirectly, lead to the disclosure of said data.

However, gender itself does not fall within "sensitive data". Therefore, a correction in the entry of gender itself does not constitute "sensitive data" that would require the granting of permission by the Authority in order for third parties to access the registry data in question. Thus, the Gender Identity Law should have adopted a clearer position as regards the provision of Article 8 of Law 344/1976, expressly amending it in relation to the publicity of registry ledgers and/or adding gender identity data to the "sensitive data" of Article 2(b) of Law 2472/1997, taking into consideration, in this event, that all processing of gender identity data must be subject to the requirement of the Authority's permission, except in the event of exemptions under Article 7A of Law 2472/1997.

According to Article 6 paragraph 2 of the Gender Identity Law, if individuals become legally incapacitated, their guardian has access to the data of the gender entry change. This is a glaring violation of Article 8 paragraph 2 of the Charter of Fundamental Rights of the European Union and Article 12 of Directive 95/46/EC concerning the right of data subjects to access the data relating to them. The right to access cannot be construed as conditional on the legal capacity of individuals, as it is a fundamental right protected under EU law.

---

[27]Council of the State Opinion 73/1994 and Opinion 689/1995 of the 3rd Chamber.

4 Developments After the Enactment of Law 4491/2017

As mentioned before, individuals who wish to correct the registry entry as to their gender and full name must follow the judicial procedure of Non-Adversarial Proceedings (jurisdictio voluntaria) at the District Civil Court of the region of the registry where their registry act of birth is located. Therefore, if an individual was not born in Greece, they cannot, according to the wording of the Law, proceed with correcting the registry gender entry, unless they have already effected the correction at a foreign registry and wish to have the foreign registry act transcribed at the Special Registry of the Ministry of Interior.

As a result, trans EU nationals, migrants, asylum-seekers and refugees residing in Greece may face an undue burden in order to obtain legal recognition of their gender identity in Greece. This is particularly worrying in light of the vulnerability of certain groups such as refugee and migrant trans women, who are particularly exposed to violence and threats of violence due to their gender identity and gender expression.[28]

By way of exception, the District Civil Courts have accepted that the court of the area where the interested party is domiciled also has jurisdiction. However, this admission by way of exception, although based on settled case-law, is unfortunately not included in the Gender Identity Law, but continues to derive from a number of court judgments on the legal recognition of gender identity.

In this respect, the District Court of Mytilene with its judgment in case 136/2018, which became final on February 19, 2019, proceeded to a change in the registered sex and the name of a trans woman who had already been recognized as a refugee by the Regional Asylum Office of Mytilene. The reasoning of the Court in this case is quite interesting. In its decision the Court explained that the most important feature of refugee status is the disruption of the refugee's relationship with his/her country of origin, where he/she is at risk of persecution as stated in the 1951 Geneva Convention and the Additional Protocol of 31 January 1967. This alienation implies that the trans refugee cannot approach the authorities of his/her country of origin in order to obtain the necessary documents for the exercise of his/her rights. At the same time, since the Greek and international legal orders recognize the human right to gender identity, the trans individual must be able to exercise this right while under the jurisdiction of the Greek authorities. Consequently, since a trans individual cannot be required to correct his/her registration documents in his/her country of origin, in order to alter the passport's details and the documents granting asylum by the Greek authorities, the alteration in the details of these documents must be made by the Greek authorities. Also, in accordance with the general principle of equal treatment of Article 26 ICCPR and the fundamental obligation of all Greek state institutions to ensure the respect for the dignity of all persons under their jurisdiction (Article

[28]See Amnesty International Public Statement "Greece: Draft law on legal recognition of gender identity must be strengthened so that trans persons enjoy human rights without discrimination, AI Index: EUR 25/6692/2017, 10 July 2017, https://www.amnesty.org/download/Documents/EUR2566922017ENGLISH.pdf. Accessed 4 July 2020.

2 paragraph 1 of the Greek Constitution), if a special procedure is provided to Greek nationals, it must be proportionately provided to asylum seekers and recognized refugees as well.[29]

The usage of the concept of human dignity by the Greek court is quite interesting. In Greek law, Article 2(1) of the Constitution of Greece stipulates that: "Respect and protection of the value of the human being constitute the primary obligations of the State". Article 2(1) may also be read in conjunction with Article 5(1) of the Constitution, which stipulates that: "All persons shall have the right to develop freely their personality and to participate in the social, economic and political life of the country, insofar as they do not infringe the rights of others or violate the Constitution and the good usages". Under Article 110(1) of the Constitution, Article 2(1) and Article 5(1) may not be revised. Consequently, the Article concerning the intrinsic value of the human being holds a prominent position in the Constitution of Greece and is inviolable. It establishes a positive obligation on the part of the State to protect it and is considered an absolute right. As a concept, human dignity is first encountered in Article 7(2) of the Constitution, which stipulates that: "Torture, any bodily maltreatment, impairment of health or the use of psychological violence, as well as any other offence against human dignity are prohibited and punished as provided by law". Both doctrine and jurisprudence, however, accept that the value of the human being and human dignity are identical from a legal standpoint.[30] Article 2 (1), combined with Article 5(1), establishes the inviolability of human dignity not only for Greek citizens but for every person, including migrants and refugees.

5 Concluding Remarks

The Gender Identity Law 4491/2017 is undoubtedly a significant step forward towards the institutionalization of gender identity rights in Greece as its aim is to end the marginalization of persons whose perceived gender identity does not correspond with that assigned at birth. Despite reactions from a number of political parties within the Greek Parliament and the Greek Orthodox Church, the Law was finally adopted as Greece had to comply with international and European standards regarding the recognition of the civil status of trans persons. Moreover, the Greek courts, even before the adoption of the Gender Identity Law, had already accepted in their recent case-law, the right of trans persons to be legally recognized without undergoing surgery.

The then Greek left-wing government (SYRIZA) managed to endorse policies that would permit persons to legally alter their names and gender marker on all official documents without undergoing surgery and sterilization. Almost the entire

[29]For some extracts of this judgments see: http://www.immigration.gr/2019/02/anagnorish-taytothtas-fylou-trans-gynaika-prosfyga.html. Accessed 4 July 2020.

[30]Tsevrenis (2012), pp. 47–58.

political opposition in Parliament, with the exception of a few small political parties (ANEL, Potami, DHSY) rejected the proposed legislation. There was great support by the LGBTQI community in Greece, and more specifically by the Transgender Association of Greece.[31] The final text of the Law did not follow all the proposals made by the draft committee, and was the result of a compromise within the Greek Parliament. There are still some grey zones that would need to be amended in the future.

One of the highly contested issues which resulted in having the major opposition party "New Democracy" withdraw its support to the legislation was the issue of extending the right to minors. The final text of the Law provided for the possibility only for persons 15 or older to undergo an alteration of their civil status as far as gender is concerned, under strict conditions, including a psycho-medical examination until the age of 17.

Removing blanket age restrictions and giving access to minors, on the basis of their best interest, taking into account their evolving capacities and their right to be heard without imposing upon them psycho-medical evaluations is an issue that needs to be resolved in the future. The Greek legal system is a civil law system and, even though court judgments are binding upon the litigants of the given case, the principle of *stare decisis* does not apply in future cases as it does in common law systems. Nevertheless, the Greek courts have recently dealt with the issue of legal recognition of the civil status of trans persons with great sensitivity basing their decisions on international and European standards, without a specific national legislative framework. Now, with the Gender Identity Law, they would need to comply to the new provisions, and may be forced to limit some of the rights previously granted to trans individuals.

Another contested issue of the Gender Identity Law is the single status requirement which, as previously mentioned, is against the right to family and private life not only for the trans persons but also for all the members of their family, spouse and children. The possibility to conclude civil partnership instead of marriage deprives trans persons from a great number of rights that cis persons have in Greece. Of course as there is no legal recognition of same-sex marriage in Greece, the entire LGBTQI community in the country faces the same problem.

The bureaucratic procedures that need to be followed before different Greek public services cost both time and money for trans persons. Trans individuals should be allowed to legally correct their name and gender, including the gender markers on all official documents issued by the state, through a quick, accessible, and transparent procedure and in accordance with the individual's sense of gender identity, without limitations on the number of instances that a gender marker can be changed.

Last but not least, other categories of persons, such as trans immigrants, asylum seekers or refugees in Greece should have been protected by the Gender Identity Law, and not simply by specific judgments issued by the Greek courts, by ensuring that legal gender recognition is not limited only to individuals holding birth

[31] See http://www.transgender-association.gr/. Accessed 4 July 2020.

certificates issued by a Greek Registry office. Also, it must be legally ensured that trans individuals who have obtained legal recognition of gender identity in another country have the relevant decision recognized in Greece, without having to undergo anew a procedure of legal gender recognition. Moreover, individuals who identify themselves as having a gender that is neither male nor female (such as intersex, non-binary, gender fluid) should be allowed to obtain official papers that reflect their gender identity by regulating in the future the abolition of gender markers on official papers or the possibility of a no gender option.

In conclusion, even if there are still some unresolved issues that need to be addressed through possible amendments of the existing legislation, Greece has, undoubtedly, moved forward in creating an institutional framework for the recognition of the civil status of trans persons. The Greek Gender Identity Law, responding to international and European standards of protection, may lead the way for a social transformation in the country. It is possible for a legal reform to change the mentality of the people, especially on issues which have remained hidden and unregulated for centuries within a given society. The best example of this is the late 20th century reform on gender equality in Greece that went hand in hand with the democratization process of the country. Society was still quite traditional but radical pro-gender equality reforms influenced by the EU legal framework managed to rapidly change mentalities.[32] Legal reform on socially sensitive matters, such as gender identity issues, usually follows societal change, but sometimes precedes it as in the case in Greece, where legal culture may act as a filter or as a means of communication between the social system and the legal system and may increase in the future the visibility and acceptance of trans individuals in Greek society. At least now trans persons legally exist.

References

European Commission, Directorate-General for Justice and Consumers (2012) Trans and intersex people: discrimination on the grounds of sex, gender identity, and gender expression. Office for Official Publications of the European Union, Luxembourg

Konsta A-M (2019) Gender Equality Law in Greece and the European Union: the trajectory from exclusion to inclusion. In: Tsakiropoulou-Summers T, Kitsi-Mitakou K (eds) Women and the ideology of political exclusion: from classical antiquity to the modern era. Routledge, London and New York, pp 293–311

Kounougeri-Manoledaki E (ed) (2017) Anagnorisi taftotitas filou: Enopsi tou sxediou nomou tis Nomoparaskevastikis Epitropis apo to Ypourgeio Dikaiosunis (Recognition of gender identity: in view of the Draft Law of the Legal Drafting Committee by the Ministry of Justice). Sakkoulas, Athens – Thessaloniki

Tsevrenis V (2012) Anthropini Axioprepia (Human dignity). Sakkoulas Publications, Athens - Thessaloniki, pp 47–58

[32] Konsta (2019), pp. 293–311.

The Law Concerning Trans Persons in Ireland

Peter Dunne

Abstract This chapter traces the civil status of trans persons in Ireland, identifying the broader legal context in which Irish trans-focused laws operate. The mechanics and consequences of trans-oriented laws in Ireland are in focus—with a detailed analysis of statute, policy and case law provided. Where appropriate, commentary on the merits of existing law and the potential for future reforms is given. Though not an exhaustive account of legal rights for trans communities in Ireland, by exploring the myriad intersections of law and trans identities, the chapter hopes to present a clear, detailed insight to the status of trans communities in contemporary Irish law.

This chapter traces the civil status of trans persons in Ireland, identifying the broader legal context in which Irish trans focused laws operate. The mechanics and consequences of trans oriented laws in Ireland are in focus—with a detailed analysis of statute, policy and case law provided. Where appropriate, commentary on the merits of existing law and the potential for future reforms is given, based on the numerous sources, including Government reports, civil society interventions and academic commentary. The chapter is not an exhaustive account of legal rights for trans communities in Ireland, and many legal matters—which directly impact upon trans lives in this jurisdiction—fall outside the scope of discussion. Yet, by exploring the myriad intersections of law and trans identities, the chapter hopes to present a clear, detailed insight to the status of trans communities in contemporary Irish law.

P. Dunne (✉)
University of Bristol, Bristol, UK
e-mail: pd17653@bristol.ac.uk

I. C. Jaramillo, L. Carlson (eds.), *Trans Rights and Wrongs*, Ius Comparatum - Global Studies in Comparative Law 54,
https://doi.org/10.1007/978-3-030-68494-5_21

1 The Civil Status of Gender

Sex and gender are legal categories in Irish law. As compared with comparable constitutions worldwide, the Irish Constitution, Bunreacht na hEireann, operates a particularly gendered dynamic.[1] Article 41(2)(1) provides that "by her life within the home, *woman* gives to the State a support without which the common good cannot be achieved" (emphasis added). In the following sub-section, "[t]he State" commits itself to ensuring that "mothers shall not be obliged by economic necessity to engage in labour to the neglect of their duties in the home" (note the conflation of "woman" and "mothers").

Article 41(2)(1) of the Constitution can be (and has been) subject to critique.[2] It is instructive that, while the Constitution defines women as mothers and homemakers, the Preamble celebrates "our fathers" who, "through centuries of trial", "heroic [ly] and unremitting[ly] struggle[d] to regain the rightful independence of our Nation." Removing (or amending) art. 41(2)(1) has been proposed on numerous occasions—most recently by a citizens' Constitutional Convention in 2013[3]—and the current Government has indicated an intention to hold a public referendum on the provision before the end of the current parliamentary session.

Under the Civil Registrations Act 2004, all children who are born in the State must be registered within three months of their birth.[4] Among the "particulars", which must be "entered in [the] register of births", is the "sex of the child."[5] Therefore, from the time they are born, all persons in Ireland must have an identifiable, state-recognised legal sex. While the importance of sex status in Irish has waned, it remains relevant in a number of key areas. For example, Ireland's primary and secondary schools remain majority single-sex. Access to specific educational institutions therefore depends on legal sex. Ireland also operates different maternity and paternity regimes.[6] The sex and parental role of a parent determines the statutory 'leave' period to which they have entitlement. The Employment Equality Act 1998 (as amended) (1998 Act) and Equal Status Act 2000 (as amended) (2000 Act) both recognise a "gender ground" of discrimination, which arises from (unjustifiable)

---

[1] Brady (2012).

[2] Second Commission on the Status of Women, *Report to Government* (1993). See also: 'Submissions to the Constitutional Convention on the Role of Women' (*The Convention on the Constitution Website, No Date Available*). Https://www.constitution.ie/Submissions.aspx?cid=60. Accessed 15 July 2017.

[3] Minihan, Mary. 2013. Convention favours gender equality and change to 'women in home' clause', *The Irish Times*, 18 February. Https://www.irishtimes.com/news/convention-favours-gender-equality-and-change-to-women-in-home-clause-1.1252785. Accessed 15 July 2017.

[4] Civil Registrations Act 2004, s. 19(1).

[5] Civil Registrations Act 2004, First Schedule, Part I.

[6] Paternity Leave and Benefits Act 2016 (Ireland); The Maternity Protections Acts 1994 and 2004.

unequal treatment between two individuals where "one is male and the other is female."[7]

When the birth of a child is registered in Ireland in accordance with the 2004 Act, a 'birth certificate' is issued. The child's legal sex is thereafter determined by reference to that birth certificate (which mirrors the information contained in the national Register of Births).[8] Although the child may (either before or after obtaining the age of majority) receive additional identity documents, legal sex remains tied to the birth certificate.[9] The primary importance of birth certificates explains the necessity of gender recognition reform in Ireland. Prior to 2015, when binary trans persons were first legally acknowledged by the Irish state (Gender Recognition Act 2015), it was possible for individuals to obtain alternative identification (particularly passports) with their preferred gender markers.[10] However, as these ancillary identifying instruments did not amend people's core legal status, it had no effect on issues, such as access to marriage and social security entitlements. In *S v An Bord Uchtála*,[11] a male-identified youth, with a female legal sex, was initially denied access to boys-only primary education because, despite his clear and consistent gender preference, his female legal status was inconsistent with school entry requirements.

In general, amendments to a birth certificate (made by way of correcting or altering data in the register of births) are rare and are only permitted in exceptional circumstances. Ireland's Department of Social Protection advises that a "birth certificate is a legal document and cannot be amended unless there are valid reasons to do so, as the Civil Registration Service has a duty to protect the integrity of the records held."[12] Section 63 of the 2004 Act provides for a process whereby—through an application to a Superintendent Registrar—an individual may formally request that either a "clerical error" or an "error of fact" be amended. As regards parentage on birth certificates, any correction or amendment can only be made pursuant to a "declaration of parentage" (i.e. a court declares that a person or persons named in an application are the applicant's mother or father) under s. 35 of the Status of Children Act 1987.

---

[7]Employment Equality Act 1998, s. 6(2)(a); Equal Status Act 200, s. 3(2)(a).

[8]'Registering the Birth of Your Baby' (*Citizens Information Website Ireland,* 22 December 2016) http://www.citizensinformation.ie/en/birth_family_relationships/after_your_baby_is_born/registering_birth_your_baby.html. Accessed 15 July 2017.

[9]*Ibid.*

[10]Passports Act 1998, s. 11.

[11](High Court, 4 December 2009).

[12]'Correction of Errors and Other Amendments' (*Department of Social Protection Website*, 21 October 2013). Https://www.welfare.ie/en/Pages/Registering_Birth.aspx#correction. Accessed 15 July 2017.

2 Regulation of Trans Identities

Since 2015, Irish law has formally acknowledged the preferred (binary) gender of trans individuals over the age of 16 years.[13] Ireland was one of the last European Union Member States to introduce comprehensive legal gender recognition. As the law currently stands (discussed in detail below), the Gender Recognition Act 2015 (2015 Act) permits persons, who are at least 18 years old, to amend their male or female gender by way of self-declaration.[14] Minors, aged between 16 and 17 years, can access gender recognition through a supervised process, requiring parental consent, medical oversight and the supervision of the Circuit Family Court.[15] Irish law does not currently recognise the preferred gender of children under 16 years.

The movement towards legal gender recognition in Ireland has been a long (and sometimes politically contentious) process.[16] In 1993, Dr Lydia Foy, an Irish trans woman, who retained her birth-assigned male sex, requested that the Registrar of Births issue her with an amended (female) birth certificate.[17] When, after a period of protracted negotiations, the Registrar ultimately refused the request, Dr Foy commenced litigation. In *Foy v Registrar General of Births, Deaths and Marriages (No 1),*[18] the High Court (McKechnie J), despite expressing considerable sympathy for Dr Foy's position, concluded that the Irish Constitution did not require the State to acknowledge her preferred gender.

Two days after the *Foy (No 1)* judgment, the European Court of Human Rights (ECtHR) issued its opinion in *Goodwin v United Kingdom.*[19] In *Goodwin*—departing from earlier case law whereby denying gender recognition had fallen within the UK's margin of appreciation—the ECtHR held that refusing to provide Christine Goodwin with an amended birth certificate violated arts. 8 and 12 ECHR.[20] From an Irish perspective, *Goodwin* was immensely important in three respects. First, as Irish birth registration procedures mirrored, in many respects, the system in England and Wales, the decision strongly implied that Irish law now contravened the European Convention. Second, *Goodwin* precipitated the introduction of comprehensive reform in the United Kingdom (Gender Recognition Act 2004). This further highlighted Ireland's outlier position within the Council of Europe, and encouraged both political and activist movements towards reform. Finally, when the Oireachtas (Irish national parliament) partially incorporated the ECHR into domestic law in 2003, the incompatibility between *Goodwin* and Ireland's legal vacuum became a catalyst to re-open the *Foy* litigation. While the

---

[13] Gender Recognition Act 2015.

[14] *Ibid.*, s. 10.

[15] *Ibid.*, s. 12.

[16] See generally, Dunne (2014), p. 70; Moynihan (2008), p. 38; Ryan (2004), p. 15; Farrell (2012).

[17] Farrell (2013), pp. 16–17.

[18] [2002] IEHC 116.

[19] [2002] 35 EHRR 18.

[20] *Ibid.*, [93] and [104].

State's failure to recognise preferred gender may not have been unconstitutional, it appeared to conflict with Ireland's international obligations under art. 8 ECHR.

In *Foy v Registrar General of Births, Deaths and Marriages (No 2)*,[21] the High Court (with McKechnie J once again presiding) issued the first 'declaration of incompatibility' under the 2003 Act.[22] Having regard to the *Goodwin* jurisprudence, McKecknie J observed a clear conflict between Irish law and the ECHR requirements.[23] The judge expressed surprise that, in the five years since his original decision in *Foy (No 1)*,[24] the legislature had taken "no steps of any significance to redress the undoubted difficulties which continue to exist"[25] for trans individuals. In consequence, according to McKechnie J, "Ireland as of now [was] very much isolated within the Member States of the Council of Europe."[26]

Despite the clear (and seemingly irrefutable) evidence that Irish law (or the lack thereof) violated Convention norms, the Government initially decided to appeal the High Court judgment.[27] In 2008, the United Nations Human Rights Committee added to the movement for reform when, in its Concluding Observations on Ireland's Third Periodic Report, it specifically recommended that the State "recognise the right of transgender persons to a change of gender by permitting the issuance of new birth certificates."[28]

In 2010 the Government announced that it would withdraw its appeal to the Supreme Court, and established a Gender Recognition Advisory Group (GRAG)[29] to provide a blueprint for acknowledging preferred gender in Ireland. GRAG's membership was comprised solely of public servants, and there was no openly trans representation on the panel. The process by which GRAG was constituted and operated (particularly its public consultation) was a source of particular discontent for Ireland's trans community. The perceived exclusion of trans voices and experiences led to widespread calls for trans participation when the Government subsequently constituted a two-year review of the Gender Recognition Act 2015 in November 2017.[30] In its 2011 Report to the Minister for Social Protection, GRAG

[21][2007] IEHC 470.

[22]*Ibid.*, [110]. For the statutory foundations of the 'Declaration of Incompatibility', see: European Convention on Human Rights Act 2003, s. 5.

[23]*Ibid.*, [85]–[105].

[24]*Ibid.*, [102].

[25]*Ibid.*, [100].

[26]*Ibid.*

[27]Farrell (2013), p. 17.

[28]UN Human Rights Committee, 'Concluding Observations of the Human Rights Committee' (30 July 2008) UN Doc No. CCPR/C/IRL/CO/3, [8].

[29]Farrell (2013), p. 17.

[30]The Gender Recognition Review Group specifically incorporated trans voices within its members. See McMahon, Aine. 2017. Moninne Griffith to chair Gender Recognition Act review. *Irish Times*, 3 November. Https://www.irishtimes.com/news/social-affairs/moninne-griffith-to-chair-gender-recognition-act-review-1.3279508?mode=amp. Accessed 10 July 2019.

adopted a conservative approach to recognising preferred gender.[31] Advocating a UK-inspired model law, GRAG's recommendations called for a diagnosis requirement, forced divorce, a gender recognition panel and the total exclusion of minors.[32]

In the years following the GRAG publication, intensive consultations took place between Government officials and representatives of trans persons and their families.[33] While the delay in enacting legislation undoubtedly reflected the (comparatively) low priority which successive governments had placed on the recognition question, it also speaks to the significant practical difficulties which all actors—state and non-state—confronted in trying to find both a politically and socially acceptable model of affirmation.

Subsequent to the GRAG Report, two members of the national parliament, Deputy Aengus O'Snodaigh (Sinn Fein)[34] and Senator Katherine Zappone (Independent Senator) both published Private Members Bills which would have provided legal gender recognition.[35] These proposed laws were promoted and supported by trans activists and organisations. In 2013 and 2014, the Government adopted a General Scheme, and then a Revised General Scheme, for a Gender Recognition Bill.[36] It was not until June 2015, however, in the wake of the Marriage Equality Referendum, that the Department of Social Protection announced that they were moving forward with legislation and that, for adults, it would be based on self-determination. The 2015 Act was passed by the Oireachtas on 15 July 2015.

Prior to the 2015 Act, trans people (or at least those who fell within the category of "gender reassignment") were already protected under Ireland's equality legislation. On the face of both statutes, neither the 1998 Act nor the 2000 Act embraced trans identities. However, in the landmark *Hannon v First Direct* case, the (former) Equality Tribunal concluded that, for the purpose of employment equality guarantees, "gender…protects transgender persons from sex discrimination, that is, discrimination arising essentially if not exclusively on the sex of the person concerned."[37] Even if the 1998 Act did not specifically reference trans communities,

[31]Ni Mhuirthile, Tanya. 2011. Long Awaited Report of the Gender Recognition Advisory Group. *Human Rights in Ireland Blog,* 15 July. Http://humanrights.ie/gender-sexuality-and-the-law/long-awaited-report-of-the-gender-recognition-advisory-group/. Accessed 15 July 2017. See also Transgender Europe. 2011. Irish Government Gender Recognition Advisory Group Report – A Missed Opportunity. *TGEU Website*, 15 July. Http://tgeu.org/irish-government-gender-recognition-advisory-group-report-a-missed-opportunity/. Accessed 15 July 2017.

[32]Gender Recognition Advisory Group (GRAG). 2011. *Report to Joan Burton TD, Minister for Social Protection,* 3–4.

[33]Transgender Equality Network Ireland. Legal Gender Recognition in Ireland. *TENI Website, No Date Available.* Http://www.teni.ie/page.aspx?contentid=586. Accessed 15 July 2017.

[34]Gender Recognition Bill 2013.

[35]Legal Recognition of Gender Bill 2013.

[36](Revised) General Scheme of Gender Recognition Bill 2014 (*Department of Social Welfare Website*) https://www.welfare.ie/en/downloads/Revised-General-Scheme-of-the-Gender-Recognition-Bill-2014.pdf. Accessed 15 July 2017.

[37]The Equality Tribunal, DEC-E2011-066 (29 March 2011), [4.3].

it did prevent Ms Hannon's employer from disfavouring her professionally because she was trans. The *Hannon* judgment is consistent with (and necessitated) by European Union case law (e.g. *P v S and Cornwall County Council*[38]) whereby the Court of Justice of the European Union affirmed that "the scope of the [employment equality] directive cannot be confined simply to discrimination based on the fact that a person is of one or other sex" but also extends to "discrimination arising. . .from the gender reassignment."[39] This statement has now also been enshrined in the recitals to the 2006 Equal Treatment Directive.[40]

There is evidence, therefore, that (at least some) trans individuals are protected under Ireland's existing non-discrimination laws. The current position is, however, unsatisfactory for two reasons. First, even if trans people implicitly come within both the 1998 and 2000 frameworks, this is practically and symbolically insufficient. It is *symbolically* problematic because, without expressly naming trans experiences, the current legislation invisibilises and marginalises non-cisgender lives. To exclude trans people from both statutes is to suggest (even subconsciously) that trans people, and the discrimination that they face, are less worthy of official recognition. The 1998 Act and 2000 Act are also *practically* insufficient because, where trans identities are not specifically mentioned, (a) trans individuals, particularly those who do not or cannot access legal advice, may not understand their rights; and (b) employers may be encouraged to believe that anti-trans conduct is not prohibited under the current framework.

Second, relying upon EU law protections risks excluding the multiplicity of trans experiences which fall outside notions of "gender reassignment". While in 1996, the CJEU's judgment in *P v S* was comparatively progressive,[41] the opinion adopts a narrow conceptualisation of trans people. Using the language of "gender reassignment", the Court's case law (and the subsequent Equal Treatment Directive) approaches trans experiences through a lens of medicalisation. Under EU law, trans persons should not experience unfavourable employment conditions because they undertake a process of medical transition. Yet, it remains unclear to what extent EU law and national legislation, such as Ireland's equality frameworks, which transposes that law, can accommodate and protect more complex and nuanced identities. Would, for example, "gender reassignment" embrace trans persons who express and live their preferred gender without altering their physical bodies? Is there protection for non-binary individuals, who confront discrimination because they situate their identities outside 'male' and 'female' norms? To the extent that Ireland's implicit coverage for trans communities requires adherence to standard binary frameworks, it has little (or no) relevance for an increasing number of Irish people.[42]

---

[38]Case C-13/94 ECR I-2143.

[39]*Ibid.*, [20].

[40]See: Directive 2006/54, Preamble, [3].

[41]Campbell and Lardy (1996), p. 412; Bell (1995), p. 63.

[42]McNeil et al. (2014), pp. 15, 22 and 34. See generally Dunne and Turraoin (2015).

With these limitations in mind, advocates for the trans community in Ireland have called for the specific inclusion of gender identity protections within domestic equality law.[43] It appeared that this recommendation was being taken up with the publication, in 2016, of the 'General Scheme of the Equality/Disability (Miscellaneous Provisions) Bill' (a proposed law to reform Ireland's disability rights framework prior to ratification of the UN Convention on the Rights of Persons with Disabilities). Heads 10 and 11 of the General Scheme would have extended the definition of 'gender ground' within the 1998 Act and the 2000 Act to "[incorporate] transgender and intersex as categories."[44] In both cases the 'Interpretations' sections in each statute (as amended) would be revised to include "gender, gender identity, intersex person, transgender man and transgender woman."[45]

The Gender Scheme, while a positive step towards trans (and intersex) protection, has been the subject of critique.[46] In particular, there was an apparent uncertainty as to what the Government was seeking to achieve with these reforms. Although the reference to 'gender identity' was welcome—and seemed to promote a broader understanding of gender inequality based on experience rather than categorisation—the inclusion of "transgender man and transgender woman" reinforced gender binarism and risked excluding persons who cannot (or would not) come within identifiable male-female norms.[47]

In addition, speaking in terms of "intersex person[s]" (a) incorrectly assumes that there is a pre-existing, universalised intersex narrative; and (b) ignores the fact that many persons, who experience intersex, define that experience as relating to sex characteristics rather than as a lived identity.[48] For trans and intersex advocates, there was a real fear that, in attempting to enhance the legal position of marginalised communities, the Government would enshrine insufficient and inaccurate protected characteristics, which did not reflect (or account for) common lived experiences. Ultimately, however, these concerns have been put on hold as, under the Disability (Miscellaneous Provisions) Bill 2016, published in December 2016, the Government no longer pursued trans and intersex equality rights within this wider reform project.

---

[43] Teni, Glen and BelongTo. 2016. Joint Submission on the Equality/Disability (Miscellaneous Provisions) Bill, 2016.

[44] See General Scheme of the Equality/Disability (Miscellaneous Provisions) Bill, Head 10 and Head 11 http://www.justice.ie/en/JELR/General-Scheme-of-the-Equality-Disability-(Miscellaneous-Provisions)-Bill-17-August-2016.pdf/Files/General-Scheme-of-the-Equality-Disability-(Miscellaneous-Provisions)-Bill-17-August-2016.pdf accessed 15 July 2015.

[45] *Ibid.*

[46] Irish Human Rights and Equality Commission, Observations on the General Scheme of the Equality/Disability (Miscellaneous Provisions) Bill (IHREC 2016) 47–50. Https://www.ihrec.ie/app/uploads/2016/11/Observations-on-the-General-Scheme-Equality-Disability-Miscellaneous-Provisions-Bill.pdf. Accessed 15 July 2017.

[47] *Ibid.*, 47–48.

[48] *Ibid.*, 48.

3 Legal Name Change

Section 10 of the Gender Recognition Act 2015 provides, *inter alia*, that, where a person applies for a Gender Recognition Certificate, and they wish to obtain a new name as part of that process, the person must provide the Minister for Social Protection with both "the forename and surname by which he or she wishes to be known"[49] and "proof of his or her identity."[50]

In response to a parliamentary question in 2017, the Minister for Social Protection explained that proof of identity may be offered in two ways. First, there can be "evidence of use or repute."[51] This requires that an applicant furnish "two documents that shows that the person is using the new name."[52] Among the documentation which the Minister will accept are drivers licences, college identification cards or school reports. Second, in the absence of such evidence, the applicant can execute a deed pool.[53] Deed polls are the standard instrument by which most Irish people change their legal name.[54] They involve an individual declaring that he or she is giving up the prior legal name and will use their new legal name for all purposes. The person must sign the deed before a witness, who is required to swear an affidavit in front of a solicitor or commissioner of oaths.[55]

In theory, as an inexpensive and comparatively straightforward process, most applicants for legal gender recognition would change their name through use of a deed poll. However, for the specific purposes of the 2015 Act, the Department for Social Protection will only accept a deed poll, which has been enrolled in the Central Office of the High Court.[56] This additional procedure not only creates greater administrative burdens for applicants. It may also expose an applicant's trans history. Where a deed poll is enrolled with the High Court, it is recorded in a publicly-accessible online database.[57] Despite the significant emphasis which the

---

[49]Gender Recognition Act 2015, s. 10(1)(b).

[50]*Ibid.*, 10(1)(c).

[51]'Written Answers – Tuesday 21 February 2017: Department of Social Protection – Gender Recognition' (21 February 2017). Https://www.kildarestreet.com/wrans/?id=2017-02-21a.749. Accessed 15 July 2017.

[52]*Ibid.*

[53]*Ibid.*

[54]'Deed Poll' (*Courts Service of Ireland Website*, 21 April 2017). Http://www.courts.ie/Courts.ie/Library3.nsf/pagecurrent/075D7770C94358068025804B005C294B?opendocument&l=en. Accessed 15 July 2017.

[55]*Ibid.*

[56]'Written Answers – Tuesday 21 February 2017: Department of Social Protection – Gender Recognition' (21 February 2017). Https://www.kildarestreet.com/wrans/?id=2017-02-21a.749. Accessed 15 July 2017.

[57]'Deed Poll' (*Courts Service of Ireland Website*, 21 April 2017). Http://www.courts.ie/Courts.ie/Library3.nsf/pagecurrent/075D7770C94358068025804B005C294B?opendocument&l=en. Accessed 15 July 2017.

2015 Act places upon privacy,[58] having to provide an enrolled deed poll (a requirement which is not specifically provided for in the statute) may disclose the fact that an applicant has renounced a legal name, associated with one gender, in favour of a legal name tied to another gender. In many cases, this will also disclose an applicant's trans status.

For at least a number of trans individuals in Ireland, the inability to provide evidence of "use or repute"—coupled with their fear that obtaining an *enrolled* deed poll will inevitably 'out' their trans identity—means that they avoid changing their legal name as part of the gender recognition process. Indeed, for some applicants, the fact that they cannot feasibly amend their legal gender without a public disclosure of their name change is enough to postpone (or to entirely forgo) legally validating their preferred gender.

4 Gender Recognition

Trans persons in Ireland have been able to obtain legal recognition of their preferred gender since 2015. As noted, the formal rules are now contained in an Act of the Oireachtas—Gender Recognition Act 2015. The 2015 Act provides for three distinct recognition regimes, depending on the age of the applicant: persons aged 18 years or above, persons aged 16 to 17 years, and persons under the age of 16 years.

4.1 Persons Aged 18 Years or Above

For applicants who have achieved the age of majority (18 years or above), legal gender recognition operates by way of self-determination. Applicants apply for a Gender Recognition Certificate (GRC) to the Minister for Social Protection[59] making a statutory declaration that (a) they have a "settled and solemn intention of living in the preferred gender for the rest of" their lives (i.e. legal gender recognition is intended to be permanent in Ireland);[60] (b) they "under[stand] the consequences of the application";[61] and (c) they are making the application "of [their] free will."[62]

Applicants must make their request "in writing in the form, including electronic form, as may be prescribed."[63] Section 8(3) of the 2015 Act provides that "the Minister shall consider an application. . .and shall decide to either (a) issue a gender

[58]See e.g. Gender Recognition Act 2015, s. 30C.

[59]Gender Recognition Act 2015, s. 8.

[60]*Ibid.*, s. 10(1)(f)(ii).

[61]*Ibid.*, s. 10(1)(f)(iii).

[62]*Ibid.*, s. 10(1)(f)(iv).

[63]*Ibid.*, s. 8(2).

recognition certificate, or (b) refuse to issue a gender recognition certificate." In considering an application, the Minister may require further information from applicants[64] and a decision must be made "as soon as practicable."[65]

Where there is a positive response to a request, the Minister must furnish the applicant with a GRC "as soon as may be after the making of a decision."[66] The Certificate will include: (a) forenames and surnames; (b) date of birth; and (c) gender.[67] Sections 14–16 of the 2015 Act establish procedures for the revocation of a GRC (either at the behest of the Minister[68] or the applicant[69]) and the correction of clerical errors.[70] Where the Minister refuses an application, he or she must offer "reasons for the decision."[71] There is also a requirement to notify the applicant that he or she has a right to appeal to the Circuit Family Court "not later than 90 days, or such longer period as a judge of the court may for good and sufficient reason determine."[72]

Section 10(1)(f)(i) of the 2015 Act (in its current form) requires applicants to offer a statutory declaration that they are "not married or in a civil partnership." Throughout the negotiations, which followed the GRAG report, the 'divorce requirement (as it has come to be known) proved to be a major stumbling block in efforts to find a politically feasible solution.[73] While, in Ireland, as in many other jurisdictions, one spouse's transition often does terminate a marital relationship, there are many Irish couples who have remained intact throughout the transition process. For these individuals, a requirement to divorce creates an impossible choice—compromise marriage and family rights or forgo an accurate legal identity.

Within Ireland's unique constitutional framework, forced divorce gives rise to additional (unforeseen) challenges. Article 41(3)(2)(i) of the Irish Constitution restricts judges to permitting divorces only where they are satisfied that there is "no reasonable prospect of a reconciliation."[74] Thus, where a court is confronted with two individuals—an applicant for gender recognition and their spouse—who remain in a committed union, and who only request a divorce to satisfy statutory

[64] *Ibid.*, s. 8(4).

[65] *Ibid.*, s. 8(5).

[66] *Ibid.*, s. 13(2).

[67] *Ibid.*, s. 13(3)(a)-(c).

[68] Gender Recognition Act 2015, s. 14.

[69] *Ibid.*, s. 15.

[70] *Ibid.*, s. 16.

[71] *Ibid.*, 8(5)(a).

[72] *Ibid.*, ss. 8(5)(b) and 17(1).

[73] Dunne (2014), p. 70. See also Gartland, Fiona. 2014. Singles Clause in Gender Bill is "Forced Divorce". *Irish Times*, 7 August. Https://www.irishtimes.com/news/crime-and-law/singles-clause-in-gender-bill-is-forced-divorce-1.1890389. Accessed 15 Jul 2017.

[74] Constitution of Ireland, art. 41(3)(2)(). In 2019, the Irish public voted to ease the constitutional requirements to access a divorce in Ireland. However, both pre [under art. 41(3)(2)(ii)] and post-referendum [under the current art. 41(3)(2)(i)], the Irish courts can only grant a divorce where they are satisfied that there is no reasonable prospect of a reconciliation between the spouses.

gender recognition procedures, it is clear that the couple are not irreconcilable.[75] In such circumstances, there is an arguable case that a judge, as a matter of constitutional law, cannot grant a legal dissolution. Therefore, compulsory divorce would have been an insurmountable hurdle for some married applicants for legal gender recognition in Ireland.[76]

The rationale behind 'forced' divorce was the perceived need to prevent same-sex marriages.[77] Where different-sex spouses enter a valid, heterosexual union, gender transition would lead to a situation where there are now two individuals, with the same legal sex, who inhabit that legal relationship. Where the Irish population voted 'Yes' in the high-profile 2015 marriage equality referendum—enshrining same-sex marriage rights in art. 41 of the Constitution[78]—any necessity for a divorce requirement would appear to have been removed (i.e. if Bunreacht na hEireann embraces same-sex marriage, there is no need for measures to avoid such unions). However, although the 2015 Act was passed after the referendum, the result of the referendum was still being challenged in the Irish Courts in July 2015.[79] The President had not yet signed the referendum legislation and, therefore, as a matter of constitutional law, same-sex unions remained impermissible. As a result, s. 10(1)(f)(i) was retained in the final draft. However, when the Oireacthas subsequently enacted marriage equality legislation (Marriage Act 2015), s. 24 thereof deleted the obligation that applicants be neither married nor in a civil partnership.

While the 2015 Act does not specifically mention intersex, there does not appear to be any reason why an applicant, who experiences intersex variance and who does not self-identify with his or her birth-assigned gender, cannot apply for a GRC.

4.2 *Persons Aged 16 and 17 Years*

The 2015 Act does make provision for trans minors who are aged between 16 and 17 years. While, as a general rule, gender recognition is limited to adult applicants, the Minister may "consider an application for a gender recognition certificate. . .on behalf of a child who has attained the age of 16 but not 18 years, if furnished with an order of the [Circuit Family] court."[80]

---

[75]Ryan, Fergus. 2012. Ryan on Gender Recognition and Marriage. *Human Rights in Ireland Website*, 19 October. Http://humanrights.ie/international-lawinternational-human-rights/ryan-on-gender-recognition-and-marriage/. Accessed 15 July 2017.

[76]*Ibid.*

[77]Ryan (2004), p. 15.

[78]Constitution of Ireland, art. 41(4).

[79]Carolan, Mary. 2015. A Marriage Referendum Appeals Rejected by the Supreme Court. *Irish Times*, 17 September. Https://www.irishtimes.com/news/crime-and-law/marriage-referendum-appeals-rejected-by-supreme-court-1.2354322. Accessed 15 July 2017.

[80]Gender Recognition Act 2015, s. 12(1).

Under s. 12 of the 2015 Act, the "next friend"[81] of a minor, aged between 16 and 17 years, may apply to the court for an exemption order permitting legal gender recognition. Although the application system for adults is grounded in self-determination, requests involving minors involve a number of additional requirements. First, there is increased medical oversight. Applications must be accompanied by a certificate from "the child's primary treating medical practitioner"[82] which confirms that "the child has attained a sufficient degree of maturity to make the decision to apply for gender recognition",[83] that "the child is aware of, has considered and fully understands the consequences of that decision",[84] that "the child's decision is freely and independently made without duress or undue influence from another person"[85] and that "the child has transitioned or is transitioning into his or her preferred gender."[86] In addition, another "endocrinologist or psychiatrist" must also certify that "his or her medical opinion concurs with the medical opinion" of the primary treating medical practitioner.[87]

Second, there is a requirement for parental or guardian consent. Under s. 12(4)(a), the Circuit Family Court must be "satisfied...[that] the child's parents, surviving parent or guardian consent or consents to the making of the application." Finally, the Court should only grant an exemption order where legal gender recognition promotes the "best interest of the child."[88] The introduction of a mechanism for 16 and 17-year-old minors to obtain gender recognition is a welcome development. It represents progress over both the GRAG Report and early government proposals, which absolutely excluded trans minors. Yet, as the law currently standards, there remains shortfalls.

The compulsory reference to medical officers works both substantively and practically against the interests of minors. To include "primary treating medical practitioner[s]", as well as endocrinologists and psychiatrists, within the youth application process gives rise to a presumption that trans identities are inevitably medicalised. Section 12 is grounded in the belief that, as all trans children medically transition, there is no undue burden in obtaining an opinion from healthcare specialists. Yet, this assumption is both inconsistent with the lived-experience for many young people and also contradicts the basis on which Ireland adopted self-determination. It was only by accepting: (a) that trans identities are not automatically medicalised; (b) that many trans people reject medical interventions; and (c) that medical transitions are distinct from legal recognition that the Irish legislature excluded healthcare professionals from the general recognition regime. If adult

[81]*Ibid.*, s. 12(2).

[82]*Ibid.*, s. 12(4)(b)(i)(I).

[83]*Ibid.*, s. 12(4)(b)(i)(II)(A).

[84]*Ibid.*, s. 12(4)(b)(i)(II)(B).

[85]*Ibid.*, s. 12(4)(b)(i)(II)(C).

[86]*Ibid.*, s. 12(4)(b)(i)(II)(D).

[87]*Ibid.*, s. 12(4)(b)(ii).

[88]*Ibid.*, s. 12(6).

trans identities are not necessarily medicalised, why would children's experiences be any different? The results of the recent National Trans Youth Forum illustrate that many young people do not prioritise medical interventions.[89] There is an irony, therefore, that, although opponents of recognition for minors (and many politicians) often raise the spectre of the premature and inappropriate medicalisation of young trans bodies, it is the Irish legislature (rather than trans advocates) who require minors to enter a medicalised pathway.

Section 12—both in terms of its medical and parental consent obligations—is likely to exclude many (often the most marginalised) trans youth. While the law presumes that trans minors have access to healthcare services and parental support, this does not reflect general trans experiences in Ireland. Indeed, rather than enjoying medical and familial affirmation, trans children often confront a healthcare system which cannot accommodate their needs and familial rejection arising out of fear and gender biases.

Numerous reports have documented the difficulty—for adults and children—of obtaining gender confirming treatments in Ireland.[90] To the extent that legal recognition is contingent upon medical support, there is a significant risk that many young people will reach the age of majority before they can satisfy the s. 12 requirements. Similarly, it is not certain that trans children in Ireland would have the backing of even one (let alone both) parents in expressing their preferred gender.[91] If youth recognition requires two-parent buy-in, this automatically excludes young people who do not enjoy familial support. While s. 12(5) provides for a limited exception to the parental consent requirement, this only applies where parents cannot or should not be approached. It makes no provision for situations where parents are present, where seeking their consent does not prevent a physical risk to the child, but where it is also clear that parents will not accede to their child's request, even though legal recognition promotes the "best interest of the child." In effect, irrespective of the merits of acknowledging a child's preferred gender (including the significant distress, which a legal birth-assigned gender can encourage) parents may, until the age of majority, act as an absolute obstacle to recognition.

Two final critiques of s. 12 arise from the way it employs the "best interest of the child" standard and from its possible exclusion of intersex variance. In negotiations prior to the 2015 Act, advocates promoted 'best interest' reasoning[92] in order to ensure that, even if the law had a presumption against acknowledging trans children, there would be a possibility for legal recognition where it served the best interests of individual children. However, under s. 12(6) of the 2015 Act, the 'best interest' standard can do nothing for young children, who although failing to satisfy the

[89] Dunne and Turraoin (2015), pp. 12–16.

[90] *Ibid.* See also McNeil et al. (2013), pp. 10–11.

[91] Dunne and Turraoin (2015), pp. 14–17.

[92] See e.g. *Advice of the Ombudsman for Children on the General Scheme of the Gender Recognition Bill 2013* (2013). Http://www.teni.ie/attachments/cac06b6d-c2d4-4d81-a8d7-8a29dffa4544.PDF. Accessed 15 July 2017; The Equality Authority of Ireland (2014), pp. 21–27.

statutory requirements (e.g. minimum age, etc.) would still benefit from a GRC. Instead, as the law currently stands, 'best interest' can only be a justification for withholding (rather than extending) youth affirmation. The Circuit Family Court can only issue an exemption order where it is satisfied that legal gender recognition would serve the best interest of 16 and 17-year-old applicants.

In terms of 'intersex variance', requiring that the primary treating medical practitioner certify that a minor applicant "has transitioned or is transitioning" gives rise to practical difficulties. Many persons, who experience intersex, do not have a narrative of 'discovering' their preferred gender.[93] While these individuals may have, at birth, been assigned a legal gender with which they are not connected, they never self-identified with that legal gender. In many cases, their families recognised their preferred gender and allowed the child to develop in accordance with their preferred gender. As such, for these individuals, there is no process of 'transition'. Although obtaining legal gender recognition is beneficial (in many cases vital) for these young people, it would not be possible for the primary treating medical practitioner to offer the necessary certification.[94] In the Draft Heads of the Gender Recognition Bill 2013, the Government had included a similar requirement for adult applicants, but removed it (at least in part) because of the challenges it presented for applicants who experience intersex variance.[95] In those circumstances, it is unclear why the Government did not realise that such a pre-requisite might also exclude intersex youth.

4.3 *Persons Aged Under 16 Years*

The 2015 Act does not permit legal gender recognition for persons under the age of 16 years. In effect, Irish law takes the position that trans children do not exist. This means that: (a) younger trans people cannot obtain state affirmation of their preferred gender; and (b) they will, in many cases, have to interact with state actors using a birth-assigned gender to which they have no connection.[96] The failure to acknowledge trans youth is compounded by the fact that, although the (now closed) Gay and Lesbian Equality Network and the Irish Department of Education has issued guidelines on 'best practice'[97] for trans youth, Irish schools currently have no legal obligation to reasonably accommodate trans primary and secondary school students within their care. In its 2018 report to the Minister for Employment Affairs and Social Protection, the Gender Recognition Act Review Group recommended that

[93]The Equality Authority of Ireland (2014), p. 35.

[94]*Ibid.*

[95]*Ibid.*, 34–36.

[96]Dunne and Turraoin (2015), pp. 18–19.

[97]GLEN (2016).

GRCs should be available to children of all ages—with an emphasis on parental consent, external support and the possibility of revocation.[98]

5 Non-binary Recognition

Ireland does not currently provide a system of non-binary recognition. Under the terms of the 2015 Act, while adult applicants may amend their legal gender through a process of self-determination, they must select either a 'male' or 'female' gender option. Referring to the effects of a GRC, s. 18(1) of the 2015 Act notes that "if the preferred gender is the male gender the person's sex becomes that of a man, and if it is the female gender the person's sex becomes that of a woman." There is no provision for applicants whose preferred gender falls outside the male-female binary. Similarly, as the law currently stands, the Irish State does not issue passport documents with an 'X' gender marker or without gender markers.[99]

While, prior to the enactment of the 2015 Act, non-binary recognition was not a central prioritisation, it has become a much greater feature of public and political debates. This perhaps reflects the sense, both within and outside Ireland's trans community, that non-binary affirmation (in addition to recognition for trans minors) remains an unresolved question arising out of the 2015 Act. It has also been precipitated by growing evidence that significant numbers of trans-identified persons in Ireland now have a gender which does not reproduce male-female norms.[100]

As in other Global North jurisdictions, non-binary identities and the concept of 'gender fluidity' are increasingly evident in various aspects of Irish society. Print media, including Ireland's leading newspapers, now regularly feature stories on gender fluidity and narratives outside 'man' or 'woman'.[101]

Drawing upon experiences and movements in other common law jurisdictions, Transgender Equality Network Ireland (the largest trans advocacy and service provider in Ireland) has, in recent years, increased its calls for non-binary identity

[98] *Review of the Gender Recognition Act 2015 - Report to the Minister for Employment Affairs and Social Protection.* 2015, 86. Http://www.welfare.ie/en/downloads/GRA%20Review%20Report.pdf. Accessed 10 July 2019.

[99] Gender Recognition Act 2015, s. 38.

[100] McNeil et al. (2013), pp. 15, 22 and 34. See generally Dunne and Turraoin (2015).

[101] Cairns, Kay. 2016. As non-binary, someone not strictly a man or a woman, I'm seen as too confusing to discuss. *The Irish Times,* 30 August. Http://www.irishtimes.com/life-and-style/people/as-non-binary-someone-not-strictly-a-man-or-a-woman-i-m-seen-as-too-confusing-to-discuss-1.2772871. Accessed 19 March 2017; McQuillan, Deirdre. 2017. Ireland's first androgynous model: "Defiance boils up within me". *Irish Times*, 22 April 2017. Https://www.irishtimes.com/life-and-style/fashion/ireland-s-first-androgynous-model-defiance-boils-up-within-me-1.3042578. Accessed 15 July 2017; O'Callaghan, Helen. 2015. Gender fluidity: Break free from being identified as male or female. *Irish Examiner*, 3 October. Http://www.irishexaminer.com/lifestyle/features/gender-fluidity-break-free-from-being-identified-as-male-or-female-356787.html. Accessed 15 July 2017.

documentation in Ireland, particularly the introduction of 'X' sex markers.[102] One of the pitfalls of advocating for non-binary communities, however, is the absence of detailed research on non-binary experiences and priorities. While non-binary identities have been included in wider reports, there remains a need for focused data, which considers community demographics and desires. The Gender Recognition Act Review Group has recommended the long-term reform of the 2015 Act in order to accommodate individuals who are neither female nor male. In the immediate future, it has called upon "[g]overnment Departments and other public bodies [to] take any positive steps they can take to improve the position of people who are non-binary."[103]

6 Consequences of Legal Gender Recognition

Under s. 18(1) of the 2015 Act, "where a gender recognition certificate is issued to a person the person's gender shall from the date of that issue become for all purposes the preferred gender." In Ireland, obtaining legal gender recognition means that an individual no longer has their birth-assigned sex and will be acknowledged as having, in law, their preferred gender. All state entities, and private actors which (permissibly) draw distinctions based upon legal gender, must treat the applicant as having the gender stated in the GRC.

There are, however, a number of exceptions under the 2015 Act. Where, prior to gender recognition, an applicant has already acquired rights and obligations as a legal father or mother, obtaining a GRC cannot deprive (or absolve) the applicant of that status.[104] Thus, where, for example, a trans man (who has a female legal sex) gives birth to a child and is formally acknowledged as the child's mother, he will not lose (and cannot renounce) that position merely because he now has a male legal gender. It is unclear in Ireland whether, if a legal male gives birth, he would still obtain the status of mother or whether he would be entitled to be registered according to a different nomenclature, such as father.

Under s. 20(1) of the 2015 Act, obtaining gender recognition does not "affect the disposal or devolution of property under a will (including a codicil) or other instrument executed before" the statute came into effect. Put simply: by amending his or her legal gender, an applicant cannot lose inheritance rights or supplant the inheritance rights of another (e.g. a will that leaves a farm to the oldest son, in circumstances, where the oldest child legally transitions from his assigned female sex).

---

[102] 2017. *Gender Recognition (Amendment) Bill 2017 Passes Second Stage in the Seanad.* TENI Website, 11 May. Http://www.teni.ie/news-post.aspx?contentid=1686. Accessed 15 July 2017.

[103] *Review of the Gender Recognition Act 2015 - Report to the Minister for Employment Affairs and Social Protection* (2015), 97. Http://www.welfare.ie/en/downloads/GRA%20Review%20Report.pdf. Accessed 10 July 2019.

[104] Gender Recognition Act 2015, s. 19.

Section 21(1) states that "[i]n the performance...of functions as a personal representative or trustee, a personal representative or trustee shall not be required to enquire, before conveying or distributing any property, whether a gender recognition certificate has been issued to any person or revoked, if that issue or revocation could affect entitlement to the property." According to sub-section (2), the personal representative or trustee will not be liable to any person for making a conveyance or distribution without such inquiry, provided that there was not "notice of the issue or revocation before the conveyance or distribution."

A particularly interesting (and somewhat controversial) exception to the effects of legal gender recognition are 'gender specific offences'. Section 23(1) provides that, where an individual commits a gender-specific sexual offence, which he or she (in law) could only have committed if he or she had their birth-assigned sex, the fact that the person has legally transitioned will not prevent a conviction for that offence. Where, for example, an accused can only be convicted of penis-vagina rape if he has a male legal sex, a trans woman, who commits that offence, cannot use her GRC as a defence. Similarly, where an accused commits an offence, which may only be perpetrated against women, the accused will not escape criminal liability because the victim has been affirmed as a legal male.

In many respects, s. 23 presents lawmakers with a complicated dilemma. On the one hand, it is welcome that the Oireacthas would close a potential loophole in the criminal justice system, and prevent applicants from using gender recognition to avoid appropriate liability. Where a trans woman commits a rape offence, she should (like male offenders) be sanctioned. It would be wrong if the 2015 Act became a defence to serious sexual offences. However, on the other hand, one must consider the mind-frame of potential victims. While many trans men, who experience gender specific offences, may desire conviction for their attacker, others may worry about the symbolic impact of what that prosecution means. To the extent that s. 23 prevents defendants from hiding behind a GRC, it also requires that trans victims be (perhaps involuntarily) drawn out from their preferred gender. Where a trans man is the victim of a gender specific offence, prosecuting his attacker implies, even for the limited purposes of the criminal law, that the man actually has a female identity. Some trans men may object to a criminal process, which (in their eyes) delegitimises their masculinity. This will particularly be the case if the man is required to give evidence as the victim of a crime that can only be committed against women.

7 Relationship Between Gay/Lesbian/Bisexual and Trans Rights

As with trans rights (but to a lesser extent), advancements for gay, lesbian and bisexual persons are a relatively recent development in Irish law. It was not until 1993, following the ECtHR judgment in *Norris v Ireland,*[105] that the Irish legislature

[105] [1986] 8 EHRR CD75.

decriminalised consensual sexual intercourse between two legal males.[106] In 2021, however, Ireland's LGB community enjoy relatively broad protections as compared with peer communities across the Council of Europe.[107]

Under the Civil Partnership and Certain Rights and Obligations of Cohabitants Act 2010, Ireland created a legal institution ("civil partnership") for same-sex relationships.[108] While, the 2010 Act did not provide for joint or second parent adoption rights, these entitlements were subsequently extended through the Children and Family Relationships Act 2015. In May 2015, Ireland became the first country in the world to adopt marriage equality by popular vote.[109] The proposal to permit 'gay' marital unions was supported by 62% of votes cast.

Gay, lesbian and bisexual persons are expressly acknowledged within Ireland's equality frameworks. The 1998 Act and the 2000 Act both include a "sexual orientation ground".[110] With limited exceptions, individuals cannot be treated unfavourably in employment or the provision of services because they are not heterosexual (or, indeed, because they are heterosexual). As originally enacted, s. 37 of the 1998 Act appeared to allow religious institutions—particularly schools and hospitals—to discriminate against employees, by possibly denying promotion or even terminating work contracts, because employees were gay, lesbian or bisexual. The justification was that institutions with a religious ethos, usually catholic, were entitled to guard against employee conduct which would undermine that ethos. In the years following the 1998 Act, s. 37 had a highly-publicised "chill factor"[111] whereby state-employed teachers, doctors and nurses were required to conceal their sexual orientation for fear of negative impacts upon their career. However, as part of the Equality (Miscellaneous Provisions) Act 2015, the Oireacthas has now clarified that publicly-funded educational and medical institutions cannot, irrespective of ethos, discriminate merely because an employee is LGB.[112] Instead, unfavourable treatment can only arise if employees are actually engaging in conduct which undermines an ethos.[113]

It is difficult to accurately gauge the relationship between trans and wider LGB advocacy, particularly the extent to which advances for sexual orientation rights have precipitated gender identity reform. In some instances, the introduction of LGB

---

[106]Criminal Law (Sexual Offences) Act 1993.

[107]Rainbow Europe Index 2017. *ILGA-Europe Website*, 17 May. Https://www.ilga-europe.org/resources/rainbow-europe/rainbow-europe-2017. Accessed 15 July 2017.

[108]Civil Partnership and Certain Rights and Obligations of Cohabitants Act 2010, ss. 3–5.

[109]See generally Tobin (2016), p. 115.

[110]Employment Equality Act 1998, s. 6(2)(d); Equal Status Act 2000, s. 3(2)(d).

[111]O'Brien, Carl. 2015. Gay Teachers Say that Law Change Removes "Chill Factor" on Sexuality. *Irish Times*, 3 December. Https://www.irishtimes.com/news/education/gay-teachers-say-law-change-removes-chill-factor-on-sexuality-1.2453556. Accessed 15 July 2017. See also O'Donovan, Darren and Mullally, Siobhan. 2011. Religion in Ireland's "public squares": education, the family and expanding equality claims'. *Public Law* 284.

[112]Equality (Miscellaneous Provisions) Act 2015, s. 11(b).

[113]*Ibid.*, s. 11(b).

rights initiatives has had a direct impact on trans communities. This can be seen both practically and symbolically in the wake of the marriage equality referendum. At a symbolic and political level, there is no doubt that the widespread public support for 'gay' marriage expressed both during the referendum campaign, and in the large 'Yes' victory, emboldened the Fine-Gael/Labour Coalition Government to include a self-determination model within the 2015 Act. Had the Government lost the referendum, or if there had been more overt public hostility toward LGB rights, it is unlikely that the parliament would have adopted the 2015 Act in its current form. From a practical perspective, as already noted, the passage of marriage equality legislation in 2015 expressly removed the statutory requirement that, in order to obtain gender recognition, spouses would have to dissolve their marital union. Indeed, the first same-sex married couples in Ireland were not cisgender persons who contracted a new union. Rather, they were trans persons, and their existing spouses, who accessed a GRC without having to divorce.

In the area of children's rights, there has also been considerable overlap between sexual orientation and gender identity advocacy. This is perhaps unsurprising as many young Irish people increasingly express identities which incorporate fluid understandings of gender and sexuality, and where labels such as gay, lesbian and trans are less important than individualised experiences and narratives.[114] BeLonGTo Youth Services[115]—an internationally recognised leader in service provision for queer youth—has played a leading role. BeLonGTo has always prioritised recognition and affirmation for trans-identified children, and it has incorporated trans voices into its wider youth projects.[116]

Yet, in many respects (as in other countries), there has been (and remains) an unequal advancement for Irish trans rights as compared with peer LGB-protections. While, in many respects, this inequality is tangibly legal, it is also fundamentally symbolic. While gay people, and their right to engage in consensual sexual activities, were finally acknowledged in 1993, it was not until 22 years later that Irish law recognised that trans people exist. Sexual orientation is now an explicitly protected ground under Ireland's equality framework. However, trans people are not mentioned in either the 1998 Act or the 2000 Act. More complicated gender identities, such non-binary and agender, may not come within the implicit guarantees which the 'gender ground' offers, particularly where those guarantees arise from the idea of "gender reassignment" in European Union law.

During the marriage equality referendum, numerous political actors and civil society advocates emphasised the impact that marriage equality would have upon

[114]See generally Dunne and Turraoin (2015).

[115]'What is BeLongTo'. *BeLongTo Youth Services, No Date Available.* Http://www.belongto.org/about.aspx?contentid=104. Accessed 15 July 2017. See also United Nations High Commissioner for Human Rights (UN HCHR). 2011. *Discriminatory laws and practices and acts of violence against individuals based on their sexual orientation and gender identity.* 17 November 2011 UN Doc No. A/HRC/19/41, [138].

[116]*IndividualiTy BeLongTo. BeLongTo Youth Services, No Date Available.* Http://www.belongto.org/group.aspx?sectionid=80. Accessed 15 July 2017.

younger generations.[117] For LGB teenagers, discovering their sexuality, it would be extremely empowering to realise that a majority of their citizens affirm and celebrate non-heterosexual identities. Yet, at almost the exact same time, the Government was consciously excluding trans youth from the 2015 Act. While LGB children were being encouraged to embrace their identity, trans youth heard the message that their identities did not (and could not) legally exist. The symbolism of these differentiated priorities is reflected in trans perceptions of their place within Irish culture. A striking feature of the National Trans Youth Forum Report was the extent to which, even among young people, there remains a sense that trans persons are second class citizens within Ireland's wider LGBT communities.[118]

References

Bell M (1995) Shifting conceptions of sexual discrimination at the Court of Justice: from P v S to Grant v SWT. Eur Law J 5(1):63

Brady A (2012) The constitution, gender and reform: improving the position of women in the constitution. National Women's Council of Ireland

Campbell A, Lardy H (1996) Discrimination against transsexuals in employment. Eur Law Rev 21 (5):412

Dunne P (2014) Divorce in the Gender Recognition Bill 2013. Irish Law Times 32(5):70

Dunne P, Turraoin C (2015) "It's Time to Hear Our Voices": National Trans Youth Forum Report 2015. TENI

Farrell M (2012) Briefing note on Lydia Foy case & transgender issues in Ireland. FLAC. Https://www.flac.ie/download/pdf/foy_case_briefing_oct_2012.pdf. Accessed 15 July 2017

Farrell M (2013) Lydia Foy's 20 year battle for legal recognition. In: O'Sullivan O (ed) Equality and identity: transgender and intersex experience in Ireland. TENI, pp 16–17

GLEN (2016) "Being LGBT in School" a resource for post-primary schools to prevent homophobic and transphobic bullying and support LGBT students. GLEN and DOE. Https://www.education.ie/en/Publications/Education-Reports/Being-LGBT-in-School.pdf. Accessed 15 July 2017

McNeil J et al (2013) Speaking from the margins: trans mental health and wellbeing in Ireland. TENI, pp 10–11

McNeil J et al (2014) Speaking from the margins: trans mental health and wellbeing in Ireland. TENI, pp 15, 22 and 34

Moynihan Y (2008) "God has given you one face and you give yourself another": the implications of transsexual recognition in matters of marriage: Dr Lydia Foy's laudable victory spawns reform in terms of same-sex unions'. Irish J Fam Law 11(2):38

Ni Mhuirthile T (2013) Afterword. In: O'Sullivan O (ed) Equality and identity: transgender and intersex experience in Ireland. TENI, p 121

[117]*"Why My Family is Voting YES" Former President Mary McAleese calls on families across Ireland to vote YES'*. BeLongTo Website. Http://www.belongto.org/attachments/250_Press_Release.pdf. Accessed 15 July 2017; *ISPCC confirms its support for a Yes Vote in the Marriage Equality Referendum*. 2015. Irish Society for the Prevention of Cruelty to Children Website, 9 April. Https://www.ispcc.ie/news-media/past-press-releases/press-releases-2015/ispcc-confirms-its-support-for-a-yes-vote-in-the-marriage-equality-referendum/12758. Accessed 15 July 2017.

[118]Dunne and Turraoin (2015), pp. 10–11.

Ryan F (2004) Marriage at the boundaries of gender: the "transsexual dilemma" resolved? Irish J Fam Law 7(1):15
The Equality Authority of Ireland (2014) Observations on the Revised General Scheme of the Gender Recognition Bill 2014. Walsh Printers, pp 21–27
Tobin B (2016) Marriage equality in Ireland: the politico-legal context. Int J Law Policy Fam 30 (2):115

The Civil Status of Trans Persons in Norwegian Law

Andrea Vige Grønningsæter and Lars Arnesen

Abstract In 2016, the Act on Change of Legal Gender came into force in Norway, giving all residents the right to change their legal gender based on self-declaration and putting an end to the previous administrative practice, which required transgender people to undergo irreversible sterilization to change their gender status. The main purpose of the Act was thus to ensure respect of trans person's human rights and to recognize individual experiences of gender identity. At the same time, the change has broader implications for how gender is understood as a legal category. In this chapter we provide a description of what the new rules regulating change of gender status in Norway entail. Moreover, the chapter looks at the legal implications of gender in various fields of law, including anti-discrimination law and laws on affirmative action. A main finding in our analysis is that while the new regulation has been successful in ensuring legal recognition of people's gender identity, it does not address potential challenges that arise due to binary divisions between men and women (and implicit understandings of these terms as being grounded in biological and physical differences).

Prior to 2016, it was not possible to change legal gender in Norway without being diagnosed with the condition F 64.0 (transsexualism) and undergoing a comprehensive medical gender reassignment programme that included irreversible sterilisation.[1] Patients who discontinued their medical treatment before the

[1] The practice is described in detail by the expert panel's 2015 report. An English summary may be found at pages 172–178 of the report. https://www.regjeringen.no/contentassets/d3a092a312624f8e88e63120bf886e1a/rapport_juridisk_kjonn_100415.pdf. Accessed 15 July 2020.

A. V. Grønningsæter (✉)
Faculty of Law, University of Bergen, Bergen, Norway
e-mail: andrea.gronningseter@uib.no

L. Arnesen
Faculty of Law, University of Oslo, Oslo, Norway

I. C. Jaramillo, L. Carlson (eds.), *Trans Rights and Wrongs*, Ius Comparatum - Global Studies in Comparative Law 54,
https://doi.org/10.1007/978-3-030-68494-5_22

sterilisation procedure were denied change of legal gender, even if they had completed all other parts of the treatment programme.[2] The Norwegian Government accepted change of legal gender in the public records upon receipt of confirmation by the gender reassignment clinic (there is only one in Norway) that full and irreversible gender reassignment had been completed. This practice was not regulated by legislation and was subject to very little parliamentary debate or public scrutiny.[3]

The practice of requiring that a change of legal gender be contingent on irreversible sterilisation was thus little known in Norway until it was first reported on by the Council of Europe's Commissioner for Human Rights in 2009.[4] Significantly, the very first action plan designed to improve the situation for trans persons in Norway, covering the period from 2009 to 2012, was silent on the issues of gender reassignment surgery and change of legal gender.[5] Due to increased attention from national human rights organisations and NGOs concerning the topic of forced sterilisation of trans persons in the years following the Commissioner's report, the Norwegian government decided to set up an expert panel in 2013 to evaluate the situation of trans persons in Norway.[6] The expert panel submitted their final report in 2015. One of the key recommendations made by the expert panel was that the act of changing legal gender should be made subject to self-declaration.[7] The government

[2]In March 2014, an application for change of legal gender was rejected because the applicant had not successfully completed gender reassignment surgery, including sterilization. The applicant filed a complaint to the Anti-Discrimination Ombud, which concluded that the practice of rejecting change of legal gender violated the Act on Anti-Discrimination based on sexual orientation, gender identity and gender expression (decision 14/840). Despite the Ombud's decision, the registration authorities did not change the applicant's legal gender until the Legal Gender Act was enacted on 1 June 2016. The Ombud's decision is available in Norwegian. Https://www.ldo.no/nyheiter-og-fag/klagesaker/2014/18840-diskriminering-pa-grunn-av-kjonnsidentitet. Accessed 15 July 2020.

[3]The Norwegian Ministry of Health. 10 April 2015. Rett til kjønn - helse til alle kjønn. Regjeringen. no., p. I. https://www.regjeringen.no/contentassets/d3a092a312624f8e88e63120bf886e1a/rapport_juridisk_kjonn_100415.pdf. Accessed 10 February 2015, pp. 63–68. The only traceable evidence of parliamentary debate is one proposal made by the parliament member Olav Gunnar Ballo from the Socialist Party in December 2000, which asked the Government to implement legislative measures to safeguard the rights of transsexuals (the proposal did not detail any suggestions in terms of requirements for change of legal gender), c.f. Norwegian Parliament (Stortinget) (19 December, 2000). The Government responded that the rights of transsexuals where adequately protected in the already existing body of health legislation, c.f. Norwegian Parliament (Stortinget) (12 January, 2004).

[4]Council of Europe - Commissioner for Human Rights. 29 July 2009. Human Rights and Gender Identity, p. 7. Https://rm.coe.int/16806da753. Accessed on 10 February 2019.

[5]The Ministry of Children and Gender Equality. 25 June 2008. Bedre livskvalitet for lesbiske, homofile, bifile og transpersoner 2009–2012. Https://www.regjeringen.no/globalassets/upload/bld/handlingsplaner/hpl_lhbt_september_2008.pdf. Accessed 10 February 2019.

[6]See note 2, p. 1.

[7]See note 2, pp. 105–106.

followed up on this recommendation by introducing the Change of Legal Gender Act in 2016.[8]

Although one of the main purposes of this Act was to remove the sterilisation requirement, the question of whether the previous practice had violated the human rights of trans persons was not addressed by the government. In 2018, two lawsuits were brought against the government concerning the previous regulation of change of legal gender.[9] The first case concerned a trans person who had been unable to change her legal gender until 2016 because she had not undergone irreversible sterilisation. The second case concerned a trans person who had felt compelled to undergo irreversible sterilisation in order to be able to change his gender status. In the first case, the District Court of Oslo[10] concluded that the refusal to allow the plaintiff to change her legal gender without undergoing gender reassignment surgery constituted unlawful discrimination in violation with the Norwegian anti-discrimination legislation.[11] However, the District Court found in favour of the state in both cases, concluding that the previous requirements for change of legal gender had not violated the human rights of either of the plaintiffs. Both judgments have been appealed to the Court of Appeal.

Change of names in the Population Register was significantly liberalised by the introduction in 2002 of the Personal Names Act.[12] The provisions of the Act do not include any rights or limitations for trans persons as regards changing personal names. However, the government issued a guidance notice specifying that trans persons are to be entitled to change their name to one typically associated with the opposite sex, even if they have not undergone gender reassignment surgery.[13] Name change procedures have consequently been available to trans persons ever since 2002, while on the other hand, trans persons were denied the right to change their legal gender without undergoing irreversible sterilisation until the enactment of the Change of Legal Gender Act on 1 July, 2016.

The expert panel offered a number of additional recommendations that have not been acted upon as of yet. The most important of these was that there should be

[8]In Norwegian: Lov om endring av juridisk kjønn (LOV-2016-06-17-46). Available in electronic format on the Lovdata platform (lovdata.no).

[9]The judgments are currently not published but may be obtained from the Oslo District Court.

[10]The District Court is the first instance in the Norwegian court system. Judgments from the District Court (tingretten) may be appealed to the Appellate Court (lagmannsretten). A small number of cases from the Appellate Court are granted leave to appeal by the Supreme Court.

[11]Nonetheless, the Court concluded that the plaintiff was not entitled to compensation for non-economic loss due to the discrimination. The judgment pointed to the fact that a requirement for granting compensation of non-economic loss is that the person who has committed the discriminatory act can be blamed for doing so. The Court concluded that the employees of the Norwegian Tax Administration could not be blamed for refusing the request to change legal gender in line with the requirements imposed by the administration practice at the time.

[12]In Norwegian: Navneloven (LOV-2002-06-07-19). The Act may be retrieved electronically on the Lovdata platform (lovdata.no).

[13]Guidance note (G-2002-20). The guidance notice is still in force and available on the Lovdata platform (lovdata.no).

further assessment of the implications of legal gender in various areas of society where legal gender is used in connection with affirmative action initiatives.[14] Norway has, for instance, rules on gender equality in the boardrooms of public companies and "gender points" for students applying to educational programmes where one gender is clearly underrepresented.[15] Under current regulations, the gender quota rules are based on the legal gender which appears in the Population Register, that is, the gender status which may be changed by self-declaration.[16]

The adoption of the Change of Legal Gender Act in 2016, together, perhaps, with the lack of further assessment of the implications of legal gender in other areas of law, has resulted in numerous editorials in the Norwegian press on the topic of legal gender and the situation of trans persons in Norway. In particular, the Change of Legal Gender Act has been criticised for undermining the interests of women, as the status of "woman" may now be claimed by means of self-declaration by persons seeking to circumvent rules on affirmative action for women, or by men who wish to gain access to women-only spaces, such as public changing rooms or shelters.[17]

The expert panel also recommended further consideration of the introduction of a third legal gender.[18] The recognition of a third legal gender has been proposed by various political parties, but was most recently rejected by the Norwegian Parliament in 2017.[19] So far, the Norwegian Government has no specific plans to follow up on any of the recommendations offered in the 2015 expert panel's report.

This Chapter covers the following topics: In the next section, we provide an account of how gender and name are recorded in the Norwegian Population Register. We thereafter describe how the data subject may change gender and name in the Population Register upon request. The legal implications of gender in various field of law, including anti-discrimination law and laws on affirmative action in relation to gender equality initiatives are then explored. A brief account of the criticisms levelled at the current act is given, both by those in favour of liberalising the procedures for changing personal name and gender, and those who would like to move back to more restrictive regulation. Lastly, we suggest some possible improvements to the current legislation.

---

[14]The Norwegian Ministry of Health (April 2015), p. I.

[15]Sections 7–9 of the regulation on admission to tertiary education programmes (FOR-2017-01-06-13).

[16]Section 6 of the Change of Legal Gender Act.

[17]In Norwegian newspaper editorials. See, for instance, editorials by Tonje Gjevjon published electronically on dagbladet.no (Available in Norwegian).

[18]The Norwegian Ministry of Health (April 2015), report by the expert panel, p. 121.

[19]Norwegian Parliament (Stortinget) (7 March, 2017). The proposal was rejected, with 9 votes in favour and 93 against. A record of the vote may be accessed at: https://www.stortinget.no/no/Saker-og-publikasjoner/Saker/Sak/Voteringsoversikt/?p=65994&dnid=1. Accessed 15 July 2020.

1 The Registration of Gender and Name

The Population Register Act states that legal gender, name and a number of other personal data *may* be recorded in the Norwegian Population Register for all persons born in Norway or residing in Norway for more than six months.[20] Legal gender and name will thus be entered in the Population Register at the discretion of the registration authorities. There is no formal duty, nor right to be registered with a legal gender or name in the Population Register. However, in accordance with the Personal Names Act, all residents in Norway are obligated to have a given name and a surname which must be used as an official personal name. Moreover, when a child is born the person(s) with parental responsibility are required to notify the authorities of the child's name within six months after the birth.[21]

Although there is no formal requirement for legal gender or name to be entered in the Population Register, it is established administrative practice for both of these to be registered. Persons born in Norway or residing in the country for more than six months are required to have a personal identification number.[22] This number contains eleven digits. The ninth digit indicates the gender of the person; an even number indicates "female", while an odd number indicates "male".[23] The registration authorities therefore need to know the legal gender in order to issue a mandatory personal identification number. Furthermore, all persons over the age of 15 who reside in Norway, either temporarily or on a permanent basis, are required to provide the registration authorities with personal data, including name and gender upon request from the authorities.[24]

Norwegian citizens have the right to a passport upon request to the issuing authorities.[25] The personal data to be recorded in the passport is not specified in Norwegian law, but is decided at the discretion of the issuing authority (organised under local police offices). The issuing authority determines the personal data to be recorded in the passport, based on the guidelines provided by the International Civil Aviation Organization (ICAO).[26] All data must be checked against the data registered in the Population Register. Hence, to the extent name and gender are recorded in the passport, this will be on the basis of the legal gender registered in the

[20]Articles 2-1 and 4-1 of the Population Register Act. In Norwegian: folkeregisterloven (LOV-2016-12-09-88). The act may be retrieved electronically from the Lovdata platform (lovdata.no).

[21]See Sect. 2.2 of this chapter.

[22]Ibid.

[23]Section 2-2-1 of the regulation accompanying the Population Register Act. In Norwegian: folkeregisterforskriften (FOR-2017-07-14-1201). The regulation may be retrieved electronically from the Lovdata platform (lovdata.no).

[24]Section 11-1 of the Population Register Act.

[25]Section 1 of the Passport Act. In Norwegian: Lov om Pass (LOV-1997-06-19-82).

[26]The Norwegian Ministry of Justice and Public Security. (13 March 2015). Prop. 66 L (2014-2015), p. 10. Https://www.regjeringen.no/contentassets/70cdf1d7444a466ebffb18bef32ee3d1/no/pdfs/prp201420150066000dddpdfs.pdf, Accessed on 10 February 2019.

Population Register.[27] The ICAO requires name to be registered in the passport, but not gender.[28] At present, the Norwegian issuing authority has chosen to record both name and gender, and so far, to our knowledge, there has been no discussion about amending the Norwegian passport guidelines.

Although Norwegian citizens have the right to apply for a passport, they have no duty to have one. Currently there are no alternative governmental ID-card schemes apart from passports.[29] The government is currently working on an alternative ID-card scheme, but at the time of writing it is still uncertain when it will be rolled out.[30] According to the proposed ID-card Act, the card will only record personal data that is regarded as "necessary" for proper identification.[31] The working group has included gender in the list of personal data regarded as "necessary" for the ID-card, alongside name, citizenship, personal identification number and various other personal data.[32]

To sum up, although name and gender are not required by law to be registered in the Population Register, they are nevertheless widely registered by the authorities. Legal gender recorded in the Population Register is needed to issue mandatory national identification numbers, which by law must contain a gender-based ninth digit (even numbers indicating "female" and odd numbers "male"). The government is currently reviewing the national identification number system, which may render the gender-based ninth digit obsolete.[33] It remains to be seen whether the registration authorities will continue to register gender if gender is no longer needed to issue mandatory national identification numbers.

[27] Section 7 of the regulation accompanying the Passport Act. In Norwegian: passforskriften (FOR-1999-12-09-1263).

[28] International Civil Aviation Organization (ICAO). (2015). Doc 9303 - Machine Readable Travel Documents, p. 14. Https://www.icao.int/publications/Documents/9303_p4_cons_en.pdf. Accessed 10 February 2019.

[29] The Norwegian government started issuing national ID-cards on 30 November 2020, after this chapter was written. Gender is included among the information given on these ID-cards.

[30] The ID-Cards Act has been adopted but is not yet in force. In Norwegian: Lov om ID-kort (LOV-2015-06-05-39).

[31] Section 6 of the ID-Cards Act.

[32] The Norwegian Ministry of Justice and Public Security (Prop. 66 L (2014-2015)), p. 34.

[33] In a Ministry of Finance consultation memorandum, the government proposes that the new national identification number system should be gender-neutral. The proposal is currently under consideration. Regardless of which solution is chosen, the new system will most likely only affect persons who are issued with a national identification number after 2032. The consultation memorandum may be accessed in Norwegian. Https://www.regjeringen.no/contentassets/c7cc56174c6645349b847c0614119e8b/h_notat_ene_personidentifikator.pdf. Accessed 15 July 2020.

1.1 *First-Time Recording of Gender in the Population Register*

There are no procedural rules set down at law on when or how the legal gender of children born in Norway should be reported to the registration authorities. Legal gender is usually reported by either the medical staff at the hospital, or by the parents themselves, for example if the child is born at home or otherwise without the assistance of medical personnel. In the case of foreign-born residents, legal gender is registered on the basis of the identity documents they present to the registration authorities.

The registration authorities must check that the data provided to them are correct before they are entered in the Population Register.[34] All persons registered in the Population Register have the right to request correction under Article 16 of the General Data Protection Act (GDPR).[35] The data in the Population Register must be corrected if there has been an "obvious" registration error or if the documentation the data is based upon proves to be incorrect.[36] The Act does not define what the registered gender should be based upon, for instance if it should be based on physical appearance, sexual organs or the self-reported gender identity of the data subject. There is thus no guidance as to how a request for correction should be handled by the registration authorities if, for example, the parents disagree with the legal gender assigned to their child by the hospital staff at birth. See Sect. 3.2 below for more details on the procedures for changing children's legal gender.

For foreign-born children, the registration authorities require the birth certificate to record gender and other personal data. Depending on the country the child is born in, the authorities may require additional proof, e.g. confirmation from the Norwegian embassy or a Norwegian representative in the country where the child is presumed to have been born.

1.2 *First-Time Recording of a Name in the Population Register*

Everyone subject to Norwegian law is required to have a name, regardless of whether they are staying in the country temporarily or on a permanent basis.[37] Parents of children born in Norway are required to report the name to the authorities

[34] Section 8-1 of the Population Register Act.

[35] Regulation (EU) 2016/679 incorporated in the Norwegian Personal Data Act enacted on July 20, 2018.

[36] Section 9-2 of the Population Register Act.

[37] Section 1 of the Personal Names Act. In Norwegian: navneloven (LOV-2002-06-07-19).

within six months of the child's birth.[38] If no surname is notified by the six-month deadline, the child will be given the mother's surname. There are no specific rules on whether the parents or legal guardian may request correction of the child's name if they failed to meet the initial six-month deadline for reporting the name to the registration authorities. Personal names may be changed, though a request to change a personal name is subject to age limitations, see further below.

For foreign-born children, the registration authorities will require a birth certificate in order to record the name and other personal data about the child, as described above. There are no specific procedural requirements for adult foreigners residing in Norway. In order to be a legal resident in Norway, a foreigner must have presented travel documents upon entering the country. The name of the foreigner will presumably be based on the name recorded in the travel documents.

2 Change of Legal Gender in the Population Register

Prior to 2016 the legal gender recorded in the Population Register could only be changed upon confirmation of full gender reassignment treatment from the National Treatment Centre for Transsexualism (NTCT).[39] Requests for change of legal gender from individuals who had cancelled their treatment at NTCT before completing the gender-reassignment procedure, including irreversibly sterilisation, were automatically rejected.[40] Following the 2016 Change of Legal Gender Act, the registration authorities started to accept requests for change of gender status based on self-declaration.

In accordance with the Change of Legal Gender Act, persons who identify as the other gender than the one they are registered as in the Population Register are entitled to change their gender status.[41] The right to change legal gender is thus based on the person's subjective experience of their gender and is not dependent on medical diagnosis, gender reassignment surgery or other documentation substantiating their gender identity. To change their legal gender, a person must contact the Norwegian Tax Administration and declare that they want to change their gender status. A leaflet containing information about the consequences of changing legal gender is then sent to the person's home address. After receiving the information, the person has to send a signed return slip, confirming that the declaration is upheld.[42]

---

[38]Section 2 of the Personal Names Act.

[39]In Norwegian: Nasjonal behandlingstjeneste for transseksualisme (NBTS).

[40]Treatment at the NTCT is dependent on the patient being diagnosed with the condition F.64.0 (transsexualism). Consequently, individuals who were not considered to fulfil the diagnostic requirements of this condition would also be unable to change their legal gender prior to 2016, since they would not be able to access gender reassignment treatment.

[41]Section 2 of the Change of Legal Gender Act.

[42]The Norwegian Ministry of Health. (18 March 2016). Prop.74 L (2015–2016) Lov om endring av juridisk kjønn, p. 36. Https://www.regjeringen.no/contentassets/3e554a9086cb431ab101efeea3f58df1/no/pdfs/prp201520160074000dddpdfs.pdf. Accessed on 10 February 2019.

During the legislative process of the Change of Legal Gender Act, it was considered whether a mandatory "reflection period" should be imposed before the application to change gender status could be approved.[43] The aim of such a period would be to prevent impulsive applications from being made and to give persons time to consider the consequences that a change of gender status would entail. In the preparatory works of the Act, however, the need for a reflection period was rejected, as it was argued that there is reason to believe that most persons who apply to change their legal gender have already given the implications of such a change due consideration. It was also stated that, for persons who have spent a lot of time considering their choice, imposing a further reflection period may be perceived as mistrust.[44]

Change of legal gender is formally only open to persons who "perceive themselves to belong to the opposite sex".[45] Hence, in principle it is not available to persons with other motives. For example, it is not permitted to change one's legal gender merely to obtain economic advantages or positions that are only available to the opposite sex. However, it is evidently impossible to monitor the motives of those who request to change their legal gender, as the criteria for changing legal gender are entirely based on the person's own feeling of belonging to the opposite sex. Accordingly, it has been argued that the system could be open to abuse, for example by men who want to obtain a seat on a board or a place in an academic programme reserved for the opposite sex. There are no limitations on how many times a person may change their legal gender.[46] Thus a man without any feelings of belonging to the opposite sex could change his legal gender to get access to a seat on a board reserved for women, and thereafter change back to his original legal gender, once the position had been secured. The system of changing legal gender on the basis of self-declaration has therefore been viewed with scepticism by some legal scholars and social commentators in the Norwegian press, as discussed further below.

2.1 Change of Legal Gender for Children and Persons Under Guardianship

The act of changing legal gender requires in principle that the applicant have legal capacity. However, the Change of Legal Gender Act makes an explicit exception from the requirement for legal capacity for persons who are legally incapacitated. Persons who are placed under guardianship are entitled to change their legal gender on their own initiative and the change is not dependent on the consent of their guardian.[47] This is due to the fact that the right to change one's gender status has

---

[43] See the expert panel's report, pp. 108–109.

[44] The Norwegian Ministry of Health (Prop. 74. L (2015-2016)), p. 20.

[45] Section 2 of the Change of Legal Gender Act.

[46] The Norwegian Ministry of Health (Prop. 74. L (2015-2016)), p. 31.

[47] Section 3 of the Change of Legal Gender Act.

been recognised as an area where it is of particular importance to protect the individual's right to self-determination.[48]

Persons under the age of 18 are regarded as minors under Norwegian law. Minors do not have legal capacity unless a clear legal exception has been made. The Change of Legal Gender Act includes a number of exceptions to enable minors to request change of legal gender.[49] The Act divide minors into three age groups:

- Minors above the age of sixteen years old
- Minors between the ages of six and sixteen years old
- Minors under the age of six years old

Children who have turned sixteen years of age are entitled to request change of legal gender without parental consent. This is the age at which children in Norway have legal capacity to consent to medical treatment. The Act thus provides children of sixteen years of age and over the same right to request change of legal gender as adults.

Children between the ages of six and sixteen years old may request a change of legal gender together with a parent or legal guardian. Where parents have joint parental responsibility for the child, the application may be accepted if it is considered to be in the best interest of the child, even if one of the parents is opposed to the application. When considering the best interest of the child, the Norwegian Constitution[50] and the Children's Act[51] state that the opinion of the child is to be weighed in accordance with their age and maturity when decisions regarding the child's personal situation is made. Consequently, children who are between six and sixteen years old must obtain consent from at least one of their parents to be able to change their gender status.

It is not possible for children under the age of six years old to change legal gender on the basis of self-declaration, even if the parents or legal guardian consent to the change. Change of legal gender for children below the age of six is subject to medical criteria alone: the child may be re-registered as the opposite sex if the child shows atypical gender characteristics, i.e. intersex conditions. However, the Act only offers two gender categories, meaning that the child must be registered as either female or male. The child's parents or legal guardians may submit an application to change the child's gender status, but such an application is only granted where documentation of the child's medical condition is provided by health personnel. It is also a condition that children who are mature enough to form their own opinion regarding the change are heard before a decision is made.

Consequently, for children below the age of six the general rule that change of legal gender is not dependent on medical assessments does not apply. During the

---

[48]The Norwegian Ministry of Health (Prop. 74. L (2015-2016)), pp. 28–29.

[49]These exceptions are regulated in Section 4 of the Change of Legal Gender Act.

[50]Article 104 of the Constitution concerns the right of children to be heard in matters concerning their own well-being.

[51]Section 31 of the Children's Act. In Norwegian: Barnelova (LOV-1981-04-08-7).

legislative process of the Change of Legal Gender Act, several actors criticised this, pointing to the fact that a central purpose of the Act was to give a right to change legal gender based on the person's individual experience of their gender identity rather than medical assessments. However, the Ministry of Health stated that the requirement to document an atypical gender development was intended to protect the youngest children, since children under the age of six were generally not considered to be mature enough to understand the consequences of changing legal gender.[52]

2.2 *Change of Personal Name*

Anyone over the age of sixteen years may apply to change their name by applying to the authority responsible for personal names. The application may be rejected if the authority deems the new name to be of "substantial disadvantage" to the applicant or if there are other "serious grounds" for rejecting the application.[53] The application could, for instance, be rejected if the applicant requests a name which violates public decency, for example a swear word or something that most persons would find offensive. Significantly, the government issued a guidance notice in 2002 on the interpretation of the Personal Names Act. It determines that parents may not choose a "boy's name" for a girl and vice versa. However, the guidance note makes an exception to the general rule regarding gendered names where the person in question is "in the process of changing their gender" or if the person has a "transgendered identity", regardless of whether the applicant is undergoing gender reassignment surgery. The guidance notice is still in force.[54]

In cases where an application to change a registered name concerns a child under the age of sixteen years old, the application must be made by the child's parents or guardians. As a general rule, both parents must consent to the change: otherwise the application should be rejected. However, if the child in question has changed gender status in accordance with the Change of Legal Gender Act, it is sufficient for one of the parents to consent to the change.[55] This exception was introduced at the same time as the Change of Legal Gender Act to ensure that children who have been allowed to change their gender status cannot be blocked from also changing their names if one parent does not support their new gender status.

A person's name may usually only be changed once every 10 years. Change of legal gender is not subject to any such limitation. During the legislative process of the Change of Legal Gender Act it was therefore considered whether an exception to the ten-year limit on changing personal names was needed in cases where a person changes their gender status more than once. However, the ten-year limit does not

[52]The Norwegian Ministry of Health (Prop. 74. L (2015-2016)), p. 28.

[53]Section 10 of the Personal Names Act.

[54]Guidance note (G-2002-20). Available in electronic format on the Lovdata platform (lovdata.no).

[55]Section 12(2) of the Personal Names Act.

apply where a person wants to change back to their previous given name. An exception to the ten-year limit may also be made if there are particular reasons for doing so. In such cases the right to change one's name is dependent on a discretionary assessment by the authorities. In the light of these provisions it was decided that it was not necessary to make any particular exceptions for persons who have changed their legal gender.[56]

3 The Role of Legal Gender in Norwegian Law

Gender is not defined in any legislative acts or other accompanying legal sources, apart from the Change of Legal Gender Act, which provides the clarification that whenever "gender" is used in law, the term is to refer to self-declared gender. The Act makes only two exceptions to this rule: for the establishment of motherhood or fatherhood and for parental custody pursuant to the Children's Act.[57] Establishment of motherhood and fatherhood and parental custody is to be based on the gender assigned at birth.

In principle, this means that the Act introduces two categories of legal genders: the gender assigned at birth and the self-declared gender. The second category, self-declared gender, is only relevant for persons who have changed legal gender through self-declaration, and excludes children under the age of six years, who may only change their legal gender with medical approval. For children under the age of six years, therefore, a change of legal gender should be regarded as a correction of the gender assigned at birth. In contrast, anyone changing their legal gender on the basis of self-declaration from the age of six years and above will be subject to two legal gender categories, namely, that of the gender assigned at birth and that of their later self-declared gender.

The Change of Legal Gender Act does not explicitly operate with two categories of legal gender. Nevertheless, the practical implication of the Act is the introduction of a two-track system of legal gender in Norwegian law, namely:

1. The gender assigned at birth which is relevant for the establishment of parenthood and parental custody under the Children's Act;
2. The self-declared gender which is applicable in all other areas of law.

It is not specifically stated in Norwegian law whether the gender assigned at birth is to still be recorded in the Population Register after a request for change of legal gender has been approved. Neither is there any specific regulation regarding whether the registration authorities shall keep a record of requests for changes, for instance, in the case of someone who has changed legal gender back and forth several times. The

[56]See section 10(2) nr. 4 and 4 of the Personal Names Act and the Norwegian Ministry of Health (Prop. 74. L (2015-2016)), p. 34.

[57]Section 6 of the Change of Legal Gender Act.

Population Register Act states that the registration authorities may keep "historical" personal data to the extent necessary.[58] In the absence of any specific rules on the topic in the Population Register Act, the registration authorities are at liberty to record the personal data deemed necessary, provided that the storage limitations of Article 17 of the GDPR are adhered to. This could then include historical data about change of name and gender.

Currently, the legislature has chosen to make the self-declared gender applicable in all laws, except for the establishment of parenthood in accordance with the Children's Act.[59] This implies that the self-declared legal gender is to be used in the context of affirmative action initiatives, for example when deciding whether a student is entitled to "gender points" when applying to educational programmes. Nevertheless, once a two-track system has been introduced: gender assigned at birth, and self-declared gender, there is nothing stopping legislators from shifting the balance between the two. For instance, legislators may choose to amend the Change of Legal Gender Act, to exclude self-declared gender from a greater number of legislative instruments, such as those related to affirmative action initiatives.

If the legislature chooses to make the gender assigned at birth relevant in other areas of law, such as affirmative action initiatives, it will presumably be necessary to routinely record both categories of gender. An employer subject to affirmative action rules would, for instance, be required to record both the gender assigned at birth and the self-declared legal gender in the employee register to ensure compliance with affirmative action rules. More extensive use of the gender assigned at birth will evidently make self-declared gender proportionately less relevant. Therefore, it may be argued that self-declared gender should be applied as broadly as possible, in order to make the act of changing legal gender meaningful.

We will now go on to explore the implications of legal gender in certain areas of law, including the establishment of parenthood, the right to health care services and anti-discrimination law, including affirmative action initiatives and the regulation of gender-divided physical spaces, such as public toilets and changing rooms.

3.1 The Establishment of Parenthood

Under current legislation, a person who is registered as "male" in the Population Register and who gives birth to a child, will be legally recognised as the child's mother, rather than the father. In accordance with the preparatory works of the Change of Legal Gender, the reason for using the birth-assigned gender in such situations is that it is necessary to establish the parenthood of the child.[60]

[58]Section 3-1 of the Population Register Act.

[59]Section 6 of the Change of Legal Gender Act.

[60]The Norwegian Ministry of Health (Prop. 74. L (2015-2016)), pp. 31 and 37.

It is not clear why introducing a two-track system of legal gender was considered necessary by the legislators to accommodate the rules on the establishment of parenthood in the Children's Act. While the provisions regarding motherhood and fatherhood currently make reference to "women" and "men", recorded gender could have been made superfluous by defining motherhood in terms of the act of giving birth (without defining this person as either male or female).[61] Likewise the establishment of fatherhood could simply be based on the relationship to the mother of the child, regardless of the person's gender status. Thus, references to "men" and "women" could have been eliminated from the definition of motherhood and fatherhood, removing the need to use a person's birth-assigned gender. However, since both "motherhood" and "fatherhood" are in themselves highly gendered words, it is possible that the legislators considered that these terms would be perceived as referring to the person's birth-assigned gender, even if the terms "women" and "men" were eliminated from the provisions.[62]

Since 2009 lesbian couples in Norway have had the right to assisted reproduction technology in order to conceive children. The term "co-mother" was introduced as an alternative to "father", to refer to the female partner of the birth mother of the child.[63] In cases where a person has changed legal gender from male to female, they may have the status of "co-mother" to the children of their female partner. Thus, there is not considered to be any need to use a person's birth-assigned gender to establish the parenthood of the child in such cases. Male-to-female trans persons may consequently be recognised as co-mothers rather than fathers, while it is impossible by law for female-to-male trans persons with biological children to be recognised as fathers.[64]

3.2 *The Right to Health Care Services for Trans Persons*

The right to health care services for trans persons is not affected by the person's legal gender.[65] The change of gender status thus has no implications for a person's entitlement to receive medical treatment. Instead, trans persons' right to treatment follows from general health care legislation. Under the Patients' and Users' Act, patients are entitled to receive "immediate and necessary health care" from the

[61] See chapter 2 of the Children's Act, including section 2 and 3.

[62] For a more in-depth analysis of the legal regulation of trans persons and parenthood, see Sørlie (2018).

[63] Section 4a of the Children's Act.

[64] The Norwegian Ministry of Health (Prop. 74. L (2015-2016)), p. 31. However, it is only in the event that the child has been conceived through the state system for assisted reproduction that the female partner of the child's birth mother can be recognised as co-mother.

[65] The Norwegian Ministry of Health (Prop. 74. L (2015-2016)), p. 32.

municipal or specialist health care services.[66] Whether a trans person is entitled to medical treatment is therefore dependent on assessments made by health care professionals concerning what constitutes "necessary health care" for the individual patient.

Health care services for trans persons are currently organised through the National Treatment Centre for Transsexualism (NTCT), located at the Oslo University Hospital.[67] In 2010, the NTCT became a national treatment service and the unit is the only public institution that offers gender reassignment treatment in Norway. The treatment offered includes psychiatric assessment, and hormonal and surgical treatment. However, the right to receive health care services at the unit is limited to patients who have been diagnosed with F 64.0 (transsexualism). If a trans patient is found not to fulfil the criteria for this diagnosis they are usually denied treatment at the NTCT. A 2012 report from the Ministry of Health found that no health care services are currently offered to patients who have been rejected by the unit.[68] As a consequence, in Norway the right to health care services for trans persons is currently dependent on being diagnosed with transsexualism.

In their 2015 report, the expert panel which was established to evaluate the situation of trans persons in Norway concluded that the medical treatment offered at the NTCT does not deliver the right to health care services for all trans persons. The panel pointed to the fact that only a minority of those experiencing gender dysphoria are diagnosed with F 64.0 (transsexualism) and that this is the only diagnosis that currently gives persons a right to receive treatment. Consequently, they recommended that the authorities should ensure that all those experiencing gender dysphoria should have access to appropriate health care services.[69] A majority of the expert panel further recommended that the treatment offered at the NTCT should be decentralised, though a minority were of the opinion that such a decentralisation would have serious consequences for the health services offered to trans patients.[70] Nonetheless, the expert panel unanimously recommended that national guidelines for the treatment available to trans persons should be developed.[71]

As of yet, the expert panel's recommendations regarding health care services have not resulted in any changes to the medical treatment provided. In January 2017 a working group was established to follow up the recommendations. The group was

[66]Section 2-1 a and 2-1 b of the Patient's and User's Rights Act. In Norwegian: pasient- og brukerrettighetsloven (LOV-1999-07-02-63).

[67]The Norwegian Ministry of Health (April 2015), report by the expert panel, pp. 39–40.

[68]The Norwegian Ministry of Health. 01 October 2012. Gjennomgang av behandlingstilbudet til transseksuelle og transpersoner. Directorate of Health, p. 13. Https://docplayer.me/4113594-Gjennomgang-av-behandlingstilbudet-til-transseksuelle-og-transpersoner.html. Accessed 28 February 2019.

[69]The Norwegian Ministry of Health (April 2015), see the summary of the report, p. V.

[70]See note 69, p. VI.

[71]See note 69, p. 147.

asked to make suggestions on how responsibility for the treatment of trans persons could be divided between the NTCT and the regional health trusts. The working group was further asked to give recommendations on how treatment for patients who do not qualify for treatment at the NTCT should be organised.[72] The group delivered their report in March 2018 but were unable to reach a consensus on what changes should be made. The members of the group disagreed on whether there should be a right to treatment that was wholly-based on the patient's experience of gender dysphoria, or if previously established diagnostic criteria should still apply. There was also disagreement on whether the health care services should be decentralised.[73]

The disagreements within both the expert panel and the working group indicate the shifting views on what the right to necessary health care services for trans persons entails and on who should be entitled to such treatment. These changes also affect the medical understanding of trans persons. In the updated version of the International Classification of Diseases (ICD-11), transsexualism has been removed from the chapter on mental illnesses, and the term 'gender incongruence' has been added to a new section on conditions related to sexual health.[74] It is unclear if, and when, the new definition will have consequences for the treatment that is offered to trans persons in Norway.

3.3 The Anti-discrimination Act and the Regulation of Gender-Specific Physical Spaces

Trans persons were first explicitly included in Norwegian anti-discrimination legislation in 2014. However, in 2008 the Equality and Anti-Discrimination Tribunal concluded that discrimination of someone undergoing gender reassignment surgery was covered by the category of gender in the current Equality Act. This means that protection against discrimination was limited to trans persons who were diagnosed as transsexual until 2014, when a separate act prohibiting discrimination on the basis of sexual orientation, gender identity and gender expression was enacted.[75]

In January 2018 the current Equality and Anti-Discrimination Act came into effect, which merged the previous four anti-discrimination acts into one general legislative act.[76] The Act prohibits discrimination and harassment on twelve

[72]The Norwegian Ministry of Health (April 2015), report by the expert panel, p. 3.

[73]Ibid., pp. 27–32.

[74]ICD-11, International Classification of Diseases for Mortality and Morbidity Statistics, chapter 17.

[75]See the Prohibition of Discrimination Act on the basis of Sexual Orientation, Gender Identity and Gender Expression (LOV-2013-06-21-58). The Act was replaced by the general Equality and Anti-Discrimination Act in 2018.

[76]The Equality and Anti-Discrimination Act (LOV-2017-06-16-51).

grounds, including gender, gender identity and gender expression.[77] While none of these terms are given a specific definition in the Act, the preparatory works state that "gender identity" concerns a person's own experience of their gender, while "gender expression" indicates the ways in which persons (consciously or unconsciously) express themselves through behaviour, clothes, appearance, language etc. It is also stated that the two protected categories aim to provide trans persons with protection against discrimination.[78]

The term "transgender people" in the context of the anti-discrimination legislation is understood as an umbrella term and is not limited to persons who have been diagnosed as transsexual or who have undergone such medical interventions as gender reassignment surgery. The protection is meant to cover discrimination against persons who do not identify with their physical sex, as well as persons who perceive themselves as neither women nor men. The decisive factor is thus the person's own subjective understanding of their gender. The protection also includes persons with a gender expression that deviates from what is expected, given their physical or biological sex.[79]

Arguably, the Equality and Anti-Discrimination Act constitutes an implicit lack of recognition of trans persons' self-determined gender. The Act distinguishes between discrimination because of a person's gender on the one hand and because of a person's gender identity and gender expression on the other. Only cisgender persons, meaning those whose gender identity matches their birth-assigned gender, are considered to be covered by the protected category of gender.[80] The term "gender" is thereby given an (implicit) biological and physical definition. Conversely, it is explicitly stated in the preparatory works of the Act that trans persons, including transsexuals who have undergone gender reassignment treatment, are not protected based on gender but rather on the grounds of gender identity and gender expression.[81] The Equality and Anti-Discrimination Act also prohibits discrimination on account of an assumed characteristic.[82] Thus, if a trans person is discriminated against because they are perceived as a cisgender person (either male or female), they would presumably be considered to have been discriminated against because of an assumed gender rather than their "actual" gender. The only group to transcend this division are persons born with an intersex condition, who are

[77]Section 6 of the Equality and Anti-Discrimination Act.

[78]The Ministry of Children and Gender Equality. 5 April 2017. Prop. 81 L (2016-2017) Lov om likestilling og forbud mot diskriminering (likestillings- og diskrimineringsloven), pp. 85–86. Https//: www.regjeringen.no/no/documenter/prop.-81-l-20162017/id2547420/. Accessed 28 February 2019.

[79]Seen note 78, p. 86.

[80]Gender is not given an explicit definition in the Equality and Anti-Discrimination Act or in the preparatory works, although the latter state that "both men and women" are covered by the category of gender.

[81]The Norwegian Ministry of Children and Equality (Prop. 81 L (2016-2017)), p. 312.

[82]See section 6 of the Equality and Anti-Discrimination Act.

considered to be covered by both gender and gender identity/gender expression.[83] While the difference is mainly academic, and is unlikely to have any consequence for the right to protection against discrimination, the example illustrates the continued importance a person's physical body has for the understanding of gender in Norwegian legislation, notwithstanding the right to change gender status given by the Change of Legal Gender Act.

3.4 Rules Regarding Positive Preferential Treatment (Affirmative Action)

In general, Norwegian legislation is formulated in gender-neutral terms and a person's gender does not affect the person's legal position. For example, the obligation to do military service applies equally to both men and women, and the current Marriage Act defines marriage as being between "two persons of the same or opposite gender".[84] There are some exceptions to this, however, for example in relation to regulations regarding parenthood, reproduction or welfare benefits connected with pregnancy. In addition to this, gender is often used as a legal category in Norwegian legislation that aims to promote gender equality. For example, the Equality and Anti-Discrimination Act allows for positive differential treatment (affirmative action) on the basis of protected categories under certain conditions.[85] This regulation has been used particularly in order to strengthen the position of women by introducing rules regarding gender quotas on boards of public companies, committees, and councils.

Rules regarding affirmative action have been introduced in several Norwegian acts. This includes the Act relating to the Court of Justice which requires there to be both men and women among the members of the Conciliation Boards.[86] The Act also requires there to be two lists of lay judges in each court's judicial district, one of

[83] It must be noted that it is somewhat unclear how discrimination against intersex persons is viewed in the new Equality and Anti-Discrimination Act. While the preparatory works of the Act explicitly state that transsexual persons are no longer considered to be covered by the category of gender, this is not said about intersex persons. Instead, reference is made to the previous anti-discrimination legislation where it is noted that intersex persons are covered by gender, gender identity and gender expression. However, in the guidance to the individual sections of the act, persons with intersex conditions are only explicitly mentioned under the headings of gender identity and gender expression.

[84] See section 6 of the Compulsory Military Service Act (although this section says that women born before 1997 are exempt from compulsory service) and Section 1 of the Marriage Act.

[85] See section 11 of the Equality and Anti-Discrimination Act. In order for differential treatment to be considered lawful, it must be designed to promote the purpose of the Act, and the negative impact on the person or persons whose position will worsen must be reasonably proportionate to the intended purpose, and the differential treatment must cease once the purpose has been achieved.

[86] See section 27 of the Act relating to the Court of Justice. The Conciliation Boards are mediation institutions with limited jurisdiction in certain civil cases.

women and one of men.[87] When a case is to be considered in court equal numbers of female and male lay judges must be drawn from the two lists.[88] Furthermore, the Equality and Anti-Discrimination Act contains detailed provisions regarding how many of each gender should be represented on public boards, and in committees and councils, depending on the total number of members.[89] The same applies to the Norwegian Public Limited Companies Act, which requires that both genders should be represented on the board of such companies (and stipulates the number of men and women).[90]

In addition to these Acts, the regulations on admission to higher education makes it possible to make use of "gender points" in order to achieve a higher degree of gender equality in educational programmes where one gender is clearly underrepresented.[91] Both male and female students may be entitled to gender points, depending on which gender is underrepresented in the educational programme to which the student is applying for. When deciding whether the rules on gender quotas have been met, or if an applicant for an educational programme is entitled to gender points, the Change of Legal Gender Act requires the self-declared gender of the person to be used.[92]

3.5 Access to Gender-Specific Spaces

Another concern that has been raised in connection with the adoption of the Change of Legal Gender Act is the issue of trans persons' access to gender-specific spaces. The debate has centred around the question of whether male-to-female trans women, who have changed their legal gender but who have not undergone gender reassignment surgery, are entitled to access women-only spaces.[93] Since the Act makes it possible to change legal gender based on self-declaration, it has been argued that the system may be misused by men who want to gain access to women's changing rooms, toilets or shelters. It has also been argued that allowing persons

[87] Sections 64 and 65 of the Act relating to the Court of Justice.

[88] Section 87 of the Act relating to the Court of Justice.

[89] Section 28 of the Equality and Anti-Discrimination Act.

[90] Section 6-1 a of the Norwegian Public Limited Companies Act.

[91] Sections 7–9 of the regulations on admission to tertiary education programmes.

[92] See below as to the criticism of the use of self-declared gender when calculating gender quotas or gender points.

[93] See, for example, newspaper editorials from different actors within the women's movement and lesbian activists: https://www.dagbladet.no/kultur/hva-avgjor-om-du-er-kvinne-eller-mann/70053234 [What decides whether you are a woman or a man?], https://www.dagbladet.no/kultur/hatkampanjen-mot-feminister/70039162 [Hate campaign against feminists], https://www.dagbladet.no/kultur/mann-kan-ikke-bli-kvinne/70040157 [Men cannot become women]. All accessed 15 July 2020. All the editorials are available in Norwegian.

with penises to use such facilities may exclude other women due to modesty considerations or fear of being assaulted.

With some exceptions, access to gender-specific spaces is not regulated in Norwegian legislation,[94] and the question was not addressed by legislators when the Change of Legal Gender Act was passed. In general, Norwegian legislation, therefore, does not provide a clear answer to the question of trans persons' right to access gender-specific spaces. However, denying a trans person access to a public changing room or toilet will constitute differential treatment, and may therefore violate the prohibition against discrimination on the basis of gender identity or gender expression.[95] Whether denying a trans person access to a public space is lawful or not will depend on an assessment of whether the differential treatment has an objective purpose, is necessary to achieve this purpose and does not have a disproportionately negative impact on the trans person who is denied access.[96] In accordance with current practice, protecting the modesty of others may be considered a legitimate objective.[97]

As of yet, neither the Norwegian courts, nor the Equality and Anti-Discrimination Ombud[98] or Tribunal has addressed the question of whether denying trans persons access to gender-specific spaces constitutes discrimination. Speaking generally, the equality and anti-discrimination Ombud has stated that the assessment must be made in practical terms, taking into account the needs of the person who is denied access, the design of the facilities in question, and what alternative solutions have been

[94]Rules regarding access to gender-specific spaces are given both in the Regulation on the design and layout of workplaces and work premises (the Workplace Regulations) and in the Act on Municipal Crisis Shelters (the Crisis Shelter Act). In accordance with section 3-4 of the Workplace Regulations, workplaces must normally be provided with separate changing rooms for men and women. Similarly, according to section 2, paragraph four, of the Crisis Shelter Act, housing that is provided to men and women should be physically separated. Presumably, when deciding who should be considered male of female after these regulations, the self-declared gender of the person should be used, since no exception has made under section 6 of the Change of Legal Gender Act. However, for a more detailed discussion of these issues, see the discussion below.

[95]Section 6 of the Equality and Anti-Discrimination Act.

[96]Section 9 of the Equality and Anti-Discrimination Act.

[97]See the summary of current practice in relation to prohibition against discrimination on the basis of sexual orientation, gender identity and gender expression from the Equality and Anti-Discrimination Ombud (2017), pp. 81–83. Available in Norwegian. Https://www.ldo.no/nyheiter-og-fag/Analyser/fagoppsummering-skk/. Accessed 15 July 2020.

[98]The Equality and Anti-Discrimination Ombud is appointed by the government for a fixed term of six years. The Ombud is an independent public administrative agency that is tasked with working to promote genuine equality and prevent unlawful discrimination in all sectors of society. Additionally, the Ombud is tasked with providing guidance on the Norwegian anti-discrimination legislation. The Anti-Discrimination is an independent public administrative agency charged with enforcing the provisions in the anti-discrimination legislation, with some exceptions. The Tribunal may make administrative decisions, including ordering stoppage or remediation, to secure the cessation of discrimination. Administrative decisions made by the Tribunal may be submitted to the courts for comprehensive review, c.f. the Equality and Anti-Discrimination Ombud Act.

attempted.[99] Whether the differential treatment is considered to be lawful will thus depend on the circumstances in the specific case. In the statement, the Ombud also pointed to the preparatory works of the Equality and Anti-Discrimination Act, which state that lack of access to neutral (unisex) toilets or changing rooms may expose trans persons to a risk of violence and harassment. A failure to meet such needs may therefore constitute discrimination.[100]

In summary, although the debate in Norway regarding trans persons' access to gender-specific spaces has centred around the Change of Legal Gender Act, access to such spaces are only rarely regulated in legislation.[101] As examples, neither access to the changing rooms at fitness centres nor swimming halls is regulated by law. Thus, when deciding whether denying a trans person access to these types of gender-specific spaces constitutes discrimination, the person's legal gender is, in principle, irrelevant. The Equality and Anti-Discrimination Act prohibits discrimination on the basis of gender identity or gender expression regardless of whether the person in question has changed their gender status or undergone gender reassignment surgery. Therefore, the question of denial of access to gender-specific public space may be considered to constitute discrimination is generally not contingent on the legal gender status of the persons concerned.

4 Criticism and Current Discussions Regarding the Regulation of Legal Gender

There had been little debate on legal gender and the possibility of changing one's gender status prior to the enactment of the Change of Legal Gender Act on 1 July 2016. The legislative proposal attracted little attention or interest from society at large and was only explicitly mentioned in the political platform of two out of eight political parties holding seats in Parliament at the time the Act was adopted.[102] The Act may have been viewed largely as a bureaucratic matter designed to accommodate a small minority of trans persons who experienced dissonance between their gender identity and the legal gender assigned to them at birth, but who did not want to undergo full gender reassignment surgery to change their legal gender, or who were unable to do so because they had not been diagnosed as transsexual. The Act may also have been viewed as uncontroversial for the broader public, as it was

[99]See note 98.

[100]The Norwegian Ministry of Children and Equality (Prop. 81 L (2016-2017)), p. 125.

[101]For example, regulations of changing rooms at workplaces and gender-separated housing in Crisis Shelters, discussed further below.

[102]The possibility of changing legal gender without undergoing sterilisation was explicitly mentioned in the manifestos of the Labour Party and the Liberal Party. All other party policy statements in the Parliamentary period of 2013–2017 were silent on the issue. Which policy issues political parties choose to include in their manifestos are an indication of how important or politically potent an issue is considered to be prior to the parliamentary elections.

largely framed as a measure to support the human rights of a minority who had previously been forced to undergo irreversible medical procedures in order to obtain legal recognition of their identity.

The relatively subdued debate preceding the enactment of the Change of Legal Gender Act is strikingly different from the debate over equal marriage, which attracted massive public interest and was considered to be highly controversial, prior to the formal enactment of equal marriage on 1 January 2009. The legal implications of the Change of Legal Gender Act are, however, arguably more far-reaching than those of equal marriage. Equal marriage merely extended the right to marry to a minority, without affecting the legal marital status of the majority.[103] In contrast, the Change Legal Gender Act constitutes a formal amendment of the definition of legal gender, which affects not just a minority group but all members of society, whenever legal gender is applied in law.

Accordingly, after its enactment the Act has been criticised for watering down the definition of what it means to be a "man" or a "woman", as the definition of "man" and "woman" is now presumably based on self-declared gender rather than the gender assigned at birth. This debate hardly existed before the enactment of the Act in 2016, but it has steadily developed over the past few years. Criticisms have to a great extent been inspired by those voiced in other countries which have either discussed or passed similar legislative changes as those in Norway. For example, opponents of the Act warn about the harmful consequences that may result from change of legal gender, for instance the possibility that violent male predators may disguise themselves as women to obtain access to women-only spaces, thus echoing warnings voiced in the United Kingdom. Affirmative action initiatives based on gender status, such as gender points for higher education programmes could also be open to abuse. However, the proponents of these criticisms are not always clear about what they view as the best alternative to the Act. Some may be sceptical about any legislation making it possible to change legal gender, for religious or ideological reasons, while others are not necessarily hostile to the concept of changing legal gender itself, but critical of how the Act is structured. In the following account we will leave the ideological debate over the definition of gender aside, limiting our scope to the supposed structural flaws of the Act and its limitations.

We have selected three issues here for further exploration. We will initially examine the critique put forward by Professor Marit Halvorsen (University of Oslo) who has focused on the deficiencies of the Act in relation to the correction of historical personal data and the regulation of access to gender-specific spaces.[104] Finally, we will address the issue of recognising a third legal gender.

---

[103]It may be noted that a lawsuit was brought against the government in 2009, arguing that the new gender-neutral Marriage Act affected the marriages of heterosexual persons by changing the definition of marriage as being between a man and a woman. The claim was dismissed by the District Court of Oslo, and appeal was denied by Oslo Appeal Court, c.f. TOSLO-2009-142711.

[104]Halvorsen (2018). Https://www.idunn.no/lor/2018/08/om_lov_om_endring_av_juridisk_kjoenn. Accessed 10 February 2019.

4.1 Correction of Historical Personal Data

Professor Halvorsen, published a paper in October 2018, in which she claimed that the Change of Legal Gender Act contains a number of errors and deficiencies. Halvorsen points out that the Act does not provide for any amendments to the administrative process for changing data in official documents issued in the past.[105] As an example, Halvorsen points to the fact that university diplomas can generally only be issued once. The regulations are silent on the question of whether new diplomas may be issued to candidates who have changed either their name or legal gender.

Although not mentioned by Halvorsen, the Personal Names Act is likewise silent on the right to correct personal data after a name change. The rules on issuances of diplomas are not regulated by statutory law, but the administrative rules of each education institution. Given that education institutions keep records of their students and alumina, they are subject to the Norwegian Personal Data Act, including the General Data Protection Regulation (GDPR). The right to correct personal data follows from Article 16 of the General Data Protection Regulation (GDPR), which passed into Norwegian law 20 July 2018.[106] Accordingly, once the legal gender and name have been formally changed, the GDPR provides for the right to correct previously recorded legal gender and personal name. Nevertheless, the right to correction of your own personal data does not necessarily accommodate a right to obtain a new original diploma. Thus, in the case of diplomas, Halvorsen is correct to point out that the education sector should evaluate whether the rules of issuing original diplomas should be amended, i.e. to safeguard the interests of persons that have changed name or legal gender. Furthermore, there may be instances where historical records, such as that of previous personal name and legal gender, need to be stored. Articles 5 and 6 of the GDPR provide for the right to store such data insofar as continued storage is justified by a legitimate purpose and a valid processing basis, for instance a legal obligation.[107] However, as a general rule, the data subject has the right to have all personal data corrected and updated in all registers where the previous name or legal gender are recorded.

Although the concerns of Halvorsen are valid, there is sound reason to believe that the problem of for instance diploma issuance will be largely mitigated by recent developments in the digitalisation of diplomas and other essential documents, as there is a range of digital tools to correct and authenticate official certificates.

---

[105]Ibid., point 2.1.

[106]Section 1 of the Personal Data Act.

[107]We assume here that personal data related to e.g. diplomas is stored by the university or other such institution. If the personal data is deleted by the institution, the data subject has no right of correction. For example, a former employee cannot ask a former employer to correct a historical certificate of employment if the employer no longer stores the relevant data. There may, then, be various real-life situations where a person who has changed legal gender or personal name will be confronted with historical data that are difficult or impossible to amend.

4.2 Regulation of Access to Gender-Specific Spaces

Another issue that Halvorsen has raised in her paper is that the Act of Change of Legal Gender does not resolve how access to gender-specific spaces, such as public toilets and changing rooms is to be regulated.[108] While Norwegian legislation generally does not regulate access to gender-specific spaces, some exceptions apply. This include the Workplace Regulations which stipulate that employers must ensure that employees have access to gender-divided toilets and changing rooms, but without specifying how employees should be divided into separate genders.[109] The same applies to the Crisis Shelter Act, which states that housing provided to women and men must be physically separated.[110]

In principle, the Change of Legal Gender Act states that the self-declared legal gender shall apply in all circumstances, unless there is an exemption. The only explicit exemption from self-declared legal gender is the establishment of parenthood in accordance with the Children's Act.[111] Employees, then, should be given access to gender-specific toilets in accordance with their self-declared gender. Similarly, where a person is seeking protection at a Crisis Shelter, their housing should be based on their legal gender. In reality, however, the issue of access criteria for gender-specific spaces has proved more complex and contentious. At present it is not clear whether persons actually have access to gender-specific rooms on the basis of their self-declared gender.

The issue of access to gender-specific spaces has not been clarified in case law or administrative practice. The Equality and Anti-Discrimination Tribunal has dealt with one case regarding access to a public changing room at a gym. However, the case did not involve the criteria for access to gender-specific spaces, but rather whether remarks made towards a trans woman by another woman at the gym constituted harassment.[112] The case originated from two confrontations in which the trans woman was accused of using the changing room reserved for the opposite gender. On the basis of the evidence presented, the majority of the Tribunal found that the statements, although uncomfortable for the trans woman, did not constitute harassment. In regard to trans women's right to access to changing rooms, the majority of the Tribunal noted in their decision that the Change of Legal Gender Act does not address the practical challenges experienced by persons who have

[108] Halvorsen (2018) point 2.2.

[109] Sections 7–9 of the Workplace Regulations.

[110] Section 2, paragraph four of the Crisis Shelter Act.

[111] Section 6 of the Change of Legal Gender Act.

[112] The Equality and Anti-Discrimination Tribunal, Case no. 68/2018. Accessible in Norwegian. Http://diskrimineringsnemnda.no/media/2218/68-2018-uttalelse-anonymisert.pdf. Accessed 15 July 2020.

changed their legal gender, and that the right to access changing rooms thus lacks legal clarification.[113]

Halvorsen argues that the issue of access to gender-specific spaces is unresolved by the Change of Legal Gender Act. The question thus remains to be dealt with as a discrimination issue under the auspices of the Gender Equality and Anti-Discrimination Act. Halvorsen points out that it is unfortunate that the criteria for access to gender-specific changing rooms are so vague, as this may give rise to confrontation and increased conflict, which is detrimental to both trans persons and members of the majority population. Halvorsen argues that the majority population may reasonably expect that gender-specific spaces should only be used by persons perceived to belong to a specific biological sex, rather than a self-declared gender.

We will argue that Halvorsen is correct in saying that the issue of access to gender-specific rooms is a contentious and unresolved issue. The Change of Legal Gender Act stipulates that self-declared gender is to be recognised in all areas of law, except when there is an exemption. Gender-specific spaces, however, are largely unregulated by law. Access to changing rooms in fitness centres, swimming pools etc. are not regulated by law. Furthermore, the expert panel's report, which forms the essential preparatory work for the Change of Legal Gender Act, does not discuss this particular issue. Instead, the expert panel points out that further work should be done to evaluate the application of legal gender in a broader societal context.[114] Where gender is used as a criterion in society without being regulated by law, people are thus free to define gender as they please, provided that they do not act in violation with the Gender Equality and Anti-Discrimination Act. At the same time, it is unfortunate that the implications of access to gender-divided spaces was not given greater attention during the legislative process, particularly in regards to access to changing rooms at the workplace and housing in Crisis Shelters. This may both have a negative impact on trans persons' safety and well-being, as well as resulting in an increased opposition towards the Change of Legal Gender Act due to concerns that the Act will undermine the rights cis-gendered women. One possible solution to the quandary of gender-specific rooms may be to increase the availability of gender-neutral spaces, as an alternative to gender-specific options. This accords with the preparatory works, which state that a lack of gender-neutral alternatives may expose trans persons to violence and could therefore, depending on the circumstances, constitute discrimination.[115] However, a physical solution requires a willingness to invest in new infrastructure.

---

[113]The Equality and Anti-Discrimination Tribunal, Case no. 68/2018. Accessible in Norwegian. Http://diskrimineringsnemnda.no/media/2218/68-2018-uttalelse-anonymisert.pdf. Accessed 15 July 2020.

[114]The Norwegian Ministry of Health (April 2015), report by the expert panel, p. I.

[115]The Norwegian Ministry for Children and Equality (Prop. 81 L (2016-2017)), p. 125.

4.3 Third Legal Gender

The expert panel recommended in its 2015 report that the recognition of a third legal gender should be given further examination. However, they regarded it as outside the scope of their mandate to consider whether a third legal gender should be acknowledged in law.[116] Following the enactment of the Change of Legal Gender Act, there has been some debate on whether a third legal gender should be adopted. A third legal gender option has been proposed in Parliament twice but rejected both times.[117]

As of yet it is still unclear what a third legal gender option would involve. In a paper published in 2017, Arnesen put forward a model of how a third legal gender option may operate in law.[118] The model features a division between negative and positive recognition. Negative recognition means freedom from being labelled as either male or female, while positive recognition means the explicit recognition of an alternative to "man" or "woman". The effects of legal gender would of course be vastly different, depending on whether the third legal gender option was considered as a reservation, i.e. the liberty not to be labelled as man or woman, or as a positive third option with legal effects.

The introduction of a third legal gender option would inevitably force the legislature to consider how and under what circumstances the third option would have effect in law, for example, whether it would be applied in affirmative action initiatives. Arnesen has argued that the negative recognition model is the most feasible option, but that persons should nevertheless have the freedom to include a self-declared gender description in identity documents, such as passports and driving licences. The third legal gender option would offer no other legal effects than the liberty not to be identified as female or male in identity documents. Anyone opting for a third legal gender option would therefore be placed in the female or male category whenever legal gender was applied in law, for instance in connection with gender quotas for higher education programmes.

An alternative to the third legal gender option in identity documents could be to leave the gender category out altogether. That would entail that the third legal gender option would have little effect unless it was positively recognized alongside male and female whenever legal gender is applied in law. In our opinion, there is little reason to include a third legal gender option in affirmative action initiatives, such as gender quotas for the boardrooms of commercial companies. The underlying justification for recognition of a third legal gender and for affirmative action initiatives are evidently different. Affirmative action in relation to boardrooms, for instance, is being taken in Norway because women are invariably underrepresented in boardrooms. Affirmative action is based on a presumption that the population at large is

---

[116]The Norwegian Ministry of Health (April 2015), report by the expert panel, pp. 119–121.

[117]A proposal for the introduction of a third legal gender option was last rejected in 2017.

[118]Arnesen (2017), pp. 84–112. Accessible in Norwegian. Https://www.idunn.no/kritisk_juss/2017/02/boer_retten_anerkjenne_merenn_to_kjoenn, Accessed 15 July 2020.

either male or female. Thus, this underlying justification runs somewhat at odds with the idea behind a third legal gender, namely, that there is greater diversity of gender than merely male and female. Although there are persons who identify as something other than male or female, it remains true that a great part of the population identifying as female are underrepresented in important areas in society, such as corporate boardrooms. The dilemma of legal gender recognition is to find the right way to acknowledge gender diversity in law, without having any detrimental effects on the rights granted to the majority that identify as either male or female.

5 Concluding Observations

While the Change of Legal Gender Act has been met with criticism based on the potential for misuse of the system there are, in our opinion, few good alternatives as to how the right to change legal gender could be regulated. A main purpose of the enactment of the Change of Legal Gender Act was to put an end to the previous administrative practice which required trans persons to undergo irreversible sterilisation in order to be able to change their gender status. As such, a central aim of the Act was to remove the link between medical treatment and the right to change legal gender, and thus to recognise a person's own individual experience of their gender identity.

Consequently, although it could be possible to expand the "two-track system" of legal gender so that a person's birth gender should be used in relation to rules on affirmative action or other legislation where a person's gender status is relevant, this would simultaneously make the Change of Legal Gender Act less meaningful. In turn, such exceptions to the use of self-declared gender would also contravene with the purpose of the Act: to ensure a legal recognition of trans persons' gender identity.

At the same time, as this Chapter has illustrated, gender remains a central category both in Norwegian legislation and in society in general. While the Change of Legal Gender Act has ensured a right to change gender status on the basis of self-declaration, it does not address the challenges trans persons face due to binary divisions between men and women (and implicit understandings of these terms as biological and physical). Uncertainties regarding trans persons' right to access gender-specific spaces has thus proven to create conflict as well as a fear that women's rights may be undermined.

One solution to this problem is to increase the access to gender-neutral spaces, such as providing separate stalls in public changing rooms and similar solutions. This would also benefit other groups than trans persons who, for various reasons, may wish to ensure their privacy in public spaces.

Finally, we are of the opinion that the 2015 recommendation of the expert panel to assess the possibility of introducing a third legal gender option should be followed. The Norwegian anti-discrimination legislation already recognises the existence of non-binary persons and that such persons are entitled to protection from discrimination. As such, we recommend that the possibility of legally recognising the gender identity of non-binary persons through a third gender option should be evaluated.

References

Arnesen L (2017) Bør retten anerkjenne mer enn to kjønn? [Should Norwegian law recognise more than two genders?]. Kritisk Juss 53(2):84–112

Halvorsen M (2018) Om lov om endring av juridisk kjønn [Regarding the change of Legal Gender Act]. Lov og Rett 57(8)

Sørlie A (2018) Governing (trans)parenthood – the tenacious hold of biological connection and heterosexuality. In: Otto D (ed) Queering international law – possibilities, alliances, complicities, risk. Routledge

The Paradox of Trans Law in Sweden

Laura Carlson

Abstract Sweden was the first country in the world to allow a person to legally change gender in 1972. At the same time, the requirements under the 1972 act for changing gender included being unmarried, a Swedish citizen and infertile. The latter in most cases entailed sterilization surgery, a requirement in place until 2013. A trend can be detected in the Swedish legal system during the period from 1972 to 2013 to a greater focus on individual rights generally, as well as specific attention being given to the legal parameters affecting trans persons. The current law has been amended to a certain degree, such as the removal of the requirement of infertility, but the lawmaker has retained several controversial aspects, the social security numbering system disclosing sex (and age), as well as a gendered concept of legal parenthood based on a mother and a father. New legislative inquiries have been called for with respect to trans issues entailing that Swedish law can be seen as still in a period of flux as to fully recognizing needs and achieving trans legal solutions.

Sweden has the longest legal timeline with respect to trans law, with the first act adopted already by 1972, the Act on Determining Sex in Certain Cases (*lag* 1972:119 *om fastställande av könstillhörighet i visa fall*), the first in the world allowing persons to legally change their gender. The path of this law recognizing trans persons, however, was not straightforward and only positive. This early recognition by Swedish lawmakers as to the situation of trans persons and invocation of preferred gender was counteracted by the requirements under the 1972 act for gender reassignment, namely to be a Swedish citizen, infertile and unmarried. The legal requirement of sterilization in order to change gender was the first such anywhere, and the Swedish 1972 act became the model for many countries. The requirement as to sterilization had a tenuous if not non-existent basis in scientific research, and would be part of the Swedish legal landscape for a period of four

L. Carlson (✉)
Department of Law, Stockholm University, Stockholm, Sweden
e-mail: laura.carlson@juridicum.su.se

I. C. Jaramillo, L. Carlson (eds.), *Trans Rights and Wrongs*, Ius Comparatum - Global Studies in Comparative Law 54,
https://doi.org/10.1007/978-3-030-68494-5_23

decades, until 2013.[1] This chapter first provides a general description of the parameters of individual rights in the Swedish legal system and the role of law, then looks at the historical treatment of trans legal issues in Sweden against the background of its legal system, civil society and the understandings of rights, discrimination protections and access to justice generally. The current state of the law is then examined in which the most recent legislative amendments are addressed.

1 The Evolution to a Rights Concept in Swedish Law

The Swedish legal system has historically not had a strong tradition of individual rights, as seen very clearly with respect to the requirement of sterilization in order to change legal gender, a requirement in effect from 1972 until 2013, when the court found the requirement to be in violation of the European Convention of Human Rights (ECHR). As a civil law country, the courts have been relegated to the role of simply interpreting the law, not creating law. As such, litigation has not been seen as a vehicle to change society until recently. The constellations created by the separation of functions as set out in the constitutional act, the 1974 Instrument of Government, entails that the Parliament is the ultimate arbitrator of the law, with the courts having only a limited power of judicial review. The design of the 1974 Instrument of Government is for a weak judicial system that would not rule over the Parliament, evincing a very strong belief in majoritarianism, and the triumph of politics over juridification. The focus on the intent of the legislator, and the courts' perception of their role as applying and not creating law, entail that Sweden considers itself a civil law (and not common law) country despite the absence of any overarching legislative codification.

As the law historically has not been perceived of as a vehicle for societal change on the individual level, the very little civil society there is in Sweden has also been litigation-adverse and generally not adopting the role of legal watchdog with respect to state action. One significant exception here however is the Swedish Federation for Lesbian, Gay, Bisexual, Transgender and Queer Rights (*Riksförbundet för homosexuellas, bisexuellas, trans personers och queeras rättigheter*, "RFSL"), a non-profit organization that has been working for LGBTQ rights for over 65 years, as further discussed below.

Historically as stated there has been no strong legal culture of individual rights or access to justice in Sweden. The argument can be strongly made that the focus instead has been on social and not legal justice. The role of the 1974 Constitutional Instrument of Government was not even clear when enacted as to whether it should simply serve as guidance for the parliament, or whether individuals could assert rights under this constitutional act. A broader individual rights cultural arguably

[1]For an exhaustive history of Swedish trans legislation and its influence outside of Sweden, see Garland (2016). See also Dunne (2017), pp. 554–581.

would not come into play until after Sweden's 1995 EU membership.[2] Only after 2018 legislative amendments could courts explicitly award damages for violations of ECHR rights as granted under the convention, over sixty years after the signing. This progression from simply a perspective of social justice to encompassing legal justice can also be seen in the developments in the legal treatment of trans issues. The historical timeline presented below is divided into three periods: the origins of trans law in Sweden, 1960's to 2007; the paradigm shift as to individual rights in 2008–2015; and the current state of the law.

1.1 The Origins of Swedish Trans Law: The 1960's to 2007

Trans legal issues highlight the forced marriage between technology/medicine and law. The first documented attempt at gender reassignment surgery was in Berlin in 1912. The first successful operation in Germany was in 1953, and in Sweden 1968. A Swedish legislative directive was issued in 1966 to form the 1968 legislative inquiry discussed below. Medicine was providing certain physical alternatives with respect to gender reassignment, while the legal aspects at that time were immutable, particularly in the form of Swedish social security numbers, sex as registered at birth by the Swedish Lutheran Church on behalf of the state, and names.

Social security numbers (also referred to as personal identity numbers), names and registered sex historically have been and still are very strongly intertwined in Sweden. These three together can be seen as forcing the issue of legal gender assignment already in the 1950's and 1960's. The Swedish social security numbering system began to be used in 1947, and even today is still based on several markers, the first the date of birth, the second place of birth (designation removed for births after 1990), and the third sex (even numbers female, odd numbers male). A typical Swedish social security number consequently is the year-month-date of birth, followed by four digits, the second to the last of which indicates whether the person is male or female, as for example, 890102-3286. From this example, the age of this woman born in Gotland is readily evident.[3] Almost all identification in Sweden occurs with the social security number. Bank accounts are often simply the social security number. In contrast to other countries, the social security number is used

[2]This skepticism with respect to individual rights can perhaps be seen most clearly with the Swedish treatment of the ECHR. Sweden was an original member of the Council of Europe and signed the ECHR already in 1951. The Swedish legislative investigation at that time determined that the ECHR would be applicable only to conflicts between private parties (and not public institutions or law), thus significantly limiting (wrongly) the scope of the ECHR. Sweden did not sign the protocol granting the European Court of Human Rights, having the mandate to interpret the ECHR, jurisdiction over Sweden until 1966. However, under the requirements of dualism, the ECHR did not become Swedish law until 1994, effective 1998.

[3]See Ludvigsson et al. (2009), pp. 659–667. The Swedish Lutheran Church had kept the population records from 1686 until the Tax Agency took over this task in 1991.

extensively, allowing for easy access to age, place of birth and sex. A typical example would be renting something as nonessential such as a dvd film, where the vendor would ask for the social security number as an identity check, and if the appearance of the individual did not reflect the sex on the number, questions can be raised.

The same is true of the legislation concerning names. Sweden adopted its first Name Act in 1901, mostly to prohibit the use of noble names by the general population, which act was in place until 1963. The 1946 Church Records Act forbade giving a child a name that would cause offense or expose the child to ridicule (a requirement in existence even today). Between these two laws, the Swedish Church, and today, the Swedish Tax Agency (*Skatteverket*), scrutinize the names submitted for children and can refuse to register them. The 1963 Name Act, replacing the 1901 act, required all Swedes to have a last name, and that any first names to be registered should not cause offense, expose a person to ridicule or otherwise be seen as not suitable. This wide margin of discretion allowed for narrow interpretations as to permissible names that often were bound to sex, for example, Michael a permitted name for males but not for females. The Swedish rules concerning social security numbers and names at that time (and even to a certain degree today) locked individuals into one sex with no room for fluidity, as reflected in the report issued by the 1968 legislative inquiry that became the basis for the 1972 act.[4]

A Swedish doctoral dissertation published in 1967 indicated that by the end of 1965, beginning of 1966, there were 110 transsexual persons over the age of 15 who had sought help from psychiatrists.[5] The 1968 legislative inquiry, citing this study, went on to discuss the substantive and formal sides of sex, the first concerning whether a person's actual sex is male or female, the second the formalities with respect to the individual's first name, records in the church book and social security number. The inquiry proposed that new legislation require that the individual not be married and have been sterilized (or unable to biologically reproduce). The requirement of sterilization perhaps seems somewhat odd. It is however strongly anchored historically in a sterilization program that was conducted in Sweden for eugenic, social or medical indications beginning with the 1934 Sterilization Act, then the more stringent 1941 Sterilization Act in place until 1976. It is estimated that approximately 63,000 persons were sterilized during this period under these two laws, and half of these against their will. Most were women, and persons diagnosed with psychological disorders were particularly vulnerable.[6]

The 1972 Act on Determining Sex in Certain Cases was adopted based on the findings of the 1968 legislative inquiry. A person under the act could legally change their sex as registered by the church if certain requirements were met. These were that the individual could not be married (or as allowed after 1995, in a registered

[4]Legislative Inquiry SOU 1968:28, *Intersexuellas könstillhörighet*, pp. 33–34.

[5]See Wålinder (1967).

[6]See Kommissionen mot antiziganism (2015), p. 28.

partnership), be a Swedish citizen, and had to be sterile. Aside from any medical rationalization for sterilization, the legislator also focused on creating legal certainty within the family structure. If transindividuals, who have been acknowledged in their preferred gender, could nevertheless procreate using their natural reproductive capacities, there was a fear that any resulting children would be confused about their genetic origins or denied important family relationships.[7] This need for legal certainty in family relationships and for a mother and a father is still evident in the 2019 amendments to the Swedish Family Code as discussed further below.

Legal amendments were also later adopted with respect to the legal treatment of homosexuality. Homosexuality was first criminalized in Sweden in 1608 with the death penalty for both men under the law concerning treasonous crimes. It remained a crime until 1944, after which it was viewed as a mental illness. Homosexuality was listed as a psychological disease until 1979, when that designation was removed. The legal age of sexual consent for homosexuals, 18 years of age, was amended in 1978 to be the same as for heterosexuals, 15 years of age. A law for cohabitating homosexual couples was enacted in 1988 (*Lag* 1987:813 *om homosexuella sambor*), and registered partnerships were created in 1995. A registered partnership enabled partners of the same sex to legally register their relationship. However, the rights of registered partners are not as extensive as those of spouses. Sexual orientation was first a protected ground with respect to employment discrimination in 1999.

The 1970's also included several other milestones in Swedish law with respect to discrimination protections. The primary constitutional act, the 1809 Instrument of Government, was remolded and adopted in its new form in 1974 (*kungörelse* 1974:152 *om beslutad ny regeringsform*). New articles were added in 1976 including explicit protections against discrimination on the basis of race, color or ethnic origins (Article 15) and sex (Article 16). Up to 1976, there were no legislative protections against discrimination on the bases of these (or any other) grounds. Neither was there any perceived need for such legislation, particularly by the labor unions, who wished to retain their power of self-regulation through collective agreements of the terms and conditions in the labor market. Labor and employment legislation were seen as anathema to this autonomy of the social partners.

The first act on parental leave (and prohibitions against discrimination at the workplace on the basis of its exercise) was enacted in 1978. The first act on Equal Treatment between Men and Women at Work was adopted in 1979, the first act prohibiting racial discrimination was enacted next (without sanctions) in 1986. Protections against discrimination on other bases were legislated thereafter; ethnic

[7]Legislative Bill Prop. 1972:6, *Kungl. Maj:ts proposition med förslag till lag om fastställande av könstillhörighet i vissa fall, m.m.*, p. 3. For a discourse analysis in Swedish of the different legislative forced sterilizations, see Magnusson, K. 2013. *Tvånget och autonomin: En diskursanalytisk undersökning av sterilisering som villkor i svensk lagstiftning*, unpublished Master Thesis, Lund University Faculty of Law. Magnusson identifies four different discourses with respect to the various state-enforced sterilization requirements: eugenics (optimizing the fabric of the Swedish people), who should be allowed to start a family (object) from societal perspectives (subject), respectability as a class issue, and heterosexuality as the norm.

origins and religion (1994), disability (1999) and sexual orientation (1999), much of which was driven by the requirements of EU law.

Recognition of past legal wrongs and individual redress began to surface more consistently around the year 2000. The Government passed special legislation for compensation to victims of sterilizations under the 1934 and 1941 acts conducted from 1935 to 1975 (*lag* 1999:332 *om ersättning till steriliserade i vissa fall*), which explicitly did not cover persons sterilized under the 1972 act. Damages in the lump sum of SEK 175,000 were to be paid to those eligible persons who filed their claims by December 2002 (a period of exactly three years in which to file claims).[8]

1.2 Paradigm Shift as to Individual Rights: 2008–2012

The perspective of discrimination protections as being broader than simply employment rights and more as human rights was clearly manifested in the legislative preparatory works to the 2008 Discrimination Act (effective 1 January 2009).[9] This act replaced the majority of ad-hoc legislation addressing discrimination protections. Protection against unlawful discrimination based on transgender was introduced for the first time (along with age protections). The objective under the Act was to create an umbrella concept, transgender identity or expression (*könsöverskridande identitet eller uttryck*), to include all trans persons, transvestites, intersexual individuals, inter- and transgender individuals. Sex, gender and sexual orientation are all separately protected grounds under the 2008 act. The scope of the protections has also been expanded, now encompassing employment, education, labor market programs, entrepreneur programs, membership in certain organizations, the sale of goods, services and residences, health care, social insurance, military service and public employment.

[8]A similar inquiry and compensation program were created with respect to the estimated at least 250,000 children removed from their homes during the period from 1920 to 1995, see Legislative Inquiry SOU 2009:99, *Vanvård i social barnavård under 1900-talet*, p. 43 and Legislative Inquiry SOU 2011:9, *Barnen som samhället svek.* A 2012 act on compensation in the lump sum of SEK 250,000 to the children neglected in social care between 1920 and 1980 was adopted (*lag* 2012:663 *om ersättning på grund av övergrepp eller försummelser i samhällsvården av barn och unga i vissa fall*). Such damage claims had to be made within two years, by December 2014. More than half of the 4000 individuals applying for compensation under this system have been denied by the Compensation Board (*Ersättningsnämnden*) whose decisions could not be appealed, see Lundström, T. 2016. *Staten lovade 250.000 kronor till vanvårdade – mer än hälften fick ingenting.* SvT Nyheter, 17 May.

[9]This can also be seen as a response to European requirements, such as for example the 2002 judgment of the European Court of Human Rights in *Goodwin v United Kingdom* [2002] 35 EHRR 18, holding that the UK's failure to offer the petitioner an amended birth certificate violated her right to private life under Article 8 ECHR. This holding by the Court can be seen as heralding greater efforts both on the international and European levels as to gender recognition and protection.

The Marriage Code was amended in 2009 to include both homosexual and heterosexual marriages. Prior to 2009 a marriage could only be entered into by a man and a woman. No new registered partnerships can be registered after this amendment in the Marriage Code. Another change in 2009 was that homosexual men could donate blood, but upon the condition that they had not had sex with another man for the year prior to the donation (which is still the requirement today).

The requirements with respect to gender reassignment under the 1972 act began to be challenged more heavily. The government formed a new legislative inquiry, SOU 2007:16, *Ändrad könstillhörighet*, which proposed removing the requirements as to not being married or in a registered partnership and being a Swedish citizen. The requirement as to sterilization was proposed to be amended to a requirement of castration to allow individuals to be able to become a parent through artificial insemination. No legislative action was however taken.

The Commissioner for Human Rights at the Council of Europe recommended in 2009 the abolishment of the state-enforced requirement of sterilization such as in Sweden.[10] The National Board of Health and Welfare (*Socialstyrelsen*) presented a 2010 report as to the societal care and support for trans persons. The Board's proposal was to entirely remove the requirements as to marriage/partnership and sterilization, and instead of Swedish citizenship, require residence in Sweden of one year. The 2010 report cited the 2006 Yogyakarta Principles[11] to combat and protect against discrimination and abuse based on sex, sexual orientation or gender identity, including abolishing sterilization requirements. The 2010 report also cited the 2009 Commissioner for Human Rights report, which also drew upon the Yogyakarta Principles, recommending the removal of compulsory medical sterilization and forced medical treatment in association with gender.

The judgments of the Swedish courts started to critically assess the lawmakers' assumptions as to trans requirements against European law requirements. The Swedish Supreme Administrative Court held in 2009 that individuals over the age of 18 years, regardless of their biological or legal gender/sex have the right to determine their first name.[12] The Tax Agency had denied the petitioner's request to change his name from Jan-Olov to Madeleine with the motivation that Madeleine was not a manly name, was not a sex neutral name, and therefore was not a suitable name for a man. Petitioner appealed, arguing that he was a transvestite and was known by both names, Jan-Olov and Madeleine, that the 1982 Name Act had no explicit prohibition reflecting the argument made by the Tax Agency and such an interpretation was in violation of an individual's right to live according to their gender identity. The Supreme Administrative Court agreed, stating that the choice of name was so personal that extensive freedom must be given to the individual in that choice, particularly when the person is an adult.

---

[10]See Commissioner for Human Rights (2009), pp. 18–19.

[11]For more information on the Yogyakarta Principles, see the website yogyakartaprinciples.org. Accessed 6 July 2020.

[12]See RÅ 2009 ref. 55.

A Stockholm trial court held in 2010 that the requirement as to not being married or in a registered partnership under the 1972 act was in violation of the ECHR. The act however was still not amended. A Stockholm administrative trial court held in 2012 that the requirement of sterilization was in violation of Article 2:6 of the Instrument of Government, and also in violation of Article 8 (protection for private and family life) and Article 14 (discrimination prohibition) of the ECHR. The Court of Appeals upheld this decision, stating that:

> The concept of forced bodily violation… is more than a mere operation that is forced in the sense that the individual cannot stop it. If the surgery is a condition to receive certain benefits or rights, it is usually considered to be forced. It has been established … that the requirement for sterilization does not follow from prerequisites of certain physical conditions as criteria for establishing one's gender belonging.
>
> Sterilization involves a very radical and irreversible physical operation for the individual. To justify a sterilization requirement solely with reference to keeping order in familial relationships can hardly be permitted to be done in light of these types of intrusions and prevailing values. In addition, the requirement to undergo the surgery cannot be considered to be voluntary. In this Court's judgment, the sterilization requirement is such an intrusive procedure that it cannot be considered consistent with Ch. 2, 6 § of the Swedish Constitution and Article 8 of the ECHR. Furthermore, the requirement is directed only toward transsexual persons. Establishment of such a far-reaching requirement for one certain group means that the requirements of the 1972 act must also be considered in conflict with the prohibition of discrimination in ECHR Article 14.[13]

To a foreign reader these judgments perhaps do not seem to be too radical from the aspect of the courts assessing the law. However, these judgments demarcate a significant shift, from the period when the Instrument of Government was seen as not bearing individual rights, and the ECHR was not to be applied in public law, to the individual successfully asserting the protections afforded by the Instrument of Government and the ECHR through litigation. The courts in these judgments are not simply interpreting Swedish law according to the intent of the Swedish legislator, but instead against the requirements of European law and human rights. The requirement of sterilization was removed the year after the decision by the Court of Appeals in 2013.

The Swedish National Board of Health and Welfare issued in 2015 the guidelines, Good care of adults with gender dysphoria—National Knowledge Support (*God vård av vuxna med könsdysfori—Nationellt kunskapsstöd*) and Good care of children and youths with gender dysphoria—National Knowledge Support (*God vård av barn och ungdomar med könsdysfori—Nationellt kunskapsstöd*) with recommendations as to the specialized care. According to the National Patient Register, 1365 individuals were in contact with Swedish health care due to gender dysphoria in 2013, of which 78 were younger than 18 years of age. Two core principles are taken up in the recommendations, multi-disciplinary teams and counselling.

[13]See citing Stockholm Administrative Court of Appeals, *Socialstyrelsen v. NN*, Case no. 1968-12 (19 December 2012), pp. 5–6. This translation is taken from Garland, pp. 161–162.

Three additional legislative inquiries were conducted in 2014, 2015 and 2017. The 2014 inquiry[14] investigated the legislative treatment of both legal and medical gender reassignment, calling for further inquiries. The 2015 inquiry[15] proposed explicitly including trans persons as groups protected against the crimes of agitation, insulting behavior, hate speech and criminal discrimination. The 2015 inquiry resulting in legislative amendments to the criminal code in 2018 now specifically including trans persons as a protected group against hate crimes and unlawful discrimination. Amendments were also made in 2019 to Article 7:6 of the 1949 constitution act concerning the freedom of the press, to include trans persons as a protected group with respect to the crime of incitement against a group of individuals (*hets mot folkgrupp*). The 2017 inquiry[16] looked at ways to promote stronger LGBTQI rights through better governmental coordination in areas of health care, education, police work, asylum procedures and employment. The alternatives of having a third gender and a gender-neutral social security number were also investigated, with the recommendation of further investigation.

The Government presented a plan for a modern trans legislation in May 2018, comprising two laws, one regarding legal gender and the other the medical procedures with respect to voluntary physical changes. Change of legal gender is to not in any way be tied to medical procedures. Cited as reason for the urgency of such changes is a 2015 report issued by the Public Health Agency of Sweden (*Folkhälsomyndigheten*) finding that one-third of all trans persons in Sweden have attempted to commit suicide at least once, with those under the age of thirty years seriously contemplating suicide several times.[17]

2 The Current State of Swedish Trans Law

Several topics are taken up in this section with respect to the current state of the law and trans issues, including the 1972 act, civil status, parenthood, the name act, the social security number and the payment of damages for the 1972 act's legal requirement as to sterilization. Though this chapter deals with the legal treatment in Sweden of trans issues, it should be noted that this progression is parallel to the changes occurring on the international and national levels. Ten principles (YP+10) were added to the Yogyakarta Principles in 2017, reflecting the "significant

[14]Legislative Inquiry SOU 2014:91, *Juridiskt kön och medicinsk könskorrigering* (Legal gender and medical gender reassignment) with an English summary.

[15]Legislative Inquiry SOU 2015:103. *Ett utvidgat straffrättsligt skydd för trans personer m.m.* (An expanded criminally sanctioned protection for trans persons) with a summary in English. This inquiry also removed the word "race" from much of the Swedish legislation despite the title of the inquiry dealing with transgender.

[16]Legislative Inquiry SOU 2017:92, *Trans personer i Sverige - Förslag för stärkt ställning och bättre levnadsvillkor* with an English summary.

[17]Folkhälsomyndigheten (2105) Hälsan och hälsans bestämningsfaktorer för trans personer.

developments both in the field of international human rights law and in the understanding of violations affecting persons of 'diverse sexual orientations and gender identities', as well as a recognition of the often distinct violations affecting persons on grounds of 'gender expression' and 'sex characteristics'." The European Court of Human Rights held in the 2017 case, *A.P and Others v. France*, that French authorities had infringed on the petitioners' right to respect for private life under Article 8 ECHR by making gender recognition conditional on undergoing an operation involving a high probability of sterility.

2.1 The Current 1972 Act

Despite the several legislative inquiries and court judgments, the 1972 Act on Determining Sex in Certain Cases as amended, is still the governing law almost fifty years later. The most recent amendment was in 2013 with respect to the removal of the requirement of sterilization to change gender. The 1972 act still regulates both legal and medical gender reassignment.

Under the current act, an individual in order to apply for legal gender reassignment is to be at least 18 years of age, declare that they have for a lengthy period believed that they belong to the other gender, have for a period had the appearance of belonging to the other gender, and will continue live in the other gender in the future. For medical gender reassignment, the individual needs to be at least 12 years old to consent, and declare that they were born with a deviation (Swedish *avvikelse)* in gender development, and that gender reassignment is consistent with the development of the gender identity and most compatible with the applicant's physical condition.

Applications for gender reassignment, legal or medical, can only be granted to persons registered in Sweden. The application cannot be granted to an individual who is a registered partner. The requirement of not being married was removed in 2012.

2.2 Civil Status

There are four categories of civil status in Sweden: Married, registered partners, cohabiting partners and no claimed relationship. A marriage ceremony is religious or civil, and the couple either homosexual or heterosexual.[18] The marriage is registered with the Tax Agency. Registered partnerships can no longer be entered into, but from the period between 1995 and 2009 a homosexual or heterosexual couple could

[18] After amendments to the Marriage Code in 2009. Civil status in Sweden historically as mentioned above was under the authority of the government agency, the Swedish National Lutheran Church,

enter into a registered partnership that then could be registered with the Tax Agency. These relationships are still valid. Cohabiting couples have no legal registration requirements and very limited legal rights with respect to each other. The legal definition of a cohabiting couple is two persons who live together continuously in a couple relationship and share a common household. Though there is no explicit requirement as to longevity, a joint child is often seen as fulfilling this requirement.

As marriages and registered partnerships are registered with the Tax Agency, an individual can simply request a statement as to civil status from the Tax Agency. Requests as to changing civil status are also made to the Tax Agency.

2.3 Parenthood

Just as the binary for gender is in need of deconstruction, so to is the binary of parenthood requiring a mother and a father no longer tenable given today's society and technology. The legal determination of a child's parents under Swedish law was until very recently quite simplistic: A woman giving birth to a child was the mother, and the man married to the woman was the father. Historically, this presumption of fatherhood, derived from Roman law, was to protect the sanctity of marriage from claims by third parties. If the biological father is not the husband, the biological father has no right to bring suit to establish paternity.

A court can find that a husband is not the father of a child under three circumstances: where it has been shown that the mother has had sexual intercourse with another man during the time the child was conceived and it is probable that the other man is the biological father, where it is genetically shown that the husband is not the father, or where the child was conceived prior to the marriage or when the spouses lived separately and it is not probable that the spouses had sexual intercourse with each other during the time the child was conceived. If the husband accepts another man's acknowledgement of paternity, the husband will be deemed to not be the father of the child. Any acknowledgement of paternity is always to be confirmed by the mother in writing.

---

which was also in charge of the national population register generally, tracking births, sex, residence, nationality and civil status. Freedom of religion was first legislated in Sweden in 1951. The National Lutheran Church, part of the Swedish state since the sixteenth century, was separated from the state by law in 2000 and then ceased to be recognized as a state administrative agency.

The right to a church marriage ceremony between a man and a woman was first enacted by law in 1686 and became obligatory in 1734. Civil marriage ceremonies instead of a church ceremony were first allowed in 1863 in those cases were one of the spouses was Jewish. A general right to civil marriage ceremonies was legislated in 1908. The right for priests of religions other than those of the Swedish Lutheran Church to conduct marriage ceremonies was created in 1951. The majority of marriage ceremonies today are still conducted by priests of the Swedish Lutheran Church (54%). When the Marriage Code was amended in 2009 to include homosexual couples, one of the compromises reached within the church and with the legislature was that individual priests could refuse to marry a couple based on grounds of conscience.

If the parents are not married, the paternity of a child is to be established either by a voluntary acknowledgement of paternity or court judgment. An acknowledgement of paternity is to be in writing, witnessed by two persons and confirmed by the mother in writing unless a guardian has been appointed for the mother. The acknowledgement of paternity must also be approved by the municipal social welfare committee (*socialnämnden*).

If paternity is to be established by court judgment, the court is to declare a man the father if such is established through genetic testing, or if it is established that the man had sexual intercourse with the woman during the period in which the child was conceived, or during the same period, the woman was artificially inseminated with his sperm, and it is probable that the child is his. Where the couple is cohabitating, the father has either to register paternity or a court issue a judgment. The presumption of fatherhood has never been applicable to cohabitating couples.

A court cannot declare a man the father of a child where the man was a sperm donor in accordance with the Act on Genetic Privacy (*lag* 2006:351 *om genetisk integritet*). Retaining the fatherhood presumption within marriage, instead of letting both parents regardless of gender register parenthood (as is the case for fathers who are cohabitees today), has led to extremely complicated legal rules in the Parental Code with respect to fatherhood particularly and artificial semination. Distinctions are now made in the law after 2018 amendments between on one hand, spouses, registered partners and cohabitees, and on the other hand, establishing parenthood for trans parents. Distinctions are also made between artificial insemination procedures done in Sweden and done elsewhere, as well as whether the insemination is done internally or externally, and with or without the consent of the other party. If a mother has been inseminated outside her body with the consent of her spouse, registered partner or cohabitee, and it is probable that the child was the result of the insemination, then the party giving the consent will be deemed to be the child's parent, as confirmed by a confirmation or judgment.

Specific rules now exist with respect to a child born to trans persons in the Parental Code. A transman who gives birth to a child is to be deemed the father of the child. However, references in other laws (outside that chapter of the Parental Code) as to the mother are to be applicable. A transwoman who donates sperm to a child is to be considered the mother of the child, but in the other laws comparable to the father. The parenthood of the other person in a couple who has not born a child is to be confirmed or determined by judgment. The parents of a child born but not genetically related to both parents has the duty under the law to inform the child of this as soon as suitable.

The legal provisions regarding artificial insemination and trans persons, as well as retention of the fatherhood presumption in marriage, reveal almost the same apprehension as to embracing different family constellations as present when the 1972 act was initially adopted. A much simpler system would instead be to have two parents who register their parenthood, regardless of whether married or trans, birth parent or not. It can be questioned whether these differentiated rules, particular on the basis of trans, are lawful in light of the discrimination protections in place. As with the ideas of a third or no gender, parenthood should instead perhaps be distinguished on different levels, such as legal parents, social parents, biological parents and genetic parents, etc. and simply avoid the very complicated system now created under the Swedish Parental Code.

2.4 The 2016 Name Act and Social Security Numbers

The pincers initially raising trans issues, the Name Act and the Social Security numbering system, have not changed significantly since the 1960's. As discussed above, first the Swedish Lutheran Church then the Tax Agency has approved first names given to children by parents or changes of name by the person themselves as to whether the proposed first names could give offence, expose a person to ridicule or otherwise not be seen as suitable. The current 2016 Names Act (*lag* 2016:1013 *om personnamn*) has retained these three requirements. Given the 2009 holding of the Swedish Supreme Administrative Court, the application of these requirements should now be more gender neutral and broader. This particularly in light of the Court stating that individuals have the right to live according to their gender identity and that the choice of name is so personal that extensive freedom must be given to the individual in that choice, particularly when the person is an adult.[19] There are no statutory limits as to how many name changes can be made. Too many however may give rise to concerns of fraud. The application is to be made to the Tax Agency, and that authority's decisions can be appealed to the courts.

Several different legislative inquiries have skirted on the issue of changing the markers in the social security number system, particularly as the last two remaining are protected grounds with respect to discrimination, age and sex. However, the conclusions drawn have been that such would be too difficult. This is interesting as it is not grounded in any deeper analysis, and can be assessed against the fact that all predictions are that Sweden has already run out of social security numbers for certain birthdates. One estimation is that by 2017, 11,000 individuals had been given false birthdates.[20] When an individual has successfully petitioned for a gender reassignment under the 1972 act, they also receive a new social security number that shows the changed gender.

2.5 Trans Specific Legislative Protections

As seen from the historical account above, civil law protections against unlawful discrimination were given at different times, parental leave (1978), sex (1979),

[19]See RÅ 2009 ref. 55.

[20]See Wikén, J. 2017. 11 000 har påhittade födelsedagar – personnumren räcker inte till. *Metro*, April 10.

sexual orientation (1999) and transgender identity or expression (2009). These three latter grounds are protected under the 2008 Discrimination Act.[21] The act describes discrimination as either direct discrimination (disparate treatment), indirect discrimination (disparate impact), harassment or instructions to discriminate. The protected grounds are defined in section 1:5 of the act. Sex is defined as that someone is a woman or a man. Transgender identity or expression is defined as where someone does not identify herself or himself as a woman or a man or expresses by their manner of dressing or in some other way that they belong to another sex. Sexual orientation is defined as homosexual, bisexual or heterosexual orientation. A person who intends to change or has changed the sex they belong to is also covered by sex as a ground of discrimination under the act. The prohibition as to discrimination and reprisals encompass working life, education, labour market policy activities, starting or running a business and professional recognition, memberships in certain organizations, goods, services and house, health and medical care, social services, the social insurance system, military service (with certain exceptions) and public employment.

Employers have additional duties under the 2008 act in the form of active measures, including equal pay between women and men based on audits. Educational providers also have a duty to conduct a more limited range of active measures. The Equality Ombudsman is charged with overseeing the enforcement of the act. Remedies under the act include discrimination damages and the voiding of certain decisions. The statute of limitations for claims under the act can be very short. Certain employment claims have to be filed within a few months of the date the discriminatory decision was made by the employer. Discrimination damage awards tend to be modest, SEK 60,000, with the losing party (statistically more often the employee) bearing the prevailing party's legal costs and fees, which typically average at a higher amount, over SEK 150,000. There are no published cases to date decided by the Labour Court citing transgender identity or expression as a basis for unlawful discrimination.

Certain conduct as directed against trans persons is specifically criminalized in the penal code. Incitement against a group of individuals is a crime in section 16:8 of the penal code whereby an individual, in a statement or other message, disseminates threats or expresses contempt against an ethnic group or other group based on race, color or ethnic origins, faith, sexual orientation or transgender identity or expression. The sanction is at the most two years imprisonment, or if minor, fines. Unlawful discrimination is where a commercial actor in its operations discriminates against a person on the basis of race, national or ethnic origins, faith, sexual orientation or transgender identity or expression. The sanction is fines or imprisonment up to one year. Including as aggravating circumstances in section 29:1(7) for any crime is where the motive of the crime is to offend a person, a folk group or another such group of persons because of race, skin color, national or ethnic origin, creed, sexual

[21] An English translation of the 2008 Discrimination Act is available at the website of the Equality Ombudsman at do.se.

orientation, transgender identity or expression or other similar circumstances. Included in the crimes listed under the Freedom of the Press Act is incitement against a group of persons on the basis of sexual orientation or transgender identity or expression.

2.6 The Payment of Damages for Sterilization

In another first, Sweden became the first country in the world to offer compensation to trans people who were forced to undergo sterilization in order to be allowed to change their sex. An act was passed in 2018 to pay a lumpsum of SEK 225,000 in compensation to those individuals who had successfully petitioned for legal gender reassignment in the period between 1 July 1972 and 30 June 2013 (*lagen* 2018:162 *om statlig ersättning till personer som har fått ändrad könstillhörighet fastställd*). It is estimated that approximately 900 individuals were be eligible to make claims for being forced to undergo sterilization for gender reassignment in the period from 1972 to 2013. There was a little over a two-year period in which to file such claims by 1 May 2020, to the Legal, Financial and Administrative Services Agency (*Kammarkollegiet*), and as of 10 December 2020, 530 of 573 applicants received this compensation.

3 The Role of Civil Society

As stated in the short description of the Swedish legal system given above, the courts and civil society generally have not acted as counterweights to the lawmakers. This is for several reasons that due to space constraints can only be briefly stated here. One primary reason is that the law has not been seen as a vehicle for societal change in the Nordic countries in the same way as for example in Anglo-American countries. Another has been the endeavor that the state, and not private organizations or even in some cases, the family, is to take care of the needs of individuals. A third can be seen as at least the façade of the need for consensus, and the faith placed in the state as a benevolent actor taking care of the needs of its people. Regardless of the truths of these reasons, the reality is that there is not a robust civil society in Sweden, with few exceptions. One of the most prominent and successful of these is the Riksförbundet för sexuellt likaberättigande (The National Organization for Sexual Equality, now The Swedish Federation for Lesbian, Gay, Bisexual, Transgender and Queer Rights, RSFL, rfsl.se).

RFSL has been very active since the backlash to the 1944 decriminalization of homosexuality. Swedish members in the Danish Association of 1948 began to hold meetings in Sweden, and by 1952 the Swedish Riksförbundet för sexuellt likaberättigande (The National Organization for Sexual Equality) was founded. RFSL began immediately to successfully lobby for legal change, such as the same age of consent for homosexuals (then 18) as for heterosexuals (then 15). Efforts were made as to requiring the Swedish UN delegate to request an investigation into the social, legal and human rights of homosexuals internationally. Another early focus already by 1953 was homosexual marriage.

RFSL has been very involved in bringing to the attention of lawmakers LGBTQ issues such as Aids, hate crimes, treatment of refugees, healthcare and family issues to name a few. RFSL has been active in providing legal opinions (*remisser*) to legislative proposals. Strategic litigation has also been used by RFLS, for example by filing a claim with the Parliamentary Ombudsman on behalf of 160 individuals harmed by involuntary sterilization for damages, which was denied. Today RFSL has 7000 members and 36 clubs distributed over Sweden. RFSL offers LGBTQ certification and internet courses on LGBTQ issues.

ILGA-Europe, a civil society organization advocating for human right and equality for LGBTI persons at the European level, invoking strategic litigation and strengthening the movement globally, has placed Sweden 10th of forty-nine countries in Europe on their Rainbow Europe 2020 map.[22] The top five countries as to LGBTI rights on the map are Malta, Belgium, Luxembourg, Denmark and Norway. The bottom five are Monaco, Russia, Armenia, Turkey and Azerbaijan. Sweden's ranking was a result of the following:

- that the 1972 Act on Determining Sex in Certain Cases still is not based on self-identification,
- that the 1972 Act on Determining Sex in Certain Cases still has the requirement of a psychological evaluation in order to change legal gender,
- that the 1972 Act on Determining Sex in Certain Cases still has age requirements with respect to changing legal gender,
- that there is no legal prohibition against surgical interventions on intersex individuals that are not medically-motivated and that occur without the consent of the individual,
- that there is no gender-neutral parental presumption,
- that there is no prohibition against conversion therapy, and
- that the Discrimination Act does not prohibit discrimination on the basis of sex characteristic (in other words, discrimination against intersex persons is permitted).

4 The Way Forward

The history of trans legal rights in Sweden clearly demonstrates that lawmakers alone cannot and should not determine the path with respect to trans rights. Sweden is perhaps one of the best examples of why "Nothing about us without us" is so

[22] ILGA Europe. 2020. Rainbow Europe 2020. Https://www.ilga-europe.org/rainboweurope/2020. Accessed 6 July 2020.

important. Civil society must challenge lawmakers as to the decisions taken (or not). The courts also need act as guarantors of human rights as the negative outcomes as generated by law should be brought to courts for remedies. As of 2018 the Swedish courts have the explicit authority to award damages for violations of the European Convention, and hopefully this can be an incentive for individuals negatively affected by the law to litigate. It is not until the law is tested that it can be assessed. The 2018 amendments to the Parental Code bring this to the fore. Based on a norm of heterosexual marriage, differential legal treatment is given to trans parents. Such treatment would not even be necessary if the marital fatherhood presumption were to be abolished and parents could simply register themselves as parents without judicial intervention except in cases where there is conflict between the parents. With the removal of more and more legal distinctions based on male/female, retaining that dichotomy with respect to parents is a step backwards. The same is true of the social security numbering system that has two markers disclosing protected grounds, sex and age.

Andrew Gilden[23] describes the Navajo approach to gender, which recognizes four genders, feminine female, masculine male, feminine male and masculine female. This approach comprises three overarching themes: child autonomy, tribal collectivism and gender egalitarianism. Under this system, children are not assigned a gender until they reach an age at which they can decide themselves, with a significant freedom to explore different alternatives. Collectivism comes into play in that the child is not raised as just a member of a nuclear family, but rather as a member of the tribal collective. Gender egalitarianism is present in that there is no increased social stigma or economic disadvantage in the child choosing birth or preferred gender. That which can be taken immediately here for further discussion is the child autonomy in choosing gender and whether there is a true need to legally identify gender at birth. The legal need for certain of these vestiges of the past, the legal distinction between mothers and father, social security numbers disclosing sex and age, as well as determining gender at birth, perhaps no longer should be ascribed the same weight as they traditionally have been attributed.

References

Commissioner for Human Rights (2009) Issue paper human rights and gender identity. Council of Europe, pp 18–19

Dunne P (2017) Transgender sterilisation requirements in Europe. Med Law Rev 25(4):554–581

Garland J (2016) On science, law, and medicine: the case of gender "normalizing" interventions on children who are diagnosed as different in sex development. Uppsala Univ. Press

Gilden A (2013) Toward a more transformative approach: the limits of transgender formal equality. Berk J Gend Law Justice 23(1):84–144

---

[23]Gilden (2013), p. 121.

Kommissionen mot antiziganism (2015) Antiziganismen i Sverige: Om övergrepp och kränkningar av romer under 1900-talet och idag. Stockholm, p 28

Ludvigsson JF, Otterblad-Olausson P, Pettersson BU, Ekbom A (2009) The Swedish personal identity number: possibilities and pitfalls in healthcare and medical research. Eur J Epidemiol 24 (11):659–667

Wålinder J (1967) Transsexualism: a study of forty-three cases. Gothenburg University